# BEHAVIOR AND ENVIRONMENT
## Psychological and Geographical Approaches

# ADVANCES IN PSYCHOLOGY

# 96

*Editors:*

G. E. STELMACH

P. A. VROON

NORTH-HOLLAND
AMSTERDAM • LONDON • NEW YORK • TOKYO

# BEHAVIOR AND ENVIRONMENT

## Psychological and Geographical Approaches

Edited by

Tommy GÄRLING
*Department of Psychology*
*Gothenburg University*
*Göteborg, Sweden*

Reginald G. GOLLEDGE
*Department of Geography*
*University of California*
*Santa Barbara, CA, U.S.A.*

1993

NORTH-HOLLAND
AMSTERDAM • LONDON • NEW YORK • TOKYO

ELSEVIER SCIENCE PUBLISHERS B.V.
Sara Burgerhartstraat 25
P.O. Box 211, 1000 AE Amsterdam, The Netherlands

ISBN: 0 444 89698 8



This book is printed on acid-free paper.

Transferred to digital printing 2007

# Contents

# Contributors

DOUGLAS AMEDEO, Department of Geography, University of Nebraska, Lincoln, Nebraska 68588-0135

W. A. V. CLARK, Department of Geography, University of California, Los Angeles, California 90024

KIRSTIN DOW, Department of Geography, Clark University, Worcester, Massachusetts 01610-1477

GARY W. EVANS, Human Ecology, Cornell University, Ithaca, New York 14853

GORDON R. FOXALL, Consumer Research Unit, Department of Commerce, The Birmingham Business School, University of Birmingham, Birmingham B15 2TT, United Kingdom

TOMMY GÄRLING, Department of Psychology, University of Göteborg, P.O. Box 14158, Göteborg, Sweden

JÖRGEN GARVILL, Environmental Psychology Research Group, Department of Psychology, University of Umeå, S-90187 Umeå, Sweden

REGINALD G. GOLLEDGE, Department of Geography, University of California, Santa Barbara, California 93106

PAUL M. W. HACKETT, Consumer Research Unit, Department of Commerce, The Birmingham Business School, University of Birmingham, Birmingham B15 2TT, United Kingdom

PERRY HANSON, Director, Information Systems and Telecommunications, Wellesley College, Wellesley, Massachusetts 02181-8201

SUSAN HANSON, Department of Geography, Clark University, Worcester, Massachusetts 01610-1477

TERRY HARTIG, Program in Social Ecology, University of California, Irvine, California 92717

STEPHEN C. HIRTLE, Department of Information Science, University of Pittsburgh, Pittsburgh, Pennsylvania 15260

P. BRYAN HEIDORN, Department of Information Science, University of Pittsburgh, Pittsburgh, Pennsylvania 15260

RACHEL KAPLAN, School of Natural Resources, University of Michigan, Ann Arbor, Michigan 48109-1115

ROGER E. KASPERSON, Department of Geography, Clark University, Worcester, Massachusetts 01610-1477

ROBERT LLOYD, Department of Geography, University of South Carolina, Columbia, South Carolina 29208

THOMAS P. MCDONALD, Learning Technology Center, Peabody College, Vanderbilt University, Nashville, Tennessee 37203

HENRY MONTGOMERY, Department of Psychology, Stockholm University, S-10691 Stockholm, Sweden

JAMES W. PELLEGRINO, Learning Technology Center, Peabody College, Vanderbilt University, Nashville, Tennessee 37203

JOHN J. PIGRAM, Department of Geography and Planning, The University of New England, Armidale, N. S. W. 2351, Australia

W. FRED VAN RAAIJ, Department of Economics, Erasmus University, P.O. Box 1738, 3000 DR Rotterdam, The Netherlands

PAUL SLOVIC, Decision Research, 1201 Oak Street, Eugene, Oregon 97401

HARRY TIMMERMANS, Urban Planning Group, Faculty of Architecture, University of Technology, P.O. Box 513, 5600 MB Eindhoven, The Netherlands

# Preface

The publication of a book with contributions by geographers and psychologists is timely for two reasons. First, the fields of psychology and geography are capable of increasing our scientific knowledge of how human behavior is interfaced with the molar physical environment. Such knowledge is essential for the solution of many of today's most urgent environmental problems. Failure to constrain use of scarce resources, pollution due to human activities, creation of technological hazards, and deteriorating urban quality due to vandalism and crime are all well known examples.

Second, although we have seen during the last three decades an influence of psychology in geographical research, only recently have psychologists recognized that they have something to learn from geography. It is a timely matter for psychologists to become involved in a two-way interdisciplinary communication. With this book we hope to further promote this process. Our conviction is that the disciplines of geography and psychology are to some extent complementary, so that their closer collaboration will have synergistic effects on both discipine's attempts to find solutions to environmental problems through an increased understanding of the many behavior-environment interfaces.

As evidence of the increasing interest in geography shown by psychologists, joint symposia were organized in 1988 at the International Congresses of Geography and Psychology in Sydney, Australia. These symposia were then followed by two others which we organized in 1990 at the International Congress of Applied Psychology in Kyoto, Japan. This book is an outgrowth of those latter symposia. Several of the participants have contributed chapters; others who did not participate in the symposia were invited to prepare chapters on topics not covered in them. As a consequence, the book deals with most of the research problems of mutual interest to geographers and psychologists. Furthermore, by asking a psychologist and a geographer to each write a chapter on a designated topic, close comparisons can be made between how the two disciplines approach the same problems.

The degree to which informed discussion of the different research problems has been achieved is due to the fact that the contributors are active researchers. We owe a great deal of gratitude to them for devoting the time and effort we requested. Some were also willing to participate in a panel discussion on the interface between psychology and geography organized by Reg Golledge at the 1992 meeting of the Association of American Geographers in San Diego, California.

Despite the undeniable importance of the authors' contributions, this book would not have materialized without the assistance of Karen Harp, who skillfully edited all the manuscripts, prepared illustrations and camera ready copy, and helped compile the index. We are most grateful to her for this.

Tommy Gärling
Reginald G. Golledge

*Behavior and Environment: Psychological and Geographical Approaches*
*T. Gärling and R.G. Golledge (Editors)*



# CHAPTER 1

# Understanding Behavior and Environment: A Joint Challenge to Psychology and Geography

**Tommy Gärling and Reginald G. Golledge**

There are many interfaces between human behavior and the environment. These have been a major concern of psychology since its inception in the last century. However, it was not until environmental psychology emerged in the 1960s that the *molar physical* environment became a focus of interest (Craik, 1970; Proshansky & O'Hanlon, 1977; Stokols & Altman, 1987). The molar physical environment has, on the other hand, long been the focal concern of geography (Gaile & Wilmott, 1989; Gould, 1985; Johnston, 1979). Yet it was not until later, with the emergence of the behavioral approach, that geography sought to understand the relationship behavior has to the molar physical environment through the study of mediating psychological processes such as perception, cognition, appraisals, and decision making (Golledge, 1982). Given this emphasis, the newly established behavioral geography adopted the same goal as environmental psychology (Gärling & Evans, 1991).

Both psychology and geography thus attempt to understand how behavior and environment are interfaced. The aim of this book is to give state-of-the-art reviews of several different areas of research on the behavior-environment interfaces within which both psychologists and geographers are actively involved. By asking both a geographer and a psychologist to contribute a review of each research area, answers are provided to the question of what each discipline contributes towards the understanding of the many behavior-environment interfaces. It is hoped that such answers will together give a fuller understanding than each discipline provides by itself.

Behavioral geography initially borrowed concepts and methods from psychology (Gold, 1980; Golledge & Stimson, 1987; Walmsley & Lewis, 1984), but has since evolved to become an independent subdiscipline

(Golledge & Timmermans, 1990, Timmermans & Golledge, 1990). It may therefore seem as if this book would not have required the participation of psychologists. However, perhaps because of the dissociation between the two areas, the psychologists have contributed something different from the geographers. Without exceptions, the psychologists chose to analyze the mediating psychological processes which explain why behavior is interfaced with the environment in the ways it is. Although not avoiding such analyses, the geographers were in contrast more likely to emphasize the real-world phenomena which need to be explained.

In the next section of this introductory chapter we give a brief overview of the different behavior-environment interfaces. In the following section, we then analyze in some detail the differences in approach of psychology and geography. Finally, we summarize what we see as areas where research would benefit from further integration of psychology and geography.

## Behavior-Environment Interfaces

Many of the effects that the molar physical environment has on people's behavior depend on where people are and what they do. Therefore, *location* and *activity* are key concepts in any analysis. Whereas geography provides descriptive answers to questions such as where certain activities take place, those working in psychology (or behavioral geography) are more likely to ask the complementary questions about why certain activities take place in certain locations and what the psychological consequences are? In answering these questions, reference is primarily made to psychological processes such as perception, cognition, appraisals (or the formation of preferences), and decision making.

Applying the explanatory schemata of psychology, everyday interactions with the molar physical environment are viewed as the outcome of choices. Choices are preceded by acquisition of information from and about the environment, information which is subjected to judgments and appraisals before being acted on. People also have motives and goals which they bring to bear on the processing of the information. Chapters 2 to 11, constituting Part I of the book, review research on the basic component processes in the behavior-environment interaction of acquiring, judging, and appraising information. Chapters 12 to 17, assembled in Part II, review research on the basic component processes entailed by behavior-environment interactions in several of their real-world contexts such as choices of residential, retail, and recreational environments. A brief summary of the contents of the chapters follows.

Chapter 2 by geographer Reginald Golledge and Chapter 3 by psychologists Thomas McDonald and James Pellegrino review research on how spatial information in environments is perceived, acquired, and used in different tasks.

Research on how nonspatial information is perceived, appraised, and acted on is then reviewed in two chapters. In Chapter 4 geographer Douglas Amedeo contributes a psychologically-oriented analysis of affective reactions to environments. In contrast, psychologist Rachel Kaplan in Chapter 5 discusses more objective, cognitively-oriented appraisals of environments. She is in particular concerned with the lack of relationship such appraisals may show with the psychological quality of life in contemporary Western societies.

Chapter 6 is written by geographer Robert Lloyd, Chapter 7 by psychologists Stephen Hirtle and Bryan Heidorn. In both chapters research is reviewed on how environments are represented mentally, and how they should be represented externally to be comprehensible, for instance in maps.

Pervasive negative appraisals of environments may follow from perceptions of potential natural disasters and technological catastrophes or accidents. An analysis of the societal effects of risk perceptions is given in Chapter 8 by geographers Roger Kasperson and Kirstin Dow. In Chapter 9, psychologist Paul Slovic reviews research showing how people judge the likelihood of such events and how such judgments influence both their wider appraisals of and choice of environments.

In the final chapters in Part I, geographers Susan and Perry Hanson (Chapter 10) review and analyze descriptive research showing where, when, and in which types of everyday activities people participate. In Chapter 11, written by psychologists Tommy Gärling and Jörgen Garvill, several cognitive and motivational theories proposed in psychology are reviewed, and their value as explanations of participation in everyday activities assessed.

Part II of the book starts with Chapter 12 by geographer William Clark, who reviews research on residential search and choice. In Chapter 13 psychologist Henry Montgomery shows how psychological research on how people make decisions may assist in understanding residential choice.

Chapter 14, written by geographer Harry Timmermans, is a review of conceptualizations, models, and empirical findings in research on choices of retail environments. In Chapter 15 psychologists Paul Hackett,

Gordon Foxall, and Fred van Raaij review consumer research on how the retail environment affects purchases and satisfaction.

Finally, in Chapter 16 geographer John Pigram broadly reviews research on recreation. From this he derives both the basis for choices of recreational environments and the benefits accrued from such choices. How appraisals of recreational environments and benefits can be understood psychologically is the topic of Chapter 17 by psychologists Terry Hartig and Gary Evans who review several theories which address the question.

## Differences in Psychological and Geographical Approaches

Examples of differences in the approaches of psychology and (behavioral) geography may not be readily apparent in the following chapters. Alerting the reader to them here will hopefully enhance the ability to appreciate the separate contributions of each discipline. At the same time, both geography and psychology are so diverse that any general statement is difficult to make. In the following chapters there are also similarities which reflect collaboration between behavioral geographers and psychologists (e.g., Downs & Liben, 1987; Golledge, Kwan, & Gärling, 1992; Kasperson et al., 1982; Klatzky et al., 1990).

Below we discuss differences in assumptions underlying or entailed by more encompassing conceptualizations of behavior and environment. These assumptions include the degree to which an individual perspective is employed in analyses of behavior-environment interfaces, how the environment is conceptualized, and how the influence of the environment itself is conceptualized. Finally, there are differences in preferred methodologies which will be discussed.

### *Definitions of an Individual Perspective*

In psychology there does not seem to be any alternative to an individual perspective. It is generally assumed by psychologists that there is an individual actor, an external environment or situation, an input from the environment to actor initializing a psychological process, and an output from actor to environment termed action (e.g., Gärling & Golledge, 1989). It is important to note that the individual perspective entails the search for nomothetic laws, or what is generally true about people. Individual differences are not denied but considered to reflect measurement errors unless invariant over time and situational contexts.

In geography there are in contrast three different definitions of an individual perspective. One of them is indistinguishable from psychology. It is reflected in most chapters by geographers in this book (see also Golledge, 1981). A second acknowledges the individual's uniqueness. Although dismissed of as being unscientific (although complementary and potentially valuable in other realms of human activity) (Blackburn, 1976), such an individualistic perspective is adopted by many geographers (Relph, 1976 Saarinen & Sell, 1980 Seamon, 1987). In the present book, Chapter 4 comes at times close to an individualistic perspective.

Almost opposite to an individualistic perspective is a third definition (e.g., Fischer, Nijkamp, & Papageorgiou, 1991; Smith & Mertz, 1980). Here the individual perspective is merely implicit. In primary focus is some higher-order unit such as a government, firm, or household. The generic term "decision making unit" may also be used. This definition shares with the individual perspective in psychology the generality assumption. However, it neither articulates the characteristics of the individual actors comprising the higher-order units nor explicitly makes assumptions about how they interact. Sociodemographic characteristics, if anything, are used for describing individuals, rather than psychological-process characteristics. In Chapters 8 and 12, the third definition is most clearly adhered to.

Although clearly different, the last definition should not be difficult to reconcile with the definition of an individual perspective in psychology. An elaboration of the individual perspective is in many cases sufficient to make it more explicit with regard to mediating psychological processes. In doing this, concepts and empirical findings in psychology may be drawn on. A good example is obtained if Chapter 13 is compared to Chapter 12. In the former chapter, decision making is conceived of as a psychological process rather than simply as a decision outcome (choice).

### *Definitions of the Environment*

The important unresolved problem in psychology was once stated to be "What is the stimulus?" (Gibson, 1960). Interest in the environment appears since to have waned in some psychological subdisciplines. An exception is environmental psychology, which has seen upsurge in research since the 1960s (Stokols & Altman, 1987). This research has highlighted the narrowness of the common conceptualization of environment in psychology as a stimulus or physical energy impinging on the individual to which his or her senses are capable of responding (e.g., Pervin, 1978). With the insight that individuals - rather than, or in addition to, reacting to physical energy - acquire information about the environment on the basis of which they act (Gibson, 1950; Ittelson, 1973), the ground was laid for the information-processing approach in cognitive psychology (Newell & Simon, 1972). All chapters by psychologists share this basic approach. Furthermore, within the information-processing approach the environment as mentally represented by the individual becomes an important target for study. Chapters 3 and 7 review such research. In other chapters (Chapters 11 and 13), the way that observable actions depend on mental representations of the environment is at issue.

Although psychology's conceptualization of the environment has been expanded, it cannot be denied that it is impoverished when compared to the conceptualization in geography. The latter is more likely to also include the nonphysical, "hidden" aspects of the environment such as cultural, political, legal, and administrative rules imposed on its use. A most clear indication of this is given in Chapter 8.

Even though focus is limited to the physical environment, the geographer places more emphasis on and defines more broadly the spatial environment. This can be seen in comparing Chapter 2 by Golledge to Chapter 3 by McDonald and Pellegrino. Starting from his broader definition, Golledge raises several interesting questions concerning the ways individuals conceptualize spatial aspects of the environment, questions which psychologists have tended to neglect. Although McDonald and Pellegrino remind us that in psychology there is a long history of research on spatial cognition, it is nevertheless true that psychologists are in general less tuned than geographers to the importance of spatial extent for *everyday human activities*. Related to this, psychologists' research on spatial cognition, as well as on space perception (Gibson, 1950), has tended to be limited to small-scale environments rather than the large-scale environments (neighborhoods, cities, regions, and nations) of interest to geographers.

Traditionally, in both geography and psychology the objective rather than the subjective environment has been emphasized. In psychology the emphasis was strongest during the heydays of behaviorism (Skinner, 1974). Observable behavior was then conceived as being the result of antecedent environmental (stimuli) and individual or organismic (need) factors. Even though such a conceptualization has been replaced by one of an information-processing individual acting on the basis of information processed, it should not be ignored that the objective environment affects the individual. A valuable contribution from geography is the emphasis on objective environmental constraints (Desbarats, 1983; Eagle, 1988; Gould, 1975; Lenntorp, 1978). Similarly, as discussed in Chapters 5 and 17, both scarce, non-renewable resources acting as constraints and stress-inducing/reducing properties of environments have direct and indirect psychological impacts on individuals, whether or not they are aware of them. Such an emphasis on the objective environment is even more pronounced in geography (O'Riordan, 1973; Manners & Mikesell, 1974; Mitchell, 1984).

### *Definitions of the Influence of the Environment on Behavior*

Different forms of environmental determinism have plagued geography in the past (Huntington, 1945; Taylor, 1951). Conceptualizing the influence of the environment as causal was also particularly common in psychology before the cognitive breakthrough. Within the cognitive, information-processing approach, it is however generally assumed that people act on the basis of decisions they make. These decisions are in turn based on appraisals of acquired information. Thus, the relationship of the observed action or behavior to the environment is mediated by psychological processes. It has been argued that decisions or intentions can be considered as (proximal) causes of actions in the same sense as physical phenomena are causally determined (Brand, 1984). In Chapter 11, Gärling and Garvill (like those psychologists cited in the chapter) draw on this philosophical standpoint.

The analysis by Gärling and Garvill should be contrasted with that of geographers Hanson and Hanson (Chapter 10), who write on the same topic. They appear to assume nothing more than that the environment imposes constraints on feasible activities. Since these constraints are primarily of a physical or physiological nature, the authors are apparently cautious about not going beyond a physicalist conception of a cause-effect relationship. A similar difference between psychologists and geographers in willingness to give inferred psychological processes causal status in explanations is evident in Chapters 12 and 13.

There are many examples of a more elaborate view in psychology where the individual and environment are interacting. Thus, actions due to the impact of the environment in turn affect the environment and modify its impact, and so on. In this vein, some psychologists (Carver & Scheier, 1981; Powers, 1973) have applied control theory. Others go even further by conceptualizing people and environments as aspects of one single, transactional process (Altman & Rogoff, 1987). The latter conceptualization is also found in geography (cf. Chapter 4).

With the exception for differences in the causal role ascribed to psychological processes, it appears that geography and psychology have undergone parallel developments in how the influence of the environment should be conceptualized. It is probably fair to say that interactionism is dominating, implying mutual causal influences over time between behavior and environment. An interest in applying systems analysis is also evident in both disciplines.

### *Methodology*

The most readily discernible difference in methodology between geography and psychology appears to be choice of research strategy. There are also differences in the modelling and data analysis techniques geographers and psychologists prefer to use. The latter difference stands out when comparing the degree of quantitative modelling of consumer choice in current geographic research (Chapter 14) to the qualitative facet-theory approach taken by consumer psychologists (Chapter 15). However, depending on research area, such a difference may or may not be observed. We prefer here to confine our comments to the difference in research strategy which we see as more consequential.

Psychologists in general consider experimentation to be superior to any other research strategy. The essence of experiments is the systematic manipulation of certain conditions, assumed to affect a phenomenon of interest, under strict control of extraneous factors. Experiments thereby possess a high degree of internal validity in making possible the precise assessment of the validity of theory-derived causal hypotheses. A drawback with experiments is that they sometimes lack external validity or similarity with the real world. Although there are several examples to the contrary in this book (see Chapters 2, 6, and 14), geographers may for this reason shy away from an experimental approach. Viewing the real world as their laboratory, geographers instead prefer to measure the phenomena as they appear there. Particularly clear examples of this approach are the research on activities described in Chapter 10, the research on residential choice described in Chapter 12, some of the research on choice of shopping locations described in Chapter 14, and the research on recreation described in Chapter 16. Those examples should be contrasted with the research described by psychologists in their companion chapters.

Experiments may sometimes be possible to conduct in real-world settings. Such field experiments have a prominent place in several subfields of psychology (e.g., consumer and marketing research, see Chapter 15; environmental psychology, see Chapter 17). Still, the selection of variables studied is a more important issue than the matter of whether the experiment is performed in the laboratory instead of in the field. However, sometimes unobtrusiveness is so important that systematic manipulation is inconceivable even in the field.

An increasing awareness seems to have emerged among psychologists of the value, or necessity, of combining the strengths and weaknesses of different research strategies. Today, case studies, correlational research designs, surveys, and the choice of more diverse subject populations are common place in psychology. At the same time the experimental approach is gaining recognition in geography. Yet it is probably still necessary to draw on research from both disciplines to extract information that is complementary with respect to internal and external validity. However, with increasing interdisciplinary communication, the preferred metho-dology will perhaps in the future be dictated more by the research problems than by disciplinary boundaries.

## Future Challenges

Although there are several signs of an increasing commonality between behavioral geography and psychology, there are yet few, if any examples of integrative research. Many subareas exist in which the potential for such research is high. Specific examples include general principles of, as well as individual differences in, spatial cognition as related to cartography and geographical information systems (GIS); locomotion, wayfinding, and navigation in actual, large-scale environments; choice and activity analysis in the context of demand modelling; resolving questions regarding the influence of scale on cognitive processes; and affective reactions to everyday environments. In the remaining part of this subsection we exemplify the kind of future challenges for psychology and geography by briefly discussing three research topics.

### *Spatial Abilities*

A critical question central to many of the problems of concern to both geography and psychology is that of the nature of spatial abilities. Research on the issue has been carried out in psychology for a long time. A large number of tests of spatial abilities and competence has been developed (Eliot & McFarlane-Smith, 1983). In contrast, geographers have been much less interested in measuring spatial abilities, or even to incorporate them into their explanatory schemata. The obvious challenge for geographers is to thoroughly explore this possibility.

A challenge for psychologists is to address questions of what relationship, if any, there is between spatial abilities and actual spatial behavior as studied by geographers. Specific questions suggesting themselves are: Do people's skills in localizing things at both a local and global scale correlate with spatial abilities? Is there any relationship between spatial abilities and people's skills in describing spatial and distributional patterns in large-scale environments? Is the use of global systems of reference, such as the cardinal compass directions, in thinking and actual behavior, indicative of high spatial abilities? How does expert spatial knowledge differ from novice spatial knowledge?

### *Locomotion, Wayfinding, and Navigation*

Moving through space is an integral part of our existence. For many years geographers focussed on the overt act of physically changing from one to another location. They searched the environment for correlates of spatial movement patterns. A high degree of coincidence between a movement pattern and a pattern of some other phenomenon was deemed sufficient to "explain" the movement pattern. In psychology, processes such as cognitive mapping of the environment, finding one's way and navigating have been studied. As behavioral geography developed, an interest was aroused in using such processes as explanations.

A joint challenge to geography and psychology is clearly to further develop process explanations of movement patterns. A most promising means of collaborative efforts to this end is the development of computational-process models (CPM) (Golledge et al., 1992; Smith, Pellegrino, & Golledge, 1982).

### *Spatial Decision Making*

As noted by, for instance, Gärling, Böök, & Lindberg (1984), there is a gap to bridge between a mental representation of a large-scale environment and actual behavior in that environment. This bridge was believed to consist of action plans.

How action plans are formed has in a more limited sense been studied by geographers interested in spatial decision making (Timmermans & Golledge, 1990), that is, consumers' choices of locations for different purposes such as shopping, recreation, etc. For the most part, this research relies more on normative principles of decision making, such as utility maximization, than on behavioral principles. However, as early as 1960, geographer Huff conceptualized the spatial-decision making process using a mix of psychological and geographic concepts. By drawing on the notion of "bounded rationality" which Simon (1957) had introduced, Huff (1960) noted the need to incorporate notions of how decision makers search for information. He developed concepts such as "behavior space perception" and "cognized movement imagery" or "travel plans." Later Golledge (1967) and Amedeo and Golledge (1975) elaborated and expanded on these concepts.

A challenge to psychologists interested in decision making is to follow up on the early attempts at introducing behavioral principles in research on spatial decision making. At the same time, geographers now working in this field should find many useful, new concepts that have been developed by psychologists undertaking behavioral research on decision making since the 1960s.

## A Final Comment

We trust this chapter, and, indeed, the whole book, will make evident the benefit psychologists would gain from becoming more familiar with geographical research, and how much geographers would benefit from becoming more familiar with psychological research. We thus hope this book is instrumental in tearing down existing communication barriers. The other barriers we leave to others to remove.

## References


Altman, I., & Rogoff, B. (1987). World views in psychology: Trait, interactional, organismic, and transactional perspectives. In D. Stokols & I. Altman (Eds.), *Handbook of environmental psychology* (Vol. 1, pp. 7-40). New York: Wiley.

Amedeo, D., & Golledge, R. G. (1975). *An introduction to scientific reasoning in geography*. New York: Wiley.

Blackburn, T. R. (1976). Sensuous-intellectual complementarity. In M. H. Marx & F. E. Goodson (Eds.), *Theories in contemporary psychology* (2nd ed., pp. 346-361). New York: Macmillan.

Brand, M. (1984). *Intending and acting*. Cambridge, MA: MIT Press.

Carver, C. S., & Scheier, M. (1981). *Attention and self-regulation: A control-theory approach to human behavior*. New York: Springer.

Craik, K. H. (1970). Environmental psychology. In T. M. Newcomb (Ed.), *New directions in psychology* (Vol. IV, pp. 3-121). Holt, Rinehart and Winston.

Desbarats, J. (1983). Spatial choice and constraints on behavior. *Annals of the Association of American Geographers, 73*, 340-357.

Downs, R. M., & Liben, L. S. (1987). Children's understanding of maps. In P. Ellen & C. Thinus-Blanc (Eds.), *Cognitive processes and spatial orientation in animal and man* (pp. 201-219). Dordrecht: Martinus Nijhoff.

Eagle, T. C. (1988). Context effects in consumer spatial behavior. In R. G. Golledge & H. J. P. Timmermans (Eds.), *Behavioral modelling in geography and planning* (pp. 299-324). London: Croom Helm.

Eliot, J., & McFarlane-Smith, I. M. (1983). *An international directory of spatial tests*. Oxford: NFER-Nelson.

Fischer, M., Nijkamp, P., & Papageorgiou, Y. (Eds.) (1991). *Spatial choices and processes*. Amsterdam: Elsevier.

Gaile, G., & Wilmott, C. (Eds.) (1989). *Geography in America*. New York: Merrill.

Gärling, T., Böök, A., & Lindberg, E. (1984). Cognitive mapping of large-scale environments: The interrelationship of action plans, acquisition, and orientation. *Environment and Behavior, 16*, 3-34.

Gärling, T., & Evans, G. W. (Eds.). (1991). *Environment, cognition and action: An integrated approach*. New York: Oxford University Press.

Gärling, T., & Golledge, R. G. (1989). Environmental perception and cognition. In E. H. Zube & G. T. Moore (Eds.), *Advances in environment, behavior, and design* (Vol. 2, pp. 203-236). New York: Plenum.

Gibson, J. J. (1950). *The perception of the visual world*. Boston: Houghton Mifflin.

Gibson, J. J. (1960). The concept of the stimulus in psychology. *American Psychologist, 15*, 694-703.

Gold, J. R. (1980). *An introduction to behavioral geography*. New York: Oxford University Press.

Golledge, R. G. (1967). Conceptualizing the market decision process. *Journal of Regional Science, 7*, 239-258.

Golledge, R. G. (1981). Misconceptions, misinterpretations, and misrepresentations of behavioral approaches in human geography. *Environment and Planning A, 13*, 1325-1344.

Golledge, R. G. (1982) Substantive and methodological aspects of the interface between geography and psychology. In R. G. Golledge & J. Rayner (Eds.), *Proximity and preference* (pp. xix-xxxix). Minneapolis, MN: University of Minnesota Press.

Golledge, R. G., Kwan, M.-P., & Gärling, T. (1992). *Computational-process modelling of travel decisions using a geographical information system*. Unpublished manuscript. Department of Geography, University of California Santa Barbara.

Golledge, R. G., & Stimson, R. (1987). *Analytical behavioral geography*. London: Croom Helm.

Golledge, R. G., & Timmermans, H. J. P. (1990). Applications of behavioral research on spatial problems I: Cognition. *Progress in Human Geography, 14*, 57-99.

Gould, P. (1975). *Spatial diffusion: The spread of ideas and innovations in geographic space* (Learning Package Series No. 11.). New York: Learning Resources in International Studies.

Gould, P. (1985). *The geographer at work*. London: Routledge & Kegan Paul.

Huff, D. (1960). A topological model of consumer space preferences. *Papers of the Regional Science Association, 6*, 159-173.

Huntington, E. (1945). *Mainsprings of Civilization*. New York: Arno.

Ittelson, W. H. (1973). Environment perception and contemporary perceptual theory. In W. H. Ittelson (Ed.), *Cognition and environment* (pp. 1-19). New York: Seminar.

Johnston, R. J. (1979). *Geography and geographers*. New York: Wiley.

Kasperson, R. E., Renn, O., Slovic, P., Brown, H. S., Emel, J., Goble, R., Kasperson, J. X., & Ratick, S. (1988). The social amplification of risk: A conceptual framework. *Risk Analysis, 8*, 177-187.

Klatzky, R., Loomis, J., Golledge, R. G., Cicinelli, J., Doherty, S., & Pellegrino, J. (1990). Acquisition of route and survey knowledge in the absence of vision. *Journal of Motor Behavior, 22*, 19-43.

Lenntorp, B. (1978). A time-geographic simulation model of individual activity programmes. In T. Carlstein, D. Parkes, and N. Thrift (Eds.), *Human activity and time geography* (pp. 162-180). London: Arnold.

Manners, I., & Mikesell, M. (Eds.). (1974). *Perspectives on environment* (Publication No. 13). Washington, D.C.: Commission on College Geography.

Mitchell, J. (1984). Hazard perception studies: Convergent concerns and divergent approaches during the past decade. In T. F. Saarinen, D. Seamon & J. L. Sell (Eds.), *Environmental perception and behavior* (Research Paper #209, pp. 33-59). Chicago: University of Chicago, Department of Geography.

Newell, A., & Simon, H. A. (1972). *Human problem solving*. Englewood Cliffs, NJ: Prentice-Hall.

O'Riordan, T. (1973) Some reflections on environmental attitudes and environmental behavior. *Area, 5*, 17-21.

Pervin, L. A. (1978). Definitions, measurements, and classifications of stimuli, situations, and environments. *Human Ecology, 6*, 71-105.

Powers, W. T. (1973). Feedback: Beyond behaviorism. *Science, 179*, 351-356.

Proshansky, H. M., & O'Hanlon, T. (1977). Environmental psychology: Origins and development. In D. Stokols (Ed.), *Perspectives on environment and behavior* (pp. 101-129). New York: Plenum.

Relph, E. (1976). *Place and placelessness*. London: Pion.

Saarinen, T., & Sell, J. (1980). Environmental perception. *Progress in Human Geography, 4*, 525-547.

Seamon, D. (1987). Phenomenology and environment-behavior research. In E. H. Zube & G. T. Moore (Eds.), *Advances in environment, behavior, and design* (Vol. 1, pp. 3-27). New York: Plenum.

Simon, H. A. (1957). *Models of man*. New York: Wiley.

Skinner, B. F. (1974). *About behaviorism*. New York: Knopf.

Smith, T. R., Pellegrino, J. W., & Golledge, R. G. (1982). Computational process modelling of spatial cognition and behavior. *Geographical Analysis, 14*, 305-325.

Smith, T. R., & Mertz, F. (1980). An analysis of the effects of information revision on the outcome of housing-market search. *Environment and Planning A, 12*, 155-174.

Stokols, D., & Altman, I. (1987). *Handbook of environmental psychology* (Vols. 1-2). New York: Wiley.

Taylor, G. (Ed.). (1951). *Geography in the Twentieth Century*. New York: Philosophical Library.

Timmermans, H. J. P., & Golledge, R. G. (1990). Applications of behavioral research on spatial problems II: Preference and choice. *Progress in Human Geography, 14*, 311-354.

Walmsley, D. J., & Lewis, G. J. (1984). *Human geography: Behavioral approaches*. New York: Longman.

# PART I

# Basic Processes of Behavior-Environment Interaction

*Behavior and Environment: Psychological and Geographical Approaches*
*T. Gärling and R.G. Golledge (Editors)*


CHAPTER 2

# Geographical Perspectives on Spatial Cognition

**Reginald G. Golledge**

Geography has as one of its major emphases the discovery and explanation of spatial patterns of specific features, functions, phenomena and interactions in environments of many scales. These patterns generally are identified at scales well beyond the perceptual domain. They may consist of things such as the locational pattern of cities in a region, patterns of crop production at a regional or national level, or patterns of shopping centers within a particular city. Since many individuals have no need to know about these spatial patterns, they do not develop an awareness of them. Once described or explained, the patterns become obvious. But few of these patterns are readily recognized by most people. Thus, knowledge of many spatial properties of an environment may be considered beyond the realm of common sense understanding, requiring an expert knowledge structure based on explicit training. The focus of this chapter is to articulate some of the fundamental or primitive elements that are embedded in the physical and built environment, that should have counterparts in cognized space. Such an emphasis helps explain the geographer's perspective in environmental cognition generally and in spatial cognition in particular.

The first goal of this chapter is to articulate some of the fundamental or primitive elements of physical reality that have been identified by geographic research, and to suggest how they should evidence themselves in the cognitive domain. A second goal is to articulate some specific properties of spatial knowledge from a geographical perspective, to advance hypotheses about the way these properties manifest themselves in the *content* of cognized space, and to provide evidence wherever possible of the explicit and implicit involvement of geographers in identifying the nature and content of spatial cognition. A third goal is to examine how geographers have used spatial cognition in dealing with real world problems.

## *Geographical Perspectives on Components of Spatial Knowledge*

In the language of the geographer, the most comprehensive spatial knowledge system should contain the following properties:

1) Individual "occurrences" of different types of spatial phenomena
2) Spatial distributions of occurrence classes of phenomena
3) Spatial processes that account for the development and patterns of spatial phenomena
4) Spatial contiguity and spatial association
5) Linkage and connectivity
6) Geographic regions
7) Spatial stratification and hierarchies
8) Spatial structure

While I have discussed some of these elements in detail elsewhere (Golledge, 1992), I shall comment briefly on each of them to emphasize both a geographic perspective on spatial knowledge and to highlight the types of questions raised by geographers in studying both natural and built environments.

## *Components of Spatial Knowledge*

***Occurrences of different types of phenomena.*** Occurrences are often referred to by terms such as "reference nodes", "landmarks" or "choice points." The geographer argues that each occurrence has a minimal number of elemental characteristics. The first of these is *identity*, which is a name or label that can be attached to an occurrence; it can be made *place specific* and *class specific*. A place-specific cue is identified by a unique place location (e.g., 7-11 store at corner of Magnolia Street and Hollister Avenue), while class specific cues are identified by a generic label (e.g., food store) (Table 2.1).

Each occurrence also has a *location* which is an elemental indicator of existence. In geographic space it is usually sufficient to provide a two-dimensional coordinate definition of location (called geo-referencing) although many less precise locational terms can be found in all natural languages (e.g., near, in front of, to the right of, far from). In cognitive space occurrences often require multidimensional coordinates to specify their existence (e.g., the location of a candy bar in a space with dimensions of nuttiness, chewiness, and sweetness). While on the surface it would seem that the multidimensional spatial definition of an occurrence should be more accurate and precise, in fact both the identification of the dimensions of such spaces and the discovery of relevant measurement systems to specify position along those dimensions makes specification of location more imprecise. Even when some of the dimensions of such multidimensional spaces are equated with dimensions of the simpler two-dimensional geographic space (e.g., north/south and east/west), there are often mismatches between the specified location in physical reality and location in a cognitive space.

TABLE 2.1

*Labelling Environmental Cues*

| Cue | Class | Place Specific Locational Label |
|---|---|---|
| Vons Supermarket | Food Store | Vons at Turnpike Road<br>Vons at Fairview Center<br>Vons at La Cumbre Center |
| Fire Station | Emergency Services | Storke Road Fire Station<br>Carrillo Street Fire Station<br>Cave Road Sheriff's Office |
| Elementary School | Education Facility | El Rancho Elementary School<br>Hollister Elementary School<br>La Patera Elementary School |

A third characteristic of a set of occurrences is a *magnitude* measure. In geographic space the magnitude of an occurrence is often measured by a simple frequency count, or its equivalent in a size or volume measurement system. Measuring magnitude in a cognitive space depends on individual subjective assessment (Holyoak & Mah, 1982). In both kinds of space the question of categorization and threshold is raised, e.g., how much of an attribute is needed before an occurrence is perceived to be a member of a common cue class defined by that attribute? How big must an urban place be before it is called a city? How distinct must a place be before it is defined as a "landmark"? And what measure defines degrees of "bigness" or degrees of distinctiveness?

Finally, each occurrence exists in *time* as well as space. Temporal existence can be identified in an absolute sense, relating to the actual or possible existence path of an occurrence, or it can be related to an arbitrary measurement system that allows expectancy to be set into a base of defined intervals of elements of the space itself (e.g., the temporal definition of longitude, or degrees of east or west measured in clock time). In geographic space we frequently assume that phenomena are fixed in space. In cognitive space, one seeks to find what features are permanent, for these anchor cognitive representations. Permanence can be measured by recall frequency and accuracy. Elsewhere I have suggested that occurrences with unambiguous identities, well specified locations, reliable and acceptable measures of magnitude, and permanence in the temporal domain, appear to have the greatest capacity for anchoring spatial knowledge structures (Golledge, 1992).

Occurrences in both geographic and cognitive space often have salience or weights added to them that reflect the functional importance of specific attributes. For example, what objectively otherwise appears to be "just another house" may be a President's birthplace. As such it accrues distinction and importance that would otherwise be absent, but requires an additional dimension to record this attribute.

***Spatial distributions.*** The above discussion treats occurrences as individual elements (e.g., single landmarks). A higher level of organization, both in physical and cognitive space, is a spatial distribution. A spatial distribution is a set of occurrences with common identity, magnitude, temporal or functional characteristics that are grouped to expose their pattern or arrangement. For example, 7-11 convenience stores in a city represent a spatial distribution even though they are usually widely scattered. Other examples of spatial distributions might include fire stations, schools, post offices, banks, and parks.

Properties of spatial distributions include density (or the ratio of the number of occurrences in the distribution to the area of the host space); arrangement (or the pattern or shape of the internal structure of the distribution); and spatial variance (the degree of spatial concentration, clustering, or dispersion of the distribution set). For the geographer, the property of density helps differentiate many features in a landscape. Housing density varies from crowded inner-city multi-family, multi-story dwellings, to single-story row houses, to single-family dwellings on small lots, to larger detached houses with spacious yards in suburbia. Patterns of schools closely reflect changes in residential densities; schools need to be more widely spaced in suburbia to capture threshold populations. Regional shopping centers often are regularly spaced around the edges of cities. Wedges and sectors of industry or commerce radiate out from city centers along major arterial roads and highways. And some features are clustered such as gas stations on corners, or fast food places near schools, while others are scattered such as parks in cities. Thus, occurrences and the distributions they form are spatial facts and should be identifiable in both geographic and cognitive space. Whether examining objective or cognitive information, defining the nature of the distributions present in the environment is a research question of considerable importance. Research has not as yet been forthcoming that defines whether people in general are aware of or store in memory such distributions.

***Spatial processes.*** Processes are responsible for chaining occurrences and their distributions into events, activities, and behaviors. Spatial processes are procedures or mechanisms for inducing changes in a system. They do not act simultaneously and in the same way at every location in a spatial system. For example, erosion by a stream varies with local gradient, channel configuration and soil type; migration is not uniform between all pairs of cities; and despite today's technology, information is not always available at different places at the same time. Specific processes include spatial interaction, spatial diffusion, migration, spread and growth, and spatial decision making, choice, and attitude towards risk. Examples of how these are modeled abound in the geographic literature (e.g., Clark, 1982; Golledge & Timmermans, 1988; Gould, 1975). Figure 2.1a illustrates how a spatial diffusion process might manifest itself in a data set, if diffusion occurred by a simple nearest neighbor contagious process. Figure 2.1b shows sets of curves that could describe how spatial processes are reflected in the distributions of distances between phenomena such as the birthplace of marriage partners (Pareto curve), the distances of residential moves in a city, or the spread of a rumor.

Perhaps the most widely used summary concept in geography is the spatial interaction model. This is based on a social equivalent of gravitational attraction theory and simply suggests that interaction between two places $(i,j)$ is a direct function of their attractive masses (e.g., populations $P_i$, $P_j$) and an indirect function of the friction between them (usually interpreted as an exponential of their distance apart). Hence, interaction ($I_{ij}$) is defined as:

$$I_{ij} = \frac{f(P_i \times P_j)}{D_{ij}^{n}} \qquad (1)$$

a)

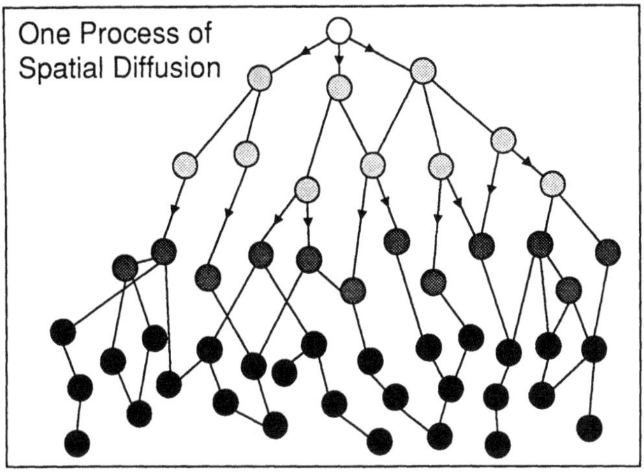


b)

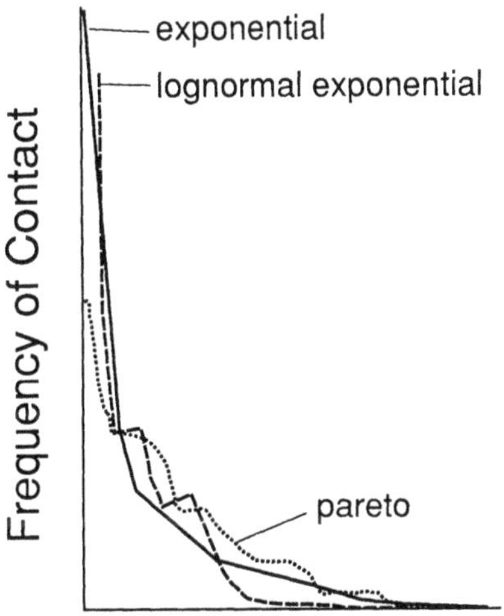


FIGURE 2.1. Types of spatial processes: a) spatial diffusion; b) distance decay.

Such a model can account for the magnitude of telephone calls between urban centers, the number of students attending a university from both home and nearby states or counties, the number of customers in an area patronizing a grocery store, or the flow of money between Federal Reserve and full service banks. Such models summarize the probability that a person living in one area has visited another and has thus been exposed to landmarks or features of the other place. Knowing such processes are at work in the environment provides insights into the types of behaviors expected or observed in different environments. Questions remain, however, as to what unique processes produce these observable behaviors and how they can be isolated and tested.

***Spatial contiguity and spatial association.*** A fundamental spatial concept is spatial separation; the elemental term used to describe this is *distance*. Whereas distance in geographic space is usually well specified in terms of one or another of the standard geometries (usually Euclidean), there is still considerable speculation as to whether or not any one particular distance metric should be used in cognitive spaces (Baird, Wagner & Noma, 1982; Golledge & Hubert, 1982; Montello, 1991).

Distance is the bond that links places together or separates them in both cognitive and geographic space. When an anchor point or line or area is identified, we look at what is nearby. Geographic law suggests that things close to each other will be more alike than those farther apart and that there will be regularity to this decay of similarity over distance that can usually be expressed by a Pareto curve or simple negative exponential function. So we look for linked occurrences, "nearest neighbors", or things "in the neighborhood." In geographic space we can identify $n^{th}$ order nearest neighbors; but in cognitive spaces can we even identify one nearest neighbor? When we rank order environmental features according to paired proximity, for example, we are in fact performing a distance ordering function of the nearest neighbor type. Most people can perform proximity rankings satisfactorily. However, when an estimate of distance is required from one place to all others, performance deteriorates. Perhaps it is the geometric implication that intrudes to diminish performance capacity. But certainly when qualitative distance is used to estimate first nearest neighbors, competent performance can be expected. What is it then about distance that makes it so fundamentally comprehensible in geographic space but so much more difficult in cognitive space? Both geographers and psychologist must explore this question further.

Another spatial concept related to separation is that of *contiguity*. Terms freely used to describe this concept in cognitive space include proximity, spatial similarity or dissimilarity, and spatial clustering; similar expressions in geography include nearest neighbor, spatial variation, and spatial heterogeneity. The notion of contiguity is clearly expressed by looking at measures of association between spatially lagged variables.

Table 2.2, for example, shows that as distance intervals (spatial lags) increase between phenomena represented in cells of a 9x9 matrix, their degree of similarity diminishes. This phenomenon is common to many features in geographic space, and search for explanations of this characteristic remains an important area of geographic investigation.

TABLE 2.2

*Correlations Between Spatially Lagged (Order Neighbor) Variables*

| Spatial lag between cell values in a 9 x 9 matrix | Correlation |
|---|---|
| 0 | .542 |
| 1 | .415 |
| 2 | .343 |
| 3 | .278 |
| 4 | .121 |
| 5 | .024 |
| 6 | .042 |
| 7 | -.015 |

Adapted from Costanzo, 1985. Reprinted by permission.

A concept central to the geographic measure of contiguity, is called spatial autocorrelation (Cliff and Ord, 1981). For any spatially located data, one can expect that there is a set of values ($x_i$) that are likely to be related in some way over space. Tobler (1970, p. 236) has defined the first law of geography as follows: Everything is related to everything else, but near things are more related than distant things. It is also implied, based on numerous empirical studies of distance decay effects in spatially distributed phenomena, that degree of relatedness or similarity will decrease exponentially with increasing distance. Given this first law, then if our set of data ($x_i$) displays interdependence over space, we say that the data are spatially autocorrelated. Figure 2.2 shows how a set of data represented in matrix form could be spatially arranged if maximum or minimal spatial autocorrelation existed. Costanzo (1985) used these data to show how conventional correlation measures ignored spatial association or confounded it with point-to-point measures of association. He further argued that people were not good at estimating spatial association, even though they can reasonably evaluate conventional correlation.

Cliff and Ord (1981) give one measure of spatial autocorrelation as:

$$X_i = P \sum_j W_{ij} X_j + \epsilon_i \tag{2}$$

where $\epsilon_i$ are independent and identically distributed variants with common variance $\sigma^2$, $W_{ij}$ are a set of weights specifying which $j$ subareas have variant values directly spatially related to $W_i$, P is a measure of overall level of spatial autocorrelation among the $\{x_i x_j\}$ pairs for $w_{ij} > 0$.

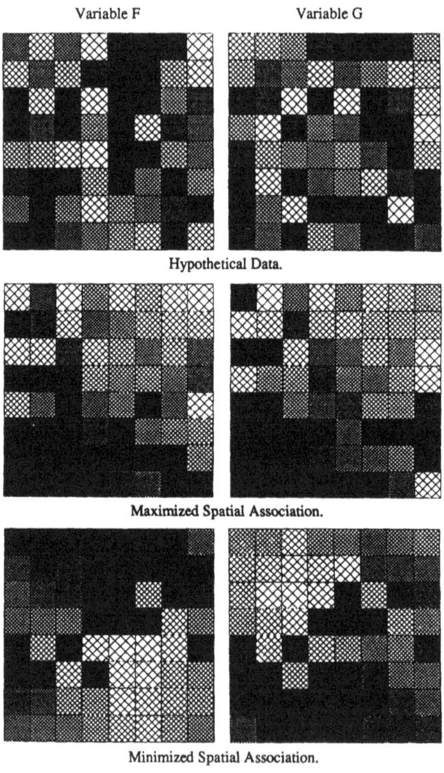


FIGURE 2.2. Rearranging of spatial patterns to show maximal and minimal spatial association. Compiled from Costanzo, 1985.

The weights used in a measure of the overall level of spatial autocorrelation amongst $(X_i\ X_j)$ pairs can have a value of 1 if $j$ is physically contiguous to *i* (or cognized as being adjacent to *i*) and 0 otherwise. Thus, Tobler's first law of geography can be expressed as:

$$W_{ij} = (c + d_{ij})^{-\alpha}$$

where $d_{ij}$ is the actual or cognized distance between points or areas *i* and *j*, $\alpha$ is a friction of distance parameter similar to that used in many spatial interaction models, or reflecting the relation between subjective and objective distance, and c is a constant greater than 0.

Another autocorrelation feature of spatial data modelled by the exponential form $y = ax^{-b}$ is called distance decay; here y is some index of frequency of occurrence at some fixed location, and x is the distance from that location. The distance decay function has been found important in the examination of spatial choices and spatial interactions. In the cognitive domain it underlies the notion that recognition capabilities are greater near anchors or reference nodes and diminish exponentially with increasing distance from such nodes. This in turn implies increased error with distance such that in, say, a route learning context, recognition errors for specific locations along a learned route should increase with distance from the origin, destination, or from important choice points. Thus, most errors will be found in the interior of routes. (Golledge et al., 1985). Distance decay is a central part of the long established gravity model (Cadwallader, 1979; Huff, 1960; Zipf, 1946) discussed earlier.

***Linkage and connectivity.*** *Connectivity* is a measure of the linkage pattern among discrete locations or line segments. Degrees of connectivity range from complete to null and are often measured and modelled by geographers using graph theoretic concepts (e.g., Kansky, 1967; Ore, 1963; Taaffe & Gauthier, 1973). Measures include those of centrality in a graph or network, circuity of a system, cyclomatic number, network diameter, and degree of connectivity. Other features of linked systems include link concatenation, spatial sequence, and spatial order. Partial connectivities are evident both in geographic space (e.g., most transportation systems), as well as in cognitive space (e.g., incomplete route representations).

Linkages occur amongst specific functions in cities or within single buildings (e.g., handbag stores near shoe stores; restaurants and bars near business offices; medical, dental and pharmaceutical activities near a hospital). While spatial linkage is a commonly recognized feature of geographic space, it is rarely examined in the domain of cognitive space.

***Regions.*** Usually defined as an area or segment of space in which the elements contained therein are more closely allied or identified with each other than they are with elements outside the designated area, a region manifests itself in both geographic reality and in cognitive representations. For example, Couclelis, Golledge, Gale, and Tobler (1987) illustrated how anchor-points can dominate regions of space, influencing location, distance, and orientation errors of other cues. They showed how minor order nodes are distorted in the same direction as the anchor point, imparting a sectoral stretching and distortion to the spatial knowledge structure.

The search for regions, both uniform and nodal, has been an important part of geography since its earliest inception. There are a complex set of models used to both define and analyze regionalization procedures (Anselin, 1988). In psychological space, various regional definitions have been determined using methods such as discriminant analysis, factor analysis, multidimensional scaling, and cluster analysis (Golledge, 1977a; Golledge and Rushton, 1972; Hartigan, 1976; Kruskal & Wish, 1978). For the geographer, the determination of regions has often been a major end point of research (Clark & Hosking, 1989; Hart, 1981; Hartshorn, 1954; King, 1969). A region, once defined, encompasses many of the spatial primitives already discussed, and it provides a spatial classification that allows one to begin interpretation and analysis of spatial phenomena contained within it and differentiated between regions. But, although regions are important concepts in both geographic and cognitive space, their occurrence, meaning, and role as organizing criteria remain largely unknown in the cognitive domain.

***Spatial stratification and hierarchies.*** *Hierarchical* concepts are firmly embedded in both natural and technical languages. A simple example in geographic space might be as follows: metropolitan areas are bigger than cities, which are bigger than towns, villages, and hamlets, in that order (King & Golledge, 1978). Semantic lists are often recalled by defining a set of anchors, and clustering nearby or related words around such anchors, geographic information (e.g., place names) is often grouped into hierarchically ordered areas such as nations, states, counties etc.

*Stratification* concepts abound in our attempts to make sense of natural, built, and cognitive environments. Such concepts are important in theories of environmental cognition (e.g., Golledge's hierarchically-based anchor point theory, 1977a, 1987) and in general discussions of the nature of environmental cognition (e.g., Hirtle & Jonides, 1985; Stevens & Coupe, 1978). While noticeably missing from early conceptualizations of spatial knowledge (including developmental theories), this organizing concept is so fundamentally a part of objective environments and the languages built to describe such environments that it cannot be ignored.

***Spatial structure.*** For the geographer *spatial structure* is most often identified on a map. By mapping macroscale phenomena one is able to observe at a glance things such as locations, distributions, densities, dispersions, patterns, connections, and hierarchies. Awareness of these characteristics often influences decision making and choice behavior and helps define sets of feasible alternatives in many episodic decision making situations. For example, knowing a set of feasible locations in the vicinity of a home base is necessary when choosing a place at which to shop.

Spatial structure, as perceived by the trained geographer, is an expert form of configurational or survey level knowledge. It includes more than just the basic (declarative) components; it also contains difficult to perceive associations and relations that have to be inferred or deduced from knowledge of the characteristics of space and the links between individual elements. It is not obvious that the ability to make such inferences and associations is widespread, and it is not certain as to the complete range of errors likely to exist in the generation or interpretation of cognized configurations.

A knowledge base contains within it the rules for attaching meaning to an experience. These rules are generally embedded in a language and contain rationalizations for recognizing, categorizing, connecting, associating, rejecting, and remembering experiential data. Spatial knowledge, then, consists of information obtained by a process of experiencing elements of and in space to which meaning can be attached. Any individual's knowledge structure depends on the unique way the net of meaning filters experience and on what meanings are consequently attached to information that passes through sensory filters for storage in memory. This, in turn, is influenced by the ability of an individual to recognize properties of phenomena (including spatial properties), and the ability to recognize, articulate, and use those properties. With this in mind, I turn now to a discussion of geographic research that has spanned both geographic and cognitive domains.

## Psychological Perspectives on the Components of Spatial Knowledge in Geography

Spatial knowledge consists of some combination of points, lines, areas, and surfaces. Individually and in combination these appear to be capable of recognition and have become accepted parts of declarative knowledge systems. Together they comprise what Kuipers (1978) called a "common sense" spatial knowledge structure. However, in both the natural environment and the transformed, or built, environment, understanding comes not only from knowing what is where, but also how different things fit together. As I pointed out in the previous section. this includes higher level concepts such as hierarchy, surface, association, connectivity, pattern, and so on. For example, with the exception of Gärling, Böök, Lindberg, and Arce (1990), psychologists have neglected height or relief in their examination of spatial phenomena. In contrast, the geographer commonly represents spatial interactions, movements, or even the basic distribution or pattern of phenomena as surfaces. These are sometimes represented in two dimensional form (e.g., contour lines representing physical relief) and sometimes represented as three dimensional surfaces (e.g., spatial distribution of population densities or a surface representing flows through space and time). As more attention in the geographical world is focused on presenting spatial data as a Geographical Information System (GIS), the tendency to use three dimensional graphs and surfaces to represent such data is increasing. In addition, the nested hierarchical structures of functional arrangement over space has produced powerful geographic theory (e.g., central place theory) which is visually represented as an overlapping two dimensional nested hierarchy. Given this enriched way of looking at environments and the data contained in them, one can postulate that geography is a spatial science and the geographer is an expert with a specific set of techniques and representational devices to unpack information contained in the spatial domain. The gap between the expert knowledge structure and the common sense understanding of environment and its more restricted and impoverished knowledge structure then becomes obvious.

It is only in the last few decades that geographers have become aware of their special skills and knowledge systems for understanding space in domains other than objective physical reality. As this awareness has grown, however, it has become more and more obvious that spatial knowledge is much more than the sensing or description of landmarks, routes and areas in an internal representation of environment. In this section, therefore, I examine some of the geographic research in the area of spatial cognition and environmental knowing to illustrate this point.

Before proceeding, however, it is essential to point out what differentiates the geographer's work in this area from that of other researchers. The answer is simple. The difference lies in the type of questions the geographer asks. To illustrate, consider the following sets of questions that are typical of geographic inquiry: Where is it? What else exists at that particular place? Why is it there? Can it be found elsewhere? Why is it found there? How much occurs at that location? How far does the phenomena extend over space? What relations are there to nearby phenomena? What is the nature of its distribution? What spatial process accounts for its distribution? Where is it in relation to others of the same kind? What are the identifying characteristics of its distribution? Does it occur in the same type of places throughout the world? Where are the distribution boundaries? What other features are spatially associated with it? Do these features usually occur together in space? Is it linked or connected to other things? Have the occurrences always been located where they are now? How has it changed spatially and through time? How can we account for its spread? And how can this knowledge be used? As I proceed in the next section, it should also become obvious that the geographer's questions are often dissimilar to those asked by psychologists.

### *Cognitive Maps*

Perhaps the most attention in past decades has been focused on the idea first of mental maps and later cognitive maps. The term mental map defined a mapped preference surface (Gould, 1973). To compile these surfaces, subjects were asked to rank order areal units such as states, cities, countries, in order of preference according to some criteria such as desirability for living. The ranked orderings were then cartographically summarized using isolines of equal attractivity. The resulting contour map highlighted regions of great desirability and showed gradients from these to the troughs or pits of lower desirability. While these were interesting visual summaries of people's preferences, usually constructed such that they covered very large areas such as countries, they proved to be of little use as explanatory or predictive devices.

Extending beyond this initial idea of mental map, geographers then adopted the notion of a cognitive map or cognitive configuration as an external representation of environmental information retrieved from memory. This information was collected either directly via techniques such as sketch mapping or verbal descriptions of places, or more indirectly by attempting to recover the latent spatial structure contained in long-term memory via an indirect judgment process used in conjunction with non-metric multidimensional scaling (Golledge & Rushton, 1972).

Much of the geographer's interest at this time was in explaining patterns of human spatial behavior. The cognitive map was assumed to be an internalized Geographic Information System (GIS) in which different strata or levels of information could be compressed, combined, manipulated, and interpreted. Thus, when asked to make judgments about proximities of individually stored landmarks that may not have previously been considered together as a holistic system (e.g., public buildings, monuments, recreational areas, grocery stores, freeway segments etc.) each individual would first invoke a function that would focus on location, and then estimate proximity in terms of, say, a scale value. It was these scale values that were manipulated via external measurement techniques to produce latent spatial structures or configurations of environmental cues. The same process guided development of distributions of phenomena. It was assumed that once recovered, these external representations would give insights into how people behaved - for they were the best representation of the information available regarding what spatial data was stored in memory. It was considered essential to determine this because volumes of geographic research had shown a lack of coincidence between overt spatial behavior and measurements made on hypothesized explanatory variables in objective reality (e.g., Euclidean distance measures between places, time transforms of actual route distances separating places, and so on). This latter literature is far too large to attempt to review here, but overviews can be obtained from many introductory human geography textbooks.

The cognitive map as an internal geographic information system did become the analytical tool that the preference surface (mental map) had failed to become. Cadwallader (1979) pointed to the increased reliability of gravity models based on cognitive information rather than objective information for predicting human movement such as consumer behavior or migration. Smith (1983) used the cognitive map concept to anchor a selection of models aimed at understanding how residential site selection decisions were made. More recently, Phipps and Clark (1988) used concepts of cognitive mapping to build computer simulations of decision processes and the sets of behaviors involved in choosing new home sites. Timmermans, van der Heijden and Westerveld (1982) have similarly used cognitive mapping concepts in his studies of consumer spatial behavior. In other research, externalizations of cognitive maps have been used in both individual and group contexts to discover locational accuracy and to throw light on the type of distortion and fuzziness that one can expect when spatial information is stored in and recalled from long-term memory (Buttenfield, 1985; Gale, 1982; Richardson, 1982). This latter work surfaced only after a significant treatise by Tobler (1976) discussing the geometry of mental maps. He suggested that location errors and the spatial variance or fuzziness associated with remembering sets of locations could be recovered and mapped cartographically using error ellipses. Such ellipses provided indexes that could then be incorporated into explanatory models of human behavior. Case studies of the use of such measures to help explain movement patterns of populations such as mentally retarded can be found in Richardson (1982) and Golledge, Rayner and Parnicky (1980).

### *Landmarks and Reference Nodes*

Perhaps the single greatest influence on geographic research on spatial cognition was Lynch's (1960) book, The Image of the City. Lynch argued that built environments (such as a city) could be decomposed into sets of two dimensional components - landmarks, nodes, paths, boundaries, and districts. Higher order geometric properties were ignored in favor of these basic components. The easiest of these components to work with were landmarks and routes. They had a well defined existence in objective space and could be designated at specific places in the environment. People could be examined with regard to their knowledge of landmarks - theoretically, the most dominant and most widely known features in an environment. Similarly, people could readily identify routes that linked locations or segments of environments, and their physical existence could similarly be pinpointed. Lynch suggested, then, that this is how complex environments were encoded and stored in long-term memory. The individual bits and pieces that were known and identifiable were stored in long-term memory and acted as a frame for organizing sensed environmental information. Thus, when people were asked to sketch what they knew of a place, they would invariably use the point/line/area conventions of standard graphic, geometric, and cartographic representation to illustrate their knowledge base. Of course, such sketches would not represent their total knowledge structures, which may include non-spatial information (e.g., feelings of habitability or danger). Despite problems that arise if one attempts to re-assemble such decomposed images (Gale, Golledge, Pellegrino, & Doherty, 1990a), this remarkable conceptualization stimulated research in many disciplines as well as geography.

For the geographer, the simplest geometric feature was the point. Each point was an occurrence with identity, location, magnitude, and time dimensions. Information on all of these could be collected and represented visually in cartographic form. Comparisons could easily be made between estimated or reproduced and actual locations, between subjective and objective and interpoint distances, and between other subjective and objective relations. Since location was perhaps the most important single concept for the geographer, and the landmark lent itself readily to locational analysis, much geographic research concentrated on these types of occurrences. Much of the research on cognitive maps, for example, involved recovering locational patterns of well known places in different environments, then comparing the recovered pattern to existing patterns (Golledge, 1977b; Buttenfield, 1985). While the psychologist or the planner/designer focused on characteristics that made a landmark easily perceivable, the geographer focused on locational accuracy. Landmarks still provide the easiest spatial form (i.e., point patterns) to work with and still dominate much of the geographically relevant cognitive mapping research.

Besides their imagibility, however, landmark definition was seen as a critical stage in the evolution of spatial knowledge. Hart and Moore (1973) discussed the evolution of spatial knowledge from egocentric to allocentric frames of reference, from topological to fully metric geometric understanding, and from landmark to route and survey types of knowledge. The latter transition was later popularized in psychology by Siegel and White (1975). Golledge (1978) postulated an anchor point theory of spatial knowledge acquisition in which landmarks acted as critical organizing nodes, dominating other environmental information in their vicinity. This theory was hierarchically organized with a critical set of landmarks acting as primary nodes or anchors and dominating segments of space (nodal regions) in which successively lower ordered sets of nodes, routes, and areas could be identified. As one went further down the hierarchy, characteristics such as locational precision, unambiguous identity, magnitude measures, or even temporal awareness, diminished. Landmarks or anchor points acted as reference nodes for spatial organization and for integrating discrete bits of information into distributions and patterns capable of being imaged, externally represented, and analyzed.

### *Routes and Paths*

Linear elements, and the sequences and orders that are associated with linear organizations, are the next most convenient orderings of spatial information. Most overt spatial behavior in humans is directed or purposive. Movement does not take place at random but usually consists of traversing a path between known origins and destinations. The bulk of such traverses take place over paths already laid down in the environment. For the geographer the interesting questions have included: Which paths are known? Which paths are chosen? Why choose them? What criteria underlies choice of paths? What patterns of movement develop in a given network? To answer such questions, objective data could be collected simply by monitoring path segments and counting the number of users, or at the individual level, having people reconstruct the paths they used in some type of commerce with the environment (e.g., journey to work, journey to school, journey to shop, journey to recreate). Paths such as street systems form an extremely complicated network in which there are numerous alternative segment combinations that could be selected. Obvious questions arise, therefore, as to why some path segments become more frequently chosen than others.

Frequency of use of path segments is readily recorded in travel flow diagrams or by simple mathematical models. The literature in geography and many other disciplines (e.g., transportation, logistics, operations research) is replete with models *designed to choose a route through a complex network according to a pre-specified criteria and a set of pre-specified constraints*. Such path selection algorithms are most often applied in objective reality and rarely have they been used in the cognitive domain. But at the same time, rarely have the decision criteria and constraints used by geographers and other transportation researchers been examined via controlled experiments to see if people are either aware of such criteria, or if they ever deliberately use them. Again, this is a fruitful area of research for both disciplines.

It is commonly accepted that the bulk of our knowledge about any given environment comes from travelling through it. Just as obviously, the segments of the environment to which we are exposed by such travel are necessarily limited. It is but a short step to make the inference that cognitive representations of environments must, therefore, be incomplete as well as being schematized and abstract. But what principles are used to select particular routes? What influences the selection of different types of routes or segment sequences? Here again the geographer's initial answer is to say that route selection is conditioned by the physical location and availability of links between selected end points. There are only a limited number of work places, shopping centers, recreational areas, industrial areas, and so on. Each of these places act as magnets attracting many workers or users. If one is motivated by hunger, there are only a limited number of locations in the environment where food can be purchased. Given this set of *feasible alternatives*, one should be able to use simple principles such as least effort, minimizing time or distance, or minimizing route complexity, to predict which route will most likely be chosen by any randomly located individual. Such criteria are built into standard network solution algorithms often derived from linear programming techniques. However, when using these algorithms, one has to make the assumption that people act according to such criteria. Very little is known about this, although psychologist Gärling and his co-workers have shown that people are not necessarily shortest path travellers (Gärling, Säisä, Böök, & Lindberg, 1986). Geographers and transportation scientists in general have not tested these hypotheses, preferring to make associational inferences based on the proportion of people travelling from an origin to a destination that *could be allocated* to a specified route.

Since the bulk of geographic interest in routes and paths is large-scale and limited to measuring and explaining quantities of flows over such paths and routes, they have paid much less attention to understanding how path selection occurs. This is the area of human wayfinding, a topic which has seen more work in psychology than in geography. Human wayfinding involves experimenting with and learning routes selected for different reasons. Learning a route also requires processes of sequence recognition and order, recognition of what occurs on and off the routes being experienced, understanding the number of segments in each route and recognizing the turn angles between such segments. Investigation of these latter concepts moves one into the laboratory to work with shorter lengths or more artificial paths than is normally the case for geographers. Consequently, little geographic effort has been expended in this area. Exceptions include research by Briggs (1972, 1973, 1976), Gale (1985), Gale, Golledge, Halperin, and Couclelis, (1990b) Golledge and Zannaras (1973), and Golledge, Gale, Pellegrino, & Doherty, (1992). In these latter works combinations of passive laboratory and active field experiments have been undertaken with subjects using both familiar and unfamiliar environments to determine how quickly routes of different complexity are learned. Information absorbed during the learning process, including choice point and landmark location and sequencing, and the ability to comprehend the distance and direction of points on a route from each other, have been examined. Some work has also been undertaken on the human use of procedures such as triangulation and trilateration in estimating locations of points and their distances from other points. However, the bulk of geographic research on routes and paths focuses on flows and emphasizes quantity, episodic interval and temporal variability, directionality, and purpose, more than attempting to understand the perceptual and motor processes related to human movement over such paths.

One area where geographers have focused on process is in the building of Computational Process Models (CPMs) of movement behavior. Smith, Pellegrino, & Golledge (1982), for example, designed a CPM that simulated the wayfinding behavior of pre-teenage children in unfamiliar environments. In this model, the physical environment was defined by one module, while the decision process required for travelling through the environment was included in another module. Decisions were formalized as productions, and a traveller learned a path by exploring the physical environment. This CPM was later operationalized as NAVIGATOR by Gopal (1989). Similar CPMs have been built by Leiser (1988) and Leiser and Zilberschatz (1989).

### *Areas and Regions*

Perhaps the most pervasive concept in geography is that of region. This is defined as an area with some internal cohesion and sets of identifying characteristics. For much of this century, regional definition was perhaps the single most important characteristic of geography. Both qualitatively and quantitatively geographers searched for areas of the environment whose internal cohesion set them apart from other areas. Such regions include natural areas such as river basins, flood planes, mountainous zones, glaciated areas, deserts, and so on. Atlases are full of attempts to summarize the variety of features on the surface of the earth in a regional context. Soil regions, climatic regions, vegetation regions, and land use regions, make up the bulk of information contained in many atlases. Many geographers regard their discipline as a science of regionalizing the earth and the human activities taking place on its surface. The region is, in one sense, geography's contribution to the processes of classification and categorization.

For many years the region was presumed to have a unique discrete *existence* (Hartshorn, 1959). Over time it has become recognized more as a method of spatially classifying phenomena. The concept of regionalism permeates much of the geographer's everyday language. In urban areas, communities, districts and neighborhoods represent the areal organizing principles (or regions) that reduce complexity to comprehension. In the environment at large, the definition of zones of feature occupancy helps us understand the range of activities that take place over the surface of the earth, helps define the reasons why such activities can be found at some places and not at others, and provides the fundamental material for theorizing about the pattern of human activities across the surface of the earth.

Perhaps the one thing that comes out of this rich research heritage is that areal classification is a difficult activity. Areas are separated by boundaries. Where exactly does a boundary lay? Must they be smooth or convoluted? Where exactly does a transition between differently defined use-areas take place? How much mixing or overlap is acceptable? How do we account for overlap objectively and subjectively? Even apparently simple questions like this convolute the process of regional definition. It is no surprise, therefore, that while the geographer has worked extensively in terms of regional definition in the environment at large, comparatively little has been done using this concept in the cognitive domain. This remains true despite the fact that one of the earliest areas of interest by geographers in environmental cognition was in terms of small area (neighborhood) perception (Downs, 1970; Zannaras, 1968). Aware of the measurement difficulties involved, geographers interested in the regional idea focused more on the affective rather than cognitive component. Emphasis was thus placed on defining emotional ties between landscapes and human occupancy, and in differentiating between environments on the basis of the feelings they aroused more than their physical or perceptual content. Much important literature has resulted from this interest, particularly the work of Amedeo (1990), Buttimer (1969, 1974), Lowenthal (1969, 1972), Tuan (1974, 1976), and Relph (1981). Interest in this area is humanistic and often phenomenological rather than analytical, objective and experimental. Nevertheless, it represents a significant part of geographic interest in subjective properties of environments. In particular, this approach has had significant input in attempts to assess or evaluate environmental quality (see Chapters 4 and 5 of this book). The outcome of this qualitative interest, however, is the specification of an ill-defined "sense of place" in which fuzzy feelings are identified with fuzzy areas, often in a loose manner, similar to the non-analytical descriptive regional approach found throughout the discipline. Questions that remain unanswered include what spatial processes underlie regional definition and how those processes are evidenced in the cognitive domain, for, despite our poor understanding of cognitive processes involved in regionalization, classification and summarization of spatial information by regions seems to be an important part of the spatial knowledge acquisition process.

### *Spatial Hierarchies*

Both implicitly and explicitly, geographers have organized environmental information into hierarchies. In the physical environment streams are differentiated and graphically represented depending on whether they are the mainstream or trunk, or one of a variety of tributaries ranging from subsidiary rivers through creeks and intermittent feeders. Size hierarchies are used to differentiate the vertical domain of the environment, with mountains being larger than hills, which may be larger than foothills, hummocks and other lower relief. Bodies of water are organized into oceans, lakes, and various types of dams and ponds. In each of these cases hierarchical classifications are used, but sub-hierarchies are not nested within higher ones; in other words, lakes are not found *within* oceans, and ponds are not found *within* lakes. In the human domain, however, nested hierarchies are common. Administratively, an entire country may be a republic or a federation, within which are located states or provinces, and within these may be found counties, cities, or other smaller local government areas. In this case, lower orders are nested or completely contained within higher orders. Non-nested hierarchies, however, may also be found, such as different levels of education (university, college, high school), although at some levels nesting might occur (e.g., within a local school district) which implies a mixed hierarchical order.

Some of geography's most powerful theories involve nested hierarchies. Central place theory (Christaller, 1966) for example, outlines what a complex settlement system would look like in terms of the number of places of different size and their distances apart, their functional complexity, and the range of service provided by each place, as it would exist on an isotropic plain with uniform population distribution and characteristics, and uniform propensities to produce and consume. The same theory applies within cities in terms of commercial hierarchies, or other structures such as branch offices, branch banks, and so on.

The notion of spatial hierarchy is essential to the comprehension of complex environmental systems. It is an topic that has only recently attracted attention in the cognitive domain, with most of the attention coming from psychology rather than geography (Hirtle & Jonides, 1985; McNamara, Hardy, & Hirtle, 1989; Stevens & Coupe, 1978). The geographer's interest in cognitive hierarchy has been limited. The essence of hierarchy has been incorporated into Golledge's anchor point theory and some empirical testing of whether hierarchies exists in spatial knowledge structures has been undertaken by Couclelis et al. (1987), Golledge (1992), and Spector (1978). This has been sufficient to raise questions as to whether people in general are aware of hierarchies embedded in spatial distributions or whether recognition and understanding of such hierarchies is latent, or is beyond the common sense level of spatial understanding and is made clear only at the expert level. This topic is of considerable relevance to geographic understanding, and it demands much further research attention.

### *Spatial Association and Relations*

Just as in the case of regional understanding, this is an area of spatial knowledge in which geographers have consistently been at the forefront. By the early 1970s geographers had accepted the premise that conventional measures of association (such as correlation coefficients) had restricted meaning in the spatial context. Later, Costanzo (1985) and Hubert, Golledge, Costanzo & Gale (1985) showed that two sets of variables, shown to be highly related by conventional product-moment correlational measures, could be reconfigured spatially to reflect either high positive or negative spatial association, or in fact zero spatial association. In other words, they showed that conventional correlational measures were *aspatial* and do not properly serve to measure relationships between data that have well defined spatial existences.

Many geographers have attempted to develop measures of geographic association that provide an index of how closely things occur in space. McCarthy Hook, and Knos (1956) provided simple measures of geographic association that allowed them to evaluate economics-based location theories which hypothesized a spatial tie between the locational pattern of manufacturing and the resource or market base with which firms were associated. Other indicators of spatial association were developed by Bachi (1963), Geary (1963), and Moran (1948). Perhaps the most powerful indicator of spatial association, however, is the spatial autocorrelation measure discussed in an earlier section (Cliff & Ord, 1973; 1981).

Despite the importance and significance of spatial association to geographic understanding generally, virtually no research has been undertaken concerning this concept in the area of spatial cognition, either by geographers or psychologists. Exceptions include seminal work by McCarty and Salisbury (1961) and Costanzo (1985). The former assessed human ability to interpret isopleth and choropleth maps and ability to make correlational map comparisons, while the latter carefully controlled a variety of map measures and degree of correlation of phenomena before having people evaluate their similarities.

An essential part of the process of defining associations between spatially distributed phenomena is the ability to recognize the patterns or configurational arrangements of the sets of phenomena being compared. Again, comparatively little research has been undertaken by geographers or psychologists on this topic. My current research is devoted to this particular question. In this research, hypothetical environments are created with a limited number of variables present (convenience stores, elementary schools, parks, arterial roads, and administrative institutions). After being given sufficient time to thoroughly peruse a map, subjects are asked to reproduce the configuration of schools or convenient stores. This reproduction is requested with and without frame of reference and anchoring information. Other questions concerning proximal or nearest neighbor relations of each point to all other points are examined, and the ability of subjects to take each point in a distribution as a node and rank order the distances of other members of the distribution from that node is also examined. This survey of ability to comprehend a distribution and its peculiar spatial properties, is to my knowledge the first of this type. Considering the overwhelming significance to geographers of recognition of distributional and spatial pattern features, it is surprising that previous work on the degree of human understanding of these concepts has not been undertaken. Results of my research show that subjects do not perform these tasks well. This has some important ramifications for general theories of the structure of spatial knowledge. If this trend proves to be widespread, it would be a clear indication that common sense spatial knowledge does not include understanding of all of the primitive elements that geographers assume are important in building spatial knowledge. Without an understanding of the notion of a distribution, it may not be reasonable to expect that configurational comprehension develops in any but an expert mode. Which returns us to perhaps the most fundamental question of all: what exactly is a spatial knowledge structure and what are the sets of components and characteristics that could feasibly be expected to be incorporated into such a structure?

## Where Do We Go From Here?

One can see how quickly it is possible to move beyond the mere description of the geometrical properties of a geographical or psychological space to the use of spatial information in a constructive, analytical manner. Many real-world spatial patterns can be objectively identified and formally modelled. Such models can then provide predictive devices for estimating what should be in a person's cognitive representation at various stages of development or after varying periods of exposure to an environment if there is one-to-one mapping of environmental information into one's cognitive map (either immediately or eventually). Differentiating between a predicted knowledge structure and a knowledge structure externally represented in some form by a subject, gives an idea of how well the subject is aware of the organizing principles that lie behind the spatial knowledge structure. But how can we account for mismatches, errors, gaps, and distortions? It is to help answer these questions that the geographer needs to interface with the psychologist.

It is not at all obvious that most people are aware of many components of the spatial system in which they live. While decades of research on developmental theories of spatial learning and cognition provide strong evidence that the *ability* to comprehend spatial information in configurational or survey level terms exists, much evidence also appears to indicate that this knowledge is difficult to articulate and externally represent. This leads me to suggest a differentiation between common sense knowledge, and an expert level spatial knowledge. The common sense knowledge is primarily what is tapped when we examine sketch maps, proximity judgments, or slide or video recall and recognition procedures; what individuals *appear to know* about a place. More often than not, analysis of the externally represented information indicates numerous distortions and errors. But sometimes in follow-up discussions, it is obvious that the individual knows more than they are able to express.

One suggestion is that they have neither the training, nor the technical language to express the sets of spatial associations, relations, connections, hierarchies and regions that are contained within their knowledge structures. I would suggest that the science of geography has at its core the explicit aim of giving people such understandings. Geography provides an established technical language for discussing spatial concepts. It contains numerous models that define the properties of spatial distributions, spatial networks, spatial interaction patterns, and spatial hierarchies (Anselin, 1988; Clark & Hosking, 1986). Learning the language and unpacking the essence of the concepts (as well as providing many examples of their existence from the everyday environment) provides the tools for understanding the level of environmental knowledge that one develops through association and experience.

There is at this time little research that has tested thoroughly whether those exposed to geographic training have greater success in understanding spatial knowledge than those who have not so been exposed. One exception is Stern (1983), who provided evidence that geography students consistently performed better than non-geography students from the time of immediate exposure to a new environment to the time of substantial experience with it (4 or more years). His work compares abilities to estimate distances, locations, and some connections. While these are primitives of spatial knowledge, they are not the most important or pervasive. They are, in fact, components of the basic declarative knowledge structure, and are often stored without an overlaying set of procedural rules for connecting them. What apparently is needed is more intensive investigation of the nature of spatial knowledge, and much more comprehensive examination of the hypothesis tended in this chapter that two levels of such knowledge exist: common sense and expert. It is only after such testing has been thoroughly undertaken that one can fully examine the relationship between spatial information embedded in geographic and psychological spaces.

## References

Anselin, L. (1988). *Spatial econometrics: Methods and models*. Dordrecht: Martinus Nijhoff.

Bachi, R. (1963). Standard distance measures and related methods for spatial analysis. *The Regional Science Association Papers, 10*, 83-132.

Baird, J. (1979). Studies of the cognitive representation of spatial relations. *Journal of Experimental Psychology: General, 108*, 90-91.
Baird, J., Wagner, M., & Noma, E. (1982). Impossible cognitive spaces. *Geographical Analysis, 14*, 204-216.
Briggs, R. (1972). *Cognitive distance in urban space.* Unpublished doctoral dissertation, Ohio State University, Columbus.
Briggs, R. (1973). Urban cognitive distance. In R. Downs & D. Stea (Eds.), *Image and environment: Cognitive mapping and spatial behavior* (pp. 361-388). Chicago: Aldine.
Briggs, R. (1976). Methodologies for the measurement of cognitive distance. In G. Moore & R. Golledge (Eds.), *Environmental knowing* (pp. 325-334). Stroudsberg, PA: Dowden, Hutchinson & Ross.
Buttimer, A. (1969). Social space in interdisciplinary perspective. *Geographical Review, 59*, 417-426.
Buttimer, A. (1974). *Values in geography.* (Resource Paper 24). Association of American Geographers, Commission on College Geography.
Buttenfield, B. P. (1985). Treatment of the cartographic line. *Cartographica,* 22, 1-26.
Cadwallader, M. (1979). Problems in cognitive distance: Implications for cognitive mapping. *Environment and Behavior, 11*, 559-576.
Christaller, W. (1966). *Central places in Southern Germany* (C. Baskin, Trans.). Englewood Cliffs, NJ: Prentice-Hall.
Clark, W. A. V. (1982). Recent research on migration and mobility: A review and interpretation. *Progress in Planning, 18*, 1-56.
Clark, W. A. V., & Hosking, P. L. (1986). *Statistical methods for geographers.* New York: Wiley.
Cliff, A., & Ord, J. (1973). *Spatial autocorrelation.* London: Pion.
Cliff, A., & Ord, J. (1981). *Spatial processes: Models and applications* (2nd ed.). London: Pion.
Costanzo, C. M., Jr. (1985) *Spatial association and visual comparison of choropleth maps.* Unpublished doctoral dissertation, University of California, Santa Barbara.
Couclelis, H., Golledge, R. G., Gale, N., & Tobler, W. (1987). Exploring the anchor-point hypothesis of spatial cognition. *Journal of Environmental Psychology, 7*, 99-122.
Downs, R. (1970). Geographic space perception: Past approaches and future prospects. In C. Board, R. Chorley, P. Haggett, & D. Stoddart (Eds.), *Progress in Geography* (Vol. 2, pp. 65-108). London: Arnold.

Gale, N. (1982). Exploring location error in cognitive configurations of a city. In R. G. Golledge & W. R. Tobler (Eds.), *An examination of the spatial variation in the distortion and fuzziness of cognitive maps* (NSF Report No. #SES81-10253). Washington, D.C.

Gale, N. (1985). *Route learning by children in real and simulated environments.* Unpublished doctoral dissertation, University of California, Santa Barbara.

Gale, N., Golledge, R. G., Pellegrino, J. W., & Doherty, S. (1990a). The acquisition and integration of neighborhood route knowledge. *Journal of Environmental Psychology 10*, 3-26.

Gale, N., Golledge, R. G., Halperin, W., & Couclelis, H. (1990b). Exploring spatial familiarity. *The Professional Geographer, 42*, 299-313.

Gärling, T., Säisä, J., Böök, A. & Lindberg, E. (1986). The spatio-temporal sequencing of everyday activities in the large-scale environment. *Journal of Environmental Psychology, 6*, 261-280.

Gärling, T., Böök, A., Lindberg, E. & Arce, C. (1990). Is elevation encoded in cognitive maps? *Journal of Environmental Psychology 10*, 341-352.

Geary, D. C. (1963). Some remarks about relations between stochastic variables. *Revue de L'Institute Internationale de Statistique, 31*, 163-181.

Gibson, E., & Schmuckler, M. (1989). Going somewhere: An ecological and experimental approach to development of mobility. *Ecological Psychology, 1*, 23-26.

Golledge, R. G. (1977a). Multidimensional analysis in the study of environmental behavior and environmental design. In I. Altman & J. Wohlwill (Eds.), *Human behavior and environment* (pp. 1-42). New York: Plenum.

Golledge, R. G. (1977b). Environmental cues, cognitive mapping, and spatial behavior. In D. Burke et al. (Eds.), *Behavior-Environment Research Methods* (pp. 35-46). Institute for Environmental Studies, University of Wisconsin.

Golledge, R. G. (1978). Learning about urban environments. In T. Carlstein, D. Parkes, & N. Thrift, (Eds.), *Timing space and spacing time* (pp. 76-98). London: Arnold.

Golledge, R. G. (1992). Place recognition and wayfinding: making sense of space. *Geoforum, 23*, 199-214.

Golledge, R. G., & Hubert, L. (1982). Some comments on non-Euclidean mental maps. *Environment and Planning A, 14*, 107-118.

Golledge, R. G., & Rayner, J. (1972). Spectral analysis of settlement patterns in diverse physical and economic environments. *Environment and Planning, 4*, 347-371.

Golledge, R. G., & Rushton, G. (1972). *Multidimensional Scaling: Review and Geographic Applications.* Washington, D.C.: Association of American Geographers.

Golledge, R. G., & Timmermans, H. J. P. (Eds.). (1988). *Behavioural modelling in geography and planning.* London: Croom Helm.

Golledge, R. G., & Zannaras, G. (1973). Cognitive approaches to the analysis of human spatial behavior. In W. H. Ittelson (Ed.), *Environmental cognition* (pp. 59-94). New York: Seminar.

Golledge, R. G., Rayner, J. N., & Parnicky, J. J. (1983). Spatial competence of the borderline retarded. *Proceedings, Environmental Design Research Association*, Lincoln, NB, 188-197.

Golledge, R. G., Smith, T. R., Pellegrino, J. W., Doherty, S., & Marshall, S. P. (1985). A conceptual model and empirical analysis of children's acquisition of spatial knowledge. *Journal of Environmental Psychology, 5*, 125-152.

Golledge, R. G., Gale, N., Pellegrino, J. W., & Doherty, S. (1992). Spatial knowledge acquisition: Route learning and relational distan-ces. *Annals of the Association of American Geographers, 82*, 223-244.

Gopal, S., Klatzky, R. L., & Smith, T. R. (1989). Navigator: A psychologically based model of environmental learning through navigation. *Journal of Environmental Psychology, 9*, 309-331.

Gould, P. (1973). On mental maps. In R. Downs & D. Stea (Eds.), *Image and environment: Cognitive mapping and spatial behavior* (pp. 182-220). Chicago: Aldine.

Gould, P. (1975). *Spatial diffusion: The spread of ideas and innovations in geographic space.* New York: Learning Resources in International Studies.

Hart, R. A. (1981). Children's spatial representation of the landscape: Lessons and questions from a field study. In L. Liben, A. Patterson, & N. Newcombe (Eds.), *Spatial Representation and Behavior Across the Lifespan* (pp. 195-232). New York: Academic.

Hart, R. A., & Moore, G. T. (1973). The development of spatial cognition: A review. In R. Downs & D. Stea (Eds.), *Image and Environment* (pp. 246-288). Chicago: Aldine.

Hartigan, J. A. (1976, May). *Statistical problems in clustering.* Paper presented at the advanced seminar on classification and clustering, University of Wisconsin, Madison.

Hartshorn, R. (1959). *Perspectives on the nature of geography.* (AAG Monograph Series). Washington, D.C.: Association of American Geographers.

Hirtle, S. C., & Jonides, J. (1985). Evidence of hierarchies in cognitive maps. *Memory and Cognition, 13*, 208-217.

Holyoak, K., & Mah, W. (1982). Cognitive reference points and judgments of symbolic magnitude. *Cognitive Psychology, 14*, 328-352.

Hubert, L. J., Golledge, R. G., Costanzo, C. M. & Gale, N. (1985). Measuring association between spatially defined variables: An alternative procedure. *Geographical Analysis, 17*, 36-46.

Huff, D. (1960). A topographical model of consumer preferences. *Papers and Proceedings of the Regional Science Association, 6*, 159-173.

Kansky, K. (1967). Travel patterns of urban residents. *Transportation Science, 1*, 261-285.

King, L. (1969). *Statistical analysis in geography.* Englewood Cliffs, NJ: Prentice-Hall.

King, L., & Golledge, R. G. (1978). *Cities, space and behavior.* Englewood Cliffs, NJ: Prentice-Hall.

Kruskal, J., & Wish, M. (1978). *Multidimensional scaling.* Beverly Hills: Sage.

Kuipers, B. (1978). Modelling spatial knowledge. *Cognitive Science, 2*, 129-153.

Leiser, D. (1987). The changing relations between representations and cognitive structures in the development of a cognitive map. *New Ideas in Psychology, 5*, 95-110.

Leiser, D., & Zilberschatz, A. (1989). The TRAVELLER: A computational model of spatial network learning. *Environment and Behavior, 21*, 435-463.

Lynch, K. (1960). *The image of the city.* Cambridge, MA: MIT Press.

McCarthy, H., Hook, J., & Knos, D. (1956). *The measurement of association in industrial geography.* Unpublished manuscript. Department of Geography, University of Iowa.

McCarty, H. & Salisbury, N. (1961). *Visual comparison of isopleth maps as a means of determining correlations between spatially disturbed phenomena.* (Research Paper No. 3). Department of Geography, State University of Iowa.

McNamara, T., Hardy, J., & Hirtle, S. (1989). Subjective hierarchies in spatial memory. *Journal of Experimental Psychology: Learning, Memory and Cognition, 15*, 211-227.

Montello, D. R. (1991). The measurement of cognitive distance: Methods and construct validity. *Journal of Environmental Psychology, 11*, 101-122.

Moran, P. A. (1948). The interpretation of statistical maps. *Journal of the Royal Statistical Society B, 10*, 245-251.

Ore, O. (1963). *Graphs and Their Uses*. New York: Random House.

Phipps, A. G., & Clark, W. A. V. (1988). Interactive recovery and validation of households residential utility functions. In R. G. Golledge and H. Timmermans (Eds.), *Behavioral modelling in geography and planning* (pp. 245-271). London: Croom Helm.

Relph, E. (1981). *Rational Landscapes and Humanistic Geography*. London: Croom Helm.

Smith, T. R. (1983). Computational process models of individual decision making behavior. In R. Crosby (Ed.), *Cities and regions as nonlinear decision systems* (pp. 175-158). Colorado: Westview.

Smith, T. R., Pellegrino, J. W. & Golledge, R. (1982). Computational process modelling of spatial cognition and behavior. *Geographical Analysis, 14*, 305-325.

Stevens, A. & Coupe, E. P. (1978). Distortions in judged spatial relations. *Cognitive Psychology, 10*, 422-437.

Stern, E. (1983). Are geography students more spatially oriented than others? *South African Geographer, 11*, 149-160.

Taaffe, E., & Gauthier, H., Jr. (1973). *Geography of transportation*. Englewood Cliffs, NJ: Prentice-Hall.

Timmermans, H. J. P., van der Heijden, R., & Westerveld, H. (1982). Perception of urban retailing environments: An empirical analysis of consumer information and usage fields. *Geoforum, 13*, 27-37.

Tobler, W. (1970). A computer movie simulating urban growth in the Detroit region. *Economic Geography Supplement, 46*, 234-240.

Tobler, W. (1976). The geometry of mental maps. In R.G. Golledge & G. Rushton (Eds.), *Spatial choice and spatial behavior* (pp. 69-82). Columbus: Ohio State University Press.

Zipf, G. (1946). Some determinants of the circulation of information. *American Journal of Psychology, 59*, 401-21.

*Behavior and Environment: Psychological and Geographical Approaches*
*T. Gärling and R.G. Golledge (Editors)*



# CHAPTER 3

# Psychological Perspectives on Spatial Cognition

**Thomas P. McDonald and James W. Pellegrino**

Human reference to space dates back at least as far as Anaximander (610-547 BC), one of the pre-Socratic Greek philosophers, who spoke of imaging the universe from outside of its boundaries, and in doing so provided one of the first known references to the mental representation of external space (Appleton, 1922). As we will show, there is evidence that both animals and humans construct mental representations of their environments. These representations, commonly known as cognitive maps, are used in planning and directing movement through the environment. In fact, these mental representations become such essential elements of orientation and navigation that organisms may in some cases come to rely on their representations more than on the actual features of the environment. Given the abundant diversity found in cognitive maps, it is the natural course of scientific endeavor to begin to define cognitive maps more formally, and to investigate their properties. A substantial amount of this work has been done by psychologists. In fact, spatial cognition and cognitive maps have been a subject of interest since the early days of psychology (e.g., Trowbridge, 1913).

Although the term has been used rather loosely by researchers in several domains, there remains a fairly clear intuitive notion of what is meant by a cognitive map. For our purposes, it is assumed that humans are capable of creating mental representations of various perceptible external events, such as smells, sounds, and sights. The cognitive map is taken to be the mental representation of portions of the three dimensional space in which we live. Although primarily a representation of the visual environment, it almost certainly incorporates data from several senses, as well as semantic and affective information. It is also assumed that such a representation is stored in the brain, although its exact form and the substratum in which it resides are not known. Finally, it is assumed that there exist some set of mental functions which operate on the representation, allowing individuals to navigate and to estimate distances, directions, and locations of external objects or places by applying these functions to the representation.

Over the past century, but especially over the past few decades, psychologists, together with researchers from other disciplines such as geography and computer science, have studied the properties of those mental representations that have come to be called cognitive maps. The purpose of their research has been in large part to clarify what people know, how they know it, and how to externalize this knowledge. Much of this work has been laboratory based using highly controlled learning and testing designs. In the course of this ongoing research, several issues have become focal, largely because the evidence has not been sufficient to support one view of an issue clearly over another. A major premise of the present chapter is that this lack of clarity is primarily due to paradigmatic and methodological differences among the many empirical studies. Important distinctions about what has been learned, how the learning took place, and how the testing was done have sometimes been slow in emerging. As we hope to show, some of these distinctions and differences turn out to be highly important with regard to understanding the varying nature of spatial cognition.

A primary goal of the present chapter is to review much of the psychological research that has been conducted on cognitive maps and spatial cognition, taking into account the critical distinctions mentioned above. Our discussion is divided into four major sections. The first of these considers the evidence for distinctly different, albeit related, forms of spatial learning and knowledge. The next section then considers the possibility that these different types of knowledge may be partially a product of how the knowledge was acquired, namely primary versus secondary forms of learning. The third and fourth sections then focus on questions about the characteristics of the knowledge and the quality of what has been learned. In the third section we consider the issue of orientation specificity - whether (and when) the knowledge contained in the cognitive map is orientation free versus orientation specific. The fourth section considers various distortions that exist in cognitive maps and why they seemingly occur. The issues discussed in each section are not independent, and thus the discussions necessarily overlap with many points appearing more than once. We have attempted to present the discussion in a sequence that minimizes redundancy and that carries forward a general set of terms, inferences and conclusions from each section to the next.

## Multiple Types of Spatial Learning and Knowledge

### *Conclusions From Research With Animals*

Near the middle of this century, Tolman and other S-S learning theorists engaged in a lively debate with Hull and other S-R learning theorists about the nature of learning. The latter maintained that in learning the correct path to a goal box in a maze, rats acquired a chain of responses, each elicited by a stimulus at a choice point along the way (e.g., Hull, 1943, 1952). In contrast, Tolman and the new "cognitive" psychologists maintained that rats acquired a mental map of the maze, which was somehow utilized in guiding their movement towards the goal (e.g., Tolman, 1932, 1948). This "place versus response" controversy came to occupy center stage for learning theorists, amidst a clamor of puzzling results. In one of the initial place learning studies, McFarlane (1930) trained rats to swim through a maze, then drained the water and found that the rats were able to run the maze with almost no errors. This confounded the Hullians, because the responses involved in running are not the same as those involved in swimming, and according to the theoretical perspective of the S-R theorist, little transfer of learning should have occurred.

Another landmark study for the place learning theorists was conducted by Tolman and Honzik (1930), who familiarized rats with a maze composed of intersecting paths, then strategically placed obstacles which blocked one or more of the paths. In the crucial condition of the study, although a response learning perspective predicted that rats would choose a short but incorrect path, the rats chose a longer path which correctly led them to the goal box, providing evidence that rats had internalized a map of the maze. There followed a series of studies by Tolman and his associates which seemed to confirm the view that rats were place learners rather than response learners (e.g., Tolman, Ritchie, & Kalish, 1946a, 1946b, 1947).

But the situation grew muddled as more researchers began investigating the phenomenon. Kendler and Gasser (1948) found that with fewer than twenty trials, rats tended to be place learners, but with additional experience in the maze, rats tended to be response learners. Other studies (e.g., Evans, 1936; Harsh, 1937; Keller & Hill, 1936) demonstrated that variables such as the width of the alleys in the maze or the enclosure of the paths determined the place or response nature of learning. Meanwhile, the response learning theorists began to find ingenious explanations, in purely S-R terms, that could account for the apparently "cognitive" behavior of the rats (e.g., Spence & Hull, 1938). But perhaps the most illuminating results were those which demonstrated that the presence and salience of extramaze cues might be the critical factors in determining whether rats learned "places" or "responses" (e.g., Blodgett & McCutchan, 1947, 1948).

After more than a decade of controversy, some of the more enlightened participants in this debate began to question the very foundation of the dispute, noting that the reification of intervening variables had led the issue into domains that were more philosophical than psychological (e.g., Kendler, 1952). The controversy was essentially laid to rest following Restle (1957), who presented compelling evidence that rats are sometimes place learners and sometimes response learners, depending upon specific attributes of the learning environment. In cue-rich environments, rats tend to be place learners, but in the absence of distinctive cues, they learn responses.

In recent years, however, amid revived interest in the topic, it has been noted that many of the classic place learning experiments confounded two types of "place," the first based on associative cues, in which the animal associates reward with the location of a particular cue, and the second based on relational cues, in which the animal learns the spatial relationships among the cues as a means of navigating to the goal. In several of the Tolman place learning experiments (e.g., Tolman, Ritchie, & Kalish, 1946a), the baited arm of the multi-arm, radial "sun-burst" maze used by the experimenters had a light bulb located just behind it, and rats may have used associative cues to learn that food was to be found in the direction of the light bulb, without learning anything of the layout of the maze. Thus a more precisely formulated version of the controversy may be said to concern response learning, relational place learning, and associative place learning, the latter pertaining to the simple association between place and reward.

It is known that rats are capable of simple response learning within a week of birth, and that they are capable of associative place learning relatively early in their development (Nadel, 1988). It has also been shown that rats are capable of relational and not just associative place learning (e.g., Suzuki, Augerinos, & Black, 1980). In general, the findings in recent research have shown that rats can be response, associative place, or relational place learners, depending on the level of the rat's development and the type of task. Several studies (Rudy, Stadler-Morris, & Albert, 1987; Schenk, 1985) have shown that response learning comes first, followed by associative place learning, and finally relational place learning. Among sufficiently developed rats, as indicated by Restle (1957), when the environment is rich with cues, rats tend to learn about places, but when there are relatively few discriminable cues in the environment, rats tend to learn response chains. The important conclusion for the present discussion is that there appear to be different learning strategies or types, and that there is evidence for a developmental trend among those types. Furthermore, these types may have qualitative as well as quantitative differences. As Tolman maintained, relational place learning would seem to require a representation of the type that has come to be called a cognitive map. Associative place learning, however, is just a special case of a simple learned association between two objects or events. It is spatial only because one of its components is a spatial object. Response learning was not considered spatial by the learning theorists, but note that it may require the discrimination of spatial choice points. These differences will be of interest again after a consideration of human data.

### *Conclusions From Research With Humans*

Developmental psychologists have been studying spatial processes in humans with particular attention to the development of route finding or wayfinding ability, as well as the development of mental representations such as cognitive maps. The principal theoretical statement was made by Siegel and White (1975), who proposed that spatial knowledge is acquired in three stages: first knowledge of landmarks, then knowledge of routes, then finally survey or configurational knowledge. Landmark knowledge is essentially familiarization with a location, a landmark, without knowledge of that landmark's position relative to other locations, nor of how to traverse between other locations and the landmark. Route knowledge is the knowledge of how to go from one location to another, but without definitive knowledge of the relative positions of locations. Most comprehensive of the three is configurational or survey knowledge, that is, a cognitive map, which is knowledge of the relative locations of objects in the environment. From this representation, landmark and route information can be derived, even for routes never before travelled. Notice that this landmark/route/map distinction corresponds roughly to associative place, response, and relational place learning as studied in rats by the learning theorists. The nature of the correspondence will continue to be of interest as the developmental and other findings are considered in turn.

Siegel and White based their theory of the acquisition of spatial knowledge in part on experimental findings which supported their distinctions, and also in part on logical considerations dictated by other developmental theories. For example, children who have not reached Piaget's formal operations stage (e.g., Piaget & Inhelder, 1967) should not be able to use configurational representations because they are not yet capable of dealing with objective frames of reference, and thus, according to the theory, young children must be relying on landmark and route knowledge to navigate.

The Siegel and White theory has received support along several lines since its initial formulation. For example, in a study using kindergarten, second, and fifth graders, Herman and Siegel (1978) demonstrated developmental differences in the ability to construct a model of the environment, a task which should require configurational knowledge. Allen (1979) presented evidence that spatial learning begins with rote memory for movements, progresses to knowledge of routes, and finally involves configurational representations. Cousins, Siegel, and Maxwell (1983) found comparable route knowledge for first, fourth, and seventh graders, but a strong developmental trend for distance and direction estimates (which should involve configurational knowledge), even after controlling for the effects of familiarity with the locations.

Some tangential studies have also been supportive of the developmental model. Scholnick, Fein, and Campbell (1990), using Piaget and Inhelder's map placement task, found that landmark placement predicted young children's performance on a wayfinding task, whereas open field placement predicted the wayfinding performance of older children, a finding which is consistent with the view that only the older children are capable of forming configurational representations. Herman, Klein, and Blomquist (1986) found that for 11 year olds, being driven around the perimeter of a city environment before being shown the interior led to better learning than being shown the interior first. For 8 year olds and 19 year olds, however, there was no difference, suggesting a developmental change around the age of 11. It may be that 11 year olds are at a stage of spatial development in which the ability to represent configurational knowledge is in its initial phase, and thus they are particularly receptive to information that enhances their ability to create a well-defined cognitive map.

The Siegel and White developmental model has been expanded to include the view that the development by adults of cognitive maps in new or unfamiliar environments parallels the development of representations in children, a sort of logical extension of the "ontogeny recapitulates phylogeny" aphorism, here reconstituted to propose that microgenetic development parallels ontogenetic development. Thus just as a child progresses from landmark knowledge to route knowledge to configurational knowledge over the course of several years, so the adult progresses through those same stages in constructing a representation of an unfamiliar environment (Golledge, Smith, Pellegrino, Doherty & Marshall, 1985). In this view, configurational knowledge is seen as the goal of spatial learning, since it provides the most complete information about the environment, incorporating both route and landmark information.

This expanded view has received support in several studies. For example, Foley and Cohen (1984) had subjects make distance and direction estimates for locations within a large, complex building, and asked subjects which type of imagery they used in making those estimates: walking imagery, images of the exterior of the building, map-like images, or three-dimensional cross-sectional images. Inexperienced subjects were more likely to report walking imagery, and experienced subjects were more likely to report map-like imagery, a finding which is consistent with the developmental model. Kirasic, Allen, and Siegel, (1984) found that subjects with moderate experience in an environment were not significantly better than inexperienced subjects at direction and distance estimates, yet the more experienced subjects were clearly better on absolute location measure, which required more explicit configurational knowledge.

Nevertheless, other experiments have cast doubt on the idea of rigid linear and sequential stages in the acquisition of spatial knowledge. Curtis, Siegel, and Furlong (1981) compared first, fifth, and eighth graders and found developmental differences in distance and direction estimates, with a significantly larger increase between first and fifth grades. This much is consistent with the developmental model, yet by using triangulation techniques rather than the more typical map construction tasks, Curtis et al. also found evidence that even the youngest children had moderately explicit configurational knowledge. This raises questions about the nature of the developmental differences found in some of the previous developmental studies, suggesting that young children may have performance rather than competence problems in carrying out tasks which require configurational knowledge. In other words, young children may have reasonably good configurational representations, but they are unable to perform the experimental tasks which measure such knowledge. Indeed, several researchers (e.g., Kosslyn, Heldmeyer, & Locklear, 1977; Siegel, 1981) have argued specifically that children with equally good mental representations may not be equal in their ability to construct maps, and this will obviously confound studies which use map construction as a measure of configurational knowledge.

Using tasks other than map construction, some developmental studies (e.g., Hazen, 1982; Hazen, Lockman, & Pick, 1978) have shown that children as young as three can infer spatial relations, which according to theory should require some form of configurational representation. In addition, Uttal and Wellman (1989) demonstrated that four and five year olds were capable of memorizing maps to locate objects in a multi-room playhouse, and Herman, Kail, and Siegel (1979) provided empirical support for the conclusion that paths are learned before or at least along with landmarks, a result which is consistent with the animal data presented above, but is inconsistent with the developmental model. Taken as a whole, these developmental findings suggest that landmark, route, and configurational knowledge may not always be acquired in the proposed order, and in fact may be acquired in concurrent rather than sequential fashion.

The evidence from adult learning studies is even more varied, with the results of several studies challenging at least the rigid version of the developmental model. In addition to Herman et. al. (1979), others (e.g., Evans, Marrero, & Butler, 1981; Lindberg & Gärling, 1983) have found evidence that paths are learned before or at least along with landmarks. In the study by Foley and Cohen (1984) mentioned above, even the inexperienced subjects reported using map-like imagery at least some of the time. Moeser (1988) found that student nurses who worked in a large, complex, irregularly shaped building for two years had very poor configurational representations of the building, yet their route knowledge was excellent. Novice student nurses, however, who studied a floor plan of the building, easily outperformed their more experienced colleagues on both wayfinding and configurational tasks. These studies indicate that different types of spatial knowledge may be acquired to different degrees, that they are not necessarily acquired in the developmental order, and that in natural settings some types of spatial knowledge may not be acquired at all. Lindberg and Gärling (1982) have in fact argued for the view that all types of spatial knowledge are developing from the beginning, but that their relative development may vary with the particular spatial environment.

In summary, the human performance data suggest that there are qualitatively different types of spatial knowledge, which are commonly referred to as landmark, route, and configurational knowledge. These may correspond to different types of spatial learning, and may involve separate knowledge structures. Moreover, although there are many indications that the development of spatial knowledge in general follows a landmark, route, configurational representation sequence, it also seems that different types of spatial knowledge may be acquired concurrently, and out of sequence as well. To some extent configurational knowledge appears to subsume the other knowledge types, since determination of routes and the placement of landmarks can be computed from a configurational representation. It is not clear, however, that individuals always strive for or attain configurational knowledge, at least for some domains of their environment, and thus different types of knowledge may exist to different degrees for different spatial environments even in the adult.

### *Summary*

The evidence presented thus far converges on some points, but remains divergent on others. Of particular interest is the apparent correspondence, on the one hand, of associative place, response, and relational place learning in animals, with landmark, route, and configurational knowledge in humans. At the same time there is an apparent lack of correspondence in sequence, since response learning precedes associative place learning in animals, but in theory landmark learning should precede route learning in humans. This is further complicated by some of the contrary findings in the developmental literature which showed that sometimes routes may be learned before landmarks. Overall, however, the animal and human performance data, as well as neurological data (see e.g., Abraham, Potegal, & Miller, 1983; Hellige & Michimata, 1989; Kosslyn et al., 1989; O'Keefe, Nadel, Keightley, & Kill, 1975; Whishaw, 1985; Whishaw & Dunnett, 1985) strongly indicate the existence of different types of spatial knowledge, which may even correspond to distinct brain structures and functions. Furthermore, the performance data suggest a general developmental sequence in the acquisition of this knowledge.

## How We Acquire Spatial Knowledge: Primary Versus Secondary Learning

Presson and Somerville (1985) have suggested a distinction between primary and secondary learning with respect to acquiring knowledge of a route. Primary learning involves actually moving along the route, whereas secondary learning involves studying a map of the route. But this distinction may also be applied to more than just routes. Thus, primary learning would involve direct experience with an environment, whereas secondary learning would involve studying a map or other symbolic representation of the environment. At first, this distinction might seem to correspond naturally to that between route knowledge and configurational knowledge. The situation is, however, more complex, because it appears that configurational knowledge may also be acquired from extensive route experience, and route knowledge could be easily acquired by studying a map.

***Procedural Versus Declarative Knowledge***

Perhaps some of this confusion can be resolved by recognizing that there seem to be two very different types of route knowledge. The first is a type of what Anderson (1982) refers to as "procedural" knowledge, and thus what shall be referred to as procedural route knowledge. It consists of well-learned response patterns which exist in a functionally compact or "compiled" form that may be relatively inaccessible to conscious processes. Procedural knowledge, as expounded by Anderson, makes little demand on attentional resources, and may be utilized very quickly and efficiently. Consider the situation in which you become deeply involved in a conversation with someone while driving a familiar daily route. You may later find yourself at your destination with little memory of any of the route-related events that took place while you were driving, and particularly with no recollection of making the decisions to follow the correct route at choice points along the way. This is an example of the use of procedural route knowledge in getting to your destination. It is reasonable to expect this type of knowledge to have motor or kinesthetic components, and indeed Gale, Golledge, Pellegrino, and Doherty (1990) have found that children who learned walking routes by studying videotaped walks could not navigate as well as children with actual walking experience, even though both groups performed about equally well on tasks that test recognition of route locations.

The second type of route knowledge is a type of "declarative" knowledge, referring to a mental database of facts and rules. Declarative route knowledge, as it shall be termed, is a predecessor of procedural route knowledge. Consider the situation in which you are told that in order to get to a previously unvisited friend's house in an unfamiliar area, you should take the first left, go right at the next light, go down three blocks, turn right, go left at the fork in the road, and then turn left at the first cross street. If you now become engrossed in conversation, you are likely to find yourself lost. This kind of route information would be learned in much the same way as any ordered list, and it is reasonable to expect well known properties of memory functioning to be in evidence. Only when this route has been followed many times will it become represented in procedural form.

One of the difficulties in making this distinction in the literature is that some "route" tasks measure only declarative route knowledge which has been acquired by means of a relatively short laboratory task, whereas others involve measurements of previously well-traveled routes, which should have strong procedural representations. This is further muddled by the interaction between task and measurement, because it is possible to infer route knowledge from a configurational representation, and thus tasks which purport to measure declarative route knowledge may simply be assessing the accuracy of an underlying configurational representation.

### *Constructing Configurational Representations*

It is the contention of the developmental theory that configurational knowledge is built up from route knowledge, and there is little doubt that configurational representations can in fact be constructed from both declarative and procedural route knowledge. Allen, Siegel, and Rosinski (1978) had subjects first learn routes by viewing slides of a neighborhood setting, then estimate distance between points on the route. Distance estimates were reasonably good, even when the slides had been presented in random order! Apparently humans are quite capable of constructing configurational representations from simple declarative route knowledge which involves no motor component. At the other extreme, Rieser, Guth, and Hill (1982, 1986) have demonstrated that blind and blindfolded subjects are able to find shortcuts in settings which they have learned by navigation alone. Furthermore, Klatzky et al. (1990) present convincing evidence that blindfolded subjects created a mental image of an environment learned by traversing paths, and Passini, Proulx, and Rainville (1990) found that visually impaired subjects created configurational representations comparable to those of sighted subjects, although acquisition time was slower. Thus it appears that some form of survey representation can be constructed from procedural route knowledge.

It is clear, therefore, that cognitive maps can in general be built up from route knowledge. But as studies such as those by Moeser (1988) have shown, individuals who study a map of an area may acquire far more comprehensive configurational knowledge than those who have travelled the area extensively. Secondary learning may also lead to superior wayfinding abilities, as Hunt (1984) found with individuals who experienced either a simulated site visit, using slides and a model, or an actual site visit to a retirement home. Once again the primary/secondary and procedural/declarative distinctions are crucial, and researchers such as Thorndyke and Hayes-Roth (1982) have emphasized these distinctions in studying learning from maps versus learning from navigating routes. They found that with moderate exposure, declarative knowledge, acquired from map learning, is superior for estimating relative locations and straight line distances, whereas procedural knowledge, acquired from navigation, is superior for estimating route distances. With extensive exposure however, any advantages associated with map learning disappear.

Obviously, the developmental hypothesis of the acquisition of configurational representations is intended to apply only to primary learning, in which individuals have direct experience with an environment. Secondary learning is a very different process, involving simply the memorization of a symbolic representation of the primary environment. However, it is also apparent that a configurational representation acquired through secondary learning can be utilized in the primary environment, as documented in the studies by Hunt (1984) and Moeser (1988), mentioned above. This realization leads to an interesting theoretical question: is the configurational representation acquired from primary learning the same as the representation acquired from secondary learning? An examination of both theoretical arguments and empirical results suggests that it is not. On the one hand, the representation acquired from studying a map would seem to be "map-like," and numerous studies (e.g., Evans & Pezdek, 1980; Presson, DeLange, & Hazelrigg, 1989; Sholl, 1987; Tversky, 1981) have shown that representations acquired from maps are subject to rotation effects, just as actual map reading, whereas representations acquired from experience do not show such effects.

In contrast, Kuipers (1982) has compiled evidence from a variety of studies which points to the conclusion that cognitive maps acquired from experience are generally not very map-like. Some of these studies (e.g., Appleyard, 1970; Kosslyn, Pick, & Fariello, 1974) have shown that cognitive maps acquired from primary learning tend to be composed of disconnected components, and others (e.g., Hazen, Lockman, & Pick, 1978; Piaget, Inhelder & Szeminska, 1960) have found that routes are sometimes represented asymmetrically, so that they can be followed in one direction, but not in the other. Along different lines, Gärling, Säisä, Böök, and Lindberg (1986) asked subjects to find a minimal travel route among several actual locations in one case, and several imaginary locations which had been displayed in map form in the other, and subjects performed significantly better on the latter task. This finding is consistent with the idea that the map-like representation acquired from secondary learning allowed subjects to make relatively accurate interlocation distance comparisons, in contrast to the primary learning subjects whose representation was apparently not as well suited for performing simultaneous comparisons among the locations.

In conjunction with these findings, both McNamara, Ratcliff, and McKoon (1984) and Thorndyke (1981) have shown that distance estimates made from representations acquired from experience are distorted by the number of points on the route, a finding that fits nicely with that of Sadalla and Magel (1980) who found that routes with more turns are estimated to be longer than comparable routes with fewer turns. These results demonstrate that representations acquired by primary learning are biased by the procedural route knowledge from which they are derived, whereas representations acquired from secondary learning do not show such effects.

Further evidence for a difference in representations was provided by McDonald and Pellegrino (1991) who asked subjects to estimate directions for environments learned either in the laboratory, from a map-like or "bird's eye" view, or through extensive direct experience (i.e., familiar locations on a college campus). Subjects first imagined themselves standing at one location, facing a second location (orientation phase), and then pointed to a third location (pointing phase). Latencies were recorded for both the orientation and pointing phases of the task. Although accuracies for the two tasks were highly correlated, and although orientation latencies were not significantly different, pointing latencies for the environment acquired from experience were roughly twice as long as for the environment learned in the laboratory. This finding was replicated in three separate experiments, each using different laboratory environments and different subject samples as well. McDonald and Pellegrino suggest that when individuals are asked to imagine themselves standing at a particular location, memory for adjacent locations is primed, and this is true for either type of environment. Thus, orientation latencies may be similar. However, mental images for the environment acquired through primary learning are detail-rich perspective views, whereas images for the laboratory environment are detail-sparse schematic overhead views. When asked to point to another location in the primary environment, subjects may have to generate several detail-rich images. For the secondary environment, subjects need only scan a mental image which is already in working memory. The difference in pointing latencies may thus reflect a difference in the complexity and number of the qualitatively and quantitatively different mental images which are generated.

### *Summary*

The cumulative weight of the evidence presented above points to the conclusion that configurational representations acquired through primary learning are different from those acquired through secondary learning. In parallel with a declarative/procedural distinction in route knowledge, there is a corresponding difference in the resulting representations. As simple as this conclusion may seem, the distinction between types of representations is often overlooked, and many past studies have simply compared "cognitive maps" with no consideration for the circumstances in which they were acquired.

But although there is evidence that the representations are at least in certain cases qualitatively different, it is still not clear that the representations must always be different, nor even if they are initially different, that they must remain different. As mentioned above, Thorndyke (1981) found that the performance advantage associated with learning from maps disappears with sufficient experience in the environment. Gärling, Böök, and Ergezen (1982) similarly found evidence that representations acquired from primary learning become more map-like with experience.

Perhaps cognitive maps acquired through direct experience with the environment are "multimedia" representations, incorporating detailed perspective views, along with additional components such as sounds, smells, tactual and affective sensations, and, eventually, also incorporating a schematic map-like representation which has been abstracted from the numerous perspective views. This interpretation, which is an extension of the "dual code" (procedural and configurational) view presented by Gärling, Böök, and Lindberg (1985), potentially clarifies a number of divergent findings. If subjects have had only a nominal amount of direct experience with an environment, or if, like Moeser's (1988) nurses, they have apparently made no attempt to construct a configurational representation, then their performance on tasks designed to measure configurational knowledge will be inferior to that of subjects who have learned an environment from a map. But with enough experience, primary learning could lead to superior performance, because of the multiplicity of cues available in addition to a schematic, abstracted, map-like representation. In this case, cognitive maps acquired through primary learning would in essence be supersets of the representations acquired through secondary learning.

## Orientation Specificity in Cognitive Maps

Presson and Hazelrigg (1984) distinguish between spatial information which is available only in the orientation in which it was encoded (orientation specific) and spatial information which is available in a range of orientations (orientation free). This is an important distinction, because it appears that in some cases cognitive maps are orientation specific, whereas in others they are orientation free. Some of the initial attention to orientation specificity came about through the work of Levine (1982), who studied "you-are-here" maps of the sort commonly found at hospitals, shopping centers, airports, college campuses, and similar locations. This work was inspired by Levine's observation that in many cases the directions on the map were not isomorphic to the actual physical directions of the mapped space. That is, a "you-are-here" map might indicate that the cafeteria is to the left and the nursery is to the right, but because the map has been placed at a 90° angle to its surroundings, the cafeteria is actually straight ahead, and the nursery is directly behind the observer. Thus the relative placement of locations is preserved by the map, but the actual directions may be rotated.

Levine used the terms "aligned" and "misaligned" to refer to these two types of map placement, and the term "contraligned" was used for a map that was misaligned by 180°. Subsequent controlled experimentation by Levine and his associates (Levine, Marchon, & Hanley, 1984) confirmed the intuitive conclusion that contraligned you-are-here maps lead to more errors and longer latencies in locating targets than aligned maps. Additional work by Rossano and Warren (1989) has shown that when subjects are asked to point to locations learned from maps which were misaligned by various amounts, errors are not random, but tend to cluster in contraligned or "mirror image" directions, relative to the correct direction. In all of these studies, the pattern of latencies and errors points to the conclusion that the representations are orientation specific.

But perhaps the definitive study on this topic was conducted by Evans and Pezdek (1980), who presented subjects with triads of names of locations, and asked whether the triad represented the correct relative placement of the locations. On individual trials, the triads were depicted in various rotations, and response latencies were recorded. When the triads were composed of U.S. state names, there was a strong rotation effect (see Shepard & Metzler, 1971), indicating that subjects' representations were orientation specific, but when the triads were composed of the names of buildings on the subjects' college campus, latencies were independent of orientation, indicating orientation free representations. Evans and Pezdek clarified this finding by having subjects who were unfamiliar with the campus learn the buildings from a map, and once again latencies were directly proportional to the degree of rotation, indicating an orientation specific representation.

The apparent conclusion is that representations constructed from map learning, that is, secondary learning, are orientation-specific, whereas representations constructed from primary learning are orientation-free. This conclusion was suggested by Evans and Pezdek (1980), and supported by subsequent studies (Sholl, 1987; Thorndyke & Hayes-Roth, 1982). Tangential support was provided by Liben and Downs (1986), who found substantial correlations between children's map reading skills and their performance on mental rotation tasks. But there is evidence that learning mode may not be the only determinant of orientation specificity.

Rieser (1989) placed subjects in typical offices or living rooms and had them learn the locations of objects around the room. In the test phase, subjects closed their eyes and responded in one of three conditions: translation, in which the subject was asked to point to a target as if standing at a particular object; imagined rotation, in which the subject was asked to point at a target as if facing a particular object; and locomoted rotation, which was the same as imagined rotation, except that the subject was actually turned by the experimenter on each trial to face in the "imagined" direction. Rieser found that subjects had little difficulty with the translation trials, suggesting an orientation-free representation. For the rotation trials, however, the response latencies for the imagined rotations displayed the typical rotation effect, whereas the latencies for the locomoted rotation showed no differences due to degree of rotation. It appears that somehow the specificity of the orientation is determined in this case not by the mode of learning, but by the task instructions and the physical movement of the individual at test time. However, there is another factor here not yet considered, namely small-scale versus large-scale spaces.

### *Small-Scale Versus Large-Scale Space*

Siegel (1981) has distinguished between small- and large-scale spaces. The former can be apprehended in a single glance, whereas the latter can be viewed only in segments, and thus information from multiple views must be integrated. A map of the United States, therefore, is a small-scale space, even though its referent space, that is, the space represented by the map, is quite large. On the other hand, the inside of a typical house is a large-scale space, because it cannot be seen all at once. In this context, the results of the Evans and Pezdek (1980) study described above can be accounted for not only by the primary or secondary mode of learning, but also by the scale of the space. Subjects demonstrated orientation-free representations for their college campus, which is a large-scale space, but orientation-specific representations for the maps, which are small-scale spaces.

This distinction of scale may also help to illuminate the findings in the Rieser (1989) study, by noting that subjects learned the layout of the room from a position approximately in the center of the room. Thus, in order to see the entire room, they had to turn in different directions, and therefore the room may have been for them a large-scale space, because they could not observe it all at once. However, in entering and leaving the room, they may in fact have been able to see it all in a single view. Perhaps Rieser's findings show that subjects created multiple representations, which were cued by the instructions and physical movement at test time.

It is important to note that the small/large scale distinction is logically independent of the primary/secondary learning distinction. A map could be so large that it would require multiple views to see it all. An obstacle course, for example, could be in such a confined area that it could be apprehended in a single view, although primary learning for such an environment might require a considerable expenditure of time and physical effort. However, though logically independent, these distinctions are rarely identified in the literature.

Furthermore, some studies seem to evade definitive classification. Palij, Levine, and Kahan (1984) had blindfolded subjects walk a simple five-point path marked on the floor of a room, after which subjects were seated in wheelchairs, wheeled to a particular location on the path, and placed in an orientation that was either aligned or contraligned with their orientation as they had walked the path. This would appear to be primary learning, but because subjects are blindfolded during learning, it is not clear whether the learned space is small or large, or even whether such a distinction can be sensibly applied. Palij et al. found that in the contraligned condition, subjects made more errors and took more time to estimate the direction of other points on the path. This is in contrast to Evans and Pezdek's (1980) results, and provides evidence that primary learning can lead to an orientation-specific representation.

In a more elaborate version of the paradigm used by Palij et al. (1984), Presson and Hazelrigg (1984) had subjects either walk blindfolded on a four point path marked on the floor of a room, look at a 1:10 scale map of the path, or view the path from a single vantage point in the room. Subjects were then wheeled in chairs to locations on the path, placed either in an aligned position or a contraligned position, and asked to point to their locations on the path. Subjects who had walked the path or viewed it performed about equally in both aligned and contraligned conditions, indicating an orientation-free representation. Note that this is in direct contradiction to the results found by Palij et al. (1984). Yet subjects who studied the map made significantly more errors in the contraligned condition, indicating that they had constructed an orientation-specific representation. Apparently the primary/secondary learning distinction must be carefully considered, at least in the context of small-scale space. Walking the path would seem to be primary learning, and studying the map was certainly secondary learning, but viewing the path from a single vantage point would seem more similar to secondary learning than primary learning. In explaining their results, Presson and Hazelrigg suggest that viewing a space directly is a type of interaction with that space, and thus a form of primary learning, whereas viewing a map entails symbolic translation, and is thus secondary learning.

In a follow-up to the study above, Presson, et al. (1989) controlled the manner in which subjects walked the path. In a multiple-orientation condition, subjects walked in a normal manner, but in a single-orientation condition, subjects always maintained the same absolute orientation while walking. This required subjects to walk sideways and backwards at times in order to complete the route. The results showed that multiple-orientation walks led to orientation-free representations, whereas single-orientation walks led to orientation-specific representations. It is tempting to conclude that it is the "imagined" scale of the space that is relevant, i.e., that although blindfolded, subjects in the multiple-orientation condition would have seen the path from several vantage points, whereas subjects in the single-orientation condition would have had only a single view. However, such an explanation would still not explain why subjects who viewed the entire room from a single vantage point in the Presson and Hazelrigg (1984) study performed as though they had orientation-free representations.

Thus it appears that neither the primary/secondary nor large/small scale distinctions are sufficient to account for all of the data in the studies just discussed. But there is yet another possibility, namely, that the absolute size of the viewed space is the determining factor in orientation specificity. Thus the map condition is the Presson and Hazelrigg (1984) study may have produced an orientation-specific representation because the map of the path was so much smaller than the path as marked on the floor of the room. Presson, DeLange, and Hazelrigg (1989) followed up on this idea in a subsequent study in which path sizes, map sizes, the sizes of the referent spaces, the degree of scale transformation, and the instructional set were systematically varied. The finding was that the absolute size of the space was indeed the critical factor. Small maps of large paths and small paths alike lead to orientation-specific representations, whereas large maps and large paths lead to orientation-free representations.

Such a simple conclusion is very appealing, but there are reasons for withholding full approbation. Most of the studies just discussed involved paths which consisted of no more than five points, connected by segments of not more than a few feet, and subjects typically walked the path only once. In spite of the sound logical basis of the small/large scale and primary/secondary learning distinctions, it is not clear that experiments which use relatively simple, artificial paths, and require only a few minutes of subject participation, can be generalized to environments of several acres or square miles, which may take weeks or months to learn.

Long before many of the studies above were conducted, Siegel, Kirasic, and Kail (1979) issued a strong caution against generalizing the results of studies conducted in "toy" environments to large-scale, real-world environments. Their caveat should once again be given consideration. Perhaps, going back to the suggestion of Ittelson (1973), the difference between small- and large-scale spaces should be considered in terms of the difference between spaces which one acts in, or explores, and spaces which one acts on, or observes. More recently, Weatherford (1985) has proposed classifying environments as model small scale, navigable small scale, or large scale. Model small-scale spaces would include maps, models, and other symbolic representations of space, whereas navigable small-scale spaces would include spaces such as rooms, which are large enough to permit movement, but which can be viewed from a single vantage point.

In this light, most of the studies discussed in this section would be considered navigable small scale, even though in some cases the subject did not or could not glimpse the entire space with a single view. And it may well be that in such small spaces, slight differences in instruction set, the size of the display, the type of locomotion, and even the procedure followed at test time can influence the orientation specificity of the subject's representation, or at least determine which of several representations the subject uses at test time. In general, however, the evidence presented thus far indicates that the mode of learning (primary or secondary), the scale of the space, and the size of the visual display are all potential determinants of the orientation specificity of a cognitive map.

### *Maps as Orienting Schemas*

There remains another important perspective on the issue of orientation specificity. Neisser (1976) offers the view that a cognitive map is first and foremost an orienting schema. Speaking from ethological and evolutionary perspectives, he posits that configurational representations of spatial information are specialized knowledge structures whose purpose is to direct perceptual and motor exploration of the environment. They are a means of providing an easily updated representation of the locations of objects relative to the observer and to each other. For this reason, a cognitive map is likely to be viewer-centered, and not particularly map-like. And because it must be able to function equally well no matter which direction the individual is facing, it should be orientation-free rather than orientation-specific. Thus in a cognitive map derived from experience, information about the relative locations of objects must be computed from perspective views, whereas in the memorized image of a map, such information is directly stored.

Speaking from a similar perspective, Kuipers (1978, 1982) has argued that reference systems in cognitive maps are likely to be local, in the sense of being aligned with the body axes, rather than global. In other words, because humans do not seem to be facile at using an internal compass mechanism, for example, it is more important for an individual to know the position of an object relative to his or her current orientation rather than in relation to a compass direction or other global reference system. For this reason, cognitive maps are useful to the extent that they are orientation free, because the individual's orientation in the environment is constantly changing. Gärling, Böök, and Lindberg (1984) have concurred with this view, noting that movement in an environment is usually goal directed, and thus the purpose of a cognitive map is to aid in planning movement. For this reason, an egocentric reference system is likely to be the most efficacious.

Empirical support for this general perspective was provided by Frederickson and Bartlett (1987), who presented subjects with pictures which had salient objects near their lateral edges. Subjects sat in a room with a door on one side and a window on the other, and were instructed to encode the objects using either an egocentric reference frame (e.g., the big tree is on the left and the barn is on the right) or an environmental reference frame (e.g., the big tree is on the door side of the room and the barn is on the window side of the room). The experiment was designed so that the reference frame at encoding time was completely crossed with the reference frame at recall, and thus some of the subjects who used an egocentric reference frame to encode the information were required to recall the information in an egocentric reference frame, but others who had encoded egocentrically were required to recall using an environmental reference frame, and so on. Frederickson and Bartlett found that recall was best when subjects were asked to recall with an egocentric reference frame, no matter which reference frame was used at encoding.

They conclude from this result that memory for orientation is, in terms of Pylyshyn (1979, 1981), cognitively impenetrable, meaning that the method of encoding cannot be influenced by conceptual or tacit knowledge, and implying that the information is stored in analog rather than symbolic form (see Anderson, 1978). That is, it appears that subjects encoded the information in an egocentric fashion, in spite of any instructions to use an environmental frame of reference. This is presumably because memory for orientation, which is the basis for the cognitive map as an orienting schema, must ultimately be coded in a viewer-centered frame of reference for a variety of physiological and ultimately evolutionary reasons.

Although Frederickson and Bartlett's (1987) results were obtained in a rather artificial setting, Sholl (1987) has provided verification of their results on a larger scale. Subjects first faced either north or west, then pointed to a specified target location, and this was done both for U.S. cities and for local landmarks. Just as with the results of Evans and Pezdek (1980), Sholl found a rotation effect for latencies on the U.S. cities task, suggesting that secondary learning had led to orientation-specific representations, but no rotation effect for the local landmarks, suggesting that primary learning had led to orientation-free representations.

Sholl's (1987) view of the cognitive map as an orienting schema led her to hypothesize additional differences in response latencies. If the purpose of a cognitive map acquired through primary learning is to direct movement, then it is reasonable to assume that objects located in front of the observer would be more quickly located than objects behind the observer. The results confirmed Sholl's predictions: for the local landmarks, locations in front of the subject were located significantly faster than objects behind the subject, but for the U.S. cities, there were no significant differences between forward and backward latencies. In a subsequent task, Sholl compared subjects whose knowledge of certain Northeastern U.S. cities was acquired predominantly through secondary learning, with subjects who had both substantial primary and secondary experience with the cities. Unlike the primary learners, the primary/secondary learners showed no differences for front and back latencies, and their response profiles were markedly different from those of either the primary or secondary learners in the previous study. This led Sholl to the conclusion that although cognitive maps for relatively small local environments function as orienting schemas, a different type of representation is used for larger areas.

### *Summary*

Overall, the acknowledgement of different scales of visual space, along with the view of configurational representations of spatial knowledge acquired through primary learning as orienting schemas, helps to clarify both the empirical and theoretical basis of orientation specificity in cognitive maps. In general, it appears that primary learning in a large-scale environment leads to an orientation-free representation, possibly due to the nature of the cognitive map as an orienting schema in this setting. Conversely, it appears that secondary learning of small, symbolic spatial arrays leads to orientation-specific representations. The picture for small-scale navigable spaces remains unclear, and it may be that factors such as the absolute size of the space and the task demands play a role in determining the orientation specificity of representations created in this type of environment.

## Distortions in Cognitive Maps

The predominance of evidence presented thus far indicates that humans create mental representations of their spatial environments, that one type of such a representation, which has come to be called a cognitive map, preserves information about the relative positions of objects in the environment, and that its properties may be at least in part determined by the manner in which it is acquired and perhaps by the scale and absolute size of the space itself. Furthermore, it has been suggested that as a functional rather than a literal representation of reality, the cognitive map may incorporate distortions of its referent space. This suggests another pertinent theoretical question: are the distortions in cognitive maps of a random nature, or are there systematic patterns of distortion? The empirical evidence indicates the latter.

It must be remembered throughout the following discussion that configurational representations acquired through primary learning may be qualitatively different from those acquired through secondary learning. As previously suggested, the former may be "multi-media" representations, affective and semantic associations, and possibly an abstracted schematic representation as well. The latter, however, may simply be mental images of a picture, specifically a picture which happens to be a map. Thus it is reasonable to expect that some types of distortion may be specific to representations acquired in one manner or the other. Nevertheless, because cognitive maps acquired through primary learning may be supersets of those acquired through secondary learning, it may also be that most types of distortion are common to configurational representations acquired through either type of learning.

### *Metric Distortion*

There is ample evidence that directions in cognitive maps acquired through both primary and secondary learning are subject to systematic and predictable patterns of distortion. Lynch (1960) found that residents of large cities displayed tendencies to misrepresent landmarks as being aligned in simple north/south or east/west configurations. Tversky (1981) confirmed this same type of alignment error for configurations acquired through secondary learning, finding that subjects misrepresented the locations of South American cities apparently because of a tendency to represent South America as lying directly south of North America, whereas in fact it is offset substantially to the east. This phenomenon has been replicated by Muller (1985). Tversky also found rotation errors, noting that residents of the San Francisco Bay peninsula demonstrated a tendency to think of the area as being aligned on a north/south axis, when in fact it runs northwest to southeast. Similar results were reported by Lloyd and Heivley (1987) for urban neighborhoods.

Rotation errors are similar to alignment errors in the sense that in the former, whole configurations are rotated into alignment with a reference system, whereas in the latter, individual components of a configuration are translated or displaced so as to be aligned with a reference system. Howard and Kerst (1981) have reported both types of errors for representations acquired through both primary and secondary learning, suggesting that such errors represent fundamental patterns of distortion in cognitive maps. Lloyd (1989a) replicated these findings, noting that rotation and alignment errors were typically smaller for representations acquired from secondary learning, and suggesting therefore that the differences between primary and secondary learning representations are more quantitative than qualitative.

Further evidence for distortion in the representation of direction was found by Moar and Bower (1983), who chose a triad of well known locations in a local environment, and asked subjects to judge the set of six possible directions between the locations. From these judgements, the three angles between the locations were derived. Moar and Bower found that angle estimates had a tendency to be biased towards 90°, and furthermore that the sum of the three derived angles typically exceeded 180°, suggesting a fundamental inconsistency in the represented directions.

There is also ample evidence for distortions in the representation of distance. For primary learning, Briggs (1973) found that the relative familiarity of landmarks along urban routes influenced distance judgements for those routes. Others (Allen, 1981; Byrne, 1979; Sadalla & Magel, 1980) have demonstrated that the number of turns in a route is also a determinant of estimated distance, with routes having more turns estimated as longer than those with fewer turns. This finding was elaborated by Allen and Kirasic (1985), who showed that subjects subdivide routes into segments, then use the segment boundaries as markers to estimate distance. When estimates cross segment boundaries, errors accumulate for each boundary crossed.

Many of these findings have been replicated for representations acquired through secondary learning. Using artificial environments learned from maps, Thorndyke (1981) also found that routes with more turns are estimated as longer than those with fewer turns, and McNamara et al. (1984) found that distance estimates were determined more by route distance than by Euclidean distance. There is also evidence for asymmetry in the representation of distances. Holyoak and Mah (1982) had subjects use a uniform distance scale to estimate how far east cities were from the Pacific coast, and how far west they were from the Atlantic coast. They found that subjects overestimated the distances in both directions, pointing to a fundamental inconsistency in their representation of distance.

### *Hierarchical Structure*

It appears that in many cases the metric distortions in cognitive maps noted above may result from a hierarchical structure of the representations. In a now classic study, Stevens and Coupe (1978) found that subjects judged Reno, Nevada, to be east of San Diego, California, even though it is actually further west. This is presumably because subjects have encoded the state of California as lying west of the state of Nevada, and thus they infer that cites in California must lie west of cities in Nevada. Stevens and Coupe suggest that this finding provides evidence for a hierarchical encoding of spatial information, in the sense that decisions about cities are made by referring to their superordinate category, that is, the states in which the cities reside. Additional evidence for a hierarchical structure in representations acquired through secondary learning was provided by Maki (1981), who demonstrated that response times to verify distance and direction judgements are faster for inter-cluster rather than intra-cluster locations, indicating that comparisons are being made at a superordinate level.

Evidence for hierarchical organization in cognitive maps acquired from primary learning was provided by Hirtle and Jonides (1985), who used a free recall paradigm to uncover subjective clusters in a well-traveled local environment. Subjects were then asked to estimate distances between points, and it was found that across-cluster distances were consistently overestimated, whereas within-cluster distances were consistently underestimated, indicating that the subjective hierarchies of the subjects influenced their estimates in a consistent fashion. Others (Canter

& Tagg, 1975; Newcombe & Liben, 1982) have shown that natural boundaries such as rivers, hills, railroad tracks, and buildings appear to influence distance estimates, such that distances across boundaries tend to be overestimated.

McNamara (1986) has distinguished between non-hierarchical theories, which propose that spatial knowledge is stored in an analog representation such as an image or network, and hierarchical theories, which propose that an environment is conceptualized as consisting of regions, and that spatial knowledge is stored in a hierarchical, compartmentalized fashion. He further distinguishes strongly hierarchical theories, which propose a minimal encoding of information such that as much as possible can be computed from the hierarchical structure, and partially hierarchical theories, which propose that some spatial relationships which can be computed will also be stored explicitly.

In an attempt to determine the hierarchical nature of cognitive maps, McNamara (1986) conducted an experiment in which some subjects studied maps of objects placed in a four quadrant space, others viewed the objects as they roamed about a navigable small-scale space which was divided into quadrants by lines on the floor, and others moved about the same navigable space but were not allowed to cross quadrant lines (instead they had to step out of the space and walk around the perimeter to another quadrant). Critical pairs of objects were either in the same or different quadrants, and they were either close together or far apart. Using a priming task for item recognition, he found that recognition was faster for items primed by same quadrant items, and using distance estimates, he found that subjects underestimated distances between objects in the same quadrant, with both results indicating a hierarchical structure to the subjects' representations. McNamara also found a reliable effect of distance on priming across quadrant boundaries, suggesting that subjects were directly encoding distance information for pairs of objects in different quadrants. As outlined above, this is evidence for a partially rather than strictly hierarchical representation, apparently for both primary and secondary learning (although it may be prudent to remember that the primary learning took place in a navigable small-scale space rather than a large-scale space).

In addition to studies which show that spatial boundaries contribute to a hierarchical organization in cognitive maps, some researchers have found evidence for clustering even in the absence of explicit spatial boundaries. Hirtle and Mascolo (1986), using maps of imaginary environments, found that semantic labels can induce clustering which seems to alter memory for spatial locations, such that subjects remember semantically related locations as being closer together than unrelated locations.

This is an important finding for the additional reason that it appears to demonstrate that verbal and spatial information may be encoded together, even in representations acquired through secondary learning. Further evidence for hierarchical clustering was provided by McNamara, Hardy, and Hirtle (1989), who had subjects learn the locations of objects on small-scale spatial layouts. Using a recognition priming task, they found evidence that subjects created their own spatial hierarchies even when no physical or perceptual boundaries were present. This provides support for the idea that hierarchical organization is a fundamental property of spatial memory.

### *Summary and Theoretical Considerations*

It appears that cognitive maps, whether acquired through primary or secondary learning, are not simply scaled-down literal images of reality. Instead, they appear to have a hierarchical organization, which is generally useful for making judgements about distances and directions in the real world. However, this organization may be the very cause of distortions in the representation, such that distances and directions are misrepresented in various systematic ways. Although this tradeoff of function may initially seem puzzling, it can also be seen as a natural consequence of an efficient system of representation. Making precise estimates of distance and direction could be computationally very expensive, and thus the hierarchical structure of the representation allows macrospatial judgements to be made quickly and in a computationally inexpensive fashion. Nevertheless, the representation must maintain a somewhat literal mapping of reality, in order to allow microspatial estimates to be made. The error due to distortion in this case may be so small that it is of no practical consequence for typical spatial operations, such as estimating the distance to the supermarket, or the direction to a friend's house.

However, the results of the studies above allow an alternative explanation. It may be that cognitive maps themselves are distortion free, but that the process of retrieving information from the representation induces distortion. Remembering the distinction between representations and the functions that operate on them, it can be seen that distortion may be inherent in the representation, in the functions, or in both. This is obviously a difficult issue to unravel, because experimental procedures cannot examine cognitive maps directly, and thus scientific knowledge of the structure of cognitive maps must come from tasks in which subjects retrieve information. For this reason Siegel (1981) has argued that tasks which measure spatial knowledge should employ response measures with a minimal cognitive load, in an effort to achieve a more accurate assessment. It is not clear, however, that any response measure can be truly non-invasive.

Some clues to the source of distortion can be discerned by comparing perceptual processes with similar judgements on mental representations. Thus, just as Allen and Kirasic (1985) and others have suggested that subjects estimate route distances in cognitive maps by marking routes off into segments, Hartley (1977, 1981) has shown that subjects use a similar "lying off" method when estimating the length of perceived lines. This apparent parallel of function suggests that the distorted distance estimates from cognitive maps are caused by the same estimation process used in perception, and thus the retrieval process rather than the representation may be the source of the distortion.

Holyoak and Mah (1982), however, propose a different mechanism for distance distortion. They argue that metric judgements on cognitive maps are made by loading relatively precise spatial information into working memory, a limited capacity buffer which may have only about seven graduated categories of distance (see Miller, 1956). These categories are scaled to fit the distance being estimated, with the result that short distances tend to be overestimated, whereas long distances tend to be underestimated. Lloyd (1989b) provided a test of this hypothesis, by comparing distance judgements for both perception and memory of a map. He found that perception subjects consistently overestimated distances, whereas memory subjects produced results consistent with Holyoak and Mah's predictions, underestimating short distances and overestimating long ones. Lloyd argues therefore that different cognitive processes are used in estimating distance from perception versus memory. However, the ultimate conclusion is once again that the process of decoding information from a cognitive map may be a source of distortion.

Although these findings demonstrate that information retrieval is a possible source of estimation error for distance in cognitive maps, they do not explain the range of results pointing to distortions in both distance and direction, nor can they explain the hierarchical findings. Furthermore, they do not rule out the possibility that some of the distortion lies in the representation, and some in the decoding process. In fact, McNamara, Hardy, and Hirtle (1989) provide several arguments against distortion due to retrieval, arguing that their priming tasks would have produced different patterns of results if subjects had imposed hierarchical structures only during the recall task. For the present, the issue of the source of distortion in cognitive map tasks must remain unresolved. Given the accumulated evidence for a variety of different types of distortion, involving diverse types of cognitive judgements, it may be best to conclude for the time being that both the representations and the recall tasks are sources of the observed distortion.

## Concluding Comments

We began this chapter by noting that the mental representation of the environment has long been a topic of interest and speculation. Much of this chapter has been devoted to objective, empirical research that has attempted to specify what we know about our three-dimensional world and how we come to learn it. It may surprise some to learn that so much work has been done in the attempt to determine mental representations of the spatial environment. Perhaps even more surprising is the fact that answers to seemingly simple questions have been elusive, with many apparent contradictions across the myriad studies conducted to date. In retrospect this should not be surprising given the various critical distinctions that we have pointed out in the different sections of this chapter. It should also not be surprising given the tremendous variety of environments that individuals interact with and within, as well as the various ways that they do so and their differing purposes. If there is a message that emerges from the psychological research on spatial cognition and cognitive maps, it is a verification of the flexibility, adaptability and power of human cognition. We seemingly learn what we need to learn when we need to learn it. It also appears that information is represented in ways that make it useful for the tasks that we need to perform. What is often perplexing is that our knowledge of the environment appears limited, especially when set in the context of objective descriptions of the environment (see Chapter 2 in this book). But that is probably an inappropriate perspective on the issue since much of what could be learned is irrelevant to the functioning of the organism unless there is a reason for acquiring that knowledge. This last point was driven home for one of us when his son turned sixteen and was eligible to drive. After obtaining his license he was preparing to drive to his high school for the first time but found himself needing to ask how to get there. This was befuddling to his parents since the route to high school had been traversed daily by car for two years. Of course, the salient point was that he had always been a passenger, never the driver and therefore never responsible for navigation. He had no effective route knowledge because he had never needed to acquire it. This problem generalized to much of the rest of his suburban environment but was rapidly overcome by the exigencies associated with actually getting somewhere that he wanted to go!

## References


Abraham, L.Potegal, M. & Miller, S. (1983). Evidence for caudate nucleus involvement in an egocentric spatial task: Return from passive transport. *Physiological Psychology, 11*, 11-17.

Allen, G. L. (1979). *A developmental perspective on the structural organization of spatial knowledge.* Unpublished doctoral dissertation, University of Pittsburgh.

Allen, G. L. (1981). A developmental perspective on the effects of "subdividing" macrospatial experience. *Journal of Experimental Psychology: Human Learning and Memory, 7*, 120-132.

Allen, G. L., & Kirasic, K. C. (1985). Effects of the cognitive organization of route knowledge on judgments of macrospatial distance. *Memory and Cognition, 13*, 218-227.

Allen, G. L., Siegel, A. W., & Rosinski, R. R. (1978). The role of perceptual context in structuring spatial knowledge. *Journal of Experimental Psychology: Human Learning and Memory, 4*, 617-630.

Anderson, J. R. (1978). Arguments concerning representations for mental imagery. *Psychological Review, 85*, 249-277.

Anderson, J. R. (1982). Acquisition of cognitive skill. *Psychological Review, 89*, 369-406.

Appleton, R. B. (1922). *The elements of Greek philosophy from Thales to Aristotle.* London: Methuen.

Appleyard, D. (1970). Styles and methods of structuring a city. *Environment and Behavior, 2*, 100-117.

Blodgett, H. C., & McCutchan, K. (1947). Place versus response-learning in the simple T-maze. *Journal of Experimental Psychology, 37*, 412-422.

Blodgett, H. C., & McCutchan, K. (1948). The relative strength of place and response-learning in the T-maze. *Journal of Comparative and Physiological Psychology, 41*, 17-24.

Bogoraz-Tan, V. G. (1940). *The Chukchee. Memoirs of the American Museum of Natural History.* New York: G. E. Stechert.

Briggs, R. (1973). Urban cognitive distances. In R. Downs and D. Stea (Eds.), *Image and environment: Cognitive mapping and spatial behavior* (pp. 361-388). Chicago: Aldine .

Byrne, R. (1979). Memory for urban geography. *Quarterly Journal of Experimental Psychology, 31*, 147-154.

Canter, D. V., & Tagg, S. K. (1975). Distance estimation in cities. *Environment and Behavior, 7*, 59-80.

Cousins, J. H., Siegel, A. W., & Maxwell, S. E. (1983). Way finding and cognitive mapping in large-scale environments: A test of a developmental model. *Journal of Experimental Child Psychology, 35*, 1-20.

Curtis, L. E., Siegel, A. W., & Furlong, N. E. (1981). Developmental differences in cognitive mapping: Configurational knowledge of familiar large-scale environments. *Journal of Experimental Child Psychology, 31*, 456-469.

Evans, G. W., Marrero, D., & Butler, P. (1981). Environmental learning and cognitive mapping. *Environment and Behavior, 13*, 83-104.

Evans, G. W., & Pezdek, K. (1980). Cognitive mapping: Knowledge of real-world distance and location information. *Journal of Experimental Psychology: Human Learning and Memory, 6*, 13-24.

Evans, S. (1936). Flexibility of established habit. *Journal of General Psychology, 14*, 177-200.

Foley, J. E., & Cohen, A. J. (1984). Working mental representations of the environment. *Environment and Behavior, 16*, 713-729.

Frederickson, R. E., & Bartlett, J. C. (1987). Cognitive impenetrability of memory for orientation. *Journal of Experimental Psychology: Learning, Memory, and Cognition, 13*, 269-277.

Gale, N., Golledge, R. G., Pellegrino, J. W., & Doherty, S. (1990). The acquisition and integration of route knowledge in an unfamiliar neighborhood. *Journal of Environmental Psychology, 10*, 3-25.

Gärling, T., Böök, A., & Ergezen, N. (1982). Memory for the spatial layout of the everyday physical environment: Differential rates of acquisition of different types of information. *Scandinavian Journal of Psychology, 23*, 23-35.

Gärling, T., Böök, A., & Lindberg, E. (1984). Cognitive mapping of large-scale environments: The interrelationship of action plans, acquisition, and orientation. *Environment and Behavior, 16*, 3-34.

Gärling, T.,Böök, A., & Lindberg, E. (1985). Adult's spatial memory representations of the spatial properties of their everyday physical environment. In R. Cohen (Ed.), *The development of spatial cognition* (pp. 141-184). Hillsdale, NJ: Erlbaum.

Gärling, T., Säisä, J., Böök, A., & Lindberg, E. (1986). The spatio-temporal sequencing of everyday activities in the large-scale environment. *Journal of Environmental Psychology, 6*, 261-280.

Golledge, R. G., Smith, T. R., Pellegrino, J. W., Doherty, S., & Marshall, S. P. (1985). A conceptual model and empirical analysis of children's acquisition of spatial knowledge. *Journal of Environmental Psychology, 5*, 125-152.

Harsh, C. M. (1937). Disturbance and "insight" in rats. *University of California Publications in Psychology, 6*, 163-168.
Hartley, A. (1977). Mental measurement in magnitude estimation of length. *Journal of Experimental Psychology: Human Perception and Performance, 3*, 622-628.
Hartley, A. (1981). Mental measurement of line length: The role of the standard. *Journal of Experimental Psychology: Human Perception and Performance, 7*, 309-317.
Hazen, N. L. (1982). Spatial exploration and spatial knowledge: Individual and developmental differences in very young children. *Child Development, 53*, 826-833.
Hazen, N. L., Lockman, J. J., & Pick, H. L. (1978). The development of children's representations of large-scale environments. *Child Development, 49*, 623-636.
Hellige, J. B., & Michimata, C. (1989). Categorization versus distance: Hemispheric differences for processing spatial information. *Memory & Cognition, 17*, 770-776.
Herman, J. F., Kail, R. V., & Siegel, A. W. (1979). Cognitive maps of a college campus: A new look at freshman orientation. *Bulletin of the Psychonomic Society, 13*, 183-186.
Herman, J. F., Klein, C. A., & Blomquist, S. L. (1986). Developmental differences in the use of an abstract reference frame to infer spatial relationships. *Developmental Psychology, 22*, 468-476.
Herman, J. F., & Siegel, A. W. (1978). The development of spatial representation of large scale environments. *Journal of Experimental Child Psychology, 26*, 389-406.
Hirtle, S. C., & Jonides, J. (1985). Evidence of hierarchies in cognitive maps. *Memory and Cognition, 13*, 208-217.
Hirtle, S. C., & Mascolo, M. F. (1986). Effect of semantic clustering on the memory of spatial locations. *Journal of Experimental Psychology: Learning, Memory, and Cognition, 12*, 182-189.
Holyoak, K. J., & Mah, W. A. (1982). Cognitive reference points in judgments of symbolic magnitude. *Cognitive Psychology, 14*, 328-352.
Howard, J. H., & Kerst, S. M. (1981). Memory and perception of cartographic information for familiar and unfamiliar environments. *Human Factors, 23*, 495-504.
Hull, C. L. (1943). *Principles of behavior*. New York: Appleton.
Hull, C. L. (1952). *A behavior system*. New Haven, CT: Yale University Press.
Hunt, M. E. (1984). Environmental learning without being there. *Environment and Behavior, 16*, 307-334.

Ittelson, W. H. (1973). Environment perception and contemporary perceptual theory. In W. H. Ittelson (Ed.), *Environment and cognition* (pp. 1-21). New York: Seminary.

Keller, F. S., & Hill, L. M. (1936). Another "insight" experiment. *Journal of Genetic Psychology,* 484-489.

Kendler, H. H. (1952). What is learned? A theoretical blind alley. *Psychological Review, 59,* 269-277.

Kendler, H. H., & Gasser, W. P. (1948). Variables in spatial learning: I. Number of reinforcements during training. *Journal of Comparative and Physiological Psychology, 41,* 178-187.

Kirasic, K. C., Allen, G. L., & Siegel, A. W. (1984). Expression of configurational knowledge of large-scale environments: Students' performance of cognitive tasks. *Environment and Behavior, 16,* 687-712.

Klatzky, R. L., Loomis, J. M., Golledge, R. G., Cicinelli, J. G., Doherty, S., & Pellegrino, J. W. (1990). Acquisition of route and survey knowledge in the absence of vision. *Journal of Motor Behavior,* 22, 19-43.

Kosslyn, S. M. (1987). Seeing and imagining in the cerebral hemispheres: A computational approach. *Psychological Review, 94,* 148-175.

Kosslyn, S. M., Heldmeyer, K. H., & Locklear, E. P. (1977). Children's drawings as data about internal representations. *Journal of Experimental Child Psychology, 23,* 191-211.

Kosslyn, S. M., Koenig, O., Barrett, A., Cave, C. B., Tang, J., & Gabrielli, J. D. E. (1989). Evidence for two types of spatial representations: Hemispheric specialization for categorical and coordinate relations. *Journal of Experimental Psychology: Human Perception and Performance, 15,* 723-735.

Kosslyn, S. M., Pick, H. L., & Fariello, G. R. (1974). Cognitive maps in children and men. *Child Development, 45,* 707-716.

Kuipers, B. (1978). Modelling spatial knowledge. *Cognitive Science, 2,* 129-153.

Kuipers, B. (1982). The "map in the head" metaphor. *Environment and Behavior, 14,* 202-220.

Levine, M. (1982). You-are-here maps. *Environment and Behavior, 14,* 221-237.

Levine, M., Marchon, I., & Hanley, G. (1984). The placement and misplacement of you-are-here maps. *Environment and Behavior, 16,* 139-157.

Liben, L. S., & Downs, R. M. (1986). *Children's production and comprehension of maps: Increasing graphic literacy* (Report to the National Institute of Education; Grant No. 6-83-0025). Washington, DC: National Institute of Education.

Lindberg, E., & Gärling, T. (1982). Acquisition of locational information about reference points during locomotion: The role of central information processing. *Scandinavian Journal of Psychology, 23*, 207-218.

Lindberg, E., & Gärling, T. (1983). Acquisition of different types of locational information in cognitive maps: Automatic or effortful processing? *Psychological Research, 45*, 19-38.

Lloyd, R. (1989a). Cognitive maps: Encoding and decoding information. *Annals of the Association of American Geographers, 79*, 101-124.

Lloyd, R. (1989b). The estimation of distance and direction from cognitive maps. *The American Cartographer, 16*, 109-122.

Lloyd, R., & Heivley, C. (1987). Systematic distortions in urban cognitive maps. *Annals of the Association of American Geographers, 77*, 191-207.

Lynch, K. (1960). *The image of the city*. Cambridge, MA: MIT Press.

McFarlane, D. A. (1930). The role of kinesthesis in maze learning. *University of California Publications in Psychology, 4*, 277-305.

Maki, R. H. (1981). Categorization and distance effects with spatial linear orders. *Journal of Experimental Psychology: Human Learning and Memory, 7*, 15-32.

McDonald, T. P., & Pellegrino, J. W. (1991). *Direction estimates following primary versus secondary spatial learning*. Unpublished manuscript.

McNamara, T. P. (1986). Mental representations of spatial relations. *Cognitive Psychology, 18*, 87-121.

McNamara, T. P., Hardy, J. K., & Hirtle, S. C. (1989). Subjective hierarchies in spatial memory. *Journal of Experimental Psychology: Learning, Memory, and Cognition, 15*, 211-227.

McNamara, T. P., Ratcliff, R., & McKoon, G. (1984). The mental representation of knowledge acquired from maps. *Journal of Experimental Psychology: Learning, Memory, and Cognition, 10*, 723-732.

Miller, G. (1956). The magic number seven, plus or minus two: Some limits on the capacity for processing information. *Psychological Review, 63*, 81-97.

Moar, I., & Bower, G. H. (1983). Inconsistency in spatial knowledge. *Memory and Cognition, 11*, 107-113.

Moeser, S. D. (1988). Cognitive mapping in a complex building. *Environment and Behavior, 20*, 21-49.

Muller, J. (1985). Mental maps at a global scale. *Cartographica, 22*, 51-59.
Nadel, L. (1988). Landmarks: Neurobiological perspectives. *British Journal of Developmental Psychology, 6*, 383-385.
Neisser, U. (1976). *Cognition and reality*. San Francisco: Freeman.
Newcombe, N., & Liben, L. S. (1982). Barrier effects in the cognitive maps of children and adults. *Journal of Experimental Child Psychology, 34*, 46-58.
O'Keefe, J., Nadel, L., Keightley, S., & Kill, D. (1975). Fornix lesions selectively abolish place learning in the rat. *Experimental Neurology, 48*, 152-166.
Palij, M., Levine, M., & Kahan, T. (1984). The orientation of cognitive maps. *Bulletin of the Psychonomic Society, 22*, 105-108.
Passini, R., Proulx, G., & Rainville, C. (1990). The spatio-cognitive abilities of the visually impaired population. *Environment and Behavior, 22*, 91-118.
Piaget, J., & Inhelder, B. (1967). *The child's conception of space*. New York: Norton.
Piaget, J., Inhelder, B., & Szeminska, A. (1960). *The child's conception of geometry*. New York: Basic Books.
Presson, C. C., DeLange, N., & Hazelrigg, M. D. (1989). Orientation specificity in spatial memory: What makes a path different from a map of the path? *Journal of Experimental Psychology: Learning, Memory, and Cognition, 15*, 887-897.
Presson, C. C., & Hazelrigg, M. D. (1984). Building spatial representations through primary and secondary learning. *Journal of Experimental Psychology: Learning, Memory, and Cognition, 10*, 716-722.
Presson, C. C., & Somerville, S. C. (1985). Beyond egocentrism: A new look at the beginnings of spatial representation. In H. Wellman (Ed.), *The development of children's spatial search*. Hillsdale, NJ: Erlbaum.
Pylyshyn, Z. W. (1979). The rate of "mental rotation" of images: A test of a holistic analogue hypothesis. *Memory & Cognition, 7*, 19-28.
Pylyshyn, Z. W. (1981). The imagery debate: Analogue media versus tacit knowledge. *Psychological Review, 88*, 16-45.
Restle, F. (1957). Discrimination of cues in mazes: A resolution of the "place-vs.-response" question. *Psychological Review, 64*, 217-228.
Rieser, J. J. (1989). Access to knowledge of spatial structure at novel points of observation. *Journal of Experimental Psychology: Learning, Memory, and Cognition, 15*, 1157-1165.

Rieser, J. J., Guth, D. A., & Hill, E. W. (1982). Mental processes mediating independent travel: Implications for orientation and mobility. *Journal of Visual Impairment and Blindness, 76*, 213-219.
Rieser, J. J., Guth, D. A., & Hill, E. W. (1986). Sensitivity to perspective structure while walking without vision. *Perception, 15*, 173-188.
Rossano, M. J., & Warren, D. H. (1989). Misaligned maps lead to predictable errors. *Perception, 18*, 215-229.
Rudy, J. W., Stadler-Morris, S., & Albert, P. (1987). Ontogeny of spatial navigation behaviors in the rat: Dissociation of "proximal"- and "distal"-cue based behaviors. *Behavioral Neuroscience, 101*, 62-73.
Sadalla, E. K., & Magel, S. G. (1980). The perception of traversed distance. *Environment and Behavior, 12*, 65-79.
Schenk, F. (1985). Development of place navigation in rats from weaning to puberty. *Behavioral and Neural Biology, 43*, 69-85.
Scholnick, E. K., Fein, G. G., & Campbell, P. F. (1990). Changing predictors of map use in wayfinding. *Developmental Psychology, 26*, 188-193.
Shepard, R. N., & Metzler, J. (1971). Mental rotation of three-dimensional objects. *Science, 171*, 701-703.
Sholl, M. J. (1987). Cognitive maps as orienting schemata. *Journal of Experimental Psychology: Learning, Memory, and Cognition, 13*, 615-628.
Siegel, A. W. (1981). The externalization of cognitive maps by children and adults: In search of ways to ask better questions. In L. S. Liben, A. Patterson, & N. Newcombe (Eds.), *Spatial representation and behavior across the life span: Theory and application* (pp. 167-194). New York: Academic.
Siegel, A. W., Kirasic, K. C., & Kail, R. V. (1979). Stalking the elusive cognitive map: The development of children's representations of geographic space. In J. F. Wohlwill & I. Altman (Eds.), *Human behavior and environment* (Vol. 3). New York: Plenum.
Siegel, A. W., & White, S. H. (1975). The development of spatial representations of large-scale environments. In H. W. Reese (Ed.), *Advances in child development and behavior* (Vol 10, pp. 9-55). New York: Academic.
Spence, K. W., & Hull, C. L. (1938). Correction versus non-correction. *Journal of Comparative Psychology, 25*, 127-133.
Stevens, A., & Coupe, P. (1978). Distortions in judged spatial relations. *Cognitive Psychology, 12*, 137-175.
Suzuki, S., Augerinos, G., & Black, A. H. (1980). Stimulus control of spatial behavior on the eight-arm maze in rats. *Learning and Motivation, 11*, 1-18.

Thorndyke, P. W. (1981). Distance estimation from cognitive maps. *Cognitive Psychology, 13*, 526-550.

Thorndyke, P. W., & Hayes-Roth, B. (1982). Differences in spatial knowledge acquired from maps and navigation. *Cognitive Psychology, 14*, 560-589.

Tolman, E. C. (1932). *Purposive behavior in animals and men.* New York: Appleton-Century-Crofts.

Tolman, E. C. (1948). Cognitive maps in rats and men. *Psychological Review, 55*, 189-208.

Tolman, E. C., & Honzik, C. H. (1930). "Insight" in rats. *University of California Publications in Psychology, 4*, 215-232.

Tolman, E. C., Ritchie, B. F., & Kalish, D. (1946a). Studies in spatial learning: I. Orientation and the short-cut. *Journal of Experimental Psychology, 36*, 13-24.

Tolman, E. C., Ritchie, B. F., & Kalish, D. (1946b). Studies in spatial learning: II. Place learning versus response learning. *Journal of Experimental Psychology, 36*, 221-229.

Tolman, E. C., Ritchie, B. F., & Kalish, D. (1947). Studies in spatial learning: V. Response learning versus place learning by the non-correction method. *Journal of Experimental Psychology, 37*, 285-292.

Trowbridge, C. C. (1913). On fundamental methods of orientation and "imaginary maps." *Science, 38*, 990.

Tversky, B. (1981). Distortions in memory for maps. *Cognitive Psychology, 13*, 407-433.

Uttal, D. H., & Wellman, H. M. (1989). Young children's representation of spatial information acquired from maps. *Developmental Psychology, 25*, 128-138.

Weatherford, D. L. (1985). Representing and manipulating spatial information from different environments: Models to neighborhoods. In R. Cohen (Ed.), *The development of spatial cognition* (pp. 41-70). Hillsdale, NJ: Lawrence Erlbaum Associates.

Whishaw, I. Q. (1985). Cholinergic receptor blockade in the rat impairs locale but not taxon strategies for place navigation in a swimming pool. *Behavioral Neuroscience, 99*, 979-1005.

Whishaw, I. Q., & Dunnett, S. B. (1985). Dopamine depletion, stimulation or blockade in the rat disrupts spatial navigation and locomotion dependent upon beacon or distal cues. *Behavioural Brain Research, 18*, 11-29.

*Behavior and Environment: Psychological and Geographical Approaches*
*T. Gärling and R.G. Golledge (Editors)*



## CHAPTER 4

# Emotions in Person-Environment-Behavior Episodes

**Douglas Amedeo**

Affective appraisals and their resulting emotional incidents are believed to exert significant influences on the nature and tone of other responses and experiences. For that reason, they are of special interest to many researchers. However, the way in which these things are usually understood makes their incorporation into investigations emphasizing environmental contexts somewhat awkward. For example, two premises underlie the work of researchers investigating the immediate significance of environments in human activities and experiences. One holds that activities and experiences ordinarily take place in environmental configurations such as settings, places, landscapes, and the like, while the other indicates that humans apprehend, interpret, appraise, evaluate, and adapt to environments within which they enact their activities and undergo their experiences.

Premises like these communicate the idea that environments constitute an external source of information necessary for the execution of human action and for undergoing experience. But they also suggest that people necessarily transact and interact with this information and, in the process, assess it for meaning. They especially imply that the informational base for activities and experiences is likely to be influenced by the presentation of that information and how it is processed. Thus, given their influences on other responses and experiences, the rational unit for visualizing both affective appraisals and their resulting emotions would, by these premises, seem to be the person-environment-behavior episode.

Currently, arguments about the causes underlying the onset, intensity, and differences in emotions span a large number of diverse subject areas and are offered by a wide variety of investigators. G. Mandler (1975), Lyons (1980), and, as of late, Strongman (1987) describe the available theories and other less extensive conceptualizations and offer their own thoughts about the nature of the emotional occurrence. But the array type (e.g., the environment) within which the context for the occurrence of the emotional experience is frequently embedded is not an issue of overwhelming concern in the general literature on affects; indeed, it receives relatively little emphasis, despite its potential ecological implications.

The discussion offered here will focus on that issue. Its aim will be to explore how the emotional experience might be contemplated when human activity and experience are viewed through a person-environment-behavior (P-E-B) perspective. The work of others will be taken into consideration in building this discussion, particularly knowledge developed about fundamental components involved in an emotional occurrence. It should be made clear that embedding the emotional experience in an environmental context, though not frequently done, is not original with this attempt. At least two other extensive conceptualizations precede the one that will be entertained here. They will be examined in some detail prior to the outlining of this discussion's rendition.

## Definitions of Emotions, Feelings, and Affect

The literature is unclear regarding the criteria to define emotion or, for that matter, affect. Standardization of meaning for terms like emotion, feeling, mood, affect, and so on has not yet taken place. Strongman (1987) describes how P. Kleinginna and S. Kleinginna (1981) categorized "hundreds of definitions" in order to derive some useful conceptual intersections and create a single definition from them. Their efforts led them to submit this interpretation of what clusters of other researchers meant by emotion:

> Emotion is a complex set of interactions among subjective and objective factors, mediated by neural/hormonal systems, which can (a) give rise to affective experiences such as feelings of arousal, pleasure/displeasure; (b) generate cognitive processes such as emotionally relevant perceptual effects, appraisals, labeling processes; (c) activate widespread physiological adjustments to the arousing conditions; and (d) lead to behavior that is often, but not always, expressive, goal-directed, and adaptive. (Strongman, 1987, p. 3)

Kleinginna and Kleinginna's interpretation suggests why severe definitional difficulties exist in the research literature on affects (see also Plutchik, 1965). Investigators involved in such research come from a large set of diverse subject-areas, including different interests in psychology (like social, cognitive, developmental, clinical, behavioral, and environmental), branches of psychiatry, sociology, education, biology, philosophy, literature, art, and aesthetics. Inquiries are made about types of emotional experiences, how those experiencing them apprehend them, the basis for and differences between them, the ways we express emotions or affective experiences, how others recognize such expressions, the stimuli that may excite or activate them, what their functions in everyday existence might be (e.g., adaptive, drives, motivations, etc.), the degree to which they influence behavior in general, and so on. Investigators approach their research equipped with different initial assumptions about how the world operates, and different perspectives influence the nature of the theories that are developed and the nature of the concepts about which generalizations are formed.

Nearly twenty years ago, Strongman (1973) pointed to our numerous theories on emotions and reviewed twenty of the leading ones. Since then, the theoretical literature has become far more voluminous. It is not surprising that definitions, basic assumptions, and research contexts often fail to correspond from one group of studies to another.

The lack of clarity in meaning persists even among the definitions of specific types of emotions. Davitz (1969, pp. 1-2), in his treatment of the language of emotion, indicates that "a review of the psychological literature dealing with emotion provides little help in understanding what people mean when they say someone is happy or sad." Eighteen years later, Strongman (1987, p. 7) suggests that little has changed; he states that "a similar lack of precision surrounds terms which refer to specific emotions, jealousy, fear, love, anger, for example (and, particularly, anxiety)."

In practice, feelings, emotions, and sometimes even moods are considered part of an emotional category. Some researchers widen the category to include preferences and aesthetic evaluations, and the broader concept "affect" appears to be more useful in describing this larger domain (see, for example, R. Kaplan, 1975, 1977; S. Kaplan 1975; Nasar, 1981, 1983, 1988; Ulrich, 1983; Winkel, Malek, & Thiel, 1969; Wohlwill, 1976). This chapter is directed at the most familiar of affects, emotions, and the feelings associated with them, and P. Kleinginna and S. Kleinginna's definition, cited earlier, reflects the essence of what is meant here by emotion. The general term "affect" here refers to both feelings and the emotions. Numerous individuals from a variety of intellectual backgrounds have investigated affects, and their efforts at least have made coherent information available about the components underlying emotion. This discussion presents some essentials about these components in order to consider their relevance to the emotional occurrence in a person-environment-behavior context.

## Central Themes in Research on Emotional Occurrences

Discussions of how emotions come about consider both the physiological and cognitive levels of human functioning (see Lyons, 1980; G. Mandler, 1975; Strongman, 1973, 1987). Sometimes theorists put greater emphasis on one or the other of these levels, but more recent descriptions make it increasingly clear that the two are likely to interact as processes.

### *The Physiological Component in Emotional Occurrences*

Physiological activities which differ from regular or usual physiological activity commonly take place in many instances of emotional occurrences. Individuals frequently report sensing physiological changes when undergoing more intense emotional experiences. Physiological changes recorded or observed during emotional episodes have been associated with adrenaline flow, blood circulation, respiration, muscular tension, gastro-intestinal activity, temperature, and secretions (Goshen, 1967).

Physiological changes associated with emotions are assumed set off by nerve cell activity in the Limbic system, which is said to be, in an evolutionary sense, an older part of the brain - one not involved in intellectual functions but in life-sustaining ones. Specific parts of the Limbic system (e.g., hypothalamus and limbic cortex) are believed to be directly involved in the nerve cell activities related to emotions, particularly those associated with the relatively more intense emotions like fear, rage, anxiety, agitation, those occurring in sexual excitation, and so on. The physiological changes which these nerve cell activities generate generally appear as deviations (e.g., increases and, in some instances, decreases) from the ordinary body actions which the autonomic nervous system regulate to maintain the individual's normal physical working state.

The two main divisions of this system, the sympathetic and parasympathetic, access and control various body organs like the lungs, heart, liver, spleen, stomach, pancreas, adrenals, kidneys, colon, intestines, and sex glands. These divisions generally create opposite effects and tend to counterbalance each other. For example, one might transmit impulses to speed the heart while the other governs its slowing down. The sympathetic division seems more involved in generating bodily activities associated with emotions and the parasympathetic with activities related to maintaining normal functioning of various parts of the body.

Some theorists have emphasized the importance of physiological changes for comprehending both the emotional occurrence itself and differences among emotions, such as the frequently cited James and Lange (1922). Their argument was that emotions were really feelings of physiological changes that occurred when individuals experienced such affects. They reasoned that bodily changes were responses to perceptions of emotion-activating stimuli and that feelings of these changes were the emotions. They also believed that evaluations (i.e., cognition) of what one felt followed from physiological changes (some cognitive theorists contend the reverse). Though James and Lange allude to perception, they do not stress that as the vital aspect of emotion. For them, the subjective experiencing or the feeling of the physiological changes associated with the emotional occurrence is the emotion. Hence, differences in feelings meant differences in bodily changes.

Cannon (1927) was one of the first to question their contentions. He reasoned that the patterning of physiological changes during an emotion was an ineffective criterion for differentiating among the emotions, particularly because the same physiological changes often occur during emotions that are very different from one another, and, in fact, even occur in non-emotional states.

The works of Schachter and Singer (1962) and Schachter and Wheeler (1962) presented another significant challenge to the James and Lange view and provided incentive for further investigations about the cognitive component in the emotional occurrence.

Schachter and Singer (1962) suspected that significant connections might exist between valuative-type cognitions of affective situations and the physiological changes experienced during an emotional occurrence. To test that hypothesis, they devised experiments in which actors, in the presence of individual subjects, pretended to be undergoing emotional states (e.g., anger and euphoria). Subjects were not aware of the real purpose of the experiment (they were led to understand it had a different intent) or that the performers were actors and a part of it. Before their encounter with the actor, subjects either had been injected with adrenaline (epinephrine) and not informed of its real substance and its physiological effects, injected and informed, or injected with a placebo. From the responses of these three types of subjects to the effects or non-effects of the injections and the scenes acted out, Schachter and Singer concluded that subjects indicated experiencing no emotions until they were put in contexts that would suggest certain affects.

This suggested that, even though subjects were experiencing pronounced physiological changes from the injected epinephrine, they did not consider themselves to be undergoing emotions until they were placed in situations from which, through appraisals, they could generate appropriate cognitions for the bodily changes. The implication is that labeling of sensations associated with physiological changes emanates out of affective meaning generated by evaluations made of situations in which changes occur - provided, of course, labelers feel that the situation had something to do with such changes.

This implication appeared re-enforced by those subjects informed of the substance in the injection and its physiological effects. When they were exposed to the contrived situations in which actors displayed euphoria and anger, they did not report feeling either of the emotions. Apparently, they did not take the situations as relevant; they knew the causes of the physiological changes they were experiencing. The adrenaline in the injection generated them.

While intensity differences have been noticed with regard to some physiological aspect or another, and while certain physiological changes seem to occur more often with some emotions than with others, no one-to-one relationship between pattern of physiological changes and specific emotion has been conclusively established. Other research findings over time have not supported the James-Lange contention satisfactorily. Lyons (1980, p. 15) for example, indicates that "the wealth of experimental evidence about the physiological aspects of emotions has yet to confirm the possibility of distinguishing emotions by reference to physiological changes alone." Later, Strongman (1987, p. 240) comes to a similar conclusion. He states that "the evidence for any physiological response patterning *(among the emotions)* is disappointingly slight" (italics added).

In sum, while there is no evidence for a correspondence between a particular pattern of physiological changes and specific emotions, it nevertheless seems evident that such changes are an important component for emotions. Their felt presence, since different from the usual bodily activity in intensity, rate, and discharge, may indicate to an individual the onset of an emotion, though not a particular one.

The important point, as critics would contend, is that other factors operating during an emotional occurrence should be considered to understand both the nature of the occurrence itself and the differences among the emotions. That is to say, physiological changes should be related to the situations that have generated them and to the evaluations of those situations by the individuals who experience them. One insurmountable problem, for example, that physiological supporters have had to face is that the *same* stimulus conditions or situation can generate different emotions in different people. This suggests, of course, that different individuals can perceive and evaluate the same situation differently. To deal with that not uncommon occurrence, some provision for a cognitive process in emotion was necessary.

### *The Cognitive Component in Emotion*

Many terms like happiness, jealousy, fear, anxiety, shame, love, hate, embarrassment, joy, elation, and others either summarize reactions to situations involving relations between self and others or, in a case like anxiety, may exemplify a focus on the self alone. The terms conceptualize what is being felt during an emotional occurrence and strongly suggest that the states they describe follow from assessments of exchanges with others in different situations or reflections about self. It thus seems reasonable that theorists concerned with affects would recommend considering a cognitive component in contemplating the nature of the emotional experience.

From the cognitive perspective, what is important in understanding a specific emotion is the nature of the mental state associated with it, the stimulus or external conditions activating the emotion, and how the individual perceives and evaluates those conditions. Cognitive theorists acknowledge the presence of physiological changes during emotions, but many of them claim that such changes follow rather than precede evaluations of the external conditions cuing a given affect.

Two points are basic in reasoning about the influence of cognition in affective experiences. One is that cognitions of situations determine *what* is felt in them, while the other is that the concepts individuals use to *label* their emotional reactions to surroundings, events, and others, grow out of their evaluations of such things. These ideas suggest that individuals employ an interpretative process to label their affective reactions to situations. If this is the case, then a person's definition of a situation and assessment of its meaning determine the nature of the affective episode the person experiences in that circumstance.

Cognitive evaluations usually are employed to integrate and endow with meaning that which is perceived of a situation. Since the relevance of situations is to individuals, such meaning is likely to be more than purely factual. It is apt also to have a strong subjective or personal component with regard to the status of the self in the perceived circumstances, and an important aspect of that component in many instances thus may be affective. Evaluation already is viewed as an integral part of the more general process of perception. Referring to it broadly, as has been done here, tends to de-emphasize its more distinctive features with regard to the way it actually proceeds during an emotional occurrence. There is some merit in treating it this way however; doing so illustrates that, like perception, the emotional occurrence depends on memory activity, the use of attention processes, cognitive structures, previous experiences, and so on (Amedeo & York, 1984; Geertz, 1969).

Of particular interest in the analysis of the emotional event itself, however, is the distinctive manner in which affective information in a situation is evaluated for its meaning. A number of individuals have reflected on how such information is processed during evaluation (Fiske, 1981; Lazarus, Averill, & Opton, 1970; G. Mandler, 1975; Peters, 1970; Shott, 1979; Strongman, 1973, 1987), but Arnold's (1970a, 1970b) thoughts appear to have set the basis for much of the work that followed hers.

In Arnold's view, the distinctive aspect of the more general evaluative process during an emotional episode is an appraisal: an assessment process that involves personal judgments about effects objects and/or people in the perceived situation may have on "us." Arnold is suggesting that objects, other people, and/or events as such do not specify an emotion; rather, what the individual thinks of these things is what matters in the labeling of an emotion. In her reasoning, perception of a situation precedes an appraisal of it, and, in turn, the appraisal evaluates the perceived situation for its affective significance to the individual.

Arnold thus maintains that the type of emotion (i.e., the feeling) experienced in a situation results from a form of cognition called an appraisal (see Arnold, 1970b; Lazarus et al., 1970; Peters 1970). Appraisals help the individual translate that which has been recognized in the situation. They involve such activities as remembering similar situations in the past and the effects they might have had on one's emotional episodes (i.e., recall from affective memory), imagining how the present situation might affect one in the light of those recalls, and estimating whether, for example, such effects will be harmful or beneficial. Appraisals are formed as individuals view situations along a variety of dimensions as being, for example, acceptable or unacceptable, agreeable or disagreeable, beneficial or harmful, interesting or boring, or even of no immediate relevance. Thus, all emotions (i.e., the feelings used to label them) have appraisals as a base, and different types of emotions have different appraisals. There are two main influences on the nature of appraisals: one generated by the activities of remembering, imagining, and estimating; the other evoked by the situation itself. That is, cues from an individual's apprehension of situational features help to stimulate and focus the individual's attention to particular channels of thought peculiar to a specific type of appraisal which, in turn, leads to a distinctly defined type of emotion. Though each particular appraisal has definite interpretations associated with it, the distinctiveness of those interpretations can be understood only in terms of what the individual initially comes to apprehend regarding the features of a situation. In other words, for an appraisal process to be initiated, some subset of cues from the apprehension of the situation must have the potential to change or modify an individual's initial state.

### *Integrating the Physiological Emphasis with the Cognitive*

Lyons' (1980) thoughts on evaluation take Arnold's reasoning a bit further. He indicates that evaluative cognitive activity plays an essential role in the experiencing of emotions, in that it both generates the physiological changes which the individual undergoing the emotion feels and also is the means by which persons differentiate the emotions.

According to his reasoning, an actual or ongoing emotional state has a number of interrelated components. These include beliefs about one's present situation, an evaluation of that situation in terms of those beliefs (particularly in relation to one's self), and a generation of wants and desires from such evaluations. Wants and desires, in turn, direct behavior, and wants and evaluation together activate both atypical physiological changes and the subjective expression of these changes or feelings. The example Lyons (1980, p. 57) uses to exemplify how these components come together in an empirical situation is vivid:

> To take a simple case of fear, the sight of a ferocious dog might cause Fred to evaluate it as threateningly dangerous to him, such that he wants to run away and escape, and so he takes to his heels. And the combination of the evaluation of the situation as threateningly dangerous, plus his urgent desire to escape, stirs up his physiological processes, increasing his adrenaline output, his blood flow, and respiration rate, so that he feels his heart thumping, the sweat on the palms of his hands and down the small of his back, a constriction around the chest, and a dryness in his mouth.

Lyons makes it clear that, although we can view either evaluation and atypical physiological changes as necessary components of an actual or ongoing emotional state, we need both to discuss the sufficient conditions to define an emotional state. Atypical or unusual bodily changes certainly may indicate an emotional state; but since an evaluation of a situation activates such changes associated with emotion both must exist before we claim that an emotional state is present.

Lyons (1980, pp. 77-78) indicates that "for most emotions if not all, what emotion, if any, will well up in a person will depend on how he 'sees' the object he has apprehended or believes he has apprehended. A man is afraid because he 'sees' the object or situation as dangerous. A man is angry because he 'sees' the situation as offensive or insulting." However, as Lyons points out, if evaluations are to arouse individuals or generate emotions, they probably should involve assessments of situations that are qualitative in a negative or positive sense. In terms of the self, the likely reference point in any emotion, such assessments would contain approvals or disapprovals of some aspects of the situation being evaluated. This would seem necessary, since a dispassionate or indifferent evaluation probably will fail to stir the individual and more likely will be an informational one.

## Conceptualizations About Emotions in Environments

What qualifications to current theorizing about emotions then do we need to make if we formally acknowledge that the domains for experiencing and "behaving" are actual environments? If theorizing was thoroughly robust, the answer probably would be none, as such provisions would have been provided for already.

But theories on emotions are not complete, and, in practice, most make no provisions for explicit considerations of environmental aspects. Statements that people experience emotions in actual environments (frequently referred to as situations, settings, places, etc.) are not uncommon in the research literature, but they usually amount to little more than casual acknowledgements of the presence of the environmental dimension. This is not to say, however, that research about emotional occurrences in actual environments is nonexistent (for reviews, see Russell & Snodgrass, 1987; Ulrich, 1983).

Those who focus on person-environment issues in their research generally suggest that emotional experiences may be related to person-environment-behavior contexts in a number of ways, depending on where in such contexts they are believed to be causally significant or are themselves influenced. Ittelson, Rivlin, Proshansky, & Winkel, (1974, p. 88) illustrate a common way of viewing emotion in their remark that "spaces and places, no less than people, can evoke intense emotional responses. Rooms, neighborhoods, and cities can be 'friendly,' 'threatening,' 'frustrating,' or 'loathsome;' they can induce hate, love, fear, desire, and other affective states."

The causal orientation exemplified in a statement of this sort moves from the environment to the emotional occurrence. In his observations about the importance of the actual environment in emotional experiences, Strongman (1987, p. 225) also emphasizes that orientation. He states that "it is indisputable that the environment has an emotional impact on the individual. By this, reference is not simply being made to stimulus-response relationships, but to the influence of the grand environment, be it natural or artificial, on the emotional state of a person."

Though experience suggests that contentions like these make sense, the integrations of ideas necessary to make them more explicit and coherent are scarce. It is often difficult, for example, to ascertain from current research just what *evoke, induce, or generate* can mean conceptually and how to construe an influence from a grand environment (Fried & Gliecher, 1961; E. Gerson & M. Gerson, 1976; Howard et. al., 1972; Sears & Auld, 1976; Wohlwill, 1966).

However, researchers working with other concerns in the person-environment realm have developed two extensive conceptualizations addressing emotional experiences in person-environment-behavior contexts. What is particularly interesting about each is their examination of the emotional state not only from the way in which it might have been influenced but also from the way it influences. One of these conceptualizations comes out of Mehrabian and Russell's (1974) efforts to develop an approach to environmental psychology, while the other is a product of Ulrich's (1983) concern for environmental aesthetics.

Mehrabian and Russell propose that the emotional state an individual actually experiences in a setting is directly influenced by the stimuli of the surroundings, the individual's initial emotional states, and affective inclinations related to the individual's personality traits. They argue that, when individuals encounter a setting, they do so with ongoing internal affective states and emotional dispositions closely associated with their personality traits. These affective preconditions, so to speak, are said to interact with the effects from the environmental encounter to generate an individual's overall emotional state.

They claim that three fundamental emotional dimensions, "pleasure," "arousal," and "dominance," effectively summarize the emotion-evoking aspects of environments and can, in different combinations, be used to characterize any individual's emotional experience at any time to any setting.

Mehrabian and Russell point to the variety of correlations found between individual instances of physical stimuli in environments (e.g., characteristics of light, color, sound, and temperature) and their two emotional dimensions of pleasure and arousal. They explain, however, that environments usually make stimuli available that activate a number of sensory receptors simultaneously and in complex combinations, and that stimulus effects on an encountering individual do vary in time. Hence, to better capture the overall external influences that can result from such inherent variances in stimulus effects, Mehrabian and Russell use information theory. They state (1974, p. 77) that "the concept of average information rate can be used to characterize complex spatial and temporal arrangements of stimuli within and across settings. It also serves as the basis for a simple, yet powerful, hypothesis: information rate is a direct correlate of arousal." In the empirical application of their work, a verbal way to measure information rate is developed using subjects' descriptions of a situation along adjective pairs of concepts reflecting the presence of or relations between macro characteristics.

To reiterate: the significance of emotions in person-environment-behavior episodes is exemplified by assigning emotions an intervening role in Mehrabian and Russell's framework. The emotional responses to the environment, expressed as pleasure, arousal, and dominance, or combinations of them, are said to influence the different behaviors that take place in the environment.

Mehrabian and Russell use the concept "approach-avoidance" to characterize behaviors in the environment. They (1974, p. 96) broadly define this concept to..."include physical movement toward, or away from, an environment or stimulus, degree of attention, exploration, favorable attitudes such as verbally or nonverbally expressed preference or liking, approach to a task (the level of performance), and approach to another person (affiliation)."

To elicit information about approach-avoidance reactions to situations, Mehrabian and Russell suggest the use of eight questions that tap such broader themes or categories as "desire to stay in the situation," "desire to explore the situation," "desire to work in the situation," and "desire to affiliate in the situation." They examine the findings in the research literature dealing with relations between emotional reactions to physical and social stimuli in the environment and approach-avoidance behaviors, and, on the basis of these results and investigations of their own, they indicate that a number of postulates regarding the connection between emotions and behavior follow from their framework. One (1974, p. 137) is "that approach to a situation is a direct correlate of the situation's pleasure-eliciting quality," and the other is "that approach to a situation is an inverted-U-shaped function of the arousing quality of (or information rate from) the situation."

It should be noted that their framework makes no provisions for cognitive appraisals of environmental information to account for the type of the emotion experienced by an individual in a setting or for differences in affective experiences of the same setting among individuals. Nor is there any emphasis on a knowing process to rationalize how an encountering individual assesses information acquired via sensory receptors for situation identification and definition.

Mehrabian and Russell use the term "direct" to refer to the influence an environment's stimuli has on an individual's emotional state; this probably rules out any consideration of an intermediate perceptual-cognitive process. It does not mean, however, that they were unconcerned with individual differences. Their above description of the emotional state noted that the immediate influence of the environment on an individual's emotional reaction is qualified by internal emotional conditions of the individual. The latter consists of "temporary" affective conditions and, of special significance to their conceptualization, "trait emotions." Mehrabian and Russell indicate that these refer to an individual's "characteristic levels of pleasure, arousal, and dominance." They (1974, p. 199) state that "a person's approach-avoidance responses to a situation are determined not only by the emotional responses that the situation typically elicits but also by the emotions with which he enters that situation." Hence, by also focusing on the emotional correlates associated with various personality traits, their framework makes available a way for accounting for individual differences in approach-avoidance to various settings by references to trait differences.

A personality trait that plays a significant role in their conceptualization is arousal-seeking tendency. They claim that a person's preference (an example of approach) for an environment is related to that person's preferred arousal level. They note that different people are inclined toward different arousal levels or some may be high stimulus seekers while others may be low. Mehrabian and Russell (1974, p. 55) illustrate their reasoning for focusing on this trait in this way: "Of particular interest was the personality trait of arousal-seeking tendency, since variations in arousal-seeking behaviors (e.g., seeking out, exploring, remaining in, or preferring a place) are accounted for by the interaction of stimulus properties (i.e., of the environment or information rate) and by individual differences in preferred arousal level" (italics added).

In his conceptualization, Ulrich (1983) contends that, once visual perception takes place, the first level of reaction to the environment is affective. He indicates that this reaction is usually a broad or highly generalized one (e.g., involving liking, disliking, interest, fear, etc.) and is a response not primarily to information but to preferenda aspects of the immediate environmental encounter (i.e., preferenda elicit them). Preferenda refer to configurations of features or stimulus characteristics in environments that are inherently nondescript and thus do not (nor, as Ulrich contends, need they) lend themselves to cognitive judgments but are nevertheless highly effective in generating affects (see Zajonc, 1980). These generalized affects, according to Ulrich, may serve directly as motivators for approach-avoidance impulses or behavior in environmental interactions or generate arousal in the electrocortical and autonomic systems and, in so doing, mobilize the individual to engage in certain types of behavior or to continue ongoing behavior.

According to Ulrich, this initial affective reaction also can interact with ongoing processes involved in the overall apprehension of the environment. These include perceptual-cognitive processes involved in the recognition and definition of the situation and cognitive appraisals of the environment with regard to assessing its significance for well-being and its beneficial or threatening implications. Ulrich contends that, if the initial affective reaction is intense, it is likely to be prominent in immediate experience, heavily influence the course of the cognitive evaluating process, and constitute a strong catalyst in memory for repeated apprehensions of such scenes. If, on the other hand, it is mild, it is not likely to have much of an affect on the ongoing evaluating process.

Ulrich indicates that the eventual affective state an individual experiences in an environmental encounter may be influenced directly by the initial generalized affective reaction, ongoing cognitive evaluation of the surroundings, and/or the interaction effects of the two. When cognitive evaluation is influenced by an intense initial affective reaction, the ultimate affective state is likely to be an elaboration of the generalized reaction and may consist of other emotions as well that are generated by appraisal aspects of the evaluation. This eventual or post-cognitive affective state may lead to further physiological arousal. This, in turn, generates motivations or action impulses which may lead to instances of adaptive behavior or functioning in the environment.

For Ulrich, then, affective reactions to "natural" environments serve some adaptive function, and, in that sense, affects and behavior are connected in the environment. This point is so distinctive to his conceptualization that it is best to note how Ulrich (1983, p. 93), himself, puts it:

> It is assumed that an individual's affective reaction motivates, or serves as an action impulse for, adaptive behavior or functioning... The individual is physiologically mobilized to undertake or sustain adaptive actions because affects in relation to the scene have produced appropriate changes in arousal... Adaptive refers here to a wide array of actions and functioning which are appropriate in terms of fostering well-being. The term action impulse reflects the notion that an action motivated internally by affect and expressed in neurophysiological arousal need not be carried out and can be suppressed or denied...For instance, a person viewing an attractive natural setting might feel strong preference and interest, and an impulse to explore the area on foot, but could suppress the behavior and simply continue looking from the same vantage point.

Some examples of adaptive behaviors said by Ulrich (1983, p. 94) to be motivated by affective/arousal reactions to the natural surroundings include exploration, approach, avoidance, vigilant attention with scanning.

Mehrabian and Russell's modeling and Ulrich's conceptualization appear to be the only extensive frameworks in the person-environment-behavior field that explicitly consider the emotional experience in an environmental circumstance (see also, however, typology by Grossbart & Amedeo, 1979). In a number of ways, they are alike. Both, for example, emphasize physiological arousal as a basis for other responses to the environment and neither treats cognition as necessary and/or prior to the onset of an emotional occurrence. Given these and other significant similarities in their outlook, it is somewhat curious that alternative frameworks employing different perspectives have not also emerged.

It is evident, for example, that there is a greater emphasis on information and cognitive processing in current discussions about emotions and person-environment-behavior relations than there had been in the more distant past. Since an emotional experience, itself, ordinarily emanates out of some kind of person-environment-behavior episode, this common emphasis should have provided the basis for an alternative way of viewing the emotional occurrence in actual environments. So far it has not. The discussion below speculates on a another way to envision the emotional experience - one that attempts to be consistent with reasoning-parallels found in thoughts on emotional occurrences and in thinking about P-E-B relations and that can be embedded within current frameworks concerned with person-environment-behavior episodes.

## The Emotional Experience Within Person-Environment-Behavior Frameworks

Strongman's (1987, p. 245) extensive review of conceptual development in the field of emotion has led him to conclude that "recent research and thought all point to the inadvisability, not to say the impossibility, of accounting for emotion without considering cognition...In my view, cognition is both central and necessary to emotion."

Strongman's conclusion (and also Lyons', 1980) regarding the importance of cognition in emotional occurrences suggests that at least two issues about emotion may be entertainable within current information-oriented, person-environment-behavior frameworks. One involves the significance of the environment, itself, for experiencing emotions, while the other concerns the impact of the emotional occurrence in any person-environment-behavior episode. The degree to which issues like these actually can be handled by P-E-B frameworks depends, of course, on whether they can be embedded within the reasoning structures of these frameworks. Current versions of information-oriented, P-E-B frameworks are examined below in order to show the extent to which that is possible.

### *Features of Information-Oriented, Person-Environment-Behavior Frameworks*

Reflections on person attributes, behavior, and the socio-cultural-physical settings that constitute surroundings have led over time to the development of frameworks that model how such fundamentals of human existence interrelate. One of these conceptualizations is said to have an interactional-constructivist viewpoint, while another is described as possessing a transactional perspective. Both, in any event, are collections of loosely-integrated hypotheses and assumptions which, when considered together, facilitate attempts to deal with such fundamental inquiries as how environments are experienced by individuals, the way in which such experiences "enter into" behavioral episodes, and the manner by which individuals establish durable relations with their environments. Despite significant differences in the way the unit of observation is construed in each, the two frameworks are actually quite similar in their reasoning (see Heft, 1981; Ittelson, 1973; Ittelson et al., 1974; S. Kaplan & R. Kaplan, 1982; Moore, 1979, 1987; Moore & Golledge, 1976; Stokols, 1978; Tibbetts, 1972, 1976; Wapner, Kaplan, & Cohen, 1973, 1987).

Their reasoning evolves out of a fundamental belief that human behavior and experience are fully intelligible only when viewed in terms of the environmental circumstances in which they happen. Under this assumption, an environment constitutes a person's surroundings - a medium for action and one that makes available to all the senses information necessary for action and integral to experience. Thus, a salient proposition common to both conceptualizations is that activity and experience in or with regard to the environment depend on the availability of information and the way it is processed. That is, in any person-environment episode, individuals engage in a knowing or a perceptual-cognitive process through which they acquire, synthesize, and integrate environmental information with internal sources of knowledge to form a contextual-arena basis for experience and behavior.

Internal sources of knowledge or cumulative integrations of previous environmental experiences are said to be involved in directing what environmental information is acquired during the environmental knowing process and in organizing its elaboration to render it informative. The terms mental representation and image frequently have been used to refer to such knowledge in these frameworks (see Downs & Stea, 1973, 1977; Evans, 1980; Heft, 1981; Moore, 1974, 1979, 1987; Moore & Golledge, 1976; Neisser, 1976; Tibbetts, 1976).

The transactional perspective, in particular, contends that individuals experience and come to know their world as a result of their actions in it, and their actions, in turn, are guided by prior experience. It suggests that environmental knowledge, whether in the form of integrated prior experience or from an immediate source, is a necessary prerequisite for action and a basis for experience. It indicates that individuals actively seek and process information about their surroundings in order to carry out their ordinary and everyday affairs. But since individuals can have contact with environments only via their senses, the transactional viewpoint contends that what is sensed has little meaning until it is related to the individual's purposes, motivations, and goals for actions.

According to this perspective, knowledge about environmental circumstances is constructed via an ongoing process of using information obtained from ongoing transactions to adjust, alter, and revise prior assumptions, anticipations, and expectancies about those circumstances. But the latter obviously evolve from prior experiences. Hence, for this framework, immediate experience is a product of mental activity arising out of person-environment transactions, and environmental knowledge is an essential for behavior.

The interactional-constructivist model subscribes to essentially the same basic reasoning as the transactional. In some respects, however, it elaborates on this reasoning by describing how previous experiences operate in environmental apprehension. It indicates, for example, that what individuals come to assume, anticipate, and expect about their surroundings while interacting with them are outcomes from a continuously ongoing perceptual-cognitive process in which information about previous environmental experiences (internal information) is combined with immediate information from surroundings. Internal information, however, is not considered to be a literal rendition of previous environmental experiences but rather mental representations of them. By that is meant that these representations are essentially environmental-type, cognitive constructions developed from a series of previous environmental experiences and stored in permanent memory. Continuously undergoing development, such constructions are susceptible to modifications whenever changes have been noted in the environmental type they represent. In other words, this model suggests that an individual's prior environmental or internal knowledge influences the selection, interpretation, and assessment of external information just as bringing in new information from external sources can change the internal information in memory.

A variety of terms have been used to refer to internal information or knowledge. As indicated, the general term has been mental representation; but other concepts have been used as well. These include environmental schemata or prototypes (Neisser, 1976), scenes (J. Mandler, 1984), cognitive maps (Downs & Stea, 1977; Golledge and Stimson, 1987), or environmental images (Lynch, 1960). Environmental schemata (to use the most general concept) are assumed to serve as the categorical rules guiding the individual's awareness and selection of external information from the environment. They are involved in the transformation of sensation into knowledge and the integration of external information with information held in memory. They function like automatic patterns in the organizing of sensory and other inputs into coherent experiences (see Amedeo & York, 1990, for a discussion of environmental schemata and prototypes and Blumenthal, 1977, for a discussion of longer-term cognitive integrations).

### *Emotions as Responses to Environmental Circumstances*

To propose that current information-oriented, P-E-B frameworks be adapted to take into account both the occurrence and influences of emotional events is to suggest that, in different ways, emotions potentially can play an important role in person-environment-behavior episodes. From everyday experiences, it is evident that they do. Consider, for example, some of the more common ways in which emotion can be of interest to those concerned with the nature of such episodes.

Emotion as a response to the external situation, itself, certainly would evoke interest, particularly because this is the type of experience that probably is most reflective of an individual's assessment of a setting's personal significance. The emotional response, itself, might be a reaction not only to context aspects of immediate surroundings but also to arena and ambiance aspects. However, context, arena, and ambiance are only facets of the larger entity generally conceptualized as an environment. Hence, because in environmental perception they probably are envisioned contingently, an emotion as a response cannot be appreciated fully if thought of as only a reaction to one of them. For example, negative feelings like threat, fear, and/or anxiety may characterize an individual's immediate responses to the context and ambiance of a certain area or section of a city. These responses may then inhibit an individual's ongoing exploration of the area. Decreased exploration of an area suggests relatively less transacting with it and, therefore, less exposure to its information. Since the development of a functionally useful cognitive map (i.e., orienting facet of the larger environmental schema) depends on, among other sources, information gathered through transacting with an area, such spatial cognitions of this part of the city probably will be malformed relative to actual structural conditions or poorly represented. Spatially negotiating those parts of the city may then turn out to be relatively awkward and ineffective because the cognitive base guiding perception of those areas is faulty. Such areas are not likely to serve as effective arenas for common everyday activities.

Feelings about a particular area can arise mainly from a direct appraisal of the circumstances depicted in its surroundings or they can be induced from some affective norm associated with a cognitive prototype of that type of area, the latter being activated by external attributes or cues. For most cases, the likelihood is that external information and norms jointly operate in affective appraisal processes. Areas in which positive affective appraisals take place usually encourage transacting with them. These areas get to be well known and thus are well represented structurally in orienting representations like cognitive maps. They are negotiated relatively more easily and serve effectively as arenas for activity. The opposite can be maintained for areas that reinforce negative responses.

Another major concern about emotion when reflecting on P-E-B episodes is the manner in which it influences the nature or quality of behavior enacted in an environment. Imagine, for example, an individual arranging to dine with another in some popularly distinguished dining place. Suppose that, upon encountering the dining place, it is perceived as having many unanticipated negative aspects like inappropriate lighting, crabby and sullen waiters, long waiting periods, water and grease-marked silverware, cold food, too much smoke, ordinary menu, crowding, etc. The emotional response to these conditions may be felt as irritation, frustration, and even anger. If these affects are somehow mixed with dining activity (say, through their influences on ongoing environmental apprehension), an entirely different enactment of that activity may occur than if one "mixes" it with excitement, pleasantness, and joy - all of which, incidentally, also can be evoked or reinforced by a dining place. In this example, there is a strong likelihood that the tone or quality of the behavior with regard to the environment has been affected by the emotions experienced. That is, if the individuals still dine, they do so in a way that is likely to be different in tone than if the emotions experienced in the place were positive. Of course, in the light of the emotions experienced, the behavior actually enacted could have been different from that intended; wants and/or desires arising out the evaluation and appraisal associated with the negative emotional responses could have served as motives for, among other things, walking out of the dining place instead of dining.

Consider the importance of perceptual-cognitive processing in this entire person-environment-behavior episode. In addition to generating the information necessary for ongoing action decisions, it provided the grounds for affective experience. Current theorizing on emotion says, for example, that emotional reactions evolve out of appraisals of perceived information.

Is it likely that the emotional experience will directly influence or cause behavior? The information on this issue is not yet conclusive. Currently, the inclination in the fields of both emotion and cognition is to treat emotion as the first level of response to a situation (Blumenthal, 1976; Ittelson et. al., 1974; Lyons, 1980). As such, it is especially influential in determining the state of an individual. Since, in the case of environmental perception, the individual doing the perceiving is nearly always a part of that which is being perceived, the emotional state of the individual should color ongoing environmental perception significantly. It seems that broader level responses to the environment, like emotion, influence ongoing perceptual-cognitive activity associated with action in the environment, and, through that means, qualify, reinforce, or change intended behavior.

In the example, the dining environment was perceived and appraised negatively. It need not have been. Other individuals having different social ends, expectations, and anticipations, for example, might have perceived and assessed the dining place differently and, possibly, experienced different affects. This points to the importance of the role of internal information in what is apprehended about the dining place. The nature of the information that an individual acquires in such a setting depends not only on what is available in the setting but also on the character of the information that the individual brings into the perceptual situation (Brown, 1972).

### *Informational Issues in Emotional Responses to Environments*

Perhaps the most salient point that can be made about this last example is that activities (i.e., the behaviors involved in dining) are understood more effectively when apprehended in the setting or the environment of which they are a part and in terms of which they generally are conceived. Despite their apparent substantial social and psychological meaning, it would be somewhat incomplete to evaluate such activities independent of the setting in which they occur (e.g., the restaurant). An important reason for this is that too many stimulus-effects potentially important to their clarification may be overlooked in the assessment of their nature. The same point, of course, can be made about the occurrences of experiences like emotions in environmental contexts.

In general, external information necessary for both the enactment of actions and the onset of experiences ordinarily appears as and is encountered in an environmental configuration. From a definition-of-the-situation perspective (Rapoport, 1978, 1982), such a configuration is a rather complex gestalt containing information about content and relations, environmental patterning-effects on both, and information about properties unique to the patterning itself. Facets of environmental information-displays like arena, context, and ambiance, when viewed interdependently, tend to exemplify this gestalt-like character of environments. Hence, since information external to individuals generally is manifested as part of environmental arrays and environmental-type schemata are believed to guide and/or direct apprehension of such arrays (Evans, 1980; Neisser, 1976), it is reasonable to expect that in general the process of perceiving the external world involves apprehending its information both ecologically and componentially.

In other words, because information external to individuals is usually an inextricable part of a physical setting, comprehension of it is influenced by that mode of its appearance. This suggests that configuration properties of environmental arrays, like details about spacing, position, connection, orientation, organization, temporality, and ambiance, to some extent may qualify how content information like social and psychological details get to be known in any environmental encounter. Thus, contemplating an emotion from the perspective of it being a response to the environment should take into account not only the way in which external information necessary to it normally appears in surroundings but also any qualifying implications those appearances might have on all aspects of such information. What this amounts to for a cognitively-oriented theory about emotion is that different external informational circumstances are encountered when the emotional occurrence is pictured as happening in environments than when it is not conceived of in that way.

From the perspective of an individual's daily, moment-to-moment activity, one thing is abundantly clear: whatever other significance the immediate environment has for the individual (e.g., biologically vital when considered as part of the broader scene and, hence, the basis for sustaining life), its chief function in activity episodes or moment-to-moment purposeful behavior is that it is an immediate and major source of information. For most of us, our daily living routine is made up of a series of person-environment-behavior episodes. We engage in a variety of activities (behavior) within different settings or situations (environments) and we do so from the perspective of what "we are" as individuals. For the vast majority of these episodes, the relevant environments are immediate or proximate, the activities are relatively ordinary or routine, and the orienting is with respect to the person (i.e., the self). Whatever constitutes experiences (e.g., emotional) for an individual for the most part will evolve from such episodes.

Emotions, in terms of their feeling aspects, are subjective experiences of an affective type. They are typically responses to objects and other people, and these are nearly always integral parts of environmental contexts. Both information-oriented P-E-B frameworks by the way they view person-environment-behavior relations, suggest that what is critical in understanding emotions are the physical-social contexts within which they are enacted, together with the nature of persons from which they emanate. Both are especially critical because each constitutes a main source of information (i.e., external and internal) for the cognitive or evaluative process associated with emotional experiences and because meaning, itself, the subjective assessment of which nearly always is reflected in the feeling that labels an emotion, depends on both sources.

Noting the emphasis that ordinarily is placed on cognitive processing (e.g. evaluation and/or appraisal) in discussions of the emotional experience and considering the main features of the two environmental frameworks described above, it could be said that current information-oriented P-E-B frameworks already contain the necessary provisions for describing how an emotional event might evolve in a P-E-B situation. They do so because they provide for cognitive processing at the perceiving and evaluating stages of environmental knowing and, most important, because they admit into such processing information from the situation as it appears empirically in environmental configurations.

However, as was evident in their description earlier, P-E-B frameworks account for experiences and behavior in environmental contexts through the use of a knowing process (i.e., perception and cognition) that considers not only external information present in environments but also internal knowledge embodied by the person and interactions between the two sources as well. When used by individuals to direct environmental knowing, internal knowledge is believed to be manifested cognitively in schematic and/or prototype forms - hence references to the role of cognitive maps, environmental images, representations, etc., in such frameworks (Amedeo & York, 1990; Evans, 1980; Heft, 1981). Such forms, being cognitive structures, generally are termed "longer temporal integrations" to reflect how they develop cognitively (e.g., schemata, concepts, images, plans, perceptual constancies, scenes, scripts, and so on). Essentially, they are involved in attention activities and the integration of information during the perceptual-cognitive process (Blumenthal, 1977).

An interesting query for the interests in this chapter is whether emotional counterparts to such integrations also are employed during environmental knowing, particularly during affective appraisals of environmental circumstances. For instance, it appears that many settings elicit essentially the same emotional response from individuals making up various groups in society, suggesting, perhaps, similar affective appraisals of their circumstances. Examples include ceremonial circumstances, funerals, places of worship and shrines, party settings, athletic events, weddings, and many other environmental situations exemplifying certain kinds of social relations. And, in some social systems, there appear to be environmental circumstances to which the emotional response is practically identical for all adults.

In their work, Amedeo and York (1984) contend that individuals do employ affective-type integrations in their appraisals of environments. They indicate that, for some environmental circumstances, internal knowledge can include emotional norms or feeling rules, and it is these, through their influence on environmental appraisals, that frequently influence peoples' emotional responses to external circumstances.

### *The Influence of Norms in Emotional Responses to Environments*

To follow their reasoning, consider that current theories on emotions maintain that individuals use a cognitive interpretative-process to label their emotional reactions. That is to say, a person's definition of a situation and appraisal of its meaning together help to determine the nature of his or her affective experience. If interpretation and the nature of affective experience are so linked, then, given the usual social-cultural influences operating in determining meaning, patterns of emotional responses to environments should reflect existing emotional norms regarding what should be felt in such environments. (Norms here suggest group standards and/or rules that imply or specify expected, appropriate, or inappropriate emotional responses to situations).

For example, if, as Rapoport (1982) indicates, the environment communicates nonverbally to those who transact with it, then the meanings attributed to its cues must be jointly determined by what the cues, themselves, suggest and by the internal knowledge individuals use in processing information. Hence, cognitive styles and cognitive integrations held in permanent memory should influence considerably the way individuals integrate environmental information and construct meanings.

In the adult, many of these integrations have been formed over a lifetime of continuing enculturation and socialization. They are essentially socially and culturally stereotyped patterns that are relatively persistent, organized, and often automatic ways of thinking, feeling, and remembering. Such patterns are believed to influence all of the processes individuals use in constructing immediate experiences, including the appraisal process involved in labeling emotional reactions to physical environments. Thus, social norms and cultural habits influence how we read (in the case of emotions, appraise) the cues in the environment when we attempt to assess meaning (Appleyard, 1979; J. Duncan & N. Duncan, 1976).

But human interpretations of environments cannot be thought of independently from the physical environment's contents (i.e., external information). Environmental components suggest certain meanings over others. They can activate, evoke, and/or arouse and thereby influence attentional integrations significantly. In general, environmental cues help to organize perspectives, suggest certain definitions or interpretations over others, and, in many cases, define appropriate responses and/or behavior to them. This is because cues or codes embedded in environments already have established meaning which is grounded in the symbolic system of the specific social/cultural context (Rapoport, 1976, 1978).

The influences of social and cultural norms, then, operate directly and indirectly in both the internal perceptual-cognitive process the individual uses to appraise the physical environment and in what the environment's cues suggest. In a given social system, this often leads to: (1) a set of criterion about appropriateness, inappropriateness, and expectancies, which guide individual interpretations of the definitions of the situations associated with settings; (2) a constancy or uniformity among individuals in their responses to many environments; and (3) a consistency in environmental response for any one individual over an interval of time. In the affective sense, this is manifested in the evolution of emotional norms or feeling rules suggesting the appropriate emotional response to certain environmental circumstances.

In a pluralistic society, the presence of emotional norms or feeling rules should lead to both widespread similarities in affective response for some environments (e.g., wilderness scenes) and subsets of response-similarity for others. In a strictly traditional society, however, emotional responses to many external situations should be uniform (i.e., general, well-known, and common); there should be strong agreement in beliefs that certain feelings constitute appropriate responses to particular surroundings and their embedded social situations (see the works of Fiske, 1981; Geertz, 1959; Kemper, 1978; Shott, 1979).

In view of the pervasiveness of social and cultural influences on knowing processes, experiences, learning, and meaning, Amedeo and York's (1984) contention - that an affective form of internal knowledge like norms or feeling rules influence peoples' emotional responses to physical environments and their associated situations - seems plausible. Though they suggest that a formal test of their assertions is currently not possible, they did search for indications that their argument possessed some credibility. Examining the reported beliefs of seventy-nine individuals (members of a pluralistic society) about their likely emotional responses to three different environments (a city street-scene, an office party, and a park scene) they found groupings in the responses to the first two environments (the presence of multiple or subnorms) and a single pattern of response for the pastoral or park scene (an indication of a universal norm, perhaps). They view their results as somewhat tentative but certainly supportive of the contention that emotional norms or feeling rules operate in affective responses to environmental circumstances.

### *The Fundamental Significance of Emotion to Person-Environment-Behavior Episodes*

But how should emotional responses to environmental circumstances be viewed: as incidental reactions to P-E-B episodes, or as decisive influences in their outcome? Discussions about related issues in a variety of fields tend to favor the contention that emotions are fundamental to such events. Indeed, Strongman's (1987) conclusion from his review of general theory strongly suggests that emotion enters into P-E-B episodes via its potential influence over the cognitive processing integral to environmental knowing.

To understand how such a role for emotion might be possible (c.f., Amedeo & York, 1988), consider first some general beliefs expressed about affect and cognitive processes in the wider research literature. Investigators suggest that affective experiences acquire significance due to their potential to control information-processing and, thereby, perception and ongoing behavior. Simon (1967), for example, recommends that motivational and emotional controls over cognition be included in a general theory of thinking and problem-solving. Blumenthal (1977) specifies why such an inclusion makes sense; he points out that "the emotional augmentation of experience links enduring needs and dispositions to the psychological present. It can direct the course of cognition -

the retrieval of memories, the structuring of thoughts, or the formation of perceptions" (pp. 101-2, 151-85).

Clark and Isen (1982) maintain that there is a relationship between feeling states and social behavior and review evidence linking such states with evaluative thinking. In experiments about the more temperament-reflecting affective states, Gilligan and Bower (1984) inquire about mood's involvement in recall of affectively toned material, its effects on the learning of mood-congruent material, how mood's intensity relates to learning, and the biases that affective states may have on cognitive processes like interpretation, free associations, and social judgments. Their results show clear and consistent relations between these things and lead them to conclude (pp. 568-69) that "emotion thus seems to be inextricably related to how we perceive and think, influencing them at every turn. Indeed, results reported throughout this chapter suggest that emotion is often a central component of cognitive processes in general."

The importance of these remarks should not be missed. When researchers argue that affect can direct the course of cognition, influence the retrieval of memories, enter into learning, and guide the structuring of thoughts or the formation of experience, they in effect claim that affect is capable of influencing in decisive ways many of the subprocesses making up information processing in general. The significance of their contentions for emotion in person-environment-behavior episodes becomes clear when we note that such subprocesses play critical roles in the reasoning used by the Interactional-Constructivist and Transactional frameworks to describe such episodes.

Recall, for example, that basic to the logic of both frameworks is the idea that information about environments is vital to behavior and experience. Hence, both perspectives stress that, in the fundamental process of environmental apprehension or knowing, external information (i.e., information available in surroundings and susceptible to being sensed by receptors) is attended to cognitively and structured in conjunction with internal information to form the percepts that make up a person's ongoing notion of his or her surroundings. They point out that internal information is in the form of an environmental representation activated from permanent memory and is, in itself, a longer-temporal, cognitive integration that has developed, from among other things, previous environmental transactions. From this sort of reasoning, it is said, the environment that is being apprehended is an ongoing construction. The important point here is that perception, cognition, memory, and learning are all necessary parts of the information-processing logic of these frameworks; and if that is so and the wider-literature claims are plausible, affect must be also. Given these conceptualizations, how then should affects like emotions be incorporated into P-E-B frameworks?

Two similar, well-developed proposals on affect offer some thoughts useful for dealing with that question. One proposal was put forth by Clark and Isen (1982) and the other by Gilligan and Bower (1984). (See also, however, Leventhal, 1982). Both propositions rely on the basic notion that, over time or through experience, emotions become associated in networks with similarly toned or thematically congruent objects, events, behaviors, beliefs, roles, themes, interpretative schemata, etc., to form memory entities.

Clark and Isen stress that it is the similarity in tone of affect and these other things that provide the bonding for their association in a network, while Gilligan and Bower emphasize thematic and/or semantic bonds. Since both proposals treat affect as central nodes in these associative networks, affect essentially guides recall. Its position in such memory associations result in affect's greater accessibility to the material in its networks and, through possible multiple linking and/or hierarchical structuring, material in other associative networks as well. Perhaps the most significant point of these affect-interfacing proposals is the idea that, when affect is activated, it induces, through these associations, the retrieval of stored related information for cognitive processing with acquired external information. Gilligan and Bower (1984, p. 568) put it this way: "...emotional mood primes and brings into readiness peripheral categories and interpretive schemata that guides what people *attend to* as well as how they *interpret it*" (italics added).

The relevance of these proposals for the Interactional-Constructivist and Transactional frameworks is evident. Given the purpose and significance of the environmental component in a person-environment-behavior event, affect should have its most decisive influence throughout the time in a P-E-B episode in which information processing contributes to the construction of an environmental representation useful for immediate functioning (i.e., judgements and decisions). This means that the affective state of a person in such an event should directly influence, in a tonal and thematic sense, what internal information is brought forth from memory to central processing for structuring a rendition of surroundings that facilitates the functioning peculiar to the ongoing P-E-B episode. Thus, if these proposals describe affect-interfacing well, congruent associations should be found between affect experienced in an environment and notions of such surroundings.

In their research, Amedeo and York (1988) looked for indications of such associations by comparing results from one study examining subjects' beliefs about their emotional responses to three different environments with those of another investigating the same subjects' what-comes-to-mind reactions to the same settings. In the first study, the emotional responses to these environments were examined for the presence of emotional norms or feeling rules (Amedeo & York, 1984, but see also Purcell, 1986). In the second, the what-comes-to-mind responses to these environments were examined for indications of underlying environmental schemata (e.g., Amedeo & York, 1990).

The incentive for comparing these results came from the finding that the emotional norms or feeling rules reflected in various groupings of subject beliefs differed significantly in terms of affective meaning and tonal quality. Since affective norms or beliefs about what one should feel in a place are likely to be memory items and since the central curiosity was with affect's influence over ongoing environmental apprehensions in P-E-B episodes, the inquiry of significance in these comparisons became something like the following: are the meaning and tonal qualities of these affective norms congruent with those of other significant memory items, particularly environmental schemata for these same places?

Examining the results obtained in their study on affective norms with those acquired from their investigation on environmental schemata, Amedeo and York (1988) indicate that there is some semantic and tonal congruence between affective norms or rules and environmental schemata. They (p. 209) conclude that:

> It is commonly believed that norms and schemata, like concepts, rules, stereotypes, etc., reflect the manner in which information is organized in long-term memory for 'later' use in cognitive processing. Thus, the associations observed here, being between memory items that are related (i.e., are with reference to the same environment), makes the hypothesis that affect influences the organization and retrieval of other memory items for use in the construction of percepts a *plausible* one.

One point certainly should not be missed in this discussion about affect's influence in environmental knowing: since the enactment of behavior and the occurrence of experience in any given situation are influenced by what becomes known about the situation, this more fundamental role of emotion may better illuminate the nature of all its others in P-E-B episodes.

## Concluding Remarks

The intent in this chapter has been to incorporate a consideration of affect, particularly emotions, into current, information-oriented, person-environment-behavior frameworks. The discussion began with the recommendation that emotions have their meaning and significance in P-E-B episodes and the observation that these frameworks currently rationalize such episodes in a way that is consistent with present general theorizing about emotion.

A fundamental point is that it makes more sense to explore emotional occurrences as they unfold in environmental configurations than to examine them in other ways, particularly because such configurations are the contexts of actual experience. Environments, as specific array-types, have particular interacting facets (e.g., arena, context, and ambiance) that in combination or alone tend to present stimulus-effects not likely to be found in nonenvironmental assessments.

A second point is that, given social-cultural influences in learning, perception, cognition, etc., social norms or feeling rules probably influence appraisals of perceived environmental circumstances and, thereby, the affective response to such surroundings.

The final and perhaps most significant point is that emotion, in addition to its being viewed as an environmental response, also should be explored for its essential role in environmental knowing, which is a fundamental process in person-environment-behavior episodes.

## References


Altman, I. (1975). *The environment and social behavior: Privacy, personal space, territory, crowding*. Monterey, CA: Brooks/Cole.

Altman, I., & Chemers, M. 1980). *Culture and environment*. Monterey, CA: Brooks/Cole Publishing Company.

Amedeo, D., & York, R. A. (1984). Grouping in affective responses to environments; indications of emotional norm influence in person-environment relations. In D. Duerk & D. Campbell (Eds.), *EDRA 15: Proceedings* (pp. 193-205). Washington, DC: Environmental Design Research Association.

Amedeo, D., & York, R. A. (1988). Affective states in cognitively-oriented person-environment-behavior frameworks. In D. Lawrence, R. Habe, A. Hacker, & D. Sherrod (Eds.), *EDRA 19: Proceedings* (pp. 203-211). Oklahoma City, OK: Environmental Design Research Association.

Amedeo, D., & York, R. A. (1990). Indications of environmental schemata from thoughts about environments. *Journal of Environmental Psychology. 10*, 219-253.

Appleyard, D. (1979). The environment as a social symbol. *Ekistics, 46*, 272-281.
Arnold, M. B. (Ed.). (1970a). *Feelings and emotions: The Loyola symposium*. New York: Academic Press.
Arnold, M. B. (1970b) Perennial problems in the field of emotion. In M. B. Arnold (Ed.), *Feelings and emotions: The Loyola symposium*. New York: Academic Press.
Barker, R. G. (1968). *Ecological psychology: Concepts and methods for studying the environment of behavior*. Stanford, CA: Stanford University Press.
Blumenthal, A. (1977). *The process of cognition*. Englewood Cliffs, NJ: Prentice-Hall.
Brown, H. (1972). Perception and Meaning. *Studies in the Philosophy of Mind: American Philosophical Quarterly Monograph Series, 6*, 1-8.
Cannon, W. B. (1927). The James-Lange theory of emotion. *American Journal of Psychology, 39*, 106-124.
Clark, M. S., Fiske, S. T. Eds.).(1982). *Affect and cognition*. Hillsdale, NJ: Prentice Hall.
Clark, M. S., & Isen, A. M. (1982). Towards understanding the relationship between feeling states and social behavior. In A. H. Hastorf & A. M. Isen (Eds.), *Cognitive social psychology*. New York: Elsevier.
Cosgrove, J. (1984). *Social formation and symbolic landscape*. London: Croom Helm.
Davitz, J. R. (1969). *The language of emotion*. New York: Academic.
Downs, R., & Stea, D. (Eds.). (1973). *Image and environment: Cognitive maps and spatial behavior*. Chicago: Aldine.
Downs, R., & Stea, D. (1977) *Maps in mind*. New York: Harper & Row.
Duncan, J. S., & Duncan, N. G. (1976). Social worlds, status passage, and environmental perspectives. In G. T. Moore & R. G. Golledge (Eds.), *Environmental knowing* (pp. 206-213). Stroudsburg, PA: Dowden, Hutchinson & Ross.
Evans, G. W. (1980). Environmental cognition. *Psychological Bulletin, 88*, 259-287.
Fiske, S. T. 1981). Social cognition and affect. In J. H. Harvey (Ed.), *Cognition, social behavior, and environment*. Hillsdale, NJ: Erlbaum.
Fried, M. & Gliecher, P. (1961). Some sources of residential satisfaction in an urban slum. *Journal of the American Institute of Planners, 27*, 305-15.
Geertz, H. (1959). The vocabulary of emotion: a study of Javanese socialization processes. *Psychiatry: Journal for the Study of Interpersonal Processes, 22*, 225-37.

Gerson, E. M., & Gerson, M. S. (1976). The social framework of place perspective. In G. T. Moore & R. G. Golledge, (Eds.), *Environmental Knowing* (pp. 196-205). Stroudsburg, PA: Dowden, Hutchinson & Ross.

Geschwing, N. (1980). Neurological knowledge and complex behaviors. *Journal of Cognitive Science, 4*, 185-193.

Gilligan, S. G. Bower, G. H. (1984). Cognitive consequences of emotional arousal. In C. E. Izard, J. Kagan, & R. B. Zajonc (Eds.), *Emotions, cognition, and behavior*. New York: Cambridge University Press.

Gold, J. R. (1980). *An introduction to behavioral geography*. New York: Oxford University Press.

Golledge, R. G. Stimson, R. (1987). *Analytical behavioral geography*. London: Croom Helm.

Goshen, C. (1967). A systematic classification of the phenomenology of emotions. *Psychiatric Quarterly, 41*.

Grossbart, S., & Amedeo, D. (1979). The process of experiencing feelings in environments: Exploratory modeling. In A. Seidel & S. Danford (Eds.), *EDRA 10 Proceedings* (pp. 18-30). Washington, D.C.: Environmental Design and Research Association.

Heft, H. (1981). An examination of constructivist and Gibsonian approaches to environmental psychology. *Population and Environment, 4*, 227-245.

Howard, R. B., Mlynarski, F. G., & Sauer, G. C. (1972). A comparative analysis of affective responses to real and represented environments. In M. J. Mitchell (Ed.), *EDRA 3 Proceedings*, (pp. 1-8) Washington, D.C.: Environmental Design and Research Association.

Ittelson, W. H. (1973). Environmental perception and contemporary perception theory. In W. H. Ittelson, (Ed.), *Environment and cognition* (pp. 1-19). New York: Seminar.

Ittelson, W. H., Rivlin, L. G., Proshansky, H. M., & Winkel, G. H. (1974). *An introduction to environmental psychology*. New York: Holt, Rinehart & Winston.

Izard, C. E. (1972). *The face of emotion*. New York: Appleton-Century-Crofts.

Izard, C. E. (1977). *Human emotions*. New York: Plenum.

James, W., & Lange, C. (1922). *The emotions*. London: Knight.

Kaplan, R. (1975). Some methods and strategies in the prediction of preferences. In E. H. Zube, G. G. Fabos, & R. Brush (Eds.), *Landscape assessment: Values, perceptions, and resources*. New York: Halsted.

Kaplan, R. (1977). Patterns of environmental preference. *Environment and Behavior, 9*, 195-216.

Kaplan, S. (1975). An informal model for the prediction of preference. In E. H. Zube, G. G. Fabos, & R. Brush (Eds.), *Landscape assessment: Values, perceptions, and resources*. New York: Halsted.

Kaplan, S., & Kaplan, R. (1982). *Cognition and environment: Functioning in an uncertain world*. New York: Praeger.

Kemper, T. D. (1978). Toward a sociology of emotions: Some problems and solutions. *The American Sociologist, 13*, 30-41.

Kleinginna, P. R., Jr., & Kleinginna, A. M. (1981). A Categorized list of emotional definitions, with suggestions for a consensual definition. *Motivation and Emotion, 5*, 345-79.

Lazarus, R. S., Averill, J. R., & Opton, E. M. (1970). Toward a cognitive theory of emotion. In M. B. Arnold (Ed.), *Feelings and emotions: The Loyola symposium*. New York: Academic Press.

Leventhal, H. (1982). The integration of emotion and cognition: A view from the perceptual-motor theory of emotion. In M. S. Clark & S. T. Fiske (Eds.), *Affect and cognition*. Hillsdale, N.J.: Erlbaum.

Lynch, K. (1960). *The image of the city*. Cambridge, MA: MIT Press.

Lyons, W. (1980). *Emotion*. London: Cambridge University Press.

Magnusson, D. (Ed.) (1981). *Toward a psychology of situations: An interactional perspective*. Hillsdale, NJ: Erlbaum.

Mandler, G. (1975). *Mind and emotion*. New York: Wiley.

Mandler, J. (1984). *Stories, scripts, and scenes: Aspects of schema theory*. Hillsdale, NJ: Erlbaum.

McKechnie, G. E. (1970). Measuring environmental dispositions with environmental response inventory. In J. Archea & C. Eastman, (Eds.), *EDRA 2, Proceedings of the Environmental Design and Research Association* (pp. 320-26). Washington, D.C.: Environmental Design and Research Association.

McKechnie, G. E. (1974). *ERI manual: Environmental response inventory*. Palo Alto, CA: Consulting Psychologists.

Mehrabian, A., & Russell, J. A. (1974). *An approach to environmental psychology*. Cambridge, MA: MIT Press.

Moore, G. T., Golledge, R. G. (Eds.). (1976). *Environmental Knowing*. Stroudsburg, PA: Dowden, Hutchinson & Ross.

Moore, G. T. (1979). Knowing about environmental knowing: The current state of theory and research on environmental cognition. *Environment and Behavior, 11*, 33-70.

Moore, G. T. (1987). Environment and behavior research in North America: History, developments, and unresolved issues. In D. Stokols & I. Altman (Eds.), *Handbook of environmental psychology* (Vol 2. pp. 1359-1410). New York: Wiley.

Nasar, J. L. (1981). Responses to different spatial configurations. *Human Factors, 23*, 439-46.
Nasar, J. L. (1983). *Affective responses to urban scenes: A field study.* Paper presented at the Environmental Design Research Association Conference, EDRA 83, Lincoln, Nebraska.
Nasar, J. L. (Ed.) (1988). *Environmental aesthetics: Theory, research, and applications.* Cambridge: Cambridge University Press.
Neisser, U. (1963). The imitation of man by machine. *Science, 139*, 193-197.
Neisser, U. (1976). *Cognition and reality.* San Francisco: Freeman.
Norman, D. A. (1980). Twelve issues for cognitive science. *Journal of Cognitive Science, 4*, 1-32.
Peters, R. S. (1970). The education of the emotions. In M. G. Arnold (Ed.), *Feelings and emotions: The Loyola symposium.* New York: Academic Press.
Plutchik, R. (1965). What is an emotion? *The Journal of Psychology, 61*, 295-303.
Purcell, A. T. (1986). Environmental perception and affect: A schema discrepancy model. *Environment and Behavior, 18*, 3-30.
Rapoport, A. (1976). Environmental cognition in cross-cultural perspective. In G. T. Moore & R. G. Golledge (Eds.), *Environmental knowing* (pp. 220-234). Stroudsburg, PA: Dowden, Hutchinson & Ross.
Rapoport, A. (1978). *On the environment and the definition of the situation.* (Working Paper WP78-1). School of Architecture and Urban Planning, Milwaukee, Wisconsin.
Rapoport, A. (1982). *The meaning of the built environment; A nonverbal communication approach.* Beverly Hills, CA: Sage.
Rapoport, A. (1990). *History and precedent in environmental design.* New York: Plenum.
Russell, J., & Snodgrass, J. (1987). Personality and the environment. In D. Stokols & I. Altman (Eds.), *Handbook of environmental psychology* (pp. 245-280). New York: Wiley.
Schacter, S., & Singer, J. (1962). Cognitive, social and physiological determinants of emotional state. *Psychological Review, 69*, 379-399.
Schacter, S., & Wheeler, L. (1962). Epinephrine, chlorpromazine, and amusement. *Journal of Abnormal and Social Psychology, 65*, 118-121.
Sears, D., & Auld, R. (1976). Design and attitudes to the environment. *Environment and Planning, 3*, 237-46.
Shott, S. (1979). Emotion and social life: A symbolic interactionist analysis. *American Journal of Sociology, 84*, 1317-1334.

Simon, M. A. (1967). Motivational and emotional controls of cognition. *Psychological Review, 74*, 29-39.
Stokols, D. (1978). Environmental psychology. *Annual Review of Psychology, 29*, 253-295.
Strongman, K. T. (1973). *The Psychology of Emotion.* New York: Wiley.
Strongman, K. T. (1987). *The Psychology of Emotion.* New York: Wiley.
Tibbetts, P. (1972). The transactional theory of human knowledge and action. *Man-Environment Systems, 2*, 37-59.
Tibbetts, P. (1976). Epistemology, perceptual theory, and the built environment. *Man-Environment Systems, 6*, 91-98.
Tuan, Y.-F. (1974). *Topophilia.* Englewood Cliff, NJ: Prentice Hall.
Ulrich, R. S. (1983). Aesthetic and affective responses to natural environments. In I. Altman & J. F. Wohlwill (Eds.), *Behavior and the natural environment* (pp. 85-125). New York: Plenum.
Wapner, S., Kaplan, B., & Cohen, S. S. (1973). An organismic-developmental perspective for understanding transactions of men and environments. *Environment and Behavior, 5*, 255-289.
Wapner, S. (1987). A holistic, developmental, systems-oriented environmental psychology: Some beginnings. In D. Stokols & I. Altman, (Eds.), *Handbook of Environmental Psychology* (Vol. 2., pp 1433-1465). New York: Wiley.
Wicker, A. W. (1979). *An introduction to ecological psychology.* Monterey, CA: Brooks/Cole.
Winkel, G. H., Malek, R., & Thiel, P. (1969). The role of personality differences in judgements of roadside quality. *Environment and Behavior, 2*, 199-224.
Wohlwill, J. F. (1966). The physical environment: a problem for a psychology of stimulation. *Journal of Social Issues, 22*, 29-38.
Wohlwill, J. F. (1976). Environmental aesthetics: The environment as a source of affect. In I. Altman & J. F. Wohlwill (Eds.), *Human Behavior and Environment; Advances in Theory and Research* (pp. 37-86). New York: Plenum.
Zajonc, R. B. (1980). Feeling and thinking: Preferences need no inferences. *American Psychologist 35*, 151-175.

*Behavior and Environment: Psychological and Geographical Approaches*
*T. Gärling and R.G. Golledge (Editors)*



# CHAPTER 5

# Environmental Appraisal, Human Needs, and a Sustainable Future

**Rachel Kaplan**

Human hope is intimately tied to environmental appraisal. The wish list, however, is more clearly articulated than the environmental analysis. Human despair too is intimately tied to environmental appraisal. Here again, the implicit environmental assumptions underlying the human condition go unnoticed. The environment that humankind has for so long taken for granted has been assaulted by actions that appeared to meet the wants and aspirations of an animal capable of planning its pleasures. Yet planful and insightful as this creature may be, the unanticipated consequences of good intentions have all too often been painfully costly. From a short term perspective such damage may be greater for some than for others; in the long run, however, we share one common world and it has to sustain us all.

The storyline of this chapter is something like this: Environmental planning and economic development depend upon environmental appraisal. The choices of what to assess and what is valued are fundamental to the decisions that are taken. Implicit in these choices are assumptions. The consequences of these assumptions often differentially affect those who make the decisions and those whose environment is impacted. Both the impacted environment and the decision process are at the root of considerable psychological malaise. The story, unfortunately, lacks a happy ending. It does, however, offer some alternatives that could improve the situation.

## Lessons from Accounting

Humans have engaged in record-keeping for many centuries. Cave paintings can be considered an early form of environmental appraisal, an accounting of existing conditions that communicated presumably important information. Individuals also keep records for personal reasons (e.g., seasonal conditions and garden developments) and to meet legislative requirements (e.g., expense records for tax purposes). Governmental units invest substantial resources in systems that track the existing situation; records are maintained of population characteristics and locations, the costs of delivering various services, revenues, crimes, miles of highway, rainfall, landfill capacity, and numerous other domains.

Accounting systems, or efforts to inventory, necessarily require decisions about what to include. The road commission, for example, needs to have information about miles of different kinds of roads in its jurisdiction and about the kind of equipment it has available. Does it need to know maintenance costs for each truck? What about the color of each truck? It is probably a reasonable assertion that the match between what is inventoried and what is found to be useful varies widely and is rarely perfect. Errors are frequently made on the side of keeping records of attributes that are easily inventoried whether or not they are pertinent. Conversely, hindsight often leads to interest in records that were not recognized as useful when they could have been obtained readily.

The question of what to include in environmental appraisals does not have, and cannot have, a straightforward answer. The many answers depend on a horde of issues, many of them much more evident in retrospect. Even with the wonders of modern technology, it is unlikely that a perfect system can be developed; nonetheless, a number of errors can be mitigated.

Substantial recent work has focused on the contrast between economic and environmental indicators (or accounting procedures) in the insights they provide about the current global condition. The purpose of this section is to review some of this material both as a way to highlight the issue of what attributes to select in an appraisal and as a prelude to the next section which will focus on yet another realm of indicators that have received far less attention in such appraisals.

### *The Economic View*

The GNP is much in the news. Gross National Product is intended as an index of the current economic outlook. It is a numeric value that summarizes a combination of factors or attributes pertaining to the current condition. What factors are included, how they are combined, and what "condition" is being summarized are not part of the news. As a barometer of the nation's economy, the gains in the GNP are proclaimed as important positive signs and the declines are generally explained in terms of financial transactions.

The GNP is based on three major components: consumer purchases, private investments, and government spending. Higher GNP, based on the assumption that growth is desirable, is taken to reflect a more positive outlook. Increased consumer spending is an important aspect of such a positive appraisal; the decline of raw materials is not considered in the equation.

Based on indicators at a larger scale, Brown (1991) reports that "growth in global economic output during the eighties was greater than during the several thousand years from the beginning of civilization until 1950. International trade, another widely used measure of global economic progress, grew even more rapidly, expanding by nearly half during the eighties" (p. 6).

In addition to established economic indices such as GNP or GDP (Gross Domestic Product) there are numerous other indicators of the current condition (Daly & Cobb, 1989). One can look at personal wealth, at the number of products available in the stores, at the number of shopping centers and malls that have been developed, or at the number of cars per capita as ways to appraise the existing economic situation.

### *Environmental Indicators*

The current condition is far less rosy when viewed from the perspective of environmental attributes. Measured in terms of loss of trees, land degradation, decline of water quality, air pollution, mineral depletion, land devoted to storage of waste products, the picture is in sharp contrast to the economic outlook. Yet resource destruction has no salience in the accounting systems that are based on economic considerations.

Hinrichsen (1991) discusses an effort, currently under way in the newly united Germany to develop a "Gross Ecological Product." The task is proving difficult for the 40 statisticians and economists assigned to it both because of the problem of putting a monetary value on environmental deterioration and because of data unavailability. Hinrichsen cites Eberhard Moths, the head of the research section on energy and the environment in the Federal Ministry of Economics: "It is my personal view that roughly two-thirds of the costs that should be included in prices are not. Most of these hidden, or external, costs are environmental" (p. 5).

Durning (1991) argues perceptively that "overconsumption by the world's fortunate is an environmental problem unmatched in severity by anything but perhaps population growth" (p. 153). In the U.S. and other developed nations, consumerism and success are ever more identified with each other. "The Japanese speak of the 'new three sacred treasures': color television, air conditioning, and the automobile" (p. 153). The consumerism that is reflected in an increased GNP in one part of the world often draws on resources from a distant portion of the globe. Consumerism in that distant, resource-providing nation, is likely to be at a substantially different scale.

The contrast in consumption patterns across different parts of the world and the consequent effects on the environment provide a powerful lesson in the choice of what attributes to include in an appraisal. For example, if one would assess transportation systems in the vast majority of countries around the world, it is unlikely that any measures of air quality would be included. Consider an appraisal of the transportation system used by the several billions of people whose transportation is mostly on foot or by bicycle! By contrast, consider the attributes that become salient when the transportation system is based on automobiles.

The relation between transportation by automobile and by airplane leads to yet another realm of issues to consider - albeit for a tiny portion of the world's people. The relative energy demands, carbon dioxide emissions, effects on acid rain, climate change, landuse implications (roads, housing locations, and retail locations), as well as costs in human life are all central to assessing the environmental impacts of these modes of transportation.

A recent newspaper article on the relative safety of driving and flying provides some vivid imagery. Some statisticians challenged the notion that flying is safer for long distances, arguing that experienced drivers wearing seat belts, driving heavy cars on interstate highways, for distances up to 600 miles, are safer than those traveling by plane. Other statisticians challenged these results and concluded that driving is safer only for distances up to 303 miles. They based their challenge on the flight information that had been used as the comparison to automobile safety, arguing that only nonstop flights should be included as they are more likely to be of comparable distances to car travel.

Imagine the data banks that were compiled for these statistical analyses. The decisions about what data to enter - what to inventory in the appraisal - are an implicit indication of what is deemed important. Judging from the brief article, auto data included age and sobriety of the driver, use of seat belts, size and weight of car, distance traveled, type of road; flight data included distance traveled and number of landings/takeoffs. Presumably the analysts are at the mercy of the agencies that record such information who, in turn, have made the decisions about what is important to assess.

Beyond the choice of variables, however, there is the question of why the analyses are performed. It is presumably not irrelevant to know that the statisticians who came up with the 600 mile answer were employed by an automobile company while the 303 mile solution was reached by academic statisticians. It is also noteworthy that these discussions, couched in terms of safety, are based on fatalities. For those who have survived automobile crashes, changed for the remainder of their lives in terms of their physical and mental states, "safety" might well connote some other criteria.

### *How to Choose an Indicator?*

One cannot perform appraisals without making a decision about the "things" that will be appraised. These attributes can then be combined in some fashion to yield a summary index (such as the GNP) or kept separate to permit examination of variation across the different indicators. The choice of attributes, however, is necessarily critical to the conclusions that will be drawn.

As we have seen, the view of the world situation (or of any nation's current outlook) is quite different depending on whether one relies on an economic set of indicators or on an environmental appraisal. Several efforts have been made to develop alternative measures that address the limitations implicit in any of the commonly used accounting systems. For example, an approach that relies heavily on consumer spending or per capita income poses problems both for nations that are heavily invested in consumerism (but where environmental costs are not included in the equation) and for those where consumerism or personal income are not salient.

The choice of alternative indicators is, necessarily, closely tied to the question of why such accounts are to be kept. The attributes that one has selected for describing the existing condition presumably reflect matters that are deemed important to the situation. But importance is often not a sufficient criterion. The attributes that are considered important are likely to vary in their perceived value. Value, in turn, brings forth the notion of a purpose for the appraisal (R. Kaplan, 1991). An analysis of traffic safety can yield very different outcomes if its purpose is to promote the automobile or to set insurance policy. As Morowitz (1991) suggested, "the answer to 'how much is a species worth?' is 'What kind of world do you want to live in?'" (p. 754).

## Toward What End?

At some level, often not clearly enunciated, the rationale for virtually all appraisals is tied to human well-being. The World Bank, in its *World Development Report 1991,* proclaims "The challenge of development, in the broadest sense, is to improve the quality of life" (p. 4). Yet links between the appraisals and the welfare of the people are often weak. Moreover, they are often misguided. Is an upturned GNP tantamount to a citizenry that is in better psychological health? Are the billions of people without motorized transportation systems in poor psychological health? What are the relationships between the economic and environmental indicators and the human condition? How is one to assess the human condition? The purpose of this section is to explore these issues in their international complexity.

It is hard to examine the human condition of the vast majority of the world population without confronting the issue of extreme poverty, starvation, sickness, and homelessness. Indicators of the economic situation in the areas where these conditions are rampant may or may not reflect this human condition because of the extreme variation between the rich and the poor within a relatively small geographical region or nation. Indicators of the environmental situation in some human-impoverished areas may also not reflect the depravity of the human condition because there are still natural resources available, the air quality may not be as bad as in the North, and the water may not be as polluted as in industrialized areas. Nonetheless, these people are unquestionably impoverished.

My intention is to focus this discussion not on the conditions related to extreme poverty, but on the human condition of the western world (or North, or developed nations) on the one hand, and of other regions that are sometimes considered the South, developing nations, or the Third World. Within this context, the choice of attributes to reflect the human condition tend toward *psychological* as opposed to social indicators (such as levels of education or provision of health care, nutritional, or social services). A full picture of well-being must, of course, include each of these aspects and many others. Since more documentation is available on the social indicators (Miringoff, 1990, monitors 17 such categories in an Index of Social Indicators and, under the rubric of "basic needs" [e.g., Lisk, 1985; Stewart, 1985], they are widely considered in the international context), I have chosen to reflect here on dimensions that are perhaps more subtle and certainly more neglected.

On many social indicators the developed world is likely to fare better than the developing nations. It is probably often assumed that this pattern would follow as well for psychological manifestations of well-being. But the two domains suggest some different outcomes. Verhelst (1987), a senior project officer with a Belgian development agency, comments that he is frequently asked whether he finds it depressing to spend so much time working in the context of "poor countries." He responds that, quite on the contrary, "it is when I land in one of those asepticized airports in Europe or North America that I am overwhelmed by sadness. Everything there is perfectly organized but the people look despondent and seem nervous. Are they happy, these Westerners whom everyone envies so?" (p. 65). Durning (1991) indicates that "many in the industrial lands have a sense that their world of plenty is somehow hollow - that, hoodwinked by a consumerist culture, they have been fruitlessly attempting to satisfy what are essentially social, psychological, and spiritual needs with material things" (pp. 153-154).

### *What Consumption Doesn't Buy*

There was a time that is sometimes described as "simpler." It entailed fewer "things," fewer technologies, a slower pace. With the simplicity came a variety of other attributes that are relatively invisible. Fortunately, there are still traces of such simpler life styles. Some people can recall the patterns of previous generations; written pieces document such times; there still exist groups and cultures that live a life that is relatively less influenced by industrialization.

Verhelst (1987) describes some of these invisible qualities in terms of "a vitality, a taste for life, human qualities and a sense of the sacred that leave a lasting impression of hope" (p. 65). He argues that the harsh social struggles do not get in the way of "a sense of celebration, human tenderness and, ultimately, the desire for social harmony" (p. 73).

There is an extensive literature on cultures whose lifestyle is directly related to ecological considerations (e.g., Goland, 1992; Jochim, 1981; Lee, 1979; Rappaport, 1984). While many of these share little with lifestyles in the developed world, Critchfield (1991, pp. 224-225) persuasively draws parallels between the villages of Asia, Africa and Latin America and the recent rural past in the United States:

> Everybody who farms, affected as they are by too much or too little rain, or wind, hail, frost, snow, or whatever, has to be fairly fatalistic. The agricultural setting reinforces religion. Churchgoing - and I mentioned 77% of rural North Dakotans go to church on Sunday - with its rituals for birth, marriage, and death, and such holy days as Christmas and Easter, confers meaning and dignity on rural lives... When it comes to religion, the fatalism I mentioned, combined with skepticism toward

> organized religion (jokes about the pastor) and deep personal faith, are as common to a North Dakota or Iowa farmer as to a Punjabi or Polish peasant. Rural people are plain, straight, and conservative in outlook the world over.

A particularly perceptive analysis of ecological impact on lifestyle is provided by Coombs (1990) with respect to the Australian Aboriginal people. His description provides a rich source of insights into issues central to human well-being that neither economic nor environmental indicators capture. Coombs describes the Aboriginal society, dependent on an "inhospitable land," as being "of extreme material simplicity" (p. 59). They live in small communities that have traditionally "engaged in little production but depended on harvesting the natural products of the land and its waters. They neither tilled nor seeded the earth; they domesticated only the dingo and their tools were few" (p. 107). In summarizing his description, Coombs highlights the following characteristics of the hunter-gatherer lifestyle:

> - direct involvement in the natural physical environment;
> - a high level of activity - physical, intellectual and aesthetic - arising from patterns of behaviour required in social relationships with the different aspects of the total environment;
> - involvement in a variety of groups of various sizes in ways which required both identification and differentiation by the performance of a personal role in relation to the group and its corporate affairs;
> - a pattern of spiritual beliefs amounting to a conception of the universe which gave coherence and justification to other aspects of a person's lifestyle; and
> - an active participatory and creative cultural life which recorded and celebrated the integrated physical, social and spiritual aspects of the lifestyle.
>
> These characteristics seemed to provide for each person a balance between a sense of security and of challenge, a personal identity - a combination of belonging and having an individual role, and a sense of contributing to the fulfillment of a cosmic purpose. (pp. 115-116)

Such aspects of the human condition find little expression in the accounting systems that update the pulse of nations. Health delivery, nutrition, education, longevity are all amply recorded in many parts of the world but are not in any direct way related to self-fulfillment, a sense of worth, or an opportunity to contribute to the well-being of others. Nor are these aspects of the quality of life necessarily contingent on economic wealth. In fact, a high level of consumerism might well be negatively related to a sense of personal identity that is separate from the material goods one acquires. As Durning (1991) points out, "when alternative measures of success are not available, the deep human need to be valued and respected by others is acted out through consumption" (p. 162).

### *In Exchange for What?*

It is widely held that development is the answer to improving the life of those who are poor. Economic development assistance is generally provided by those who have more on behalf of those who are needy. Such efforts are often well intended; their consequences, however, are often not comparably positive. As indicated on the back jacket of Verhelst's (1987) book, "far from eliminating mass poverty, (development) often destroys the very environment on which people depend for their livelihood and uproots them from their traditional ways of life."

Using traditional economic indicators it is easy to see the disparity between nations. In the eyes of development experts, "Growing productivity is the engine of development" (World Bank, 1991, p. 4). Environmental assessments are also central to planning strategies for economic development. It is the local environmental resources that are pivotal to the decision about what to develop and how to go about it. While the availability of resources is important to the development decision, the depletion of the natural resources that might be part and parcel of the development strategy is less likely to be acknowledged in the assessment.

In addition to the economic and environmental assessments, economic development also includes a social appraisal, although the absence of documentation often makes this more difficult. But the social appraisal (e.g., infant mortality, nutrition, literacy) is unlikely to include the subtle indicators of the more fragile and vulnerable aspects of the human condition. It is hardly surprising that these are not assessed since the experts who help with the appraisal are not cognizant of these subtleties themselves. So, in good faith and with positive intentions, there is the hope of betterment - less poverty, a firm economic base for employment, a market for the unique resources of the land. The betterment, if any, may come in exchange for the very soul of the culture. The failures of appraisal can go deep. Misplaced envy of the western world continues, even as the wealthy nations begin to realize that their wealth has come at great costs.

### *A Summary*

Assessments derive from decisions about what is important and what is valued. The purpose of the appraisal, whether stated or not, has direct consequences in the selection of the attributes that constitute the appraisal. The outcomes of appraisals are what is characteristically communicated; hidden from view, however, are the attributes that were used to generate the appraisal and even its purpose.

Changes in economic outlooks are in the news persistently. Implicitly they are calculated as an index of human welfare. What factors enter into the equation (e.g., the close ties between consumption and GNP) and the relation between these and human welfare are not widely discussed. Closer examination, however, suggests that an apparently positive economic outlook (say, in the United States) does not necessarily mean (1) greater human welfare for many people living in United States, (2) greater human welfare for people living in countries whose resources have been exported to the United States, or (3) a likelihood of greater economic prosperity in the future as resources that are not incorporated in the equation are depleted, degraded, discarded, or otherwise violated.

Changes in the environmental outlook are also receiving more attention. It is no longer some fringe minority that speaks of an environmental crisis. Complex and uncertain consequences of lifestyles that had been taken for granted (e.g., automobile use or the relationship between rain forests and meat consumption) are as much part of the media diet as is the GNP. The ozone layer, global climate, fuel emissions, and aquifers are relatively recent additions to the popular vocabulary.

Recognition of the cultural crisis in the developed world is also increasingly evident. Crime, substance abuse, violence against friends and family, unemployment, homelessness are not restricted to a few geographic regions or a select segment of the citizenry in many nations of the North. The expectation of wealth, health and happiness pervades the human condition and contributes to a psychological malaise as so many hopes are rarely fulfilled: The lottery is not won (and if won, still does not bring joy [Brickman, Coates & Janoff-Bulman, 1978]), the technology that permits greater longevity does not bring dignity with the increased years, the exposure to ever-more products and competing brands brings confusion and waste, rather than opportunity and satisfaction.

What is less clear is that all these realms are intertwined and that a network of hidden assumptions has helped create a situation with worldwide ramifications. A seemingly rational process, a reliance on a multitude of carefully-formulated assessment tools, a headlong drive to improve the lot of humanity - these have all contributed to consequences that undermine the very conditions they were intended to salvage.

## Elements of Solutions

Having painted a dire, all too depressing picture of the condition of North and South, it is time to consider ways to keep the process from continuing on its downward path. If a rational process, carefully-formulated tools, and a desire to improve the lot of humanity have brought us to our present condition, what can one possibly do to change course?

Even if we restrict our quest to issues related to appraisal, there is surely no single answer. Nor can the solutions be universally applicable. I can hardly claim to have even modest knowledge in the many interrelated domains that must be brought together in altering the path. Nonetheless, a psychological perspective of the situation suggests some important elements that need to be incorporated in the solutions.

Three interdependent domains are discussed in this section as a way to highlight some aspects that must be considered in taking stock of the complex relationships between the environment and human functioning. The first of these focuses on the environmental resources in terms of their vulnerability. The second domain explores the many ways in which any solutions must be cognizant of the enormous amount of knowledge that is available. Knowledge resides not only in the great technological expertise of the western world, but equally in the expertise with the local situation of people in the less-developed world. The third domain concerns some ways that take advantage of the needs humans have of each other. The plight of the world, after all, is a shared concern and its amelioration depends on shared perspectives.

### *Finite Resources*

The notion that resources are finite is discomforting. They had for many centuries seemed endless. Technological sophistication made extraction of resources ever more feasible and the confidence in technological salvation remains strong and firm for many.

Somehow, with the aid of technological prowess and with the knowledge that there will always be more, there has been monumental destruction. Savory (1988, p. xx) documents some of these patterns:

> Nowhere is the problem of environmental deterioration more apparent than in the United States. America, with her great

> concentration of wealth, brainpower, modern technology, and educational infrastructure, has no solutions. Despite excellent prices and the lowest input costs in the world, thousands of farmers leave the land every year, bankrupt. America's deserts continue to advance as relentlessly as those of any country. Water supplies deteriorate in volume, stability of flow, and quality. Probably no nation in the history of the world has destroyed its agricultural base of soil and water faster than America is doing.

With the situation at home not encouraging, the United States and other western nations have contributed to the resource demise of many developing countries. These nations are increasingly aware that their own situation is intimately tied to the resource patterns of the North. "To combat hunger injustice and ecological imbalance, the West must change" (Verhelst, 1987, p. 66). The imbalance in global use of resources is a vital component in the disparities between the well-being of the world's peoples.

Discomforting though it may be, there is increasing acknowledgement that resources are finite (Daly & Cobb, 1989; Korten, 1990; Orr, 1991). There is also increasing recognition that these finite resources must be managed in a way that not only meets present needs, but can also meet the needs of future generations. This theme of *sustainable* development is at the heart of the Brundtland Report (World Commission on Environment and Development, 1987), *Our common future*, and has been incorporated in many public statement since (Starke, 1990). It is a call for stewardship that implies care as opposed to ownership (S. Kaplan & R. Kaplan, 1982), respect for resources rather than rampant consumption, and greater comprehension of the imbalances caused by resource depletion.

### *Sharing Knowledge*

In contemporary jargon, one can describe the process of appraisal, or inventorying, as a problem of data-base management. In other words, appraisal is necessarily a matter of extracting, storing, and accessing what often turn out to be vast amounts of information. The prevalence of and enormous investment in such appraisals provide vivid indication that humans depend on and even crave information, often for its own sake. In the larger picture, this is hardly surprising since we are an information-oriented organism (S. Kaplan & R. Kaplan, 1978; r. Lachman & J. Lachman, 1979; Pfeiffer, 1978). The centrality of knowledge or information to human functioning is a bond common to the species. People are constantly and continuously assessing the world around them and drawing on past appraisals to make decisions (R. Kaplan, 1991). Much of the information we depend on is not acquired through formal education, nor even through verbal means; noticing, observing, listening to the patterns of life entails processing vast amounts of information.

While information may well be a common coin among humankind, there are important differences among people in the value they ascribe to different sources and kinds of information. Presumably, in all cultures some individuals are considered to have more information, or more pertinent information, at least in the context of specific situations. Such people of wisdom, experience, or spiritual insight often are accorded special standing by virtue of their different knowledge. In less developed countries it is likely that these are the individuals who play key roles in negotiating arrangements for accepting offers of economic development. The individuals who come from the wealthy nations with offers of assistance may be experts by virtue of their political standing, assumed power, scientific knowledge, entrepreneurial talents, technological skills, insights into community development, or a host of other factors that draw on their experience.

Experts, whether in the North or South, play a special function by virtue of qualities that are assumed to be inherent in expertise. They are sought not only for their greater knowledge, but for their ability to "see" (or understand) a situation more fully. Experts are expected to manage uncertainty (at least within the domain of their expertise) in ways that others cannot achieve (S. Kaplan & R. Kaplan, 1982). In many contexts, they are presumed to know what is best.

While experts are essential to many decisions, it is also the case that their very expertise has been central to many poor decisions. Laski (1930, cited in S. Kaplan & R. Kaplan, 1982, p. 170) recognized this quite a few decades ago in the context of foreign policy:

> Expertise, it may be argued, sacrifices the insight of common sense to intensity of experience. It breeds on inability to accept new views from the very depth of its preoccupation with its own conclusions... Above all, perhaps, and this most urgently where human problems are concerned, the expert fails to see that every judgment he makes not purely factual in nature brings with it a scheme of values which has no special validity about it. He tends to confuse the importance of his facts with the importance of what he proposes to do about them.

Given these pitfalls of experts, an antidote is hardly optional. A way to benefit from the strengths of expert knowledge while offsetting some of the limitations is to acknowledge that wisdom is not uniquely lodged with the expert. In fact, a great deal of wisdom and knowledge are available at the local level, in the observations and lore of the people. Participation by the citizenry is thus an essential tool for incorporating the more vulnerable aspects of quality of life in the decision making process. In many parts of the world, participatory development (Lineberry, 1989) is becoming a recognized approach to achieving the aims of development with fewer of the dilemmas. "When matched to careful external assistance, this indigenous intelligence can result in projects which are manageable in scope, do not rely unduly on imported technology, have low recurrent cost expenses and which beneficiaries themselves can voluntarily maintain after the project has been completed" (Alamgir, 1989, pp. 5-6).

The tradeoffs between the knowledge of experts and of the people is, of course, not limited to economic development between the richer and poorer nations. The limitations of expertise that Laski cited are just as prevalent in the context of environmental assessment in economic development of any American city. In fact, it may be easier for many to witness the potential damage, concomitant with expertise, in this more familiar context. It seems likely, for example, that the abundance of shopping malls on the American landscape is not the result of citizen input. It is no longer a rare event that "local wisdom" expresses its "intensity of experience" to block efforts to further mall the countryside.

Korten (1990) defines development as a "process by which the members of a society increase their personal and institutional capacities to mobilize and manage resources to produce sustainable and justly distributed improvements in their quality of life consistent with their own aspirations" (p. 67). This definition is fascinating for its intentional innocence about economic output, rather emphasizing that "only the people themselves can define what they consider to be improvements in the quality of their lives" (p. 68).

Korten's (1990) notion of a "People-Centered Vision" thus acknowledges the indigenous intelligence as well as local values that have so frequently been violated in failed efforts to provide assistance or apparent betterment. While economic and environmental indicators are vital, and expertise is essential to the choice and measurement of these attributes, it is reliance on local knowledge that is most likely to highlight the requirements of human well-being. Building upon such local insights is an essential element in increasing the likelihood of appropriate assessments.

## *Adversity and Hope*

Amongst the many problems that human activities have generated, one receiving increasing attention is the rapid and massive decline in biodiversity. Whole species are disappearing and the conditions for survival of others are increasingly endangered. As human populations proliferate, many wildlife populations have declined. The count of the species that have been lost, the proposals for appraising the damage (e.g., inventory of millions of species), and suggested approaches for solving the crisis have varied considerably. A recent issue of *Science* featured several articles on this subject. As Koshland (1991) summarizes in his editorial, "what emerges from these papers ... is that the diversity of species is worth preserving because it represents a wealth of knowledge that cannot be replaced" (p. 717).

The importance of preserving cultural diversity seems to me defensible on strikingly similar grounds. The headlong drive to westernize, urbanize, and increase productivity have come at the expense of local values and cultural roots. Just as with declining wildlife species, the lost cultural knowledge has been detrimental both from a local and a universal stance. People in the wealthy nations have little imagery about lifestyles of the very recent past. The average 30 hours a week that Americans are said to spend watching television must have been consumed by other activities a few decades ago. Lacking so much that the North takes for granted, how is it that people of the South manage to maintain a vitality, find joy in life, and cause for celebration?

Cross-cultural studies can provide great insight into patterns of coping with adversity and sustaining hope. Triandis' (1988) discussion of "collectivism v. individualism" portrays one axis for exploring such patterns. He cites a list of attributes proposed by a Thai psychologist, Wichiarajote, "to contrast between 'an achieving' (individualistic) and an 'affiliative' (collectivist) society" (p. 70). The list (see Table 5.1) is striking in a number of respects: it highlights a rich assortment of qualities that contribute to the intangible aspects of life satisfaction, and juxtaposes attributes in novel ways. At the same time, the strict division made along cultural lines is surprising since the patterns one knows best consist of a mixture from both camps.

Several of these attributes are consistent with the descriptions others have used to characterize the anonymity of encounters among the industrial nations as opposed to the intensely social life among developing nations. Money and goods have replaced exchange based on human contact (Durning, 1990; Foa, 1971). Face-to-face encounters foster a sense of community and remind one of the need people have for each other. The sense of futility, of having no part to play in the larger scheme of things, that pervades the younger generation of wealthy nations is likely to be a close corollary of the facelessness of much of their life. There is of course great irony in a situation that finds the nations of the South envying the material riches of the North. Such riches are not, however, correlated with a sense of hope, fulfillment, or spiritual strength.

TABLE 5.1
*Wichiarajote's Attributes that Distinguish Different Societies*

| Achieving (individualistic) | Affiliative (collectivist) |
|---|---|
| self-assertion | respectfulness |
| equalitarian | hierarchical organization |
| peer influences | parental influences |
| free exchange of ideas | fear to express ideas |
| self-orientation | other-orientation |
| autonomy | mutual dependence |
| casual-spontaneous | inhibited-restricted expression |
| fear of failure | fear of rejection |
| principle-centeredness | person-centeredness |
| organizational loyalty | small group loyalty |
| encouragement of evaluation | fear of loss of face |
| achievement criteria (for selection & promotion) | ascriptive criteria |
| fairness | sacrifice |
| opportunistic use of others | loyalty and obligation |
| frankness | *krengchai* (approximately = not telling what you feel) |
| high on achievement motivation | affiliation |
| future-oriented | present-oriented |
| delay of gratification | immediate gratification |
| self importance | self-effacement |
| responsibility | having fun |
| creative | conforming |
| material concern | spiritual |
| efficiency | peace of mind |

Adapted from W. Wichiarajote, 1975, "A theory of the affiliative society vs. the achieving society", mimeographed paper, as cited by Triandis, 1988, p. 70.

## Appraisal and Decision Making

A first crucial step toward the resolution of the crises the world is facing is recognizing their complexity. The actions of the western nations profoundly and persistently impact the lives of people through- out the world. Fortunately, there are signs of increasing recognition of these realities. Not only does the daily news provide vivid images of demise, despair, destruction, depletion, or dissatisfaction, but there are also growing efforts to counter some of the environmental degradation. Green movements are increasing around the world and numerous governmental units are issuing statements that acknowledge the importance of appropriate actions (ANGOC, 1990; Dobson, 1991). The faith in economic indicators is showing signs of eroding (Brown, 1991; Garbarino, 1988; Starke, 1990).

Appraisal is more important than ever. Experience has repeatedly shown that values not appraised are ultimately ignored in the planning process. The questions of what to assess and how to incorporate these in decision making are far from resolved. Some common tendencies in appraisal have been misguided and some important considerations have been ignored. Some of these issues are discussed in this section. In particular, I will briefly explore three themes: the problems inherent in the search for the Best Index, participation and ties to local wisdom, and a human scale, sensitive to human inclinations and needs.

### *Too Few / Too Many: The Choice of Indicators*

Perhaps because of the reliance on the GNP and indices patterned on it, decision makers have favored development of an index that combines the separate assessments of attributes into a single value. The Human Development Index, devised by the United Nations (see Brown, 1991), Daly and Cobb's (1989) Index of Sustainable Economic Welfare, and the German's effort to develop the Gross Ecological Product (Hinrichsen, 1991) are examples of such quests. If the underlying rationale for such combinatorial efforts is the assumption that it is difficult for humans to juggle several values, the goal of achieving a single best index is misguided. Decision makers as well as humans without professional training have considerable experience with juxtaposing incommensurate qualities. Trade-offs are the stuff of life, not only within a given economy (e.g., money, time, space), but also among them.

If the rationale for seeking a single index is the assumption that it provides a valid summary of the combined attributes, the effort is not merely misguided but misled. The process of combining attributes requires assumptions which necessarily impact the solution. One such assumption in the case of many economic analyses is that a monetary value can be used as a common coin. How much is clean air worth in yen or dollars? Another assumption is that two assessments, yielding the same value on the index, are equivalent. It is not hard to imagine situations where one assessment involves mid-range values on each of the attributes while another is based on values that are at both extremes. If the index is based on averaging the components, the two could be identical although the underlying situations have nothing in common with respect to the measured attributes. A further assumption is that the separate significance of each of the components of the equation is the same across all situations. The amount of money spent on clothes and fuel, for example, might not mean the same in frigid or temperate parts of the country. The use of such attributes in an index of Affluence, or even worse, Quality of Life, while ignoring climate, would be totally misleading.

There are thus many problems with creating an index that yields a single value. There are also problems with having so many separate attributes that they exceed the human capacity for "juggling" the pieces. If one takes seriously the complexity of the interrelatedness among the multitude of issues that are at the root of environmental and human crises, the list of potential attributes to include in an appraisal is overwhelming. The difficulty in this case is one of managing the volume of information. Even if two situations were relatively similar, the capacity to recognize the similar patterns would be costly and burdensome.

The reliance on a single summary value as well as the insistence on a vast collection of potentially important attributes are both unlikely to be appropriate appraisal goals. Environmental appraisal requires consideration of different domains and each of these domains may entail a number of attributes. The failure to include a domain, such as Intangibles, in the appraisal automatically signifies that it is not valued. The various domains that are included, however, need not be combined. Their interdependence and relative importance, depending on circumstances, are far more likely to be acknowledged if they are maintained as separate accounts.

There are various approaches to maintaining such separation yet enabling comparison. McHarg (1969) effectively used overlays as a way to track different domains while also comparing them. For example, a decision concerning interstate highway route selection might include an appraisal of recreation value, scenic value, and historic value as well as economic and ecological considerations. It is important to note that no attempt is made to express these noneconomic dimensions of value in monetary units, nor is such a translation required for the decision making process. The separate layers can thus be examined individually; it may turn out that a single layer plays an overriding role in a particular situation (e.g., identification of a toxic waste disposal site). By placing the layers together, other comparisons can become apparent, such as areas where several domains lead to a common conclusion (e.g., fragile environment). A tabular format can have similar advantages of providing a spatial analysis, permitting examination of both the separate domains and their trade-offs. The temptation to array too much information comes at the considerable cost of exceeding information-processing capacity (Simon, 1990), or, perhaps phrased more usefully, exceeding the powers of "eye-and-brain" (Gregory, 1966).

### *Participation and Anticipated Regret*

Only by being mindful of all the pieces of a puzzle can one put it together. Thus a comprehensive perspective is vital to appraising the human and environmental condition. At the same time, however, such a holistic perspective is at best relative. The complexity of even seemingly simple situations has prevented holistic approaches from being the dominant mode (Savory, 1988). Not only does a holistic analysis require a huge amount of assessment, it must draw on many kinds of experts to select the attributes to appraise. And even with all the expertise that can be brought to the situation, it is likely that some very basic questions will have been ignored.

Inventories readily become standardized; one is modeled after another, and the attributes that are included, though substantial in number, may be inappropriate to particular situations. Economic develop-ment projects have often involved appraisal of local natural resources and economic potentials. The similarity of solutions despite dissimilar local conditions has come at the expense of cultural roots and psychological well-being.

When people in a small community work together, when neighbors come to each other's assistance, when bureaucracy is relatively absent - one rarely speaks of participation. Nor does one take notice of local wisdom in the many contexts where people share their insights in the absence of someone who is cast as expert. As soon as the assistance is imported or when a distinction, such as power or knowledge, is evident between the provider and the recipient, the issues of participation and the recognition of local knowledge become pertinent.

The participation literature is vast. There are numerous examples of approaches to international development that have shown that such projects need not sacrifice local wisdom (ANGOC, 1990; Korten, 1990; Lineberry, 1989; Starke, 1990; Verhelst, 1987; Wisner, Stea, & Kruks, 1991). Gathering such examples, sharing success stories, is in itself an important contribution. Knowledge of how something was done elsewhere provides necessary imagery and it is such imagery that is often lacking.

We have argued that the provision of multiple images of alternative solutions can be a critical aspect of participation (S. Kaplan & R. Kaplan,

1989). The purpose of such images is not to have citizens vote on the one that meets majority endorsement. Rather they offer a sampling of the realm of the possible. Given a sense of that realm citizens can more readily engage in the process. The final outcome may be a totally different alternative or one that combines elements of the alternatives that were presented.

When local individuals react to alternatives and express their preferences, the result is the very sort of holistic appraisal that one often wishes experts could generate. Thus to return to the McHarg (1969) approach, the appraisal of scenic or recreation value could be obtained through the efforts of experts in these areas. But it is often less expensive, more locally responsive, and of higher validity to obtain them as the outcomes of a participatory process.

In addition to the importance of participation as a way to build on local knowledge and talent, it is an essential process for other reasons as well. Lisk (1985) suggests that "the participation of people in the making of decisions which affect them is a basic human need in its own right" (p. 28). Furthermore, he argues that "it is widely believed that genuine participation increases confidence of individuals or groups in their own ability to initiate actions in defence of their interests" (p. 28).

The confidence to initiate such actions could be an important factor in guiding people-compatible development. Development brings change and change is not value-free. It is unlikely that many changes brought by development would have occurred if the people who were sold on all the benefits that would accrue, had also been cognizant of what would be lost. The downside of progress repeatedly emerges in hindsight. It is time that people were encouraged to foresee what gains and what losses a project might bring. The concept of *anticipated regret* captures this notion of helping people to consider, before it is too late, what trade-offs will be made.

### *Human Scale*

A phenomenon that is repeated with some regularity involves the public response to a major catastrophe accompanied by many casualties, when a small handful of survivors is found in the rubble. The names of these few individuals become common knowledge, their condition is updated frequently on media reports, they receive outpourings of good wishes. These are people, rather than the anonymous numbers lost in a casualty. These individuals give a small sense of hope amidst news of despair and crisis.

The problems of the world are bigger than any of us can fathom. Many environmental appraisals depict a dire situation of mammoth global proportions. The poverty and malnutrition, homelessness and sense of futility are of an enormity that is beyond comprehension. It is little wonder that people feel hopeless and helpless. These threats, like major catastrophes, are at a scale that people find difficult to grasp. By contrast, the plight of a little girl, a lone survivor of a plane crash that killed her parents, is at a human scale.

The inability to comprehend problems of a global dimension is hardly an indication that humans are incapable animals. It is an indication that approaches to solving these problems must take into account the scale which humans can handle. When people do understand a situation, when it can draw on their knowledge, they can be competent and reasonable collaborators (S. Kaplan & R. Kaplan, 1989). When the quest for a solution calls upon humans skills and inclinations, there can be remarkable outcomes, perhaps not outcomes that have universal applicability, but outcomes that are workable in certain situations.

Workable solutions are likely to come from patterns that acknowledge such a human scale. S. Kaplan (1990) speaks of "adaptive muddling" as an approach that "draws upon the insight, the enthusiasm, the curiosity, the dedication, the restlessness, and the diversity of ordinary people" (p. 23). Encouraging such solutions requires a willingness to permit small experiments that fit local circumstances (De Young & S. Kaplan, 1988). And the imagery of results of successful experiments is an essential ingredient in encouraging further attempts in another place.

Given the magnitude of the world crisis and human malaise and the awesome loss of human resources when people do not have a sense of being needed, it would seem that encouraging such small solutions would be an appropriate path. The very strengths of humankind that are now so readily ignored and violated would be central to these small steps. If we can incorporate human needs and preferences in planning and decision making, we will have an environment at a scale in which humans can and will want to employ their substantial talents and energies:

> Love of the earth is not altogether dead within the human heart. There is still concern that children and grandchildren inherit a livable world. There is still a willingness to live a frugal and disciplined life if that can be seen as truly meaningful in relation to the massiveness of the problem. Capacity for sacrifice is not altogether gone. In short there is a religious depth in myriad of people that can find expression in lives lived appropriately to reality. That depth must be touched and tapped, and it must be directed by an honest and encompassing view of reality. If that is done, there is hope. (Daly & Cobb, 1989, p. 374)

## Acknowledgements

This paper constitutes an adventure into many areas that are new to me. The extensive and current collection of the University of Michigan library system has made this quest a great pleasure. Suggestions and comments by James E. Crowfoot, Abram W. Kaplan, and William C. Sullivan III have been most helpful. Stephen Kaplan's encouragement of and enthusiasm for the project have made it seem a reasonable and appropriate challenge.

## References

Alamgir, M. (1989). Participatory development: The IFAD experience. In W. P. Lineberry (Ed.), *Assessing participatory development: Rhetoric versus Reality*. Boulder, CO: Westview.

ANGOC (1990). *People's participation and environmentally sustainable development*. Metro Manila, Philippines: Asian NGO Coalition for Agrarian Reform and Rural Development.

Brickman, P., Coates, D. & Janoff-Bulman, R. (1978). Lottery winners and accident victims: Is happiness relative? *Journal of Personality and Social Psychology, 36*, 917-927.

Brown, L. R. (Ed.). (1991). *State of the world 1991: A Worldwatch Institute report on progress toward a sustainable society* (pp. 3-20). New York: Norton.

Coombs, H. C. (1990). *The return of scarcity: Strategies for an economic future*. Cambridge: Cambridge University Press.

Critchfield, R. (1991). *Trees, why do you wait: America's changing rural culture*. Washington, D.C.: Island.

Daly, H. E. & Cobb, J. B., Jr. (1989). *For the common good: Redirecting the economy toward community, environment, and a sustainable future*. Boston: Beacon.

De Young, R. & Kaplan, S. (1988). On averting the tragedy of the commons. *Environmental Management, 12*, 273-283.

Dobson, A. (Ed.). (1991). *The green reader: Essays toward a sustainable society*. San Francisco: Mercury House.

Durning, A. (1991). Asking how much is enough. In L. R. Brown (Ed.), *State of the world 1991* (pp. 153-169). New York: Norton.

Foa, U. G. (1971). Interpersonal and economic resources. *Science, 171*, 345-351.

Garbarino, J. (1988). *The future as if it really mattered*. Longmont, CO: Bookmakers Guild.

Goland, C. A. (1992). *Cultivating diversity: Field scattering as agricultural risk management in Cuyo Cuyo, Dept. of Puno, Peru.* Ann Arbor, MI: University Microfilms International.

Gregory, R. L. (1966). *Eye and brain.* New York: McGraw-Hill.

Hinrichsen, D. (1991). Economists' shining lie. *Amicus Journal, 13,* 3-5.

Jochim, M. A. (1981). *Strategies for survival: Cultural behavior in an ecological context.* New York: Academic Press.

Kaplan, R. (1991). Environmental description and prediction: A conceptual analysis. In T. Gärling & G. Evans (Eds.), *Environment, cognition and action: An integrated approach* (pp. 19-34). New York: Oxford University Press.

Kaplan, S. (1990). Being needed, adaptive muddling and human-environment relationships. In R. I. Selby, K. H. Anthony, J. Choi & B. Orland (Eds.), *Coming of age* (pp. 19-25). Oklahoma City, OK: Environmental Design and Research Association.

Kaplan, S., & Kaplan, R. (1978). *Humanscape: Environments for people.* Ann Arbor, MI: Ulrich's.

Kaplan, S., & Kaplan, R. (1982). *Cognition and environment: Functioning in an uncertain world.* New York: Praeger.

Kaplan, S. & Kaplan, R. (1989). The visual environment: Public participation in design and planning. *Journal of Social Issues, 45,* 59-86.

Korten, D. C. (1990). *Getting to the 21st Century: Voluntary action and the global agenda.* West Hartford, CT: Kumarian.

Koshland, D. E. Jr. (1991). Preserving biodiversity. *Science, 253,* 717.

Lachman, R. & Lachman, J. L. (1979). Comprehension and cognition. In F. I. M. Craik & L. S. Cermak (Eds.), *Levels of processing in human memory.* Hillsdale, NJ: Erlbaum.

Lee, R. B. (1979). *The Kung San: Men, women, and work in a foraging society.* New York: Cambridge University Press.

Lineberry, W. P. (Ed.). (1989). *Assessing participatory development: Rhetoric versus reality.* Boulder, CO: Westview.

Lisk, F. (1985). The role of popular participation in basic needs-oriented development planning. In F. Lisk (Ed.), *Popular participation in planning for basic needs: Concepts, methods and practices.* Hampshire, UK: Gower.

McHarg, I. L. (1969). *Design with nature.* New York: Natural History.

Miringoff, M. L. (1990). Monitoring the social well-being of the nation. *Public Welfare, 48,* 34-38.

Morowitz, H. J. (1991). Balancing species preservation and economic considerations. *Science, 253,* 752-754.

Orr, D. W. (1991). *Ecological literacy: Education and the transition to a postmodern world.* Albany, NY: State University of New York Press.

Pfeiffer, J. E. (1978). *The emergence of man.* New York: Harper & Row.

Rappaport, R. A. (1984). *Pigs for the ancestors: Ritual in the ecology of a New Guinea people.* New Haven: Yale University Press.

Savory, A. (1988). *Holistic resource management.* Washington, D.C.: Island.

Simon, H. A. (1990). Invariants of human behavior. *Annual Review of Psychology. 41*, 1-20.

Starke, L. (1990). *Signs of hope: Working towards our common future.* New York: Oxford University Press.

Stewart, F. (1985). *Basic needs in developing countries.* Baltimore, MD: Johns Hopkins Press.

Triandis, H. (1988). Collectivism v. individualism: A reconceptualisation of a basic concept in cross-cultural social psychology. In G. K. Verma & C. Bagley (Eds.), *Cross-cultural studies of personality, attitudes and cognition (*pp. 60-95*).* London: Macmillan.

Verhelst, T. G. (1987). *No life without roots: Culture and development.* (Trans. B. Cumming, 1990). London: Zed Books.

Wisner, B., Stea, D., & Kruks, S. (1991). Participatory and action research methods. In E. H. Zube & G. T. Moore (Eds.), *Advances in environment, behavior and design* (Vol. 3, pp. 271-295). New York: Plenum.

World Bank (1991). *World Development Report 1991: The challenge of development.* New York: Oxford University Press.

World Commission on Environment and Development (1987). *Our common future.* Oxford: Oxford University Press.

*Behavior and Environment: Psychological and Geographical Approaches*
*T. Gärling and R.G. Golledge (Editors)*



# CHAPTER 6

# Cognitive Processes and Cartographic Maps

**Robert Lloyd**

Geographers have always been interested in exploring environments and representing them on maps. Our interest in spatial cognition is a natural extension of this tradition. We share theoretical interests with psychologists that focus on the processes used to encode spatial information into memory, the nature of the internal representation, and the decoding processes used with internal representations for making decisions (see Chapter 7 in this book). In addition to theoretical concerns, geographers usually have a distinct interest in the specific environment being represented and in the behavior of persons who have the environment represented in their memory. Geographers have always aspired to represent environments on maps and have been concerned with how effectively their maps communicated information about environments. It is this desire to communicate spatial information effectively that has caused geographers to be interested in the cognitive processes people use when interacting with cartographic maps. Some environments have unique characteristics that make their representations especially interesting.

The map of New Orleans represented in Figure 6.1 was published in The Times-Picayune (June 30, 1991) with the Sunday classified advertisements. The map is represented in the conventional manner with north at the top. It is a rather simple map showing a lake in the north and a river that flows west to east across the map. The lake and river go unlabeled, but some areas in the city and streets are identified. The map is obviously intended for use by readers who are familiar with the local environment. It is an unusual map in that it presents propositional information used by experienced navigators on a cartographic map. The verbal coding used on the map would seem to be at odds with the frame that encompasses it. Since no north arrow is provided, an outsider might incorrectly conclude that east is at the top of the map. The map communicates in terms that make sense to those persons who navigate through the city and the river's influence on this process is apparent. The area between the lake and the river is on the same side of the river as the Eastern United States. Extending this notion makes the West Bank in the south a reasonable concept. It is common for the word up to be used for north and down for south. Clearly above and below are not equivalent terms. The flow of the river is the critical information. Above a street that intersects the river is upstream and below is downstream. Location is simply communicated by the side and flow of the river. Lewis (1976) has explained how the residents of New Orleans describe their urban environment.

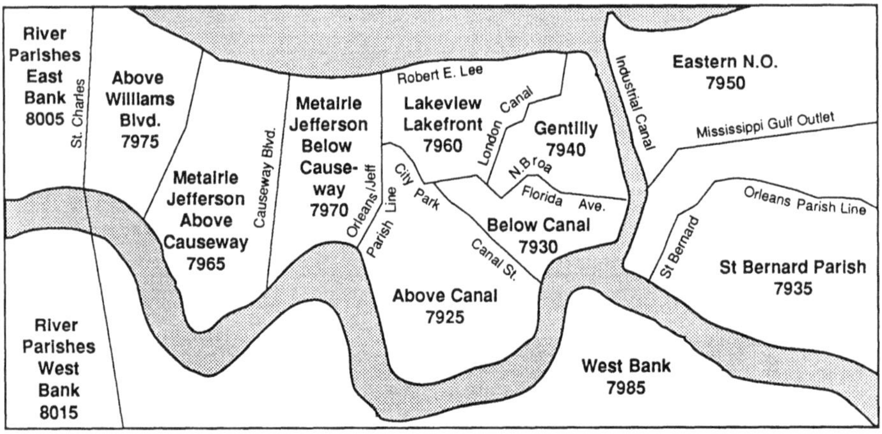


FIGURE 6.1. Map of New Orleans published by The Times-Picayune in the classified advertisement section of the Newspaper (June 30, 1991). Reprinted with permission.

This chapter will focus on cognitive issues that are specifically related to processing cartographic maps. The direct visual processing of cartographic maps represented on paper or monitors is considered as is the processing of cognitive maps in memory that were encoded from cartographic maps. My goal in writing this chapter was to discuss specific ideas related to processing spatial information represented on cartographic maps and to relate these ideas to the broader cognition literature.

Some studies have compared cognitive maps generated from studying cartographic maps with those encoded while navigating through an environment. One difference between these two processes is how the information is encountered. A typical cartographic map provides all the information at the same time, usually expressed with a north at the top orientation, a vertical vantage point, and a parallel perspective (Muehrcke, 1980). The typical navigation experience is a sequence of encounters, on foot or in some surface conveyance, that enables one to encode different parts of the environment each time. The information encoded from the environment, therefore, has multiple orientations, a horizontal vantage point, and, assuming normal vision, a stereographic perspective. Less typical are navigation experiences above the surface that could have either a vertical or oblique vantage point. One also could close one eye for a central perspective. Differences in cognitive representations might be related to parallel versus serial processing, single versus multiple orientations, vertical versus horizontal vantage points, and parallel versus stereographic perspectives. These differences are related to decisions made by the cartographer to represent the environment on the cartographic map.

## Navigation Versus Map Reading

Cognitive maps encoded from cartographic maps are different from those encoded during navigation. Researchers have studied these differences in a number of ways. Evans and Pezdek (1980) performed experiments that had subjects do the same tasks using different environmental representations. Landmarks on a college campus were learned by navigation and states of the United States were learned from cartographic maps. An experiment that asked which of two pairs of locations was closer together in the real world produced very similar results for the campus landmarks and the states. There was a linear relationship between reaction time and the ratio of the inter-pair distances in both cases. In both cases subjects also reported using imagery to make the comparisons.

Another experiment had subjects determine if triads of campus landmarks or states were presented in their correct relative position in geographic space or in a mirror image of these positions. Subjects processing states showed the usual strong positive linear relationship between reaction time and degrees of rotation (Shepard & Cooper, 1983). Subjects processing campus landmarks took about the same time to answer for all orientations. The authors argued that the difference was obtained because state locations were learned from maps with a single north at the top orientation and campus landmarks were learned with multiple orientations during navigation. Other subjects, who were not familiar with the campus and learned the landmarks from a map, showed a strong linear relationship between reaction time and degrees of rotation. The authors concluded that the multiple perspectives of a navigation experience was one important variable, but other variables, motoric navigation, functional concerns, etc., may also be important (Evans & Pezdek, 1980).

Thorndyke and Hayes-Roth (1982) have defined procedural and survey knowledge as distinctly different types of information in cognitive maps. Knowledge about an environment acquired directly by navigating through the environment was called procedural knowledge. The authors argued that procedural knowledge is stored as verbal information related to the process of going from one location in the environment to another. The proportion of a person's cognitive map encoded as procedural knowledge should change dramatically with variations in geographic scale. As the proportion of an environment represented as procedural knowledge decreases with geographic scale, the proportion represented as survey knowledge should increase. Survey knowledge is represented as visual imagery, provides more holistic impressions, and can easily be acquired from cartographic maps. Clearly, environments that cover large areas, for example, continents, are mostly encoded from cartographic maps.

Presson and Hazelrigg (1984) made a distinction between spatial knowledge acquired from primary and secondary sources to study what they called the "alignment effect." In their study primary spatial knowledge was acquired directly either by viewing from a single vantage point or navigating through the environment. Secondary knowledge was acquired indirectly by studying a map. Their results supported an alignment effect for map learning with performance being enhanced by a subject being aligned with the environment as the encoded cartographic map was aligned and diminished when the reverse was true. The results did not, however, support previous suggestions that the effect was caused by differences in viewing versus navigating in the environment, simultaneous (survey knowledge) processing versus successive (procedural knowledge) processing, or on having a single versus multiple vantage point. What did predict the alignment effect was whether information was directly or indirectly encoded.

Sholl performed experiments that considered Neisser's (1976) view that cognitive maps are not like pictures in the head, but "orienting schemata, cognitive structures specialized to direct both perceptual and motor exploration of the environment" (Sholl, 1987, p. 16). If cognitive maps are functioning like pictures (Levine, Jankovic, & Palij, 1982), then all regenerated information should be equally accessible (the equiavailability principle) and be represented in a specific orientation (the specific-orientation hypothesis).

Orienting schemata would give special status to things in front of a person because we are primed to respond to what we are ready to perceive (Shepard, 1978). Given a particular orientation, information in front of a person could be responded to faster than information behind the person. Unlike the fixed orientation of maps or map-like images, orienting schemata have a flexible alignment and all orientations can be responded to in an equal amount of time.

Sholl's (1987) experiments had subjects point to campus landmarks (primary knowledge) or cities in the northeastern part of the United States (secondary knowledge). Results indicated campus landmarks were not represented in a fixed orientation and were not equally accessible when in front or behind the subjects. Cities in the northeastern United States were represented in a specific orientation and equally accessible when in front or behind the subjects. A group of subjects with both primary and secondary knowledge of cities appeared to rely upon a representation with north at the top and did not consistently respond faster to cities in front of them. This suggested that orienting schemata were not in effect during the judgments at this geographic scale, even though subjects had some direct contact with the city locations.

Carpenter and Just (1986) presented an interesting view of the relationship between a person and the environment related to orientation and imagery. They argued that objects encoded with respect to larger or stable frames of reference will be rotated to change orientation. Objects encoded as part of a stable frame of reference will cause a change of perspective for the person, that is, the person is rotated instead of the object. When the frame of reference is internal to the object, encoded information is independent of an object's orientation. This latter case is why very familiar objects can be recognize in any orientation.

## Neisser's View

Neisser (1976) argued that information is picked up from the environment in a perceptual cycle. His view of the cognitive mapping process provides a meaningful structure for understanding differences in primary and secondary spatial information. Important elements of the perceptual cycle are anticipatory schemata that direct the information pick up (Figure 6.2). "A schema is that portion of the entire perceptual cycle which is internal to the perceiver, modifiable by experience, and somehow specific to what is being perceived. The schema accepts information as it becomes available at sensory surfaces and is changed by that information; it directs movements and exploratory activities that make more information available, by which it is further modified" (p. 54). Schemata developed by experiences with the environment would be used by the person in Figure 6.2 to acquire primary information directly from the environment. Different schemata, developed by reading experiences, would direct the acquisition of secondary information from a book. And yet other schemata, developed by map reading experiences, would direct someone acquiring secondary information from a cartographic map. A schema is thought to be a format, like a format in a computer language, for picking up information and a plan for obtaining more information. Schemata accept information from the environment or objects and direct actions.

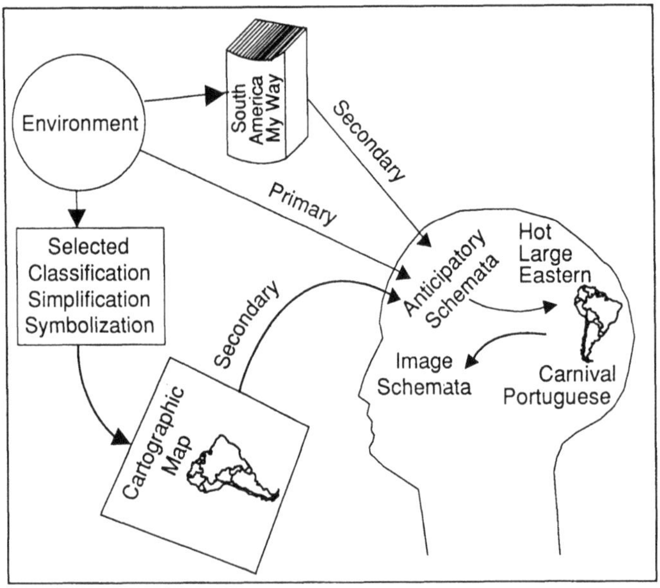


FIGURE 6.2. Sketch illustrating the encoding of information about the environment from primary and secondary sources.

Neisser's consideration of cognitive maps is limited to primary information acquired directly while interacting with the immediate environment. Primary activities produce cognitive maps that are orienting schemata because one's ego is involved. As Neisser (1976) explains:

> Information about oneself, like all other information, can only be picked up by an appropriately tuned schema. Conversely, all information that is picked up, including proprioceptive information, modifies a schema. In the case of movement through the environment, this is an orienting schema or cognitive map. This means that the cognitive map always includes the perceiver as well as the environment. Ego and world are perceptually inseparable. (pp. 116-117)

Although Neisser did not discuss spatial information picked up from cartographic maps, an extrapolation of his view might argue that the schemata used to acquire information from a cartographic map would not involve the ego. The cartographic abstraction process has constructed an object that represents the environment. Object schemata are used to accept information from them and direct future map-reading actions. For familiar large-scale environments, certainly at the urban scale and larger, we may have both orienting schemata based on primary experiences and object schemata, based on map-reading experiences.

Given a particular situation that requires the use of the schemata, the appropriate one is initiated to accept information. When we are considering the immediate environment, for instance, deciding to turn left or right at the next traffic light, the cognitive map as orienting schema with the embedded ego is used. This can happen when actively involved in navigation or when using imagery to provide directions to someone over the telephone. Neisser (1976, p. 130) argued that "the experience of having an image is just the inner aspect of a readiness to perceive the imagined object, and that differences in the nature and quality of people's images reflect differences in the kind of information they are prepared to pick up." This view rules out that images are pictures in the head. They are, instead, plans for obtaining information from potential environments or potential cartographic maps. The imagery experience is a state of visual readiness to perceive an environment or object and the image is our expectations of what will be seen.

## Representing the Environment on a Cartographic Map

Cartographers can represent the environment in many ways. Their job is to sort through the numerous possibilities and decide which is best for a particular situation. Muehrcke (1980) describes a process called cartographic abstraction which is used by cartographers to transform physical reality into a map. He represented this process as including four types of activities: (1) selection, (2) classification, (3) simplification, and (4) symbolization.

Selection involves determining what specific information should be mapped to represent the environment. The cartographer must make a series of decisions that lead to a focused representation of the environment. Muehrcke presented these decisions as questions concerning where, when, and what. In addition to a specific location, time, and information set, a geographic scale and perspective must be considered. If the entire earth is to be represented, the choice of map projection becomes very important. The classification of the information being mapped results in labeled categories that can be more easily verbalized. Maps usually have legends that attach formal labels to categories of information, for instance, roads, water wells, or high elevations. The use of classified information on maps presents a less complex and, therefore, easier to understand message. The labeled categories of information make it easier for map users because labels can be processed with more abstract language systems.

Simplification is similar to classification in that its goal is to reduce complexity. This is accomplished by eliminating details. A typical thematic map focuses on a single variable, for instance, elevation or population density, eliminating the details of all other information associated with the locations on the map. Another example of simplification is the smoothing of lines that represent rivers or political boundaries. A river represented on a small scale map is usually simpler than the same river represented on a large scale map.

Features of the environment are represented on the map by graphic symbolization. Houses might be represented by red squares, rivers by blue lines, and forests by patches of green. The choice of the best shape or color for symbolizing points, linear, or areal features on maps is often decided by conventional wisdom.

Current Geographic Information Systems (GIS) have immediate access to data files, numerous menus for quick decision making and execution, and high resolution color monitors to display the final representation of the environment. These systems are rapidly replacing draftsmen with paper, pen, and ruler, but the basic goals and processes remain the same. A GIS does the labor for the cartographer. Once a map exists, it matters little to the person using the maps whether a GIS or a draftsman with colored pencils constructed it.

## Representing the Environment in Cognitive Maps

The formal definition of cognitive mapping offered by Downs and Stea (1973, p. 9) suggested that individuals use some processes similar to those used by cartographers: "Cognitive mapping is a process composed of a series of psychological transformations by which an individual acquires, codes, stores, recalls, and decodes information about the relative locations and attributes of phenomena in his everyday spatial environment." Most cognitive mapping studies have focused on structural knowledge about the environment such as distances and directions between locations. In addition to where places are located we also encode into memory other important information about locations (Lloyd & Hooper, 1991).

Figure 6.2 above illustrates a person thinking about Brazil. Information about Brazil has previously been encoded as both verbal propositions (Portuguese is the language in Brazil) and visual images (map of South America). Verbal information could have been acquired directly through contact with the environment on an earlier visit, for instance, a carnival celebration in Rio de Janeiro. Verbal information also may have been encoded from secondary sources, for instance, reading Brazil described as the largest country in South America. Map reading also may provide verbal information, for instance, a map of South America showing average temperatures may lead one to conclude that Brazil has a .hot climate. Although it might be possible to encode enough verbal propositions to describe the complete visual details of an environment, most people are not likely to have enough direct experiences to do this with a continent. Being typical in this respect, the person in Figure 6.2 is shown as acquiring his or her map image of South America from a cartographic map. This was made much easier because of the selection, classification, simplification, and symbolization processes performed by the cartographer to produce the cartographic map of South America. Both the cartographer and the cognitive mapper selectively acquire information about the environment. The cartographer's information is likely to be more accurate, precise, and complete. Cognitive mappers may selectively acquire only certain information and only for parts of the environment (Lloyd & Hooper, 1991). Cartographers make a conscious effort to obtain specific information. Cognitive mappers may acquire information about the environment without even knowing it (Lewicki, 1986; Lewicki, Hill, & Bizot, 1988).

Both cartographers and cognitive mappers use classification to reduce complexity. We classify objects in the environment as large, green, or faraway. The person in Figure 6.2 might further process the encoded information through higher-order image schemata to determine the meaning of the information so some decision could be made (Johnson, 1987). Cognitive mappers, like cartographers, use simplification processes to deal with the complexities of the environment (Byrne, 1979). Tversky (1981) has documented what she called rotation and alignment heuristics used to encode spatial information. One of her experiments indicated that subjects' cognitive maps of South America were encoded in a rotated position so the continent's major axis had an incorrect north-south orientation. Another of her experiments indicated subjects' cognitive maps of South America were moved westward to align the continent with North America. Arguments that the same processes effect urban cognitive maps have been made by Lloyd (1989a), Lloyd and Heivley (1987), and Nicholson (1990).

## Visual Processing of Cartographic Maps

This part of the chapter selectively discusses cognitive processes associated with typical map reading tasks. In general, map reading is a very complex operation that often uses multiply cognitive processes to solve even simple problems. Typical experimental designs focus attention on only part of a larger process. Only recognition, distance estimation, and search processes are considered here.

### *Orientation and the Recognition Process*

Since most cartographic maps are represented with north at the top, people have difficulty recognizing shapes on maps that are encountered in orientations other than this conventional one. Results from studies that have focused on the recognition of maps have been consistent with other studies on the rotation of images of objects (Shepard & Cooper, 1983). This supports the notion that cognitive maps encoded from small scale cartographic maps are cognitive representations of objects. Since they are not based on actual movement through the environment they represent, they are detached from the ego. In a study by Steinke and Lloyd (1983), maps of states viewed in unfamiliar orientations were typically rotated to north at the top before being identified as correct or mirror images. The strong relationship between reaction time and degrees of rotation from north at the top indicated that subjects were forming an image of the basic shape, rotating it to north at the top, and then comparing the image to a north at the top representation in memory. Distributions of graduated circles or dots on the same basemap found the same relationship between reaction time and degrees of rotation from north at the top (Lloyd & Steinke, 1984). The graduated circle maps, which had more complex information, had longer average reaction times for all orientations. This indicated that maps are like other objects learned at fixed orientations. Images of the same basemap that contained more information required more time to generate. Once these different map images were formed, however, they apparently could be rotated at the same rate.

Conerway (1991) considered the complexity of the outline forming a state boundary and how this affected the identification of state outlines and their mirror images. She found the same basic relationship between reaction time and degrees of rotation from north at the top. The mean reaction times were, however, significantly slower for states that had less complex boundaries. States with more complex boundaries were thought to provide more information that could be used to determine the identity of a trial state. This was an important part of the overall process that determined if a particular trial was a correct or mirror image of a state outline. She also determined that the rate of rotation was not significantly different for maps of varying complexity. This again supports the notion that the rate of rotation of map images is not affected by characteristics of the map that may otherwise affect the total time needed to respond.

The identification of maps represented as three dimensional surfaces also has been investigated (Rice, 1989). Prism maps presented at particular rotations may have counties in the foreground higher than those in the background. Reaction times varied with degree of rotation from north at the top, but also were affected by particular orientations of the surface that obscured prominent outline features. Holmes (1984) studied the horizontal and vertical angular separation of pairs of maps represented as three dimensional fishnet surfaces. His study differed from those discussed above in a number of ways. Subjects looked at two maps and decided if they were the same or different. There was no correct map in memory at a fixed orientation. One surface represented an area with a small, medium, and large mountain and the other a mirror image of the first surface. The surfaces rotated freely as the subjects examined them and no correct orientation was specified. Subjects studied the two surfaces so they could identify the two versions, but were not instructed to use any particular method. Subjects were presented with randomly selected pairs of the various combinations and asked to determine if the maps were the same or different. Interesting results were that horizontal rotational difference between pairs of maps significantly affected reaction time for subjects using imagery, but vertical differences in vantage points did not. Another interesting result was that some subjects used imagery to solve the task and others used verbal coding related to the relationship of three mountains having a clockwise progression on one version of the map and a counterclockwise progression on the other version. Subjects using verbal methods were faster than those using imagery and were able to respond in the same amount of time regardless of the vantage points or orientations associated with pairs of maps.

### *Estimating Distances on Maps with Scales*

Since maps provide information for making decisions, how the information is acquired and its accuracy are of some practical importance. The cognitive processes used to determine the distance between locations on a map provide an interesting example. A graphic scale on a map is a line marked to indicate the distance on the earth represented on the map by the length of the line. Verbal scales such as "one inch equals one hundred miles" are also frequently found on maps. A number of studies have shown that people use imagery processes with such scales to estimate distances.

Hartley (1977, 1981) performed a number of experiments that had subjects judge the length of lines. Subjects were provided visual or verbal standards that were shorter than the judged lines. Most subjects used what Hartley (1977) called the "laying off process" to estimate distances. They would form an image of the standard and imagine it moving along the length of the line. By counting the number of standards needed to cover the line one can estimate the length of the line. Results consistently indicated a strong linear relationship between response times and estimated distances. This is because longer distances take more layoffs and this takes more time. When the length of the standard was increased, the reaction times decreased because fewer layoffs were required. The slopes of the regression lines relating reaction time and estimated length for shorter and longer standards were, however, the same. This indicated that the length of the standard did not affect how fast the image of the standard could be moved along the line. Error patterns indicated a tendency to overestimate the lengths of lines. The layoff process caused error to accumulate with each layoff. This caused errors in length estimates to increase as the lengths of lines increased.

If a distance is exactly a multiple of a standard, it is possible to count the number of layoffs and obtain an accurate estimate of the distance. Since locations on maps may be separated by distances that are not exact multiples of the graphic or verbal scale, precise distance estimates require a second process to determine the fraction of the standard remaining after the number of whole units have been counted. Holzapfel (1985) presented some distances to subjects that were exact multiples of the standard and some distances that were not multiples of the standard. The latter distances were associated with reaction times that were longer than the next longer regular distances. He argued that an additional interpolation process had to be used for irregular distances. His data also supported Hartley's notion that error accumulates during the layoff process. He suggested maps with incremented graphic scales, substantially larger than those typically used, could provide faster and more accurate estimates. Such a graphic scale would allow an image of the distance on the map to be transferred to the larger graphic scale. All distance estimates should require the same amount of time because no layoffs or interpolations would be required. Since layoffs would not be necessary, error would not increase as distances became longer. A study by Lloyd (1989b) supported this argument. Subjects who were viewing routes on a street network were asked to estimate the distance between points on either end of the route by marking a line with a digitizing pen. The line was physically separated from the map and longer than any of the routes. Although errors indicated a consistent overestimation of the distances, they did not increases with longer distances.

Eboch (1985) performed an experiment that compared distance estimates performed with a set of isolated lines with estimates made with a set of similar lines that collectively represented a road network on a map. The results supported Hartley's argument that most subjects spontaneously decided to use a layoff process. Some subjects were able to perform the distance estimation task faster when the lines were represented together on the road map. When lines were considered one at a time in a random order information learned during previous decisions cannot easily be used for later decisions. When a map was always visible during the experiment, subjects were able to encode information they had computed during earlier trials and use it in subsequent trials.

### *Searching Maps and Feature Integration Theory*

Searching is probably the task most closely associated with using maps (Dobson, 1985). It is part of many map-reading activities. We may need to find a map symbol, a name, a color, or a combination of features, for instance, a blue line named the Monongahela River, as part of an activity designed to solve a larger problem. The search may be an initial or intermediate step toward some ultimate goal, for instance, planning a route to an unfamiliar destination. The ideal map search finds the correct information quickly.

Treisman's feature integration theory of attention assumes that features are encoded early, automatically, and in parallel across the visual field, while objects, which are constructed from features, are identified at a later stage in the process using focused attention (Treisman & Gelade, 1980). This preattentive level of visual processing has not received a great amount of attention from cartographers with the exception of eye-movement studies that considered the selection of the next fixation location (Dobson, 1979, 1980; see Steinke, 1987 for review). The cartographer can design maps that help or hinder the important initial preattentive stage of processing. As Dobson (1983) argued:

> Searching for targets, as a consequence, is significantly influenced by the contrast between alternative target choices. Emphasizing conspicuity in the targets (distributions) of the display should promote more accurate and efficient processing of the distinguishing graphic characteristic. In this sense, fine

> tuning the interface between the human perceptual mechanism and the graphic characteristics used to distinguish elements of the stimulus image should be a primary task of cartographic researchers.

Someone visually processing a map that just appeared on a monitor would initially encode information along a number of separable dimensions (Dobson, 1983; Garner, 1974; Shortridge, 1982). A dimension is "the complete range of variation which is separately analyzed by some functionally independent perceptual subsystem" (Treisman & Gelade, 1980, p. 99). Examples would be color, brightness, orientation, texture, size, location, and spatial frequency. A feature is "a particular value on a dimension" (Treisman & Gelade, 1980, p. 99).

Examples would be red, dark, vertical, coarse, small, central, and few. "In order to recombine these separate representations and to ensure the correct synthesis of features for each object in a complex display [like a map], stimulus locations are processed serially with focal attention" (Treisman & Gelade, 1980, p. 98). "If the dimensions comprising a stimulus can be visually pulled apart and seen as unrelated, the stimulus dimensions are considered separable....Those stimuli whose dimensions cannot be separated, but are perceived as a single dimension have integral dimensions" (Shortridge, 1982, p. 162). A circle's size and its shade of grey would be features on separable dimensions. A dot's hue and brightness would be features on integral dimensions.

Treisman and Gormican (1988) used a search paradigm that tested pairs of stimuli along a common dimension separated by a single separable feature. A display would have 1, 6, or 12 distractors (long or short lines) and a single target (a long or short line). Results indicated that targets that were more extreme on a dimension were found faster among distractors than where those less extreme on a dimension. Additional experiments indicated that targets that deviated from a prototype could be found faster than the prototypes. Prototype color targets (red, green, or blue) resulted in slower search times among deviation color distractor (magenta, lime, or turquoise) than when the situation was reversed. The "pop out" effect for deviation colors was explained as follows (Treisman & Gormican, 1988, p. 31):

> When the target is a prototype [red], it activates its own channel more than any individual distractor [magenta] does, but the increase must be detected against a high background level produced by pooled distractors. When the target is the deviating stimulus [magenta], it activates the prototype channel less than the prototype [red], but in addition it produces activity on another channel [blue] on which the prototype distractors produce little or no effect. The asymmetry then follows from Weber's law: Detecting *some* against a background of *none*

should be easier than detecting *more* against a background of *some*.

Treisman and Gelade (1980) argued that the search process used to find a target defined by one of its separate features (a color or shape) was different from the process used to find targets defined by conjunctive features. When targets were defined by both color and shape (conjunctive targets), a serial self-terminating search process was used. Both positive (target present) and negative (target not present) answers had a strong linear relationship with display size and the slope for negative responses was approximately twice as steep as the slope for positive answers (Lloyd, 1988; Pashler, 1987; Sternberg, 1969). The results "suggested that focal attention, scanning successive locations serially, is the means by which the correct integration of features into multidimensional percepts is insured. When this integration is not required by the task, parallel detection of features should be possible" (Treisman & Gelade, 1980, p. 106). It is interesting to note that conjunctive map symbols have been shown to enhance performance on other types of map-reading tasks (Dobson, 1983).

Feature integration theory explains why map designers can create a "pop out" effect for a symbol marking an important location that needs immediate attention from map readers. Single-feature symbols that are defined by a feature that is not shared by other symbols on the map enables map readers to use parallel processing to find it. Map readers should be able to find such symbols in a minimum amount of time no matter how many other symbols are competing for attention. Feature integration theory relates to the initial preattentive stage of map reading. Following this stage, focused attention can be used for map-reading tasks involving the identification or comparison of an object on the map. Experimental results also have been reported that suggest some conjunctive targets can "pop out" of displays provided the values on each dimensions are highly discriminable (Downing & Pinker, 1985; McLeod, Driver, & Crisp, 1988; Nakayama & Silverman, 1986a, 1986b; Steinman, 1987; Wolf, Cave, & Franzel, 1989). Some dimensions considered have been related to the motion and stereographic depth of target and distractor elements.

Cave and Wolf (1990) described a guided search theory that has two stages. A parallel stage with top-down and bottom-up components determines how likely it is that the stimulus at each location is the target. The bottom-up component is similar to Treisman's "pop out" effect. It is based on the contrast between the target and background when nothing is known about the target. They argued that prior information known about the target also aids search. This top-down information makes any locations with characteristics similar to the target a more likely candidate. If the target is known to be red, then any location that is red is possibly the target. Treisman and Sato's (1990) feature inhibition strategy makes a similar assumption, but focuses on our ability to ignore low probability locations.

Gallinaro (1991) performed an experiment that considered the cognitive processes used to search for boundaries on choropleth maps. Her results supported the guided search model suggested by Cave and Wolf (1990). Subjects searched maps for targets that were a unique boundary condition, for instance, a red county adjacent to a blue county. Reaction times increased as the number of boundaries with colors matching either of the target boundary colors increased. Reaction times did not increase as the number of boundaries with colors not matching either of the target boundary colors increased. Subjects were apparently able to ignore boundaries that were not potential targets and serially searched boundaries that were potential targets. Results indicated that boundaries with certain color combinations could be processed faster than other combinations. The opponent process theory of color vision provided the best explanation of the results (Eastman, 1986; Overheim & Wagner, 1982; Varley, 1983). Red/blue and green/yellow boundary targets, which, according to the theory, have colors that can be processed on independent receptors, were significantly faster than cyan/magenta or magenta/green boundary targets.

## Encoding Information from Cartographic Maps

Cartographic maps are objects with fixed orientations and are encoded in memory using the same processes used to encode other objects with fixed orientations, that is, information is equally accessible, orientation specific, and the ego is not involved in the process. Are cartographic maps special in any other ways? Information that we might be interested in encoding about objects is related to if the object has a certain characteristic and where such a characteristic is located. Most familiar objects have a structure that makes it possible to presume where the characteristic will be found. If a person is described as wearing glasses or shoes, we can safely assume where these items are located. A map of a country might be consulted to determine if the country had oil reserves. Since there is no standard location for oil reserves, we would have to encode in our cognitive maps not only the existence of the reserves but also their spatial location. To the extent that spatial location is generally a more important issue for cartographic maps compared to most other objects, it might be considered a special class of object. Locations may be encoded into memory using verbal or visual information.

Map descriptions analyzed by Shimron (1978) indicated that subjects used words that indicated positional relationships, identified familiar shapes, and associated some locations, for instance, cities, with other classes of map elements, for instance, highways. Such hierarchical structures in cognitive maps have been investigated by a number of researchers (Eastman, 1985; Hirtle & Jonides, 1985; McNamara, 1986; Stevens & Coupe, 1978; Wilson, 1990).

Coordinate positions were indicated by terms such as left/right, east/west, top/bottom, or north/south. Map elements were compared to well known geometric figures or other shapes, for instance, the highway was shaped like an S. Knowledge of the relative positions of a map's symbols was thought to be related to an ability to associate specific locations with verbal labels and classes of map elements. Visual imagery was thought to be important for integrating all the information together. The importance of verbal labels for remembering the locations of map elements has also been demonstrated by Pezdek and Evans (1979).

Shimron (1978) considered several systems of memory organization for encoding cartographic maps into memory and evaluated their effectiveness. An experiment that controlled the time available for encoding a map suggested that some processes were done before others. For example, local connections were known before integrated knowledge of positional information. Another experiment controlled the presentation of either classes of map elements in layers or sections of the map. Layers of information, for instance, sets of cities or highways, were presented one at a time on panels representing the upper, middle or lower third of the map they presented. Subjects learning sections performed better on memory tests than subjects learning layers. Another experiment considered the effect of verbal information that provided a context for the map-learning experience. An experimental group listened to a story related to the map, while a control group sketched the map. Results indicated that the associations between map elements, for instance, cities and highways, were strengthened by the verbal propositions of the story.

Gilmartin (1986) considered the effect maps had when supplementing a text. One group of subjects read an unillustrated text, a second group read the text accompanied by two maps, and a third group read the text and were instructed to use imagery to visualize the information they were reading. Test scores related to recalling spatial information were highest for the text plus maps group and lowest for text only group. An interesting finding was that men benefitted more than women from the presence of the maps. Women scored the same as men on standardized spatial ability tests and also when instructed to use visual imagery. This may indicate a preferred style difference between the genders. Apparently, most men spontaneously decided to integrate the maps with the text, while most women decided not to.

Thorndyke and Staz (1980) considered the relative success of methods used to acquire knowledge from maps. They argued that maps are more complex than most materials used in the typical experiment and many possible techniques could be used to memorize them. A first experiment had subjects memorize maps and think aloud about how they were acquiring information from the map. Analyses of these learning protocols and observations of subjects' behavior while learning the maps indicated that four general types of processes were important. Some procedures were frequently used by good learners and others were used by poor learners. Good learners tended to use a more systematic approach. They used partitioning techniques, systematic sampling in the early stages of learning, and memory-directed sampling in the final stages. Subjects were not very different in their use of verbal learning procedures, but subjects who were good learners tended to use visual imagery as a rehearsal device. All subjects evaluated what they had learned, but good learners focused more on evaluating recently learned information and were better at correctly evaluating how well they knew the information on the maps. Good learners would adopt a technique for acquiring information and stay with it until they had achieved their goal. Poor learners tended not to make good control choices of which procedures to use and when to switch procedures. Unexpectedly, previous experience with maps was not a good predictor of successful learning.

Subjects in a second experiment were trained to use the most successful procedures to learn the maps. The training resulted in improved recall of spatial attributes, but not of verbal attributes. The effectiveness of the training appeared to be dependent on the subject's ability to create and hold visual imagery in memory.

## Patterns on Maps

It would appear that both verbal propositions and visual imagery can be used to encode information from maps into memory. The maps used in the experiments discussed in the previous section were what cartographers would call reference maps. They were a basemap marked with symbols that indicated something existed in space, for instance, cities, highways, lakes, rivers, etc., at particular locations. Other types of maps, thematic maps, present the distribution of some variable within a space. Studies related to the processing of information represented on thematic maps have focused on patterns symbolized on the maps.

### *Visual Processes and Color*

Heyn (1984) investigated how attributes of color were used to process visual information on maps. She tested five different color schemes that varied in both hue and brightness. Maps were presented to subjects that were constructed using one of the schemes. Questions were asked related to either estimating quantities or recognizing patterns. Subjects answered the questions while looking at the maps. Reaction times were analyzed to determine good and poor color schemes. For estimation of quantities, color schemes with large variations in hue were found to be the most efficient. For pattern recognition, schemes that varied in brightness were most successful.

Dannatt (1984) considered the use of dual-hued color schemes to represent data on choropleth maps that have a natural zero break point. Values were either plus, if an area had gained population through migration, or minus, if an area had lost population. The dual-hued color schemes had different hues representing classes of data on either side of the break point. The classes became darker in both directions as they deviated more from the break point. Performance comparisons were made with progressive color schemes. Hues were selected for these schemes so they progressed through some spectral order. They had darker colors representing higher values and lighter colors representing lower values. Subjects validated true/false statements related to maps they were viewing. Statements described the net migration for a particular location or compared the net migration for pairs of locations. Subjects were found to be more efficient when using maps constructed with dual-hued color schemes. For example, one statement simply indicated a marked area had gained or lost population. The mean reaction time for both color schemes plotted for each level (class) of data indicated that subjects could respond to all levels of the dual-hued maps in the same amount of time. Since the progressive scheme did not have a distinct change in the hue at the zero point, subjects using these maps required more time to answer when judging central values.

*Memory Processes*

When a thematic map like those discussed above is encoded into memory, both verbal and visual processes can be used. Studies that have evaluated the relative success of such processes have provided some interesting results. Skipper (1989) had subjects memorize patterns of colors distributed on maps of South America and later reconstruct them from memory. The complexity of the pattern on the maps significantly affected both encoding and decoding times. The colors associated with larger countries were correctly recalled more frequently than for smaller countries. Although these map characteristics impacted processing, they were determined primarily by the data rather than the cartographer. The color scheme used to assign colors to classes of data was also found to be important. By testing color schemes that varied only in hue, only in brightness, and a dual ended scheme that varied in both hue and brightness, accuracy was found to be lowest for maps that only varied in brightness. It was more difficult to process patterns if the hue was constant and the classes only varied in brightness.

The task required subjects to associate 13 countries with one of four possible colors. The countries had names that were familiar to the subjects and were distinctive in both size and shape. It was not surprising that most subjects used some form of verbal coding to memorize the associations. The few subjects who exclusively used imagery processes were significantly faster at encoding and decoding their cognitive maps, but were significantly less accurate in recalling the patterns of colors.

Reagan (1990) considered processes used to learn bi-variate maps. This type of map simultaneously presents two variables by manipulating two separable dimensions. Subjects were instructed to memorize graduated circle maps of Mongolia. Unlike the above experiment, that used a basemap representing familiar and easily named country locations, this basemap was not familiar and names were unknown. The two dimensions that visually varied over the map were the size of circles and the brightness of the color filling the circles. It was hypothesized that subjects would perform a reconstruction task from memory more efficiently when size and brightness were strongly correlated. When this was true the redundant coding would provide the same message from both dimensions, for instance, large circles would be dark and small circles would be light. When the variables were not strongly correlated, the two messages would conflict. Results indicated that the correlation between the dimensions significantly affected encoding times, but had no effect on either accuracy or decoding times. The important conclusion from this is that the benefits from redundant coding occurred when the information is being encoded from the cartographic map into memory. Once the information is encoded into memory, the speed and accuracy related to reconstructing the size, brightness, or both distributions is no longer related to the correlation of the dimensions.

It has been argued that focal color, those that are prototypes of categories, can be encoded and decoded faster and more accurately than nonfocal colors (Rosch, 1973). Focal red is the one that people would select as the best example of red when considering all possible colors that might be associated with the hue named red. Other researchers have found that focal colors were not superior to nonfocal colors in a search process if the nonfocal colors' separation within the color spectrum was equal to the focal colors' separation (Boynton & Smallman, 1990).

McNiff (1991) found the blue that was thought to best represent the category was not the same blue that people selected as the best to represent water on a map, the best example of green also was not the best example to represent forests on maps, and the best example of red was not the best to symbolize urban areas on maps. She performed experiments that had subjects memorize landuse patterns on maps and later indicate the correct landuse for a selected location. Three set of colors were compared. Focal colors were those selected as the best examples of colors named red, green, and blue. Associative colors were those selected as the best to use on maps for urban red, forest green, and water blue. False colors were nonfocal colors often used in remote sensing. The false color representing urban was bright blue, forest was a bright red, and water was a dark blue. This provided a frequently used set of colors that varied in both hue and brightness. The focal and associative colors did not vary in brightness.

Results indicated that maps produced with focal colors were generally not processed faster or more accurately than maps made with other color schemes. False colors here consistently performed better than focal colors with faster study times, response times, and higher accuracy. Associative colors were efficient for subjects who used verbal processes to encode the maps, but were not efficient for subjects who used visual imagery processes. The better performance of the false colors was thought to be related to their variation in both hue and brightness while the other schemes varied only in hue. The extra dimension was particularly an advantage for subjects who used visual imagery. Subjects assigned to the false color maps that encoded the maps using visual imagery produced the best overall performance.

The interaction of the strategy used by the subject and the complexity of the maps indicated that study times generally increased with map complexity for both strategies, but verbal strategies always took longer than visual strategies. Reaction times were not related to complexity for both strategies, but verbal processors always took longer to respond. The relationship between accuracy and complexity indicated that both strategies were relatively successful when map complexity was low. As complexity increased to moderate levels, accuracy dropped for both groups with verbal processors maintaining an advantage. Visual processors actually increased slightly with higher levels of complexity while accuracy for verbal processor decreased severely.

## Error in Cognitive Maps

Studies have shown that cognitive maps are not a perfect reflection of the environments they represent. Errors have been linked to encoding processes, storage systems, and decoding processes (Holyoak & Mah, 1982; Stevens & Coupe, 1978; Tversky, 1981). This part of the chapter focuses on studies at the urban scale related to error. The urban scale is of particular interest because this geographic scale is likely to have multiple encoding systems operating. Both primary and secondary spatial information can be encoded (Presson & Hazelrigg, 1984). Spatial knowledge can be acquired as both procedural knowledge, that is, verbal propositions and survey knowledge, that is, visual imagery (Thorndyke & Hayes-Roth, 1982). Neisser's (1976) view that cognitive maps are orienting schemata is another valid view at this scale, but has received relatively little attention from geographers (Tuan, 1975).

Studies have shown that economic status, length of residence, and mobility had an impact on urban residents' cognitive maps (Golledge, 1978; Golledge & Spector, 1978; Orleans, 1973). Lloyd and Heivley (1987) attempted to hold these variables constant while studying the cognitive maps for subjects in three different neighborhoods in a city. Their goal was to determine if a neighborhood's relative position within the urban space affected its residents' cognitive maps. Results indicated an overestimation of shorter distances and underestimation of longer distances for all three neighborhoods. This result supported Holyoak and Mah's (1982) argument that a decoding process they call implicit scaling produces distance errors when cognitive maps are used to estimated distances. Note that this error pattern is different from the one found when cartographic maps were used to estimate distances (Hartley, 1981). Subjects from the three neighborhoods had different error patterns when estimating directions. Cognitive maps appeared to be rotated to align the major transportation axis connecting the neighborhood with the CBD with a cardinal direction. This supported Tversky's (1981) argument that alignment and rotation heuristics are used during encoding to simplify environments.

Lloyd (1989a) compared cognitive maps of subjects who had lived in a city for a long time with those subjects who learned the city only by studying a map. The experimental task required that subjects located landmarks using reference points. Absolute and relative errors were examined using a Euclidean regression algorithm (Waterman & Gordon, 1984). Absolute error is related to systematic translation, rotation, and scaling of locations in a cognitive map. Relative error is not systematic and is thought to be caused when information about specific locations is inaccurate or incomplete. The author argued there are some fundamental differences between cognitive maps encoded by navigating through the environment and those encoded from cartographic maps. Navigation subjects had significantly more absolute and relative errors in their cognitive maps than map- reading subjects. They also took significantly longer to make their locational decisions. The pattern of the error suggested a quantitative rather than a qualitative difference. The orientations of individual cognitive maps were much more consistent for subjects who learned from the cartographic map. This indicated that the fixed orientation of the cartographic map was encoded into these subjects' cognitive maps and supported similar results reported by Evans and Pezdek (1980).

The above study considered cognitive maps encoded from primary and secondary sources. In that study primary sources provided verbal propositions or procedural knowledge through navigation, and the map, a secondary source, provided visual-imagery information or survey knowledge through map reading. Another study (Lloyd, 1989b) considered encoding verbal and visual information from maps. Perception subjects made decisions concerning distances and directions between pairs of landmarks while viewing a map. Memory subjects learned about the landmarks either by writing verbal descriptions or sketching drawings to provide information about how to move between pairs of landmarks. Error patterns suggested that the processes used to estimate distances were similar for both sets of memory subjects, but different from perception subjects. It was argued that memory subjects used the implicit scaling model to estimate distances (Holyoak & Mah, 1982), and that perception subjects used the laying-off process (Hartley, 1981). The experiment indicated that using visual or verbal experiences to encode a cartographic map into memory resulted in the same processes being used to decode the distances and produced the same error pattern. This supported, in a cartographic map context, the notion that distinctions between primary versus secondary learning is more important than the distinction between verbal versus visual.

## Conclusion

Maps are important in our daily life. The efficiency of the cognitive processes used by people interacting with maps has been a key issue for geographers. Research on the cartographic map has naturally focused on their construction. The selection, classification, simplification, and symbolization decisions made by cartographers shape their maps. Cognitive maps are, in turn, shaped by these cartographic products. A good example of this relationship is the impact of map projections on our impressions of countries. A recent controversy has centered around the relative sizes of countries represented on world maps. The debate has concentrated on a popular map projection that exaggerates the relative sizes of higher-latitude countries (Robinson, 1985). The sizes and shapes of countries in a person's cognitive map undoubtedly are related to how that information was represented on frequently encountered cartographic maps. The studies discussed above have shown that other variables, such as a map's complexity, orientation, and color design, also impacted people's ability to efficiently use the map.

Research on the map reader has measured reaction times and error patterns. They have focused on differences between cognitive maps encoded as primary or secondary information and using verbal or imagery processes. The relative efficiency of a type of information or an encoding process seems to be dependent on the task being performed. Sometimes verbal coding is more successful (Holmes, 1984; Skipper, 1989) and sometimes imagery coding is more successful (Lloyd, 1989a; Thorndyke & Staz, 1980) There is also some evidence that subjects do not always select the most efficient procedures for encoding spatial information and that they have preferences for strategies (McNiff, 1991). Finally, Neisser's (1976) view of cognitive maps is both interesting and challenging. Many types of spatial information can now be easily and efficiently represented as map animations (Gersmehl, 1990). The information map readers can encode from such animated maps may be quite different from the information typically encoded from static maps. Cartographers who wish to effectively communicate with animations will have to understand the cognitive processes used by map readers interacting with animated maps. Could cartographic maps be produced that would allow the ego to be encoded with the spatial information, for instance, by creating, as part of the map, an animated object to represent the self? Could cartographic maps be produced that do not have the limitation of a fixed orientation by using multiple vantage points and orientations?

## References

Boynton, R. & Smallman, H. (1990). Visual search for basic versus non-basic chromatic targets. In M. Brill (Ed.), *Perceiving, measuring, and using color* (pp. 9-18). Bellingham, WA: The International Society for Optical Engineering.

Byrne, R. (1979). Memory for urban geography. *Quarterly Journal of Experimental Psychology, 31*, 147-154.

Carpenter, P., & Just, M. (1986). Spatial ability: An information processing approach to psychometrics. In R. Sternberg (Ed.), *Advances in the psychology of human intelligence* (pp. 221-252). Hillsdale, NJ: Erlbaum.

Cave, K., & Wolf, J. (1990). Modeling the role of parallel processing in visual search. *Cognitive Psychology, 22*, 225-271.

Conerway, V. (1991). *The effects of complexity on the mental rotation of map images.* Unpublished master's thesis, University of South Carolina.

Dannatt, L. (1984). *The evaluation of color schemes for bi-polar choropleth maps.* Unpublished master's thesis, University of South Carolina.

Dobson, M. (1979). The influence of map information on fixation location. *The American Cartographer, 6*, 51-65.

Dobson, M. (1980). The influence of the amount of graphic information on visual matching. *The Cartographic Journal, 17*, 26-32.

Dobson, M. (1983). Visual information processing and cartographic communication: The utility of redundant stimulus dimensions. In D. Taylor (Ed.), *Graphic communication and design in contemporary cartography* (pp. 149-175). New York: Wiley.

Dobson, M. (1985). The future of perceptual cartography. *Cartographica, 22*, 27-43.

Downing, C., & Pinker, S. (1985). The spatial structure of visual attention. In M. Posner & O. Marin (Eds.), *Attention and performance XI* (pp. 172-287). Hillsdale, NJ: Erlbaum.

Downs, R., & Stea, D. (Eds.). (1973). *Image and environment: Cognitive mapping and spatial behavior.* Chicago: Aldine.

Eastman, J. (1985). Graphic organization and memory structures for map learning. *Cartographica, 22*, 1-20.

Eastman, J. (1986). Opponent process theory and syntax for qualitative relationships in quantitative series. *The American Cartographer, 13*, 324-333.

Eboch, M. (1985). *The cartographic scale: A cognitive investigation.* M. A. Thesis. The University of South Carolina.

Evans, G., & Pezdek, K. (1980). Cognitive mapping: Knowledge of real-world distance and location information. *Journal of Experimental Psychology: Human Learning and Memory, 6*, 13-24.

Gallinaro, N. (1991). *Searching choropleth maps for boundaries: The cognitive process.* M. A. Thesis, University of South Carolina.

Garner, W. (1974). *The processing of information and structure.* Potomac, MD: Erlbaum.

Gersmehl, P. (1990). Choosing tools: Nine metaphors of four-dimensional cartography. *Cartographic Perspectives, 5*, 3-17.

Gilmartin, P. (1986). Maps, mental imagery, and gender in the recall of geographical information. *The American Cartographer, 13*, 335-344.

Golledge, R. G. (1978). Learning about urban environments. In T. Carlstein, D. Parks, & N. Thrift (Eds.), *Timing space and spacing time* (pp. 76-98). London: Arnold.

Golledge, R. G., & Spector, A. (1978). Comprehending the urban environment: theory and practice. *Geographical Analysis, 10*, 403-426.

Hartley, A. (1977). Mental measurement in the magnitude estimation of length. *Journal of Experimental Psychology: Human Perception and Performance, 3*, 622-628.

Hartley, A. (1981). Mental measurement of line length: The role of the standard. *Journal of Experimental Psychology: Human Perception and Performance, 7*, 309-317.

Heyn, B. (1984). *An evaluation of map color schemes for use on CRT's.* Unpublished master's thesis, University of South Carolina.

Hirtle, S., & Jonides, J. (1985). Evidence of hierarchies in cognitive maps. *Memory and Cognition, 13*, 208- 217.

Holmes, J. (1984). *Cognitive processes used to recognize perspective three-dimensional map surfaces.* Unpublished master's thesis, University of South Carolina.

Holzapfel, D. (1985). *Estimating distances using a scale: The interpolation process.* M. A. Thesis. University of South Carolina.

Johnson, M. (1987). *The body in the mind: The bodily basis of meaning, imagination, and reason.* Chicago: The University of Chicago Press.

Levine, M., Jankovic, I., & Palij, M. (1982). Principles of spatial problems solving. *Journal of Experimental Psychology: General, 111*, 157-175.

Lewicki, P. (1986). Processing information about covariations that cannot be articulated. *Journal of Experimental Psychology: Learning, Memory, and Cognition, 12*, 135-146.

Lewicki, P., Hill, T., & Bizot, E. (1988). Acquisition of procedural knowledge about a pattern of stimuli that cannot be articulated. *Cognitive Psychology, 20*, 24-37.

Lewis, P. (1976). *New Orleans: The making of an urban landscape.* Cambridge: Ballinger.

Lloyd, R. (1988). Searching for map symbols: The cognitive process. *The American Cartographer, 15*, 363- 377.

Lloyd, R. (1989a). Cognitive mapping: Encoding and decoding information. *Annals of the Association of American Geographers, 79*, 101-124.

Lloyd, R. (1989b). The estimation of distance and direction from cognitive maps. *The American Cartographer, 16*, 109-122.

Lloyd, R. & Heivley, C. (1987). Systematic distortions in urban cognitive maps. *Annals of the Association of American Geographers, 77*, 191-207.

Lloyd, R., & Hooper, H. (1991). Urban cognitive maps: Computation and structure. *The Professional Geographer, 43*, 15-28.

Lloyd, R., & Steinke, T. (1984). Recognition of disoriented maps: The cognitive process. *The Cartographic Journal, 21*, 55-59.

McLeod, P., Driver, J., & Crisp, J. (1988). Visual search for a conjunction of movement and form is parallel. *Nature, 332*, 154-155.

McNamara, T. (1986). Mental representations of spatial relations. *Cognitive Psychology, 18*, 87-121.

McNiff, M. (1991). *Memory for land use categories on maps: A comparison of focal, associative, and false color schemes.* Unpublished master's thesis, University of South Carolina.

Miller, G. (1956). The magic number seven plus or minus two: Some limits on our capacity for processing information. *Psychological Review, 63*, 81-97.

Muehrcke, P. (1980). *Map use: Reading, analysis, and interpretation.* Madison, WI: JP Publications.

Nakayama, K., & Silverman, G. (1986a). Serial and parallel encoding of visual feature conjunctions. *Investigative Ophthalmology and Visual Science, 27*, 182.

Nakayama, K., & Silverman, G. (1986b). Serial and parallel processing of visual feature conjunctions. *Nature, 320*, 264-265.

Neisser, U. (1976). *Cognition and reality: Principles and implications of cognitive psychology.* San Francisco: Freeman.

Nicholson, T. (1990). *Cognitive maps for recreational environments: Myrtle Beach, South Carolina.* M. A. Thesis, University of South Carolina.

Orleans, P. (1973). Differential cognition of urban residents: Effects of social scale on mapping. In R. Downs & D. Stea (Eds.), *Image and environment: Cognitive mapping and spatial behavior* (pp. 115-130). Chicago: Aldine.

Overheim, R., & Wagner, D. (1982). *Light and color.* New York: Wiley.

Pashler, H. (1987). Detecting conjunctions of color and form: Reassessing the serial search hypothesis. *Perception & Psychophysics, 41*, 191-201.

Pezdek, K., & Evans, G. (1979). Visual and verbal memory for objects and their spatial locations. *Journal of Experimental Psychology, 5*, 360-373.

Presson, C., & Hazelrigg, M. (1984). Building spatial representations through primary and secondary learning. *Journal of Experimental Psychology: Learning, Memory, and Cognition, 10*, 716-722.

Reagan, B. (1990). *The effects of correlation on multidimensional symbol encoding.* Unpublished master's thesis, University of South Carolina.

Rice, K. (1989). Disoriented prism maps: A recognition experiment. *Cartographic Perspectives, 4*, 32.

Robinson, A. (1985). Arno Peters and his new cartography. *The American Cartographer, 12*, 103-111.

Rosch, E. (1973). Natural categories. *Cognitive Psychology, 4*, 328-350.

Shepard, R. (1978). The mental image. *American Psychologist, 33*, 125-137.

Shepard, R., & Cooper, L. (1983). *Mental images and their transformations.* Cambridge: MIT Press.

Shimron, J. (1978). Learning positional information from maps. *The American Cartographer, 5*, 9-19.

Sholl, M. (1987). Cognitive maps as orienting schemata. *Journal of Experimental Psychology: Learning, Memory, and Cognition, 13*, 615-628.

Shortridge, B. (1982). Stimulus processing models from psychology: Can we use them in cartography? *The American Cartographer, 9*, 155-167.

Skipper, L. (1989). *Patterns on cognitive maps: Encoding and decoding processes.* M. A. Thesis, University of South Carolina.

Steinke, T. (1987). Eye movement studies in cartography and related fields. *Cartographica, 24*, 40-73.

Steinke, T., & Lloyd, R. (1983). Images of maps: A rotation experiment. *The Professional Geographer, 35*, 455-461.

Steinman, S. (1987). Serial and parallel search in pattern vision. *Perception, 16*, 389-399.

Sternberg, S. (1969). Memory scanning: Mental processes revealed by reaction-time experiments. *American Scientist, 57*, 421-457.

Stevens, A., & Coupe, P. (1978). Distortions in judged spatial relations. *Cognitive Psychology, 10*, 422-437.

Thorndyke, P. (1981). Distance estimations from cognitive maps. *Cognitive Psychology, 13*, 526-550.

Thorndyke, P., & Hayes-Roth, B. (1982). Differences in spatial knowledge acquired from maps and navigation. *Cognitive Psychology, 14*, 560-581.

Thorndyke, P., & Staz, C. (1980). Individual differences in procedures for knowledge acquisition from maps. *Cognitive Psychology, 12*, 137-175.

Treisman, A., & Gelade, G. (1980). A feature integration theory of attention. *Cognitive Psychology, 12*, 97- 136.

Treisman, A., & Gormican, S. (1988). Feature analysis in early vision: Evidence from search asymmetries. *Psychological Review, 95*, 15-48.

Treisman, A., & Sato, S. (1990). Conjunction search revisited. *Journal of Experimental Psychology: Human Perception and Performance, 16*, 459-478.

Tuan, Y. (1975). Images and mental maps. *Annals of the Association of American Geographers, 65*, 205-213.

Tversky, B. (1981). Distortions in memory for maps. *Cognitive Psychology, 13*, 407-433.

Varley, H. (1980). *Colour*. London: Marshall.

Waterman, S., & Gordon, D. (1984). A quantitative-comparative approach to analysis of distortion in mental maps. *The Professional Geographer, 36*, 326-337.

Wilson, R. (1990). *The relationship of error in cognitive maps to the visual hierarchy in map design.* Unpublished master's thesis, University of South Carolina.

Wolf, J., Cave, K., & Franzel, S. (1989). Guided search: An alternative to the modified feature integration model for visual search. *Journal of Experimental Psychology: Human Perception and Performance, 15*, 419-433.

*Behavior and Environment: Psychological and Geographical Approaches*
*T. Gärling and R.G. Golledge (Editors)*


## CHAPTER 7

# The Structure of Cognitive Maps: Representations and Processes

**Stephen C. Hirtle and P. Bryan Heidorn**

Research on spatial representations, from the point of view of psychology, has focused on the internal representation that is acquired during spatial interaction, either directly with an environment or indirectly with a description or rendition of the environment. In this regard, there are three important levels of spatial constructs. The first level is the actual three-dimensional space, which in many cases may be approximated quite accurately by a two-dimensional surface.[1] The second level is a description of the environment, which may be spatial, such as a map, linguistic, such as a verbal description, or a combination of both spatial and linguistic, such as an annotated map. In many cases, people interact with either the actual space or a description of the environment, but not both. Through interaction the third level, a mental representation of space, is created. These three levels of representation can be seen in Figure 7.1, where the internal representation can be achieved through one of two paths, as indicated.

When psychologists speak of an internal representation, they are referring to a mapping from (selective) aspects of the real, or represented, world to the internal, or representing, world (Rumelhart & Norman, 1985). The representation, or internal code, might resemble a specific modality, such as visual or acoustic, and it might contain, or omit, certain pieces of information (Bower & Clapper, 1989). In addition, it makes little sense to discuss a representation without discussion of the process that acts upon the representation (Rumelhart & Norman, 1985). The process and representation together provide a representational system. Furthermore, there is a certain degree of indeterminacy in defining a representational system, in that different representations might be behav-

[1] In fact, with the exception of a few studies in environmental psychology (Gärling et al., 1991) and related research on imagery (e.g., Pinker, 1980), there has been little effort at understanding the role of the vertical dimension in cognitive maps.

Furthermore, there is a certain degree of indeterminacy in defining a representational system, in that different representations might be behavioral indistinguishable, if there is freedom in the process that acts upon that representation (Anderson, 1978; Pylyshyn, 1989).

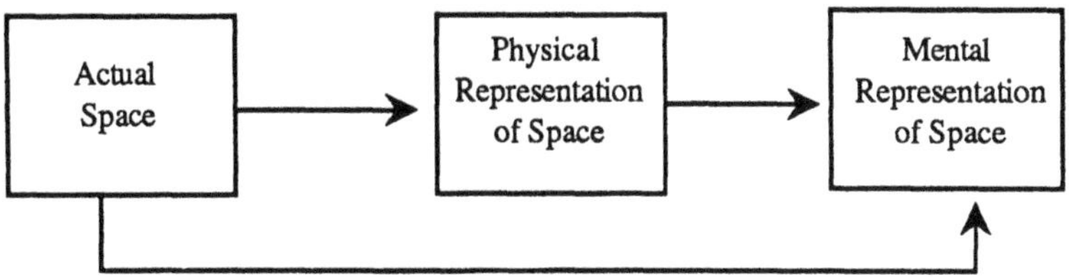


FIGURE 7.1. Schematic diagram of the three levels of representation.

The three general problems discussed in this chapter are (1) describing the internal representation of space as acquired from physical representations that are also spatial in nature, such as maps, (2) describing the representations inherent in computational models of space, and (3) describing the interaction with linguistic representations. Before discussing these issues in detail, we start by reviewing, in the next two sections, some critical distinctions and discuss tasks that have been used to uncover the mental representation. Next, we discuss how the internal representation is structured as a result of structure in the external representation. We follow this by a discussion of computational models and the representations that they adopt. In most cases a computational model is at the heart a computer program. Next, we discuss linguistic analyses from the point of representation. Linguistics provides techniques for studying the language people use to describe the environment. Finally, we close with a discussion of implications of this research for future geographic information services and uses.

## General Issues

One of the earliest theoretical distinctions was that of Lynch (1960), who developed a taxonomy consisting of landmarks, paths, nodes, districts, and edges. This line of research has lead to careful analysis in the laboratory of the role of landmarks (e.g., Holyoak & Mah, 1982), routes (e.g., McNamara, Altarriba, Bendele, Johnson, & Clayton, 1984), neighborhoods (e.g., Hirtle & Jonides, 1985) and other physical and cognitive structures, as organizing principles of cognitive maps.

mark knowledge is characterized by the ability to recognize landmarks, but with little understanding of the routes between landmarks. Route knowledge is characterized by the knowledge of sequential locations, or routes, without knowledge of a general spatial framework, such as orientation. Finally, survey, or configurational, knowledge is characterized by the ability to generalize beyond learned routes and locate objects within a general frame of reference. Thus, configurational knowledge is more holistic and is said to incorporate Euclidean, as opposed to purely topological, relationships (Hirtle & Hudson, 1991). Experimental evidence has supported the notion that these three levels are distinct and that spatial acquisition in most cases proceeds in acquiring landmark knowledge first, followed by route knowledge, and finally, in some cases, survey knowledge. Several researchers since have refined these concepts and shown that survey knowledge may be acquired early in the acquisition process in addition to, or even instead of, route knowledge (Gärling, Böök, & Ergezen, 1982; Moar & Carleton, 1982; Stern & Leiser, 1988).

A third and final distinction that is important to define is between local and global representations. While a single representation may hold at both the local and global level, there is no need to make such a strong assumption. For example, it might be quite reasonable to assume that the local level is Euclidean, whereas knowledge at the global level is only topological. Such a dichotomy can result in distortions, such as found by Moar & Bower (1983), where subjects were unable to reconstruct the correct angles in cases where city streets from a triangle.

## Measurement Procedures

Given that one is interested in the mental representation of space that a subject has either stored in long-term memory or that one has acquired recently, the question arises of how to infer the nature of the representation. Recent reviews of the literature on cognitive mapping (Gärling & Golledge, 1989; McNamara, 1991), in addition to the chapters by Golledge (Chapter 2 in this book), Pellegrino (Chapter 3 in this book), and Lloyd (Chapter 6 in this book), provide additional details of many of the points made here.

After some early attempts to tap directly the mental representation of space using sketch maps (e.g., Lynch, 1960), interest shifted to the use of indirect measures, such as distance estimation (e.g., Baird, 1979; MacKay, 1976), angular bearings (e.g., Hardwick, McIntyre, & Pick, 1976), both distance estimation and angular bearings (e.g., Kirasic, Allen, & Siegel, 1984), or comparative distance judgments (e.g., Baum &

Jonides, 1979; Hirtle & Jonides, 1985). Such methods are less likely to be biased by artistic skills of the subject and provide a degree of vulnerability. That is, whereas distances within a hand drawn map must, by definition, conform to the laws of two dimensional Euclidean space, distance judgments have no set constraints. Therefore, only the indirect measures can be used to test principles, such as the existence of non-Euclidean cognitive maps.

In more recent experimental work, two additional techniques have emerged for the study of cognitive mapping. These are the use of spatial priming (McNamara, 1986; McNamara, Hardy, & Hirtle, 1989b) and the use of the ordered tree clustering algorithm (Hirtle & Jonides, 1985; McNamara et al., 1989b). As these techniques are rather novel and somewhat controversial, they are reviewed in detail below.

### *Priming*

McNamara has provided the most compelling evidence of how spatial priming may be used to deduce the structure of cognitive maps starting with a study published in 1984 (McNamara, Ratcliff, & McKoon, 1984). The basic finding is that the recognition time for an object in a spatial layout will be faster if the object is preceded by another object that is closer in terms of the cognitive distance. Specifically, locations will be primed by locations on the same route (McNamara et al., 1984) or in the same region or cluster (McNamara, 1986; McNamara et al., 1989b).

It is important to note that the priming that occurs from spatial relations occurs independently of any nonspatial associations. In a critical study, McNamara and LeSueur (1989) had subjects learn maps in which pairs of objects were related semantically (e.g., cup-saucer). The results showed that targets preceded by close primes were recognized faster than targets preceded by far primes, for both related and unrelated pairs, with related pairs faster overall. These results, with the additional manipulations reported, lead McNamara and LeSueur (1989) to conclude that non-spatial associations between items increase the likelihood of encoding the spatial relationship between two items, as was found by Hirtle and Mascolo (1986). That is, if a cup is next to a saucer the obvious semantic relationship will lead to the formation of a spatial cluster and to a priming effect, and, thus, the priming reflects the both functional and Euclidean distance between locations, and not just the semantic association between the words.

There has been two sources of conflict with the basic interpretation above (McNamara, 1991). First, it is possible when studying naturally acquired spatial memories not to observe any spatial priming unless the judgment requires a specific spatial judgment (Clayton & Chattin, 1989; McNamara et al., 1989a). For example, asking subjects whether a building is on a university campus or not resulted in a lack of spatial priming, but asking subjects whether a building is on part of a university campus (in one college or another) did result in spatial priming (McNamara et al., 1989a). Second, there is some evidence that temporal contiguity is the critical variable in creating a spatial priming effect (Clayton & Habibi, 1991). However, in a rejoinder to this work, McNamara (1991) reports an alternative result in which spatial and temporal effects were additive. Therefore, at present, it still appears that a priming paradigm can provide a valuable tool for tapping into the mental representation of spatial knowledge.

### *Ordered Trees*

A second recent development has been the use of techniques for discovering hierarchical clusters in areas without predefined clusters. Of course, in many cases there is no need to determine clusters experimentally, as the clusters are formed by an obvious division such as state membership (Stevens & Coupe, 1978), explicit boundaries (McNamara, 1986), or distinct semantic relationships (Hirtle & Mascolo, 1986). However, for cases in which there are no clear boundaries or clusters, one must produce independent evidence of what the spatial clusters might be. One solution is to ask subjects to recall the objects, or landmarks, in the space, repeatedly. The order of the recall can be used to produce an ordered tree (Reitman & Rueter, 1980), in which the items are grouped in a tree where the branches may be ordered in addition to nested hierarchically. Thus, the ordered tree, as derived from an independent free-recall task, can be used to deduce a potential clustering of locations. Hirtle and Jonides (1985) showed that performance on map drawing, map reconstruction, comparative distance judgments, and absolute distance judgments can be predicted from the ordered trees. Specifically, within-cluster pairs were judged closer than equally distant between-cluster pairs. McNamara et al. (1989b) showed that distance judgments and spatial priming can be predicted from the ordered trees, in a similar way. Finally, Hirtle and Hudson (1990) showed that configurational and route knowledge can be distinguished from the order information within an ordered tree. Thus, the ordered tree algorithm also provides a useful tool for inferring the mental representation that a subject has of a spatial domain.

## Acquisition of Spatial Mental Representations

The question remains of how spatial concepts are represented in long-term memory and how that representation arises from experiences with either the actual space or the physical representation of the space. The next three sections review research examining characteristics of the mental representation depending on how spatial knowledge is acquired.

### *Structured Representations*

A number of studies within psychology have tried to isolate the effect that various structured representations would have on the mental representation that is acquired during learning. For example, rather than present rich maps with complete details, a common strategy has been to present impoverished maps to subjects, highlighting a single feature. Using this approach, McNamara et al. (1984) had subjects learn locations on a map connected a sparse network of routes. Locations on the map, which were given a set of fictitious city names, could be classified as being close in both Euclidean and route distance, close in Euclidean but far in route distance, or far in both Euclidean and route distance. (The fourth logical condition of far in Euclidean distance, but close in route distance is geometrically impossible.) Subjects then participated in a recognition task, to measure spatial priming, and asked to estimate distances between locations. The results indicated that route distance alone is the critical determinant of priming data. That is, recognition time was about 50 msec faster if a location was preceded by another location that was close in route distance, rather than far in route distance, and at the same time the difference in recognition time between the two far route conditions was nonsignificant. The pairs that were close in both route and Euclidean distance were underestimated relative to those that were far in route distance, but close in Euclidean distance. Together, the results suggest that either the mental representation or the process that act upon the representation is influenced by the route network, such that locations on the same route are judged subjectively closer.

McNamara (1986) showed a related effect using a map consisting of 32 locations, which was divided into four quadrants. Critical pairs of items could be classified as being either close or far, and in the same region or neighboring regions. Recognition times were faster for locations that were preceded by locations that were close in distance or that were in the same region. Furthermore, these effects were additive, so that the fastest time were for locations that were preceded by a locations that were both close in distance and in the same region. Here, the structure is based on regions rather than paths, but the results point to a similar conclusion. That is, the representation, or process acting on the representation, is altered by the external structure.

In a recent paper, Munro and Hirtle (1989) created a connectionist architecture to model the effects found in the two studies just described (McNamara, 1986; McNamara et al., 1984). This was done by creating three sets of units: place nodes, grid nodes, and category nodes. There is one place node for each location on the map, which are then connected to both the grid nodes and the categories nodes. The (x,y) coordinates of a location are represented in the connections between the place nodes and the grid nodes using a form of coarse coding, as described by Hinton, McClelland, & Rumelhart, (1986). Here, the 30 grid nodes can be thought to form a 6 by 5 rectangular grid across the map and the activation are determined by a Gaussian peak centered at the coordinates. Thus, the place and grid nodes alone specify the Euclidean information about locations. The third set of nodes, the category nodes, are needed to represent the additional information inherent in the cognitive map due to the routes or cells. Thus, in modelling the McNamara et al (1984) study, there were seven categories nodes, one for each route. In modelling the McNamara (1986) study, there were four category nodes, one for each cell. For both cases, Munro and Hirtle (1989) were able to show how the connectionist model could account for the empirical data obtained earlier. It is interesting to note that one connectionist architecture could account for both seemingly distinct studies, suggesting that in both cases the bias is due to an additional propositional structure (e.g., category nodes) interacting with a Euclidean space (e.g., grid nodes).

It is important to note that the structure imposed by the physical representation needs not be explicit. Hirtle and Mascolo (1986) showed a constriction effect for distance judgments, such that locations in the same semantic, or functional, cluster were judged closer that identically distant locations in different clusters. In this case, the maps lack explicit boundaries, but the points could be classified into two distinct, and spatially separate, groups. As before, the implicit structure resulted in a constriction effect, where locations given similar semantic labels were judged as closer than locations in distinct clusters.

### *Study of Unstructured Representations*

McNamara et al. (1989b) questioned whether similar effects could be found for spaces where there was no inherent structure. Using a method of study similar to McNamara (1986), they presented a map to subjects, where the distribution of objects was homogenous and formed no obvious perceptual groups. Despite this lack of organization, McNamara et al. (1989b) found that subjects imposed a hierarchical structure, which they were able to recover using the ordered tree algorithm. Furthermore as in previous studies, within-cluster pairs both resulted in greater priming in a recognition task, and judged closer than identically distant between-cluster pairs.

Recently, Huttenlocher, Hedges, & Duncan, (1991) reports an interesting variant in which subjects are asked simply to study the location of a dot in a circle, then locate the dot in a blank circle 8 sec later. Subjects showed a systematic shift in their placement of the dot away from 0, 90, 180, or 270 degrees and towards 45, 135, 225, 315 degree, even though no such axis lines appeared within the circle. Huttenlocher et al. further showed that the effect of misplacement could be accounted for by a judgment process acting upon an unbiased representation. The judgment process results in a recall bias towards the four inherent quadrants of the circle. Thus, even in one of the most impoverished stimulus sets, a hierarchical structure results in a bias in the relocation of dots.

### *Summary*

McNamara et al. (1989b) review two general classes of theories: hierarchical and non-hierarchical. Non-hierarchical theories of cognitive maps comprise a class of theories that lack nested levels of representation. Most non-hierarchical theories have assumed instead a holistic, map-like representation, akin to a mental image (Birnbaum, Anderson, & Hynan, 1989; Kosslyn, Ball, Reiser, 1978; Levine, Jankovic, & Palij, 1982; Thorndyke, 1981). In contrast, an alternative class of theories suggest that a hierarchical model is more appropriate (Couclelis, Golledge, Gale, & Tobler, 1987; Hirtle & Jonides, 1985; McNamara, 1986; Stevens & Coupe, 1978). This class of theories is best characterize by the inclusion of distinct patterns of encoding at local and global levels. The hierarchies may arise due to explicit structure, such as state boundaries (Stevens & Coupe, 1978), or they may arise due to implicit structure, such as city neighborhoods (Hirtle & Jonides, 1985). More importantly, as was just discussed, hierarchical structure will arise even in cases where there is no inherent structure (Huttenlocher et al., 1991; McNamara et al., 1989b).

Evidence presented in this section most decisively points in favor of a hierarchical model. Furthermore, the research of Huttenlocher et al. (1991) suggests that the effects of the hierarchical structure are due to processes acting upon an unbiased representation. While their data are encouraging, additional research is needed on this question. For example, it is unclear how the recall of a single dot will generalize to the greater storage problem of an entire cognitive map. One might conclude that as a natural cognitive map is recalled, or reconstructed, it becomes biased from the processes discussed by Huttenlocher et al. (1991), so that the processes of recall and reconstruction result, in turn, in a biased representation.

Finally, it is important to realize that the hierarchical structure need not be complete. McNamara (1991) and McNamara et al. (1989b) discuss the notion of partial hierarchies that can account for the findings as well. By this notion, McNamara and his colleagues simply mean the clusters can overlap as well as being nested.

## Computational Models

As an alternative to traditional experimental methods, there has been a recent increase in the development of computational models of spatial cognitive processes (e.g., Gopal, Klatzky, & Smith, 1989; Kuipers & Levitt, 1988; Leiser & Zilberschatz, 1989; Munro & Hirtle, 1989; Yeap, 1988). It is important to recognize the distinction between computational models of human cognitive process and computational systems. Computational systems are designed to perform the same task as the human system, but with little attention to how humans perform the task. In contrast, computational models facilitate theory formation. The goal of the model is to remain consistent with empirical data in the field. In so doing, they integrate current theories. The computational instantiation of theories also makes any assumptions, or theoretical gaps, explicit. When multiple hypotheses are possible, the qualitative consequences of each may be tested directly in the model. The outcomes can be compared to existing data or help guide human experimental work.

The medium used to express the theory provides a fresh perspective on the phenomena being studied. Dynamic and interacting systems can be developed, rather than expressing theories in words, static equations, or lists of principles. These systems express the ideas of a theory in a way that augments the more traditional forms of theory expression. In particular, the computational models are better at allowing scientists to view the processing dynamics of the theory (for example, which components require the greatest resources, or the effects of process order or parallelism). Likewise, the issue of representation, which is often overlooked in other types of models, is made explicit in these models.

The form and content of the representation chosen for a particular computational model is influenced by the task to be performed. For example, the model CITYTOUR (Andre, Bosch & Rist, 1987; Retz-Schmidt, 1988) is designed to answer natural language questions about the spatial relationship between objects in a city. There are three object types represented in the system: Stationary objects, moving objects, and the listener (on a moving bus). Moving objects are represented by a series of centroid-time stamp pairs. The centroid is based on absolute horizontal plane coordinates. Stationary objects are represented by a centroid, closed polygon, prominent front and delineative rectangle (based on the observers position). It is assumed that the system already "knows" the city since it knows the location of each object. When the system is asked the question, "Is the post office behind the church?", the system uses the intrinsic front of the church to determine the area defined by the word "behind" in the question. "Behind" is defined as the half-plane bounded by the side of the delineative rectangle opposite from the intrinsic front. The system answers deictic questions like "Is the post office behind the church from here?" by projecting a new half-plane that is opposite the side of the building the observer can see.

Other computational models like TOUR (Kuipers & Levitt, 1988), NAVIGATOR (Gopal et al., 1989) and that developed by Yeap (1988) explain how an area can be learned. None start with the fixed locations of objects that are available in CITYTOUR. These models differ from one another partly because of the parts of the problem they focus on. For example, Yeap (1988) includes an analysis of how the bounds of a room can be recognized. For that task he assumes a vision system that provides lists of line segments that represent the walls of the current room, sections of other rooms as seen through portals in the current room and occluding objects that hide parts of the room's boundaries. It is only after the evaluation of these line segments that the system generates a hypothesis of something like the closed polygon provided to CITYTOUR. Since Yeap's model does not address the applicability of spatial prepositions, it avoids the problem of calculating areas such as the delineative rectangle.

Finally, Munro and Hirtle (1989) and Wender (1989) have developed connectionist models of cognitive maps, in contrast to the symbolic approaches listed above. Here the representation is implicit in the interaction of small computational units, akin to neural cells. Together, the computational models highlight how the internal representation is dependent, not only on the external stimuli, but also on their intended use.

## Linguistic Analysis

A final mode of spatial interaction to discuss is knowledge that is expressed or conveyed through language. There are at least two ways that the study of language will expand our understanding of human spatial representation. Language is an overt behavior, which can act as a window into the underlying internal representations. What is said and how it is said can provide important information about what needs to be communicated about spatial relations. We can infer that what needs to be communicated is important. Second, natural language is often the medium of choice for conveying spatial information, while other times it is a necessity, such as during a telephone conversation. However, even in face-to-face conversation, when strangers are asked for directions, the response is usually verbal with some gestures added (Freundschuh et al., 1990).

Whenever someone uses natural language to describe a spatial relationship they are faced with the task of converting an internal representation, a cognitive map, into a stream of discrete words, which an intelligent listener will be able to convert back into another cognitive map. Both listener and speaker rely on a set of linguistic conventions. The conventions that are agreed upon, particularly those which are used in many languages, may tell us something about the information that is being communicated.

The language stream is very sparse in relation to information being conveyed. It points to concepts in the listener that are most important for the task at hand. This means that the words and constructs of the natural language are key features of the cognitive map. This does not mean that the cognitive map is linguistic in nature, only that the components, which a speaker selects to code into language, are just those which will be important to the listener. The language users need not be conscious of this selection process since the task is controlled in part by the structure of natural language, the culture and the similar perceptual and possibly cognitive apparatus of the speaker and listener.

We will focus here on one particular analysis of the linguistic description of space. The discussion is limited to the question of how we describe the location of an object. The linguistic mechanism often used for this purpose (Herskovits, 1985, 1986; Talmy, 1983) is to first identify the object of interest, then select a reference object known to the listener, and finally specify the relationship between the known location and the location of the target object from some specific point of view. The point of this discussion is to examine important aspects of the linguistic interaction, which will highlight characteristics of the mental representation. The language stream specifies what objects and spatial relationships in the environment are most important to both the speaker and listener. Conversely, this specifies the aspects of the environment that may be ignored, or at least underrepresented, in the internal representation.

### *Primary and Reference Objects*

Locations are by their very nature relative to some frame of reference. Whenever an object's location or orientation is specified it is done in relation to some other object. Talmy (1983) and Herskovits (1986) call this relationship figure/ground. Retz-Schmidt (1988) calls it primary object and reference object and provides an extensive list of other terms used to describe the relationship. Primary/reference object is the nomenclature used here.

For example, the location and orientation of a bicycle can be determined in relation to a number of reference objects: (1a) The bike stood near the driveway; (2b) The bike stood in the driveway; (1c) The bike stood across/along the driveway; (1d) The bike rolled across/along the driveway. In (1a) "near" puts the bike proximal to the driveway. In (1b) "in" specifies a containment and co-location relationship but does not specify the orientation of the bike in relation to the driveway. In (1c) "across" and "along" specify the orientation and location of the bike either perpendicular or horizontal to the driveway (Talmy, 1983). As in (1d), the verb can modify the subject or primary objects representation.

The heuristics used to select a reference object specify the cognitively salient properties of the objects and relations. Talmy (1983) identifies some of these features, such as preference for reference objects that are permanently located and that are larger or equal in size to the primary object, and preference for reference objects with intrinsic directional characteristic or upon which one can be easily imposed so that the listener can be oriented properly within the frame of reference.

As an example of reference object selection, we might consider the problem of constructing queries in a geographic information system (GIS). In GIS there is an exchange of information between a human user and the computer system. The user's query specifies the information need, then the system responds. Both the query and the response are spatial expressions and follow the same rules as to what must be specified.

Queries are formulated in such a way as to specify the referent object and request further information on instances of primary objects that fit a particular relationship to that reference object. Consider the following queries: (2a) Show (Where is) the oil well with highest output within

50km of Kuwait; (2b) Show all pipelines crossing Kuwait. As is often the case for geographic databases, query (2a) asks for locations in a particular area (Kuwait). "Kuwait" is then the reference object. The primary object for the response is given in the question, "the well." The verb "show" indicates that a graphical output is requested, but interestingly the linguistic (communicative) principles still apply. An effective system must display the reference object, Kuwait, and the primary object, the well, in relation to that reference object. Plotting the well on a screen without the outline of Kuwait would be unacceptable. This requirement of a frame of reference is consistent with arguments of Haviland and Clark (1974) and Grice (1974).

A non-graphical system would be forced to answer the query with a different frame of reference, as there is no linguistic mechanism to specify easily the location in relation to an irregular area like Kuwait, which has no intrinsic directionality. Spatial relations like "in front of/left of/behind Kuwait" will not work. A previously agreed upon frame of reference can be inherited from the earth in this case. It might make sense to respond, "The well is east of Kuwait," and adopt a relation based on the larger, earth-based framework. However, at that point, there is no longer a need for the reference object, and the new reference becomes the earth based frame. Now, the response would be given in latitude and longitude. Reference object selection is in part determined by the relational description tools available in the medium of communication. Similar arguments can be made for reference object selection in direction giving (Riesbeck, 1980).

### *Spatial Linguistic Schemata*

Up to this point we have discussed the primary and reference objects but not the relationship between them. Individual spatial relationship markers of a language, like locative prepositions in English, are signals of idealized spatial relationships between idealized representation of the objects. Talmy (1983) called these relation schemata. Herskovits (1985, 1986) calls them ideal meanings. Only some aspects of a spatial scene are actually represented by linguistic elements. Other aspects of the scene are irrelevant. Each spatial expression represents a large class of relationships between objects that share a set of common features. The feature set, which identifies a specific linguistic construct (in, on, left of, etc.), is not absolute and is more closely related to Rosch's (1977) notion of a prototype (Herskovits, 1986). Extending this reasoning to the cognitive map we may suspect that it may only store schematic relations between objects, not a "realistic" picture of spatial relations.

Spatial schemata "are largely built up from such rudimentary spatial elements as of points, bounded and unbounded lines, bounded and unbounded plains, and the like, ..." (Talmy, 1983, p. 258). The application of a schema to a scene can be viewed as a pattern matching operation, which can include processes such as idealization and abstraction.

Idealization is a form of generalization that occurs when some aspect of a rich real world object is distilled to a simple linguistic relation, as seen in the following examples: (3a) Cleveland is west of Pittsburgh; (3b) The water is in the volcano/bird bath/bowl; (3c) The ant crawled along the pencil. Directions can be simplified, in seen in (3a). The preposition "in" can be applied to anything held up within a concave volume like a volcano, bird bath or bowl, as seen in (3b). Idealization can also result in the simplification of three-dimensional objects into a two-dimensional line, as seen in (3c).

Abstraction is the process of ignoring aspects of a scene, which are irrelevant for the schema. For the preposition "in," the color or size of the containing volume does not matter to the application of the schema.

Linguistic schemata can be used to determine what is important to be represented in a cognitive map. For example, some relations between objects may be unimportant for future uses of the map. The exact alignment of fronts of buildings is generally unimportant so when a scene is being stored that detail may be "idealized away" leading to an inaccurate, but nonetheless useful representation of the environment. You can still travel down a street and find your house, even if you do not remember how the fronts of the buildings are aligned.

This analysis is consistent with the view that the cognitive map uses processes based on these idealized forms and relations. These idealizations can be observed through the systematic distortions created by them. As discussed above, one interpretation of these findings is that spatial memory is organized hierarchically (Hirtle & Jonides, 1985; McNamara, 1986). A cognitive map may represent that California is west of Nevada (Stevens & Coupe, 1978). In this representation, both states are treated as point objects or idealized rectangles. When we must decide if San Diego is west of Reno, we are mislead by the idealized relationship of their associated states.

The use of schemata also allows some degree of indeterminacy with regard to the size or shape of the objects. For example, in English, the size of the primary and reference objects are irrelevant to the containment use of the preposition "in," as long as the primary object is smaller than the referent (Talmy, 1983). Consider, for example: The fruit sat in the bowl; The house sat in the valley; The black hole sat in the galaxy. Similar arguments can be made for the irrelevance of shape (Talmy, 1983). Thus, we see that language can use locative prepositions, to cover a very large range of phenomena.

However, the selection of the proper language element to designate a relation is language specific. Some languages make finer distinctions between the idealized schema than others. The distinction is often in the properties of the objects required to apply a spatial schema. This type of difference occurs between English "in" and Polish "w/na" (Cienki, 1989). "in the country" would use "w," whereas "in the meadow" would use "na." It appears that the use of "w" in Polish is more restrictive than English "in." Polish requires a frame-like bounded area to apply "w," otherwise "na" is used.

Talmy (1983) points out a similar distinction in the California Indian language, Atsugewi. This language uses about 50 suffixes on the verb to mark distinctions on reference object geometry for what in English is covered by the one word "into."

The variations of schema between languages tell us about what information must be represented in the cognitive map. In spite of the variations between English and Polish for the use of "in" there are important consistency. There is a concept of containment in both languages. The variation is around detail features of the reference object that are deemed important in subcategorizing the containment relationship. In all cases we have an idealized point object(s) lying on the surface of a plane. Languages provide more or less detail to specify the kind of plane.

A city can be represented in the cognitive map as an unbounded or bounded plane or a point depending on the context. If we state "Crime is bad in Chicago," then we might decide to move to the suburbs to avoid the high crime rate. However, if we state "Traffic is bad in Chicago," then we imply the entire Chicago metropolitan area and would not expect to avoid heavy traffic by avoiding the city limits.

In terms of the theory, we might suspect that changing the idealization will change how the representation is used. If we draw a boundary around a region of a city map we simultaneously affect the representation of the objects within the bounds. These objects will be contained in a more specific and maybe definitive manner forming a more coherent conceptual group.

### *Selecting the Point of View*

The selection of a preposition to describe a scene also determines the point of view of the scene. There are two points of view that will be discussed here: intrinsic and deictic. Extrinsic cases are more complicated and will not be discussed. Intrinsic use is dependent on the biased geometry of the reference object (Andre et al., 1987; Retz-Schmidt, 1988; Talmy, 1983). Objects like buildings and people have fronts that are independent of the point of view of the speaker or listener. In the sentence "The statue is in front of the town hall," we understand the statue to be located on the forward-facing side of the town hall.

Deictic view is assigned from either the perceptual point of view of the speaker or the listener. This view can be applied unambiguously for objects without intrinsic bias. This includes objects like trees in the example: "The ball is in front of the tree." The view that is selected is often a function of the application and culture.

Since most geographic information systems are earth based, the view is determined to be intrinsic to the earth, which has a definite biased geometry. There are some special cases where local geometry determines the view, as in the DIME representation of street geometry (Cooke & Maxfield, 1967). The DIME representation specifies two road intersection points in a fixed order, thus specifying a directed path. Paths and direction of motion have intrinsic fronts. The representation also specifies lateral directions of left or right. This is only possible if the path is assumed to be lying on the surface of the earth or on an idealized plane. This plane provides a surface along which the path travels allowing the assignment of an up and down. Any natural language instructions generated from this database would have to select prepositions that describe this path-oriented geometry. These include signals to the listener as to the direction of motion.

The cognitive map must be usable for different tasks, with different points of view and detail. For instance, recent work by Bryant, Tversky, & Franklin, (1992) has shown that people can interact with a scene from the point of view of being on the scene, or observing it from a distance. The selection of view affects their speed of processing spatial relations like front/back, left/right, and up/down. As we have seen, an examination of the language which people use to describe spatial relations can be used to help us understand experimental data and to suggest future direction for research into the process and structure of the cognitive map.

*Summary*

Compared to research on map study and on computational models, language use of spatial terms is more dynamic and the spatial representations for linguistic use are more dependent on characteristics such as the point of view. The linguistic mechanisms that people use to describe their environment provide insight into the internal mechanisms people use for spatial memory and processing. People select reference objects and reference frames to localize other objects in space. The specification of spatial relations and objects are idealized. Objects become point-like, plane-like, etc. Relations like "in" do not specify exactly where inside the reference object the primary object may be found. This is consistent with recall and reaction time data where people tend to be biased toward the ideal or prototype (Hirtle & Jonides, 1985; Huttenlocher et al., 1991). Examination of a linguistic point of view tells us about the potential ways the mental representation may be used.

## Conclusions

One of the most critical debates within cognitive psychology has been whether or not the representation of spatial information is structured by non-spatial information. If non-spatial information can influence spatial information in a selective manner, then any representational system that includes only a spatial analog will yield an incomplete theory. Research reviewed on the study of maps clearly points to the importance of structure, and the creation of structure by subjects when none exists. Research on linguistic representations suggests that point of view and a reference framework are also important. Finally, research on computational models provides insight into the data requirements to implement the theoretical and empirical issues brought forth in the other sections.

One might ask what are the lessons to be learned from a decade of research on mental representations of spatial knowledge for applications, such as GIS design? We think that it is clear that space is not perceived, stored, or processed in a homogeneous manner. Structure and orientation within the space are used to organize the space, and in cases where no structure is available, one will be created. Therefore, in presenting information to people, it is important to present redundant, structured information. It is also critical to allow subjects to converse in a language of topology that allows for relations such as containment or adjacency, rather than strict Euclidean terms (see Pipkin, 1982, for further discussion on this point).

Specifically, we can envision several classes of geographic information systems, which can be enhanced by consideration of the psychology of spatial relations. One would be in-car navigation systems designed to give guidance or information to the driver in real-time conditions (e.g., Freundschuh et al., 1990). A second class would be geographic information retrieval systems, where individuals are seeking information from an on-line retrieval system that includes a geographical component, such a geological references (e.g., Hill & Rasmussen, 1992). In each case, the critical interaction is between an individual and a computer system. In the first class, information is being transmitted primarily to the individual (in the form of instructions), whereas in the second class, information is being transmitted primarily from the individual (in the form of a query). However, in both cases, there is a need to express statements in general but meaningful terms, such as "turn left at the next major intersection" or "off the coast of Louisiana," without stating the explicit geographic relationship.

Perhaps most interesting would be a potential future use for GIS, of combining a knowledge-based geographic information system (e.g., Smith, Peuquet, Menon, & Agarwal, 1987), with something akin to a knowbot (Dertouzos, 1991), which search a network of databases for useful information to the user, without explicit commands or instructions. That is, the knowbot would, in effect, monitor the GIS system and communicate when necessary to users. Applications of such a system might be useful in the regulating of hazard wastes, tracking demographic shifts or municipal development, or monitoring consumer trends. However, such a system would be dependent on a geographic vocabulary that is consistent with the user's cognitive map and would require the melding of an intelligent interface with conceptual representation of spatial knowledge.

## References


Anderson, J. R. (1978). Arguments concerning representations for mental imagery. *Psychological Review, 85*, 249-277.

Andre, E., Bosch, G. & Rist, T. (1987). Coping with the intrinsic and Deictic uses of spatial prepositions. In P. Jorrand & V. Sgurev (Eds.), *Artificial intelligence II, Proceedings of the second international conference on artificial intelligence: Methodology, systems, applications, Varna, Bulgaria* (pp. 375-382). Amsterdam: North Holland.

Baird, J. C. (1979). Studies of the cognitive representation of spatial relations. *Journal of Experimental Psychology: General, 108*, 90-106.

Baum, D. R., & Jonides, J. (1979). Cognitive maps: Analysis of comparative judgments of distance. *Memory & Cognition, 7*, 462-468.

Birnbaum, M. H., Anderson, C. J., & Hynan, L. G. (1989). Two operations for "ratios" and "differences" of distances on the mental map. *Journal of Experimental Psychology: Human Perception and Performance, 15*, 785-796.

Bower, G. H., & Clapper, J. P. (1989). Experimental methods in cognitive science. In M. I. Posner (Ed.), *Foundations of cognitive science.* Cambridge, MA: MIT Press.

Bryant, D. J., Tversky, B., & Franklin, N. (1992). Internal and external spatial frameworks representing described scenes. *Journal of Memory and Language, 31*, 74-98.

Cienki, A. J. (1989). *Spatial cognition and the semantics of prepositions in English, Polish, and Russian.* München: Sagner.

Clayton, K., & Chattin, D. (1989). Spatial and semantic priming effects in tests of spatial knowledge. *Journal of Experimental Psychology Learning, Memory, and Cognition, 15*, 495-506.

Clayton, K., & Habibi, A. (1991). The contribution of temporal contiguity to the spatial priming effect. *Journal of Experimental Psychology: Learning, Memory, and Cognition, 17*, 263-271.

Cooke, D. F., & Maxfield, W. F. (1967). The development of a geographic base file and its uses for mapping. In *Urban and Regional Information Systems for Social Programs: Proceedings of the 5th annual conference of the urban and regional information systems association* (pp. 207-218). Kent, OH: Kent State.

Couclelis, H. Golledge, R. G., Gale, N., & Tobler, W. (1987). Exploring the anchor-point hypothesis of spatial cognition. *Journal of Environmental Psychology, 7*, 99-122.

Dertouzos, M. L. (1991). Communications, computers, and networks. *Scientific American, 265*(3), 62-71.

Freundschuh, S. M., Mark, D. M., Gopal, S., Gould, M. D., & Couclelis, H. (1990). Verbal directions for wayfinding: Implications for navigation and geographic information and analysis systems. In *Proceedings of the 4th international symposium on spatial data handling* (pp. 478-487). Columbus, OH: International Geographical Union.

Gärling, T., Böök, A., & Ergezen, N. (1982). Memory for the spatial layout of the everyday physical environment: Differential rates of acquisition of different types of information. *Scandinavian Journal of Psychology, 23*, 23-35.

Gärling, T., & Golledge, R. G. (1989). Environmental perception and cognition. In E. H. Zube and G. T. Moore (Eds.), *Advances in environment, behavior, and design* (Vol. 2, pp. 203-236). New York: Plenum.

Gopal, S., Klatzky, R. L., & Smith, T. R. (1989). Navigator: A psychologically based model of environmental learning through navigation. *Journal of Environmental Psychology, 9*, 309-331.

Grice, P. H. (1974). Logic and Conversation. In P. Cole & J. L. Morgan (Eds.), *Syntax and Semantics* (vol. 3, pp. 42-58). New York: Academic.

Hardwick, D. A., McIntyre, C. W., & Pick, H. L. (1976). The content and manipulation of cognitive maps in children and adults. *Monographs of the Society for Research in Child Development, 41*, (3, Serial No. 166).

Hart, R. A., & Moore, G. T. (1973). The development of spatial cognition: A review. In R. M. Downs & D. Stea (Eds.), *Image and environment* (pp. 246-288). Chicago: Aldine.

Haviland, S. E., & Clark H. H. (1974). What's new? Acquiring new information as a process in comprehension. *Journal of Verbal Learning and Verbal Behavior, 13*, 512-521.

Herskovits, A. (1985). Semantics and pragmatics of locative expressions. *Cognitive Science, 9*, 341-378.

Herskovits, A. (1986). *Language and spatial cognition: An interdisciplinary study of the prepositions in English.* Cambridge, UK: Cambridge University Press.

Hill, L. L., & Rasmussen, E. M. (1991). Geographic indexing terms as spatial indicators. In *Studies in multimedia: State of the art solutions in Multimedia and Hypertext* (ASIS Monograph Series, pp. 9-20). Medford, NJ: Learned Information.

Hinton, G. E., McClelland, J. L., & Rumelhart, D. E. (1986). Distributed representations. In D. E. Rumelhart & J. L. McClelland (Eds.), *Parallel distributed processing: Explorations in the microstructure of cognition*, (Vol. 1, pp. 77-109). Cambridge, MA: Bradford.

Hirtle, S. C., & Hudson, J. (1991). sAcquisition of spatial knowledge of routes. *Journal of Environmental Psychology, 11*, 335-345.

Hirtle, S. C., & Jonides, J. (1985). Evidence of hierarchies in cognitive maps. *Memory & Cognition, 13*, 208-217.

Hirtle, S. C., & Mascolo, M. F. (1986). The effect of semantic clustering on the memory of spatial locations. *Journal of Experimental Psychology: Learning, Memory and Cognition, 12*, 181-189.

Holyoak, K. J., & Mah, W. A. (1982). Cognitive reference points in judgments of symbolic magnitude. *Cognitive Psychology, 14*, 328-352.

Huttenlocher, J., Hedges, L. V., & Duncan, S. (1991). Categories and particulars: Prototype effects in estimating spatial location. *Psychological Review, 98*, 352-376.

Kirasic, K. C., Allen, G. L., & Siegel, A. W. (1984). Expression of configurational knowledge of large-scale environments: performance of cognitive tasks. *Environment and Behavior, 16*, 687-712.

Kosslyn, S. M., Ball, T. M., Reiser, B. J. (1978). Visual images preserve metric spatial information: Evidence from studies of image scanning. *Journal of Experimental Psychology: Human Perception and Performance, 40*, 47-60.

Kuipers, B. J. & Levitt, T. S. (1988). Navigation and mapping in large-scale space. *AI Magazine, 9*(2), 25-43.

Leiser, D., & Zilberschatz, A. (1989). The TRAVELLER: A computational model of spatial network learning. *Environment and Behavior, 21*, 435-463.

Levine, M., Jankovic, I. N., & Palij, M. (1982). Principles of spatial problem solving. *Journal of Experimental Psychology: General, 111*, 157-175.

Lynch, K. (1960). *The image of the city*. Cambridge, MA: MIT Press.

MacKay, D. B. (1976). The effect of spatial stimuli on the estimation of cognitive maps. *Geographical Analysis, 8*, 439-452.

McNamara, T. P. (1986). Mental representations of spatial relations. *Cognitive Psychology, 18*, 87-121.

McNamara, T. P. (1991). Memory's view of space. In G. H. Bower (Ed.), *The psychology of learning and motivation: Advances in research and theory* (Vol. 27, pp. 147-186). New York: Academic Press.

McNamara, T. P., Altarriba, J., Bendele, M., Johnson, S. C., & Clayton, K. N. (1989a). Constraints on priming in spatial memory: Naturally learned versus experimentally learned environments. *Memory & Cognition, 17*, 444-453.

McNamara, T. P., Hardy, J. K., & Hirtle, S. C. (1989b). Subjective hierarchies in spatial memory. *Journal of Experimental Psychology: Learning, Memory and Cognition, 15*, 211-227.

McNamara, T. P., & LeSueur, L. L. (1989). Mental representations of spatial and nonspatial relations. *The Quarterly Journal of Experimental Psychology, 41A*, 215-233.

McNamara, T. P., Ratcliff, R., & McKoon, G. (1984). The mental representation of knowledge acquired from maps. *Journal of Experimental Psychology: Learning, Memory, and Cognition, 10*, 723-732.

Moar, I., & Bower, G. H. (1983). Inconsistency in spatial knowledge. *Memory and Cognition, 11*, 107-113.

Moar, I. & Carleton, L. R. (1982). Memory for routes. *Quarterly Journal of Experimental Psychology, 34A*, 381-394.

Munro, P. & Hirtle, S. C. (1989). An interactive activation model for priming of geographical information. In *The proceedings of the 11th annual conference of the cognitive science society* (pp. 773-780). Hillsdale, NJ: Erlbaum.

Pinker, S. (1980). Mental imagery and the third dimension. *Journal of Experimental Psychology: General, 109*, 354-371.

Pipkin, J. S. (1982). Some remarks on multidimensional scaling in geography. In R. G. Golledge & J. N. Rayner (Eds.), *Proximity and preference* (pp. 214-232). Minneapolis, MN: University of Minnesota Press.

Pylyshyn, Z. W. (1989). Computing in cognitive science. In M. I. Posner (Ed.), *Foundations of cognitive science.* Cambridge, MA: MIT Press.

Reitman, J. S., & Rueter, H. R. (1980). Organization revealed by recall orders and confirmed by pauses. *Cognitive Psychology, 12*, 554-581.

Retz-Schmidt, G. (1988). Various views on spatial prepositions. *AI Magazine, 9*(2), 95-105.

Riesbeck, C. K. (1980). "You can't miss it!": Judging the clarity of directions. *Cognitive Science, 4*, 285-303.

Rosch, E. (1977). Human categorization. In N. Warren (Ed.), *Advances in cross-cultural psychology* (Vol. 1, pp. 3-49). London: Academic Press.

Rumelhart, D. E., & Norman, D. A. (1985). Representation of knowledge. In A. M. Aitkenhead & J. M. Slack (Eds.), *Issues in cognitive modeling* (pp. 15-62). Hillsdale, NJ: Erlbaum.

Siegel, A. W. & White, S. H. (1975). The development of spatial representations of large-scale environments. In H. W. Reese (Ed.), *Advances in child development and behavior* (Vol. 10, pp. 9-55). New York: Academic Press.

Smith, T. R., Peuquet, D. J., Menon, S., & Agarwal, P. (1987). KBGIS II: A knowledge based geographic information system. *International Journal of Geographical Information Systems, 1*, 149-172.

Stern, E., & Leiser, D. (1988). Levels of spatial knowledge and urban travel modeling. *Geographical Analysis, 20*, 140-155.

Stevens, A., & Coupe, P. (1978). Distortions in judged spatial relations. *Cognitive Psychology, 10*, 422-437.
Talmy, L. (1983). How language structures space. In H. Pick & L. Acredolo (Eds.), *Spatial orientation: Theory, research and application* (pp. 225-282). New York: Plenum.
Thorndyke, P. W. (1981). Distance estimation from cognitive maps. *Cognitive Psychology, 13*, 526-550.
Wender, K. F. (1989, November). *Connecting analog and verbal representations for spatial relations.* Paper presented at the 30th Annual Meeting of the Psychonomic Society, Atlanta, Georgia.
Yeap, W. K. (1988). Toward a computational theory of cognitive maps. *Artificial Intelligence, 34*, 297-360.

*Behavior and Environment: Psychological and Geographical Approaches*
*T. Gärling and R.G. Golledge (Editors)*



# CHAPTER 8

# Hazard Perception and Geography

**Roger E. Kasperson and Kirstin Dow**

Perception plays a central role in explaining how risk, uncertainty, and values enter into the ways by which societies and individuals debate and cope with existing natural hazards and the introduction of new hazards associated with technological change. From an initially narrow focus on individual perceptions and decision making about natural hazards, scholarly critiques, and public controversies over technological hazards have progressively enlarged the societal context within which perception is examined. Throughout, hazards research in geography has remained consistent in its goal to elucidate differences among individuals, cultures, and societies in the perception of hazards and how society might best respond to them.

One of the remarkable features of the intellectual history of hazard analysis is the large proportion of all research devoted to understanding how individuals and various groups evaluate and respond to the hazards of nature and technology. The indicators of this concerted attention are several: perception studies have been central in natural hazards research (Burton, Kates, & White, 1978; Whyte, 1977, 1986) in his literature review of perception studies of technological hazards, Covello (1983) could list some 166 scholarly references; perception research constituted some 15-20% of all articles in *Risk Analysis* since its inception in 1981; an analysis of some 59 books on comparative risk analysis in the mid-1980s found that 35 included substantial attention to risk perception (Kates & Kasperson, 1983); *Risk Abstracts* regularly recognizes a major section on Psychological Aspects; and funding for risk perception studies has constituted a priority for both the natural hazard and risk analysis programs of the National Science Foundation throughout the 1970s and 1980s. Perception research cuts across academic investigations to hazard management practices where issues of preparedness, warning and evacuation, facility siting, and regulatory controversies must consider public concerns as well as technical risk assessments in a variety of political arenas.

Conflicts over risk management among publics, management agencies, and industries bring into sharp relief underlying differences in world views, values, concepts of justice, definitions of risk, and types of knowledge. Natural hazards research first posed the questions of differences in individual rationality in decision making over hazards. From these early inquiries, it became clear that significant differences exist among people, particularly between experts and publics. Explaining these differing perceptions and how they are incorporated into broader policy and decision processes has occupied much of hazard perception research, particularly on technological hazards, over the past decade.

Thus, the current base of understanding of hazard perception is at once impressive and uneven, with accumulated evidence in depth in some areas but gaps in knowledge in others. At the same time there are grounds for encouragement as broader and more socially grounded approaches to hazard perception emerge. This chapter reviews the current state of understanding, highlights key geographical contributions, assesses the broadening of perception research that is in process, and explores prospects for a more integrative understanding.

## Perception Studies of Natural Hazards

Geographers have approached nature-society relationships from a variety of perspectives, ranging from environmental determination (Huntington 1915, 1945), to humanism (Tuan, 1967), and to political economy (Smith, 1984; Watts, 1983). Two subfields of geography - cultural ecology and what is called "hazards" - have particularly emphasized hazards, risks, and uncertainty. Palm (1990) presents a useful overview of hazards as addressed from differing perspectives on nature-society relationships within geography, while Saarinen, Seamon, & Sell (1984), Whyte (1986), and Mitchell (1984) have examined perception studies in hazards research over time. Throughout it is apparent that the term "perception" has been used in a multitude of ways, ranging from awareness of environmental hazards to the adoption of responses or coping actions.

Cultural ecologists have generally considered natural hazards as one of a broad set of questions about the dynamics of nature-society relations in the development of cultures and societies. The types of societies investigated have typically, though not exclusively, been rural, agriculturally-based, and less developed (Butzer, 1989). Working closely with anthropologists, the research has maintained a local, contextual specificity while contemplating the potential of search for general principles and cross-society perception findings. Patterns of livelihood and environmental conditions (Kroeber, 1939), human transformation of the environment (Sauer, 1956), adaptation and coping strategies, and the influence of environmental conditions on livelihood strategies (often agricultural) have received particular attention. These themes have been addressed from a variety of theoretical perspectives (Butzer, 1989; Ellen, 1982), while largely rejecting neoclassical economic models of decision making. Among other factors, the role of risk and uncertainty associated with variation in environmental conditions such as drought (Wisner & Mbithi, 1974) and frost (Waddell, 1975) have been investigated. Scott (1976), working in a related discipline, examines agricultural innovation while arguing that a safety-first strategy dominates decision making for peasants living near the subsistence level.

Others have inquired into the role of social organizations in managing risk and providing a form of insurance, whether through reciprocity, kinship relations, loans, or other means. Waddell (1975) analyzes how the Enga, a people living in the New Guinea Highlands, through agricultural practices and social networks, cope with frost threats to agriculture. He later reports on the transformation of these practices through government intervention (Wadell, 1983). One dimension of this research has centered on examining constraints on, rather than choices among, options to avoid or cope with hazards. Drawing on a neo-Marxist analysis of development problems, some researchers (e.g. Susman, O'Keefe, & Wisner, 1983) have viewed hazards as primarily products of underdevelopment and processes creating social vulnerability. Torry (1979a), for example, points to a long history of anthropological work among groups facing severe ecological stresses. While noting the limited treatment given hazards impacts in the anthropological research of the 1970s, he finds much in the accumulated work that contributes to the topic. In their efforts to elucidate the economic, political, and social influences that mediate relationships between extreme events and people, Marston (1983) sees materialist and political economy perspectives related to cultural ecology opening the door to a broader social scope of explanation. Whyte, in reflecting on natural hazards research from the perspective of a geographer, sees the need for more reflection on earlier models and assumptions and concludes that "such a reevaluation of the field will lead us back into the fold of human ecology" (Whyte, 1986, p. 264).

Unlike the cultural ecologists, hazard geographers, or the so called "Chicago School" in hazards research, built on an initial interest in resource management problems in the United States. The seminal work was White's dissertation *Human Adjustment to Floods* which addressed floods as part of the overall human adjustment to and management of floodplain resources. Identifying hazards as part of the broader fabric of nature-society relationship which includes an array of potential human adjustments provides an interpretation of flood losses as largely acts of people rather than as "acts of God" (White, 1945). In a way that would become characteristic of much geographical work on hazards, this dissertation specifically confronted the implications of research for public policy on floods and for securing greater protection for endangered people by decision makers.

This conception of the environment as a source of hazard as well as of resource was a major intellectual contribution to both hazards and geographical inquiry and appears to be one of few developments in the intellectual history of geography that is not simply derivative theory from other fields of inquiry. The earliest research in the hazards field, also a dissertation, was the investigation of the social and psychological responses to a fire and explosion of a French munitions vessel that took approximately 2,000 lives, caused about 6,000 injuries, and left some 10,000 people homeless (Prince, 1920). This analysis was perhaps the first in what was later to become the "disaster sociology" research tradition. In its use of disasters to examine society, this tradition never fully incorporated analyses of natural processes as creators of natural hazards or the social choices that led to occupancy of hazard-prone areas. As O'Riordan (1986) points out, geographical research did effectively address many of these shortcomings. More recently, shared interests in natural hazard warning systems and response efforts have brought geographers and sociologists together on specific problems (Mileti, 1987; Saarinen, 1982; Sorenson & Mileti, in press; White, 1973).

In the 1950s, research by White and colleagues (1958) revealed that, while federal funding for floodplain protection had increased significantly, damages due to flooding had also increased. Upstream protection and flood control work were obviously failing to keep up with human encroachment and development of the floodplain outside the protected areas. It was clear, from the results of this research, that people did not behave in the economically rational manner assumed in the cost-benefit analyses for flood control projects. But why people had chosen to move into and to remain in the floodplains remained unclear. Optimism, perceptions of flood events, and low awareness of floods seemed fertile grounds for explanation, and perception studies became a focal point of research.

In 1961, White authored *The Choice of Use in Resource Management*, perhaps the most theoretical of statements written during the early stages of natural hazards research, which introduced research questions and a framework of analysis that was to characterize natural hazards research in geography over the next two decades (Kates & Burton, 1986). This work specifically rejects models of decision making based on economic rationality and introduces behavioral models of decision making into resource and hazard management questions. While it was clearly a major intellectual departure in resource theory at the time, it was also part of a growing dissatisfaction in geography with the dominant model of "man" as rational economic decision makers. Humanistic, phenomenologial, and behavioral approaches have offered further critiques and alternatives to the positivist assumptions (Cloke, Philo & Sadler, 1990; Jackson & Smith, 1984).

In the "choice of use" model, perception and awareness are central to the bounds on a manager's range of choice. At the first of three levels of analysis, the physical environment managed at a level of technology, sets the "theoretical range of choice." Since options are invariably limited by culture and institutions, no manager has that full theoretical range of choice open. As a result, a more limited subset of choice - the practical range of choice - actually exists for the resource manager. Decisions within the limits of theoretical and practical range of choice depend on the manager's analysis of options. This stress on individual perception, evaluation of hazards, and choice among options provided the framework for an impressive body of empirical studies that shed much light on hazard management in the USA and abroad.

Underlying this work were, of course, a distinctive set of assumptions. First, the research presupposed a dynamic relationship among society, nature, and technology. As Kates and Burton (1986) note, this three-dimensional interactive model stands in contrast to one- and two-dimensional (and more deterministic models) of the nature-society relationships that were widespread at the time. The approach to hazards also explicitly viewed natural resources as culturally defined (Zimmerman, 1951) and accepted the cultural relativism that accompanied that perspective. What is valued, and hence what constitutes a threat, was seen to differ among cultures along with human abilities and strategies for coping with environmental variability. As White (1966) put it (in the vocabulary of that time) after the first decade of natural hazards research:

> At the heart of managing a natural resource is the manager's perception of the resource and of the choices open to him in dealing with it. At the heart of decision on environmental quality are a manager's views of what he and others value in the environment and can preserve or cultivate. This is not a conclusion. It is a definition: natural resources are taken to be culturally defined, decisions are regarded as choices among perceived

> alternatives for bringing about change, and any choice presumes a view of the resource together with preferences in outcome and methods. (pp. 220)

This cultural context to hazards research carried it closest to research in cultural ecology that focuses on societal differences and local specificity, to questions of tolerability of risk in debates over risk management, and to the cultural school of risk theorists that eventually emerged in research on technological hazards. It was, in fact, these latter theorists that later developed a broad theoretical structure for analyzing such hazards and human behavior in the late 1970s and 1980s.

When environmental perception first emerged as a specialty within the Association of American Geographers in 1965, the papers presented ranged from perception of urban highways (Appleyard, Lynch, & Myer, 1967) to environmental perception in the Arctic (Sonnenfeld, 1967), and to perception of coastal storms (Kates, 1967). The presenters included geographers, psychologists, and city planners (Lowenthal, 1967). Other interdisciplinary collaborations soon became characteristic of hazards research, as indicated by the joint 1966 effort of Kates (a geographer) and Wohlwill (a psychologist), White's 1973 paper drawing on collaboration with a group of social psychologists at the University of Chicago, psychologist Schiff's (1970, 1971) contributions to perception research at the University of Toronto, and the publications of geographer Baumann and psychologist Sims (Baumann & Sims, 1974, 1975, 1985; Sims & Bauman, 1972). Not surprisingly, this interdisciplinary approach to hazards involved an active exploration of new methods and data bases, including opinion polls, textual and content analysis, and the use of scenarios. From the mid-1960s to early 1970s, geographers and psychologists examined such diverse techniques as the Thematic Apperception Test (Sims & Saarinen, 1969), a modified Rosenzweig Picture-Frustration Test (Barker & Burton, 1969), semantic differential techniques (Golant & Burton, 1969), and other methods reviewed in Burton, Kates, & White (1968) and Saarinen (1969). Sims and Baumann (1975) explored in some depth the difficulties of interdisciplinary, cross-cultural research as well as possible remedies. In her 1977 and 1986 reviews, Whyte provides a fuller discussion of methodological development and issues in hazards research. As the breadth of Research methods increased, so did the types of natural hazards investigated, to include drought (Saarinen, 1966), tornadoes (Sims & Baumann, 1972), coastal flood hazards (Burton et al., 1969), cyclones (Islam, 1971), and some of the early technological, or as they were called at the time, "quasi-natural" hazards such as water quality (Hewings, 1968) and air pollution (Auliciems & Burton, 1970).

In the early 1970s two large research projects proved to be an important stimulus for hazard perception studies. An assessment of natural hazards in the United States generated a broad set of research papers. Workshops involving experts from government agencies and universities supplemented the research. By 1975, an impressive body of research was available on drought, earthquake and tsunami, flood, hurricane, severe local storms, volcano, coastal erosion, frost landslides, snow avalanches, local windstorms, and urban snow hazards as well as papers on methodology and managerial approaches. The assessments followed a fairly standard format addressing the physical characteristics of the system, possible human adjustments, and research opportunities. These studies formed the basis of *Assessment of Research on Natural Hazards* (White & Haas, 1975), a comprehensive assessment designed to guide future research and policy development[1].

In 1970 Suggestions for Comparative Field Observations on Natural Hazards (N. A., 1970) demarcated the directions for a second major collaborative effort, a comparative international study on natural hazards and human coping. The project, which eventually formed the basis for *Natural Hazards: Global, National, and Local* (White, 1974), involved 28 field sites, 9 different hazards, and 16 nations. Each of the case studies adapted the same questionnaire for research and collaborators sought a test of methodology as well as a test of various hypotheses (Saarinen, 1974). The case studies covered topics ranging from drought in Australia to earthquakes in San Francisco looking at the biophysical characteristics of the region, the hazard perceptions, and the decision making regarding choices of adjustments to perceived hazards. The research focussed heavily on factors, such as experience, perception of probability, and education identified in behavioral research in looking for explanations of adjustment. The more open-ended questions, often those related to questions of cultural issues, were more frequently modified and, in some cases, omitted based on the researchers' assessments of situations. The effort was forcefully criticized for the methodological limitations in addressing cross-cultural differences and environmental variability in the broad context of social and economic developments (Torry, 1979b; Waddell, 1977).

Generally, the model of hazard (risk) adjustment that emerged from the studies of hazard perception and behavior undertaken in these two large projects defined a four step process: (1) assessment of the probability of an extreme event, (2) identification of the perceived options

[1]At time of writing, initial efforts for a Second Assessment of natural hazards were in progress under the direction of Dennis Mileti.

available to mitigate hazard, (3) evaluation of the possible consequences of adjustment alternatives, and (4) the choice of adjustment (Slovic, Kunreuther, & White, 1974). Hazard perception, as well as the characteristics of the hazard manager and the influence of other groups and institutions, occupied a key place in the overall decision process. The legacy of these perception studies carries on in four lines of current research interest: (1) investigation of the human factors contributing to particular perceptions, (2) exploration of the linkages between perception and action, (3) assessment of plans for increasing the effectiveness of hazard warning, and (4) identification of educational approaches to increase hazard awareness (now typically called risk communication). Mitchell (1984) judges the major successes in hazard perception research over two decades as: (1) investigating a large set of research techniques, (2) investigating major theoretical proposals from psychology, including cognitive dissonance and locus of control theory, (3) identifying systematic mechanisms of perceptual bias, (4) introducing the concept of perception to a wide audience of hazards researchers in the English-speaking world, and (5) bringing insights in perception to bear on practical issues in the design of more effective public information and hazard warning schemes.

The importance of these contributions should not be underestimated. The annual natural hazards workshops at Boulder, Colorado, provide persuasive evidence of the widespread use of these research results by practitioners of hazard management and by scholars dealing with hazards across diverse fields. At the same time, it is apparent that significant work on hazard perception remains to be done, including a better understanding of the factors contributing to perceptions of risk, their relative significance in the formulation of a perception, and how these factors appear in differing circumstances. Mileti (1980) has developed an overall model treating the causes and consequences of risk perception (Figure 8.1). This model developed out of an effort to synthesize the findings of then recent research in natural hazards and decision making. Mileti identified six categories of factors that contribute to the formation of risk perceptions: the ability of a social unit to estimate risk, perceived causes of environmental extremes, experience, propensity of people to deny risks, the size of the unit of analysis, and access to information. The perceived risk is considered together with the images of damage, the perceived costs and benefits of the event, and the degree of risk mitigating adjustment required. This model does not distinguish among social units, individuals, or groups, and while the influences of various factors are qualitatively expressed, their interaction (and perception itself) remains something of a black box. Efforts to unpack the contents of that box have made only limited headway. Mitchell in 1984 found the model still essentially untested by empirical research. Indeed, research over the past decade has generally focused on only two of the factors - the role of experience and propensity to deny or distort risk assessments, and cognitive heuristics and biases - identified by Mileti.

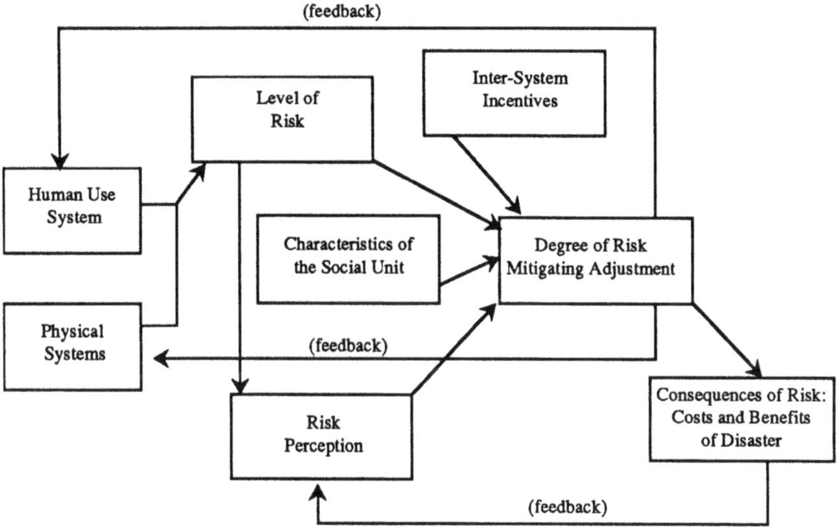


FIGURE 8.1. Key concepts in the emerging theory of risk mitigating adjustment. Adapted from Mileti, 1980.

Throughout these efforts, perception has remained a "central, but nebulous and controversial concept in hazard research" (Mitchell, 1984, p. 33). The controversy appears at two levels: first, in the understanding of factors contributing to perception and the links between awareness and response, and second, in a broader critique of the limitations on explanations based on decision making and choice at the individual level. These issues are taken up in the discussion of technological hazards below.

In addition to factors such as the roles of experience and heuristics cited by Mileti (1980), Drabek (1986) finds more mixed evidence for the inclusion of personality factors and increased significance of age, gender, ethnicity, rural and urban residency, occupation, and socioeconomic status. How best to link perception with responses (i.e. adoptions of mitigating adjustments following evacuation warnings) remains elusive. Efforts thus far have led to something of a consensus on the main characteristics important in effective warning systems. They must (a) be personally relevant, (b) specify the appropriate response, (c) be perceived as coming from a credible source, and (d) be reinforced socially and at the local level (Sims & Baumann, 1985). Efforts at developing educational programs to increase hazard awareness have shared some of these difficulties but have achieved at least some mixed success in linking awareness with response.

These explanatory and applied efforts have met with a variety of responses. Mitchell (1984, pp. 58-59) sees the task ahead of investigators as "the more difficult - and less glamorous - task of fleshing out the existing skeletal understanding of hazard perception principles in the context of hazard adjustment processes." Others argue that twenty years of effort on this line of inquiry has only made a dent in links between attitudes and behavior, offering for instance only fairly general insights about the characteristics of effective warning (Sims & Baumann, 1985). Indeed, they may be quite correct in arguing that the cumulative work on human response to natural hazards, resting as is does not a model of rational and purposeful behavior, is nearing the limits of what can be reasonably learned from this line of inquiry. Continuing to press this model for deeper understandings rather than broadening the inquiry into the cultural values that propel different rationalities and the social and economic forces that structure choice may return only limited results. Thus, we agree with Baumann and Sims that the task is to expand the conceptual framework itself, giving up the assumption of exclusionary rationality:

> Not to give up the ideas that man can be and often is rational, nor to give up those practices and programs directed at rationality, but to go beyond, to enter the realms of culture and personality, of values, attitudes, and beliefs, and there to begin to identify variables that hold the practical promise of informing policy (Sims & Baumann, 1985, p. 360).

In fact, collectively research seems to be moving down a middle path incorporating elements of both criticisms and encouragements. In technological hazards, this increased reach has moved the investigations away from an individual orientation in interviews and surveys to settings of social controversy and group dynamics.

## Perception Studies of Technological Hazards

Research on technological hazards is often dated to the seminal article by Starr (1969) comparing the risks and benefits of different technologies. Initially as a response to Starr's focus on the marketplace as a definer of risk and benefit, psychologists examined public perceptions of both risks and benefits, tradeoffs between them, and preferences for risk reduction (Fischoff et al., 1978; Otway & Fishbein, 1977; Slovic, Fischoff, & Lichtenstein, 1985). This approach, which became known as the "expressed preference" approach or the "psychometric paradigm" (Slovic, Fischoff, & Lichtenstein, 1986), has provided important insights into public perceptions and preferences for risk. This work has become widely known in the policy and practitioner communities as well as the scholarly world and serves as an antidote to more narrowly based approaches drawing solely on technical and economic assessments of risk. The work has also served to stimulate other social scientists to address public responses. One interesting result of this broader engagement of perception questions has been over time to shift the focus of research to societal processes for coping with risk and to see risk as one of several components operating in differing political arenas.

A particular interest in the psychometric research on technological hazard perception has been the marked differences between how publics and experts assess a wide range of hazards frequently within the context of broad political controversies. This is an important question less explicitly confronted in natural hazards research. Democratic processes are predicated on the assumption that the public is sufficiently rational to support political institutions and public policy processes. The prevailing view among many technical experts (for example, Lewis, 1990) is that the public, because it responds to hazards differently than experts, must be irrational in its assessment and coping. Contrary to this view, perception studies have effectively demonstrated that public assessments are imperfect but basically rational.

Psychometric research has certainly revealed that the public has problems coping with the complexity posed by technical risks. It has been widely noted, for example, that members of the public have difficulty assessing probabilities of infrequent but high consequence hazards. So while the catastrophic risks of a particular technology may be quite rare, individuals have difficulty scaling them along a proportionately divided probability scale including more commonly experienced risks (Slovic et al., 1985). Experience in siting hazardous waste facilities or cleaning up existing wastes speaks to the volatile public reaction, and strong sense of danger, of risks that are highly feared and that have been imposed without the individual's knowledge. Meanwhile, the substantial hazards posed by some technologies with which the public is more familiar and which it believes (rightly or wrongly) to be under personal control (e.g., automobile driving, alcohol, and smoking) often are significantly underestimated with respect to experts (Slovic et al., 1985).

The key studies in pointing to these limitations are the psychometric analyses of the relationship between the judged frequency of death and the actual numbers for diverse causes of death pioneered by Paul Slovic and colleagues (see Chapter 9 in this book). The results show a systematic distortion, with well publicized but rare hazards (such as botulism, tornadoes, and homicide) substantially overestimated and serious but chronic hazards such a diabetes, emphysema, and heart disease substantially underestimated. Accidents were judged to cause as many deaths as disease, whereas disease actually kills 15 times as many people as accidents. This performance, as noted above, has led some to conclude that the public is incapable of dealing with risk complexities and/or that its views on risk questions should be discounted (e.g. Lewis, 1990).

A more careful look at these results, however, provides grounds for optimism. Although members of the public obviously have problems dealing with very large and very small numbers - the public apparently compresses the risk scale that varies over an enormous range - it does quite well in rank-ordering the risks. Generally, publics know quite well what are the big and the small risks are. Moreover, they tend to make the same kinds of errors as experts do (i.e., to overestimate very small risks and underestimate very large risks), only more so. This ability to order risks, on a compressed scale to be sure, provides some evidence that the public perception of risk is basically rational, and that the resolve to increase public understanding may bear fruit if the effort is sustained and realistic. Do errors suffice to explain the differences between expert and public perceptions? Cognitive psychology in particular points to the limitations to publics coping with complexity and uncertainty that are inherent in perception heuristics (i.e., judgement rules). People simplify hazard problems and in doing so introduce various biases into their judgements. Prominent among these heuristics are availability - the extent to which a particular risk event is easy to imagine or recall - and representativeness - the tendency to assume that similar activities or technologies have equivalent risk levels or characteristics (Slovic et al., 1985). These factors help to explain why well-publicized rare hazard events are easier to recall, whereas chronic hazards that occur regularly and receive less publicity tend to be less memorable.

From anthropology and political sciences comes the argument that culture and differing world views extensively shape public perceptions and responses to hazards. According to this perspective, people select hazards to worry about according to different types of cultural bias or agenda, world view, or broad social values. Some see such selections of risk as part of broader social preferences (Douglas & Wildavsky, 1982), others as part of an overall approach to particular cultures emerging in differing experiences (Rip, 1991), and still others as values activated in social movements (Mazur, 1981).

One noteworthy version of this argument that risk perceptions, risk taking, and risk aversion are socially constructed is that of Douglas and her followers (Douglas & Wildavsky, 1982; Thompson, Ellis, & Wildavsky, 1990). Drawing upon Durkheim, this cultural theory of risk perception argues that social prescriptions that constrain individual behavior also shape characteristics of personal identity. A grid/group matrix is proposed to explain why various cultural groups give rise to distinctive views of nature, differing types of risk rationality, and alternative preferred risk management strategies. Five major types of cultural groups are identified: hierarchical, individualist, egalitarian, fatalist, and hermit. Each, it is argued, has a distinctive way of looking at the world and a differing risk agenda. While this natural view of risk provides a competing theory of risk perception bases and formation, it has also been extensively criticized (e.g., Johnson & Covello, 1987).

While none of these analytic approaches to hazard perception has shaped an authoritative answer, they have added significantly to our understanding. It is clear that judgement, heuristics, qualitative aspects of risk, and cultural interpretations provide important insights to complement the earlier, natural hazards work. Major findings include:

- public perceptions are typically based upon concern over a different and broader set of hazard consequences than those treated by experts in technical risk assessments.
- qualitative attributes of hazards often assume greater importance than the numerical level of risk, suggesting that departures in expert and public assessment may reflect a different (and perhaps broader) assessment process by publics. Multidimensional measures of risk, therefore, are a much better predictor of public response than are simple measures of consequences, such as mortality (Hohenemser, Kates, & Slovic 1983).
- as indicated by the von Winterfeldt and Edwards' (1984) taxonomy of technological controversies, volatile social conflicts over risk all involve axes of public response that include both perceived risk and values conflicts. The interrelationships between values and risk perception are not well understood but appear to be central to the acceptability (or unacceptability) of differing risks.

The book *Perilous Progress: Managing the Hazards of Technology* (Kates, Hohenemser, & Kasperson, 1985) illustrates some of the continuity in geographical contributions to hazard perception. The organization of collected essays develops a "causal model" of technological hazards that includes the genesis of risks and the roles of individual and societal decision making within a management-oriented framework of analysis. The causal model begins with the role of human wants and needs in driving technology choices and goes on to treat associated initiating events, releases, exposures, and consequences resulting from those choices. Building from this base, the collected, interdisciplinary works take up such topics as estimating consequences, assessing hazards, and examining the social processes of hazard management through a number of case studies of hazards and management institutions, including automobile safety (Bick, Hohenemser, & Kates, 1985), contraceptives (Lavine, 1985), PCBs (Goldman, 1985), and the role of the Consumer Product Safety Commission (Kasperson & Bick, 1985) and Congress (Johnson, 1985).

## Broadening Risk Perception Studies: Values, Trust, and Social Justice

Earlier we noted that perception studies have often focussed on people abstracted from their social context, community, and culture. Too often perception research has failed to relate risk to the processes that endanger people. Yet, public perceptions of risk are very different in situations in which decision processes are viewed as fair than in ones in which the risks are hidden, the risk-bearers not informed, or the risks imposed without opportunity for redress (for a discussion of "hidden" hazards, see Kasperson & Kasperson, 1990). The vehement response of publics to newly discovered hazardous waste dumps or the siting of weapons depots often says as much about the inadequacies of the institutional processes in handling a variety of social controversies over responsibility and fairness as about the risks themselves. Surely the public outrage over how risk occurs contributes to the perception of the risks themselves. Just as surely, the fairness, openness, and the disposition towards political processes in general influences the extent to which publics are willing to accept or tolerate risks or, conversely, how much risk reduction must occur. One major development in risk perception research over the past decade has been a broadening of the scope of perception studies to include how trust, values, equity, and notions of social justice enter into and interact with risk perceptions. A second development has involved studies of a broader range of social groups (Johnson & Covello, 1987; Kreps, 1989; Vaughan, 1989).

Research on technological hazards has focussed new attention on the relationships between institutional trust or distrust and public perception of risk. Three Mile Island and Chernobyl were crises of confidence in institutions as much as crises of the perception of risk. The long term erosion of public confidence in the institutions responsible for management risk (as well as other social institutions in the United States) is one of the dramatic social changes of our time. This loss of social trust certainly contributes to heightened perceptions of risk, and to greater risk aversion in the public. It also greatly complicates efforts to provide risk information or to seek acceptance of societal decisions involving judgments of "acceptable risk" (Fischoff et al., 1978). The processes by which people come to experience risk have only recently come under close research scrutiny, so that an evaluation of their effects on risk perceptions must await a broader array of research on differing political arenas and political cultures. Perceptions of risk acceptability, as well as the risk itself, have also received attention in this broader approach to perception. Lowrance (1978) argues that a thing is safe if its attendant risks are judged to be acceptable. Setting aside for the moment the important questions how well-known the risks are and by whom such judgements are made, probably no risk is acceptable if it is not accompanied by significant benefits and if it can easily be reduced further. To suggest otherwise is to invoke moral justification for readily trading practical constraints against human lives, a position that most risk managers will wisely evade. The marketplace, then, is a poor guide to what risks are publicly acceptable - witness the century-long struggle by workers to reduce workplace risks. The past existence of a risk may suggest more about the balance of political forces that prevailed at the time of decision(s) than about its acceptability to those who bore the risk.

Determining risk acceptability is characteristically an evolutionary process in society rather than a finite decision. Most hazards proceed through a series of judgements related to the growing knowledge about the causal structure of the hazard, assessments of the degree of threat posed by the consequences, and changes in the pattern of contending political forces. It is only a minority of risks for which the public approaches anything like full information and understanding. This is not irrational, for, given the relentless parade of risks that confront the individual, limited information is undoubtedly a prerequisite for warding off hypochondria if not despair. There are also large classes of risks, including many of those most feared by the public, that are involuntary in nature. Chemicals are ubiquitous in the environment, modern armaments and large-scale energy systems have global effects, and mass communication systems erode old social values and shape new ones. Many technological risks, it is apparent, are not accepted; they are imposed, often without warning, information, or opportunity for redress.

Since many technological risks are imposed on a less than fully informed people, public response is more properly thought of as tolerance or acquiescence rather than acceptance. With limited choice and imperfect knowledge, the individual usually does not resist the imposition of the risk. As knowledge of the risk and the individual's range of choice expand, the individual often becomes more risk averse. Paradoxically, the actual degree of risk acceptance achieved will also probably increase. The area between the tolerated and the accepted risk is the latitude available to the decision maker for standard-setting (Figure 8.2). This structure of risk response is, of course, time-specific and should be expected to change. Values, trust, and visions of social justice, in short, underlie definitions of risk acceptability or tolerability.

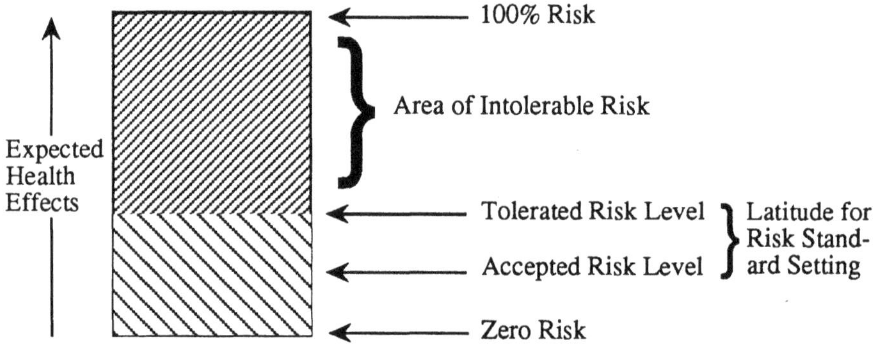


FIGURE 8.2. Schematic diagram of individual response to risk.

The complexity of perceptions of risk acceptability increases at the societal level as the diversity of perspectives on risk expands. There is little reason to expect consensus among individuals in their perceptions of and attitudes toward risk. Levels of tolerability and acceptability vary among individuals. In fact, some of the most difficult risks to manage are those in which individual structures of risk tolerance tend to be divergent rather than convergent. Such appears to be the case, for example, with nuclear power where there are notable gender differences in the response to the hazard. In such cases, the current regulatory tendency in the United States is to set the standard at the level deemed appropriate by the expert accommodating a broad public concern by adjusting the probability or exposure level. As often as not, this type of adjustment does not match the source of public concern and does not resolve the issue, leaving the decision maker and members of the public perplexed, frustrated, and irritated. And the means for communicating between anxious publics and well-intentioned public officials fail, leaving the public distrustful of the expert and the public official convinced of the public's irrationality.

The exploration of these differences within society have tended to focus on public political debates over risks. In these debates, the various positions and types of groups involved, the role of the media, and they style of government involvement have been examined for insights into social functioning as well as cultural influences. As suggested above, it is increasingly apparent that ethics and politics extensively shape risk preferences and perceptions of risk acceptability. Such judgements cannot be objective but are necessarily subjective and political, for they unavoidably (and rightfully) entail considerations of the society desired, how risks may responsibly be imposed upon others, and what risk apportionments are socially just. Attention to the underlying ethical problems is essential, and studies of risk behavior are increasingly exploring their interaction with risk perceptions.

Since the determination of risk preferences and tolerability involves consideration both of levels and of *configurations* of risk, equity is a major objective of the societal processing of risk. Characteristically, those who enjoy the benefits of a technology are not the same as those who bear the risks. Risks are rarely distributed evenly throughout society and they are sometimes exported to future generations. Attempts to control risks may benefit groups different from those who pay the control costs.

Previously, we have identified four major types of inequity that impinge on perceptions of risk tolerability (Kasperson, 1983). First is the potential inequity between workers and publics. It is easy to displace some societal risks - the toxic waste cleanup comes to mind - to workers who need jobs. Second is the inequity among generations. Concern has mounted over the export of risks to the future, particularly where the effects may be irreversible. Stratospheric ozone depletion and radioactive waste disposal are prominent examples. Third is the geographical inequity often referred to as the backyard problem. Traditionally our society has located noxious facilities and hazardous activities in the backyards of vulnerable and politically powerless people. Finally, a more general analysis is required to assess impacts across societal groups, including minorities, social classes, and native peoples.

In evaluating alternative distributions over these population groupings, principles of justice are needed to determine the moral preferability of some risk distributions over others. Four major principles - utility, ability, compensation, and consent - relevant to risk allocation issues exist:

- UTILITY: An allocation or risks is just if, and only if, it maximizes the summed welfare of all members of the morally relevant community. If summed welfare is understood collectively, the roots of this principle can be traced to the earliest documents of our civilization. If summed welfare is understood distributively, as simply adding up individual welfares, the principle takes its classical formulation from the work of the Utilitarians, Bentham and Mill.

- ABILITY: An allocation of risks is just if, and only if, it is based upon the ability of persons to bear those risks. Since need for protection mirrors ability to bear risk, this principle is simply a special case of the more general claim that allocations are just if, and only if, they treat people according to their needs.
- COMPENSATION: An allocation of risks is just if, and only if, those assuming the allocated risks are rewarded (compensated) accordingly. This principle is derived from the somewhat more general one that an allocation is just if, and only if, it is made according to the actual productive contributions of persons.
- CONSENT: An allocation of risks is just if, and only if, it has the consent of those upon whom the risks are imposed. Typical formulations of the principle are found in the Nuremberg Code and in guidelines for experimentation on human subjects.

All four principles are relevant to perceptions of equity and social justice, depending upon the distribution of risk and the associated circumstances.

Just as considerations of fairness enter into public perceptions of alternative distributions of risk, so they relate to the process by which society allocates risks. Imposing risk upon others entails responsibilities and obligations, often described as requirements of procedural justice. People who bear the risks, for example, certainly have the right to all information on the risk, as well as its associated uncertainties, and to due process in the decision. Participation of the risk bearer is needed to ensure that all aspects of the risk, and alternative opportunities for its control, are thoroughly aired and discussed. Ensuring participation involves consideration extending beyond the provision of opportunities (such as the generally ineffective public hearings) to the requisites for transforming opportunities into realities. Central to this are early and continuing public involvement, the creation of an independent technical and financial capacity by which risk bearer may challenge the risk imposer, and means of redress. Also important is how the burden of proof is allocated between the risk imposer and the risk bearer.

Experience with risk controversies suggest that social conflict typically centers as much on perceptions of the credibility of the institutions that manage risks and related issues of power relationships as on perceptions of the risks themselves. Statistical evidence supporting arguments that low-income, rural, and minority communities bear a disproportionate burden of the risks and costs of waste management, to understate the case, stress interactions among publics and agencies (Bullard, 1990; United Church of Christ, 1987). Risk preferences and perceptions of acceptability, in short, are as much a question of the process leading to the decision as what happens to the risk itself. This suggests that a broader benchmark for viewing risk perception and behavior is essential.

## The Social Amplification of Risk: An Integrative Framework

To develop a more holistic approach to hazard perception and behavior and to place such phenomena directly in societal context, Clark University researchers and Slovic in 1988 proposed a new framework of analysis termed the social amplification of risk (Kasperson et al., 1988). This approach is premised on the thesis that hazards and hazard events interact with psychological, social, institutional, and cultural processes in ways that can heighten or attenuate perceptions of hazard and shape risk behavior (Figure 8.3). Behavioral responses, in their turn, generate secondary and tertiary social or economic consequences. These consequences extend far beyond direct harms to human health or the environment to include significant indirect impacts such as liability, insurance costs, loss of confidence in institutions, stigmatization, or alienation from community affairs. In Chapter 9, Slovic outlines some of these amplified effects in more detail.

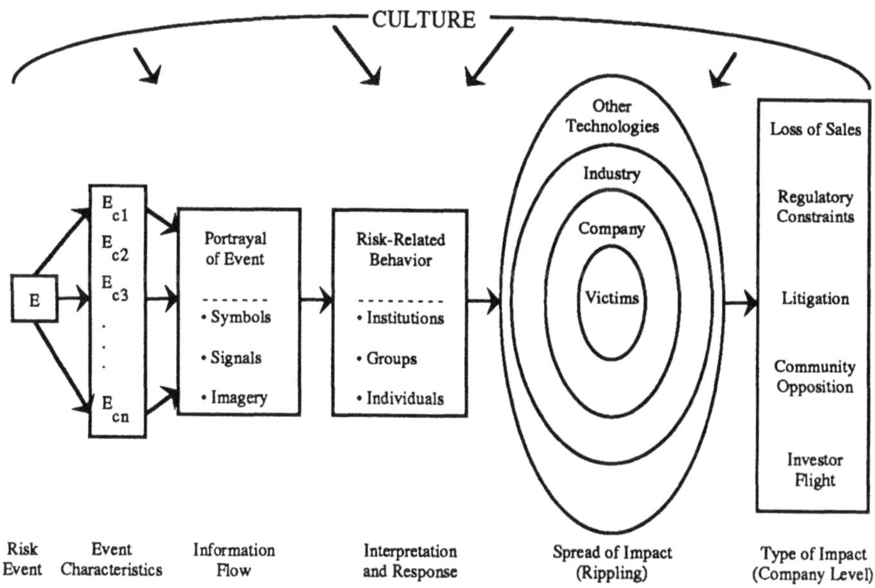


FIGURE 8.3. Highly simplified representation of the social amplification of risk and potential impacts. Example based on a corporation.

Such secondary effects often (in the case of risk amplification) trigger demands for additional institutional responses and protective actions, or, conversely (in the case of risk attenuation), place impediments in the path of needed protective actions. In our usage, amplification includes both intensifying and attenuating signals about risk. These alleged overreactions of people and organizations receive the same attention as alleged down-playing.

As used in this conception, risk is in part an objective threat of harm to people and in part it is socially constructed, that is, it is also a product of culture and social experience. Hence, hazards and hazardous events are real - they involve transformations of the physical environment of human health as a result of continuous or sudden (accidental) releases of energy, matter, or information, or involve disruptions in or threats to social and value structures. Hazard events remain limited in the social context, however, unless they are observed by human beings and communicated to others (Luhmann, 1986). The consequences of such social communication and other social interactions may lead to further physical transformations, such as changes in technologies, changes in methods of land cultivation, or changes in the composition of water, soil, and air. The experience of risk is, therefore, both an experience of physical harm and the result of cultural and social processes by which individuals, groups, and institutions acquire or create interpretations of hazards. These interpretations reflect rules as to how to select, order, and explain signals from the physical world. Additionally, each cultural or social group selects certain risks for attention and concern even as it selects out other risks as not meriting immediate concern.

The amplification process starts with either a physical event (such as an accident) or a report on environmental or technological events, releases, exposures, or consequences. Social groups and individuals actively monitor the world of experience, searching for hazards and hazard events related to their agenda of concern. Such individuals, groups, and institutions select specific characteristics of hazards or hazard events and interpret them according to their previous perceptions and mental schemes. They also communicate these interpretations to other individuals and groups and receive interpretations in return. Social groups and individuals process the information, locate the hazards in their agenda of concerns, and judge whether they should respond. Some may change their previously held beliefs, gain additional knowledge and insights, and be motivated to take actions; others use hazards as a window of opportunity to compose new interpretations about society and polity that they send to the original sources or other interested parties. Still others find evidence that the hazards confirm long-held views of the world and its order.

The individuals or groups who collect information about risks communicate with others and through behavioral responses act, in our terminology, as social amplification stations. Amplification stations can be individuals, groups, or institutions. It is obvious that social groups or institutions can amplify or attenuate signals only by working in social aggregates and participating in social processes. But individuals in groups and institutions do not act or react merely in their roles as private persons, but rather according to the role specification associated with their positions. Amplification of risk differs, therefore, among individuals in their roles as private citizens and in their roles as employees or members of social groups.

Role-related considerations and membership in social groups shape the selection of information that individuals regard as significant. Interpretations or signals that are inconsistent with previous beliefs or that contradict the person's values are often ignored or attenuated; they are intensified if the opposite is true. The process of receiving and processing risk-related information by individuals is well researched in the risk perception literature (Freudenberg, 1988; Slovic, 1987). But this is not sufficient; individuals also act as members of cultural groups and larger social units which co-determine the dynamics and social processing of risk. Individuals in their roles as members or employees of social groups or institutions not only follow their own personal values and interpretative patterns, but perceive risk information and construct the risk problematique according to cultural biases and the rules of their organization or group (Johnson & Covello, 1987). Cultural biases and role-specific factors are internalized and reinforced through education and training, identification with the goals and functions of institutions, beliefs in the importance and justification of social outcomes, and rewards (promotion, salary increase, symbolic honors) and punishments (demotions, salary cuts, disgrace). Meanwhile, conflicts between personal convictions and institutional obligations evoke psychological stress, potentially leading to alienation or anomie.

Both the information flow depicting the hazard or hazard event and the associated behavioral responses by individual and social-amplification stations generate secondary effects that extend beyond the people directly affected by the original hazard event or report. Secondary impacts include such effects as:

- enduring mental perceptions, images, and attitudes (e.g., anti-technology attitudes, alienation from physical environment, social apathy, or distrust of risk management institutions);

- impacts on the local or regional economy (e.g., reduced business sales, declines in residential property values, and drops in tourism);
- political and social pressure (e.g., political demands, changes in political climate and culture);
- social disorder (e.g., protesting, rioting, sabotage, terrorism);
- changes in risk monitoring and regulation;
- increased liability and insurance costs; and repercussions on other technologies (e.g., lower levels of public acceptance) and on social institutions (e.g., erosion of public trust).

Secondary impacts are, in turn, perceived by social groups and individuals so that additional stages of amplification may occur to produce higher order impacts. The impacts thereby may spread, or "ripple," to other parties, distant locations, or future generations. Each order of impact not only disseminates social and political impacts but may also trigger (in risk amplification) or hinder (in risk attenuation) positive changes for risk reduction. The concept of social amplification risk is hence dynamic, taking into account the continuing learning and social interactions resulting from societal experience with hazards.

The analogy of dropping a stone into a pond (cf. Figure 8.3) illustrates the spread of these higher order impacts associated with the social amplification of risk. The ripples spread outward, first encompassing the directly affected victims or the first group to be notified, then touching the next higher institutional level (a company or an agency), and in more extreme cases, reaching other parts of the industry or other social arenas with similar problems. This rippling of impacts is an important element of risk amplification since it suggests that the processes can extend (in risk amplification) or constrain (in risk attenuation) the temporal and geographical scale of impacts.

In Chapter 9, Slovic explores several applications of the social amplification framework. Meanwhile a number of empirical studies have explored hazard perception and behavior within this framework's terms (Burns et al., 1990; Machlis & Rosa, 1990; Kasperson, in press; R. Kasperson & J. Kasperson, 1990; Renn, 1991).

## The Future of Hazard Perception Studies

Hazard perception studies have over three decades created a rich basis for analyzing how individuals, social groups, institutions, and cultures have assessed, processed, and responded to hazards. From initial geographical and psychological studies of hazard, much became known of human perception of a wide range of natural hazards. More recent efforts have extended the analysis from natural to technological hazards, from choice-centered to constraint-centered analyses, from cognitive psychology to anthropology and political science, and from disciplinary to more integrative perspectives. The interaction between notions of perception and broader concerns of social interpretation, trust, values, social justice, and democratic processes is increasingly the subject of broader inquiry. Meanwhile, the long existing concern in geography to understand how human societies behave in their encounters with diverse physical and cultural environments with sensitive appreciation for the rich fabric of social meaning and complex of hazards at particular regions and places remains an enduring goal.

## References


Appleyard, D., Lynch, K., & Myer, J. (1967). The view from the road. In D. Lowenthal (Ed.), *Environmental perception and behavior* (pp. 75-88). Chicago, IL: University of Chicago.

Auliciems, A., & Burton, I. (1970). *Perception and awareness of air pollution in Toronto* (Natural Hazard Working Paper No. 13). Boulder, CO: University of Colorado.

Barker, M., & Burton, I. (1969). *Differential response to stress in natural and social environments: An application of a modified Rosenzwieg Picture-Frustration test* (Natural Hazard Working Paper No. 5). Boulder, CO: University of Colorado.

Baumann, D. D., & Sims, J. H. (1974). Human response to the hurricane. In G. F. White (Ed.), *Natural hazards: Global, national, and local* (pp. 25-29). New York: Oxford University Press.

Bick, T., Hohenemser, C., & Kates, R. W. (1985). Regulating automobile safety. In R. W. Kates, Hohenemser, C., & Kasperson, J. X. (Eds.), *Perilous progress* (pp. 311-344). Boulder, CO: Westview.

Bullard, R. D. (1990). *Dumping in Dixie: Race, class, and environmental quality*. Boulder, CO: Westview.

Burns, W., Kasperson, R. E., Kasperson, J. X., Renn, O., Emani, S., & Slovic, P. (1990). *Social amplification of risk: An empirical study*. Carson City, NV: Yucca Mountain Socioeconomic Project.

Burton, I., Kates, R. W., & White, G. F. (1968). *The Human ecology of extreme geophysical events* (Natural Hazard Working Paper No. 1). Boulder, CO: University of Colorado.

Burton, I., Kates, R. W., & Snead, R. E. (1969). *The Human ecology of coastal flood hazard in megalopolis* (Department of Geography Research Paper No. 115.) Chicago, IL: University of Chicago.

Burton, I., Kates, R. W., & White, G. F. (1978). *The Environment as hazard*. New York: Oxford University Press.

Butzer, K. (1989). Cultural ecology. In G. L. Gaile & C. J. Willmott (Eds.), *Geography in America* (pp. 192-208). Columbus, OH: Merrill.

Cloke, P., Philo, C., & Sadler, D. (1991). *Approaching human geography*. New York: Guilford.

Covello, V. T. (1983). The perception of technological risks: A literature review. *Technological Forecasting and Social Change*, *23*, 285-297.

Douglas, M., & Wildavsky, A. (1982). *Risk and culture*. Berkeley: University of California Press.

Drabek, T. E. (1986). *Human systems response to disasters*. New York: Springer.

Ellen, R. (1982). *Environment, subsistence, and system*. Cambridge: Cambridge University Press.

Fischoff, B. (1985). Managing risk perceptions. *Issues in Science and Technology*, *11*, 83-96.

Fischoff, B., Slovic, P., Lichtenstein, S., Read, S., & Combs, B. (1978). How safe is safe enough? A psychometric study of attitudes towards technological risks and benefits. *Policy Sciences, 8*, 127-152.

Fischoff, B., Lichtenstein, S., Slovic, P., Derby, S. L., & Keeny, R. L. (1987). *Acceptable risk.* New York: Cambridge University Press.

Freudenberg, W. (1988). Perceived risk, real risk: Social science and the art of probabilistic risk assessment. *Science, 242*, 44-49.

Golant, S., & Burton, I. (1969). *The meaning of a hazard-application of the semantic differential* (Natural Hazard Working Paper No. 7). Boulder, CO: University of Colorado.

Goldman, A. (1985). Controlling PCBs. In R. W. Kates, C. Hohenemser & J. X. Kasperson (Eds.), *Perilous progress* (pp. 345-370). Boulder, CO: Westview.

Hewings, J. M. (1968). *Water quality and the hazard to health: Placarding public beaches* (Natural Hazard Working Paper No. 3). Boulder, CO: University of Colorado.

Hohenemser, C., Kates, R. W., & Slovic, P. (1983). The nature of technological hazard. *Science*, *220*, 378-384.

Huntington, E. (1915). *Civilization and climate*. New Haven, CT: Yale University Press.

Huntington, E. (1945). *Mainsprings of civilization*. New York: Arno.

Islam, M. A. (1971). *Human adjustment to cyclone hazards: A case study of Char Jabbar* (Natural Hazard Working Paper No. 18). Boulder, CO: University of Colorado.

Jackson, P., & Smith, S. J. (1984). *Exploring social geography*. London: Allen and Unwin.

Johnson, B. B. (1985). Congress as hazard manager. In R. W. Kates, C. Hohenemser & J. X. Kasperson (Eds.), *Perilous progress* (pp. 455-476). Boulder, CO: Westview.

Johnson, B. B., & Covello, V. T. (Eds.). (1987). *The social and cultural construction of risk.* Dordrecht: Reidel.

Kasperson, R. E. (1983). Acceptability of human risk. *Environmental Health Perspectives, 52*, 15-20.

Kasperson, R. E. (in press). The social amplification of risk: Progress in developing an integrative framework of risk. In S. Krimsky, & D. Golding (Eds.), *Theories of risk.* New York: Praeger.

Kasperson, R. E., & Bick, T. (1985). The Consumer Product Safety Commission. In R. W. Kates, C. Hohenemser, & J. X. Kasperson (Eds.), *Perilous progress* (pp. 371-394). Boulder, CO: Westview.

Kasperson, R. E., Renn, O., Slovic, P., Brown, H. S., Emel, J., Goble, R., Kasperson, J. X., & Ratick, S. (1988). The social amplification of risk: A conceptual framework. *Risk Analysis, 8*, 177-187.

Kasperson, R. E., & Kasperson, J. X. (1990). Hidden hazards. In D. C. Mayo & R. Hollander (Eds.), *Acceptable evidence: Science and values in hazard management* (pp. 9-28). Oxford: Oxford University Press.

Kates, R. W. (1967). The perception of storm hazard on the shores of megalopolis. In D. Lowenthal (Ed.), *Environmental perception and behavior* (pp. 60-71). Chicago, IL: University of Chicago.

Kates, R. W., & Burton, I. (1986). *Geography, resources, and environment: Themes in the work of G. F. White*. Chicago: University of Chicago Press.

Kates, R. W., & Kasperson, J. X. (1983). Comparative risk analysis of technological hazards (a review). *Proceedings of the National Academy of Sciences, 80*, 7027-7038.

Kates, R. W., & Wohlwill, J. F. (Eds.). (1966). Man's response to the physical environment. *Journal of Social Issues, 22*, 1-140.

Kates, R. W., Hohenemser, C., & Kasperson, J. X. (Eds.). (1985). *Perilous progress.* Boulder, CO: Westview.

Kreps, G. (1989). *Social structure and disaster.* Durham: Duke University Press.

Kroeber, A. L. (1939). *Cultural and natural area of native North America* (University of California Publications in American Archeology and Ethnology 38). Berkeley: University of California Press.

Lavine, M. P. (1985). Contraceptives: Hazard by choice. In R. W. Kates, C. Hohenemser & J. X. Kasperson (Eds.), *Perilous progress* (pp. 395-426). Boulder, CO: Westview.

Lewis, H. W. (1990). *Technological hazards*. New York: Norton.

Lowenthal, D. (Ed.). (1967). *Environmental perception and behavior*. Chicago: University of Chicago.

Lowrance, W. W. (1976). *Acceptable risk: Science and the determination of safety*. Los Altos, CA: Kaufmann.

Luhmann, N. (1986). *Ökologische kommunikation*. Opladen: Westdeutscher.

Machlis, G. E., & Rosa, E. A. (1990). Desired risk: Broadening the social amplification of risk framework. *Risk Analysis, 10*, 161-168.

Marston, S. A. (1983). Review Essay, "Natural hazards: Towards a political economy perspective." *Political Geography Quarterly, 2*, 339-348.

Mazur, A. (1981). *The dynamics of technical controversy*. Washington, DC: Communication.

Mileti, D. S. (1980). Human adjustment to the risk of environmental extremes. *Sociology and Social Research, 64*, 327-347.

Mileti, D. S., & Sorenson, J. H. (1987). Natural hazards and precautionary behavior. In N. D. Weinstein (Ed.), *Taking care: Understanding and encouraging self-protective behavior* (pp. 189-207). Cambridge: Cambridge University Press.

Mitchell, J. K. (1984). Hazard perception studies: Convergent concerns and divergent approaches during the past decade. In T. F. Saarinen, D. Seamon, & J. L. Sell (Eds.), *Environmental perception and behavior: An inventory and prospect* (pp. 33-59). Chicago, IL: University of Chicago.

N.A. (1970). *Suggestions for comparative field observations on natural hazards* (Natural Hazard Working Paper No. 16). Boulder, CO: University of Colorado.

O'Riordan, T. (1986). Coping with environmental hazards. In R. W. Kates & I. Burton (Eds.), *Geography, resources, and environment: Themes from the work of G. F. White* (pp. 272-309). Chicago, IL: University of Chicago Press.

Otway, H., & Fishbein, M. (1977). *Public attitudes and decision making*. (Research Memorandum 77-54). Laxenburg, Austria: International Institute for Applied Systems Analysis.

Palm, R. I. (1990). *Natural hazards: An integrative framework for research and planning*. Baltimore, MD: The Johns Hopkins University Press.

Prince, S. H. (1920). *Catastrophe and social change*. Unpublished Ph.D. dissertation. New York: Columbia University.

Renn, O. (1991). Risk communication and the social amplification of risk. In R. E. Kasperson & P. J. Stallen (Eds.), *Communicating risks to the public: International perspectives* (pp. 287-324). Dordrecht: Kluwer.

Rip, A. (1991). The danger culture of industrial society. In R. E. Kasperson & P. J. Stallen (Eds.), *Communicating risks to the public: International perspectives* (pp. 345-366). Dordrecht: Kluwer.

Saarinen, T. F. (1966). *Perception of the drought hazard in the Great Plains* (Department of Geography Research Paper No. 106). Chicago, IL: University of Chicago.

Saarinen, T. F. (1969). *Perception of the environment*. Washington, D.C.: Association of American Geographers, Commission on College Geography.

Saarinen, T. F. (1974). Problems in the use of a standardized questionnaire for cross-cultural research on the perception of natural hazards. In G. F. White (Ed.), *Natural hazards: Global, national, and local* (pp. 180-186). New York: Oxford University Press.

Saarinen, T. F., (Ed.). (1982). *Perspectives on increasing hazard awareness* (Program on Environment and Behavior Monograph No. 35). Boulder, CO: Institute of Behavioral Science, University of Colorado.

Saarinen, T. F., Seamon, D., & Sell, J. L. (Eds.). (1984). *Environmental perception and behavior: An inventory and prospect* (Department of Geography Research Paper No. 209). Chicago: University of Chicago.

Sauer, C. O. (1956). The agency of man on the earth. In W. L. Thomas (Ed.), *Man's role in changing the face of the earth*. Chicago, IL: University of Chicago Press.

Schiff, M. R. (1970). *Some theoretical aspects of attitudes and perception* (Natural Hazard Working Paper No. 15). Boulder, CO: University of Colorado.

Schiff, M. R. (1971, April). *Psychological factors relating to the adoption of adjustments for natural hazards in London, Ontario*. Paper presented to Association of American Geographers, Boston, MA.

Scott, J. (1974). *The moral economy of the peasant*. New Haven, CT: Yale University Press.

Sims, J. H., & Baumann, D. D. (1972). The tornado threat: Coping styles of the north and south. *Science, 176*, 1386-92.

Sims, J. H., & Baumann, D. D. (1975). Interdisciplinary, cross-cultural research: Double trouble. *The Professional Geographer, 27*, 153-159.

Sims, J. H., & Baumann, D. D. (1985). Natural hazard research and policy: Time for a gadfly. *The American Statistician, 39*, 358-362.

Sims, J. H., & Saarinen, T. F. (1969). Coping with environmental threat: Great Plains farmers and the sudden storm. *Annals of the Association of American Geographers, 59*, 677-86.

Slovic, P. (1987). Perceived Risk. *Science, 236*, 280-285.

Slovic, P., Kunreuther, H., & White, G. F. (1974). Decision processes, rationality, and adjustment to natural hazards. In G. F. White (Ed.), *Natural hazards: Global, national, and local* (pp. 187-205). New York: Oxford University Press.

Slovic, P., Fischoff, B., & Lichtenstein, S. (1985). Characterizing perceived risk. In R. W. Kates, C. Hohenemser, & J. X. Kasperson (Eds.), *Perilous progress* (pp. 91-125). Boulder, CO: Westview.

Slovic, P., Fischoff, B., & Lichtenstein, S. (1986). The psychometric study of risk perception. In V. T. Covello, J. Menkes, & J. Mumpower (Eds.), *Risk evaluation and management* (pp. 3-24). New York: Plenum.

Sonnenfeld, J. (1967). Environmental perception and adaptation level in the Arctic. In D. Lowenthal (Ed.), *Environmental perception and behavior* (pp. 42-53). Chicago, IL: University of Chicago.

Sorenson, J., & Mileti, D. (in press). Pre-emergency information programs. In D. Golding, J. X. Kasperson, & R. E. Kasperson (Eds.), *Preparing for nuclear power plant accidents: Selected papers*. Boulder, CO: Westview.

Starr, C. (1969). Social benefit versus technological risk. *Science, 165*, 1232-1238.

Susman, P., O'Keefe, P., & Wisner, B. (1983). Global disasters, a radical interpretation. In K. Hewitt (Ed.), *Interpretations of calamity* (pp. 263-283). Boston: Allen & Unwin.

Thompson, M., Ellis, R., & Wildavsky, A. (1990). *Cultural theory*. Boulder, CO: Westview.

Torry, W. I. (1979a). Anthropological studies in hazardous environments: Past trends and new horizons. *Current Anthropology, 20*, 517-540.

Torry, W. I. (1979b). Hazards, hazes, and holes: A critique of the environment as hazard and reflections on disaster research. *Canadian Geographer, 23*, 368-383.

Tuan, Y. (1967). Attitudes toward the environment: Themes and approaches. In D. Lowenthal (Ed.), *Environmental perception and behavior* (pp. 4-17). Chicago, IL: University of Chicago.

United Church of Christ (1987). *Toxic wastes and race in the United States: A national report on the racial and socio-economic characteristics of communities with hazardous waste sites.* New York: Commission for Racial Justice.

Vaughn, C. (1989, August). *Farmworkers and pesticide exposure: Perceived risk, psychological distress, and health.* Paper presented to the Annual American Psychological Association Meetings, New Orleans.

von Winterfeldt, D., & Edwards, W. (1984). Patterns of conflict about risky technologies. *Risk Analysis, 4* , 55-68.

Waddell, E. (1975). How the Enga cope with frost: Responses to climatic perturbations in the central highlands of New Guinea. *Human Ecology, 3,* 249-273.

Waddell, E. (1977). The hazards of scientism: A review article. *Human Ecology, 5* , 69-76.

Waddell, E. (1983). Coping with frosts, governments and disaster experts: Some reflections based on a New Guinea experience and a perusal of the relevant literature. In K. Hewitt (Ed.), *Interpretations of calamity* (pp. 33-43). Boston: Allen & Unwin.

Watts, M. (1983). On the poverty of theory. In K. Hewitt (Ed.), *Interpretations of calamity* (pp. 231-262). Boston: Allen and Unwin.

White, G. F. (1945). *Human adjustment to floods* (Department of Geography Research Paper No. 29). Chicago, IL: University of Chicago.

White, G. F., et al. (1958). *Changes in urban occupance of flood plains in the United States* (Department of Geography Research Paper No. 57). Chicago, IL: University of Chicago.

White, G. F. (1961). The choice of use in resource management. *Natural Resources Journal, 1,* 23-40.

White, G. F. (1966, 1986). Formation and role of public attitudes. In R. W. Kates & I. Burton (Eds.), *Geography, resources, and environment: Themes from the work of G. F. White* (pp. 219-245). Chicago: University of Chicago Press. Reprinted from *Environmental quality in a growing economy essays from the sixth RFF forum* (pp. 105-27). Baltimore: Johns Hopkins Press

White, G. F. (1973). Natural hazards research. In R. J. Chorley (Ed.), *Directions in geography* (pp. 193-216). London: Methuen.

White, G. F. (Ed.). (1974). *Natural hazards: Global, national, and local.* New York: Oxford University Press.

White, G. F. (1984). Environmental perception and its uses: A commentary. In T. F. Saarinen, D. Seamon, & J. L. Sell (Eds.), *Environmental perception and behavior: An inventory and prospect* (pp. 93-96). Chicago, IL: University of Chicago.

White, G. F., & Haas, J. E. (1975). *Assessment of research on natural hazards*. Cambridge, MA: MIT Press.

Whyte, A. V. T. (1977). *Guidelines for field studies in environmental perception*. (MAB Technical Notes 5). Paris: UNESCO.

Whyte, A. V. T. (1986). From hazard perception to human ecology. In R. W. Kates & I. Burton (Eds.), *Geography, resources, and environment: Themes from the work of G. F. White* (pp. 240-271). Chicago: University of Chicago Press.

Wildavsky, A., & Dake, K. (1990). Theories of risk perceptions: Who fears what and why? *Daedalus, 119*, 41-60.

Wisner, B., & Mbithi, P. (1974). Drought in Eastern Kenya: Nutritional status and farmer activity. In G. F. White (Ed.), *Natural hazards: Global, national, and local*. (pp. 87-98). New York: Oxford University Press.

Zimmerman, E. W. 1951. *World resources and industries* (Rev. ed.). New York: Harper.

*Behavior and Environment: Psychological and Geographical Approaches*
*T. Gärling and R.G. Golledge (Editors)*



# CHAPTER 9

# Perceptions of Environmental Hazards: Psychological Perspectives

**Paul Slovic**

The ability to sense and avoid harmful environmental conditions is necessary for the survival of all living organisms. Survival is also aided by an ability to codify and learn from past experience. Humans have an additional capability that allows them to alter their environment as well as respond to it. This capacity both creates and reduces risk.

In recent decades, the profound development of chemical and nuclear technologies has been accompanied by the potential to cause catastrophic and long-lasting damage to the earth and the life forms that inhabit it. The mechanisms underlying these complex technologies are unfamiliar and incomprehensible to most citizens. Their most harmful consequences are rare and often delayed, hence difficult to assess by statistical analysis and not well suited to management by trial and error learning. The elusive and hard to manage qualities of today's hazards have forced the creation of a new intellectual discipline called risk assessment, designed to aid in identifying, characterizing, and quantifying risk (Ricci, Sagan, & Whipple, 1984).

Whereas technologically sophisticated analysts employ risk assessment to evaluate hazards, the majority of citizens rely on intuitive risk judgments, typically called "risk perceptions." For these people, experience with hazards tends to come from the news media, which rather thoroughly document mishaps and threats occurring throughout the world. The dominant perception for most Americans (and one that contrasts sharply with the views of professional risk assessors) is that they face more risk today than in the past and that future risks will be even greater than today's (Harris, 1980). Similar views appear to be held by citizens of many other industrialized nations. These perceptions and the opposition to technology that accompanies them have puzzled and frustrated industrialists and regulators and have led numerous observers to argue that the

American public's apparent pursuit of a "zero-risk society" threatens the nation's political and economic stability.

Over the past 15 years, a small number of researchers have been examining the opinions that people express when they are asked, in a variety of ways, to evaluate hazardous activities, substances, and technologies. This research has attempted to develop techniques for assessing the complex and subtle opinions that people have about risk. With these techniques, researchers have sought to discover what people mean when they say that something is (or is not) "risky," and to determine what factors underlie those perceptions. The basic assumption underlying these efforts is that those who promote and regulate health and safety need to understand the ways in which people think about and respond to risk.

This research attempts to aid policy makers by improving communication between them and the lay public, by directing educational efforts, and by predicting public responses to new technologies (e.g., genetic engineering), events (e.g., a good safety record, an accident), and new risk management strategies (e.g., warning labels, regulations, substitute products).

## Risk Perception Research

Important contributions to our current understanding of risk perception have come from geography, sociology, political science, anthropology, and psychology. Geographical research focused originally on understanding human behavior in the face of natural hazards, but it has since broadened to include technological hazards as well (Burton, Kates, & White, 1978). Sociological research (Freudenberg, 1988; Short, 1984) and anthropological studies (Douglas, 1966) have shown that perception and acceptance of risk have their roots in social and cultural factors. Short (1984) argues that response to hazards is mediated by social influences transmitted by friends, family, fellow workers, and respected public officials. In many cases, risk perceptions may form afterwards, as part of the ex post facto rationale for one's own behavior. In a similar vein, Douglas and Wildavsky (1982) assert that people, acting within social groups, downplay certain risks and emphasize others as a means of maintaining and controlling the group. Psychological research on risk perception, which is the focus of this chapter, originated in empirical studies of probability assessment, utility assessment, and decision making processes (Edwards, 1961). A major development in this area has been the discovery of a set of mental strategies, or heuristics, that people employ in order to make sense out of an uncertain world (Kahneman, Slovic, & Tversky,

1982). Although these rules are valid in some circumstances, in others they lead to large and persistent biases with serious implications for risk assessment. In particular, laboratory research on basic perceptions and cognitions has shown that difficulties in understanding probabilistic processes, biased media coverage, misleading personal experiences, and the anxieties generated by life's gambles cause uncertainty to be denied, risks to be misjudged (sometimes overestimated and sometimes underestimated), and judgments of fact to be held with unwarranted confidence. Unfortunately, experts' judgments appear to be prone to many of the same biases as those of laypersons, particularly when experts are forced to go beyond the limits of available data and rely upon their intuitions (Henrion & Fischoff, 1986; Kahneman et al., 1982). Research further indicates that disagreements about risk should not be expected to evaporate in the presence of evidence. Strong initial views are resistant to change because they influence the way that subsequent information is interpreted. New evidence appears reliable and informative if it is consistent with one's initial beliefs; contrary evidence tends to be dismissed as unreliable, erroneous, or unrepresentative (Nisbett & Ross, 1980). When people lack strong prior opinions, the opposite situation exists - they are at the mercy of the problem formulation. Presenting the same information about risk in different ways (for example, mortality rates as opposed to survival rates) alters their perspectives and their actions (Tversky & Kahneman, 1981).

### *The Psychometric Paradigm*

One broad strategy for studying perceived risk is to develop a taxonomy for hazards that can be used to understand and predict responses to their risks. A taxonomic scheme might explain, for example, people's extreme aversion to some hazards, their indifference to others, and the discrepancies between these reactions and experts' opinions. The most common approach to this goal has employed the psychometric paradigm (Fischoff, Slovic, Lichtenstein, Read, & Combs, 1978; Slovic, Fischoff, & Lichtenstein, 1984), which uses psychophysical scaling and multivariate analysis techniques to produce quantitative representations of risk attitudes and perceptions. Within the psychometric paradigm, people make quantitative judgments about the current and desired riskiness of diverse hazards and the desired level of regulation of each. These judgments are then related to judgments about other properties, such as (i) the hazard's status on characteristics that have been hypothesized to account for risk perceptions and attitudes (for example, voluntariness, dread, knowledge, controllability), (ii) the benefits that each hazard provides to society, (iii) the number of deaths caused by the hazard in an average year, (iv) the number of deaths caused by the hazard in a disastrous year, and (v) the seriousness of each death from a particular hazard relative to a death due to other causes.

Numerous studies carried out within the psychometric paradigm have shown that perceived risk is quantifiable and predictable. Psychometric techniques seem well suited for identifying similarities and differences among groups with regard to risk perceptions and attitudes (see Table 9.1). They have also shown that the concept "risk" means different things to different people. When experts judge risk, their responses correlate highly with technical estimates of annual fatalities. Lay people can assess annual fatalities if they are asked to (and produce estimates somewhat like the technical estimates). However, their judgments of risk are related more to other hazard characteristics (for example, catastrophic potential, threat to future generations) and, as a result, tend to differ from their own (and experts') estimates of annual fatalities.

Another consistent result from psychometric studies is that people tend to view current risk levels as unacceptably high for most activities. The gap between perceived and desired risk levels suggests that people are not satisfied with the way that market and other regulatory mechanisms have balanced risks and benefits. Across the domain of hazards, there seems to be little systematic relationship between perceptions of current risks and benefits. However, studies of expressed preferences do seem to support Starr's claim (1969) that people are willing to tolerate higher risks from activities seen as highly beneficial. But, whereas Starr concluded that voluntariness of exposure was the key mediator of risk acceptance, further studies have shown that other (perceived) characteristics such as familiarity, control, catastrophic potential, equity, and level of knowledge also seem to influence the relationship between perceived risk, perceived benefit, and risk acceptance (Fischoff et al., 1978; Slovic, Fischoff et al., 1980).

Various models have been advanced to represent the relationships between perceptions, behavior, and these qualitative characteristics of hazards. As we shall see, the picture that emerges from this work is both orderly and complex.

### *Factor-Analytic Representations*

Psychometric studies have demonstrated that every hazard has a unique pattern of qualities that appears to be related to its perceived risk. Figure 9.1 shows the mean profiles across nine characteristic qualities of risk that emerged for nuclear power and medical x-rays in an early study (Fischoff et al., 1978). Nuclear power was judged to have much higher risk than x-rays and to need much greater reduction in risk before it would become "safe enough." As the figure illustrates, nuclear power also had a much more negative profile across the various risk characteristics.

TABLE 9.1

*Ordering of perceived risks for 30 activities and technologies. The ordering is based on the geometric mean risk ratings within each group. Rank 1 represents the most risky activity or technology.*

| Activity or Technology | League of Women Voters | Active College Students | Club Members | Experts |
|---|---|---|---|---|
| Nuclear power | 1 | 1 | 8 | 20 |
| Motor vehicles | 2 | 5 | 3 | 1 |
| Handguns | 3 | 2 | 1 | 4 |
| Smoking | 4 | 3 | 4 | 2 |
| Motorcycles | 5 | 6 | 2 | 6 |
| Alcoholic Beverages | 6 | 7 | 5 | 3 |
| General (private) aviation | 7 | 15 | 11 | 12 |
| Police work | 8 | 8 | 7 | 17 |
| Pesticides | 9 | 4 | 15 | 8 |
| Surgery | 10 | 11 | 9 | 5 |
| Fire fighting | 11 | 10 | 6 | 18 |
| Large construction | 12 | 14 | 13 | 13 |
| Hunting | 13 | 18 | 10 | 23 |
| Spray cans | 14 | 13 | 23 | 26 |
| Mountain climbing | 15 | 22 | 12 | 29 |
| Bicycles | 16 | 24 | 14 | 15 |
| Commercial aviation | 17 | 16 | 18 | 16 |
| Electric power (non-nuclear) | 18 | 19 | 19 | 9 |
| Swimming | 19 | 30 | 17 | 10 |
| Contraceptives | 20 | 9 | 22 | 11 |
| Skiing | 21 | 25 | 16 | 30 |
| X-rays | 22 | 17 | 24 | 7 |
| High school and college football | 23 | 26 | 21 | 27 |
| Railroads | 24 | 23 | 20 | 19 |
| Food preservatives | 25 | 12 | 28 | 14 |
| Food coloring | 26 | 20 | 30 | 21 |
| Power mowers | 27 | 28 | 25 | 28 |
| Prescription antibiotics | 28 | 21 | 26 | 24 |
| Home appliances | 29 | 27 | 27 | 22 |
| Vaccinations | 30 | 29 | 29 | 25 |

From Slovic 1987. 

Many of the qualitative risk characteristics that make up a hazard's profile tend to be highly correlated with each other, across a wide range of hazards. For example, hazards rated as "voluntary" tend also to be rated as "controllable" and "well-known;" hazards that appeared to threaten future generations tend also to be seen as having catastrophic potential, and so on. Investigation of these interrelationships by means of factor analysis has indicated that the broader domain of characteristics can be condensed to a small set of higher-order characteristics or factors.

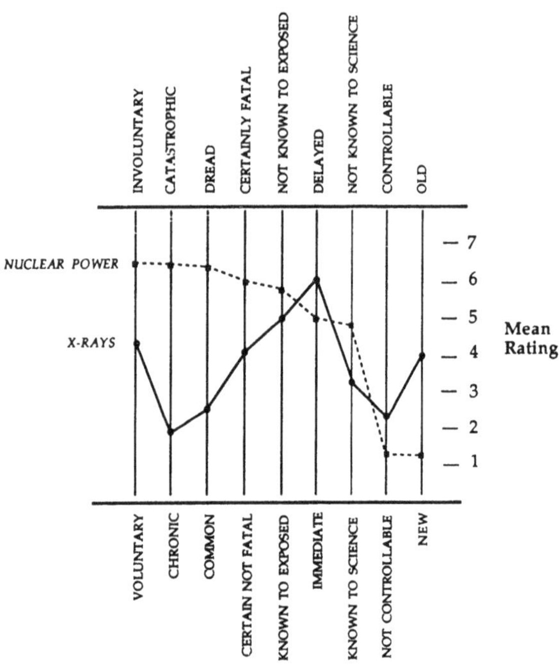


FIGURE 9.1. Profiles for nuclear power and x-rays across nine risk characteristics.

Figure 9.2 presents a spatial representation of hazards within a factor space which has been replicated across numerous groups of laypeople and experts judging large and diverse sets of hazards. The factors in this space reflect the degree to which a risk is understood and the degree to which it evokes a feeling of dread.

Research has shown that laypeople's risk perceptions and attitudes are closely related to the position of a hazard within the factor space. Most important is the factor "Dread Risk." The higher a hazard's score on this factor (i.e., the further to the right it appears in the space), the higher its perceived risk, the more people want to see its current risks reduced, and the more they want to see strict regulation employed to achieve the desired reduction in risk. In contrast, experts' perceptions of risk are not closely related to any of the various risk characteristics or factors derived from these characteristics. Instead, experts appear to see riskiness as synonymous with expected annual mortality (Slovic et al., 1979). As a result, many conflicts about risk may result from experts and laypeople having different definitions of the concept. In such cases, expert recitations of risk statistics will do little to change people's attitudes and perceptions.

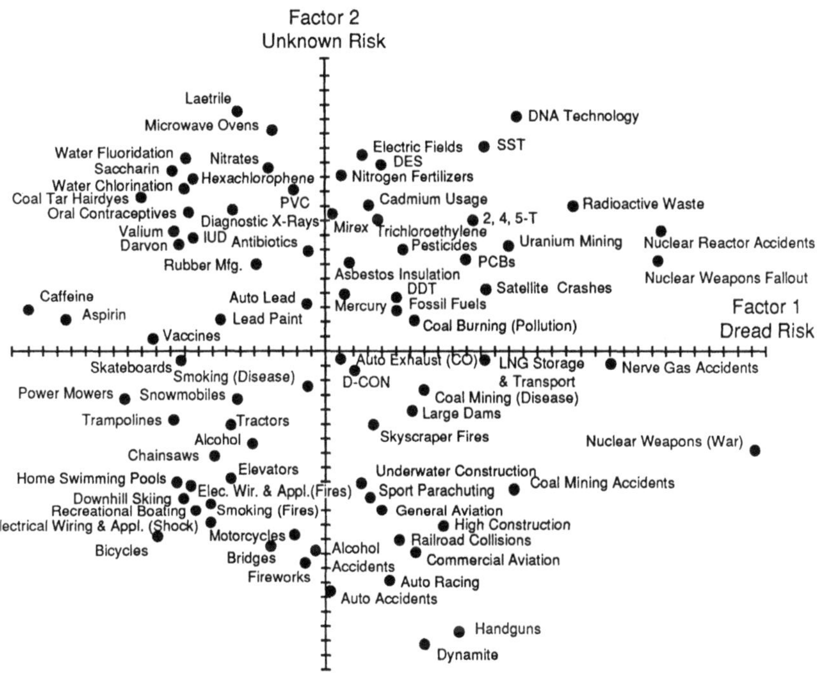


FIGURE 9.2. Location of 81 hazards on Factors 1 and 2 derived from the interrelationships among 15 risk characteristics. Each factor is made up of a combination of characteristics, as indicated by the lower diagram. (From Slovic, 1987. Copyright by the AAAS. Reprinted by permission.)

The representation shown in Figure 9.2, while robust and informative, is by no means a universal cognitive representation of the domain of hazards. Other psychometric methods (such as multidimensional scaling analysis of hazard similarity judgments), applied to quite different sets of hazards, produce different representations (Johnson & Tversky, 1984;

Slovic et al., 1984). The utility of these models for understanding and predicting behavior remains to be determined.

## Perceptions Have Impacts: The Social Amplification of Risk

Perceptions of risk play a key role in a process labeled social amplification of risk (Chapter 10 this book; Kasperson et al., 1988). Social amplification is triggered by the occurrence of an adverse event, which could be a major or minor accident, a discovery of pollution, an incident of sabotage, and so on. Risk amplification reflects the fact that the adverse impacts of such an event sometimes extend far beyond the direct damages to victims and property and may result in massive indirect impacts such as litigation against a company or loss of sales, increased regulation of an industry, and so on. In some cases, all companies within an industry are affected, regardless of which company was responsible for the mishap. Thus, the event can be thought of as a stone dropped in a pond. The ripples spread outward, encompassing first the directly affected victims, then the responsible company or agency, and, in the extreme, reaching other companies, agencies, or industries. Examples of events resulting in extreme higher-order impacts include the chemical manufacturing accident at Bhopal, India, the disastrous launch of the space shuttle Challenger, the nuclear-reactor accidents at Three Mile Island and Chernobyl, the adverse effects of the drug Thalidomide, the Exxon Valdez oil spill, and the adulteration of Tylenol capsules with cyanide. An important feature of social amplification is that the direct impacts need not be too large to trigger major indirect impacts. The seven deaths due to the Tylenol tampering resulted in more than 125,000 stories in the print media alone and inflicted losses of more than one billion dollars upon the Johnson & Johnson Company, due to the damaged image of the product (Mitchell, 1989).

It appears likely that multiple mechanisms contribute to the social amplification of risk. First, extensive media coverage of an event can contribute to heightened perceptions of risk and amplified impacts (Burns et al., 1990). Second, a particular risk or risk event may enter into the agenda of social groups, or what Mazur (1981) terms the partisans, within the community or nation. The attack on the apple growth-regulator "Alar" by the Natural Resources Defense Council demonstrates the important impacts that special-interest groups can trigger (Moore, 1989).

A third mechanism of amplification arises out of the interpretation of unfortunate events as clues or signals regarding the magnitude of the risk and the adequacy of the risk-management process (Burns et al., 1990;

Slovic, 1987). The informativeness or signal potential of a mishap, and thus its potential social impact, appears to be systematically related to the perceived characteristics of the hazard. An accident that takes many lives may produce relatively little social disturbance (beyond that caused to the victims' families and friends) if it occurs as part of a familiar and well-understood system (e.g., a train wreck). However, a small accident in an unfamiliar system (or one perceived as poorly understood), such as a nuclear waste repository or a recombinant DNA laboratory, may have immense social consequences if it is perceived as a harbinger of future and possibly catastrophic mishaps.

The concept of accidents as signals helps explain our society's strong response to mishaps involving nuclear power and nuclear wastes. Because the risks associated with nuclear energy are seen as poorly understood and catastrophic, accidents anywhere in the world may be seen as omens of disaster everywhere there are nuclear reactors and wastes, thus producing responses (e.g., increased regulation, public opposition) that carry large socioeconomic impacts.

### *Stigmatization*

Substantial socioeconomic impacts may also result from the stigma associated with the perception of environmental contamination or risk. The word stigma was used by the ancient Greeks to refer to bodily marks or brands that were designed to signal infamy or disgrace - to show, for example, that the bearer was a slave or a criminal. As used today, the word denotes someone marked as deviant, flawed, limited, spoiled, or generally undesirable in the view of some observer (Goffman, 1963). When the stigmatizing characteristic is observed, the person is denigrated or avoided. Prime targets for stigmatization are members of minority groups, the aged, homosexuals, drug addicts, alcoholics, and persons afflicted with physical deformities or mental disabilities.

Jones et al. (1984) attempted to characterize the key dimensions of social stigma. The six dimensions or factors they proposed were as follows:

1) CONCEALABILITY. Is the condition hidden or obvious? To what extent is its visibility controllable?
2) COURSE. What pattern of change over time is usually shown by the condition? What is its ultimate outcome?
3) DISRUPTIVENESS. Does the condition block or hamper interaction and communication?

4) AESTHETIC QUALITIES. To what extent does the mark make the possessor repellent, ugly, or upsetting?
5) ORIGIN. Under what circumstances did the condition originate? Was anyone responsible for it, and what was he or she trying to do?
6) PERIL. What kind of danger is posed by the mark and how imminent and serious is it?

Dimension 6, peril, is the key link between stigma and perceived risk, but other dimensions may also come into play in the stigmatization associated with hazards. It seems evident that stigmatization can be generalized from persons to products, technologies, and environments. For example, nuclear and chemical waste disposal sites may be perceived as repellent, ugly, and upsetting (Dimension 4) to the extent that they become visible (Dimension 1). Such waste sites may also be perceived as disruptive (Dimension 3). They are certainly perceived as dangerous (Dimension 6).

Stigmatization resulting from pollution by a toxic substance is described by Edelstein (1986), who analyzed a case in which a dairy's cows become contaminated with PCBs for a short period of time. Once this contamination became known (a visible mark) the reputation of the dairy was discredited and its products became undesirable, even though the level of PCBs was never sufficiently high to prohibit sale of those products. Edelstein showed, step by step, how this incident meets the various criteria of stigmatization put forth by Jones et al.

Although Edelstein's case of stigma involved dairy products, only a short leap is required to extend the concept to environments that have been contaminated by toxic substances (Edelstein, 1988). Times Beach, Missouri, and Love Canal, New York, come quickly to mind.

A dramatic example of stigmatization involving radiation occurred in September 1987, in Goiania, Brazil, where two men searching for scrap metal dismantled a cancer therapy device in an abandoned clinic. In doing so, they sawed open a capsule containing 28 grams of cesium chloride. Children and workers nearby were attracted to the glowing material and began playing with it. Before the danger was realized, several hundred people became contaminated and four persons eventually died from acute radiation poisoning. Publicity about the incident led to stigmatization of the region and its residents (Petterson, 1988). Hotels in other parts of the country refused to allow Goiania residents to register; airline pilots refused to fly with Goiania residents on board; automobiles driven by Goianians were stoned; hotel occupancy in the region dropped 60% for six weeks following the incident and virtually all conventions were canceled during this period. The sale prices of clothing and other products manufactured in Goiania dropped by 40% after the first news reports and remained depressed for a period of 30-45 days, despite the fact that none of these items was ever shown to have been contaminated.

## Empirical Studies of Environmental Risk Perception and Stigma

In recent years we have applied the concepts of perceived risk, social amplification of risk, and environmental stigma in an attempt to assess the potential economic impacts of the proposed national repository for disposing of high-level nuclear wastes.

In December 1987, the U.S. Congress amended the Nuclear Waste Policy Act and authorized the Department of Energy to determine whether Yucca Mountain, Nevada, is a geologically sound and technically feasible site for disposal of high-level nuclear waste. If the site passes a set of prescribed technical criteria, a repository will be constructed there to dispose of nuclear waste from the nation's commercial power plants.

Much effort has been, and will continue to be, devoted to characterizing the physical and biological risks associated with construction and operation of this unique facility, which must safely contain a large volume of highly radioactive material for a time period that is twice as long as recorded human history. Socioeconomic risks, though less studied, are also important. The remainder of this chapter describes a study in which my colleagues and I attempted to answer the following question pertaining to social impacts: What is the potential for a high-level nuclear waste repository at Yucca Mountain to have adverse economic effects on the city of Las Vegas and the State of Nevada during the period of constructing and filling the repository (approximately 40-60 years)?

The economic impacts of concern to us included reduction in short-term visits to the city and state by vacationers or conventioneers, effects on long-term residents (moving out of the region, reduced in-migration of retirees), and reduced ability to attract new businesses. Assessment of these impacts is obviously important to citizens and officials of Nevada, who need to know what economic consequences to expect if Yucca Mountain is developed as the repository. Information about possible economic impacts may also be relevant to the final decision itself, regarding the acceptability of the Yucca Mountain site.

Empirical research on this topic faces some major obstacles, however. Changes in scientific knowledge and changes in public opinion are inherently difficult to forecast. For example, both scientific and public views about the risks of nuclear energy have changed dramatically since the "Atoms for Peace" program began in the 1950s. An obstacle to survey research is the fact that people may not really know how the repository will affect their future preferences and decisions or the decisions of their successors. As a result, asking people to project the repository's impacts on vacation decisions to be made many years hence may, in effect, be asking them to "tell more than they can know" (Nisbett & Wilson, 1977). Studies by Baker, Moss, West, and Weyant (1977) and West and Baker (1983) indicate that answers to questions about the impact of nuclear facilities on future behavior may not be trustworthy.

Despite these difficulties, there are theoretical reasons, based upon perception of risk, social amplification processes, and stigmatization, to expect that the repository may produce adverse economic impacts. In our studies we developed a method for assessing impacts that is not dependent on direct questioning of people. We then used this method to assess the potential impacts from a repository at Yucca Mountain.

In order to avoid the problems of relying upon answers to hypothetical questions, our studies employed an indirect strategy, based on the notion of environmental imagery. Studies of environmental imagery appear to have the potential to provide a sound and defensible theoretical framework from which to understand and project possible impacts of a nuclear-waste repository on tourism and other important behaviors. Accordingly, the present studies were designed to demonstrate the concept of environmental imagery and show how it can be measured, assess the relationship between imagery and choice behavior, and describe economic impacts that might occur as a result of altered images and choices.

The concept of imagery is not new to the study of environment and behavior. Geographers, cognitive and environmental psychologists, marketing strategists, and consumer theorists have written at length about the importance of images in our environmental consciousness and our behavior (see, e.g., Boulding, 1956; Kearsley, 1985; McInnis & Price, 1987; Paivio, 1979; Saarinen & Sell, 1980; Weart, 1988). However, to our knowledge, no one has used a design such as ours to link imagery to the behaviors of concern here.

Our research was designed to test the following three propositions: (1) Images associated with environments have diverse positive and negative affective meanings that influence preferences (e.g., in this case, preferences for sites in which to vacation, retire, find a job, or start a new business); (2) A nuclear-waste repository evokes a wide variety of strongly negative images, consistent with extreme perceptions of risk and stigmatization; and (3) The repository at Yucca Mountain and the negative images it evokes will, over time, become increasingly salient in the images of Nevada and of Las Vegas. If these three propositions are true, it seems quite plausible that, as the imagery of Las Vegas and of Nevada becomes increasingly associated with the repository, the attractiveness of these places to tourists, job seekers, retirees, and business developers will decrease and their choices of Las Vegas and Nevada within sets of competing sites will decrease.

Support for these three propositions, therefore, would demonstrate the mechanism whereby the repository could produce adverse affects upon tourism, migration, and business development in Nevada and this demonstration would occur without having to ask people to make introspective judgments about their future behaviors.

### *Survey Design*

In order to test the propositions described above, we first conducted three surveys of imagery and preference. Studies 1 and 2 surveyed representative samples of residents in Phoenix, Arizona. Study 1 elicited images for four cities and asked people to indicate their preferences among these cities as places to vacation, take a new job, or retire. Study 2 did the same for four states. Study 3 surveyed a national sample of business executives, asking for their images of each of four cities and their preferences among these cities as places to open a new business or expand an existing business. All three surveys were conducted by telephone. Each survey had a sample size of about 400 persons.

The survey questions in Studies 1 and 2 were nearly identical. The cities questionnaire asked respondents to provide images for San Diego, Las Vegas, Denver, and Los Angeles. The states questionnaire elicited imagery for California, Nevada, Colorado, and New Mexico. These cities and states, in addition to Las Vegas and Nevada, were chosen for the study because they are important vacation destinations for residents of Phoenix.

The images were elicited using a version of the method of continued associations (Szalay & Deese, 1978), adapted for use in a telephone interview. Image elicitation was always the first task in the survey. In the cities survey, the elicitation interview proceeded as follows:

> My first question involves word association. For example, when I mention the word baseball, you might think of the World Series, Reggie Jackson, summertime, or even hot dogs. Today, I am interested in the first SIX thoughts or images that come to mind when you hear the name of a PLACE. Think about [CITY] for a minute. When you think about [CITY], what is the first thought or image that comes to mind? What is the next thought or image you have when I say [CITY]? Your next

thought or image? What is another thought or image you have about [CITY]?

This continued until six associations were produced or the respondent drew a blank. Then the procedure was repeated for the next city. The order of the cities was rotated across respondents. The procedure was identical for the states and business location surveys.

Following the elicitation of images, respondents were asked to rate each image they gave on a scale ranging from very positive (+2), somewhat positive (+1), neutral (0), somewhat negative (-1), or very negative (-2).

Respondents in Studies 1 and 2 were then asked to rank the cities/states according to their preference for a vacation site (long weekend vacation for cities; week or longer vacation for states). Subsequent questions asked for a preference ranking among these cities or states as retirement sites or places to move to assuming equally attractive job offers in each place, much in the same manner as vacation preferences were elicited. Next, up to six images were elicited to the stimulus "underground nuclear waste storage facility" and the stimulus "nuclear test site."

The survey also asked "In which state has the federal government proposed to build an underground facility for storing radioactive wastes?" and "In which state is the nuclear test site located?"

The survey of corporate decision makers first elicited images for each of four cities - Phoenix, Las Vegas, Denver, and Albuquerque - and then asked the respondents to evaluate these images on the -2 to +2 rating scale, as in the other surveys. Respondents were then asked to rank the cities in order of preference as a location for opening or expanding a business, assuming that market conditions and cost conditions were about equal.

### *Results: Cities Survey*

***Images.*** In response to "Las Vegas," images associated with gambling, casinos, hotels, bright lights and entertainment were dominant, followed by imagery pertaining to the climate and physical landscape, money, crime, and immorality. Imagery related to nuclear waste and the nuclear test site was very infrequent (only 2 images out of more than 1500 responses). Table 9.2 presents the hierarchy of images elicited by the phrase "underground nuclear waste storage facility." This imagery was overwhelmingly negative. The most frequent associations by far were dangerousness and death and their synonyms, followed by pollution, negative concepts, and radiation. Although we did not ask people to score these images, it seems likely that most of them would have been judged "very negative," a -2 on our five-point scale. Although some images pertaining to "necessity" came at the 17th position, they were very few in number (17) and included the phrase "necessary evil" given by two respondents. The words "Nevada" and "Las Vegas" were weakly associated with the repository, which was not surprising, given the low level of awareness of where the site is proposed to be located. Images of the nuclear test site were similarly negative and exhibited considerable overlap in content with the images of a nuclear-waste storage facility. Major test-site images included radiation, death, danger, cancer, destruction, and Nevada. More people associated Nevada with the test site (82 mentions) than with the repository.

TABLE 9.2

*Hierarchy of images associated with an "underground nuclear waste storage facility."*

| | Category | Frequency | Images Included in Category |
|---|---|---|---|
| 1. | Dangerous | 179 | dangerous, danger, hazardous, toxic, unsafe, harmful, disaster |
| 2. | Death | 107 | death, sickness, dying, destruction |
| 3. | Negative | 99 | negative, wrong, bad, unpleasant, terrible, gross, undesirable, awful, dislike, ugly, horrible |
| 4. | Pollution | 97 | pollution, contamination, leakage, spills, Love Canal |
| 5. | War | 62 | war, bombs, nuclear war, holocaust |
| 6. | Radiation | 59 | radiation, nuclear, radioactive, glowing |
| 7. | Scary | 55 | scary, frightening, concern, worried, fear, horror |
| 8. | Somewhere Else | 49 | wouldn't want to live near one, not where I live, far away as possible |
| 9. | Unnecessary | 44 | unnecessary, bad idea, waste of land |
| 10. | Problems | 39 | problems, trouble |
| 11. | Desert | 37 | desert, barren, desolate |
| 12. | Non-Nevada Locations | 35 | Utah, Arizona, Denver |
| 13. | Storage Location | 32 | caverns, underground salt mine |
| 14. | Government/Industry | 23 | government, politics, big business |

From Slovic et al., 1991. Copyright by Plenum. Reprinted by permission.

***Predicting preferences from images.*** To predict preferences among cities from images, we developed a scoring rule, the summation model, which simply sums the ratings for all the images a respondent produced for each city. A person's preferences among cities are hypothesized to be predictable from these sums. An example, illustrating the application of the summation model to the data of one respondent, is given in Table 9.3. For this respondent, the rank order of summation scores exactly matched the preference order for vacation sites.

TABLE 9.3

*Images, ratings, and summation scores for respondent 132.*

| City | Image No. | Image Rating | |
|---|---|---|---|
| SAN DIEGO | 1 | 2 | very nice |
| SAN DIEGO | 2 | 2 | good beaches |
| SAN DIEGO | 3 | 2 | zoo |
| SAN DIEGO | 4 | 1 | busy freeway |
| SAN DIEGO | 5 | 1 | easy to find way |
| SAN DIEGO | 6 | 2 | pretty town |
| | | Sum = 10 | |
| LAS VEGAS | 1 | -2 | rowdy town |
| LAS VEGAS | 2 | -1 | busy town |
| LAS VEGAS | 3 | -1 | casinos |
| LAS VEGAS | 4 | -1 | bright lights |
| LAS VEGAS | 5 | -2 | too much gambling |
| LAS VEGAS | 6 | 0 | out of the way |
| | | Sum = -7 | |
| DENVER | 1 | 2 | high |
| DENVER | 2 | 0 | crowded |
| DENVER | 3 | 2 | cool |
| DENVER | 4 | 1 | pretty |
| DENVER | 5 | -2 | busy airport |
| DENVER | 6 | -2 | busy streets |
| | | Sum = 1 | |
| LOS ANGELES | 1 | -2 | smoggy |
| LOS ANGELES | 2 | -2 | crowded |
| LOS ANGELES | 3 | -2 | dirty |
| LOS ANGELES | 4 | -1 | foggy |
| LOS ANGELES | 5 | 0 | sunny |
| LOS ANGELES | 6 | -2 | drug place |
| | | Sum = -9 | |

Note: Based on these summation scores, this person's predicted preference order for a vacation site would be: San Diego, Las Vegas, Denver, and Los Angeles.

When ranks generated by the summation model were compared to the actual ranks generated by the respondents when they stated their preferences, the model did quite well, correctly predicting 55% of the number 1 ranked vacation cities and 56% of the fourth ranked cities, with somewhat less accuracy in predicting intermediate ranks (if the model lacked predictive validity, we would expect a 25% hit rate by chance). The exact rank order of four cities generated by the summation model matched the exact rank order of the respondent 26.4% of the time (perfect matching of ranks would be expected by chance only 4.2% of the time).

A second set of tests was conducted with the summation model. Each of the four cities was paired with every other cities - making six pairs in all. For every respondent and every pair, the image score for city B was subtracted from the image score of city A. The resulting 2,346 A-B scores across all respondents were ordered from extreme negative to extreme positive and this distribution was partitioned into five subsets, as equal in size as possible (419 to 511 comparisons in each subset). Finally, within each subset, the percentage of respondents who ranked city A more favorably than city B as a vacation site was calculated. For the pairs where the mean A-B difference was most negative (mean = -6.2), A was preferred as a vacation site for only 27.4%. For those in which the mean difference was most in favor of A (mean = +11.4), 90.7% of the preferences favored A. Figure 9.3 illustrates the performance of the summation model across all pairs of cities. The choice proportions for specific pairs of cities (e.g., Las Vegas vs. Denver) were found to be quite similar to the combined plot. The data show that imagery and preference for vacation cities are strongly related. If city B has a more positive set of images than city A (as indicated by simply summing the affect ratings across images produced for each city), then city B is more likely to be preferred as a vacation site. If city A has more positive imagery, then city A is more likely to be preferred as a vacation site.

Predicting job and retirement preferences. The summation model was applied in similar fashion to the prediction of job preferences and retirement preferences for the cities survey. The hit rates were similar to those reported earlier for vacation preferences and the functional relationships relating job and retirement preferences to image scores were almost identical to the relationship shown in Figure 9.3.

### *Results: States Survey*

As in the cities survey, more people (41.0%) knew the location of the nuclear weapons test site than knew the location being considered for the repository (24.5%). The summation model was found to be about as accurate in predicting vacation, job, and retirement preferences among states as it was for predicting preferences among cities.

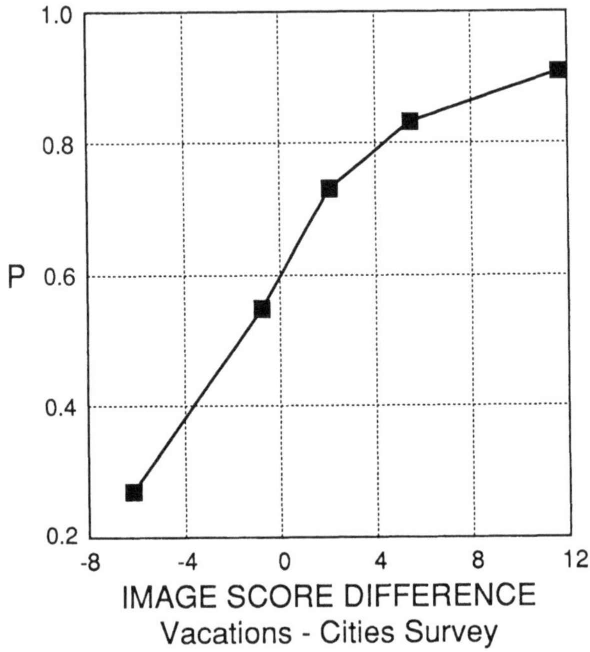


FIGURE 9.3. Proportion of times (P) City A was ranked higher than City B in the respondent's preference rankings for vacation sites as a function of mean image score differences (City A-City B). From Slovic et al., 1991. Copyright by Plenum. Reprinted by permission.

Imagery associated with "a nuclear waste storage facility" and the "nuclear test site" was extremely negative for respondents in the states survey and was almost identical to the imagery obtained in the cities survey. Whereas few people in the cities survey expressed nuclear-related imagery in response to Las Vegas, about 10% of respondents in the states survey produced nuclear imagery in response to Nevada. Such images included the terms nuclear testing, nuclear bomb, nukes, explosions, and radiation. The mean image score for Nevada for these persons was 0.18. The mean image score for persons who did not associate Nevada with things nuclear was 2.56 (a statistically significant difference; $p < .001$). As expected, persons with nuclear imagery assigned lower (poorer) preference rankings to Nevada than did persons without such images (see

Table 9.4). These findings are important because they suggest that Nevada has already undergone some stigmatization as a nuclear place.

TABLE 9.4
*Preference for Nevada as a vacation site among respondents who do and do not exhibit nuclear imagery.*

| | Nevada Preference Rank | | | | |
|---|---|---|---|---|---|
| | 1 | 2 | 3 | 4 | Mean Rank |
| Nuclear Imagery Present (N = 39) | 3 | 3 | 46 | 49 | 3.41 |
| Nuclear Imagery Absent (N = 354) | 6 | 16 | 51 | 27 | 2.98 |

Note: Cell entries are percentages within each row.

From Slovic et al., 1991.

### *Results: Corporate Decision Makers Survey*

Parallel analyses were carried out with the images and preferences of the corporate decision makers. The summation model correctly predicted 47% of the first-choice locations for siting a new business and the functional relationship between image scores and preferences for pairs of cities looked much like the relationship for vacation preferences in Figure 9.3.

In summary, three separate surveys totaling more than 1200 respondents demonstrated that a simple summation model applied to sets of images did a good job of predicting expressed preferences for cities and states in which to vacation, take a new job, retire, or site a business. The slopes of the best-fitting lines relating preferences among pairs of cities/states to differences in image values were quite steep, indicating that a change in one or two images could imply a substantial shift in preference probability.

## Effects of Repository Knowledge and Test-Site Knowledge

Additional analyses were conducted using the states survey data to determine the impact of knowledge about the state being considered for the nuclear waste repository and knowledge about the state in which the nuclear-test site is located upon images and preferences for Nevada as a vacation site. These two types of knowledge were found to be related. Persons who knew that the repository was being considered for Nevada were somewhat more likely to know that the test site is in Nevada (71%) as compared to those who lacked knowledge of the repository (55%). Similar results were obtained in the cities survey, where the corresponding values were 70% and 41%.

Additional analyses showed that the presence of a nuclear image in one's image set for Nevada was determined more by knowledge of the test-site location than by knowledge of the repository location. Nuclear imagery was produced by 15% of those persons who knew the test-site location compared to 2% of those who did not know the location. Corresponding figures associated with knowledge and lack of knowledge of the proposed repository were 12% and 9%.

Summarizing the results from these analyses, we see that the proposed Yucca Mountain repository has not yet infiltrated people's images of Nevada and has not yet had much effect on their stated vacation preferences. The test site, which has been a feature of Nevada for many years, has had a stronger influence on images and preferences. Knowledge that the weapons test site is in Nevada appears to have led to an increase in nuclear-related imagery for Nevada and nuclear imagery is associated with decreased preference for Nevada as a vacation site.

### *Imagery and Vacation Behavior*

The previous analyses demonstrated that images could predict expressed preferences for vacation sites. Can image scores also predict actual vacation trips? To address this question we attempted to resurvey the 802 respondents from our 1988 Phoenix surveys some 16-18 months later (October - December 1989). We were successful in re-interviewing about 130 persons in each of the two samples (cities survey and states survey) studied earlier. Again, we elicited word associations to each of the same four cities or four states and asked for positive/negative ratings of each image produced. In addition, we asked the respondents to indicate in which of these cities (or states) they had vacationed since the previous survey was conducted.

The predictive capability of the word-association image scores was tested by means of logistic regression analysis using a person's 1988 image score for a state or city to estimate the probability that that person would vacation in a place during the subsequent 16-18 months (until the date of the repeat survey). The estimated probabilities for both cities and states are presented in Figures 9.4 and 9.5. These data show that the affective qualities of a person's images of a place were clearly related to the probability that the person would subsequently vacation there, with the relationship being stronger for states than for cities.

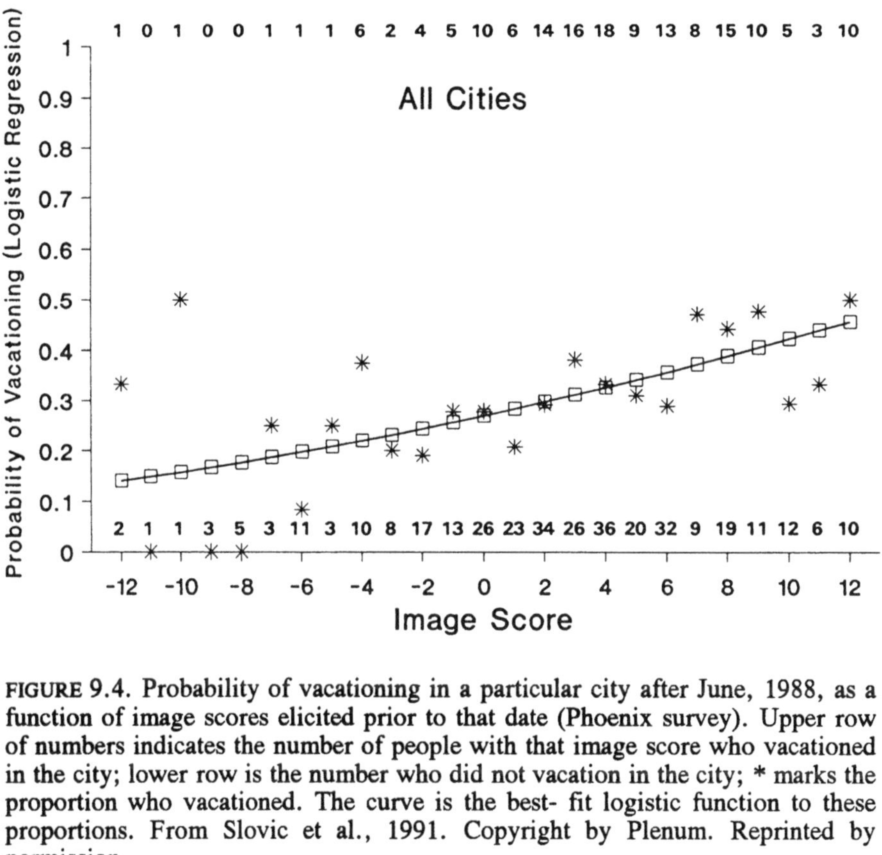


FIGURE 9.4. Probability of vacationing in a particular city after June, 1988, as a function of image scores elicited prior to that date (Phoenix survey). Upper row of numbers indicates the number of people with that image score who vacationed in the city; lower row is the number who did not vacation in the city; * marks the proportion who vacationed. The curve is the best- fit logistic function to these proportions. From Slovic et al., 1991. Copyright by Plenum. Reprinted by permission.

### *Discussion*

The results supported the three propositions that the study aimed to test: Images of cities and states, derived from a word-association technique, exhibited positive and negative affective meanings that were highly predictive of preferences for vacation sites, job and retirement locations, and business sites (Proposition 1). The concept of a nuclear-waste storage facility evoked extreme negative imagery (Proposition 2). The nuclear-weapons test site, which has been around far longer than the Yucca Mountain nuclear-waste project, has led to a modest amount of nuclear imagery becoming associated with the state of Nevada. This provides indirect evidence for Proposition 3, which asserts that nuclear-waste related images will also become associated with Nevada and Las Vegas if the Yucca Mountain Project proceeds. Nuclear imagery, when present in a person's associative responses, was found to be linked with much lower preference for Nevada as a vacation site. The verification of these propositions implies that the repository also has the potential to cause an increase in nuclear imagery which, in turn, will produce adverse impacts on tourism and other economically important activities in Nevada.

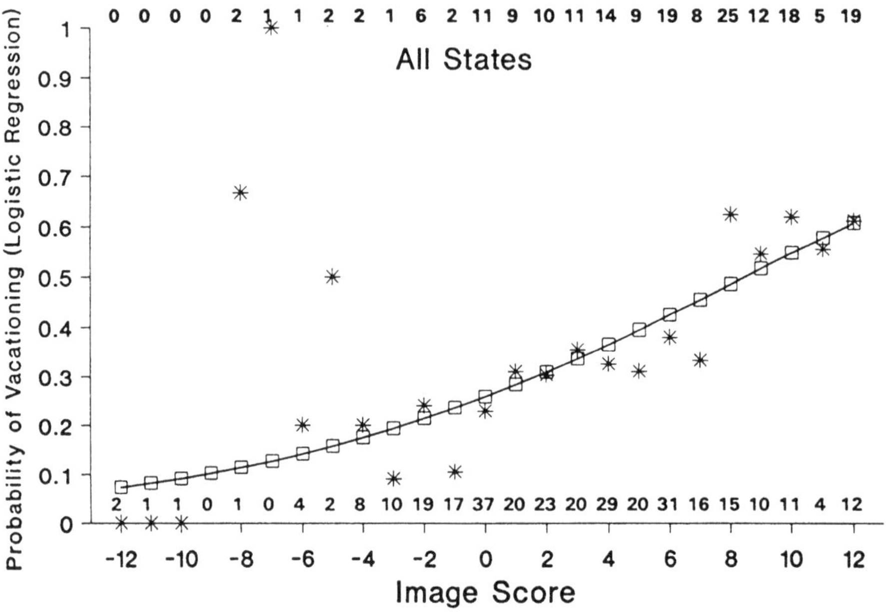


FIGURE 9.5. Probability of vacationing in a particular state after June, 1988 as a function of image scores elicited prior to that date (Phoenix survey). Upper row of numbers indicates the number of people with that image score who vacationed in the state; lower row is the number who did not vacation in the state; * marks the proportion who vacationed. The curve is the best-fit logistic function to these proportions. From Slovic et al., 1991. Copyright by Plenum. Reprinted by permission.

These findings provide a partial answer to the question that motivated the inquiry. The mechanisms of perceived risk, social amplification, and stigma are observable in the record of past experience with nuclear and other types of hazards. In the context of the Yucca Mountain Repository, these mechanisms appear to have the potential to cause substantial losses to each of the various economic sectors at risk. It would be unwise and unfair for development of the nation's high-level nuclear waste repository to proceed without taking these potential economic impacts into consideration.

Although this research has clarified the mechanisms by which adverse economic impacts can be generated, predicting the precise magnitude and duration of those impacts is impossible. The uncertainties involved in repository development make it inevitable that the actual impacts - physical, biological, social, and economic - will differ from the best of impact projections.

In sum, this analysis indicates that the development of the Yucca Mountain Repository will, in effect, force Nevadans to gamble with their future economy. The nature of that gamble cannot be specified precisely, but it appears to include credible possibilities (with unknown probabilities) of substantial losses to the visitor economy, the migrant economy, and the business economy. Because of the uncertainty inherent in projecting these impacts, reasonable people may differ greatly in their estimates. Actions may or may not appear warranted, based upon assessment of these special impacts. But the important implication of this study is that the possibility of such impacts cannot be ignored.

## Broader Implications

The research described in this chapter has implications for social-impact analysis that transcend the conflicts and concerns surrounding the proposed Yucca Mountain repository. The processes of social amplification and stigma appear relevant also to the analysis of impacts from any major facility that produces, uses, transports, or disposes of hazardous materials. The numerous proposed sites for disposal of low-level radioactive wastes and the many sites being considered for chemical-waste incinerators and landfills will face similar problems of perceived risk and its impacts, though probably to a lesser degree than the problems posed for Nevadans by a Yucca Mountain Repository. The study of socioeconomic impacts at Yucca Mountain has demonstrated that the so-called "standard effects" of large engineering projects on local employment, housing, and transportation have the potential to be dwarfed by the "special effects" of risk perception and stigma. However, just as physical or technical risks can be mitigated by proper safety design and management, effects of perceived risk may be mitigated by means of management processes that instill and maintain trust and that work to protect the economic base of those individuals and communities whom the project puts at risk.

## References

Baker, E. J., Moss, D. J., West, S. G., & Weyant, J. K. (1977). *Impact of offshore nuclear generating stations on recreational behavior at adjacent coastal sites* [NUREG-0394]. Washington, DC: U.S. Nuclear Regulatory Commission.

Boulding, K. E. (1956). *The image.* Ann Arbor, MI: University of Michigan.

Burns, W., Kasperson, R., Kasperson, J., Renn, O., Emani, S., & Slovic, P. (1990). *Social amplification of risk: An empirical study* (Technical report). Eugene, OR: Decision Research.

Burton, I., Kates, R. W., & White, G. F. (1978). *The environment as hazard.* Oxford: Oxford University Press.

Douglas, M. (1966). *Purity and danger: An analysis of concepts of pollution and taboo.* London: Routledge.

Douglas, M., & Wildavsky, A. (1982). *Risk and culture.* Berkeley: University of California Press.

Easterling, D., & Kunreuther, H. (1990). *The vulnerability of the convention industry to the siting of a high-level nuclear waste repository.* Unpublished manuscript, University of Pennsylvania, Wharton Risk and Decision Processes Center.

Edelstein, M. (1986). *Stigmatizing effects of toxic pollution* Unpublished manuscript, Ramapo College, Department of Psychology.

Edelstein, M. (1988). *Contaminated communities: The social and psychological impacts of residential toxic exposure.* Boulder, CO: Westview.

Edwards, W. (1961). Behavioral decision theory. *Annual Review of Psychology, 12,* 473-498.

Fischoff, B., Slovic, P., Lichtenstein, S., Read, S., & Combs, B. (1978). How safe is safe enough? A psychometric study of attitudes towards technological risks and benefits. *Policy Sciences, 9,* 127-152.

Freud, S. (1924). *Collected papers.* London: Hogarth.

Freudenberg, W. R. (1988). Perceived risk, real risk: Social science and the art of probabilistic risk assessment. *Science, 242,* 44-49.

Goffman, E. (1963). *Stigma.* Englewood Cliffs, NJ: Prentice-Hall.

Harris, L. (1980). *Risk in a complex society* [Public opinion poll]. New York: Marsh and McClennan.

Henrion, M., & Fischoff, B. (1986). Uncertainty assessment in the estimation of physical constants. *American Journal of Physics, 54*, 791-798.

Johnson, E. J., & Tversky, A. (1984). Representations of perceptions of risks. *Journal of Experimental Psychology: General, 113*, 55-70.

Jones, E. E., et al. (1984). *Social stigma: The psychology of marked relationships.* New York: Freeman.

Kahneman, D., Slovic, P., & Tversky, A. (Eds.). (1982). *Judgment under uncertainty: Heuristics and biases.* New York: Cambridge University Press.

Kasperson, R. E., Renn, O., Slovic, P., Brown, H. S., Emel, J., Goble, R., Kasperson, J. X., & Ratick, S. (1988). The social amplification of risk: A conceptual framework. *Risk Analysis, 8*, 177-187.

Kearsley, G. W. (1985). Methodological change and the elicitation of images in human geography. *Journal of Mental Imagery, 9*, 71-82.

Mazur, A. (1981). *The dynamics of technical controversy.* Washington, DC: Communications Press.

McInnis, D. J., & Price, L. L. (1987). The role of imagery in information processing: Review and extensions. *Journal of Consumer Research, 13*, 473-491.

Mitchell, M. L. (1989). The impact of external parties on brand-name capital: The 1982 Tylenol poisonings and subsequent cases. *Economic Inquiry, 27*, 601-618.

Moore, J. A. (1989, May-June). Speaking of data: The Alar controversy. *EPA Journal*, pp. 5- 9.

Nisbett, R., & Ross, L. (1980). *Human inference: Strategies and shortcomings of social judgment.* Englewood Cliffs, NJ: Prentice-Hall.

Nisbett, R., & Wilson, T. D. (1977). Telling more than we can know: Verbal reports on mental processes. *Psychological Review, 84*, 231-259.

Paivio, A. (1979). *Imagery and verbal processes.* Hillsdale, NJ: Erlbaum.

Petterson, J. S. (1988). Perception vs. reality of radiological impact: The Goiania model. *Nuclear News, 31(14)*, 84-90.

Ricci, P. F., Sagan, L. A., & Whipple, C. G. (1984). *Technological risk assessment.* The Hague: Nijhoff.

Saarinen, T. F., & Sell, J. L. (1980). Environmental perception. *Progress in Human Geography, 4*, 525-548.

Short, J. F., Jr. (1984). The social fabric at risk: Toward the social transformation of risk analysis. *American Sociologist Review, 49*, 711-725.

Slovic, P. (1987). Perception of risk. *Science, 236*, 280-285.

Slovic, P., Fischoff, B., & Lichtenstein, S. (1979). Rating the risks. *Environment, 21(3)*, 14-20, 36-39.

Slovic, P., Fischoff, B., & Lichtenstein, S. (1980). Facts and fears: Understanding perceived risk. In R. Schwing & W. A. Albers, Jr. (Eds.), *Societal risk assessment: How safe is safe enough?* (pp. 181-214). New York: Plenum.

Slovic, P., Fischoff, B., & Lichtenstein, S. (1984). Behavioral decision theory perspectives on risk and safety. *Acta Psychologica, 56*, 183-203.

Slovic, P., Layman, M., Kraus, N., Flynn, J., Chalmers, J., & Gesell, G. (1991). Perceived risk, stigma, and potential economic impacts of a high-level nuclear waste repository in Nevada. *Risk Analysis, 11*, 683-696.

Starr, C. (1969). Social benefit versus technological risk. *Science, 165*, 1232-1238.

Szalay, L. B., & Deese, J. (1978). *Subjective meaning and culture: An assessment through word associations.* Hillsdale, NJ: Erlbaum.

Tversky, A., & Kahneman, D. (1981). The framing of decisions and the psychology of choice. *Science, 211*, 453-458.

Weart, S. A. (1988). *Nuclear fear: A history of images.* Cambridge: Harvard University Press.

West, S. G., & Baker, E. J. (1983). Public reaction to nuclear power: The case of offshore nuclear power plants. In R. F. Kidd & J. M. Saks (Eds.), *Advances in applied social psychology* (Vol. 2, pp. 101-129). Hillsdale, NJ: Erlbaum.

Wundt, W. (1883). Über psychologische Methoden. *Philosophische Studien, 1*, 1-38.

*Behavior and Environment: Psychological and Geographical Approaches*
*T. Gärling and R.G. Golledge (Editors)*



## CHAPTER 10

# The Geography of Everyday Life

**Susan Hanson and Perry Hanson**

> Names and locations - social connections - formed the fabric of Martha's diary (Ulrich, 1990, p. 91).

Long before the advent of social scientists or transportation planners, Martha Ballard (1735-1812) kept a diary of her daily activities near what is now Augusta, Maine. Every day for 27 years Martha recorded the details of her life as a midwife, a mother of nine and grandmother of dozens, the wife of a surveyor, a gardener, trader, and neighbor. Ulrich (1990) has ingeniously restored Martha Ballard to life for 20th century readers by drawing threads from Martha's diaries to weave a rich tapestry depicting everyday life in late 18th and early 19th century northern New England. Ulrich notes in her introduction that the existence of Martha Ballard's diaries had been known for more than a century but that they had been dismissed as dealing with no more than domestic trivia. As if in defiance of that view, Ulrich's book vividly demonstrates how any understanding of the political or economic history of the time requires a firm grasp on the largely unseen and unrecorded everyday lives of women and men. She mines the richness of one woman's diary to illuminate, *inter alia*, changing medical practices, relationships between women and men, and what we now call time budgets and travel activity patterns.

## What Are Activity Patterns?

Martha Ballard lived 200 years ago in a rural environment and had no social scientist to guide her diary keeping. Yet she faithfully recorded all the aspects of daily life that are usually included in the late 20th century studies of urban activity patterns. Growing out of a dissatisfaction with transportation studies that provided very little real insight about people's everyday lives or about people's everyday decision making, studies of urban activity patterns emerged in the 1960s and 1970s.

Activity patterns studied differed from the transportation studies that preceded them by emphasizing activities rather than travel, by being sensitive to the interconnectedness of various activities (both for one person and for members of a household), and by stressing the role of constraints on people's behavior. Usually based on carefully structured records of behavior for one day for a large sample of people, studies of urban activity patterns are studies of what people do, where they do it, and when they do it. Often researchers also attempt to answer at some level the question of why they do it.

Just as "names and locations" formed the fabric of Martha's diary, locations and the activities done there form the basis of contemporary travel-activity diaries. Unlike Martha's diary, which frequently mentions doings within the household (quilting, bread-making, spinning), modern activity diaries do not usually include details of activities that take place at home. What an activity study does provide is a fine picture of the everyday life lived outside of the home in a particular city at a particular time; and as the site of more and more traditionally domestic activities (cooking, childcare, laundry, entertainment, work) has moved away from the home, activity studies have come to describe a fuller portion of people's lives. In fact, in grappling with how to define and describe the contemporary city, Fishman (1990) has suggested that activity patterns might be seen as defining what the city actually is for each person or household; that is, each household concocts its own city in the set of places incorporated into its activity pattern.

Three universal principles underlie daily activity patterns: (1) everyone - rich and poor, men and women, young and old - has 24 hours in a day; (2) no one can be in more than one place at a time; and (3) no one can move instantaneously from one place to another. People are bound by time and space. Hägerstrand (1970) and his colleagues (e.g., Carlstein, Parkes, & Thrift 1978; Lenntorp, 1976) proposed the concept of a space-time prism to illustrate graphically the impact of these constraints on people's daily lives (Figure 10.1). The height of the prism, indicating the time-dimension, is always the 24 hours in a day, but its width, representing the spatial reach of the individual's activities, varies with the transportation modes used and the amount of time spent *in situ* as opposed to travelling between places.

How and where will people spend their 24 hours? Why might geographers and other social scientists care about how and where people spend their time? These are some of the questions we shall tackle in this chapter. In the following section we provide a rationale for studying activity patterns by outlining several reasons for the scientific interest in them. Next, we describe how social scientists have gone about studying activity patterns and sketch out the complexities involved in such empirical work. We then review geographers' explanations for observed patterns and assess what activity studies have learned. Finally, we sketch out some needs for future research.

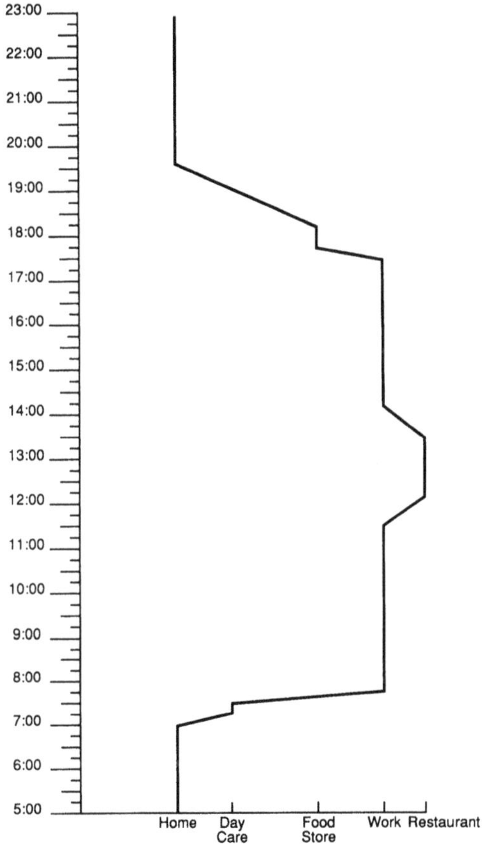


FIGURE 10.1. Hypothetical daily space-time path. In this example the person leaves home at 7 o'clock, drives to the day care center, where she drops off her child and then continues on to work, arriving at work at about 7:40. From 11:30 to 12:00 she walks to a restaurant where she has lunch and then returns to work. At the end of her work day she drives to a food store, stops there briefly to pick up a few items before returning home, her husband having retrieved the child from day care. Note that the slope of the line indicates speed of travel. Rotating this space-time path around the home axis creates the individual's space-time prism.

## Why Study Activity Patterns?

The motivation for studies of travel/activity patterns has ranged from a desire to improve predictions of travel demand to a yen for a better understanding of the complex relationships between people and the urban environment. One of the pioneers of contemporary activity pattern studies, urban planner Chapin (1974) saw studies of households' activities as providing a window on urban life, revealing how people actually made use of the city, and thereby shedding light on the quality of life enjoyed or endured by different groups of urban residents. He thought such studies would be particularly valuable for urban planners as they sought, through intervening in the built environment, to improve the quality of life.

Among the motivations drawing geographers to studies of travel behavior and activity patterns in the late 1950s and 1960s was the desire to understand the processes giving rise to urban spatial structure and to discover universal laws of human spatial behavior (Marble, 1959; Rushton, 1969). This search for universal truths about behavior, transcending particular spatial environments, was part of the then-prevailing paradigm that saw geography as a spatial science. It now seems clear that the real contribution of activity studies lies not so much in making universal pronouncements (these have not yet successfully been made) but rather in small-scale qualitative as well as quantitative inquiries into human behavior in specific spatial contexts. While the desire to generalize has not been abandoned, the difficulties of transferring findings from one spatial context to another, particularly in a policy setting, are acknowledged.

The transportation analysts who became involved in activity-based approaches in the 1970s initially did so in the quest for improved predictive travel-demand models for transportation planning. For a variety of reasons, however, activity analysis has not been widely adopted in travel forecasting and policy analysis (Hartgen, 1988; Kitamura, 1988a; Mahmassani, 1988). Instead, such analysts now see an alternative benefit of activity studies: "there is a general agreement that the activity-based approach has enriched our understanding of travel behavior" (Pas, 1988, p. 8).

How has activity analysis enriched our understanding of travel behavior and, more generally, of everyday urban life? What kinds of questions can it help answer that other approaches cannot? What promise do activity studies hold for the future? We outline here a number of reasons for pursuing the study of activity patterns, reasons that have motivated studies in the past and reasons that have yet to generate empirical work.

Just as Ulrich's (1990) main motivation for analyzing Martha Ballard's diaries was to gain insight into the everyday life of a particular time and place, so too perhaps the main motivation for studying urban activity patterns in the 20th century has been to understand daily life. And just as historian Ulrich used the specifics of that one diary to draw out many general points about life in northern New England at that time, so too do social scientists use activity studies to draw attention to general aspects of life in contemporary cities. The diary data on which such studies are based are unusually rich in that, again like Martha Ballard's diaries, they can serve to generate and to help answer a wide array of questions, many of them posed only long after the data have been collected.

One of the main reasons, then, for undertaking activity studies is that they enable scholars and practitioners such as urban planners to address a wide range of questions about daily life in cities. Moreover, activity studies often stimulate additional questions. These questions are seemingly quite simple and straightforward: How and where do people spend their time? Put another way, what is the nature, the spatial extent, and the diversity of people's activity patterns? How are the activity patterns of particular social groups (women, men, the elderly, teenagers, Latinos, African-Americans) different from each other? What are the reasons for and implications of these differences? Answering questions like these sheds light on the diversity of urban experience and can help identify the likely impacts of changes in service provision on the daily lives of different kinds of people (Hanson, 1977). Activity studies might also stimulate practitioners to consider how the service needs of certain groups of people are not being met with planning approaches that are deaf to activity patterns.

A second motivation for studies of activity patterns has been to gain insights into the relation between people's behavior and the urban environment, particularly, how behavior shifts with changes in the travel environment. The focus here is precisely on the interactions between behavior and local context. In contrast to the earlier quest for universals, therefore, most recent studies place great importance on the particulars of local conditions. Difficulties in accurately predicting behavioral change in the wake of an environmental change (e.g., reducing the headways on a bus line, adding a diamond lane to a highway, increasing parking costs in a particular town) led to an interest in learning more about how individuals and households make activity-related decisions, and, in particular, how such decisions are related to specific aspects of the local travel environment. The Household Activity Travel Simulator (HATS) developed by travel researchers at Oxford University in the mid-1970s, aimed explicitly at just this. The HATS technique has been used with small samples of households to explore people's possible reactions to various changes in the external environment such as a change in school hours or the termination of bus service (Jones, 1979). The researchers have been able to show how a seemingly simple and innocent change such as a shift in school hours entails complex behavior changes for all the adults as well as the children in a household.

We all know that people do not stay put in one place all day, and yet our understanding of a wide variety of urban problems is based in analyses that essentially assume just that: that the spatial distribution of residences represents the spatial distribution of the population. For example, studies of people's exposure to air pollution (Greenland & Yorty, 1985) or to other environmental hazards (Cutter & Tiefenbacher, 1991) assume that a night-time population distribution, when everyone is at home, holds around the clock. Similarly, studies of how much members of one racial group are exposed to people from another racial group (Farley, 1984) are based on census data describing the racial characteristics of the residential populations of census tracts. Schwab (1988) has illustrated how incorporating daily travel/activity patterns into analysis of air pollution exposure can alter our picture of exposure considerably, and Mahmassani (1988) has argued that activity analysis, with its focus on the spatial and temporal nature of people's activities, could contribute a great deal to the analysis of service provision, such as the demand for water within cities. A third reason for activity analysis is, then, that by incorporating people's daily movements outside of home, activity studies lead to more accurate assessments of exposure to or interactions with various aspects of the physical and social environment.

One of the initial motivations for studies of activity patterns in geography was as a way to measure Hägerstrand's concept of the mean information field and understand better the social and spatial context of information diffusion (Hägerstrand, 1967). Marble, Pitts, and Hanson (1972), for example, used activity data from rural Korea to examine the spatial pattern of social interactions. Recently, geographers have renewed this interest in the spatial context of information exchange, particularly in the arena of employment (Hanson & Pratt, 1991), housing, and child care (Gilbert, 1991). The framework of activity studies offers enormous potential for understanding how information flows through personal contacts, most of which are at once both mobile and rooted in space.

Finally, studies of travel/activity patterns and some of the approaches developed for studying activity patterns hold potential for increasing our understanding of the likely impacts of advances in telecommunications. With highway congestion growing daily more acute, transportation planners and policy makers, in particular, need a fuller understanding of the relationship between transportation and communication: under what conditions can or will telecommunications be substituted for travel? If one type of travel (the journey to work) is eliminated through telecommunications (in this case telecommuting), will people simply expand their participation in other out-of-home activities? How are telecommunications likely to affect travel? As Salomon (1986) has shown, research on these questions can yield counterintuitive results. Carefully designed studies of activity patterns (like the State of California study described in Kitamura, Pendyala, & Konstadinos, 1991) are the most likely to provide worthwhile insights on questions surrounding the trade-offs between travel and communication.

In sum, the reasons for studying activity patterns are rooted in, but not limited to, the practical concerns of planning urban environments. Through studies of activity patterns, scholars and practitioners have indeed gained an understanding of everyday life in cities. As we have suggested, this understanding, though perhaps not used in predictive models, is needed for tackling many different kinds of policy-related problems and pragmatic issues. Because public policy decisions (e.g., the provision or alteration of transportation facilities, suburbanization) affect activity patterns, an understanding of these patterns should inform such decisions. In view of these reasons for undertaking studies of activity patterns, we turn now to the question of how to undertake such studies.

## How to Study Activity Patterns: Methodological Concerns

Imagine that a video camera follows you incessantly (tape rolling) for a day, a week, a month, a year, or several years. This video record might approximate a complete picture of your activity pattern. Now imagine that a still camera follows you incessantly, taking snapshots at regular or random intervals, recording in each snapshot, the time, place, activity, and so on. How much is lost between the video and the snapshot? *A Midwife's Tale* is based on the record of one person's daily behavior over 27 years. Certainly it is a partial, if in one sense continuous, record. Martha's entries for most days were only a few lines long. Contemporary social scientists seek to obtain pictures of everyday life by collecting selected information about the daily activities of a much larger sample of people over a much shorter span of time.

Describing people's daily activity patterns may seem like a straightforward - even trivial - exercise. But our descriptions, explanations, and understandings of activity patterns depend on how we choose to measure them, and this choice, in turn, depends on what we see as important. In other words, measurement depends on theory. For example, the desire to predict auto travel in order to plan highway development led early transportation studies to collect data only on motorized trips and to emphasize travel (time, distance, and mode) over activities. In contrast, the 1949 travel diary data collected in Cedar Rapids, Iowa, was commissioned by outdoor advertisers who wanted to know about the frequency with which different kinds of people passed by different locations. This focus led the study designers to ask the diarists to record *all* movements made outside the home, even those made on foot over very short distances (the Cedar Rapids data set is described in Marble, 1959).

Martha Ballard's diary was self-designed. Today's activity diarists are responding to and interacting with structured questions posed by social science researchers. As is the case in any data collection effort, investigators designing a study of activity patterns must confront a host of questions. Among these are: over how long a time period will we collect information on behavior? What behaviors are we interested in? What do we want to know about these behaviors? Do we want simply to record overt behavior, or do we want to see how behaviors might change as something else changes?

In sketching out how researchers have tackled questions like these in designing activity studies, we shall draw examples from several studies but rely most heavily on the Uppsala Household Travel Survey, because it is the one with which we are most familiar. In this study, carried out in 1971 in Uppsala, Sweden, all adults in more than 300 households kept travel/activity diaries for 35 consecutive days. The households were randomly selected from a sampling frame stratified into six life cycle groups (S. Hanson & P. Hanson, 1981a). The Baltimore Travel Demand Data set, collected in Baltimore, Maryland in 1977, contains one-day travel/activity records for the adults in roughly 1,000 households (Ryan & Stahr, 1980). The most recent large-scale activity study is the Dutch National Mobility Panel, in which a large sample of households (initially more than 1,700) kept seven-day diaries at roughly six-month intervals from 1984 to 1989. The households lived in 20 different communities in the Netherlands and were stratified by stage in the life cycle, income, and community type (Golob & Meurs, 1986; Kitamura & Bovy, 1987).

Studies of activity patterns commonly track behavior over the course of (at least) one day, and view the daily pattern as a series of episodes (e.g., went to work, went out to lunch, returned to work, went home, went shopping, returned home). As mentioned earlier, geographers have tended to include only out-of-home activities and have emphasized both the activities themselves and the movement over space that ties the activities together into an activity pattern. In Chapter 11 in this book, Gärling and Garvill note that an important concern is how to classify behaviors into episodes: how to decide when to break into the flow of a day's activities and declare that a particular behavior is a separate episode. As the above example of one day's episodes suggests, geographers have taken a rather pragmatic approach to this problem by using a shift of location to signify a change of episodes.

But the classification question is not confined to the definition of episodes; it shoots through almost all aspects of designing an activity study. If a change of location signifies a new episode, what constitutes a change of location? Often the answer to this question is left to the discretion of the diarists, but in the Uppsala study we asked respondents to signal the beginning of a new episode whenever they went to a new street address. For each episode - or stop at a different activity site - what information should be collected? The following are invariably included: the *time* of the episode (time of arrival at and time of departure from each activity site); the *location* of the episode; the *activity* undertaken there; and the *mode* of travel to the activity site. Also, the episodes over the day are recorded so as to retain their temporal sequence so that links and interdependencies between and among different episodes can be seen.

In addition to these five basics, researchers have asked diarists to record other information for each episode. In the Uppsala study, for example, we asked respondents to note the amount of money spent at each stop, to record the land use type at each activity site (a park, a department store, a bank), and to list who else from the household accompanied the diarist to this site. Respondents in the Baltimore study were asked to record what packages, tools, or paraphernalia they were carrying to each stop (to assess impact on mode choice). Using the HATS technique, Jones, Dix, Clarke, and Heggie (1983) asked respondents to trace out the impact of a policy change (e.g., a change in bus service) on each of the episodes in the daily pattern. Of interest to a study focussing on information flows in space and time might be data on a range of variables pertaining to any face-to-face communication that took place during an episode.

Perhaps the most persistent question permeating the design of an activity study concerns the level of detail at which information on such things as time, location, activity, and mode will be collected. Again, these are basic classification questions, but the potential power (or weakness) of an activity study lies in how such questions are resolved. Measuring time, for example, may appear obvious, but are respondents to record arrival and departure times to the nearest second, minute, five minutes, ten minutes, quarter hour? Some studies (e.g., HATS) provide people with a daily time line, broken into 15-minute segments and ask respondents to record the "dominant activity" for each segment throughout the day. Others (e.g., the Uppsala study) ask people to note times to the nearest minute.

Classifying activities is also clearly a challenge, one that holds great potential for ensnaring both respondent and analyst in a morass of detail. Activities are most often measured in terms of four or five simple categories: work, social, recreation, personal business, or shopping (social and recreation are often combined into a single category). Of course, these general categories mask a wealth of detail that, depending on the goals of the study, the analyst may wish to tap. In the Uppsala case we chose to code activities at a fairly detailed level (within the recreation category, for example, were activities such as walk in a park, see a movie, go cross country skiing), but we have subsequently used the five general categories for most of the analysis.

The level of detail at which location has been recorded is of particular interest to geographers. At what spatial resolution should the location of episodes be captured - the street address, the city block, the census tract? Clearly, many movements will simply be washed out if too gross a level is chosen. In our view the aim should be to pinpoint the location of activity sites in urban space with great accuracy, and in the Uppsala Survey, street address coordinates were coded to the nearest meter. With the advent of sophisticated geographic information systems and the availability of address coding files from the U.S. Bureau of the Census, street addresses in the United States can now readily be geocoded to the nearest block face.

Although most activity studies have been concerned to measure the location of activities sites with care and precision, few have asked respondents to record the actual routes taken between activity sites. Instead, the airline distance between sites is simply measured from the map (or computed from the point coordinates). Exceptions are studies specifically aimed at illuminating the interactions between activity patterns and route choice such as the recent California effort to understand the linkages between telecommuting, overall activity patterns, and freeway use (Kitamura et al., 1991). Here the portion of the route on surface streets is distinguished from the portion on the freeway. Another recent exception is a study looking at day-to-day variability in the journey to work, including the specific path followed through the street network (Mahmassani, Hatcher, & Caplice, 1991).

All of these classification issues link up ultimately with questions of aggregation. Data are collected for individuals within households. Yet the reasons for undertaking activity studies - the questions such studies seek to answer - have to do not with individuals or households, but with groups and with places. Aggregation is necessary. The advantage, of course, in collecting disaggregate and detailed data is the flexibility such data afford the analyst in devising aggregation schemes. No single basis for aggregation is likely to be effective for answering all questions, and the finer the level of detail in the data, the more responsive aggregation schemes can be to tackling particular research questions. This point also relates to the fact that activity data are often called upon to answer questions that materialize only after the data have been collected. So, for example, the Uppsala data were collected on the basis of population groups defined in terms of stage in the life cycle, but because the households were selected randomly and because sex of respondent was recorded, the data have provided considerable insight into gender differences in urban activity patterns.

A final question to confront in studying activity patterns is the time period for which the activity diaries will be kept. The minimum, one 24-hour day, is also the most frequently used time slice in contemporary studies. Collecting data on a large sample for more than one day not only is costly but also poses problems of response bias (Golob & Meurs, 1986) that only careful study design can overcome (Hanson & Huff, 1982). Yet recently researchers have devoted increasing attention to some of the problems posed by relying on one-day data, particularly in a policy context (the extensive collection of references in Jones, 1990, addresses these issues). If people's behavior were entirely habitual - that is, if any day's activity pattern looked exactly like every other day's pattern - then a one-day snapshot would provide an excellent picture of a person's behavior at a particular time. Although most people seem to think that activity patterns are indeed habitual, identifying habitual patterns empirically has proved difficult (Hanson & Huff, 1988a).

In fact, from the 35-day Uppsala travel-activity records we know that a person's activity pattern is extremely variable in the short run. This variability poses a variety of problems for classifying activity patterns (Hanson & Huff, 1988b) . It also complicates attempts to assess how people's behavior changes after a change in the travel environment (e.g., a fare change on public transit, an increase in the price of fuel) or in the household context (e.g., the birth of a child, the emptying of the nest). If the researcher seeks to detect such changes in activity patterns by comparing two one-day snapshots (one taken before the change, the other after), there is no way of knowing if an observed behavioral change is in fact structural (signifying an enduring shift in behavior) or simply due to the day-to-day variability that was present but not captured in the before measure. By measuring activity patterns for a full week at each of several six-month intervals, the Dutch National Mobility Study has sought to provide a basis for distinguishing between real and random changes in activity patterns over time (Kitamura, 1988b).

## Explanatory Factors: What Shapes Activity Patterns?

Ulrich (1990) puts Martha Ballard's diaries in context by providing numerous maps encompassing the places she visited, by describing the prevailing transportation system and the conditions of travel (the Kennebec River - easily crossed when frozen but impassible after the spring thaw, the saddled or saddle-less horse), and by portraying the family and household circumstances in which Martha forged her daily activities. If contemporary analysts want to understand activity patterns, they must likewise go beyond simply collecting data on daily travel-activity behavior to include information on the household and environmental contexts in which those behaviors are developed. In some cases the search for explanation leads analysts to collect information on people's perceptions and attitudes as well.

Travel behavior and activity participation have long been viewed as the outcome of choices made within constraints (Chapin, 1974), but geographers have tended to emphasize constraints over choice. Hägerstrand (1970), in particular, saw individuals' time-space paths over the day as shaped by various types of constraints, including the nature of available transportation, the locations of possible destinations, the need to conduct certain activities in certain locations at certain times with certain other people, and the hours that activity sites are open. Studies of urban activity patterns have focused on two general sets of explanatory factors, each of which can be seen as affecting both choice and constraints. One set has to do with the household/family context and the other is related to local geographic context, including characteristics of the transportation system.

### *The Household/Family Context*

The standard urban transportation planning process forecasts travel (beginning with trip generation) as a function of household variables, including household size, number of people employed, household income, and car ownership. Studies of urban activity patterns have verified that these household characteristics are indeed related to patterns of movement and activity participation, but, by looking within the household, activity studies have deepened and extended our understanding of the relationship between individual/household characteristics and activity patterns. In particular, activity studies have identified the importance of household structure and of the individual's role within the household.

Several studies have documented that a household's stage in the life cycle strongly affects their activity patterns. In particular, children have an impact on the activity patterns of adults in the household (S. Hanson & P. Hanson, 1981a; Jones et al., 1983; Pas, 1984; Townsend, 1991). Thus, a measure of household size needs to be supplemented with information on people's ages as well. Usually life cycle stage is measured in a nominally scaled variable that classifies households according to the number, ages, and marital status of adults and the ages of children present.

Similarly, the individual's role within the household, usually measured by employment status and gender, have proved critical to any understanding of the development of and changes in activity patterns. Employment status (the level of a person's involvement in the paid labor force) affects the frequency of participation in different activities (S. Hanson & P. Hanson, 1981a), but gender has perhaps the strongest effect on activity patterns of all the individual and household level variables. Women's travel distances are more abbreviated than those of men, and their patterns of mode use and activity participation differ significantly from men's (S. Hanson & P. Hanson, 1981b; Pas, 1984). Moreover, women's activity patterns are more variable from day to day than are men's (Jones & Clarke, 1988; Pas, 1988). The data giving rise to these findings are dated (for the most part they were collected in the 1970s) and reflect the gender relations and gender-based roles prevailing in particular places at particular times. As long as gender remains a basis for divisions of labor at both home and work, however, the activity patterns of women and men will differ significantly, tracing out the different choices made and constraints faced by each group.

Through an ingenious use of simulation, Goulias and Kitamura (1992) have been able to show how shifts in the household/family context lead to changes in mobility. Drawing upon data from six different waves of the Dutch National Mobility Panel collected between 1984 and 1989, Goulias and Kitamura use observed changes in household type, employment situation, income, and car ownership to establish parameters describing longitudinal change in these factors. These parameters are then used to simulate first demographic and then mobility changes (e.g., weekday vehicle kilometers travelled and transit passenger kilometers travelled) at the individual and household level. By spinning travel forecasts from an activity study and testing those forecasts with data from a later wave of the panel, Kitamura is disproving his declaration of a few years ago that "no activity-based model has been offered that can be readily applied to a wide range of planning and policy problems" (1988, p. 27).

### *Spatial Context*

Clearly activity patterns are shaped not only by the household context but also by the opportunities and constraints present in the local environment. Although there are doubtless contemporary North American households that match Martha Ballard's household in terms of ages and number of children and husband's and wife's employment status, their activity patterns will invariably differ from those of the Ballard household because the local context is so radically different. Key aspects of the local context that are likely to affect activity patterns are characteristics of the transportation system, patterns of land use, weather, and threats to personal safety. While analyses have shown the importance of each of these to activity patterns, no single study has assessed all concurrently.

Virtually all dimensions of an activity pattern (what, where, when, how frequently, and by what travel mode people participate in activities) are affected by local context. The nature of the transportation system, beyond simply the cost and availability of transit relative to the auto, is crucial. For example, places that accommodate bicycles (the Netherlands; China; Davis, California) will have a larger proportion of activities undertaken by bike than places that do not (Boston or London). The cost structure of the transit system itself can affect activity patterns: is it a distance-based fare or a region-wide flat fare? Does the user pay or, as is the case in Japan, does the employer pay for transit? In a study of carless housewives in four suburbs of Christchurch, New Zealand, Forer and Kivell (1981) highlighted the interaction of transportation and the location of facilities in affecting the ease with which people can reach public services. They focus particularly on the way in which the quality of public transportation service in different areas affects the accessibility of facility locations.

The land use patterns in the vicinity of a household's residence and work locations have also been seen as having a bearing on activity patterns. Of particular interest, perhaps reflecting the influence of the gravity model in every geographer's education, has been the density of activity sites around the residence (and the workplace). The frequency of travel or activity participation has traditionally been deemed especially sensitive to such densities. Hanson and Schwab (1987) reviewed the research that examines the relationship between an individual's accessibility to activity sites and his/her activity patterns. They also measured that relationship in the Uppsala context, finding that mode use and travel distance are more sensitive to a person's accessibility level than is travel frequency. That is, an individual's overall level of trip making did not vary substantially with her/his accessibility to activity sites. The density of urban land use does affect various aspects of activity patterns, but, *within* urban areas, accessibility to activity sites has less impact on activity patterns than do various measures of the household context (Hanson, 1982; Pas, 1984; Recker & Schuler, 1982; Wermuth, 1982).

Depending on the purpose of an activity study, other aspects of local context may be important to measure. Lenntorp (1976) and others have included information on the hours that stores and other activity sites are open. Schwab (1988) used data on the spatial distribution of carbon monoxide in Washington DC in order to assess the differential air pollution exposure of socioeconomic groups in view of their daily activity patterns. S. Hanson and P. Hanson (1977) used daily weather (temperature and precipitation) data to demonstrate the impact of weather on mode use and trip frequency. The Baltimore study collected information on the availability and cost of parking at home and work. Finally, fear for personal safety, especially after dark, is one aspect of local context that is receiving increasing attention. Focas (1989) and Atkins (1989) showed that in London women's activity patterns are affected by their perceptions of how safe different travel modes are, and a participant observer study of elderly single-room occupancy hotel tenants in Chicago found that safety fears were a major constraint on activity patterns (Rollinson, 1991). Surprisingly little is currently known about how activity participation (e.g., the timing and location of episodes) is related to concerns about personal safety.

In sum, a variety of factors pertaining to both the household context and the particular urban context have been seen as important to understanding how activity patterns become established and change. Although in theoretical discussions of how activity patterns develop, geographers have placed considerable emphasis on the nature of the local context, in practice relatively few empirical studies have explored the relationship between activity patterns and the attributes of the local environment. Undoubtedly one reason for this dearth of attention is the difficulty and expense of collecting data on the relevant environmental variables. The few studies that have set out to establish the relative importance of household context and spatial context have found that household context explains more of the variance in activity patterns than does spatial context (Hanson, 1982; Kutter, 1973). Although the psychological factors affecting activity choice have also long been touted as key to understanding observed activity patterns (they were central to Chapin's 1974 conceptual framework), few geographers or transportation analysts have ventured onto this terrain in their analyses. Notable exceptions are studies that have focused on mode choice (e.g., Golob, Horowitz, & Wachs, 1979) or destination choice (e.g., Burnett, 1973).

## What Do We Know About Activity Patterns?

What we know is a difficult question to answer. On the one hand we know a lot about activity patterns in specific places at particular times. Just as Martha Ballard's diaries tell us much about life in Hallowell, Maine, between 1785 and 1812, contemporary activity studies have a great deal to say about life in Uppsala, Sweden in 1971, in Reading, England, in 1973 (Pas, 1988), or in Washington, D.C. in the late 1960s (Chapin, 1974). On the other hand, primarily because different investigators have employed different study designs, generalizations about the details of activity patterns (e.g., the frequency of different daily patterns) are hard to come by.

Because the data-collection phase of an activity study is expensive, relatively few such studies have been undertaken. Tracking the same individuals over several years, the Dutch National Mobility Panel is the only activity study that provides insights into change over time in the middle to long run. Generalizations, particularly about people's response to change, doubtless could be more readily made if we had many such data sets. The generalizations that have emerged - such as those mentioned earlier about gender differences in activity patterns - are based on findings from the relatively few roughly comparable data sets that have been collected.

Does the dearth of generalizations mean activity studies have been worthless? Not at all. It is no accident that the State of California chose an activity-based approach when recently it sought increased understanding of the likely impacts of telecommuting on highway use. Activity analysis is extremely well-suited to probing the likely outcomes of various policy alternatives. Will the outcomes predicted from the California study be transferrable to Boston or Miami? At some level, they probably will be, but one reason that activity studies are valuable to policy makers lies precisely in their sensitivity to variations in local conditions.

The U.S. national trends in travel suggest a growing need for data on activity patterns, in that work trips, once the premier focus of transportation studies and generally considered the most predictable component of travel, comprise an ever-diminishing portion of total urban travel (Giuliano, 1991; Richardson & Gordon, 1989). Moreover, work trips no longer account for the majority of even peak-period travel (Richardson &

Gordon, 1989). One implication of this decline in the relative importance of work travel is an increase in the overall complexity of activity patterns. Another is that since road congestion is no longer brought about simply by the journey to work, strategies to alleviate congestion will have to focus on the overall activity pattern, not simply on the journey to work as they have in the past through, for example, encouraging car pooling to work.

## Future Research Directions

The geography of everyday life fascinates. It fascinates us as people because the everyday lives of others, like Martha Ballard, shed light on our own lives. It fascinates us as geographers because people's activity patterns help to shape and in turn are shaped by place, space, and location. The geography of everyday life also fascinates because it is thoroughly enmeshed in a range of pragmatic issues facing those charged with running cities and improving the quality of life in cities. The geography of everyday life will continue to fascinate, and the need for activity studies will not abate because the questions they seek to answer and the reasons for studying activity patterns have not disappeared.

In the second section of this chapter, we outlined a number of reasons for interest in activity studies. We noted there that such studies are valued as a window on everyday life, can help planners understand how behavior is likely to change following a change in the travel environment, provide information on people's exposure to selected aspects of the physical environment (e.g., environmental hazards) and the social context (e.g., job information), and can clarify relationships between travel and telecommunications. These are questions and problems that have motivated activity pattern research. They will continue to motivate activity studies because so many of these questions remain unanswered and problems remain unsolved.

Future activity studies are most likely to be undertaken to answer particular questions that arise in particular contexts. Such small-scale, focused studies can of course be cumulative if they share a common methodology. We have described the features common to most activity studies and noted the variabilities as well. Future studies will be strengthened by including more information on the local context than has normally been included in the past. Because our present understanding of the relationship between activity patterns and environmental context is patchy at best, systematic inclusion of data on the local environment would contribute significantly to explanations of activity patterns. Linking activity studies with environmental analysis, to tackle questions such as the exposure to hazards, also seems promising. For some purposes, like that of understanding the activity impacts of telecommuting, data on in-home as well as out-of-home activities should probably be included to permit assessment of the tradeoffs involved. Finally, activity studies can doubtless benefit from linking with the work of psychologists, like that described in the following chapter. We have yet to learn of the power to be had in combining both geographic and psychological factors in explanations of activity patterns.

## References

Atkins, S. (1989). Women, travel and personal security. In M. Grieco, L. Pickup, & R. Whipp (Eds.), *Gender, transport and employment* (pp. 169-189). Brookfield, VT: Gower.

Burnett, P. (1973). The dimensions of alternatives in spatial choice process. *Geographical Analysis, 5*, 181-204.

Carlstein, T., Parkes, D., & Thrift, T. (1978). *Timing space and spacing time II: Human activity and time geography.* London: Arnold.

Chapin, F. (1974). *Human activity patterns in the city: What people do in time and space.* New York: Wiley.

Cutter, S. L., & Tiefenbacher, J. (1991). Chemical hazards in urban America. *UrbanGeography, 12*, 417-430.

Farley, J. E. (1984). P*-segregation indices: What can they tell us about housing segregation in 1980? *Urban Studies, 21*, 331-336.

Fishman, R. (1990). America's new city. *The Wilson Quarterly, 14*, 25-45.

Focas, C. (1989). A survey of women's travel needs in London. In M. Grieco, L. Pickup, & R. Whipp (Eds.), *Gender, transport and employment* (pp. 150-168). Brookfield, VT: Gower.

Forer, P. C., & Kivell, H. (1981). Space-time budgets, public transport, and spatial choice. *Environment and Planning A, 13*, 497-509.

Gilbert, M. (1991). *Ties to people, bonds to place: the urban geography of low-income minority women's survival strategies.* Dissertation proposal, Graduate School of Geography, Clark University.

Giuliano, G. (1991). Is jobs housing balance a transportation issue? *Transportation Research Record, 1305*, 305-312.

Golob, T. F., & Meurs, H. (1986). Biases in response over time in a seven-day travel diary. *Transportation, 13*, 163-181.

Golob, T., Horowitz, A., & Wachs, M. (1979). Attitude-behavior relationships in traveldemand modelling. In D. A. Hensher and P. R. Stopher (Eds.), *Behavioral travel modelling* (pp. 739-757). London: Croom Helm.

Goulias, K. G., & Kitamura, R. (1992, January). *Travel demand forecasting with dynamic microsimulation.* Paper presented at the Transportation Research Board, Washington, D.C.

Greenland, D., & Yorty, R. (1985). The spatial distribution of particulate concentrations in the Denver metropolitan area. *Annals of the Association of American Geographers, 75*, 69-82.

Hanson, P. (1977). The activity patterns of elderly households. *Geografiska Annaler, 59*, 109-124.

Hanson, P., Marble, D., & Pitts, F. (1972). Individual movement and communication fields: A preliminary report. *Regional Science Perspectives, 2*, 80-94.

Hanson, S. (1982). The determinants of daily travel-activity patterns: Relative location and socio-demographic factors. *Urban Geography, 3*, 179-202.

Hanson, S., & Hanson, P. (1977). An approach for evaluating the impact of weather on bicycle use. *Transportation Research Record, 629*, 43-48.

Hanson, S., & Hanson, P. (1981a). The travel-activity patterns of urban residents: Dimensions and relationships to sociodemographic characteristics. *Economic Geography, 57*, 332-347.

Hanson, S., & Hanson, P. (1981b). The impact of married women's employment on household travel patterns. *Transportation, 10*, 165-183.

Hanson, S., & Huff, J. (1982). Assessing day-to-day variability in complex travel patterns.*Transportation Research Record, 891*, 18-24.

Hanson, S., & Huff, J. (1988a). Systematic variability in repetitious travel. *Transportation,15*, 111-135.

Hanson, S., & Huff, J. (1988b). Repetition and day-to-day variability in individual travelpatterns: implications for classification. In R. G. Golledge & H. J. P. Timmermans (Eds.), *Behavioral modeling in geography and planning* (pp. 368-398). London:Croom Helm.

Hanson, S., & Pratt, G. (1991). Job search and the occupational segregation of women. *Annals of the Association of American Geographers, 81*, 229-253.

Hanson, S., & Schwab, M. (1987). Accessibility and intraurban travel. *Environment and Planning A, 19*, 735-748.

Hartgen, D. (1988). Viewpoint. *Transportation, 15*, 47-48.

Hägerstrand, T. (1967). On Monte Carlo simulation of diffusion. In W. Garrison and D. Marble (Eds.), *Quantitative geography, part I: Economic and cultural topics* (pp. 1-32). Evanston, IL: Northwestern University Press.

Hägerstrand, T. (1970). What about people in regional science? *Papers and Proceedings of the Regional Science Association, 24*, 7-21.

Jones, P. (1979). 'HATS': a technique for investigating household decisions. *Environment and Planning A, 11*, 59-70.

Jones, P. (Ed.). (1990). *Behavioral modelling in geography and planning.* Brookfield, VT: Gower.

Jones, P., & Clarke, M. (1988). The significance and measurement of variability in travel behavior. *Transportation, 15*, 65-87.

Jones, P., Dix, M., Clarke, M., & Heggie, I. (1983). *Understanding Travel Behavior*. Aldershot, UK: Gower.

Kitamura, R. (1988a). An evaluation of activity-based travel analysis. *Transportation, 15*, 9-34.

Kitamura, R. (1988b). An analysis of weekly activity patterns and travel expenditure. In R. G. Golledge, R. & H. J. P. Timmermans (Eds.), *Behavioral modeling in geographyand planning* (pp. 399-423). London: Croom Helm.

Kitamura, R., & Bovy, P. (1987). Analysis of attrition biases and trip reporting errors for panel data. *Transportation Research A, 21*, 287-302.

Kitamura, R., Pendyala, R., & Goulias, K. (1991, November). *Impact of telecommuting on workers' action space: an analysis of state of California telecommute pilot project data.* Paper presented at the thirty-eighth North American meetings of the Regional Science Association International, New Orleans, LA.

Kutter, E. (1973). A model for individual travel behavior. *Urban Studies, 10*, 235-258.

Lenntorp, B. (1976). *Paths in time-space environments: A time geographic study of movement possibilities of individuals.* Lund: Gleerup.

Mahmassani, H. (1988). Some comments on activity-based approaches to the analysis and prediction of travel behavior. *Transportation, 15*, 35-42.

Mahmassani, H., Hatcher, S., & Caplice, C. (1991, May). *Daily variation of trip chaining, scheduling, and path selection behavior of work commuters*. Paper presented at the 6th International Conference on Travel Behavior, Quebec, Canada.

Marble, D. (1959). Transport inputs at urban residential sites. *Papers of the Regional Science Association, 5*, 253-266.

Pas, E. (1984). The effect of selected sociodemographic characteristics on daily travel-activity behavior. *Environment and Planning A, 16*, 571-581.

Pas, E. (1988). Weekly travel-activity behavior. *Transportation, 15*, 89-110.

Pas, E. (1988). Introduction. *Transportation, 15*, 7-8.

Recker, W., & Schuler, H. (1982). An integrated analysis of complex travel behavior and urban form indicators. *Urban Geography, 3*, 110-120.

Richardson, H., & Gordon, P. (1989). Counting nonwork trips: The missing link in transportation, land use, and urban policy. *Urban Land, 48*, 6-12.

Rollinson, P. (1991). The spatial isolation of elderly single room occupancy hotel tenants. *The Professional Geographer, 43*, 456-464.

Rushton, G. (1969). Analysis of spatial behavior by revealed space preference. *Annals of the Association of American Geographers, 47*, 391-400.

Ryan, J., & Stahr, M. (1980). *Baltimore travel demand dataset (user's guide)*. Washington, D.C.: U.S. Department of Transportation, Federal Highway Administration: Urban Mass Transportation Administration.

Salomon, I. (1986). Telecommunications and travel relationships: A review. *Transportation Research A, 20*, 223-238.

Schwab, M. (1988). *Differential exposure to carbon monoxide among sociodemographic groups in Washington, D.C.* Worcester, MA: Graduate School of Geography, Clark University.

Townsend, T. A. (1991, May). *Classification and analysis of the multi-day travel/activity patterns of households and their members*. Paper presented at the 6th International Conference on Travel Behavior, Quebec, Canada.

Ulrich, L. T. (1990). *A midwife's tale: The life of Martha Ballard, based on her diary, 1785 -1812*. New York: Knopf.

Wermuth, H. (1982). Hierarchical effects of personal, household, and residential location characteristics on individual activity demand. *Environment and Planning A, 14*, 1251-1264.

*Behavior and Environment: Psychological and Geographical Approaches*
*T. Gärling and R.G. Golledge (Editors)*


# CHAPTER 11

# Psychological Explanations of Participation in Everyday Activities

**Tommy Gärling and Jörgen Garvill**

The understanding of how people adjust to different environmental conditions, of interest to both geographers and psychologists, would be incomplete if it only included how environments are perceived, cognized, and evaluated. A complete understanding of the adjustment process also requires the study of what people do (Gärling, Lindberg, Torell, & Evans, 1991).

The everyday activities in which people engage much of the time is the topic of this chapter. These activities are presumably primary means by which goals important for adjustment are attained (Gärling Lindberg, & Montgomery, 1989). Other means, more often highlighted by psychologists, include dramatic ones occurring on one or a few occasions during a life time, such as career choice, marriage, and divorce (Stewart, 1982). These are not of immediate interest here.

Following a discussion of problems in defining and measuring everyday activities, the bulk of the chapter is devoted to explanations of why people participate in different such activities. Of course, it has already been said that everyday activities are means by which goals are attained. At least to psychologists, the mechanism by which this is accomplished is nevertheless of interest to reveal. Furthermore, social scientists, planners, and policy-makers ask what benefits people gain, in terms of meaning in their lives and subjective well-being, from participating in everyday activities (e.g., Campbell, Converse, & Rodgers, 1976; Chapter 10, this book). The forecasting by planners of future capacity requirements of transportation, waste disposal, and energy-supply systems raise additional, more specific questions such as when, where, for how long, and with whom people participate in everyday activities (e.g., Schipper, Bartlett, Hawk, & Vine, 1989).

Four types of answers to both the general question and the more specific questions are presently covered in equally many sections. We begin with a brief review of nonpsychological explanations. A section on psychological explanations then follows. In this section we first discuss theories which emphasize motivational factors without explicitly assuming cognitive control. Cognitive control is the focus of explanations based on the assumption that deliberate decisions precede activity participation, reviewed and discussed in the next subsection. Even in such cognitive explanations, deliberate decisions need not always be important, as when the performance of an activity becomes routine. Automatization of everyday activities is discussed in a final subsection.

Examples from the authors' own ongoing research are in a final section used to demonstrate the important role of psychological factors in determining how much time is devoted to everyday activities, as well as to show how this role may be conceptualized.

## Everyday Activities: Definitions and Measurements

A concise definition of everyday activities may seem superfluous. After all, such activities are simply what we typically (or sometimes only occasionally) do. This is something we know from previous experience. However, inferences may come too easily, about one's own activities, and, in particular, about others' activities.

Activities constitute a stream of events, involving one, or, often, several persons, objects, and places. In this stream, units must be identified, classified, and counted or measured. The natural language provides an invariably available and often easily accessible classification system. It has been utilized in many studies of time budgets (Michelson & Reed, 1975). In such studies interviewees are asked to indicate what they did on some earlier occasion (e.g., from 6 am to 10 pm the day before). As noted by Barker (1963) who has conducted research in ecological psychology with the aim of identifying naturally occurring activities (termed behavior episodes), there is probably no substitute for the language. Nevertheless, it is essential to be aware of several fallacies entailed. For instance, the language encodes our naive theories of ourselves and other people (Rips & Conrad, 1989) which may be inaccurate. Scientific theories, in contrast, require more precise, quantitative terms than natural languages provide. There are some beginnings of relevant research focusing on the vocabulary people use for describing their activities (e.g., Vallacher & Wegner, 1989).

A distinction is made between temporal-dynamic properties of activities and their content (Barker, 1963; Birch, 1986). The former is based on breaks in the stream of activities, the latter refers to a classification, on some basis, of what is going on between breaks. It is interesting to note in this connection that it has seldom been salient to psychologist, in contrast to geographers, that activities have spatial as well as temporal organization. An exception is the interest documented by environmental psychologists in the mapping of activities in space (Ittelson, Rivlin, & Proshansky, 1976). At any rate, the fact is that, over time, activities change location. Spatiotemporal-dynamic properties of activities may thus form the basis for exact measurements, certainly in the laboratory but also in situations which are more similar to real life (e.g., Birch, 1986). An important question is what relationships these properties have to content.

In the painstaking, careful work by Barker and his colleagues (Barker, 1963; Barker & Wright, 1955) to classify activities according to content, a hierarchical system of classification is proposed. Thus, an observed activity is classified at several molar levels. In addition to the molar levels, there is a molecular level entailing simple movements. Because of the apparent arbitrariness of the choice of levels, as well as, in fact, of activity categories, we doubt the truth of Barker's (1963) claim that a classification is naturally given. The question therefore arises whether certain ways of classifying activities are more relevant than others, and, if so, why they are?

Any content classification seems difficult to make unless some theoretical structure is imposed. Indeed, it may even be difficult to find breaks between activities which are independent of how content is classified (Newtson, Rindner, Miller, & LaCross, 1977). A common general such theoretical structure is entailed by the view that persons engage in activities because they pursue different goals (e.g., Kuhl, 1986a; Nuttin, 1984). Some activities are directly consummatory, others are instrumental. That many of our daily activities may be performed routinely without much deliberation (Ronis, Yates, & Kirscht, 1989) seems to be inconsistent with this argument. As will be discussed further below, it is however not necessarily so.

Time-budget research often employs rather broad activity categories such as regular work, child care, personal hygiene, relaxing, and so forth (e.g., Szalai et al., 1972). Implied by the way the activity categories are named, the classification is based on assumptions about what goals are attained. Furthermore, these goals appear to consist primarily of psychological endstates, although important societal goals may also play some role. In the examples mentioned, the activities may be classified at a higher level as, for instance, obligatory or discretionary. In general, the level at which the activities are classified is part of any theoretically guided classification system.

If objective measures based on spatiotemporal properties of activities are at all possible to obtain, for instance through the recording of traces, through direct observations by observers, or through self-reports[1], they may nevertheless be useless for inferring content. The same activity (say, travel from home to work) clearly differs in its spatiotemporal properties, even for the same person from day to day. Conversely, if two activities can be found whose spatiotemporal properties are identical, their content may nevertheless be different. To reiterate, everyday activities are either consummatory or instrumental for the attainment of goals pursued by persons, and a content classification, as well as measurement procedure, in some way need to be based on this assumption.

A solution to the content-classification problem appears to have been sought along two lines. One is to provide the categories which an observer (who often must be the person being observed) uses instead of leaving to him or her to invent own categories. Even though this procedure is likely to increase objectivity, it only makes more obvious that some basis for constructing the activity categories is needed. The other solution is to use very general categories. This should again increase objectivity (but decrease precision). However, as already stated, the choice of level at which to classify activities is no less theory-dependent.

Our solution is almost contrary to the last procedure: Instead of making the categories more general, we propose that they are made more specific. We also propose that additional information is collected about the activities being performed, including information about the goals the persons pursue. A time-sampling technique has been developed for this purpose (Hormuth, 1986; Sjöberg & Magneberg, 1990). As will be described later, conventional survey interviews may also be used. The rationale behind our solution is that the kind of data collected will provide the basis for classifying activities with respect to how they are perceived to be related to goals.

---

[1] All these means of data collection are here considered to be objective to the extent they are reliable and unbiased. In general, recording of traces may in this sense be more objective than direct observations which in turn are likely to be more objective than self-reports. However, examples of when self-reports are more objective should not be too difficult to find.

## Overview of Nonpsychological Explanations

The aim of much empirical research in geography has been to find regularities in spatiotemporal patterns of activities (Golledge & Stimson, 1987; S. Hanson & P. Hanson, Chapter 10, this book). It is therefore understandable that explanations focus on the role of external circumstances. However, this does not preclude an interest in psychological factors. In particular, the theory of Cullen (1976) should be mentioned because of its similarity to the psychological explanations reviewed later. Each day in a person's life is in this theory assumed to consist, in various proportions, of the performance of activities which are routine or habitual, arranged in advance (e.g., appointments), planned, and impulsive. It is believed that activities should be classified accordingly. Furthermore, a distinction is made between activities depending on how fixed they are in time and space. Those activities which a person is committed to perform and which are fixed in time and space will tend to act as pegs in the daily scheduling of activity programs. Highlighted is also the importance for the daily activity schedule of long-term deliberated choices, of where to live, what job to take, and so forth.

Another influential approach has become known as time geography (Hägerstrand, 1970). This approach is responsive to the criticism that geographers (in contrast to psychologists) have tended to neglect changes over time in favour of spatial changes. In the time-geographic approach, each person is assumed to be engaged in projects which are defined as interrelated series of activities undertaken at different times in different locations. Engagement in projects defines an person's space-time path. To explain such paths or trajectories in space-time coordinates, primary emphasis is given to basic constraining factors. Again, this does not mean that awareness is lacking of the significance of psychological factors. Such factors are, however, considered both difficult to define and to measure. Since the underlying motivation is to find explanations with a high degree of invariance over time, it may also be the case that physical and biological factors are considered to be better candidates for such explanations.

Constraints are derived from a few basic premises about the physical world, such as that people cannot be in different places at the same time, and that performance of activities and movement take time. Further constraints are imposed by basic biological (and, presumably, psychological) needs - as well as socially imposed requirements - for persons to interact with each other. In contemporary societies, and perhaps in every human society, there are furthermore rules, laws, and power relationships which constrain the use of space for various activities.

The time-geographic approach should be acknowledged for highlighting constraining factors, that is, those things which stop us from engaging in activities. Nevertheless, the particular constraining factors may not be as absolute as originally thought. Furthermore, people always have options (at least of not performing an activity). Thus, an explanation solely in terms of constraints is at best incomplete.

In passing it may be noted that there exists research in economics dealing with households' allocation of time to everyday activities (Winston, 1982). Its application to so-called activity-based analyses of travel demand was reviewed by Axhausen and Gärling (in press). In contrast to the explanations presented here, the economic approach is more similar to the psychological ones to be discussed next.

## Psychological Explanations

Explanations of participation in everyday activities based on psychological theories encompass external circumstances (situations, opportunities, constraints, and consequences), personality traits and abilities, motivational states (needs, drives, and goals), and information processing (judgments, evaluations, and decisions). At the same time, there is a clear awareness of how complex the determination of human activities is, and that it will hardly be possible to specify all determinants. In psychology, as in the other life sciences, probably the best one can hope for is qualitative laws (Simon, 1990). Yet, under limited circumstances, rather exact quantitative predictions of activity participation have been possible to achieve (e.g., Ajzen & Fishbein, 1980).

Alluding to our previous discussion of levels of classification, explanations may also be distinguished depending on whether they are molar or molecular. Molecular, or reductionist, explanations would, for instance, evoke physiological principles. It is our contention that reductionist explanations of psychological phenomena are insufficient (see Horgan, 1976). In support thereof, even activities thought to be closely related to biological needs, such as eating, sleeping, and sexual activity, have empirically been found to be quite complex in their determination.

Our selection in this section of psychological explanations to be reviewed is furthermore guided by the theoretical framework alluded to earlier. Thus, only explanations in which goal attainment (or, equivalently, need reduction) is viewed as basic are reviewed. Recently, Kuhl (1986a) has pointed out that there are three different subsystems of interest to study: A cognitive subsystem which acquires, transforms, and represents knowledge about the environment (including metaknowledge about the person himself or herself); an emotional subsystem which evaluates the knowledge processed by the cognitive subsystem; and a separate motivational subsystem which represents and processes goals and activity tendencies. Our review takes as its starting point explanations emphasizing the motivational and emotional subsystems, then those explanations which solely or to a greater extent evoke the cognitive subsystem are reviewed.

### *Motivational Theories*

Current motivational theories (e.g., Weiner, 1980) show a strong cognitive direction in their conceptualization of the person as choosing between activity alternatives on the basis of judgments of likelihood of and evaluations of salient outcomes. Some of these theories will therefore be discussed later. An exception is the theory proposed by Atkinson and Birch (1970, 1986). Overt activities, as well as covert, mental activities, are in this theory assumed to be determined by motivational forces which in turn vary in strength depending on external circumstances as well as what activities the person is engaged in. In addition, this theory differs in its emphasis on explanations of the persistence of and change in activities over time. Whereas the bulk of motivational theories have focussed on the determinants of performance of particular (broadly defined) single activities such as, for instance, achievement (e.g., McClelland, Atkinson, Clark, & Lowell, 1953), the Atkinson and Birch theory thus extends the focus to the temporal characteristics of the process through which motivational factors affect activities. In contrast to other motivational theories, which have been termed episodic, Atkinson and Birch's dynamic theory may be more apt to provide a motivational explanation of the stream of everyday activities. The theory is capable of accounting both for changes in activities in an unchanging environment and persistence of activities in a changing environment.

According to Atkinson and Birch (1986), the traditional problems posed for motivational theories to explain - initiation of an activity, persistence of an activity, intensity of an activity, and choice among activities - are entailed by the simple change from one activity to another in the ongoing stream. Accounting for this change should shed light on both activity choice and time use. In Atkinson and Birch's theory, activities have tendencies to be performed. These tendencies vary in strength, and at each point in time the person engages in the activity having the strongest tendency with an intensity which is proportional to that strength. Changes in strength of tendency to perform an activity are not random but depend on the difference in the contribution of an instigating and a consummatory force. The former is a function of exposure and attendance to opportunities in the environment, the latter is a function of the degree to which the tendency is expressed in an actual activity. The rate of change of the instigating force may vary depending on what opportunities are attended. Similarly, the rate of the consummatory force varies depending on which activity a person performs. Activities vary along a continuum from being solely consummatory to being solely instrumental. A few examples illustrating this are given in Figure 11.1. The first example may, for instance, correspond to a change from reading the newspaper to answering the ringing telephone, the second starting to read the newspaper after having finished the dinner, and the third starting to have dinner after having had an appetizer (Atkinson & Birch, 1986).

There is also a tendency not to engage in an activity, based on the expectation that some negative outcome will result. Underlying resistance is an inhibitory force which is evoked by the environment (e.g., punishment). A force of resistance decreases when the activity is not performed. Whether an activity will be performed or not is determined by the difference between the tendency to participate and the tendency not to participate.

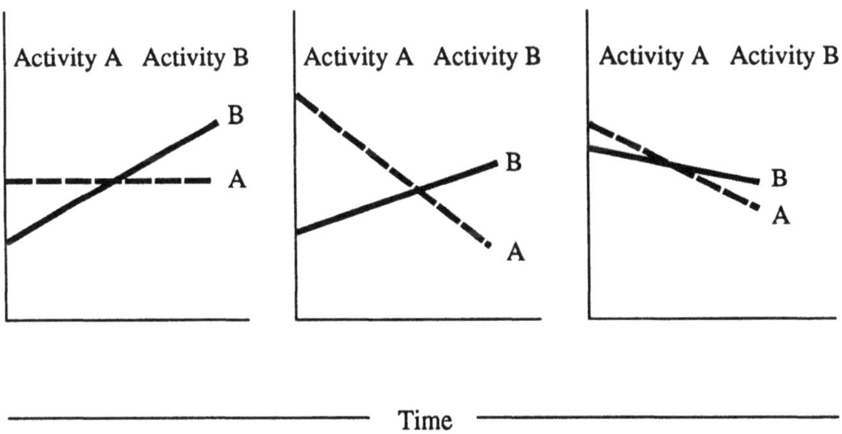


FIGURE 11.1. Three examples of change of activity due to changes in activity tendencies. Adapted from Atkinson and Birch, 1986.

Two other principles should be mentioned. One is called substitution and refers to the capacity of one activity to reduce the tendency to perform another activity. The substitute value of an activity depends on the consummatory force of the substituting activity and its similarity to the activity it substitutes for. The other, related principle is called displacement. In this case an instigating force may spread to several activities. An everyday example is that encountering a certain kind of food may also increase one's appetite for other kinds. Underlying these principles is the idea that tendencies to perform activities are organized in families on the basis of functional similarities. Similar activities may be referred to by their family names, for instance, eating, achieving, affiliating, and so forth.

In Atkinson and Birch's theory deliberate decisions play no explicit role. This is also true of choices among activities. Even though it is acknowledged that a person may experience it differently whether attempting to initiate/cease an activity or make a choice among activities, the same explanatory principles are evoked. The choice is assumed to simply be made of the activity which at the moment has the strongest tendency to be performed. A problem with this assumption is that it may lead to too frequent alternations between activities. A mechanism of selective attention is therefore postulated. The implication is that an instigating force will, in a certain environment, always be stronger when the activity is performed than when it is not. There are also lags in the consummatory force, both in its initiation and cessation. These lags favour the continuation of a newly initiated activity when it otherwise would be most susceptible to change.

Before discussing further the advantages and disadvantages of the Atkinson-Birch theory in accounting for the stream of everyday activities, some comments are needed on the problem of operationalizing the theoretical concepts. In experimental studies which have supported the theory (e.g., Kuhl & Geiger, 1976), subjects have typically participated in laboratory experiments in which they are given a free choice between several activities. Frequency, time, and quality of performance of the optional activities are measured. The environmental conditions assumed to affect the tendencies to engage in the activities are controlled or systematically varied. In contrast, a critical task in everyday life is to identify the activity alternatives and to characterize them. Furthermore, the environmental conditions need to be identified and measured.

Even though the Atkinson-Birch theory thus does not easily lend itself to specific explanations of why people engage in different kinds of everyday activities, it still provides several worthwhile possibilities deserving attention. One such possibility is, for instance, to characterize persons with respect to the strengths of their activity tendencies. An alternative in line with recent theorizing would be to evoke the concept of personal projects (Little, 1981) in explaining such individual differences. The idea is that people have current projects or goals which they are pursuing and which may determine what activities are important for them to engage in. Such goals may be tangible ones, such as a job promotion, but also less tangible ones such as becoming more responsive. Of interest here is also that activity tendencies may be grouped in families with regard to their relationships to goals. Thus, a theoretically derived superordinate classification of activities may be feasible.

The theory which has been reviewed in this subsection has other limitations. One is that it assumes that the activities are well learned. It thereby excludes situations where a person faces the problem of finding out how to attain a salient goal. Furthermore, even though the alternative activities are given, a person may go through a deliberate process of making choices, taking into account benefits and costs. Birch, Atkinson, & Bongort, (1974) attempt at introducing cognitive control in their theory does not seem to go far enough. In essence, they assume that instigating forces change, and thus activity tendencies, as a result of mental activity. A more prominent role has been ascribed to the cognitive subsystem in other theories to be described next.

### *Cognitive Theories: Decision Making*

In cognitive motivational theories, also called expectancy-value theories (Feather, 1982), the valence or utility of an alternative activity is proportional to the product of the expectancy (usually defined as the subjective probability) and the subjective evaluative value of the outcome of choosing the activity. These theories have a counterpart in subjective expected utility (SEU) theories which have been proposed in decision making research to more generally account for how people choose between alternatives (Edwards, 1954; Chapter 13 in this book). Although expectancy-value theories do not always explicitly try to explain choices between alternative activities, it is tacitly assumed that choices are made of the activity for which the expectancy-value product is maximal (Heckhausen, 1977).

In their theory of reasoned action, Fishbein and Ajzen (1975) propose that performance of actions or activities are contingent on the formation of intentions to perform them. Furthermore, even though some intentions certainly are possible to implement immediately, the existence of constraining factors often necessitates that intentions are incorporated in plans (Ajzen, 1985; Nuttin, 1984). In everyday life intentions are perhaps thus often formed in connection with a planning process (Gärling, Böök, & Lindberg, 1984; B. Hayes-Roth & F. Hayes-Roth, 1979; Miller, Galanter, & Pribram, 1960). The theory of reasoned action, or its successor the theory of planned behavior (Ajzen, 1985), specifies the determinants of the intention to perform a particular activity as the attitude towards performing the activity and the perceived social pressure to perform it. Noting that the performance of an activity is under volitional control in varying degrees depending on the presence of opportunities or possession of adequate resources such as skills, money, time, and the cooperation of other people, Ajzen (1985) proposes that perceived control over performance is another determinant of the intention. An advantage of the theories of reasoned action and planned behavior is that they prescribe methods for how to measure the different components, the intention to perform an activity, the attitude towards performing the activity, the perceived social pressure to perform it, and the perceived control over performance of the activity. These methods have been used in natural settings both to test the validity of the theory and with the practical aim of predicting performance of activities. A large number of such studies which in general have tended to support the theory is summarized in, for instance, Ajzen and Fishbein (1980) and Ajzen (1985). In a study by Ajzen and Madden (1986), perceived control was found to contribute to the prediction of intentions to perform activities which were not under volitional control. Similar results were obtained by Gärling (in press a) for a more representative set of everyday activities.

In the Fishbein and Ajzen theory, the degree to which the attitude is positive toward an activity is assumed to be proportional to the sum of the products of the subjective probability and value of the salient outcomes of performing the activity. Thus, everything else being equal, a person forms (and presumably attempts to implement) an intention to perform a certain activity whose strength is linearly related to the degree his or her attitude is positive toward performing it. The degree of positive attitude is in turn proportional to the product of how likely and valuable salient outcomes of its performance are perceived to be. Of course, a person may intend to act on the basis of mistaken beliefs. It is not certain then that the outcomes will be as expected. Such experiences presumably form the basis for corrections of beliefs (Fishbein & Ajzen, 1975). Furthermore, if an activity is not under volitional control and if the degree of control exerted over its performance is misperceived, the intention formed may never be possible to implement (Ajzen, 1985).

A similar expectancy-value theory of motivation proposed by Heckhausen (1977) is worth mentioning here because its elaboration of the expectancy and value concepts. In this theory, deciding not to perform an activity in a certain situation, rather than to perform it, is explained by assuming that the factor affecting the tendency to perform the activity is the difference in expectancy (subjective probability) that the outcome will occur when the activity is performed and that it will occur when it is not performed. Furthermore, expectations of to what extent the situation will facilitate or impede performance of the activity are also assumed to affect the tendency to perform the activity.

Heckhausen (1977) furthermore makes a distinction between the immediate outcome of performing an activity and the later consequences this outcome may have. It is actually so-called instrumentally beliefs about how the outcome's causal relation to future consequences which may make it desirable. A similar distinction is made by Triandis (1977), but he assumes that performance of the activity may sometimes in itself be desirable. Thus, whether an activity is performed or not may depend on both how desirable it is to perform and how positive or negative the consequences of its performance are. There is an abundance of examples in everyday life where the immediate outcome of an activity is more or less desirable than the future consequences; in fact, one serious problem people seem to have, for instance in health-prevention programs, in energy-conservation programs, or in programs aiming at improving the environment, is to take more into account the future consequences of their activities (Björkman, 1984).

Whereas we noted previously that the problem is to explain the stream of everyday activities, the cognitive motivational theories are limited to single activities. Even so, it seems insufficient to assume that participation is dependent on a single decision or choice. First of all, one may decide to participate in a given activity or not (or, rather, to choose one activity over one or several competing activities). Furthermore, decisions may be made of where, when, for how long, and with whom to perform the chosen activity. Still other decisions concern transportation mode, how to dress, things to bring, etc. Planning or scheduling is a more appropriate term when referring to the process of making such interrelated decisions (Gärling et al., 1984; B. Hayes-Roth & F. Hayes-Roth, 1979; Miller et al., 1960).

The research on planning most frequently recognized in psychology is that by B. Hayes-Roth and F. Hayes-Roth (1979). Their work is particularly relevant in the present context because they studied how people plan a day's errands. Furthermore, it clearly demonstrates that planning is not possible to reduce to a linear sequence of single decisions.

To study planning Hayes-Roth and Hayes-Roth used both the think-aloud technique (Ericson & Simon, 1984) and other techniques such as chronometry and analyses of errors (R. Lachman, J. Lachman, & Butterfield, 1979). On the basis of empirical results, they furthermore developed a computer simulation of planning. In contrast to some previous artificial intelligence research (Sacerdoti, 1977), this simulation entails assumptions about a heteroarchical planning process. Rather than proceeding hierarchically from a global, schematic plan to a more refined plan, people are modelled as opportunistic in their planning. For instance, decisions about how to perform some initial activities may illuminate constraints on the planning of later activities and cause a refocussing on planning of these later activities. In fact, the plans formed develop in the direction which at the time seems most promising. Of course, this less orderly way of proceeding creates the need for revisions during plan development, something which people are observed to be frequently engaged in.

A person may decide that there is not time to plan ahead, to only do some rudimentary planning, or to plan meticulously. Furthermore, some people deliberately avoid to plan to maintain the option of acting spontaneously. Such choices of how much to plan are also an integral part of planning. During planning people are furthermore likely to change forth and back between the different levels of abstraction, rather than always proceeding orderly from the more to the less abstract. Other similar decisions concern by what criteria to evaluate the plan, what types of decisions to make, and by what heuristics to make the decisions. All these higher-order, strategic decisions which explain the way people plan are incorporated in the model.

It is assumed that planning comprises the independent actions of many "cognitive specialists" who record their decisions in a common data structure called the "blackboard" (B. Hayes-Roth & F. Hayes-Roth, 1979). On the basis of the available information on the blackboard, each specialist makes tentative decisions to be incorporated in the plan. As illustrated in Figure 11.2 showing the blackboard, different specialists make different types of decisions: concerning the plan itself; concerning what data are useful in generating the plan; concerning desirable attributes of plan decisions; and concerning how to approach the planning problem (meta-plan decisions). Some of the specialists suggest high-level, abstract additions to the plan, while others suggest detailed sequences of specific operations. In the figure it is indicated that each type of decision may be made at several levels of abstraction. An executive furthermore control the process by making decisions about how to allocate cognitive resources, what types of decisions to make at certain points in time, and resolving conflicts if there are competing decisions.

Expectancy-value theories take some steps toward integrating motivational theories with those cognitive theories which assume that decision making and planning play a crucial role for people's engagement in activities. A further step is taken by Kuhl (1986b, 1987) in his information-processing approach to motivation. As noted in the beginning of this section, Kuhl maintains that a distinction needs to be made between a cognitive, an emotional, and a motivational subsystem. In particular, it is a mistake to equate emotions and motivational states with their cognitive representations. However, he argues that

> ...since most theories of human motivation assume a close interaction between cognitive and motivational processes, a more detailed account of cognitive processes [in such theories] should facilitate the elaboration of models of the interaction between cognition and motivation. (Kuhl, 1986b, p. 404).

He also believes that an information-processing approach should not necessarily be confined to an analysis of cognitive determinants of motivation.

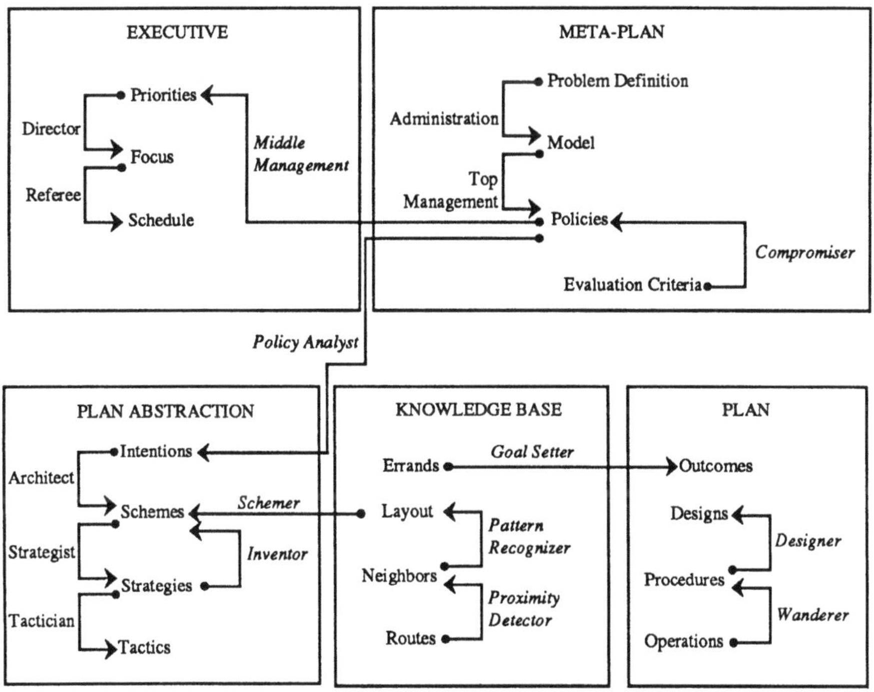


FIGURE 11.2. The blackboard where decisions are recorded. From B. Hayes-Roth and F. Hayes-Roth, 1979. Copyright by Ablex. Reprinted by permission.

Figure 11.3 illustrates hypotheses offered by Kuhl (1987) about the many possible links between the cognitive, emotional, and motivational subsystems which activity participation engages. The sequence of events starts with the activation of a memory representation in the cognitive subsystem, an emotional state, or a plan to carry out a certain activity or sets of activities aiming at attaining some goal. If the memory representation includes a commitment to execute the plan, the motivational subsystem is activated. This subsystem gives access to an executive subsystem which carries out the plan. Several different mechanisms have also been identified by means of which the motivational subsystem shields the execution of the plan from competing plans.

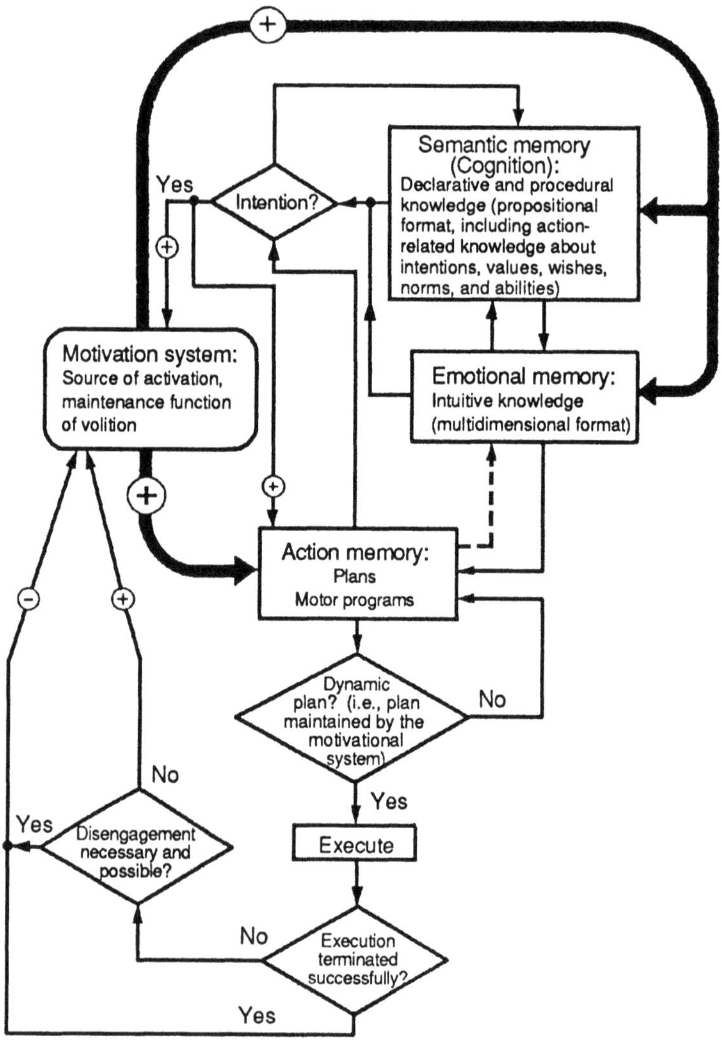


FIGURE 11.3. The different subsystems and their links which activity participation engages. From Kuhl, 1987. Copyright by Springer. Reprinted by permission.

Even though some integration thus appears possible between motivational theories which do not assume that deliberate decisions are made, cognitive theories of decision making and planning, and expectancy-value theories of motivation, it is still the case that these different theories make conflicting basic assumptions. A key issue is what role conscious decisions should be assumed to play. Obviously, analyzing the performance of activities with the aim of defining all conceivable preceding decisions may lead to overemphasizing the role of decision making. At least after some experience, people do not seem to deliberate to the same extent. This is certainly true in laboratory experiments, and informal observations suggest that our daily lives are largely made up of routines. Below we will review cognitive theories which do not assume that all activities are necessarily preceded by deliberate decisions, or that not all decisions preceding activities are deliberate.

### *Cognitive Theories: Routinization*

An attempt to empirically verify that routine or habit determines performance of activities, rather than deliberate decisions (or intentions), is reported by Bentler and Speckart (1979, 1981). Taking as their point of departure Fishbein and Ajzen's theory of reasoned action, they hypothesized that there would be a direct influence on the performance of an activity from the previous frequency with which the same activity had been performed. In Bentler and Speckart (1979), a sample of college students' attitudes towards use, social pressure to use, and actual use of alcohol, marijuana, and hard drugs were measured twice with an interval of two weeks in between. Among other things, it was found that past use influenced subsequent use. However, in Bentler and Speckart (1981) the results differed depending on whether the activity was dating, studying, or exercise.

In a theoretical explanation, Ronis et al. (1989) argued that routine activities are performed automatically. The concept of automaticity is borrowed from cognitive psychology where it denotes automatic processing of information (Schneider & Shiffrin, 1977). The latter is distinguished from its opposite in being fast, effortless, stereotypic, and unavailable to conscious awareness (Hasher & Zacks, 1979; Logan, 1988). Evidence furthermore indicates that automatic processing is acquired after extensive practice in an unchanging environment. According to Logan (1988), automaticity depends on the degree to which needed information is retrieved from memory. The novice begins with an available, general algorithm which is sufficient for performing a particular task. As experience amasses, specific solutions are learned which subsequently is possible to retrieve from memory. When performance depends solely on retrieval from memory, processing is automatized. Thus, according to this account, automatization reflects a transition from algorithm-based to memory-based processing.

Anderson (1982) proposes another conceptualization of automatization. In his general theory of acquisition of cognitive skills, three stages of skill acquisition is envisaged: the declarative stage, the knowledge compilation stage, and the procedural stage. In the first stage knowledge of facts is acquired. However, these facts cannot directly guide action unless interpreted. Because interpretation requires rehearsal of the facts in a working memory, the person is consciously aware of them. With repeated practice, the facts are transformed into procedural knowledge directly guiding actions. This is the stage of knowledge compilation. The conscious attention is then gradually reduced. Finally, in the procedural stage, a routine has been formed which can be executed without conscious control.

An important implication of Anderson's theory, as well as of that of Logan (1988), is that even if an activity has become automatized, a person is still able to gain conscious control over its performance. In Logan's theory, the algorithm is still available to be used, whereas in Anderson's theory, the declarative knowledge may still be subjected to the interpretative process. Norman and Shallice (1986) suggest that a supervisory attentional system monitors cognitive control. Thus, a person has the choice between the options of implementing a routine or to take conscious control over an activity. Another implication is that an activity only gradually become automatic. Since automaticity thus forms a continuum along which activities vary, it is difficult to know whether or not an activity should be classified as automatic.

It should at this point be clear that cognitive theories of automatization primarily deal with skill in performing everyday activities. Apparently, practising an activity leads to skill in its performance. As a consequence, fewer deliberate decisions are made. However, the role played by the motivational subsystem is not made explicit. Why should a skill or plan, however well practised, be executed unless the person is committed (intend) to do so? Entailed by the concept of automatization is that performance of activities is dependent on situational cues. Thus, it is conceivable that motivational components, such as goals, play an increasingly minor role, the more automatized an activity is. The fact that we frequently perform actions which are not intended (action slips) is evidence of this (Reason & Mycielska, 1982), although Heckhausen and

Beckman (1990) offer an alternative interpretation in the form of a hierarchy of intentions from a lowest molecular to a highest goal level.

A remaining question is why a person chooses to take conscious control over an activity? The distinction between intentional or consciously controlled activities and automatic or routine activities does not necessarily contradict the assumption that people engage in activities because they pursue different goals. Persons have many goals, all of which are not salient at a certain point in time. It is possible that those goals which a person is uncertain about how to attain are currently salient. This could be either because the goals are new and the person does not know how to achieve them, or because the well-learned activities by which the goals are attained for some reason must be replaced with less well learned activities. In such situations, the person has to evaluate different activities, decide which to implement, and closely monitor their implementation to achieve the desired outcomes (Carver & Scheier, 1981). If successful, the activities may be repeated until they eventually become automatized. As the activities needed to attain the goal become more routine and automatic, the goal becomes less salient and the person is likely to allocate his or her conscious capacity to the fulfillment of other, more salient goals.

Another possibility is that the person acquires some new goals. These goals are then likely to become salient. If routine activities are found to be useful for the attainment of the new goals, they will probably nevertheless be performed more deliberate. Empirical evidence that intentional activities are more related to salient goals than routines are, will be presented in the following section.

## Research Examples

### *Study 1*

A theoretically important question is whether many typical everyday activities are performed routinely. To the extent they are, one should not expect planning and the formation of intentions to play any major role for the performance of these activities. As mentioned above, Bentler and Speckart (1979, 1981) addressed this question. However, they chose rather nontypical, or, at least, limited sets of typical everyday activities. Therefore, we decided to replicate their studies with a more representative sample of activities which people typically perform in their leisure time.

As described in Gärling (in press b), the procedure was similar to that used by Bentler and Speckart (1979, 1981). Subjects were 64 students at University of Umeå, an equal number of men and women, who were paid for taking part in a study at the Department of Psychology. Only general information was provided about the study until subjects were debriefed the last time they attended. The participating subjects were requested on one occasion to report, in counterbalanced order, how frequently they had performed ten different activities (see Table 11.1) the preceding week and how frequently they intended to do it a following week. For a randomly selected half of the subjects the target week was the immediately following week, whereas for the other half of the subjects it was the week after that week. All subjects were asked after the target week to report how frequently they had performed the activities that week.

TABLE 11.1

*Correlations Between Performance of Everyday Activities on 1st ($F_1$) and 2nd Occasions ($F_2$), Correlations of Performance with Intentions (I), and Correlations of Performance on 1st and 2nd Occasions with Intentions Partialled out, Respectively (Study 1).*

| | Following week | | | Week after following week | | | Difference | | |
|---|---|---|---|---|---|---|---|---|---|
| Activity | $r_{F_1F_2}$ | $r_{IF_2}$ | $r_{F_1F_2.I}$ | $r_{F_1F_2}$ | $r_{IF_2}$ | $r_{F_1F_2.I}$ | $r_{F_1F_2}$ | $r_{IF_2}$ | $r_{F_1F_2.I}$ |
| Cleaning | .35* | .17 | .32 | .49** | .60*** | .50** | –.14 | –.43 | –.18 |
| Taking a shower | .86*** | .67*** | .74*** | .85*** | .89*** | .52** | .01 | –.22 | .22 |
| Running | .94*** | .78*** | .85*** | .71*** | .47** | .60*** | .23 | .31 | .15 |
| Having wine | .58*** | .37* | .52** | .32 | .44* | .17 | .26 | –.07 | .35 |
| Talking to parents | .62*** | .59*** | .48** | .49** | .81** | .01 | .13 | –.22 | .47 |
| Inviting friends | .53** | .56*** | .50** | .43* | .27 | .35* | .10 | .29 | .15 |
| Dining out | .65*** | .76*** | .30 | .36* | .10 | .35* | .29 | .66** | –.05 |
| Going to disco | .29 | .41* | .12 | .40* | .24 | .35* | –.11 | .17 | –.24 |
| Going to movies | .17 | .40* | .11 | .29 | .11 | .27 | –.12 | .29 | –.26 |
| Watching TV news | .79*** | .60*** | .67*** | .74*** | .66*** | .45** | .05 | –.06 | .22 |

*$p<.05$ **$p<.01$ ***$p<.001$

From Gärling, in press b. Reprinted by permission.

The way data were collected made it possible to determine which one of the stated intention or the previous frequency of performance was the best predictor of actual performance of the activities. Of course, if intention plays no role, previous frequency should predict actual performance better. Furthermore, if previous frequency reflects routine performance, one may expect it would predict actual performance equally well after two as after one week. Because intention, on the other hand, are likely to change more over time (e.g., Ajzen, 1985), it should predict actual performance worse after two than after one week.

The results are given in Table 11.1 in the form of product-moment correlations between the different measures calculated across subjects in each subgroup. Although not shown in the table, previous frequency of performance tended to correlate with intention. Partial correlations were therefore calculated between the former and actual performance keeping intention constant. With some exceptions, the partial correlations remained significant, thus suggesting that previous frequency may be the better predictor. Except for dining out, where intention better predicted actual performance the following week than the week after, there were no statistically reliable differences depending on for which week predictions were made. Activities for which intention seemed to play a mediating role were, in the condition where subjects reported their intentions for the following week, dining out, going to a disco, and going to the movies, in the other condition having wine and talking to parents.

Thus, the results suggested that some typical everyday activities are routinely performed, others are not. Apart from demonstrating a method suitable to determine how routinely activities are performed, the results raise the intriguing question of why certain activities, but not others, are thus performed. There may be a correlation with the frequency with which people engage in the activities. However, frequency of performance cannot in itself be an explanation.

### *Study 2*

The question of why some everyday activities are routinely performed, whereas for others intention plays a more important role, was raised in a second study. Our analysis of the question indicated that the degree of nonroutine performance of an activity is dependent on its perceived relationship to goals which are currently salient. Most everyday activities, if not all, are related to important goals, such as survival, remaining healthy, feeling pride in oneself, being satisfied, etc. (Gärling et al., 1989). However, at a certain point in time, not all these goals are salient, and only if they are, the performance of activities perceived as instrumental for their attainment become nonroutine. An example is that if the goal of weight loss becomes salient, eating (which may be routine despite its relationship to survival) is likely to become more controlled by intentions. The frequency with which the activity is performed may or may not for that reason change.

Some recent research has investigated the current goals, current concerns, or current strivings people pursue (e.g., Klinger, Barta, & Maxeiner, 1981). In this research current concern is defined as a person's state from he or she becomes committed to pursuing a particular goal until it is attained or abandoned. Little (1983) introduced the concept of personal project which is similarly defined. He also proposed a method of finding out about what personal projects people pursue as well as their characteristics. Our procedure (Gärling, 1991) was modelled after this method.

In Study 2 a correlation was sought between a measure of how related a set of everyday activities are perceived to be to the attainment of current goals and whether performance of the activities is determined by intentions to perform them. A measure was also obtained of how routinely the activities are performed in order to investigate the converse claim that if everyday activities are unrelated to current goals, they are routinely performed.

Another two groups of 24 students at the University of Umeå, equally many men as women, participated as subjects. When coming to the laboratory to participate in another study, the subjects were asked to fill out a brief questionnaire. In that questionnaire subjects first listed their five most important current goals. In counterbalanced order subjects were then asked to indicate what they intended to do (in one group on the following day, in the other group the following day one week later), and what they expected to do without intending it[2]. Finally, each listed activity was rated by the subjects with respect to how much it was related to their current goals and with respect to how routinely it was currently performed.

Except for graduation, most current goals subjects listed were nonacademic, shorter-term goals such as improve physical shape, improve personal economy, etc. Consistent with what had been hypothesized, Table 11.2 shows that intended activities were rated by subjects as more related to their goals and less routine, whereas the reverse was true of

---

[2] The correlation observed in Study 1 between previous frequency of performance of an activity and the intention to perform it at a certain frequency suggested that subjects may try to recall what they usually do when asked to indicate what they intend to do. Asking subjects what they expected to do was then supposed to induce them to recall their routine activities. If subjects also recalled their routine activities when indicating what they intended to do, no difference in results for these tasks should be expected.

activities they expected to perform. Whether or not an activity was intended was also possible to predict from the ratings by means of discriminant analyses. In these analyses the ratings of routine tended to predict intention better for the subjects who indicated what they intended to do the following day, whereas the ratings of goal-relatedness were a better predictor of intention in the other group of subjects. As one should expect, intention was also somewhat better predicted overall in the former group.

TABLE 11.2

*Mean Ratings of Routine and Goal-Relatedness of Activities Which Were Intended (I) and Not Intended (NI), Respectively, and Standardized Regression Weights (B) and Multiple Correlations (R) for Discriminant Functions Predicting Intentions*

| | Routine | | | Goal-Relatedness | | | |
|---|---|---|---|---|---|---|---|
| | NI | I | B | NI | I | B | R |
| Following day ($n$=22) | 72.6 | 38.4 | -0.64*** | 45.4 | 50.6 | -0.05 | .63*** |
| Next week ($n$=17) | 61.8 | 42.4 | -0.27 | 41.1 | 63.6 | 0.42* | .52** |

$^{*}p<.05$ $^{**}p<.01$ $^{***}p<.001$

The results also showed which activities subjects intended and which they did not intend but expected to perform. Some activities stood out as more often intended, such as studying, attending class, working extra, going to the movies, and, to a lesser extent, physical exercise. A few other activities such as shopping also appeared to be most often intended but usually closer in time to their performance. Still other activities such as personal reading, playing/listening to music, watching TV, and relaxing were performed more routinely. There were, finally, activities which were both intended and routinely performed, such as housework, having meals/snacks, and socializing with friends.

One implication of the results is that whether an activity is routinely performed or not varies across persons and over time. Thus, any classification of activities which fail to take this into account will be inaccurate. Does this imply that any classification is useless? As stated before, if data are collected about the current goals people have, in addition to what activities they are engaged in, other possibilities become available. Further research is desirable for working out these possibilities in more detail.

## Summary and Conclusions

The present chapter addressed the questions of why people participate in everyday activities, what meanings they ascribe to such participation, and what the consequences are for their subjective well-being. An approach to the task of classifying and measuring everyday activities was furthermore proposed.

Nonpsychological explanations (cf. Chapter 10) were first briefly reviewed, followed by a more thorough review of psychological explanations. In many cases the latter are, in contrast to the former, scarcely possible to directly generalize to everyday activities. It is in particular difficult to build the necessary bridges between the relatively simple activities studied in the laboratory and the complex everyday phenomena we have been concerned with in this chapter. There are however exceptions such as, for instance, the theorizing of Fishbein and Ajzen (1975). Furthermore, mechanisms studied in the laboratory, for instance many of those postulated in the theory of Atkinson and Birch (1970, 1986), should govern the everyday phenomena.

Although the review of psychological explanations emphasized cognitive processes entailed by judgment, decision, and planning, it spanned the range from ecological through motivational to cognitive psychology. Of particular interest to note is the recurrent theme that activities are goal-related (Kuhl, 1986a; Nuttin, 1984). Furthermore, the participation in everyday activities is not likely to only involve cognitive processes but to be driven by the activation of a motivational subsystem. This has most clearly been expressed in the theorizing of Kuhl (1986b, 1987), which may be seen as a synthesis of the dynamic motivational theory of Atkinson and Birch (1970, 1986) and cognitive motivational theories (Weiner, 1980).

Although a cognitive approach ascribing an important role to conscious decisions is presently highlighted, it must be acknowledged that the performance of everyday activities entails the formation of habits or routinization. The role of the latter appears however to be difficult to disentangle. Empirical research in cognitive psychology demonstrates that learning profoundly affects performance by making it more automatic and effortless (Logan, 1988). However, it seems to be less recognized, but in the present context highly important, that routinization also seems to involve changes in goal saliency. Even important goals may, for instance, become temporarily less salient, thus causing activities related to these goals to be performed more routinely. We used our own empirical results to illustrate this point.

Given that motivational components such as goals are so closely related to what activities people perform and how they perform them, any system of classifying and measuring everyday activities needs to take this into account. We suggest tentatively that a more intensive methodology be tried, entailing measurements not only of spatiotemporal-dynamic properties of everyday activities but of how the activities are related to goals. As demonstrated above in Study 2, such a methodology may reveal individual differences making it difficult to impose a rigid system of classification. In our opinion, ways of handling this complexity must be developed in future research. The new methodology may appear less objective than a classification based on physical variables. However, as was noted above (footnote 1), there is no ground for such a belief. On the contrary, we feel that such a methodological reorientation is both acceptable according to stringent scientific criteria, and also important if research on participation in everyday activities should continue to make contributions to the social sciences and to their applications in planning.

## Acknowledgements

The chapter was in part written while the first author, during the 1990/91 academic year, visited the Program in Social Ecology, University of California, Irvine. The visit was made possible by a Fulbright grant. The research reported in the chapter, as well as its writing, was financially supported by grants to the first author from the Swedish Council for Research in the Humanities and Social Sciences. We would like to express our gratitude to Kay Axhausen, Reginald G. Golledge, and Terry Hartig who provided valuable comments on drafts.

## References

Ajzen, I. (1985). From intentions to actions: A theory of planned behavior. In J. Kuhl & J. Beckman (Eds.), *Action control: From cognition to behavior* (pp. 11-39). Berlin: Springer.

Ajzen, I., & Fishbein, M. (1980). *Understanding attitudes and predicting social behavior*. Englewood Cliffs, NJ: Prentice-Hall.

Ajzen, I., & Madden, T. J. (1986). Prediction of goal-directed behavior: Attitudes, intentions, and perceived control. *Journal of Experimental Social Psychology, 22*, 453-474.

Anderson, J. R. (1982). Acquisition of cognitive skill. *Psychological Review, 89*, 369-406.

Atkinson, J. W., & Birch, D. (1970). *The dynamics of action*. New York: Wiley.
Atkinson, J. W., & Birch, D. (1986). Fundamentals of the dynamics of action. In J. Kuhl & J. W. Atkinson (Eds.), *Motivation, thought, and action* (pp. 16-48). New York: Praeger.
Axhausen, K., & Gärling, T. (in press). activity-based approaches to travel analysis: Conceptual frameworks, models, and research problems. *Transport Reviews*.
Barker, R. (1963). The stream of behavior as an empirical problem. In R. Barker (Ed.), *The stream of behavior* (pp. 1-22). New York: Appleton-Century-Crofts.
Barker, R. G., & Wright, H. F. (1951). *One boy's day*. New York: Harper.
Bentler, A., & Speckart, G. (1981). Attitudes "cause" behaviors: A structural equation analysis. *Journal of Personality and Social Psychology, 40*, 226-238.
Bentler, P. M., & Speckart, G. (1979). Models of attitude-behavior relations. *Psychological Review, 86*, 452-464.
Birch, D. (1986). From the dynamics of action to measuring the stream of behavior. In J. Kuhl & J. W. Atkinson (Eds.), *Motivation, thought, and action* (pp. 49-75). New York: Praeger.
Birch, D., Atkinson, J. W., & Bongort, K. (1974). Cognitive control of action. In B. Weiner (Ed.), *Cognitive views of human motivation* (pp. 71-84). New York: Academic Press.
Björkman, M. (1984). Decision making, risk taking, and psychological time: Review of empirical findings and psychological theory. *Scandinavian Journal of Psychology, 25*, 31-49.
Campbell, A., Converse, P., & Rodgers, W. (1976). *The quality of American life*. New York: Russell Sage Foundation.
Carver, C. S., & Scheier, M. (1981). *Attention and self-regulation: A control theory approach to human behavior*. New York: Springer.
Cullen, I. G. (1976). Human geography, regional science, and the study of individual behavior. *Environment and Planning A, 8*, 397-409.
Edwards, W. (1954). The theory of decision making. *Psychological Bulletin, 51*, 380-417.
Ericson, K. A., & Simon, H. A. (1984). *Protocol analysis: Verbal reports as data*. Cambridge, MA: MIT Press.
Feather, N. (1982). Expectancy-value approaches: Present status and future directions. In N. Feather (Ed.), *Expectations and actions: Expectancy-value models in psychology* (pp. 395-420). Hillsdale, NJ: Erlbaum.

Fishbein, M., & Ajzen, I. (1975). *Belief, attitude, intention and behavior: An introduction to theory and research.* Reading, MA: Addison-Wesley.

Gärling, T. (1991). *The impact of goals on everyday routines* (Umeå Psychological Report No. 204). Umeå, Sweden: Department of Psychology, University of Umeå.

Gärling, T. (in press a). Determinants of everyday time allocation. *Scandinavian Journal of Psychology.*

Gärling, T. (in press b). The importance of routines for the performance of everyday activities. *Scandinavian Journal of Psychology.*

Gärling, T., Böök, A., & Lindberg, E. (1984). Cognitive mapping of large-scale environments: The interrelationship of action plans, acquisition, and orientation. *Environment and Behavior, 16*, 3-34.

Gärling, T., Lindberg, E., & Montgomery, H. (1989). Beliefs about attainment of life satisfaction as determinants of preferences for everyday activities. In K. G. Grunert & F. Ölander (Eds.), *Understanding economic behavior* (pp. 33-46). Dordrecht, The Netherlands: Kluwer.

Gärling, T., Lindberg, E., Torell, G., & Evans, G. W. (1991). From environmental to ecological cognition. In T. Gärling & G. W. Evans (Eds.), *Environment, cognition and action: An integrated approach* (pp. 335-344). New York: Oxford University Press.

Golledge, R. G., & Stimson, R. J. (1987). *Analytical behavioral geography*. London: Croom Helm.

Hägerstrand, T. (1970). What about people in regional science? *Papers of the Regional Science Association, 24*, 7-21.

Hasher, L., & Zacks, R. T. (1979). Automatic and effortful processes in memory. *Journal of Experimental Psychology: General, 108*, 356-388.

Hayes-Roth, B., & Hayes-Roth, F. (1979). A cognitive model of planning. *Cognitive Science, 3*, 275-310.

Heckhausen, H. (1977). Achievement motivation and its constructs: A cognitive model. *Motivation and Emotion, 1*, 283-329.

Heckhausen, H., & Beckman, J. (1990). Intentional action and action slips. *Psychological Review, 97,* 36-48.

Horgan, T. (1976). Reduction and the mind-body problem. In M. H. Marx & F. E. Goodson (Eds.), *Theories in contemporary psychology* (2nd ed., 223-231). London: Macmillan.

Hormuth, S. (1986). The random sampling of experiences in situ. *Journal of Personality, 54*, 262-293.

Ittelson, W. H., Rivlin, L. G., & Proshansky, H. M. (1976). The use of behavioral maps in environmental psychology. In H. M. Proshansky, W. H. Ittelson, & L. G. Rivlin (Eds.), *Environmental psychology: People and their physical settings* (2nd ed., pp. 340-351). New York: Holt, Rinehart and Winston.

Klinger, E., Barta, S. G., & Maxeiner, M. E. (1980). Motivational correlates of thought content frequency and commitment. *Journal of Personality and Social Psychology, 39*, 1222-1237.

Kuhl, J. (1986a). Introduction. In J. Kuhl & J. W. Atkinson (Eds.), *Motivation, thought, and action* (pp. 1-15). New York: Praeger.

Kuhl, J. (1986b). Motivation and information processing: A new look at decision making, dynamic change, and action control. In R. M. Sorrention & E. Tory Higgins (Eds.), *Handbook of motivation and cognition* (pp. 404-434). Chichester: Wiley.

Kuhl, J. (1987). Action control: The maintenance of motivational states. In F. Halisch & J. Kuhl (Eds.), *Motivation, intention, and volition* (pp. 279-291). Berlin: Springer-Verlag.

Kuhl, J., & Geiger, E. (1986). The dynamic theory of the anxiety-behavior relationship: A study on resistance and time allocation. In J. Kuhl & J. W. Atkinson (Eds.), *Motivation, thought, and action* (pp. 76-93). New York: Praeger.

Lachman, R., Lachman, J., & Butterfield, E. C. (1979). *Cognitive psychology and information processing: An introduction.* Hillsdale, NJ: Erlbaum.

Little, B. R. (1983). Personal projects: A rational and method for investigation. *Environment and Behavior, 15*, 273-309.

Logan, G. D. (1988). Toward an instance theory of automatization. *Psychological Review, 95*, 492-527.

McClelland, D. C., Atkinson, J. W., Clark, R. A., & Lowell, E. L. (1953). *The achieving society.* New York: Appleton-Century-Crofts.

Michelson, W., & Reed, P. (1975). The time budget. In W. Michelson (Ed.), *Behavioral research methods in environmental design* (pp. 180-234). Stroudsberg, PA: Hutchinson Ross.

Miller, G. A., Galanter, E., & Pribram, K. H. (1960). *Plans and the structure of behavior*. New York: Holt, Rinehart & Winston.

Newtson, D., Rindner, R., Miller, R., & LaCross, K. (1978). Effects of availability of feature changes on behavioral segmentation. *Journal of Experimental Social Psychology, 14*, 379-388.

Norman, D. A., & Shallice, T. (1986). Attention to action: Willed and automatic control of behavior. In R. J. Davidson, G. E. Schwartz, & D. Shapiro (Eds.), *Consciousness and self-regulation: Advances in research and theory* (Vol. 4, pp. 1-18). New York: Plenum.

Nuttin, J. (1984). *Motivation, planning, and action.* Hillsdale, NJ: Leuven University Press and Erlbaum.
Reason, J., & Mycielska, K. (1982). *Absent-minded? The psychology of mental lapses and everyday errors.* Englewood Cliffs, NJ: Prentice-Hall.
Rips, L. J., & Conrad, F. G. (1989). Folk psychology of mental activities. *Psychological Review, 96*, 187-207.
Ronis, D. L., Yates, J. F., & Kirscht, J. P. (1989). Attitudes, decisions, and habits as determinants of repeated behavior. In A. R. Pratkanis, S. J. Brecker, & A. G. Greenwald (Eds.), *Attitude structure and function* (pp. 213-239). Hillsdale, NJ: Erlbaum.
Sacerdoti, E. D. (1977). *A structure for plans and behavior.* New York: Elsevier.
Schipper, L., Bartlett, S., Hawk, D., & Vine, E. (1989). Linking lifestyles and energy use: A matter of time. *Annual Review of Energy, 14*, 273-320.
Schneider, W., & Shiffrin, R. M. (1977). Controlled and automatic human information processing: I. Detection, search and attention. *Psychological Review, 84,* 1-66.
Simon, H. A. (1990). Invariants of human behavior. *Annual Review of Psychology, 41,* 1-19.
Sjöberg, L., & Magneberg, R. (1990). Action and emotion in everyday life. *Scandinavian Journal of Psychology, 31*, 9-27.
Stewart, A. J. (1982). The course of individual adaptation to life changes. *Journal of Personality and Social Psychology, 42,* 1000-1113.
Szalai, A., Converse, P., Feldheim, P., Scheuch, E., & Stone, P. (Eds.). (1972). *The use of time.* The Hague: Moulton.
Triandis, H. C. (1977). *Interpersonal behavior.* Monterey, CA: Brooks/Cole.
Vallacher, R. R., & Wegner, D. M. (1987). What do people think they're doing? Action identification and human behavior. *Psychological Review, 94*, 3-15.
Weiner, B. (1980). *Human motivation.* New York: Holt, Rinehart and Winston.
Winston, G. C. (1982). *The timing of economic activities.* Cambridge: Cambridge University Press.

# PART II

# The Real-World Contexts of Basic Processes of Behavior-Environment Interaction

*Behavior and Environment: Psychological and Geographical Approaches*
*T. Gärling and R.G. Golledge (Editors)*


## CHAPTER 12

# Search and Choice in Urban Housing Markets

**W. A. V. Clark**

Studies of residential search and choice now form a substantial and coherent body of knowledge (Clark, 1981, 1982a, 1982b, 1986). Methodological developments in discrete choice models (Wrigley, 1985), research in conjoint measurement (Phipps & Clark, 1987) and investigations of scaling models of choice (Timmermans, 1984) continue to stimulate studies of search and choice at local and aggregate scales. It is not possible to do justice to the whole of this literature. The focus of this chapter is narrowed to studies which have explicitly incorporated the spatial context or a spatial structure into the research design.

It is useful to examine what is still a reasonable structure for examining residential search choice questions and to place the more recent explicitly spatial contributions into that larger research context. The larger context is one in which the residential relocation process is divided into a decision to move, a decision to view alternatives (search), and the actual relocation behavior (the choice outcome itself). The decision to move is now accepted as a process of adjusting a (perceived) disequilibrium, sometime viewed as stress (Huff & Clark, 1978) but in every case a tradeoff between a current and an alternative residential location. The search process is driven by households falling out of adjustment and into disequilibrium as their housing composition changes. The search process is less clearly specified although there is a substantial body of empirical results which suggests a wide range of approaches to house search. The final choice is seen in the context of matching household needs to housing characteristics. (Figure 12.1)

The investigations of search and choice in geography now have a two and a half decade history and the analytical and empirical contributions have provided a rich understanding of the dimensions of the search process (Clark 1981, 1983) However, as Montgomery notes (Chapter 13 of this book), we are still a good distance from being able to predict the likelihood of a move or the actual choice of a dwelling. The work that has been accomplished as sketched out in Figure 12.1 suggests a set of models which parallel the division of research into the likelihood of a move, the decision to search and the search process itself and the actual dwelling

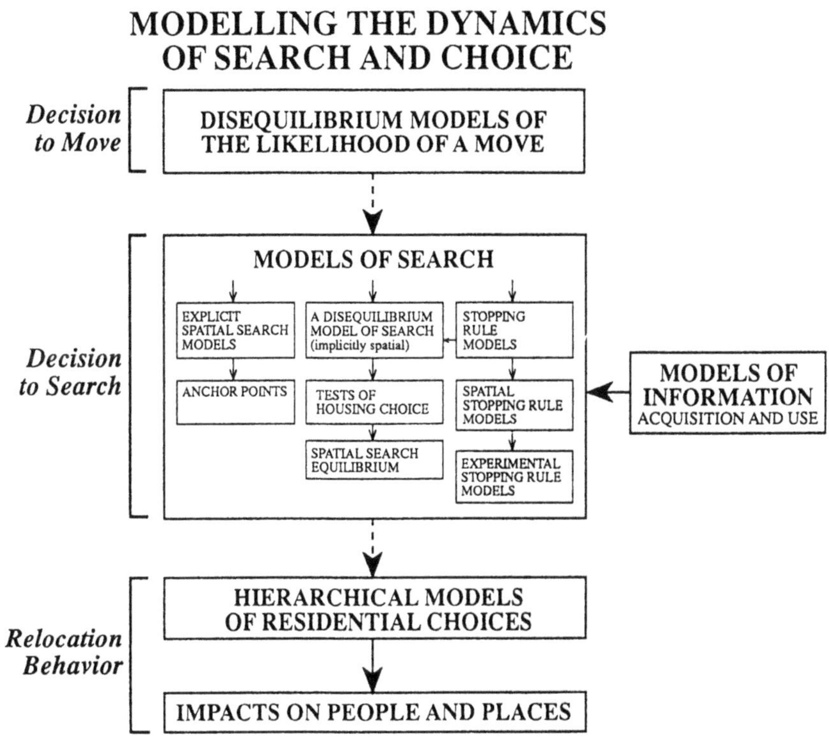


FIGURE 12.1. The structure of research on search and choice in residential mobility.

choice. The complexity involved in modelling choice and search has tended to generate research and models within one of these contexts and as yet there are no overarching models which truly link models of the decision to move and the search process. Hence it is better to think of the decision to move and the choice itself as the structure with the search process embedded within the overall mobility decision making. The multinomial hierarchical choice models (McFadden, 1978; Lerman, 1979; Lierop, 1981, 1986; Porell, 1982; Clark & Onaka 1985) have come closest to providing a decision making structure in which the choice to move is the primary choice, followed by the choice of area to search followed by the choice of house to select but empirical testing has been limited.

## Why Study Residential Search and Choice?

For at least two decades the emphasis in behavioral studies of residential relocation was on why people moved and occasionally on the impacts of mobility on individuals and on the urban structure. Slowly, however, it became apparent that we needed to know much more about the complex interconnections between the urban structure and human behavior. It was no longer enough to show that people often moved short distances in neighborhoods that they were familiar with, that they moved to bring their housing consumption nearer to equilibrium consumption, that younger households moved more often or that tenure was important, (that renters moved more often and owners less often). It was important to relate mobility to the built environment and to ask questions about the interaction of search, choice, and impacts both on the changing neighborhoods of cities and, by extension, on the population composition of neighborhoods. The focus on mobility and choice for its own sake was replaced by a concern with the integration of the processes of search, choice, and urban structural change. The focus moved from studies of why people moved to what were the processes and impacts of population relocation. In turn it created a bipolar approach to understanding relocation behavior. Simple questions of why people move were replaced either with studies of the socio/psychological processes of decision making or studies of geographic outcomes.

Understanding how people make decisions and understanding the choices that they make enriches our understanding of the general processes of behavior in the city and, by extension, our understanding of how neighborhoods change in the city. Just as studying activity patterns provides a way of assessing the relationship between environment and behavior, so studies of the search patterns and the choices that households make provides a link between the built environment, the neighborhoods of the city, and the people who live in them. Why do certain households end up in certain locations, and how are choices of locations affected by search and selection? These are questions which arise from a focus on residential search and choice when those topics are linked to the urban built environment.

A concern with residential search and choice is more than a way of linking behavior and urban structure. It also allows us to raise important questions about how housing opportunities are known and used, and on the spatial extent of peoples' experiences of the built environment. Even more important, the search and relocation behaviors raise questions about the extent to which choices are exercised freely or are constrained by household factors and factors of the market. For a time investigations of residential migration emphasized household preferences and unconstrained choices (Clark, 1981; Rossi, 1955). A counterbalancing perspective (Murie, 1974; Barrett & Short, 1979) emphasized the constraints on the mobility process which arise from the structure of the housing market itself and the actions of institutional actors in the housing market. To some, the actions of individual households were better explained by the nature of the housing system than consumer preferences (Barrett & Short, 1979), to others the individual choice process was still the primary explanation (Clark, 1986). Now, most research takes a middle ground with the actions of individuals grounded in the structure of the housing market. While individual households are necessarily constrained by the availability of housing by tenure, price and location, at the same time there is considerable evidence of individual choices in both controlled and less controlled housing markets (Dieleman, Deurloo, & Clark, 1989), and that the same processes are at work in both controlled and uncontrolled markets (Dieleman et al., 1989).

Even though there are still vigorous debates about choice and constraint, in the end studies of search and choice in the housing market will be important to the extent that they inform policy. While the extent of the spatial search for new housing is probably only peripherally related to questions of housing provision, a better understanding of the preferences for particular tenures, a better understanding of locational preferences and how those preferences are formed and how they influence choices in the housing market are an important part of understanding how the urban structure will evolve. Current interests in urban restructuring, in polycentric urban forms and the spatial organization of a pluralistic urban form will be better served by a theoretically informed understanding of residential search and choice.

## The State of Knowledge

To reiterate, initial studies of residential migration revolved around "why did a household move" and "who got what" in the housing market when they moved.The emphasis was on choice of tenure, choice of housing composition (size, amenities and so on) and choice of location. The studies were designed to explore the question of why people moved, and why they chose a given location and a given house. The research from this approach documented that people moved to improve their housing situation, to increase their space, to own rather than rent, and to improve their accessibility within their locational context. A quantitative evaluation of the choices emphasized the housing context as the explanation of their choice rather than the neighborhood or the environment. But even though this initial research has now provided a rich documentation and understanding of residential choices, and serviceable models of the way in which disequilibrium in housing consumption leads to the decision to move, the "moving process" itself was at least initially neglected. However, by the end of the decade of the 80s, studies of search had provided a set of new conceptualizations and documentation of the empirical nature of search.

### *Implicit Spatial Models of Search*

There are two sources for much of the initial research on residential search and choice. On the one hand, marketing and economics provided basic models of "search", and, on the other hand, psychology focused on choosing among alternatives. While marketing has some similarities with the psychological approaches, economics built a strong theoretical approach to the process of "stopping search". Such models focus on the issue of when to accept an offer (usually a job offer), versus continuing to search and to incur the associated costs. The job search literature (Clark & Flowerdew, 1982) emphasizes the influence of information and the way in which uncertainty and the flow of information influence the decision to continue searching. As in other work by economists, the emphasis has been on the nature of optimum search strategies within utility-maximization frameworks (Phipps & Laverty, 1983). There have been attempts to frame housing search in this context (Ioannides, 1979). The large literature in psychology is more concerned with choice among alternatives (which of course implies the existence of a search and evaluation process).

The emphasis in the psychological literature is on how alternatives are evaluated rather than how they are collected and identified. The focus extends to the role of information and opinion revision rather than identification. To psychologists, choice emphasizes individual judgments. These are often judgments of sets of alternatives conveyed to a panel and do not include identification of alternatives. The latter may be more central in the residential decision making environment. (For a discussion of the psychological approach, see Slovic, Fischoff, & Lichtenstein, 1977; Clark & Flowerdew, 1982.)

Geographers borrowed from this work and evaluated the use of stopping rule models (Flowerdew, 1976) and disequilibrium approaches to residential mobility in general (Smith, Clark, Huff, & Shapiro, 1979). But, again as in the economic approaches, these models were only implicitly spatial and there was a tendency to treat space or location as simply one attribute of the alternatives to be considered. Even so, in the Smith et al. (1979) presentation, although space was implicit it was an important component of the model. The expected utility attached to search for a dwelling in "a given neighborhood" is based upon the household's prior estimates of the housing characteristics in the area and the expected costs of search in that area (Smith et al., 1979). Thus, neighborhoods are clearly a part of the model but are the context in which search occurs rather than the defining characteristics of the process itself. These notions of the search process as a utility-equilibrium process emphasize that an individual's decision to search is a function of the difference between the expected utility of further search and the utility of the best vacancy found to date (Clark & Smith, 1982). As the model is neighborhood (or community) based, individuals compute the locational stress of neighborhoods in the city and search in the neighborhood which gives rise to the largest positive stress value, that is the neighborhood where the likelihood of success is greatest. A vacancy with greater utility than the current house (or vacancy) becomes the best alternative, and search continues until stress is driven to non-positive values in all neighborhoods. A test of the model in a section of Los Angeles provided some support for the process described by the model.

***Models of spatial residential search.*** In contrast to the Clark/Smith equilibrium approach, Huff (1986) provided two classes of models which are truly spatial, focusing on the nature of selection from areas and in relationship to search constraints (Figure 12.2). The area-based search model is the outcome of considering the search process as one in which households make the decision to visit a particular vacancy conditional on the area containing that vacancy. Areas with large numbers of vacancies have a greater chance of being included in the search space. But at the same time the prior search experience of the household influences the likelihood of visiting particular areas. Selecting an area is followed by a more intensive activity in that area with high probabilities of visiting vacancies near the last vacancy visited. Huff (1986) provides a formalized model of these observations, and in a test of the model in a part of the Los Angeles region, shows that households tend to persist in submarket search once an area has been identified and "provides strong behavioral evidence of the existence of geographically defined submarkets that limit the domain of search for individual households" (Huff, 1986, p. 217).

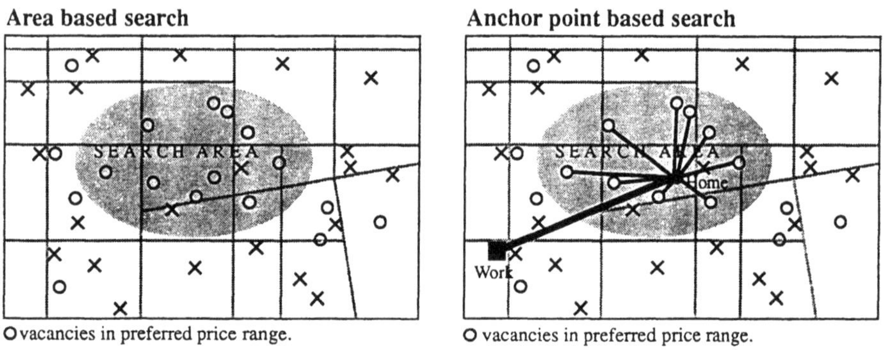


FIGURE 12.2 The spatial context of search based on Huff (1986).

The anchor-points search model also assumes that the observed search pattern reflects the underlying distribution of vacancies. However, in this case the bias in the spatial pattern of search is related to locational preferences of the household and specifically of the way in which a household concentrates search in a small area around a focal point. Search declines in intensity around the focal point. The empirical basis for this model suggests that a subset of households employ a locationally persistent search strategy by which they concentrate effort near the mean center of the search pattern. That the anchor-points model was able to match the observed search distribution over 50% of the time is convincing evidence of the importance of anchor or reference points in the search process. Both the area-based and the anchor-point models provide evidence of the strong spatial regularities in residential search. These models demonstrate that it is possible to build operational search models which build space into the search process in such a way that we can predict where households will search and, by extension where they will move.

### *The Intersection of Search, Choice and the Housing Market Environment*

An important element of the Huff (1986) search models is the recognition of variation in the housing market. Housing markets are differentiated spatially. They are differentiated by tenure and by price. It is this differentiation which underlies the creation of residential environments which are reflected in the search and choice process of individual households. Households do not search and choose in a vacuum. They are able to segment the housing market by these important variables which then enter into the search and choice process (Bourne, 1981).

A generally accepted view is that submarkets for housing do exist but at the same time there is only a limited literature devoted to defining their structure, and even less on the way in which these submarkets influence search and choice. Even so, some form of spatial segmentation is at the heart of the discussions that we have introduced in this chapter. There are clearly identifiable areas (by price, quality, accessibility, and so on), and it is these areas which help define the search process. Bourne (1981) has suggested that at the smallest spatial scale, the neighborhood scale, the only distinguishing feature of the housing market is that of limited spatial entity. Of course the difficulty is in defining that spatial entity. To date the definitions of submarkets are pragmatic statistical decisions and not theoretically based interpretations of the links between households and the housing stock. Beyond that we need additional studies of the links between the submarkets and the way they influence the search process. The models introduced by Huff (1986) are a beginning.

## Empirical Observations on Search

While the models have been developed to conceptualize the process of housing search there has been a number of studies designed to document the dimensions and characteristics of search. These empirical investigations have evaluated the length of search, the spatial extent of search, and the information used in the search process.

Economists have identified these factors as measures of search effort and search costs. For geographers there has been an attempt to create a picture of the search activities of households. Another way of thinking of these factors is to think in terms of the dimensions that they represent. They are dimensions of time, (length of search; how may alternatives does a household view? and how long do they search before making a decision? what rules does the household use to make the decision?), space (the spatial pattern and extent of search; where does the household look?) and information (the nature and use of information in the search process) (Huff 1986).

To some extent these dimensions have been discipline specific. Economists have focused on the issues of stopping, hence on issues of the length of search. Psychologists have emphasized the role of information processing, and geographers have been more concerned with empirical estimates of the spatial nature of the search. On each of these topics however, there is a substantial body of empirical information.

***Length of search.*** The surprising finding that housing search is a relatively short process still stands. Barrett (1973) in studies in Toronto, Canada and Hempel (1969) in Connecticut in the United States, pointed out that a third of all home buyers and half of all renters consider only one alternative. Clark (1982) found that recent home buyers in the Los Angeles area searched less than a month, within an area of about 3 miles radius, and looked at about 15 houses. Mackett and Johnson (1985) reported that three quarters of the searches by owners were completed in six months and half within three months. Of course, length of search and the number of units searched are closely related. An important part of the search for housing is the relationship with the urban environment and the necessity, despite recent telemarketing of houses, to visit neighborhoods and houses within neighborhoods.

Measures of search intensity - houses visited, neighborhoods and communities searched, the distance of search and the length of search all confirm the limited time and narrow spatial context of search (Figure 12.3). The diagrams reported for Los Angeles in the figure can be replicated for other metropolitan areas and in other cultural contexts. They provide an important empirical basis for the area and anchor point search models designed by Huff (1986).

There have been numerous suggested explanations for the relatively short search time. These hypotheses are drawn from economic approaches to search. Until now they have not been examined within psychological approaches to choice and decision making. The first explanation assumes that households are satisficers and are quite risk averse in their selection of alternative houses. Smith et al. (1979) suggested that the satisficing behavior leads households to stop search when they have found a unit with certain minimal conditions. A second explanation calls on the cost of search as a constraint in the search process. If we include within the cost of search the personal energy cost as well as foregone earnings and real dollar outlays for travel and other activities, this hypothesis can be a compelling explanation for the shortness of search especially when, in the case of renters the choices can be further modified within a relative short period of time. That renters search much shorter periods and examine fewer alternatives is direct evidence that households are aware of the search cost to returns ratio. Although some have suggested that data collection may not have identified all the alternatives and that prior to active search there may be a sifting of alternatives, this is less easily tested. Goodman (1976), in particular, has identified a series of testable propositions concerning the optimal length of search and the nature of the stopping rule employed by households given that the search model accurately describes search behavior. Three of the propositions may be directly related to the general explanations of limited search. If $G$ is the

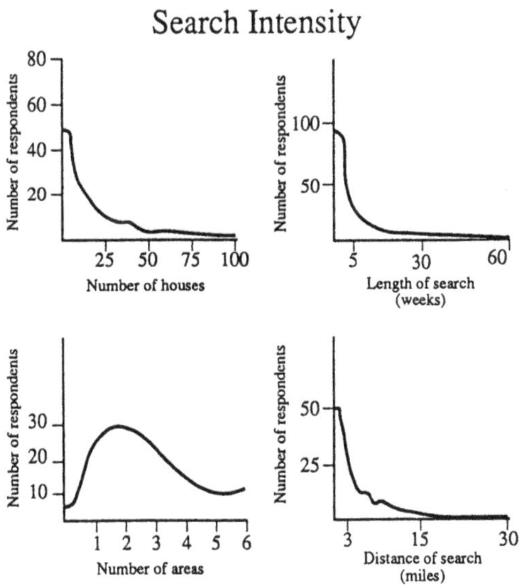


FIGURE 12.3 Distributions illustrating intensity.

distribution of net gains to the household for all vacancies (or areas) in the domain of search (gains relative to the household's current living condition), then the following propositions should be true (Huff, 1982):

1) Given the known costs of search and the expected utility or net gain from search, there is some minimum net gain, $g$, such that any vacancy found with a net gain $g$ greater than or equal to $g$ will be selected even though further search might uncover a better alternative;
2) the greater the variance of the $G$ distribution, the greater is the expected number of units searched; and
3) the lower the costs of search relative to the expected value of $G$, the greater is the expected number of units searched.

Although there are no direct tests of the propositions, the available evidence offers general confirmation. If the gains are smaller and the distribution has less variance (rental units versus houses), then renters should search for shorter periods. This has been confirmed (Michelson, 1979; Rossi, 1955, Speare, Goldstein, & Frey, 1975). Meyer (1980) has shown that the size of the household's choice set is likely to be a function of the amount of variance which exists in the population of alternatives (Meyer, 1980). For proposition (3), the support seems to come in the main from studies of the search behaviors of low-income households. Their search behavior is constrained by resource limitations including poor access to private transportation (Cronin, 1982). They face higher search costs relative to the total resources available and hence curtail search.

***The spatial context of search.*** There is still only a small group of studies which have effectively measured the nature of search in and across residential neighborhood contexts. The approaches to spatial search have been divided by Huff (1986) into studies, first, which focus on the areas searched and more particularly on the number of housing units examined in a set of neighborhoods and, second, studies which identify a point pattern of houses and locations which are in the search space. In addition to these two conceptual approaches, prior empirical contributions have been largely descriptive. They provide detail on the more limited areal searches conducted by low income and minority households and more extensive search patterns of higher income households. The combination of a restricted set of vacancies available to low income and minority households, and the general likelihood of searching in familiar areas (especially for lower income households) explain the spatially biased patterns that emerge.

The spatial context within which search occurs has also been of some concern to policy makers and especially those concerned with the increasing inner city suburban dichotomy. Deurloo, Clark, and Dieleman (1990) have provided evidence of the constrained nature of residential-relocation behavior. The latter study showed how in The Netherlands household choices reflect their initial locations. Households relocate by making choices in residential environments very similar to those in which they originate, while owners (with generally higher incomes) can effect less constrained choices. In general, search and choice are constrained processes.

***Information and search and choice.*** It has long been established that the availability, amount, and quality of information have a direct influence on the nature of the choice process. Detailed information of relative prices and the prices of alternative units will enable the decision maker to make a more informed decision. However, while there is valuable data on information use in general (Table 12.1), the application or linking of information and residential search is still fragmentary. Most empirical studies have been concerned with the amounts and types of information available to searchers in the housing market, but even these studies have in the main provided only general information on the differences in information use by income. Barrett (1973) provides support for Rossi's (1955) observation that lower-income households rely more heavily on personalized information sources such as friends and family. Palm (1976) has shown that real estate agents spatially bias the information provided to searchers. Other studies stress the changing nature of the information source over time (MacLennan & Wood, 1982). As search proceeds, the importance of personal knowledge and the use of friends and relatives decline and newspapers increase in importance. In the later stage, general areal information is replaced with specific data on housing availability. Mackett and Johnson (1986) use survey data to show that ideas change during the search process, perhaps as the result of information processing.

Several empirical studies focused on the relative roles of different sources of information. Sources varied from real estate and newspapers to signs, building contractors, and co-workers. But how are the sources used? What is the sequence of use? Although some information is provided by Clark and Smith (1979), the role and impact of information channels is still a largely unexplored area. Clark and Smith (1979) showed in a simulation study that searchers are sensitive to the cost of information and their search efficiency is significantly less with high cost information.

Of some interest to realtors is the (not unexpected) result that good agents speed up the process of search.

Other approaches focus on the provision of information rather than on its consumption. Such studies highlight another important dimension of trying to understand the process of search and choice. An analysis of real estate advertisements by both realtors and homeowners provides very different conceptions of the provision and use of information. In short, while both owners and realtors provided detailed price information (though fluctuating over time), in general owners provided much more exact location information than realtors. While realtors wish to take buyers to houses and to "sell houses", owners clearly wish to give buyers the opportunity for independent non-involved inspection (Smith, Clark, & Onaka, 1982). Of course, it is also more efficient for owners who need not show the house to every possible purchaser. The study was not able to provide definitive conclusions of the way in which information varied over time, but there was some evidence of changing information provision in stable and price escalating markets (Smith et al., 1982).

TABLE 12.1

*Relative Weighting of Information Sources Used in Housing Choice*

| | Source type | | | | | | | |
|---|---|---|---|---|---|---|---|---|
| Citation | Real Estate | News-paper | Relative/ friend | Walking/ riding around | Signs | Contractors | Did not search | Other |
| Rossi (1955) | 11 | 15 | 38 | 15 | - | - | - | 20 |
| Hempel (1970) | 38 | 25 | 12 | 6 | - | 4 | - | 15 |
| Barrett (1973) | 24 | 15 | 21 | 25 | 12 | - | - | 3 |
| Herbert (1973) | 18 | 18 | 36 | 11 | - | - | - | 17 |
| Speare (1975) | 5 | 17 | 19 | 32 | 10 | - | - | 3 |
| Michelson (1977) | 25 | 26 | 15 | 28 | - | 6 | - | -- |
| Goodman (1978) | 21 | 16 | 22 | - | 35 | 4 | - | 6 |

Finally, there is still only limited research on residential utility functions, yet such research may be central to understanding the way in which households choose particular dwellings. Moreover it is this research which brings closer links between the work of psychologists, geographers and economists. Phipps and Clark (1988) were able to document an adaptation process of residential preference formation which may account for some of the difficulty in generating models of the search and selection process. The work suggests that innate residential utilities of households are being modified by their experiences in their local housing markets. The interaction of preferences and the local housing market are a critical element of understanding search behavior.

## New Directions: Where Do We Go From Here?

Recent analyses of hierarchial search have been somewhat concerned with mathematical specificity rather than empirical evaluation and both these and previous works do not yet have an overarching organizing theme (Jayet, 1991). However, research on residential search and choice can be fitted into a developing theme which has been suggested as a way to view the processes of moving, locational and housing choice.

Within the last decade the concern to develop a conceptual structure within which the notions of housing choice and residential mobility can be embedded has led to a focus on the housing career and the life course as approaches to understanding the complex interrelated activities of search and choice. Kendig (1984, 1990) used the notion of housing careers as an organizing principle to examine the intersection of housing choices and family composition. Kendig (1990) attempts to form a link between the housing tenure decision on the one hand and the family life cycle on the other. To do this, he suggests that housing careers are the means for linking mobility and the life cycle. In this sense he is building on the work of Michelson (1977) who suggested that households pass through a series of dwellings that increasingly meet their long term housing aspirations. The paths of individual households through the housing stock are influenced by broader social changes as well as life transitions and local housing markets. In this sense the notions of housing demography link the life course (path of the individual), the housing career (the housing units that the household occupies), and the social economic changes in the household itself.

The life course is an even broader context in which the housing career can be situated. Mayer and Tuma (1990) have summarized the notion of the life course as a concept for viewing the progress of an individual or groups of individuals (or even institutions) through their lives. This process though life can be viewed as a sequence of events. The event list includes a wide range of occurrences from events related to education, to family formation, to career decisions, and not the least to housing and shelter decisions, in turn interrelated with the decisions about family and career. Much of the research in life course analysis has focussed on the individual life span and the way in which it is shaped and organized, not just by the decisions of individual actors but by the cultural beliefs of the individual and both the social and spatial context in which the individual is situated. The aim of life course analysis is to look at individual life events and the patterns of life trajectories (the terminology of housing careers is quite similar) in the context of the social processes that generate these events and trajectories.

In the past there was much attention directed to the issue of spatial mobility as such and search behavior was simply an associated activity which might create greater understanding of the mobility process. Increasingly however, the focus is not on spatial mobility as such, nor on the relationship of search behavior as related to spatial mobility; rather the focus is on the analysis of the dynamics of the separation between work and residential locations. Search then becomes important to the extent that it provides an understanding of how work and residence relationships influence mobility and housing choice.

New work will necessarily address the complexity of the decision making process in which spatial change both in the city and between regions is the process whereby households link work and residence and the processes of mobility, migration, and commuting are used to effect that linkage. The life course can be used to study the events and the timing between the events of the decisions to search, to move or commute, and/or to change jobs, as events in a trajectory of change over time. This conceptualization may provide the structure for a dynamic and interactive approach to choice and decision making in space.

## References

Barrett, F. (1973). *Residential search behavior.* (Geographical Monograph No. 1) Toronto, Canada: York University.

Bourne, L. (1981). *The geography of housing.* London: Arnold.

Brummel, A. C. (1979). A model of intraurban mobility. *Economic Geography, 55*, 338-352.

Clark, W. A. V. (1981). On modelling search behavior. In D. Griffiths & R. McKinnon (Eds.), *Dynamic spatial models* (pp. 102-131). Alphen aan de Rijn, The Netherlands: Sijthoff and Noordhooff.

Clark, W. A. V. (1982a). Modelling housing market search. London: Croom Helm.

Clark, W. A. V. (1982b). Recent research on migration and mobility: A review and interpretation. *Progress and Planning*, 18, pp. 1-56.

Clark, W. A. V. (1986). *Human migration*. Newbury Park, CA: Sage.

Clark, W. A. V., & Flowerdew, R. (1982). A review of search models and their application to search in the housing market. In W. A. V. Clark (Ed.), *Modelling housing market search* (pp. 4-29). London: Croom Helm.

Clark, W. A. V., & Onaka, J. (1985). An empirical test of a joint model of residential mobility and housing choice. *Environment and Planning A, 17*, 915-930.

Clark, W. A. V., & Smith, T. R. (1979). Modelling information use in a spatial context. *Annals of the Association of American Geographers, 69*, 575-588.

Clark, W. A. V., & Smith, T. R. (1982). Housing market search behavior and expected utility theory II: The process of search. *Environment and Planning A, 14*, 717-737.

Clark, W. A. V., & Van Lierop, W. (1986). Household location. In P. Nijkamp & E. S.. Mills (Eds.), *Handbook in regional and urban economics*. pp. 97-132.

Cronin, R. (1982) Racial differences in the search for housing. In W. A. V. Clark (Ed) *Modelling housing market search* (pp. 81-105). London: Croom Helm.

Dieleman, F. M., Deurloo, M. C., & Clark, W. A. V. (1979). A comparative view of housing choices in controlled and uncontrolled markets. *Urban Studies, 26*, 457-468.

Deurloo, M. C., Clark, W. A. V., & Dieleman, F. M. (1990). Choice of residential environment in the Randstad. *Urban Studies, 27*, 335-351.

Flowerdew, R. (1978). Search strategies and stopping rules in residential mobility, *Transactions of the Institute for British Geographers, 1*, 47-57.

Golledge, R. G. (1982). Substantive and methodological aspects of the interface between geography and psychology. In R.G. Golledge & J. Rayner (Eds.), *Proximity and preference* (pp. xix-xxxix). Minneapolis, MN: University of Minnesota Press.

Goodman, J. (1976). Housing consumption disequilibrium and local residential mobility. *Environment and Planning A, 8*, 855-874.

Hanushek, R. & Quigley, J. (1978b). Housing market disequilibrium and residential mobility. In W. A. V. Clark & E. G. Moore (Eds.), *Population mobility and residential change* (pp. 51-98). Evanston, IL: Northwestern University.

Hempel, D. J. (1970). *A comparative study of the home buying process in two Connecticut markets.* Storrs, CT: Center for Real Estate and Urban Economic Studies, University of Connecticut.

Huff, J. O. (1984). Distance decay models of residential search. In G. Gaile & C. Wilmott (Eds.) *Spatial Statistics and Models,* (pp. 345-366). New York: Reidel.

Huff, J. O. (1986). Geographic regularities in residential search behavior. *Annals of the Association of American Geographers, 76,* 208-227.

Huff, J. O. & Clark, W. A. V. (1978). Cumulative stress and cumulative inertia, a behavioral model of the decision to move. *Environment and Planning A, 10,* 1101-1119.

Ionnides, Y. M. (1979). Market allocation through search: Equilibrium adjustment and price dispersion. *Journal of Economic Theory, 11,* 247-249.

Jayet, H. (1991). Spatial search process and spatial interaction: 2, Polarization of concentration, and spatial search equilibrium. *Environment and Planning A, 22,* 719-732.

Kendig, H. (1984). Housing careers, life cycle, and residential mobility: Implications for the housing market. *Urban Studies, 4,* 271-283.

Lerman, S. R. (1979). Neighborhood choice and transportation services. In D. Segal, (Ed.), *The economics of neighborhoods* (pp. 83-118). New York: Academic Press.

Lierop, Van W. F. J. (1986). *Spatial interaction modelling and residential choice analysis.* Aldershot, England: Gower.

Mackett, R. L. & Johnson, I. (1985). Residential search behavior: The implications for survey and analytical design. *Tijdschrift voor Economishe en Sociale Geografie, 76,* 173-179.

MacLennan, D. & Wood, G. (1982). Information acquisition: patterns and strategies. In W. A. V. Clark (Ed.), *Modelling housing market search.* (134-159). London: Croom Helm.

Mayer, K., & Tuma, N. (1990). *Event history analysis in life course research.* Madison, WI: University of Wisconsin Press.

McCarty, K. (1982). An analytical model of housing search. In W. A. V. Clark (Ed.), *Modelling housing market search* (pp. 30-53). London: Croom Helm.

McFadden, D. (1978). Modelling the choice of residential location in spatial interaction theory and planning models. In A. Karlquist, L. Lundquist, F. Snickars & J. W. Weibull (Eds.), *Spatial interaction theory and planning models* (pp. 75-96). Amsterdam: North-Holland.

Meyer, R. (1980). A descriptive model of constrained residential search. *Geographical Analysis, 12*, 21-32.

Michelson, W. (1979). *Environmental choice, human behavior and residential satisfaction.* New York: Oxford University.

Murie, A. (1974). *Household movement and housing choice.* Birmingham, England: Center for Urban and Regional Studies.

Palm, R. (1976). Real estate agents and geographical information. *The Geographical Review, 66*, 266-280.

Phipps, A. G. & Carter, J. E. (1984). An individual-level analysis of the stress-resistance model of household mobility. *Geographical Analysis, 16*, 176-189.

Phipps, A. G., & Clark, W. A. V. (1988). Interactive recovery and validation of households' residential utility functions. In R. G. Golledge & H. J. P. Timmermans (Eds.), *Behavioural modelling in geography and planning* (pp. 245-271). London: Croom Helm.

Phipps, A. G. & Laverty, W. J. (1983). Optimal stopping and residential search behavior. *Geographical Analysis, 15*, 187-204.

Pollakoski, H. (1982). *Urban housing markets and residential location.* Lexington, MA: Lexington Books.

Porell, F. W. (1982). *Models of intraurban residential relocation.* The Hague: Kluwer.

Quigley, J. M. . (1983). Estimates of a more general model of consumer choice in the housing markets. In R. E. Grierson (Ed.), *The urban economy in housing* (pp. 125-140). Lexington, MA: Lexington Books.

Rossi, P. (1955). *Why families move.* Glenco, IL: The Free Press.

Schneider, C. H. P. (1975). Models of space searching in urban areas. *Geographical Analysis, 7*, 173-185.

Slovic, P., Fischoff, B., & Lichtenstein, S. (1977). Behavioral decision theory. *Annual Review of Psychology, 28*, 1-39.

Smith, T. R., Clark, W. A. V., Huff, J. O., & Shapiro, P. (1979). A decision making and search model for intraurban migration. *Geographical Analysis, 11*, 1-22.

Smith, T. R., Clark, W. A. V. & Onaka, J. (1982). Information provision: An analysis of newspaper real estate advertisements. In W. A. V. Clark (Ed.), *Modelling housing market search* (pp. 160-186). London: Croom Helm.

Speare, A., Goldstein, S. & Frey, W. (1975). *Residential mobility and migration and metropolitan change*. Cambridge, MA: Ballinger.

Timmermans, H. J. P. (1984). Decompositional multi-attribute preference models in spatial choice analysis. *Progress in Human Geography, 8*, 189-221.

Weibull, J. W. (1978). A search model for microeconomic analysis with spatial application. In A. Karlquist, L. Lundquist, F. Snickars, & J. W. Weibull, (Eds.), *Spatial interaction theory and planning models* (pp. 47-73). Amsterdam: North-Holland.

Wrigley, N. (1985). *Categorical data analysis*. London: Longmans.

*Behavior and Environment: Psychological and Geographical Approaches*
*T. Gärling and R.G. Golledge (Editors)*
*1993 Elsevier Science Publishers B.V.* 

# CHAPTER 13

# The Choice of a Home Seen From the Inside: Psychological Contributions to the Study of Decision Making in Housing Markets

**Henry Montgomery**

Psychological research on human decision making has been conducted for some 40 years (Payne, Bettman, & Johnson, 1992). Roughly, this research may be divided into three time periods. The research in each of these periods could be characterized in terms of its relationship to normative models of decision making which have been developed in non-psychological disciplines such as economics and statistics.

The first psychological studies of decision making relied heavily on normative decision models, using them as a point of departure for measuring subjective utilities and probabilities in choice situations (e.g., Friedman & Savage, 1952). In those years, psychologists were often optimistic about people's capacity for making rational decisions. It was taken for granted that human decision making could be modelled by theories of rational decision making (Edwards, Lindman, & Phillips, 1966).

In the second period, human decision making was contrasted with the normative models. Limitations in people's computational capacity were highlighted (Simon, 1955). Systematic deviations between predictions from normative models on probability judgments (e.g., Bayes' theorem), on preferences (e.g., the transitivity axiom), and on information integration (e.g., the subjective expected utility model) were focused in a large number of studies. Typically, these deviations were regarded as illusions or biases (e.g., Kahneman, Slovic & Tversky, 1982; see Hogarth, 1987 for a comprehensive list of biases in judgment and decision making). In other words, it was assumed, more or less explicitly, that the normative models provided the objectively correct standards for human decision making and that people simply were unable to conform consistently to these standards.

In today's research on human decision making, the link to normative decision models is less pronounced. The validity and/or relevance of some of these models have been questioned (Gigerenzer, Hoffroge & Kleinbölting, 1991). Moreover, recent research often concerns aspects of human decision making that fall outside their realm. Normative decision theory stresses the importance of consistency in decision making across situations, which implies that adaptive and constructive aspects are not highlighted. In contrast, a number of recent studies show that human decision making is adaptive to the situation at hand and that people construct their preferences for and beliefs about objects or events in response to a choice or judgment task (see the review by Payne et al., 1992). The constructive activities studied in today's research partly coincide with the biases studied earlier. However, the change of terminology may be seen as expressing a focus on the adaptive rather than on the maladaptive aspects of the examined phenomena.

The emphasis in current psychological research on adaptive aspects of human decision making obviously is in line with the purpose of the present book, that is, to understand how behavior and environment are interfaced. The behavior-environment interface could be studied from two angles. In some disciplines, such as geography and economics, people's behavior in a given environment tends to be seen from the outside. The actual behavior and its relationship to the environment are registered and modelled. Examples of such research are given in Clark's companion chapter (Chapter 12 in this book). By contrast, in psychological research decision makers are viewed from the inside. The research is focused on the decision maker's goals or values in a given environment and his or her understanding of the relevant environment. Unfortunately, the relationship between the inside and outside perspectives, that is, the link between the actor's conceptions and his or her actual behavior is rarely studied in psychological research on decision making. A research project, the aim of which was to examine not only people's conceptions and preferences of housing alternatives, but also how these conceptions and preferences are related to actual choices in the market, is reviewed below. More precisely, the project focused on how people's residential choices are related to their beliefs about how housing options may lead to the attainment of personally important values or goals. This project will be denoted as the RCBVS (Residential Choices and Belief Value Structures) project. Before reviewing this project, some distinctions in current psychological research on human decision making are briefly discussed.

## Distinctions in Current Psychological Research on Decision Making

### *Decisions vs. Choices*

Decisions concern choices among action alternatives. A decision implies that the individual has committed him/herself to act in a certain way (Montgomery, 1989a). Put differently, the result of a decision is that the individual intends to perform some action. This intention is not necessarily implemented. For example, the decision maker may change his or her mind before the decision is implemented or he or she may be unable to implement tthe decision. However, there is necessarily a link between decision and action inasmuch as decision always points to some action. By contrast, choices are not necessarily linked to actions. Choices are related to preferences. If an individual chooses alternative *a* over alternatives *b* and *c*,he or she has indicated that he or she prefers *a* to *b* and *c*. However, the alternatives need not be action alternatives, which always is true in decision situations. (For a more penetrating discussion of the distinction between decision and choice, see Karlsson, 1988).

In the literature on behavioral decision making, it appears that the terms "decision" and "choice" tend to be used synonymously. The reason may be that the great majority of studies in this research tradition have been conducted under laboratory conditions (e.g., by presenting subjects with hypothetical choice problems). In these studies the subjects usually do not need to commit themselves to act in line with their choices since no implementation of the choices is required. In other words, the link between choice and action is not made salient, and, hence, there may be no need to distinguish between choice (weak emphasis on choice-action) and decision (strong emphasis on choice-action). However, the distinction is important in the RCBVS project to be reviewed below, since in this project we studied both hypothetical preferences and choices, on the one hand, and real decisions in a housing market, on the other hand.

## Aspects, Attributes, and Attractiveness

In normative as well as in descriptive models of decision making it is typically assumed that decisions are based on the attractiveness of particular aspects or features which characterize each alternative (e.g., Svenson, 1979; von Winterfeldt & Edwards, 1986). For example, a central location of a certain housing alternative may be viewed as an attractive aspect which speaks in favor of choosing that alternative. Commonly, it is also assumed that aspects correspond to levels of attributes or dimensions, which could be used for comparing alternatives with each other. The aspect "central location" could be a level of the attribute "distance to downtown." The alternatives in a decision situation are thus seen as consisting of more or less attractive aspects on a common set of attributes which may differentiate more or less clearly between the alternatives.

In so called multiattribute-utility theory (MAUT) models of decision making, which form the basis both for normative (e.g., von Winterfeldt & Edwards, 1986) and descriptive models (e.g., Anderson, 1981), the overall attractiveness (utility) of an alternative is assumed to be a function (typically a weighted sum) of the attractiveness of the attribute levels (aspects) characterizing the alternative. The alternative with the highest overall attractiveness is to be chosen.

MAUT models have been challenged from different angles. One type of challenge concerns the role of aspects. Tversky (1969) reported data indicating that the attractiveness of differences between alternatives with respect to their aspects on an attribute, rather than the attractiveness of single aspects, may be the basis for a decision. This implies in turn that the overall attractiveness of an alternative will be dependent on aspects of the other alternatives in a decision situation (see also Tyszka, 1983).

Another challenge concerns the idea that the attractiveness of aspects (or differences between aspects) are aggregated into an overall attractiveness measure. Usually, the aggregation function is assumed to be additive. This implies that the attractiveness of single aspects contribute in a compensatory way to the decision. In the overall attractiveness measure the negative impact of unattractive aspects are compensated by the positive impact of the attractive aspects. In contrast, non-compensatory decision making models assume that decisions are based on the pattern of single attractiveness values of single aspects rather than on some total attractiveness measure. For example, the so-called conjunctive model prescribes that a to-be-chosen alternative should exceed a certain threshold value on all attributes. Hence, this model implies that if the pattern of attractiveness values are distributed in such a way that only one alternative exceeds all the relevant threshold values, then this alternative will be chosen.

Empirical research indicates that both compensatory and non-compensatory decision models do an acceptable job in describing how decisions are formed (Svenson, 1979). The occurrence of compensatory vs. non-compensatory information integration in decision making may depend on a trade-off between the effort required (in general lower effort for non-compensatory information integration) and the need for making a correct decision (there is presumably greater chance to meet this need when compensatory information integration is carried out) (Beach & Mitchell, 1978; Payne, Bettman, & Johnson, 1988).

A third challenge to MAUT models concerns the stability of attractiveness of aspects in a given situation. In MAUT models it is taken for granted that the attractiveness of a given aspect is fixed. However, several studies of the cognitive processes preceding a choice have shown that decision makers may change their evaluations of aspects in such a way that the to-be-chosen alternative becomes more clearly differentiated from its competitors (Dahlstrand & Montgomery, 1984; Montgomery & Svenson, 1989; Tyszka & Wielochowski, 1991, see also Svenson, in press, for a general discussion of differentiation processes). Montgomery (1983) described this differentiation process as a search for a dominance structure, that is, a cognitive representation in which one alternative is dominant (more attractive than other alternatives on at least one attribute and not worse on other attributes). The decision maker may make several attempts to form a dominance structure by starting out from different candidates for the final choice. The search for a dominance structure may be particularly relevant in situations where the decision implies commitment to action (Montgomery, 1989a, 1989b). This is because a dominance structure may help the decision maker to act consistently in line with his or her decision.

### *Multi-Attribute Utility Theory and the Expectancy-Value Model*

Typically, MAUT models do not emphasize that the outcomes of a decision are more or less uncertain. In contrast, this is the key idea in the so-called expectancy-value model. This model does not only apply to decision making, but also to attitude formation and motivational theories (see Chapter 11 in this book). It is assumed that a person's evaluation of an option (or object or activity) will be more or less positive as a function of the extent to which the person believes that positive or negative outcomes will occur if the option is implemented. More precisely, it is assumed that a person's evaluation of an option is determined by the sum of the products of the person's belief in and evaluation of each possible outcome of the option. In a choice situation, the decision maker will choose the alternative having the highest sum of products. This choice model is commonly called the subjective expected utility (SEU) model (Edwards, 1954).

The expectancy-value model has been found to yield fairly accurate predictions of people's attitudes (e.g., Fishbein & Ajzen, 1975). Also choices are predicable from these models (Anderson & Shanteau, 1970; Lopes & Ekberg, 1980). However, systematic deviations between predicted and actual choices have been identified and formalized in Prospect Theory (Kahneman & Tversky, 1979). Prospect Theory retains the basic structure of the SEU model, but assumes in addition (a) that outcomes should be seen as gains or losses in relation to a reference point, (b) that evaluations of gains and losses are not consistent with each other, and (c) that beliefs have different weights that are a function of but not proportional to the strength of the belief. Prospect Theory takes account of the fact that people's choices are adaptive to the situation at hand. For example, by assuming that reference points vary across situations, the theory may explain why identical outcomes *are* evaluated differently in different situations.

## *Judgment vs. Choice*

According to normative decision theory, choice is equivalent to selecting the most preferable alternative among a given set of alternatives. However, empirical research has shown that preference judgments (numerical ratings or matching judgments) sometimes are inconsistent with people's choices (Montgomery, Gärling, Lindberg, & Selart, 1990; Slovic, 1975; Tversky, Sattah, & Slovic, 1988). For example, Tversky et al. (1988) asked subjects to choose between two options that had been matched as equally preferable. The options were described on two attributes, one of which was more important than the other one. According to normative decision theory, the choice probability of each of the two options should be 0.50. In contrast, it was found that subjects consistently chose the alternative which was superior on the more important attribute. Montgomery, Gärling, Lindberg, & Selart (1990) obtained the same results for choices between options that were equally preferable according to attractiveness ratings. Tversky et al. (1988) explained their results by assuming that choice is more qualitative than judgment. More exactly, they assumed that weighing of information is less natural in choice than in judgment, which implies that choice tasks more than judgment tasks invite considering just one attribute.

The relationship between judgment and choice does not only have theoretical implications (i.e., for the interpretation of the axiom that choice is based on preferences). To the extent that choices cannot be predicted from preference judgments, the usefulness of judgments for predicting real-world decisions will be diminished. On the other hand, it would be of great practical value if such predictions are possible since preference judgments of each object in a given set could be used for predicting choices among any combination of objects within the set (i.e., by predicting that the object receiving the highest preference judgment in a given combination of objects will be chosen). It should be remembered, however, that the possibility of predicting decisions in the real world may also be hampered by a greater commitment to action in real world decisions than in choices or preferences with no clear link to action. Montgomery (1989a) hypothesized that such a commitment would imply that the individual elaborates more on given information (e.g., by searching for means to reduce the disadvantages of a promising alternative).

### *The RCBVS project*

The research project presented in this section attempted to solve two problems. The first one was to develop and to operationalize a theoretical framework which goes beyond MAUT in trying to reveal measurable psychological attributes underlying utilities related to housing alternatives. The second problem was to reveal factors which are related to the information integration rules (e.g., compensatory and non-compensatory decision rules) used by decision makers in a housing market and to find out what consequences the rules used in different conditions have for the predictability of housing preferences and choices.

The RCBVS project was recently summarized and discussed by Gärling, Garvill, Lindberg, & Montgomery (1991). The present account partly overlaps with *that*, but will also present some additional meta analyses integrating results from the studies carried out within the project.

## *Theoretical Framework*

A basic assumption behind the theoretical framework underlying the RCBVS project is that housing choices are made to attain goals, that is, to avoid unattractive states or to strive to attain attractive states. More specifically, it is assumed that people strive to achieve some limited set of fundamental goals, that is, goals which are relevant for how people evaluate their life situation. Such goals may be denoted as *life values* (Montgomery & Johansson, 1988). Examples of life values are happiness, freedom, togetherness, inner harmony, and security.

It is further assumed that people acquire *cognitive structures* which represent their beliefs about how goals can be attained (Axelrod, 1976; Biel & Montgomery, 1986). The beliefs may be based on particular aspects (attribute levels) of an object. For example, a person confronted with housing alternatives may believe that a central location (aspect) leads to an exciting life (life value). In some situations, however, an object as a whole or configurations of aspects characterizing an object may be associated with beliefs about value attainment. For example, a number of attributes may be related to the life value "security" (e.g., the attributes "closeness to friends" and "reputation") and a person may believe that all of these attributes should exceed certain levels in order to be seen as leading to security.

Finally, it is assumed *that* the cognitive structures associated with different objects are evoked when people judge their preferences of the objects or when they choose among them. Hence, preference judgments and choices are assumed to be based on people's beliefs about how alternatives are related to life values. On the basis of these assumptions, three models were derived for predicting preference judgments and choices. These models differ in their assumptions concerning the rule for combining different attribute evaluations, as well as in their reliance on beliefs about the attainment of life values for predicting preference judgments and choices. The first model is:

$$E_{Alt_j} = b\sum_{j}\sum_{k} P_{Attr_{jk}} E_{V_k} + a \qquad (1),$$

where $E_{ALT}$ represents the evaluation of housing alternative *i*; $p_{Attr}$ is the extent to which the particular level of housing alternative *i* for that alternative is believed to lead to the attainment of life value *k* (or counteract it, in which case $p$ assumes a negative value); $E_v$ is the evaluation of life value $k$; and $b$ and $a$ are arbitrary scale constants.

Equation 1 thus assumes that belief-value structures exist for each housing attribute, and that value fulfillment is simply summed across all attributes to yield the evaluation of given housing alternative. This model may be regarded as a combination of MAUT (the decomposition of alternatives into attributes) and an expectancy-value model (the belief component). Note however, that the model assumes a multi-dimensional utility concept (with each dimension corresponding to the perceived attainment of a given life value). Equation 1 was contrasted with the following *model*:

$$E_{Alt_i} = b\Sigma P_{Alt_{ik}} E_{V_k} + a \qquad (2).$$

Except for the term $p_{Alt}$, representing how much alternative $i$ (as a whole) isbelieved to affect the attainment of value $k$, the notations are the same as in Equation 1.

While retaining the assumption about the importance of belief-value structures (and in this sense being an expectancy-value model), Equation 2 does not specify the rule for how different attributes contribute to the overall value-fulfillment perceived in a given housing alternative. It thus allows for the possibility that the attributes may combine in a non-linear fashion, and that some attributes may even be neglected. In other words, Equation 2 needs not be consistent with MAUT.

The third model does not entail any assumption about the role of belief-value structures. It merely states that the evaluation of an alternative is obtained by summing the evaluation of its attributes, regardless of how the latter evaluations are arrived at:

$$E_{Alt_i} = b\Sigma E_{Attr_{ij}} + a \qquad (3).$$

$E_{Attr}$ is the evaluation of attribute $j$ possessed by the alternative $i$.

Equation 3 corresponds to a simple form of MAUT (no weighting of attributes) but need not be consistent with expectancy-value models.

It should be noted that if both the assumption about the role of life values and about additivity across attributes are valid, then Equations 1, 2, and 3 should all be expected to perform well. If only the former assumption is correct, Equation 2 should perform better than Equations 1 and 3. Where only the latter assumption is valid, Equation 3 should perform better than Equations 1 and 2.

***Empirical Results***

The research in the RCBVS project is reported in 14 separate papers comprising a total of 19 empirical studies. The first three studies (Montgomery & Svenson, 1989; Gärling, Lindberg, & Montgomery, 1989; Lindberg, Gärling, Montgomery, & Waara, 1987) were focused on the identification of the components in the theoretical framework described above, and on how subjects perceive relations between these components (e.g., between attributes and life values). Studies were also performed of how subjects perceive activities in relation to housing attributes and life values (cf. Chapter 10 in this book). In two subsequent studies the validity of Equations 1, 2, and 3 were tested for preference judgments and choices (Lindberg, Gärling, & Montgomery, 1988; Lindberg, Gärling, & Montgomery, 1989c). Equations 1 and 2 were also tested for choices and/or preference judgments in many other studies in the project. There were two field studies of choice behavior in a housing market (Lindberg, Gärling, & Montgomery, 1987a, 1990a). The effect of task variables on information integration (according to Equations 1 or 2) were investigated in several studies. These task variables included number of alternatives (Lindberg, Gärling, & Montgomery, 1987b), simultaneous or sequential presentation of information (Lindberg et al., 1989b), numerical vs. verbal information (Lindberg et al., 1991), incomplete vs. complete information (Lindberg et al., 1989a), cost differences among alternatives (Garvill, Gärling, Lindberg, & Montgomery, 1990), and level of travel costs (Lindberg et al., 1990b). Finally, we tested the dominance structuring hypothesis by examining the prevalence of restructuring of beliefs in connection with preferences or choices (Lindberg et al., 1989a, 1990a; Garvill et al., 1991).

***Beliefs About Relationships Between Attributes and Values***

Virtually all studies of the RCBVS project bear on the idea that choices and/or preferences are based on beliefs about relationships between alternatives or attributes and a set of life values. In this section we will examine what beliefs people have about the relationships between housing attributes (for rented apartments) and life values. Data from two studies will be used (Lindberg et al., 1987b, 1988). Practically all features of subjects' task were identical in the two studies. Students attending a college for adults in a Swedish medium-sized town (80,000 inhabitants) were asked to give a number between -6 and +6 to rate the extent different attribute levels of each of 12 housing attributes facilitated or counteracted the attainment of each of 12 life values. For each combination of attribute and life value an index of the perceived effects of each attribute on the possibility of attaining the 12 life values was computed by subtracting, for each respondent, the ratings of the effects of the "worst" level from the ratings of the "best" level.

To get an overview of the structure in the resulting attribute-value matrices, the following data analysis was carried out. First, the two attribute-value matrices were collapsed into one matrix by taking the means of the data in each attribute-value cell. Each row in the resulting matrix corresponded to mean ratings of values for a given attribute and each column to mean ratings of attributes for a given value. Second, the rows (attributes) and the columns (values), respectively, of the resulting matrix were subjected to cluster analysis based on correlations among rows and columns. The following clusters were identified for attributes: reputation, closeness to friends, transportation and location (neighborhood facilities, distance to friends, distance to schools, distance to work, transportation), intrinsic attributes (cost, size, standard), noise, distance to recreation facilities. The following clusters of life values were identified: freedom (freedom, excitement, leisure), togetherness, security, well being (family, pleasure. happiness, inner harmony, health), comfort, and money. Third, the attribute and value correlation matrices were subjected to non-metric multidimensional scaling (two-dimensional solutions). The clusters identified in the cluster analyses were found to be ordered in a circular fashion in line with a circumplex structure (Figure 13.1). Hence, each cluster bordered on each side to another cluster. Fourth, in clusters consisting of more than one variable means of the variables in the cluster were computed resulting in a 6 x 6 attribute type value type matrix.

Figure 13.2 presents plots of the rows (attributes) of the 6 x 6 attribute type - value type matrix across value clusters arranged in line with the circular order identified in the multidimensional scaling analysis. However, for reasons to be given below, plots of the life value "money" are shown separately in the figure. The values on the x-axis go more than one lap around the value-circle implying that some values are repeated. The point of this arrangement was to examine whether the form of the distribution of beliefs in value attainment was similar for different attribute types. As can be seen, the forms of the distributions are indeed similar although they cover different values. That is, for each attribute

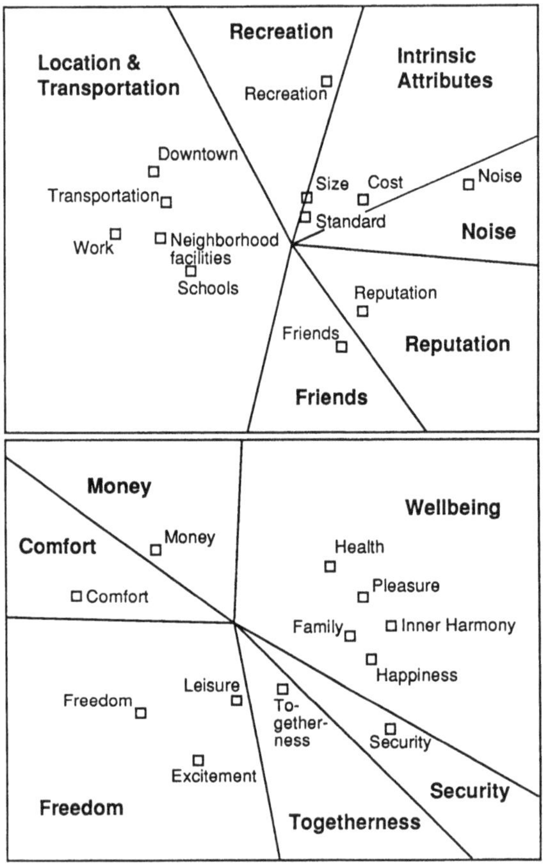


FIGURE 13.1. Multidimensional scaling of housing attributes and life values.

type a unimodal or approximately unimodal distribution across value types could be identified. Three attribute types, that is, transportation/location, intrinsic attributes, and noise, have their peaks at comfort, although noise is also strongly related to the adjacent value type of well being. The three remaining attributes have peaks at different value types: reputation at security, friends at togetherness, and recreation at freedom. The patterns now described imply that in order to get a reasonably good attainment of each value type, certain patterns of attribute levels are seen as more effective than others. For the present subjects it will be important to live in an area with a good reputation, with closeness to friends, and with good recreation facilities. Low levels of these attributes cannot easily be compensated by high levels of other attributes with peaks at other values. On the other hand, a low level of an intrinsic attribute or with respect to an attribute related to a convenient location could more easily be compensated by high levels of other attributes. This is because these types of attributes include several attributes that are seen as being related to values in a similar way.

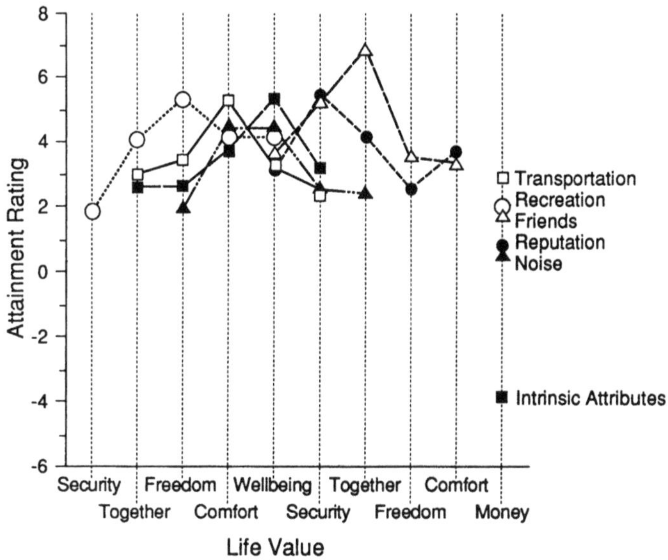


FIGURE 13.2. Means of ratings of perceived attainment of value types for different types of housing attributes.

The life value "money" in several cases did not fit the unimodal distributions of attribute types. In general, the level of beliefs in attainment of "money" was weaker than in the attainment of other value types. In one case the subjects even perceived a negative relation to attainment of money, that is, with respect to intrinsic attributes (size and standard). The subjects evidently realized that attainment of good levels of these attributes cost money. Despite the generally low levels in the beliefs in attainment of money, there are interesting differences in these beliefs among different value types. As noted above, subjects perceive that size and standard cost money, but they perceive that they may *earn* money by having access to good transportation and a convenient location of their apartment. This finding reflects facts about the Swedish market for rented apartments. Public regulations of housing rents almost prohibit charging tenants for a good location and for good transportation possibilities.

The data analysis described here suggests that people's beliefs about relations between attributes and value attainment behave in a quite orderly and meaningful fashion. It is also suggested that economic aspects play a role of their own in perceived attribute-value relations.

It may be noted that evaluations of alternatives based on the type of reasoning exemplified above (i.e., in terms of whether attributes are seen as linked to the same or to different values) is not consistent with Equation 1. According to this equation, all equally strong beliefs about attribute-value relations have the same impact on the evaluation of alternatives regardless of whether the relations concern the same or different values. In contrast, such evaluations are consistent with Equation 2 which is open for many types of perceived relationships between attributes and values. The validity of Equations 1 and 2 is examined in the next section.

### *Predictability of Preference Judgments and Choices*

In many of the studies in the RCBVS project, the possibility of predicting preference judgments and choices from Equation 1 (summation of perceived attribute-value links across attributes and values) and Equation 2 (summation of perceived alternative-value links across values) was tested. Equation 3 (summation of perceived attribute evaluations) was tested in fewer studies. In this section we examine overall patterns across studies in the predictability of preferences and choices from the three equations. The predictability was operationalized as the correlation between predicted and empirical values. Usually, product moment correlations were computed for preference judgments and biserial correlations for choices. In some studies the predictability was computed as proportions of correct predictions. In the present data analysis these proportions were transformed to tetrachoric correlations in order to make comparisons across studies possible.

Table 13.1 shows that the mean of the correlations across type of equation and preference/choice range from .351 to .603. In other words, the overall predictability tended to be moderately high across equations and preferences/choices. The table also presents mean differences between the prediction of preferences or choices according to different equations. It can be seen that Equation 2 tended to give more accurate predictions than Equation 1, both for preference judgments and for choices. Equation

1 yielded more accurate predictions of preference judgments than of choices. However, when Equation 2 was used, the difference in prediction was small and non-significant. Equation 3 yielded predictions in between those found for Equations 1 and 2 with a tendency to come very close to those found for Equation 1. The similar fit of Equations 1 and 3 supports the assumption that evaluations of attributes reflect perceived links between attributes and values. The relatively good fit of Equation 2 indicates that values are important for people's preferences and choices in a housing market.

TABLE 13.1

*Differences between fit of equations 1, 2, and 3 (correlations between predicted and observed values) and means of fit of each equation for preference judgements and choices note degrees of freedom for t-test are given within parentheses.*

| | Preference judgments | | Choices | | | |
|---|---|---|---|---|---|---|
| | eq. 2 | eq. 3 | eq. 1 | eq. 2 | Eq. 3 | Mean |
| Pref. | | | | | | |
| Eq. 1 | -.112** | -.025 | .112 | -.049 | .005 | .489 |
| Eq. 2 | | .093* | .223 | .040 | .118 | .603 |
| Eq. 3 | | | .103 | -.065 | .083 | .547 |
| Choices | | | | | | |
| Eq. 1 | | | | -.127** | -.065 | .351 |
| Eq. 2 | | | | | .103 | .508 |
| Eq. 3 | | | | | | .493 |

* $p < .05$
** $p < .01$

We will now examine in some detail the pattern of predictions found for Equations 1 and 2 for preference judgments and choices, respectively. The better predictions yielded by Equation 2 as compared to Equation 1 may be related to the fact the former equation only is based on values, whereas the latter is based on values and attributes. Earlier research has shown that expectancy-value models yield their best predictions when a limited number of attributes (assumed to be those attributes that are salient to the respondent) are entered into the model (Fishbein & Ajzen, 1975).

This implies that the validity of Equation 1 should be expected to be more sensitive to the number of attributes considered by subjects than is the case for Equation 2. More precisely, it may be expected that Equations 1 and 2 will give equally accurate predictions when the number of attributes is small, but that Equation 2 will yield better predictions than Equation 1 when the number of attributes becomes larger. To test this expectation, the differences between predictability-correlations according to Equation 1 and Equation 2 were plotted against number of attributes which varied between 4 and 15 in different studies. The plot is shown in Figure 13.3. The relation between the difference in predictability yielded by the two equations and number of attributes follows the expected pattern, although the scatter around the fitted line is quite large. It *may* be concluded that the differential success of Equations 1 and 2 is because the respondents base their judgements or choices on a limited number of attributes.

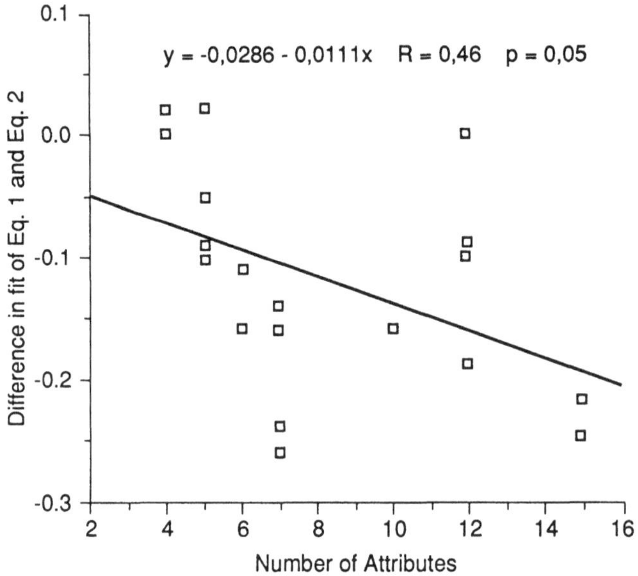


FIGURE 13.3. Differences between predictability-correlations according to Equation 1 and Equation 2 plotted against number of attributes.

Why were preference judgments better predicted than choices from Equation 1 but not from Equation 2? To answer this question, an explanation may be given that is similar to the one offered to explain the generally better fit of Equation 2. Lindberg et al. (1989b) reported data suggesting that choice tasks more than preference judgment tasks cause subjects to use simplifying heuristics, that is, to base the response on a limited fraction of the given information. Choice subjects often seemed to restrict their attention to only one type of attribute (e.g., economic or intrinsic attributes) whereas this rarely happened for preference judgment subjects. This choice strategy would be consistent with the so-called lexicographic decision rule (Tversky, 1969) - a non-compensatory rule, which prescribes the choice of the alternative which is more attractive than other alternatives on the most important attribute. As already noted, the validity of Equation 1 is more dependant on the extent to which subjects use the available information about alternatives than is true of Equation 2. Hence, using simplifying heuristics will lower the validity of Equation 1, whereas this need not happen for Equation 2. To conclude, a greater prevalence of simplifying heuristics in choice than in preference judgments may explain the variations in the predictability of preference judgments and choices by means of Equations 1 and 2, respectively.

Let us now examine how the predictability of preference judgments and choices is related to features of the situation in which subjects gave their responses. Of particular interest is to shed light on the possibilities of making predictions of choices in real-world situations. In the two field studies conducted within the RCBVS project (Lindberg, Gärling, & Montgomery, 1987a, 1990a) it was found that Equation 1 yielded low choice predictions with correlations being .15 and .21 between predicted and actual choices. Equation 2, which was tested only in one of the two studies (Lindberg et al., 1990), yielded a definitively higher correlation of.43 between predicted and actual choices. Preference judgments were generally better predicted than choices, correlations being .46 and .42 (Eq. 1) and .66 (Eq. 2).It may be noted that also for preference judgments Equation 2 clearly outperformed Equation 1.

The pattern of predictions found in our field studies may be explained in terms of two features of many real-world choice situations, namely their complexity and the existence of constraints. The complexity stands for the fact that real housing alternatives vary on a great number of attributes which in turn may be described in various ways. As noted above, it appears that decision makers in a housing market respond to this complexity by using various simplifying heuristics. The discrepancy between objective features and the decision maker's simplified representation of the choice alternatives should generally be greater in a real-world situation than in hypothetical judgement or choice tasks. This may explain why Equation 2, which in contrast to Equation 1 may account for usage of simplifying heuristics, clearly outperforms Equation 1 in real-world situations.

In a real-world choice situation, external constraints such as the availability of a preferred alternative may prevent the decision maker from implementing his or her preferences. In support of this notion Lindberg et al. (1990a) found that their respondents often were dissatisfied with decisions to reject alternatives that they preferred to their present dwelling. In contrast, the respondents were quite satisfied with alternatives which they did not prefer but nevertheless chose. Obviously, constraints in the possibilities of choosing a preferred alternative will make it harder to predict choices than preference judgments from the respondents' belief value-structures. More specifically, data in the Lindberg et al. (1990a) study suggested that the predictability of choices may have been reduced by constraints resulting from the fact the decisions were made jointly by members of the household.

In studies of hypothetical housing alternatives, the following factors were found to enhance the predictability of preferences and choices: numerical information as opposed to verbal information (Lindberg et al.,1991), variations in the cost of housing alternatives (Garvill et al., 1990), and closeness in time between belief/value ratings used for predictions and the predicted preferences/choices (Lindberg et al., 1989b). In line with the latter finding, subjects' inferences of missing information was only related to preference judgments or choices when the inferences were made simultaneously (Lindberg et al., 1989a). These results illustrate the image of the adaptive and constructive nature of decision makers. When precise information (numerical data) or particularly important information (variations in cost) is available, the subjects concentrate on that information. Evaluations and beliefs as well as inferences of missing information are constructed in the judgement or choice situation at hand. Constructive features in housing choices are further discussed in the following section.

### *The Role of Dominance Structuring*

It has been mentioned that the decision makers may feel a pressure to commit themselves to act in line with their choice. This process may involve restructuring given information in order to increase the support for the selected alternative. It will be assumed that such restructuring is equivalent to dominance structuring (Montgomery, 1983). There may exist other types of restructuring which increase the support for the specified alternative (Svenson, in press). However, in practice it is probably very hard to discriminate between dominance structuring and other types of restructuring, especially if dominance structuring is defined somewhat loosely as *attempts* (which need not be entirely successful) to find an alternative-attribute structure which makes one alternative dominant (Montgomery, 1989a).

The evidence for dominance structuring was not unequivocal in the RCBVS project. Let us first examine the evidence speaking in favour of the assumption that choices among housing alternatives are backed up by dominance structuring. As already mentioned, Lindberg et al. (1989a) asked their subjects to infer missing information about housing alternatives. The data showed very clearly that in a choice situation, subjects inferred information which favored the specified alternative. In a non-choice situation, inferences about the same alternative were more balanced. In their second field study, Lindberg et al. (1990a) conducted a follow-up interview. It was found that the respondents had re-evaluated attributes as well as changing their beliefs about attribute-value relations in line with their decision. However, it is not known to what extent these re-evaluations and belief changes occurred before or after the decision. On the other hand, Montgomery & Svenson (1989) found clear evidence for dominance structuring before the choice in think-aloud data concerning hypothetical choices between housing alternatives that existed in the market.

Let us now exemplify data which did not clearly support dominance structuring. In two studies, subjects in choice and preference judgment situations, respectively, rated the extent to which housing alternatives facilitated or counteracted each of five life values (Lindberg et al., 1989c; Garvill et al., 1991). The ratings were also made in situations requiring no choices or preference judgments. There was no clear evidence that the ratings were closer to a dominance structure in the choice situation as compared to non-choice situations. These data show that choice situations need not differ from non-choice situations with respect to the extent to which dominance structuring occurs. However, if a dominance structure exists before the choice process starts, then there is no reason to expect that choice and non-choice tasks will differ with respect to dominance structuring. Garvill et al. (1991) found that at the level of life values (but not *at* the level of attributes) there indeed often existed a dominance structure supporting the specified alternative. Hence, subjects may not need to *re*-structure their beliefs about value attainment to find a dominance structure. It may only be a question of "picking up" a dominance structure which already exists.

The data collected so far suggest that the role of dominance structuring, or of using already existing dominance structures, cannot be neglected in housing choices. However, further research is needed to identify factors which facilitate or constrain dominance structuring.

## Conclusions

The research carried out so far on behavioral decision making in general and housing choices in particular does not seem to be very useful for predicting housing choices. For planners of housing it would be helpful to know how people's preferences and choices are related to various housing attributes. However, the research reviewed above suggests that such predictions are difficult to make from psychological data (see also Rohrman & Borcherding, 1988). In our discussion we have examined how subjects may arrive at their choices by simplifying or restructuring available information. Both these activities suggest that people to some extent in an adaptive way construct their preferences and choices as a function of characteristics of the choice situation. Obviously, such adaptive activities reduce the possibilities of predicting people's choices. We also discussed how the predictability of actual-world choices is counteracted by external constraints which prevent the decision maker from implementing his or her preferences.

Predictions are perhaps often easier made on a group level from relations between objective housing attributes and actual choices in the market, implying that psychological data (e.g., attribute-value ratings) are not used. In such predictions "noise" due to adaptive activities and the existence of external constraints in single choice situations is averaged out. Such predictions are, however, limited by the availability of relevant behavioral data. Moreover, they presume that the relations between attributes and preferences/choices are stable. This presumption may often be false in today's society where different fashions and life-styles come and go. To account for such changes in the societal climate when making predictions of individuals' choice behavior, psychological knowledge is needed of principles for how values and beliefs are related to behavior.

Behavioral decision making research may be more useful for understanding housing choices. Such understanding could be valuable in at least two contexts. First, it could be useful for developing decision aids for consumers in housing markets. For example, the theoretical framework in the RCBVS project may be used for developing a computerized decision aid that will help people to think through the consequences that choosing a subset of housing alternatives will have for the attainment of particular life values. Second, behavioral decision making research may on a general level increase the understanding of how housing choices are shaped by values and beliefs as well as by internal and external constraints. Although such knowledge in a short term perspective may be of limited use for predicting actual choices, it may in the long term help planners, developers, and politicians in the housing area to be more sensitive to people's wishes.

## Acknowledgement

*Research reported in* this chapter was supported by grants from The Swedish Council for Building Research and from The Swedish Council for Research in the Humanities and Social Sciences.

## References

Anderson, N. H. (1981). *Foundations of information integration theory*. New York: Academic Press.

Anderson, N. H., & Shanteau, J. C. (1970). Information integration in risky decision making. *Journal of Experimental Psychology, 84*, 1155-1170.

Axelrod, P. (Ed.), (1976). *Structure of decision*. Princeton, NJ: Princeton University Press.

Beach, L. R., & Mitchell, T. R. (1978). A contingency model for the selection of decision strategies. *Academic Management Review, 3*, 439-449.

Biel, A., & Montgomery, H. (1986). Scenarios in energy planning. In B. Brehmer, H. Jungermann, P. Lourens, & G. Sevon (Eds.), *New directions in research on decision making* (pp. 205-18). Amsterdam: North Holland.

Dahlstrand, U., & Montgomery, H. (1984). Information search and evaluative processes in decision making: A computer based process tracing study. *Acta-Psychologica, 56*, 113-123.

Edwards, W. (1954). The theory of decision making. *Psychological Bulletin, 51*, 380-417.

Edwards, W., Lindman, R., & Phillips, L. P. (1966). Emerging technologies for making decisions. In T. Newcombe (Ed.), *New directions in psychology II* (pp. 261-325). New York: Holt.

Fishbein, M., & Ajzen, I. (1975). *Belief, attitude, intention, and behavior: An introduction to theory and research.* Hillsdale, NJ: Erlbaum.

Friedman, M., & Savage, L. J. (1952). The expected utility hypothesis and the measurability of utility. *Journal of Political Economy, 60*, 463-475.

Gärling, T., Lindberg, E., & Montgomery, H., (1989). Beliefs about the attainment of life values. In K. G. Grunert & F. Ölander (Eds.), *Understanding economic behavior* (pp. 33-46). Dordrecht: Kluwer.

Gärling, T., Garvill, J., Lindberg, E., & Montgomery, H. (1991). *Residential choices and beliefs about future life satisfaction. Test of a modified multiattribute utility (MAU) framework.* (Document D6). Stockholm: Swedish Council for Building Research.

Garvill, J., Gärling, T., Lindberg, E., & Montgomery, H. (1990). Economic and non-economic motives for residential preferences and choices. *Journal of Economic Psychology, 13*, 39-56.

Garvill, J., Gärling, T., Lindberg, E., & Montgomery, H. (1991, August). *In search of evidence for dominance structuring in decision making.* Paper presented at the 13th European Research Conference of Subjective Probability, Utility, and Decision Making, Fribourg, Switzerland.

Gigerenzer, G., Hoffroge, U., & Kleinbölting, H. (1991). Probabilistic mental models: A Brunnswickian theory of confidence. *Psychological Review, 95*, 506-528.

Hogarth, R. M. (1987). *Judgement and choice* (2nd ed.). New York: Wiley.

Kahneman, D., Slovic, P., & Tversky, A. (Eds.). (1982). *Judgement under uncertainty: Heuristics and biases.* New York: Cambridge University Press.

Kahneman, D., & Tversky, A. (1979). Prospect theory. *Psychometrica, 47*, 263-291.

Karlsson, G. (1988). A phenomenological psychological study of decision and choice. *Acta Psychologica, 68*, 7-25.

Lindberg, E., Gärling, T., & Montgomery, H. (1987a). *Intra-urban residential mobility: Beliefs about the attainment of life values as determinants of subjective evaluations of housing alternatives* (Umeå Psychological Reports No. 190). Umeå: Department of Psychology, University of Umeå.

Lindberg, E., Gärling, T., & Montgomery, H. (1987b). *Prediction of residential preferences and choices from beliefs about the attainment of life values* (Umeå Psychological Reports No. 189). Umeå: Department of Psychology, University of Umeå.

Lindberg, E., Gärling, T., & Montgomery, H. (1988). People's beliefs and values as determinants of housing preferences and simulated choices. *Scandinavian Housing and Planning Research, 5*, 181-197.

Lindberg, E., Gärling, T, & Montgomery, H. (1989a, August). *Decisions with incompletely described alternatives*. Paper presented at the 12th European Research Conference of Subjective Probability, Utility, and Decision Making, Moscow, SSSR.

Lindberg, E., Gärling, T., & Montgomery, H. (1989b). Differential predictability of preferences and choice. *Journal of Behavioral Decision-Making, 2*, 205-219.

Lindberg, E., Gärling, T., & Montgomery, H. (1989c). Subjective belief-value structures as determinants of preferences for and choices among housing alternatives. *Journal of Consumer Policy, 12*, 119-137.

Lindberg, E., Gärling, T., & Montgomery, H. (1990a). *Intra-urban residential mobility: Subjective belief-value structures as determinants of residential preferences and choices.* (Umeå Psychological Reports, No. 197). Umeå: Department of Psychology, University of Umeå.

Lindberg, E., Gärling, T., & Montgomery, H. (1990b). *The impact of travel cost and travel time on residential preferences and choices.* (Umeå Psychological Reports, No. 199). Umeå: Department of Psychology, University of Umeå.

Lindberg, E., Gärling, T., & Montgomery, H. (1991). Prediction of preferences for and choices between verbally and numerically described alternatives. *Acta Psychologica, 76*, 165-176.

Lindberg, E., Gärling, T., Montgomery, H., & Waara, R. (1987). People's evaluation of housing attributes: A study of underlying beliefs and values. *Scandinavian Housing and Planning Research, 4*, 81-103.

Lopes, L., & Ekberg, P.-H. (1980). Test of an ordering hypothesis in risky decision making. *Acta Psychologica, 45*, 161-167.

Montgomery, H. (1983). Decision rules and the search for a dominance structure: Towards a process model of decision making. In P. C. Humphreys, O. Svenson, & A. Vari (Eds.), *Analyzing and aiding decision processes* (pp. 343-369). Amsterdam: North Holland.

Montgomery, H. (1989a). From cognition to action: The search for dominance in decision making. In H. Montgomery and O. Svenson (Eds.), *Process and structure in human decision making* (pp. 23-49) Chichester: Wiley.

Montgomery, H. (1989b). The search for a dominance structure: Simplification versus elaboration. In D. Vickers and P. L. Smith (Eds.), *Human information processing: Measures, mechanisms and models* (pp. 471-483). New York: Elsevier.

Montgomery, H., Drottz, B.-M., Gärling, T., Persson, A.-L., & Waara, R. (1985). Conceptions about material and immaterial values in a sample of Swedish subjects. In H. Brandstätter and E. Kirchler (Eds.), *Economic psychology: Proceedings of the tenth IAREP annual colloquium* (pp. 427-437). Linz: Trauner.

Montgomery, H., Gärling, T., Lindberg, E., & Selart, M. (1990). Preference judgments and choice: Is the prominence effect due to information integration or information evaluation? In K. Borcherding, O. I. Larichev, & D. M. Messick (Eds.), *Contemporary issues in decision making* (pp. 149-157). Amsterdam: North Holland.

Montgomery, H., & Johansson, U. S. (1988). Life values: Their structure and relation to life conditions. In S. Maital (Ed.), *Applied behavioral economics*. (vol. 1, pp. 420-437). Brighton: Wheatsheaf.

Montgomery, H., & Svenson, O. (1989). A think aloud study of dominance structuring in decision processes. In H. Montgomery and O. Svenson (Eds.), *Process and structure in human decision making* (pp. 135-150). Chichester: Wiley.

Payne, J. W., Bettman, J. R., & Johnson, E. J. (1988). Adaptive strategy selection in decision making. *Journal of Experimental Psychology: Learning, Memory, and Cognition, 14*, 534-552.

Payne, J. W., Bettman, J. R., & Johnson, E. J. (1992). Behavioral decision research: A constructive processing perspective. *Annual Review of Psychology, 43*, 87-131.

Rohrman, B., & Borcherding, K. (1988, August). *The cognitive structure of residential decisions: A longitudinal field study*. Paper presented at the XXIV international congress of psychology, Sydney, 1988.

Simon, H. A. (1955). A behavioral model of choice. *Quarterly Journal of Economics, 69*, 99-118.
Slovic, P. (1975). Choice between equally valued alternatives. *Journal of Experimental Psychology: Human Perception and Performance, 1*, 280-287.
Svenson, O. (1979). Process descriptions of decision making. *Organizational Behavior and Human Performance, 23*, 86-112.
Svenson, O. (in press). Differentiation and consolidation theory of decision making. *Acta Psychologica.*
Tversky, A. (1969). Intransitivity of preferences. *Psychological Review, 76*, 31-48.
Tversky, A., Sattah, S., & Slovic, P. (1988). Contingent weighting in judgement and choice. *Psychological Review, 95*, 371-384.
Tyszka, T. (1983). Contextual multiattribute decision rules. In L. Sjöberg, T.Tyszka, & J. A. Wise (Eds.), *Human decision making* (pp. 243-256). Lund: Doxa.
Tyszka, T., & Wielochowski, M. (1991). Must boxing verdicts be biased? *Journal of Behavioral Decision Making, 4*, 283-295.
von Winterfeldt, D., & Edwards, W. (1986). *Decision analysis and behavioral research.* Cambridge: Cambridge University Press.

*Behavior and Environment: Psychological and Geographical Approaches*
*T. Gärling and R.G. Golledge (Editors)*



## CHAPTER 14

# Retail Environments and Spatial Shopping Behavior

**Harry Timmermans**

The interplay between aspects of retail environments and consumer spatial shopping behavior has traditionally been an area of major concern in geography, urban planning and related disciplines. It reflects an interest in explaining the relationship between locational and nonlocational attributes of stores or shopping centers and consumer choice behavior either for theory development or as a fundamental component of planning models that are used to predict the likely impact of retail planning decisions on consumer behavior and store performance measures. The purpose of this chapter is to review this literature to evaluate the state of the art and identify future research directions. The chapter focuses on both theo-retical and empirical studies involving analytical as well as modeling approaches.

The chapter is organized into seven major sections. The second section presents a conceptual framework underlying most research on consumer shopping behavior. This is followed by discussions of analytical studies of consumer perception and cognition, attitudes and preference structures, and choice of shopping centers in sections 3, 4, and 5, respectively. The sixth section traces the development of predictive models of store or shopping center choice. Finally, some directions for future research are discussed.

## A Conceptual Framework of Consumer Spatial Decision Making in Retail Environments

Over the years a number of different conceptualizations of consumer decision making and choice processes has been suggested in the literature. While there are some clear differences between them, they nevertheless share a set of common elements (Timmermans, 1982). Spatial shopping behavior is considered to be the outcome of an individual decision making process. Individuals are assumed to choose a single alternative from a choice set such as to optimize individual welfare or utility. Each shopping alternative is characterized by a set of objective attributes. Individuals attach some utility value to each of these attributes, given the decision problem at hand and their values, motivations, information levels, etc. It is assumed that individuals have perceptions of the objective attributes. This perceptive act typically involves a subjective filtering based upon imperfect information, the result of which is a cognitive space. It is assumed that individuals are only familiar with a subset of the shopping alternatives. Moreover, it is assumed that individual decision making is based upon only a few, not necessarily perfectly known attributes. It is assumed that this cognitive space rather than the objective physical space determines individual choice behavior.

Individuals are assumed to discriminate between the shopping alternatives on the basis of a set of attributes. They are assumed to combine their evaluations of the attributes according to some utility function which they use to form an overall evaluation of the shopping alternatives. This involves a subjective weighting and results in a subjective preference scale on which the shopping alternatives are positioned. Finally, individuals are assumed to use some decision rule to relate their preferences to actual choice behavior. Often, it is assumed that individuals will choose the shopping alternative with the highest preference, but more sophisticated, probabilistic rules have been suggested as well.

Different conceptualizations may differ on some aspects, but as will become evident in subsequent sections, most analytical studies and mathematical models of consumer spatial shopping behavior address components of this conceptual framework, or even strictly adhere to it.

## Consumer Perception and Cognition of Retail Environments

Analysis of the perception of stores or shopping centers has received considerable attention in the retailing literature. Different approaches to the measurement of retail images have been applied (Jenkins & Forsyth, 1980; Marks, 1976), the most important of which are a univariate analysis of respondents' evaluations of the attributes of the stores or centers, a multivariate analysis of respondents' evaluations of stores or centers, and a multivariate analysis of similarity or perceptual proximity data. The univariate analyses typically result in direct descriptions of the shopping alternatives. The aim of most of the multivariate analyses has been to identify the basic dimensions underlying the perception of retailing structures.

One of the first geographic studies in this tradition in the literature was conducted by Garner (1968) who examined 17 female students' attitudes towards 10 clothing stores in Bristol using the semantic differential technique. Another study on the cognitive dimensions of retailing alternatives was conducted in Sydney by Burnett (1973). The aim of her study was to determine the attributes of stores relevant to consumer choice behavior and to incorporate these attributes into a general cognitive-behavioral theory of spatial choice processes.

In terms of research design, Burnett's study should be viewed as an important step forward in measuring consumer perception of retailing structures. The main advantage of this approach is that respondents are not requested to respond to a set of attributes a priori selected by the researcher. In contrast, the aim is to identify the constructs used by the respondents when ranking the shopping centers in terms of overall preference. This approach therefore became the standard in the late 1970s. Other studies conducted along similar lines can be found amongst others in Singson (1975), and Spencer (1978, 1980).

Although multidimensional scaling was considered a more valid approach compared to the semantic differential technique in analyzing consumer perceptions of retailing structures, the approach still had one major drawback: the interpretation of the constructs was still largely subjective. To avoid this subjectivity, some researchers used the repertory grid to identify the dimensions underlying the perception of shopping centers. The method is based on Kelly's personal construct theory (Kelly, 1955) who assumes that individuals base their decisions on conceptual models of reality. These models are strictly personal. The repertory grid (e.g., Downs, 1970; Fransella & Bannister, 1977; Hudson, 1974) involves presenting real-world objects in triads and asking respondents in what way two objects are alike and thereby different from the third object. Once the constructs are obtained, the objects may be positioned on each construct using rating scales. Standard multivariate techniques may be used to analyze the data. Hudson (1974) was one of the first to use the repertory grid in a retailing context, while Timmermans, van der Heijden and Westerveld (1982a, 1982b) applied the repertory grid to analyze consumers' cognitions of a shopping center. The results reconfirmed the basic findings obtained in earlier studies. The repertory grid technique has found increasing popularity since these initial studies (e.g., Coshall, 1985; Hallsworth, 1985; Opacic & Potter, 1986).

Recently, Louviere and Johnson (1990) suggested using conjoint measurement to examine retail images. They used store names as the levels of the attributes of interest. The positioning of the stores can be accounted for by describing the attributes such as "prices like x", "service like y", etc. Respondents are then asked to express their opinion about the resulting profile. A model that represents the way in which respondents arrive at such overall opinions, often a linear additive model, is assumed. These data are then analyzed using multiple regression analysis. The approach was illustrated in a study of supermarket images in Edmonton, Canada. Their results indicated that consumers' perceptions were primarily driven by price differences, followed by selection, convenience, quality and friendliness. The market shares predicted by the model proved to be consistently, monotonically related to the market shares observed in a follow-up survey. The result was replicated in a second study (Louviere & Johnson, 1990). This so-called brand-anchored conjoint analysis approach seems to be very promising in the study of retail image.

A specific aspect of perception concerns the issue whether consumers know the various shopping centers in their environment. Consumers are generally not familiar with all shopping opportunities in their direct environment, nor will they patronize them all. The concepts "spatial informational field" (Potter, 1979; Smith, 1976) and "awareness space" (Horton & Reynolds, 1971) have been suggested to express the notion that consumers will only be familiar with a subset of shopping opportunities within a zone. Likewise, concepts such as activity space, action space, and spatial usage field have been introduced to identify the subset of shopping opportunities a consumer actually patronizes.

Smith (1976) examined two properties of spatial information fields: the total number of supermarkets a consumer is familiar with and the average distance between a consumer's residence and the locations of the known shops. He concluded that the number of years at the present address and social status were important variables explaining variability in spatial information fields. Hanson (1977) also concluded that consumers have limited information about shopping opportunities and that this information is unequally distributed across urban space. The level of information tends to drop with increasing distance from one's residence, albeit not symmetrically. The spatial distribution of the stores tends to have an effect on information levels; stores located in areas of a higher density are better known. Potter (1977) arrived at similar conclusions, as did Timmermans, van der Heijden, & Westerveld (1982c). Consumer information fields also tend to be reasonably predictable (van der Heijden & Timmermans, 1984).

## Consumer Attitudes and Preference Structures for Retail Environments

In our conceptual framework, we explicitly distinguished a phase of preference formation in consumer decision making. While this may have some analytical advantages, it should be noted that it is difficult to find studies in the retailing literature that are restricted to consumer attitudes or preferences per se. In most cases, the measurement of attitudes or preference is part of a wider approach that attempts to relate them to subsequent choice behavior. For example, while Rushton's (1969) preference scaling model was originally focused at deriving preference scales from overt shopping patterns, his approach was later extended into a model of choice behavior. Likewise, while conjoint measurement has been used to analyze consumer preferences (see, e.g., Timmermans, 1980b), these measurement can be linked to overt shopping behavior to generate a model that can be used for impact assessment and predictions of consumer spatial shopping behavior.

The majority of the seminal research on consumer attitudes has relied on attitude statements and rating scales. Jonassen (1955), for example, examined attitudes towards downtown versus suburban shopping by asking shoppers to indicate how much they agreed or disagreed with various statements on a five point rating scale. Williams (1981) used 27 attitude statements that expressed a particular aspect of shopping predispositions. Three groups of consumers were identified on the basis of these data. Group 1 had a predominantly economic character. The second group comprised the social aspects of shopping, while the third group was made up of two statements which related to limited time available for shopping. These attitude statements appeared to be related to aspects of shopping choice behavior (see also Ezell & Russell, 1985).

Over the years, more studies have adopted the attitudinal theories developed by Rosenberg and Fishbein. Attitudes are held to be a function of the strength of beliefs about a store or shopping center and an evaluation of these beliefs. A typical example of the approach is given in James, Durand, and Dreves (1976) who tested the predictive ability of the multi-attribute attitude model with respect to men's clothing stores. Six attributes were selected: assortment, personnel, atmosphere, service, quality, and price. Respondents were asked to rate each of these six attributes on a seven point scale in terms of importance. They were also requested to evaluate each store along each attribute. Attitudinal scores were then computed and a preference ranking derived. Traditionally, studies in this tradition have adopted this straightforward methodology.

More recently, structural equation models have grown in popularity (e.g., Korgaonkar, Lund, & Price, 1985).

## Consumer Spatial Shopping Behavior: Empirical Regularities

Underlying most studies of spatial shopping behavior is the assumption that the utility consumers derive from a shopping opportunity is a function of the attractiveness of that opportunity and some distance factor. If it is assumed that the functional relationship between a shopping center's utility and some combination of attractiveness and distance is multiplicative, the above notion can be expressed as

$$U_{ij} = A_j^{\alpha} D_{ij}^{-\beta} \quad (1),$$

where $U_{ij}$ is the utility of shopping opportunity *j* for consumers located at *i*; $A_j$ is the attractiveness of the *j*-th opportunity, $D_{ij}$ is the distance between *i* and *j*, and $\alpha$ and $\beta$ are parameters ($\alpha + \beta = 1$). It should be noted that the assumption of a multiplicative functional relationship is not crucial for the subsequent discussion. There is, however some empirical evidence (e.g., Louviere & Wilson, 1978) supporting this assumption.

Two extreme postulates of spatial shopping behavior can be derived from equation (1). If it is assumed that $\alpha = 0$, a consumer's utility for a shopping center is determined only by distance. If, in addition, it is assumed that consumers maximize their utility, they will invariably choose the nearest shopping opportunity. This is the case of distance-minimizing behavior. In contrast, if it is assumed that $\beta = 0$, and hence $\alpha = 1$, utility will depend on attractiveness only. Again, if utility-maximizing behavior is assumed, consumers will choose the shopping opportunity with the highest attractiveness. This is the case of spatial indifference.

The postulate of distance-minimizing behavior has been subject of empirical verification, especially in the context of central place theory. According to this postulate, consumers will choose the nearest store or shopping center that offers the required good. Therefore, this postulate was often referred to as the nearest town hypothesis (Clark & Rushton, 1970; Golledge, Rushton, & Clark, 1966; Rushton, Clark, & Golledge, 1967). The validity of this postulate was tested both at the interurban and intraurban level. It did not get much empirical support at the interurban scale, except that a few studies indicated that the distance-minimizing postulate might have some empirical validity in developing countries (Lentnek, Lieber, & Sheskin, 1975; Lentnek, Charnews, & Cotter, 1978;

Wood, 1974). Rushton et al. (1967) concluded that in Iowa only 35% of all trips to grocery stores were made to the nearest center.

Surprisingly, the results obtained at the intraurban scale are less consistent. Tennant (1962) and Brush and Gauthier (1968) concluded that consumer shopping behavior in Chicago and Philadelphia, respectively, was generally consistent with the postulate of distance-minimizing behavior. In contrast, Marble (1959) found in Cedar Rapids and Sussex respectively, that the postulate of distance-minimizing behavior does not describe spatial shopping behavior very well.

The lack of empirical support for the nearest-center postulate led some researchers to introduce different concepts for explaining consumer spatial shopping behavior. Some authors suggested that it is not distance per se that is of interest, but rather the difference or ratio between the distance to a shopping opportunity and the distance to the nearest opportunity. Clark and Rushton (1970), for example, found that the greater the distance to the nearest shopping opportunity, the less the impact of distance on consumer choice. Others suggested that consumers are inclined to choose other than the nearest shopping opportunity if distance is compensated by higher attractiveness as exemplified by, for example, lower prices or larger assortment. This very assumption is consistent with the assumptions underlying models of spatial consumer behavior reviewed below.

The most extreme concept in this respect is that of spatial indifference which suggests that distance does not have an impact at all on consumer choice, but rather that choice is dictated only by attractiveness considerations. The postulate of spatial indifference is however very difficult to operationalize. Perhaps one of the few real attempts to test the validity of this postulate can be found in Timmermans (1980a). He found that the overall subjective evaluation of the attractiveness of shopping areas correctly predicted 70% of shopping destination choices. The concept of reasonable travel time was used to measure a zone of spatial indifference (Timmermans, 1979, 1980a) to reflect the notion that at least within certain limits, distance does not affect consumer spatial choice behavior. Thus, although very few studies indeed have attempted to test the validity of the postulate of spatial indifference, there is ample empirical evidence suggesting that the attractiveness of shopping opportunities has some influence on consumer shopping choice behavior (e.g., Hudson, 1976; Wood, 1974).

## Predictive Models of Consumer Spatial Shopping Behavior

### *Spatial Interaction Models*

Urban planning and geography have traditionally been concerned with predicting the impact of new retailing developments on the existing retail structure. Especially in many European countries, planning authorities ask for information on the likely effects of changes in the retail environment in order to reach intelligent decisions regarding approval of new retail proposals. The predictions typically concern the impact new developments would probably have on turnover levels in existing shopping centers, consumer satisfaction, and accessibility of shopping centers. In general, approval for new developments is granted only if there would be no adverse effects.

The most widely used models are the spatial interaction models. The first applications of this type of model appeared in the late 1950s and early 1960s. Spatial interaction models, and especially the gravity model, were developed in analogy with Newton's law of gravity which states that the gravitational force or interaction between two bodies of masses $m_1$ and $m_2$ and a distance $d_{12}$ between them equals

$$F_{ij} = \frac{Km_1m_2}{d_{12}^2} \qquad (2).$$

Underlying spatial interaction models is the analogous assumption that the share of customers that a shopping center attracts from its environment is inversely proportional to distance and proportional to the attractiveness of the shopping center. This is consistent with Reilly's Law of Retail Gravitation (Reilly, 1931), further developed and confined by Converse (1949). The gravity principle was used to delimit retail market areas. It was assumed that two cities attract customers from an intermediate town in direct proportion to the populations of the two cities and in inverse proportion to the squares of the distances from these two cities to the intermediate town.

In the early 1960s, the focus of interest shifted from the delimitation of market areas to probabilities of interaction. Huff (1963, 1964) was one of the first to propose a spatial interaction model for predicting shopping trips. He suggested that the probability of choosing a shopping center is positively related to its size and decreases with some function of distance. Although this formulation is consistent with the gravity principle, Huff used Luce's choice axiom to derive his model. Luce's axiom states that when faced with several choice alternatives, the probability of an individual choosing a particular alternative is equal to the ratio of the utility of that alternative to the sum of the utilities of all alternatives considered by the individual. Applied to the problem of choice of shopping centers, this axiom implies that the probability of a consumer visiting a particular shopping center is equal to the ratio of the utility of that store to the sum of utilities of all the stores considered by the consumer:

$$p_{ij} = \frac{F_j \ / \ d_{ij}^{\beta}}{\sum_{j'} F_{j'} \ / \ d_{ij'}^{\beta}} \qquad (3),$$

where $p_{ij}$ is the probability of a consumer at $i$ visiting shopping center $j$, $F_j$ is a measure of attractiveness of shopping center $j$, $d_{ij}$ is the distance between $i$, and $j$, and $\beta$ is a distance decay parameter. Utility is thus conceptualized as a trade-off between attractiveness and distance decay. Attractiveness in turn was measured in Huff's model as a function of size.

Working independently, Lakshmanan and Hansen (1965) modified a traffic model to arrive at a similar model of spatial shopping behavior. Although much empirical work has been conducted on spatial interaction models in the context of shopping behavior since this seminal work, no major conceptual breakthroughs have been achieved. Instead, most of the relevant literature concerned problems of application and operational definitions. For example, different measures of distance and attractiveness have been suggested. Distance has been measured as straight-line distance, city-block distances, or as travel time. Likewise, attractiveness has been measured as square footage of retail space, number of establishments, etc. (see, e.g., Haines, Simon, & Alexis, 1972). In the early applications, attractiveness was typically measured by a single surrogate indicator, representing some objective measure of shopping center size. However, attractiveness is a multidimensional concept (e.g., Nevin & Houston, 1980), while, in addition, people may have imperfect impressions of these objective attributes. In order to deal with this problem, Stanley and Sewall (1976), for example, used a multidimensional scaling procedure to incorporate the effect of differing store images. This significantly improved predictive performance. Gautschi (1981) found that including additional measures of accessibility (such as availability of mass transit) in addition to image also improved the model's predictive performance. Likewise, different functions for representing the distance decay effect have been proposed. Power, exponential, and even more complex functions have been used to represent distance separation effects.

The traditional version of the spatial interaction model assumed that the probability of choosing a shopping center is proportional to its attractiveness. Later versions of the model, however, included an exponent in the specification of attractiveness to allow for the fact that the larger shopping centers tend to have an extra level of attraction beyond their greater size because of the increase in choice of goods and benefits of economies of scale.

The estimation of spatial interaction models is typically based upon aggregate, zonal data of shopping flows. Once the study area is delineated carefully to avoid large external flows, the area is divided into a number of smaller zones which are as homogeneous as possible in their demographic and socioeconomic characteristics. Consumer shopping patterns are then observed for this zonal system. The spatial interaction model is calibrated using these observations of shopping trips among the zones. This involves finding the parameter values of the spatial interaction model that provide the best fit between the observed spatial pattern of shopping trips in the study area and the pattern of trips predicted by the model. These parameter values are typically derived using iterative optimalization methods that systematically evaluate different combinations of parameter values to find the ones that give the best fit between actual and predicted trip patterns (see, e.g., Stetzer, 1976). A multitude of goodness-of-fit statistics is available to quantify the correspondence between observed and predicted flows (Timmermans & Borgers, 1985b). Much of the literature in the 1960s and 1970s has dealt with these operational problems of design of the zoning system, model calibration and goodness-of-fit. The conceptual underpinnings of the models did not change however.

Wilson (1967, 1971) improved the theoretical underpinnings of the spatial interaction models by deriving an entropy-maximizing interpretation. He showed that the spatial interaction model is consistent with principles of entropy-maximization if the distance decay function is exponential. Consequently, for some time, most shopping models based upon the spatial interaction model used this formalization (see, e.g., Gibson & Pullen, 1972), whereas many previous models used a power function (see, e.g., Murray & Kennedy, 1971; Turner, 1970). Other authors supplied different ad hoc theoretical underpinnings of the spatial interaction model. Some conceptualized travel costs as a constraint (e.g., Niedercorn & Bechdolt, 1969), or as a negative stimulus (Golob & Beckmann, 1971; Nijkamp, 1975; Smith, 1976). Still others derived the spatial interaction model from psychological theories of choice behavior (Smith, 1975; Okabe, 1975). Although this improved the basis of these models substantially, many applied researchers were not attracted by these ad hoc rationalizations (Williams, 1977; Sheppard, 1978). Especially the fact that the model was still based on zonal orientation patterns and the finding that parameters of the spatial interaction model were highly influenced by the geometry of the study area (see, e.g., Cliff, Martin, & Ord, 1976; Curry, 1972; Ewing, 1974; Sheppard, 1979a, 1979b; Sheppard, Griffith, & Curry, 1976) caused a search for improvements of the model, or even for different modelling approaches based on different assumptions. A simple improvement is to use the ratio of distances to the closest and farthest shopping centers or stores as a measure of distance separation (Ghosh, 1984; Timmermans & Veldhuisen, 1979). This has led some authors to derive models that estimate the effect of attraction variables endogenously (Baxter, 1979; Baxter & Ewing, 1979; Cesario, 1975, 1976; Ewing, 1978). Hence, these models do not include attraction variables, but rather an attraction parameter. In a separate modelling step, the estimated attractiveness terms are regressed on a series of variables that are assumed to account for the attractiveness of the destination. To some extent, these models represent an attempt to derive attractiveness independently of spatial structure. Most of these models have however not been applied in a retailing context with the exception of the model suggested by Timmermans and Veldhuisen (1979). This is not to say that there are any reasons why these models cannot be applied to problems of spatial shopping behavior.

Another way of dealing with this problem was to incorporate some measure of spatial structure into a spatial interaction model. The so-called competing destinations model, originally suggested by Fotheringham (1983) to study migration, but later also applied in a retailing context (Fotheringham, 1988a; Guy, 1987) is based on this notion. When applied to spatial shopping behavior, the choice behavior of interest is conceptualized as a hierarchical choice process in which individuals first select a part of their environment or a shopping center, and then select the shopping center within that environment or a store within a shopping center. This hierarchical choice process is modelled by incorporating the accessibility of a shopping alternative to all the other potential shopping alternatives in the attractiveness argument. The simplest approach to the specification of this additional term is the use of a Hansen-type accessibility measure. The competing destinations model was with applied mixed results by Guy (1987) to data on food and grocery shopping behavior in the Cardiff area. The improvement in fit over a conventional spatial interaction model was small but led to improvements in the aggregated predictions of shopping flows. However, the sign of the parameter was counterintuitive in that shopping centers facing greater competition tend to attract more trade. Thus, agglomeration effects appeared to be present, which is unexpected for food and grocery shopping. Including a competing destinations term on origin-specific distance decay estimates resulted in more negative distance decay parameters. This finding was at variance with that of Fotheringham (1983), suggesting that more research is needed into the application of the competing destinations model to spatial shopping behavior.

The versions of the spatial interaction model discussed in this section are all static. This field of study gained a new impetus by Wilson's attempts to develop dynamic models (see, e.g., Wilson, 1988). This was done by adding a submodel of retailer behavior. The revenues, $D_j$, at a particular site are known from the spatial interaction model. If the costs, $C_j$ of supplying facilities at site $j$ are given, the total amount of floorspace at $j$ is assumed to grow; and vice versa. Equilibrium exists if revenues at site $j$ equal retailer's cost. This specification led to some important insights (Harris & Wilson, 1978). There is a global equilibrium which maximizes consumer surplus, but there are also other stable equilibria. It can also be shown (Wilson & Oulton, 1983) that small parameter changes may lead to jumps in the type of patterns of critical parameter values. A formal dynamic representation of the basic hypothesis is:

$$W_j^{\cdot} = \epsilon \, (D_j - c_j) \, F(W_j) \tag{4}$$

where $W_{\cdot j}$ is the rate of change of $W_j$. The factor $F(W_j)$ determines the form of the trajectory to equilibrium and is usually equal to 1 or $W_j$.

This model has received much interest probably because it fits well into popular bifurcation and chaos theory. Simulation experiments showed that realistic retail structures can be generated (see, e.g., Clarke & Wilson, 1983). This work has not been restricted to size dynamics and the production constrained spatial interaction model. Fotheringham and Knudsen (1986), working with the competing destinations model, modelled location dynamics and discontinuous change in both the size and the spacing of retail establishments.

### *The multiplicative competitive interaction model*

One of the limitations of conventional shopping models derived from spatial interaction models is their restriction to a single variable operationalization of attractiveness. Obviously, in many contexts more than one attribute is of interest. This has led to attempts to specify the attractiveness component in terms of multiple variables. One of these more general forms of the spatial interaction model is the Multiplicative Competitive

Interaction model which has its roots in marketing where it has been used initially for the description of competitive market behavior, determining brand share, and the measurement of advertising and promotion effectiveness. The model has gained increasing popularity since Nakanishi and Cooper (1974, 1982) demonstrated how this model could be estimated by weighted or generalized least-squares analysis. The model is expressed as:

$$p_{ij} = \frac{\prod_{k=1}^{K} X_{kij}^{\alpha_k}}{\sum_{j'=1}^{J} \prod_{k=1}^{K} X_{kij'}^{\alpha_k}} \quad (5),$$

where $p_{ij}$ is the probability that an individual located at $i$ will choose shopping alternative $j$, $X_{kij}$ is the value of the $k$-th attribute of shopping alternative $j$ for individuals located at $i$, J is the total number of shopping alternatives, K is the total number of attributes considered, and $\alpha_k$ is a parameter for the $k$-th attribute.

In this model, multiple attributes of shopping centers are considered along with size as determinants of attractiveness. Jain and Mahajan (1979) in their study of food retailing, for example, used consumer evaluations of appearance, price, service level, and store image, as well as objective measures like the number of checkout counters, employee composition, location at an intersection, and availability of credit card services as components of the attractiveness function. Timmermans (1981b) used number of parking facilities, number of shops, variety of shops/functional complexity, number of employees, and number of superstores. Proximity to shopping centers was included by Hansen and Weinberg (1979). Black, Ostlund and Westbrook (1985) developed an outlet specific model. Often the variables of interest are highly intercorrelated. Consequently, the estimates may have high variances and be far removed from the true population values. They may even be of the wrong sign. The use of ridge regression analysis has been suggested to avoid this problem of near-multicollinearity (Mahajan, Jain, & Bergier, 1977; Timmermans, 1981b).

### *The Revealed Preference Model*

As we have seen, a potential disadvantage of the spatial interaction model is its dependence on the geometry of the study area. To avoid this problem, Rushton (1969, 1971) developed a preference scaling model. Shopping centers are classified into so-called locational types which are based on a combination of an attractiveness variable and a distance category. Shopping choice behavior is assumed to reflect a trade-off between attractiveness and distance separation. Pairwise choice data are then used to calculate the proportion of times a particular locational type is chosen given that both are present. The locational types are positioned on a unidimensional preference scale using a nonmetric multidimensional scaling algorithm.

The basic model has been extended over the years in a number of important respects. First, Rushton (1974) showed how graphical methods, trend surface analysis or conjoint analysis can be used to decompose the preference scale into the contributions of the two basic variables. This is an important step forward if the model is used for prediction or impact assessment. Second, the model focuses on preferences, not on choice. Girt (1976) therefore suggested to link the preference function to overt behavior by relating distances on the preference scale to choice probabilities. Third, Timmermans (1979) suggested to derive individuals' choice sets from data on information fields and consumer attitudes.

Although Rushton's preference scaling model has considerable appeal, it never received the attention it deserved. One of the reasons might be that the model is based on only two explanatory variables, while heterogeneity in preferences is not accounted for. The model has also been criticized for its conceptual basis. It has been suggested that the model may not represent preferences but rather (in)consistencies of choice (MacLennan & Williams, 1979 1980; Pirie, 1976; Timmermans & Rushton, 1979). Some successful applications have been reported in the literature of consumer shopping behavior (Lentnek et al., 1975; Timmermans, 1979; 1981a).

### *Discrete Choice Models*

The spatial interaction model has been criticized for its reliance on aggregate, zonal shopping flows. It has led to the development of disaggregate discrete choice models that are based on individual choice behavior, although it should be noted that many authors have used the term rather loosely in the past.

Discrete choice models focus on discrete choices made by consumers on individual shopping trips rather than on aggregate proportions of trips made from the various zones. Conventional discrete choice models may be derived from at least two formal theories: Luce's strict utility theory (Luce, 1959) and Thurstone's random utility theory (Thurstone, 1927). Strict utility theory can be considered an extension of constant utility theory to account for intransitivities in choice. In particular, Luce extended the weak and strong utility model for binary choices to the multiple alternative choice case. His theory assumes that the probability of choosing some alternative, say a shopping center, is equal to the ratio of the utility associated with that alternative to the sum of the utilities for all the alternatives in the choice set. Luce thus assumed deterministic preference structures and postulated a constant ratio decision rule. In contrast, random utility theory assumes that an individual's utility for a choice alternative is assumed to consist of a deterministic component and a random utility component. In addition, random utility theory assumes a utility-maximizing decision rule which implies that the probability of choosing some choice alternative is equal to the probability that the utility associated with a particular choice alternative exceeds that of all other choice alternatives included in a choice set. The specification of the choice model then depends on the assumptions regarding the distributions of the random utility components. If it is assumed that the random utility components are independently and identically normal distributed with zero mean, the independent multivariate probit model can be derived. If, however, it is assumed that these random components are independently, identically Type I extreme value distributed, the multinomial logit (MNL) model is derived. It may be expressed as

$$p_{ik} = \frac{\exp[U(X_k,S_i)]}{\sum_j \exp[U(X_j,S_i)]} \qquad (6),$$

where $U(X_k,S_i)$ is the deterministic part of the utility of choice alternative $k$ of individual $i$ with socioeconomic characteristics $S_i$. This model has become very popular in many fields of application including modelling consumer spatial shopping behavior.

Under strict utility theory, many different utility functions are allowed provided they are unique (except for multiplication by a positive constant). Under random utility theory many specifications are still possible, but for ease of estimation a deterministic utility component, linearity is usually assumed. The estimation of the parameters of discrete choice models typically involves establishing the functional relationship between (the evaluation of) the choice alternatives' attributes and overt choice behavior. Applications of the MNL model in retailing can be found in Richards and Ben-Akiva (1974), Recker and Stevens (1976), Timmermans (1984c), and Fotheringham (1988b).

One of the most important criticisms of the MNL model concerns the fact that the utility of a shopping center is independent from the attributes of other shopping centers in the choice set (Independence from Irrelevant

Alternatives [IIA] property): this implies that the model cannot account for so-called substitution. This assumption appears to be counterintuitive when two or more shopping centers show a high degree of similarity and hence may be substitutes. Under such circumstances, the introduction of a new, similar shopping center will not reduce market shares in direct proportion to the utility of the existing shopping centers as is implied by the MNL model, but will reduce market shares proportionally more from similar shopping centers. In recent years, various alternative models have therefore been developed which attempt to relax the IIA assumption (see Timmermans & Golledge, 1990, for a review).

Substitution models which impose more general conditions on the variance-covariance matrix differ in terms of their assumptions regarding the type of distribution of the error terms (negative exponential distribution, extreme value distribution or normal distribution), and assumptions on the error terms. To understand these models, it should be realized that increasing the error variance of a choice alternative implies that the probability of choosing that alternative increases, even if the deterministic part of the utility function is equal to that of other alternatives. Likewise, the effect of introducing covariances between the error terms of two alternatives is that, ceteris paribus, they draw more shares from each other. Only few of these more sophisticated models have actually been applied in a retailing context; hence we will restrict our discussion to these models.

Meyer and Eagle (1982) suggested capturing substitution effects by defining a single overall substitution measure. Thus, they developed a substitution model with an extended logit formula that explicitly incorporates the degree of similarity between shopping centers. The model introduced by Borgers and Timmermans (1987, 1988) avoids some of the negative aspects of the Meyer-Eagle model in that substitution for each attribute can be estimated separately and that a more direct measure of substitution is used. This model can be considered as the multinomial logit equivalent of Fotheringham's competing destinations model that is derived from the spatial interaction model, although it also includes substitution effects.

A problem with the model, and Fotheringham's competing destinations model as well, is that it does not predict spatial choice behavior as theoretically expected when the choice alternatives are located at more than three different locations. Following an idea introduced in the marketing literature by Kamakura and Srivastava (1984), Borgers and Timmermans (1985a, 1985b) developed a second model that allows the estimation of substitution and spatial structure effects. Similarity and spatial structure effects are incorporated into the variance-covariance matrix of the random disturbance terms of the utility function of the logit model. The covariance structure is modelled explicitly in terms of distances in the attribute space between the shopping centers as a measure of substitution.

An analysis of consumer choice data for hypothetical structures (Borgers & Timmermans, 1986b) indicated that when two shopping centers are located close to each other, choice probabilities of the remaining shopping centers decrease (agglomeration effects). When, in addition, both centers differ in terms of their attractiveness, the choice probability of one shopping center may increase while the choice probability of the other center decreases (redistribution effects). The predictive ability of both models was tested and compared to that of other substitution models using data on the choice of 34 shopping centers in the Maastricht region, The Netherlands (Borgers & Timmermans, 1986a). The substitution/spatial structure effects models performed only slightly better than the conventional MNL model: a finding consistent with the results obtained for simulated data sets (Borgers & Timmermans, 1987). The models that accounted for spatial structure effects produced the best results. Similar results were obtained in a follow-up study in the Eindhoven region (Borgers & Timmermans, 1992). This study also led to the conclusion that the spatial transferability of the substitution and spatial structure models is slightly better than that obtained for the MNL model.

An alternative approach to the issue of context effects is to let the degree of attribute similarity among choice alternatives directly influence the overall utility of alternatives. Meyer and Eagle (1982) and Eagle (1984, 1988) have argued that consumers shift weights associated with the attributes of alternatives. More specifically, attributes with little variation are less important. Empirical support for this hypothesis was accumulated in laboratory experiments.

Another way of avoiding the IIA-property is to develop hierarchical models, the best known model of which is probably the nested logit model. Like the MNL model, this model assumes that an individual evaluates shopping centers according to a utility function. Unlike the MNL model, the shopping centers which are supposed to be correlated are grouped into nests. Each nest is represented by an aggregate alternative with a composite utility consisting of the so-called inclusive value and a parameter to be estimated. To be consistent with utility-maximizing behavior, the inclusive values should lie in the range between 0 and 1, and the values of the parameters should change consistently from lower levels to higher levels of the hierarchy.

### *Compositional Attitudinal Models*

The compositional approach involves measuring, explicitly and separately, an individual's evaluations of the shopping centers and the importance weights he attaches to the attributes. The overall utility of a shopping center is then computed by combining these self-explicated quantities according to some combination rule. Often, a linear additive rule, which represents a compensatory decision making process, is assumed. Thus, overall utility is composed using attribute-specific measurements. Sometimes, these importance weights are not measured explicitly, but are estimated by multiple regression analysis. The overall evaluations of the shopping centers then constitute the dependent variable of the regression equation, while the independent variables consist of the self-explicated evaluations of the various attributes of the shopping centers. This would be an example of a so-called hybrid model. Because these more sophisticated models have not found any application in retailing, the present discussion is limited to the simpler versions.

Cadwallader (1975) used a compositional model that was derived in analogy with conventional spatial interaction models. He used the following model:

$$p_j = \frac{\sum_{k=1}^{K} W_k A_{jk}}{d_j} I_j \qquad (7)$$

where $p_j$ is the proportion of consumers choosing store $j$, $A_{jk}$ is the aggregate subjective attractiveness of store $j$ on attribute $k$, $W_k$ is the relative importance of attribute $k$, $d_j$ is the aggregate cognitive distance to store $j$, $I_j$ is the proportion of consumers familiar with store $j$. Note that both attractiveness and distance are measured in subjective terms. Choice probabilities are thus calculated without any calibration. Cadwallader assumed that the attractiveness of supermarkets is determined by speed of service, assortment, number of sold items and price. Respondents evaluated each of these four factors on a seven point scale. The median of these four scales was used as input to the model. Respondents were also requested to rank the four factors in order of importance. These data were used to calculate the relative importances. Distance was measured as the median of the subjectively estimated distances and information level was used as a dichotomized variable: consumers were familiar with a supermarket or not. Although the results of the application indicated that this model produced better results than a conventional spatial interaction model, it is obvious that this model can be heavily criticized on the basis of the simplistic way in which the variables are measured. Cadwallader's model was also used by Lloyd and Jennings (1978) with an extended number of attractiveness variables.

In a study of spatial shopping behavior in Eindhoven, The Netherlands, Timmermans (1980a) assumed that consumers will choose the shopping center of highest subjective attractiveness after screening the centers in terms of travel time. Thus, travel time is not used as a negative attribute in a compensatory decision making process, but as a noncompensatory screening variable. Different rules can be used to represent the integration of attribute evaluations into some overall measure of subjective attractiveness. Timmermans (1980a) compared weighted and unweighted versions of additive and multiplicative rules in terms of predictive success and found that the models performed almost equally well. In a later study, Timmermans (1983) compared the predictive success of these compositional models to that of noncompensatory decision rules. Noncompensatory decision rules assume that consumers do not arrive at some overall evaluation or preference by combining their attribute evaluations according to some algebraic rule, but that they arrive at some choice by screening the shopping centers on an attribute-by-attribute basis (see, e.g., Timmermans, 1984b). For example, a dominance rule states that a shopping center will be chosen only if it is evaluated more positively than all other shopping centers on all attributes. The conjunctive rules states that each shopping center which fails to meet a minimum value on each attribute will be eliminated from a consumers' choice set. In contrast, the disjunctive rule involves an evaluation of the shopping centers on the basis of the maximum rather than the minimum values of each attribute. Only shopping centers which meet or exceed at least one of these maximum values are accepted for further consideration. Finally, the lexicographic rule assumes that the decision making process proceeds sequentially. Shopping centers are first ranked on the basis of the most important attribute. If a single shopping center exhibits the highest evaluation score on this attribute, it will be chosen. If some shopping centers are tied on the most important attribute, the process proceeds to the next most important attribute. This process proceeds sequentially using different attributes until all shopping centers are ranked and a single shopping center remains. Although these rules sound appealing, their predictive success was much less than that of the compositional models.

### *Decompositional Multiattribute Preference and Choice Models*

Decompositional multiattribute preference models have in common with discrete choice models the assumption that individuals cognitively integrate their evaluations of a shopping center's attributes to derive the utility for a shopping center and arrive at a choice by selecting that center with the highest utility. However, unlike discrete choice models, the parameters of the decompositional multiattribute preference models are not derived from real-world data, but from experimental design data. Decompositional models differ from compositional models in that overall preferences for shopping centers are measured rather than calculated. Part-worth utilities associated with attribute levels are derived by decomposing overall preferences into attribute contributions rather than by measuring them explicitly and separately (e.g., Timmermans, 1984a).

Decompositional models involve the following steps when applied to problems of spatial shopping behavior. First, each shopping center is described by its position on a set of attributes relevant to the consumer or of planning interest. Decompositional decision models are based on the assumption that consumer choices are the result of a decision making process which involves a subjective evaluation of the positions of each shopping center on each attribute, an integration of the separate subjective evaluations of each attribute position into an overall evaluation of each shopping center, and development of a rule for translating the overall evaluations of competing shopping centers into a single choice. Decompositional decision models have in common procedures for simultaneously measuring the joint effects of two or more attributes on the individual's overall evaluations of a statistically designed set of multiattribute alternatives. In order to do so, the second step of the approach involves a definition of the attributes of interest in terms of a set of attribute levels. One then creates an experimental design to generate a set of hypothetical shopping centers that varies the positions of the attributes in a controlled manner. The creation of an appropriate design is largely determined by the model that one assumes to describe how the separate attribute positions are integrated into an overall preference or choice. Once the design is created, an evaluation task is developed in which individuals rank order or rate the hypothetical shopping centers with respect to preference. The individuals' overall evaluations of the designed shopping centers are decomposed into a set of part-worth utilities associated with every level or position of each attribute. The ability of the estimated part-worth measures to recover an individual's observed evaluation responses is assessed by a goodness-of-fit measure. The best fitting conjoint model for a given decision task is identified by comparing these goodness-of-fit measures for alternative models.

Once part-worth utilities have been estimated, a choice rule is postulated to predict the choices that an individual is likely to make given the estimated preference function. A simple, commonly used postulate is that an individual will choose the shopping center with the highest overall evaluation. Alternatively, different probabilistic rules can be postulated (e.g., Timmermans & van der Heijden, 1984). Individual choice behavior can then be simulated by defining real-world shopping centers in terms of their positions or levels on each attribute varied in the experimental task, calculating each individual's overall utility score for each shopping center on the basis of the estimated preference function, and applying the postulated choice or decision rule to map an individual's estimated overall preference or utility into choices. Applications of this approach to retailing can be found in Prosperi and Schuler (1976), Schuler (1979), Recker and Schuler (1981), Louviere and Meyer (1981), Timmermans (1980b, 1982), Verhallen and de Nooij (1982), Moore (1990). Decompositional preference models are not necessarily restricted to the domain of experience, but they can be used also to examine the potential market shares of new innovations, such as teleshopping (Timmermans, Borgers, & Gunsing, 1991). Their transferability properties seems to be promising (van der Heijden & Timmermans, 1988).

Most current decompositional multiattribute decision models applied to problems of spatial shopping behavior try to predict real-world choice behavior by assuming that the shopping center with the highest predicted overall utility will be chosen. This approach is theoretically inadequate because a deterministic rule is used to predict a probabilistic phenomenon. Furthermore, the statistical properties of the part-worth and overall utility measures derived from rankings of hypothetical shopping centers are unknown and may be inappropriate for predicting choice behavior. Some of these problems may be avoided by making explicit assumptions regarding the distribution of the error of the derived utility measures (see e.g., Timmermans & van der Heijden, 1984). Unfortunately, while distributional assumptions allow for probabilistic choice processes, they do not allow one to test the validity of the assumptions except with respect to some external criterion like real-world choice behavior. Current models typically require a fairly rigorous and restrictive set of assumptions.

Another approach that has received some attention in the retailing literature is the exploded logit model (Chapman & Staelin, 1982; Moore, 1990). This model is based on the Luce and Suppes Ranking Choice Theorem.

Given the rigorous and often limited assumptions underlying these approaches, Louviere and Woodworth (1983) suggested an approach that examines the preference formation and choice processes simultaneously. As with more traditional decompositional approaches, a set of decision attributes together with appropriate positions or levels for those attributes is first identified. Multiattribute choice alternatives are then generated by means of fractional factorial experimental designs in which each attribute is treated as a factor with varying numbers of levels. If the number of alternatives among which individuals will choose is constant (say n), and each alternative has M attributes with L levels, one can construct choice sets that satisfy the MNL or Luce choice model by designing an $L^{N*M}$ main effects, orthogonal, fractional factorial experimental design to create joint combinations of attribute levels. Choice sets created in this way have a fixed number of alternatives, but the positions of these alternatives on the decision attributes vary from choice set to choice set. Often a constant choice alternative is added to each choice set to set the origin of the utility scale.

In contrast to the rating or ranking tasks of traditional decompositional models, the Louviere and Woodworth (1983) approach involves choice tasks in which individuals select one and only one alternative in each of several experimentally designed choice sets. That is, consumers are asked to indicate which shopping center in a set is the one that they would be most likely to patronize for a particular product class. Alternatively, consumers may be asked to estimate the proportion of their total patronage that they would be likely to allocate to each center, or, in general, to allocate some fixed set of resources (e.g., dollars, points, trips, etc.) to the available alternatives. If the MNL choice model is approximately correct, a sufficient condition for estimating the part-worth utilities for the shopping centers is that the independence of alternatives across choice sets be preserved. If one has reason to expect that the MNL model will provide a reasonable approximation to the choice data, one can also construct choice designs by first using separate fractional factorial designs to generate attribute combinations for each shopping alternative. The separate fractional designs for each shopping alternative are then randomly assigned without replacement to each choice set. The effect of competitive environments might be studied along similar lines (Louviere, 1984b).

A major advantage of this design approach is that one can test for the validity of various MNL model properties, such as testing IIA by including the cross-effects of an alternative on another alternative in the utility arguments. This specification which has been referred to as the universal or mother logit model allows one to generalize the MNL model to account for violations of the IIA property due to nesting of or similarities among alternatives. It is also possible to test for the effect of choice set composition on utilities. $2^N$ designs are appropriate in this case. First, the hypothetical choice alternatives are constructed in a way similar to traditional decompositional preference models. These profiles are then placed into choice sets of varying size and composition. Timmermans and Borgers

(1985) used this approach to estimate a choice model involving generic alternatives and generic effects in shopping for groceries. Price and distance were assumed to be the most important decision attributes in grocery shopping and were each assigned two levels. Four combinations or hypothetical shopping alternatives were produced from the two levels of the two attributes. A one-half fraction of the $2^2$ factorial was used to place the four price/distance combinations into choice sets. The design permitted the estimation of some of the two-way interaction effects among the alternatives. A constant base alternative was added to each choice set, and weighted least-squares regression analysis was used to estimate the parameters of a generalized MNL choice model. The statistical results indicated that the cross-effects between alternatives were not significant, suggesting that the simple MNL model was a good approximation for these data. Timmermans, Borgers and van der Waerden (1991a) used this approach also to predict the impact on consumer choice of major changes in an existing shopping center. In a follow-up, before-after study, Timmermans, Borgers and van der Waerden (1991b) found the mother logit model predicted actual shopping choice behavior after the changes were implemented slightly better than conventional revealed choice models.

Perhaps the most important problem associated with decompositional preference models is that task demands for individual respondents become more and more onerous as the number of attributes and/or the number of levels of attributes increase. A possible solution to this information overload problem has been suggested by Louviere (1984). This so-called Hierarchical Information Integration method is based on the hypothesis that in complex decisions involving many influential attributes, individuals first group the attributes in sets. Each set defines a separate, higher-order decision construct. The idea is to structure an experimental preference or choice task in such a way to allow to study and analyze each of these integration processes separately. Louviere and Gaeth (1987) provide an example of this approach applied to an analysis of supermarket shopping behavior.

Disadvantages of the hierarchical information task are that it is restricted to preferences. In addition, the assumed hierarchical structure cannot be tested. Louviere and Timmermans (1990) showed how this method can be extended to problems of spatial choice behavior by replacing the overall preference task with a choice task. Oppewal, Timmermans, and Louviere (1991) suggested to use multiple choice experiments to test the implied hierarchical structure. Their method involves using in each subdesign the attributes of the higher-order decision construct of interest plus overall evaluations of the remaining decision constructs.

Although this work is still in a developing stage, decompositional preference and choice models can also be used to simulate the dynamics of retail systems. First, one predicts consumer shopping choice behavior by assuming some choice simulator or applying a choice model directly. Then, retailers' reactions are modelled as a function of the estimated demand for retail locations. Their behavior may influence the objective or perceived attributes of the shopping centers, resulting in possible adjustments in consumer choice of shopping centers. In this way, the dynamics may be simulated (Oppewal & Timmermans, 1988, 1989; Timmermans & van der Heijden, 1987).

## Conclusions

The interplay between retail environments and consumer spatial choice behavior constitutes a longstanding field of research in geography and urban planning. The objective of this chapter has been to summarize the main research approaches in the field. The discussion has necessarily been restrictive, both in terms of depth of coverage and the various approaches that have been discussed. The discussion has been concentrated on descriptive analytical studies on shopping behavior and static models of single shopping choices. Other important areas such as dynamic models of shopping behavior, trip chaining and pedestrian movement, and normative location/allocation models have not been discussed in any detail at all. The reader is referred to Timmermans and Borgers (1989), O'Kelly (1981), Borgers and Timmermans (1986a, 1986b), and Craig, Ghosh and McLafferty (1984) respectively.

If the existing literature is examined, one cannot escape the conclusion that most of this literature aims at finding facts about consumer shopping behavior. The interest focuses primarily on describing determinants and patterns of consumer shopping behavior. Theories are not very well developed. At best, theories are directly applied from other disciplines without much modification. The geographical component is treated as just another variable of interest that can be accommodated in the analysis in similar ways as the other non-spatial variables are incorporated. It is difficult to speak of any theoretical progress. Too often, the same phenomenon is examined, the difference only being the use of different research methods.

The only exception in this respect is the area of the modelling of spatial shopping behavior. Over the years, the theoretical underpinnings of the models have improved considerably. Moreover, one can really speak of accumulation of knowledge. The spatial dimension has been given special treatment as exemplified, for instance, by the inclusion of competition, agglomeration, and spatial structure effects. It is also in this subfield of spatial shopping behavior that more progress is to be expected. Two research themes come to mind if one thinks about avenues of future research. One is the area of modelling multiple-purpose shopping trips, and related developments such as sequential choice behavior, trip-chaining, and activity analysis. Although these topics have received some attention in the past, it is difficult to speak of accumulated knowledge. Now that the major operational problems of models of single choice behavior have been solved, the time seems ripe to tackle the much more complicated problem of multiple choice behavior with the same rigor. This problem is currently being examined by various scholars working in any one of the mentioned modelling approaches, and the first major publications are expected in the next couple of years.

Second, existing models of single choice behavior are expected to be improved even more by incorporating competitive structures into the utility functions assumed to underlie shopping choice behavior. Scholars working in different modelling traditions are currently developing models of this type. For example, Timmermans, Borgers and van der Waerden (1991) have tested such a model in the decompositional framework, Laroche and Brisoux (1989) have developed such structures in attitudinal models of consumer behavior, Borgers and Timmermans (1992) developed and tested such models in the discrete choice tradition, and Fotheringham's competing destinations model (Fotheringham, 1988a) has been advanced using the spatial interaction approach.

Finally, it is expected that the issue of developing dynamic models of spatial shopping behavior will receive more attention in the near future. As briefly indicated, this topic is now being addressed by all modelling approaches. It is very likely though, that most of this research will remain theoretical as the costs and effort of collecting reliable time-series data are often prohibitive. Yet, developments like these, and the fact that spatial shopping behavior is a field of study that is approached by scholars from different disciplinary backgrounds, continue to make consumer spatial shopping behavior an exciting field of inquiry.

## References

Baxter, M. J. (1979a). The interpretation of the distance and attractiveness components in models of recreational trips. *Geographical Analysis, 11*, 311-315.

Baxter, M. J., & Ewing, G. O. (1979). Calibration of production constrained trip distribution models and the effect of intervening opportunities. *Journal of Regional Science, 19*, 319-331.

Black, W. C., Ostlund, L. E., & Westbrook, R. A. (1985). Spatial demand models in an intrabrand context. *Journal of Marketing, 49*, 106-113.

Borgers, A. W. J., & Timmermans, H. J. P. (1985a). Context effects and spatial choice models. Paper presented at the 25th Regional Science Association Conference, Budapest.

Borgers, A. W. J., & Timmermans, H. J. P. (1985b). *Effects of spatial arrangement and similarity on spatial choice behavior.* Paper presented at 4th Colloquium on Theoretical and Quantitative Geography, Veldhoven.

Borgers, A. W. J., & Timmermans, H. J. P. (1986a). *Testing the performance of several discrete choice models in a spatial context: An empirical study.* Paper presented at the 18th British Regional Science Conference, Bristol.

Borgers, A. W. J., & Timmermans, H. J. P. (1986b). *Effects of spatial arrangement on spatial choice behavior: Some experiments.* Paper presented at the Meeting of the IGU Working Group on Mathematical Models and Systems Analysis, Madrid.

Borgers, A. W. J., & Timmermans, H. J. P. (1987). Choice model specification, substitution and spatial structure effects: A simulation experiment. *Regional Science and Urban Economics, 17*, 29-47.

Borgers, A. W. J., & Timmermans, H. J. P. (1988). A context-sensitive model of spatial shopping behavior. In R.G. Golledge, & H. J. P. Timmermans (Eds.), *Behavioural Modelling in Geography and Planning* (pp. 159-179). London: Croom Helm.

Borgers, A. W. J., & Timmermans, H. J. P. (1992). *Context-sensitive spatial choice models: Empirical application and spatial transferability.* Unpublished manuscript. University of Technology of Eindhoven..

Brush, J. E., & Gauthier, H. L. (1968). *Service centers and consumer trips.* (Research Paper 113). Department of Geography, University of Chicago.

Burnett, P. (1973). The dimensions of alternatives in spatial choice processes. *Geographical Analysis, 5*, 181-204.

Cadwallader, M. T. (1975). A behavioral model of consumer spatial decision making. *Economic Geography, 51*, 339-349.

Cesario, F. J. (1975). Linear and nonlinear regression models of spatial interaction. *Economic Geography, 51*, 69-77.

Cesario, F. J. (1976). Alternative models of spatial choice. *Economic Geography, 52*, 363-373.
Chapman, R. G., & Staelin, R. (1982). Exploiting rank ordered choice set data within the stochastic utility model. *Journal of Marketing Research, 19*, 281-299.
Clarke, M., & Wilson, A. G. (1983). The dynamics of urban spatial structure: Progress and problems. *Journal of Regional Science, 23*, 1-18.
Clark, W. A. V., & Rushton, G. (1970). Models of intra-urban consumer behavior and their implications for central place theory. *Economic Geography, 46*, 486-497.
Cliff, A. D., Martin, R., & Ord, J. K. (1976). A reply to the final comment. *Regional Studies, 10*, 341-342.
Converse, P. D. (1949). New laws in retail gravitation. *Journal of Marketing, 14*, 378-384.
Coshall, J. (1985). The form of micro-spatial consumer cognition and its congruence with search behavior. *Tijdschrift voor Economische en Sociale Geografie, 76*, 345-355.
Craig, C. S., Ghosh, A., & McLafferty, S. (1984). Models of retail location process: A review. *Journal of Retailing, 60*, 5-36.
Curry, L. (1972). A spatial analysis of gravity flows. *Regional Studies, 6*, 131-147.
Downs, R. M. (1970). The cognitive structure of an urban shopping center. *Environment and Behavior, 2*, 13-39.
Eagle, T. C. (1984). Parameter stability in disaggregate retail choice models: Experimental evidence. *Journal of Retailing, 60*, 101-123.
Eagle, T. C. (1988). Modeling context effects: Application of a weight shifting model in a spatial context. *Tijdschrift voor Economische en Sociale Geografie, 79*, 135-148.
Ewing, G. O. (1974). Gravity and linear regression models of spatial interaction: A cautionary note. *Economic Geography, 50*, 83-87.
Ewing, G. O. (1978). The interpretation and estimation of parameters in constrained trip distribution models. *Economic Geography, 54*, 254-273.
Ezell, H. F., & Russell, G. D. (1985). Single and multiple person household shoppers: A focus on grocery store selection criteria and grocery shopping attitudes and behavior. *Journal of the Academy of Marketing Science, 13*, 171-187.
Fotheringham, A. S. (1983). A new set of spatial interaction models: The theory of competing destinations. *Environment and Planning A, 15*, 15-36.

Fotheringham, A. S. (1988a). Consumer store choice and choice set definition. *Marketing Science, 7*, 299-310.

Fotheringham, A. S. (1988b). Market share analysis techniques: A review and illustration of current US practice. In N. Wrigley (Ed.), *Store choice, store location and market analysis* (pp. 120-159). London: Routledge.

Fotheringham, A. S., & Knudsen, D. C. (1984). Critical parameters in retail shopping models. *Modeling and Simulation, 15*, 75-80.

Fotheringham, A. S., & Knudsen, D. C. (1986). Modelling discontinuous change in retailing systems: Extensions of the Harris-Wilson framework with results from a simulated urban retailing system. *Geographical Analysis, 18*, 295-312.

Fransella, F., & Bannister, D. (1977). *A manual for the repertory grid technique*. London: Academic.

Garner, B. J. (1968). The analysis of qualitative data in urban geography: The example of shop quality. In *Proceedings of the Institute of British Geographers Urban Study Group Conference, Salford University*.

Gautschi, D. A. (1981). Specification of patronage models for retail center choice. *Journal of Marketing Research, 18*, 162-174.

Gibson, M., & Pullen, M. (1972). Retail turnover in the East-Midlands: A regional application of a gravity model. *Regional Studies, 6*, 183-196.

Girt, J. L. (1976). Some extensions to Rushton's spatial preference scaling model. *Geographical Analysis, 8*, 137-152.

Ghosh, A. (1984). Parameter nonstationarity in retail choice models. *Journal of Business Research, 12*, 425-436.

Golledge R. G., Rushton, G., & Clark, W. A. V. (1966). Some spatial characteristics of Iowa's dispersed farm population and their implications for the grouping of central place functions. *Economic Geography, 42*, 261-272.

Golob, T. F., & Beckmann, M. J. (1971). A utility model for travel forecasting. *Transportation Science, 5*, 79-90.

Guy, C. M. (1987). Recent advances in spatial interaction modelling: An application to the forecasting of shopping travel. *Environment and Planning A, 19*, 173-186.

Haines, G. H., Simon, L., & Alexis, M. (1972). An analysis of central city neighborhood food trading areas. *Journal of Regional Science, 12*, 95-105.

Hallsworth, A. G. (1985). *Consumer perceptions of hypermarkets and superstores*. Paper presented at the Colloque International Geographie des Activites Commerciales, Universite de Paris I.

Hansen, M. M., & Weinberg, C. B. (1979). Retail market share in a competitive environment. *Journal of Retailing, 55*, 37-46.

Hanson, S. (1977). Measuring the cognitive levels of urban residents. *Geografiska Annaler B, 59*, 67-81.

Harris, B., & Wilson, A. G. (1978). Equilibrium values and dynamics of attractiveness terms in production-constrained spatial interaction models. *Environment and Planning A, 10*, 371-388.

Heijden, van der R. E. C. M., & Timmermans, H. J. P. (1984). Modelling choice-set generating processes via stepwise logit regression procedures: Some empirical results. *Environment and Planning A, 16*, 1249-1255.

Heijden, van der R. E. C. M., & Timmermans, H. J. P. (1988). The spatial transferability of a decompositional multiattribute preference model. *Environment and Planning A, 20*, 1013-1025.

Horton, F. E., & Reynolds, D. R. (1971). Effects of urban spatial structure on individual behavior. *Economic Geography, 47*, 36-48.

Hudson, R. (1974). Images of the retailing environment: An example of the use of the repertory grid methodology. *Environment and Behavior, 6*, 470-494.

Hudson, R. (1976). Linking studies of the individual with models of aggregate behaviour: An empirical example. *Transactions of the Institute of British Geographers, 1*, 159-174.

Jain, A. K., & Mahajan, V. (1979). Evaluating the competitive environment in retailing using multiplicative competitive interactive models. In J. Sheth (Ed.), *Research in marketing* (pp. 217-235). Greenwich, CN: JAI.

James, D. L., Durand, R. M., & Dreves, R. A. (1976). The use of multi-attribute attitude models in a store image study. *Journal of Retailing, 52*, 23-32.

Jenkins, R. L., & Forsyth, S. M. (1980). Retail image research: State of the art review with implications for retail strategy. In J. C. Olson (Ed.), *Advances in consumer research VII* (pp. 189-194). Provo, UT: Association for Consumer Research.

Jonassen, C. T. (1955). *Shoppers attitudes.* (Highway Research Board, Publication 273a). Washington, D.C.: National Academy of Sciences.

Kamakura, W. A., & Srivastava, R. K. (1984). Predicting choice shares under conditions of brand interdependence. *Journal of Marketing Research, 21*, 420-432.

Kelly, G. A. (1955). *The psychology of personal constructs*. New York: Norton.

Korgaonkar, P. K., Lund, D., & Price, B. (1985). A structural equations approach toward examination of store attitude and store patronage behavior. *Journal of Retailing, 61*, 39-59.

Lakshmanan, T. R., & Hansen, W. A. (1965). A retail market potential model. *Journal of American Institute of Planners, 31*, 134-143.

Laroche, M., & Brisoux, J. E. (1989). Incorporating competition into consumer behavior models: The case of the attitude-intention relationship. *Journal of Economic Psychology, 10*, 343-362.

Lentnek, B., Charnews, M., & Cotter, J. V. (1978). Commercial factors in the development of regional urban systems: A Mexican case study. *Economic Geography, 54*, 291-308.

Lentnek, B., Lieber, S. R., & Sheskin, I. (1975). Consumer behavior in different areas. *Annals of the Association of American Geographers, 65*, 538-545.

Lloyd, R. E., & Jennings, D. (1978). Shopping behavior and income: Comparisons in an urban environment. *Economic Geography, 54*, 157-167.

Louviere, J. J. (1984a). Hierarchical information integration: A new method for the design and analysis of complex multiattribute judgment problems. In T. C. Kinnear (Ed.), *Advances in consumer research XI* (pp. 148-155). Provo, UT: Association for Consumer Research.

Louviere, J. J. (1984b). Using discrete choice experiments and multinomial logit choice models to forecast trial in a competitive retail environment: A fast food restaurant illustration. *Journal of Retailing, 60*, 81-107.

Louviere, J. J., & Gaeth, G. J. (1987). Decomposing the determinants of retail facility choice using the method of hierarchical information integration: A supermarket illustration. *Journal of Retailing, 63*, 25-48.

Louviere, J. J., & Johnson, R. D. (1990). Reliability and validity of the brand-anchored conjoint approach to measuring retailer images. *Journal of Retailing, 66*, 359-382.

Louviere, J. J., & Meyer, R. J. (1981). A composite attitude-behavior model of traveller decision making. *Transportation Research B, 15*, 411-420.

Louviere, J. J., & Timmermans, H. J. P. (1990). Hierarchical information integration applied to residential choice behavior. *Geographical Analysis, 22*, 127-145.

Louviere, J. J., & Wilson, E. (1978). Predicting consumer response in travel analysis. *Transportation Planning and Technology, 4*, 1-9.

Louviere, J. J., & Woodworth, G. (1983). Design and analysis of simulated consumer choice or allocation experiments: An approach based on aggregate data. *Journal of Marketing Research, 20*, 350-367.

Luce, R. (1959). *Individual choice behavior.* New York: Wiley.

MacLennan, D., & Williams, N. J. (1979). Revealed space preference theory: A cautionary note. *Tijdschrift voor Economische en Sociale Geografie, 70*, 307-309.

MacLennan, D., & Williams, N. J. (1980). Revealed space preference theory and spatial choice: Some limitations. *Environment and Planning A, 12*, 909-919.

Mahajan, V., Jain, A. K., & Bergier, M. (1977). Parameter estimation in marketing models in the presence of multicollinearity: An application of ridge regression analysis. *Journal of Marketing Research, 14*, 586-591.

Marble, D. F. (1959). Transport inputs at residential sites. *Papers and Proceedings of the Regional Science Association, 5*, 253-266.

Marks, R. B. (1976). Operationalizing the concept of store image. *Journal of Retailing, 52*, 37-46.

Meyer, R. J., & Eagle, T. C. (1982). Context-induced parameter instability in a disaggregate stochastic model of store choice. *Journal of Marketing Research, 19*, 62-71.

Moore, L. (1990). Segmentation of store choice models using stated preferences. *Papers of the Regional Science Association, 69*, 121-131.

Murray, W., & Kennedy, M. B. (1971). Notts/Derbys: A shopping model primer. *Journal of the Royal Town Planning Institute, 57*, 211-215.

Nakanishi, M., & Cooper, L. G. (1974). Parameter estimates for multiplicative competitive interaction models-least squares approach. *Journal of Marketing Research, 11*, 303-311.

Nakanishi, M., & Cooper, L. G. (1982). Simplified estimation procedures for MCI models. *Marketing Science, 1*, 314-322.

Niedercorn, J. H., & Bechdolt, B. V. (1969). An economic derivation of the gravity law of spatial interaction. *Journal of Regional Science, 9*, 273-282.

Nijkamp, P. (1975). Reflections on gravity and entropy models. *Regional Science and Urban Economics, 5*, 203-225.

Nevin, J. R., & Houston, M. J. (1980). Image as a component of attractiveness to intra-urban shopping areas. *Journal of Retailing, 56*, 77-93.

Okabe, A. (1975). A theoretical comparison of the opportunity and gravity models. *Regional Science and Urban Economics, 6*, 381-398.

O'Kelly, M. (1981). A model of the demand for retail facilities incorporating multistop, multipurpose trips. *Geographical Analysis, 13*, 134-148.

Opacic, S., & Potter, R. B. (1986). Grocery store cognitions of disadvantaged consumer groups: A Reading case study. *Tijdschrift voor Economische en Sociale Geografie, 77*, 288-289.

Oppewal, H., & Timmermans, H. J. P. (1988, August). *Urban retail sector dynamics and conjoint-based choice systems.* Paper presented at the Regional Science Association Conference, Stockholm, Sweden.

Oppewal, H., & Timmermans, H. J. P. (1989). Conjoint-based choice simulators: A completely disaggregate approach to study spatial choice behaviour. In G. Braun, & R. Schwarz, (Eds.), *Theorie und quantitative Methodik in der Geographie* (pp. 8-15). Meta Heft 1, Berlin: TEAS.

Oppewal, H., Timmermans, H. J. P., & Louviere, J. J. (1991, March). *An integrated approach to modeling hierarchical information integration using multiple choice experiments.* Paper presented at the Marketing Science Conference, Wilmington, DE.

Pirie, G. (1976). Thoughts on revealed preference and spatial behaviour. *Environment and Planning A, 8*, 947-955.

Potter, R. B. (1977). The nature of consumer usage fields in an urban environment. *Tijdschrift voor Economische en Sociale Geografie, 68*, 168-176.

Potter, R. B. (1979). Perception of urban retailing facilities: An analysis of consumer information fields. *Geografiska Annaler B, 61*, 19-129.

Prosperi, D. C., & Schuler, H. J. (1976). An alternate method to identify rules of spatial choice. *Geographical Perspectives, 38*, 33-38.

Recker, W., & Schuler, H. (1981). Destination choice and processing spatial information: Some empirical tests with alternative constructs. *Economic Geography, 57*, 373-383.

Recker, W., & Stevens, R. (1976). Attitudinal models of modal choice: The multinomial case for selected nonwork trips. *Transportation, 5*, 355-375.

Reilly, W. J. (1931). *The law of retail gravitation.* New York: Knickerbocker.

Richards, M., & Ben-Akiva, M. (1974). A simultaneous destination and mode choice model for shopping trips. *Transportation, 3*, 343-356.

Rushton, G. (1969). Analysis of spatial behavior by revealed space preference. *Annals of the Association of American Geographers, 59*, 391-400.

Rushton, G. (1971). Preference and choice in different environments. *Proceedings of the Association of American Geographers, 3*, 146-150.
Rushton, G. (1974). Decomposition of space preference structures. In R. G. Golledge, & G. Rushton (Eds.), *Spatial choice and spatial behavior* (pp. 119-133). Columbus, OH: Ohio State University Press.
Rushton, G., Golledge, R. G., & Clark, W. A. V. (1967). Formulation and test of a normative model for spatial allocation of grocery expenditures by a dispersed population. *Annals of the Association of American Geographers, 57*, 389-400.
Schuler, H. J. (1979). A disaggregate store-choice model of spatial decision-making. *The Professional Geographer, 31*, 146-156.
Sheppard, E. S. (1978). Theoretical underpinnings of the gravity hypothesis. *Geographical Analysis, 10*, 386-402.
Sheppard, E. S. (1979a). Notes on spatial interaction. *The Professional Geographer, 31*, 8-15.
Sheppard, E. S. (1979b). Gravity parameter estimation. *Geographical Analysis, 11*, 120-133.
Sheppard, E. S., Griffith, D. A., & Curry, L. (1976). A final comment on misspecification and autocorrelation in those gravity parameters. *Regional Studies, 10*, 337-339.
Singson, R. L. (1975). Multidimensional scaling analysis of store image and shopping behavior. *Journal of Retailing, 51*, 38-52.
Smith, G. C. (1976). The spatial information fields of urban consumers. *Transactions of the Institute of British Geographers, 1*, 175-189.
Smith, T. E. (1975). A choice theory of spatial interaction. *Regional Science and Urban Economics, 5*, 137-176.
Smith. T. E. (1976). Spatial discounting and the gravity hypothesis. *Regional Science and Urban Economics, 6*, 331-356.
Spencer, A. H. (1978). Deriving measures of attractiveness for shopping centers. *Regional Studies, 12*, 713-726.
Spencer, A. H. (1980). Cognition and shopping center choice: A multidimensional scaling approach. *Environment and Planning A, 12*, 1235-1251.
Stanley, T. J., & Sewall, M. A. (1976). Image inputs to a probabilistic model: Predicting retail potential. *Journal of Marketing, 40*, 48-53.
Stetzer, F. (1976). Parameter estimation for the constrained gravity model. *Environment and Planning A, 8*, 673-683.
Tennant, R. J. (1962). *Shopping patterns of urban residents*. Unpublished manuscript. Department of Geography, University of Chicago.
Thurstone, L. (1927). A law of comparative judgement. *Psychological Review, 34*, 273-286.

Timmermans, H. J. P. (1979). A spatial preference model of regional shopping behaviour. *Tijdschrift voor Economische en Sociale Geografie, 70*, 45-48.

Timmermans, H. J. P. (1980a). Consumer spatial choice strategies: A comparative study of some alternative behavioural spatial shopping models. *Geoforum, 11*, 123-131.

Timmermans, H. J. P. (1980b). Unidimensional conjoint measurement models and consumer decision-making. *Area, 12*, 291-300.

Timmermans, H. J. P. (1981a). Spatial choice behaviour in different environmental settings: An application of the revealed preference approach. *Geografiska Annaler B, 63*, 59 -67.

Timmermans, H. J. P. (1981b). Multi-attribute shopping models and ridge regression analysis. *Environment and Planning A, 13*, 43-56.

Timmermans, H. J. P. (1982). Consumer choice of shopping centre: An information integration approach. *Regional Studies, 16*, 171-182.

Timmermans, H. J. P. (1984a). Decompositional multiattribute preference models in spatial choice analysis: A review of some recent developments. *Progress in Human Geography, 8*, 189-221.

Timmermans, H. J. P. (1984b). Decision models for predicting preferences among multiattribute choice alternatives. In G. Bahrenberg, M. M. Fischer, & P. Nijkamp, (Eds.), *Recent developments in spatial data analysis: Methodology, measurement, models* (pp. 337-355). Aldershot: Gower.

Timmermans, H. J. P. (1984c). Discrete choice models versus decompositional multiattribute preference models: A comparative analysis of model performance in the context of spatial shopping behaviour. In D. E. Pitfield (Ed.), *Discrete choice models in regional science* (pp. 88-102). London: Pion.

Timmermans, H. J. P., & Borgers, A. W. J. (1985). The assessment of model performance in spatial choice analysis. In J. Deiters & G. Bahrenberg (Eds.), *Methodology, models and methods in regional science* (pp. 33-63). Osnabruck: OSG-Materialien Nr. 5.

Timmermans, H. J. P., & Borgers, A. W. J. (1989). Dynamic models of choice behaviour: Some fundamentals and trends. In J. Hauer, H. J. P. Timmermans, & N. Wrigley (Eds.), *Urban dynamics and spatial choice behaviour* (pp. 3-27). Boston: Kluwer.

Timmermans, H. J. P., Borgers, A. W. J., & Gunsing, M. (1991). The potential adoption of teleshopping in a spatial context: A decompositional choice experiment. *International Review of Retailing, Distribution, and Consumer Research, 2*, 549-567.

Timmermans, H. J. P., Borgers, A. W. J., & van der Waerden, P. J. H. J. (1991a). Mother logit analysis of consumer shopping destination choice. *Journal of Business Research, 23*, 311-323.
Timmermans, H. J. P., Borgers, A. W. J., & van der Waerden, P. J. H. J. (1991b). *Revealed vs. decompositional choice models: A before-after study of consumer choice of shopping centre.* Unpublished manuscript, University of Technology of Eindhoven.
Timmermans, H. J. P., & Golledge, R. G. (1990). Applications of behavioural research on spatial choice problems II: Preference and choice. *Progress in Human Geography, 14*, 311-354.
Timmermans, H. J. P., & van der Heijden, R. E. C. M. (1984). The predictive ability of alternative decision rules in decompositional multiattribute preference models. *Sistemi Urbani, 5*, 89-101.
Timmermans, H. J. P., & van der Heijden, R. E. C. M. (1987). Retail change and individual choice dynamics: A conjoint-based choice simulator experiment. In A. Metton, & L. Cassassas (Eds.), *Commercial Change* (pp. 413-446). Barcelona: Universidad de Barcelona.
Timmermans, H. J. P., Heijden van der, R. E. C. M., & Westerveld, H. (1982a). Cognition of urban retailing structures: A Dutch case study. *Tijdschrift voor Economische en Sociale Geografie, 73*, 2-12.
Timmermans, H. J. P., Heijden van der, R. E. C. M., & Westerveld, H. (1982b). The identification of factors influencing destination choice: An application of the repertory grid methodology. *Transportation, 11*, 189-203.
Timmermans, H. J. P., Heijden van der, R. E. C. M., & Westerveld, H. (1982c). Perception of urban retailing environments: An empirical analysis of consumer information and usage fields. *Geoforum, 13*, 27-37.
Timmermans, H. J. P., & Rushton, G. (1979). Revealed space preference theory: A rejoinder. *Tijdschrift voor Economische en Sociale Geografie, 70*, 309-312.
Timmermans, H. J. P., & Veldhuisen, K. J. (1979). Het ruimtelijk koopgedrag van consumenten in de context van multiattribuut planning: Een mathematische modelformulering en calibratie procedure. *Planning, 9*, 11-20.
Turner, C. J. (1970). *Severnside shopping model.* (Discussion Paper No. 4). London: Nathaniel Lichfield & Associates.
Verhallen, T. M. M., & de Nooij, G. J. (1982). Retail attribute sensitivity and shopping patronage. *Journal of Economic Psychology, 2*, 39-55.

Williams, H. C. W. L. (1977). On the formation of travel demand models and economic evaluation measures of user benefit. *Environment and Planning A, 9*, 285-344.

Williams, N. J. (1981). Attitudes and consumer spatial behaviour. *Tijdschrift voor Economische en Sociale Geografie, 72*, 145-155.

Wilson, A. G. (1988). Store and shopping-centre location and size: A review of British research and practice. In N. Wrigley (Ed.), *Store choice, store location & market analysis* (pp. 160-186-186). London: Routledge.

Wilson, A. G., & Oulton, M. J. (1983). The corner shop to supermarket transition in retailing: The beginnings of empirical evidence. *Environment and Planning A, 15*, 265-274.

Wood, L. J. (1974). Spatial interaction and partitions of rural market space. *Tijdschrift voor Economische en Sociale Geografie, 65*, 23-34.

*Behavior and Environment: Psychological and Geographical Approaches*
*T. Gärling and R.G. Golledge (Editors)*


## CHAPTER 15

# Consumers in Retail Environments

**Paul M. W. Hackett, Gordon R. Foxall, and W. Fred Van Raaij**

To understand consumer behavior within retail environments, situational factors are of great import. As Kakkar and Lutz (1981, p. 204) stated, "... a comprehensive understanding and accurate prediction of behavior in the market-place demands a situational perspective." The relatively few studies within this area have been motivated by the fact that both attitudes and personality variables, when taken alone, have been found to be relatively poor predictors of consumer behavior. As a consequence, situational variables have been investigated in an attempt to provide a better understanding of the consumer within the retail environment (e.g., Belk, 1975). In this research there has been a need to define the consumption environment and through this definition to impose a structure on the constituent variables of this environment. There has long been a recognition of the fact that human behaviors within and experience of environments, situations, locations, settings, and places are complex, multidimensional phenomena (e.g., Canter, 1977; Marans & Spreckelmeyer, 1982; Peled, 1974). This is equally true of the consumer in the retail environment. In considering a specified place, or place type, and how social or psychological processes affect and are affected by an environment, a multi-disciplinary perspective has often been employed. This is reflected in the term arcology derived from the combination of the words architecture and ecology. This term is used by Soleri (1969) to describe the city in a way which reflects the synergetic relationship between humans and their built environments. The term also serves as a reminder that many disciplines are concerned with human behavior in situ. Synergy is a term particularly apposite in this context as human beings and their environments form a complex interplay.

The question may then be asked, how does the environment exert influence on cognitions, affect, and behaviors (Troye, 1985). Does it cause, permit, facilitate, activate or direct behavior? Does a merchandise display cause consumers to buy? Or is this to overstate the direct effect of the environment on behavior, as it is more likely that environmental effects come about through interaction with other salient variables?

In this chapter, we consider the consumer in the retail environment. Research drawn from environmental and consumer psychology, and from marketing is reviewed. One of the problems in attempting such an enterprise is the problem of integration. Research in the mentioned areas in general, and that which has considered the consumer in retail environments in particular, has tended to be fragmented and to some extent lacking in common theoretical orientation. In view of the inherent complexity, it is not surprising that no single approach has dominated.

The complexity of the subject matter arises from the two subject areas of the "consumer" and the "environment," both of which are by no means simple entities. In considering the latter of these, one is faced with the enormous number of environmental features which may affect human behavior. Features of the consumer setting, such as lighting, heating, and crowdedness, have been investigated in isolation. The findings of some of this research will be reviewed. Along with the physical aspects of the retail environment, social, psychological, and economic features will also be dealt with. Several models exist to explain consumer behavior in the retail environment. An approach in the social sciences which has attempted to form a common theoretical framework within which human behavior may be investigated and understood as an integrated whole is that of facet theory (e.g., Borg & Lingoes, 1987; Canter, 1985). In concluding the chapter, this approach is applied to the retail environment to provide the basis for integrating our review.

## Environment and Situation

Environment is wider than either location, situation, or behavioral setting. A situation is a point in space and time, while location simply specifies a point in space. As people move through time and space, the number of situations they find themselves in is innumerable. The situation corresponds to a single behavior or act that takes place at that place and moment. A behavioral setting is a somewhat larger unit of analysis. A dinner setting or a commuting setting are examples of behavioral settings, because each involves an interval in space and time in which certain behaviors may be expected regardless of the particular persons present (Belk, 1975). These behaviors may be called a behavioral category, as they have a common label, goal, or value (Verhallen & Pieters, 1984).

Situations and behavioral settings are sub-units within an environment. Belk (1975, p. 158) defines the environment in the context of consumer behavior as "all those factors particular to a time and place of observation, which do not follow from personal (intra-individual) and stimulus (object or choice alternative) attributes and which have a demonstrable and systematic effect on current behavior." One may criticize the imposition by Belk of the condition of the effect on behavior as this leads to a circularity of reasoning. Environmental factors cannot, á priori, be assumed to affect consumer behavior. This is an empirical question.

Belk (1975) proposes that the following five groups of situational characteristics may be distinguished in the consumer setting:

1) Physical surroundings, such as, for instance, geographical and institutional location, decor, sounds, lighting, weather, aromas, signs, visible merchandise, and object and/or background stimuli. (Note that merchandise may be stimulus and background as well.)
2) Social surroundings, for instance, other persons, their attributes, roles, and interactions.
3) Temporal perspective, that is, time of day, season, time constraints, and time commitments.
4) Task definition, that is task orientation and definition, intent, and role, for instance searching for a specific good.
5) Antecedent states, such as temporary moods and conditions which are immediately antecedent to and which directly affect perceptions and evaluations of a given environment; for instance, anxiety, happiness, excitation, cash in hand, fatigue, and illness.

Mehrabian and Russell (1974) emphasize the affects elicited by properties of environments. These properties cause dimensions of primary emotional response, such as pleasure-displeasure, degree of arousal, and dominance-submissiveness. The emotions are defined as being the average emotional response elicited along one of the dimensions in a representative sample of respondents. The importance of this model here rests in the fact that Mehrabian and Russell include primary emotional responses as intervening between person and environment, on the one hand, and behavior, such as approach-avoidance, on the other hand (Mehrabian & Russell, 1974; Russell & Mehrabian, 1975, 1976).

Russell and Mehrabian (1978) report the results from two studies investigating the role played by primary emotional qualities elicited by an environment and the effects of these on the behaviors of approach toward a setting, desire to affiliate, and arousal-seeking tendency. Higher levels of arousal were preferred in pleasant environments, whilst lower levels were preferred in unpleasant ones. Respondents were also found to approach submissiveness-eliciting situations more than those which elicited dominance. Affiliation was desired in dominance-eliciting settings if they were pleasant. Arousal facilitated affiliation in pleasant settings but inhibited it in unpleasant settings.

Mehrabian and Russell then showed that whilst the primary emphasis may be separately defined (and to some extent separately controlled), they exert much of their influence on behavior in combination. These findings provide a framework which may be used to design studies of the retail environment and consumer behavior therein.

Troye (1985) integrates the frameworks of Belk (1974) and Mehrabian and Russell (1974). In Figure 15.1, Troye's approach is combined with our own ideas regarding situation and environment. The environment in the broadest and distal sense includes the historical, cultural, legal, and economic environment. It is an abstract, almost metaphorical use of the concept. The physical, social, and temporal environments (on which we will concentrate in this chapter) are more proximal, concrete, and observable. Consequently, they are more amenable to investigation and understanding within the context of behavior in the retail setting.

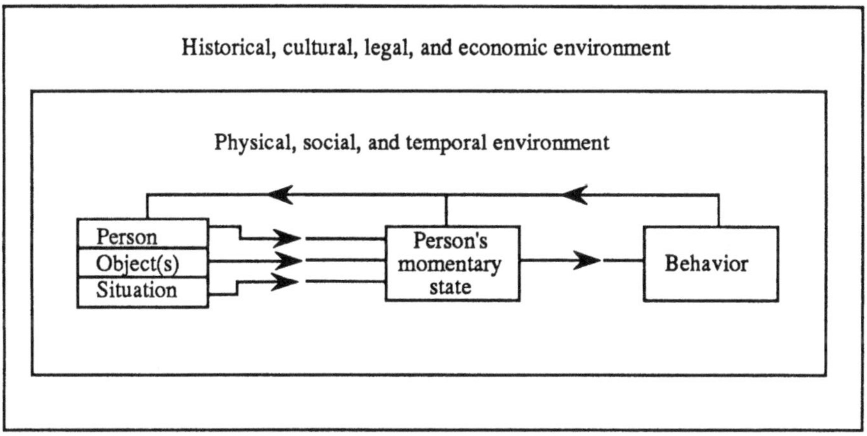


FIGURE 15.1. Environment and situation.

Foxall (1990) expands the Mehrabian and Russell framework through offering operational definitions of analogous affectual concepts. Foxall posits a three-dimensional consumer environment which facilitates and selectively reinforces consumer behavior. The three dimensions are hedonic reinforcement, informational reinforcement, and openness of setting. Within this tripartite, individuals behave as consumers. These actions, which can be of both the overt and covert types, are then selectively reinforced or punished resulting in situation-specific consumer behavior.

Between person, object, and situation exist interactions of many kinds. An individual's momentary state is the result of these direct and indirect effects. Note that the momentary state is not necessarily emotional, as in the Mehrabian and Russell approach. The momentary state influences behavior. The outcomes of behavior may have feedback effects on the person's state, his or her perceptions and evaluations of the objects and situation, and on the persons themselves.

Persons bring their relatively enduring characteristics and antecedent states to the environment. Together with the objects and the situation these factors exert influence upon behavior. Persons are not necessarily the victims of situation. According to the interactionist approach, persons select, avoid, and create situations for themselves and for others (Bowers, 1973). The result of the feedback of behavior will affect both the person and his or her momentary state.

Belk's (1975) distinctions are useful for further defining the consumer retail environment by requiring a restriction of outlook to the physical, social, and temporal surroundings. The variables in these groups can be objective and subjective. The objective physical surroundings are as recorded by a camera, before being interpreted by the actors. The subjective surroundings are as perceived, defined, and interpreted by the actors. In general, subjective rather than the objective surroundings are expected to exert influence on consumer behavior. However, some environmental influences, such as subtle cueing effects (smell, temperature) may operate at an almost subliminal level.

## The Retail Environment

The importance of consumer behavior in the retail environment has long been recognized and, as a consequence, many texts have appeared on the subject. This recognition has often occurred with the expressed intention of attempting to manipulate consumer behavior in such a manner so as to increase the demand for the services or goods offered by an organization. We are not primarily interested in the physical retail environment as it may be manipulated to achieve organizational ends. Rather, we are concerned with the manner in which the consumer and retail environment interact.

Environmental psychologists have viewed many aspects of the retail environment including both human/social and physical features and their meaning for consumers. Under the heading of human/social features influential in retail situations, research has considered the effects of crowding on the consumer. Physical aspects internal to the retail outlet such as fixture and merchandise layout, display, intra-store wayfinding and external features such as store location and inter-store wayfinding have been considered in terms of their behavioral consequences. Retail environments, speaking the language of consumption, constitute meanings to consumers (Sack, 1988).

Each of these components will be considered hereunder. Wayfinding will receive special attention as, it will be argued, this forms a convenient conceptual link between the somewhat artificially dichotomous internal/personal and social/physical components of the retail structure and setting. Firstly however, physical and social features of the retail environment will be considered as they have been studied in terms of their effects on consumer behavior.

### *Retailing Structure*

At the most general level, retailing infrastructures differ between countries. This is obviously the case along the north-south dimension, comparing developed with developing countries. It is also true of the west-east dimension, comparing market economies with what were until recently centrally planned economies. These differences are based on the economic development and system and cultural environments of abundance versus scarcity.

However, even between western countries retailing structures may differ. Douglas (1976) investigated, in a comparative study of France and the U.S.A., the grocery and clothing shopping behavior of working and non-working housewives. The behavioral differences between the two countries proved to be more significant than the differences in employment. The between-country differences were largely due to differences in retail environments.

In comparison with French housewives, their American counterparts were found to have a tendency to more frequently do their shopping in large supermarkets and less often in neighborhood and corner stores. This finding reflects the fact that shopping malls are common in the U.S.A., whereas small traditional stores are more commonly found in France. Similar patterns emerged in relation to women's clothing purchases. American housewives tended to shop more frequently in department and discount stores as opposed to the boutiques typically frequented by French housewives.

Differences in shopping behavior were thus found to predominantly reflect the retailing structure of the two countries. The high proportion of small independent grocery retailers in France perpetuated the pattern of fragmented purchasing. However, it is also possible to argue in the converse that the differences in retail environments reflected underlying differences in consumer attitudes and preferences present in the two countries. The built environment may thus be seen as both instigating adaptive behaviors and reflecting social, cultural, and societal preferences. Douglas (1976) suggested that the role of retail-environment factors should be viewed to understand consumer response patterns, rather than underlying attitudes and preferences. Focusing on apparent differences in attitudes and behaviors may be misleading, especially when this leads to negative conclusions regarding the feasibility of influencing behavior patterns.

The retailing structure is not only a product of cultural factors, but also of historical development. The department store and the shopping mall originated in the U.S.A. and later came to Europe. These retailing structures both possess their own life cycles. The classical department store is now more than one hundred years old and seems to be in the last stage of its life cycle, showing signs of decline. New retailing forms have come into existence, such as the discount department store (since 1955), the fast-food restaurant (since 1960), and the textile supermarket (since 1975) (Van Raaij & Floor, 1983).

Shopping-center and shopping-mall perceptions and preferences are a well researched topic. Van Raaij (1983) investigated six shopping areas within the city of Rotterdam, The Netherlands. As may be expected, customers were found to prefer roofed-over, pedestrian shopping areas compared to open-air high-street shopping areas with their incumbent car and truck traffic. Cleanliness, safety, friendly personnel, variety and quality of stores, atmosphere, and good connections with public transportation, along with arrangement of stores in the shopping center were found to be the most important attributes. Shopping centers are often designed with popular stores at both ends attracting many customers. This increases the flow of people passing the stores in between.

Van Raaij (1983) also performed principal components analysis of shopping-center variables. He obtained five components, namely: (1) General evaluation, including quality, variety and arrangement of shops, friendly personnel and safety; (2) physical environment, including traffic noise, other customers, shelter, and cleanliness; (3) efficiency, including distances between shops, distances from home, and crowding; (4) accessibility, including parking and ease of access to public transit; (5) and social environment, including atmosphere and friendly personnel. It should be noted that retail structure-variables are inherent in four of the five factors (the exception being the social factor). The general evaluation factor consists largely of the arrangement and evaluation of the stores: it embodies the content of the shopping area. The environment factor relates to customer well-being and the attractiveness of the area: the form of the shopping area. The third and fourth factors are efficiency factors, related to efficiency of accessing and using the shopping area.

The above results provide an empirical structure for consumer evaluations of the retail environment. They also indicate that social factors and in-store atmosphere individually play both an important role in, and separately identifiable component of, experience within retail environments. Models of spatial shopping behavior may be found in Timmermans (Chapter 14, this book).

Atmospherics is a concept conceived of in studies of environmental factors which may be designed, or manipulated in retail space to produce certain effects on consumer behavior. It was first commented on by Kotler (1973) in his seminal article. It is made up of in-store physical attributes and subjective perceptions which together comprise the locations' atmosphere. However, Donovan and Rossiter (1982) have noted that these components are (1) antecedents (rather than components) of store atmosphere, and (2) that the usual univariate conceptualization of store atmosphere is inappropriate with such an obviously multidimensional concept. Notwithstanding these caveats, atmospherics are intuitively (and empirically, see Van Raaij, 1983) an important aspect of shopping center and store design and experience.

## *Physical features of the retail setting*

Physical features of the retail location have received attention. Essentially they have been considered in the role of "behavior-triggering devices." Buttle (1984) provided a thorough consideration of this area. Of those features he lists the most common are, store fronts, display units, name signs, display cards, dump bins, window stickers, open/shut signs, door stickers, leaflets, price tickets, store layout, shelf positioning, music, demonstrations, shelf space allocation and lighting.

From this list it can be seen that a common aim is to increase visibility and appeal. These objectives rest on the assumptions that the more visible an item is the more likely it is to be seen and consequently purchased, and the more appealing a manufacturer or retailer is able to make an item appear, again, the greater the likelihood of purchase. These features are made all the more important by the fact that goods for purchase are seldom displayed in isolation. Consequently, manufacturers are faced with attracting attention to their products from among competing brands. Moreover, once having attracted the uncommitted customer, the brand must be appealing in order to become the target of purchase.

The store environment may induce consumers to impulse buying. There are degrees of impulse buying. After entering a retail location, some customers will buy from a purchase category they had no á priori intention of purchasing. Other consumers will have preformed intent upon entry to buy from a specific product category but have not yet chosen the brand. Other customers will have decided on the brand prior to store entry but will subsequently change to a competitive brand or a different product category. Due to these forms of uncertainty present in the potential purchaser, various aspects of the physical retail environment may have a lesser or greater effect upon consumer purchase choice. Some of the important physical features will now be reviewed.

Merchandising is one activity through which those who manage retail outlets may manipulate features of the retail environment to help facilitate organizational goals. Merchandising has been called the "silent salesperson" and has been identified as the much neglected cousin of advertising (Buttle, 1984). Buttle likens the roles of advertising and merchandising in claiming that they have great power and are both cost-effective means of ensuring a vital pre-purchase exposure of customers (or potential customers) to persuasive and/or informative material.

Buttle (1984) allocated merchandising techniques to one of five categories, traffic flow, shelf positioning (location of product categories and brands), allocation of limited shelf space between competing claims, use of point-of-sale material, and the mounting of special displays. He considered how each of these techniques could be profitably used by retailers and manufacturers. Much of this material will be included in our review. However, as we are less interested in these as profitable techniques and more as psychological processes, a different emphasis will be present. At this stage, it is worth noting the important role merchandising techniques play in helping to define the retail environment, and also to note the important effect factors which are often considered to be somewhat peripheral to the selling process may have on the consumer.

***Display.*** The manner in which goods/items are displayed within a store has been found to influence consumer behavior. Displays are non-personal forms of selling and represent one of the most important forms of communication devices available to retail management. Through the use of displays, in the form of window displays, signs and fixtures, attention may be attracted, and interest created to prompt the shopper to enquire about, and hopefully purchase, the products on display. As was noted by Cohen (1981) the display of items within a store may affect the purchase.

Displays may be of two broad types, window displays and interior displays. The importance of both of these forms of marketing tools has been acknowledged. Much has been written in the merchandising literature concerned with the various types of display stands, their relative and specific usefulness, their inter-store positioning, seasonal use, and their overall effectiveness. Floor displays have been found to significantly increase the number of units of the displayed product sold (Gagnon & Osterhaus, 1985). Merchandising displays of promotional goods placed at the ends of aisles may increase the purchasing of these goods. However, the same goods are then not browsed for in the store and this may negatively affect the sales of other items. It has also been found that the placing of goods at eye level increases sales of that item, and essential or regularly purchased goods which are placed at the rear of the store attract customers to them (Leed & German, 1973). Furthermore, stores which are perceived by users to be clean are more attractive to customers (Patricious, 1979).

The retail environment may thus have an effect on customer information processing. This is clearly so for signs and here-you-are maps in shopping malls, hospitals, airports, and office buildings. It is also true for the way the merchandise has been placed on the shelves. The store interior and the presentation of the assortment may affect consumers' momentary states, such as moods, desires, and orientations. In department stores, these moods may vary for the different departments and assortments. In the do-it-yourself department, a customer may get into a practical, problem-solving orientation, and judge products through this frame. In the cosmetics department, the same customer may think about personal care, luxury, self-esteem, and social acceptance. The type of orientation may affect decisions, especially in the case of "unplanned" purchases.

***Store layout.*** The layout of retail locations is another component of the store which has been studied by consumer and environmental psychologists. The way in which a store is laid-out has been found to determine the perceptions of stores' "personalness." In turn, these perceptions have been found to be an important component of customers' experience of retail settings (Gifford, 1987). The size of a store has not been found to have a similar effect on all shoppers. Simply increasing the size of a retail outlet does not produce a unified, negative or positive effect. For instance, larger stores offer better brand and goods choice (a positive feature) but are less personal (a negative feature) (Gifford, 1987).

R. Sommer, Herrick, & T. Sommer (1981) considered the properties of store layout in their research. They noted that several aspects of the layout of a supermarket (e.g., aisle orientation, linearity of check-out arrangements) were key factors in improving store traffic efficiency. However, this improvement produced reductions in perceptions of store friendliness. Other research has taken the layout of store fixtures and fittings as its subject matter. For instance, in his research, May (1969) discovered that aisle length to be an important behavioral determinant. He found that if aisles were short in length, shoppers tended to simply look down the aisle in attempting to locate their desired goods. As a consequence, customers within short-aisled areas were not attracted to impulse purchases.

Van der Ster and Van Wissen (1983) summarize studies on consumer traffic patterns in stores. Customers spending more time in the self-service store, pass and see more products, and have thus a higher probability of purchasing these products, either by impulse or by remembering the need for the product at that moment. Managers use the store layout and background music to keep customers longer in the store, hopefully without irritating them. Other studies have considered the role of background music in stores and restaurants (Milliman, 1982).

***Location and wayfinding***. It has often been claimed that location is the most important determinant of the success of a retail outlet. Perhaps as a consequence of this perceived importance, location is also a widely researched variable. When a potential shopper is choosing where to go shopping, if all other influential factors are equal (e.g., cost, availability of goods) then purchases will be made at the nearest shop which stocks the desired product. If a choice of such local shops is available, then the largest near shop will be selected (Hawkins, Best, & Coney, 1983). However, the two variables of nearness and store size have a lesser effect on the choice of purchase location as the desired target product becomes more attractive, and, as a consequence, the cost of the desired product rises. Williams (1981) for instance discovered that as the target of purchase increases in cost so did the willingness to travel to make the purchase.

A variable which is closely linked to location is wayfinding. Wayfinding and consumers' ability to locate retail facilities and thus enable purchasing, is a neglected variable associated with buying. An example of this is that features of the cognitive mapping process have received little consideration. For instance, it has been found that providing paths (channels along which a person moves or may potentially move), edges (linear elements not used or considered for use as paths), districts (sections of a region which have a two-dimensional extent and into which a person considers they can enter), nodes (strategic spots in a region such as path junctures), landmarks (other focal points which are not entered into but which are observed), and other features such as locational legibility (the degree of ease with which a location's parts may be recognized and can be organized into a coherent pattern or map) are all important for the development and subsequent use of cognitive maps (Golledge, 1987; Lynch, 1960). Little research has, however, been conducted in order to reveal the manner in which these features may affect consumer behavior in retail settings.

A number of studies have been conducted viewing consumer cognitive maps of retail locations (MacKay & Olshavsky, 1975; Olshavsky, MacKay, & Sentell, 1975). A cognitive map is an internal representation of an external geographical reality. The cognitive map or spatial image is an essential of the discipline of environmental cognition (Golledge, 1987). MacKay and Olshavsky (1975) found that cognitive maps generated by multidimensional scaling are better related to shopping preferences and frequencies than actual maps. We should, however, not conclude that consumers store cognitive maps in their heads. From wayfinding research it may be concluded that people use paths, edges, nodes, and landmarks to find their way in shopping environments. Foxall and Hackett (1992) investigated the types of stores and features of the retail location which were remembered. They found that stores which were located at nodal positions (at path junctions) were better remembered. Those retail units which formed landmarks, were used as reference points in shoppers' cognitive maps of shopping centers, and were also better remembered than units which were placed in other positions. It is of interest to note that this relationship was found in both traditional high-street and modern shopping mall locations. Furthermore, the authors discovered that large supermarkets were used as landmarks, while stores placed at the intersections of pathways and roads were used as nodal reference points. These two features were both used by shoppers as reference points in their understanding of the spatial structure of the retail environment.

The complexity of retail locations has been noted to have an effect on the development of cognitive maps (Moeser, 1988). Foxall and Hackett, (1992) reported a similar finding in a shopping mall. In their study, they compared performance of cognitive mapping and wayfinding abilities in two retail settings of differing degrees of physical complexity: The first of these being a traditional high street which is spatially arranged along two dimensions, the other a shopping mall which possessed the same two dimensions and in addition had a third, vertical, dimension in its configuration of stores. They discovered that the location of store units within the complex retail mall was less accurately and less completely remembered than the location of stores within the relatively simple high street. However, wayfinding ability (as measured by requiring respondents to either walk to, or to verbally report an imagined walk, to specified stores) was found to be a task which could be performed with much greater success in both locations than the abstract cognitive mapping exercise. Performance on the wayfinding tasks was also discovered to be more accurate in the mall than in the high street.

These findings suggest that for customers in retail environments, the ability to find their way and to find stores employs different processes than the skill to form a cognitive map. Furthermore, due to mapping being better performed in high streets and wayfinding being better performed in shopping malls, it would appear that the format and usage of cognitive maps and the experience of retail locations in these two settings constituted different psychological processes.

It has already been noted that research has found the location of stores to be of great importance in determining the success of a retail enterprise. Positioning of stores has also been cited as being influential in its effect upon recall and wayfinding abilities in retail locations. However, the subject area of cognitive mapping processes as they relate to actual consumer behavior is under-researched. Future investigations should more fully consider the effects of store position on consumer behavior.

### *Social Factors: Crowding*

Crowding, due to the physical density of shoppers within a retail location, is a component of the social setting which has been found to affect consumer behavior (Harrell, Hutt, & Anderson, 1980). In crowded stores, it has been discovered that shoppers often leave earlier than they had originally planned and that they often develop negative attitudes toward the store. For instance, Saegert (1973) found that shoppers in a crowded shoe department, located in a department store, remembered less detail about either the departments merchandise or layout than did incumbents in similar but less crowded settings. They concluded that high levels of crowdedness were able to negatively affect both consumers' satisfaction and the resulting image that they acquired of the crowded store.

Harrell et al. (1980) claimed that crowding may have negative effects on behavior as also found by Saegert (1973). However, they too found that the effects were mediated by the adaptation strategies employed by the individual (e.g., how the individual learned to cope with being in crowded situations). As a consequence, both store satisfaction and store image may be improved by either reducing crowding or by store management and design which aids the consumer in adapting to crowded conditions. An alternate interpretation was that managers could learn to anticipate changes in consumer shopping patterns and processes under varying levels of crowding and to adjust promotion and merchandising policy accordingly.

Crowding is a function of the density of the population in a particular retail setting. Crowding may impede the individual's goal-directed striving. It may interfere with his or her perceived capacity to control interpersonal relationships. Finally, it may affect individual state variables such as susceptibility to anxiety and aggressiveness. The perception of crowding may be influenced by prior experience of crowding and its effects (Harrell & Hutt, 1976). Consumers may adapt to or cope with a crowded environment by allocating less time to each environmental stimulus that reaches their senses, for instance, by visiting fewer stores before making a purchase decision. They may also postpone or cancel the purchase of low-priority products and services, delegate shopping to others, avoid crowded shopping malls, and limit social interaction with acquaintances and strangers in the purchase situation (Harrell & Hutt, 1976; Milgram, 1970). Harrell and Hutt (1976) present a model of consumer behavior under conditions of crowding which details the kinds of adaptive behavior consumers are likely to engage in: restriction of shopping time, conversation, delaying of some purchases, reducing information processing, and increasing store and brand loyalty.

Crowding may cause distraction and time pressure. With regard to information processing, Wright (1974) finds that under conditions of distraction or time pressure consumers simplify information processing and rely more on direct evidence and elimination rules than otherwise.

However, while crowding has some deleterious consequences for consumers, such as being jostled and having to put up with noise and movement over which they have no control, there are retail situations in which the presence of some or many others is a positive stimulus. A restaurant which is empty except for oneself or one's party offers little reassurance that the food and service are of high quality. A football match lacks atmosphere if only a few hundred supporters turn up. Moreover, the subjective experience of crowding may vary according to the efficiency and effectiveness of the retail operation. In other words, the customers' satisfaction with a crowded retail setting depends on the level of service provided by the staff which in turn is a function of staffing level. Ecological psychologists studied over- and undermanning in a variety of retail environments including stores, restaurants, and natural parks. Both staff and customers may experience stress as a result of under- and overstaffing in a retail setting and reduce this by altering the throughput of people in the environment, the capacity of the setting to accommodate and serve them, or the operational efficiency of the organization (Wicker & Kirmeyer, 1977).

## Consumer Satisfaction

Kakkar and Lutz (1975), in their investigation of the effects of behavioral measures in relationship to situational effects, were able to provide some information regarding environment-behavior relationships. However, they suggested that "... indices of cognitive processes and the like may be more appropriate than the specific behavioral intention statements .... [and that by] .... focusing on processes rather than outcome further insights into the nature of situational influence may be forthcoming" (p. 209). Expressions of satisfaction within consumer environments are specific cognitive processes in the retail setting. As such, these have started to receive attention.

Research which has been concerned with consumer satisfaction with service and sales environments has most recently been conducted within a framework which has attempted to both depict and to understand the multiplicity of dimensions of user experience. The approach employed has been that of facet theory (Borg, 1981; Canter, 1985; Shye, 1978). This orientation to social research uses multiple-component design and analyses in an attempt to capture all specified relevant variables within a complex social situation within a research design (Canter, 1982, 1983a).

In a review, Donald (1985) reported a common three-dimensional model of evaluation which has been developed. Hackett (1985) and Hackett and Foxall (1992) conducted a study using this approach to investigate customer satisfaction with flight, catering, and retail services at a recently opened international airport. Three dimensions were discovered, similar to those previously reported, to account for differences in reported satisfaction levels within this consumer setting.

The three dimensions differentiated the setting in terms of the social, spatial, service, or aesthetic qualities, and in terms of the centrality of importance each of these qualities had in facilitating the effective achievement of consumer purpose within the location. A third dimension was also present in satisfaction judgments. This was a dimension that differentiated the physical scales present in the airport (e.g., the air terminal, the airport, airport access services). It has been found that when place users have clearly specified goals, the scale dimension becomes a level dimension which reflects the degree or level of interaction with various aspects of the location needed to achieve objectives in the setting (Canter, 1983b).

These findings illustrate that users of consumer environments experience these environments not as a unity but rather as a divisible entity. Understanding of consumer satisfaction must consequently be gauged within this framework. Environments are furthermore experienced in terms of consumer purpose. This purpose may be of greater or lesser centrality to the experience and judgments of satisfaction. Purposiveness also implies that the physical scale of, or the level of contact with, a setting will also be subdivided. The implication is that research on consumer satisfaction with retail environments must employ these experiential dimensions in the design and interpretation of their enquiries in order to represent the consumer in their behavioral location in a way which is meaningful and which may provide comparable and cumulative results.

The findings of the above research suggest that alterations to the retail environment may affect satisfaction along one or more, but not necessarily all, dimensions. Consequently, such alterations may not improve overall levels of satisfaction associated with consumer experience within retail settings. For instance, improvements in the aesthetic qualities of a building may improve satisfaction with this aspect of the setting but may not alter overall satisfaction with the setting or with the service facilities (Hackett, 1985).

## Summary and Integration

Foxall (1983, 1990, 1992), and Fennell (1980) have presented integrative models of the situational context of consumer behavior based upon the view that the individual and his or her current setting define the situation which, in turn, accounts for behavior.

To simply identify the retail environment as possessing physical and psychological attributes is insufficient, when attempts are being made to understand the consumer within this environment. Kakkar and Lutz (1981) stated that research into the consumption location should address the conceptual boundaries of the location, and the dimensions of the situation such that a taxonomy may be built. The development of a taxonomy of the consumption situation is impelled by the desire to predict and to manipulate consumer behavior.

Any model or taxonomy of consumer behavior within the location of consumption behavior which attempts to understand this form of behavior or the effects of situation upon behavior must be psychological in nature.

It is not enough to include a psychological component in a model of consumption location. Dimensions of this model which person (consumer) - location (retail environment) relations may be understood.

Within the facet theory approach, a research content is addressed and an attempt is made to identify relevant variables. Having done this, the next step is the specification of these variables through a mapping sentence format which includes salient content variables along with connective phrases which may suggest inter-variable relationships (Levy, 1976). Defining a specific area for a research project thus allows close inspection of variable effect relationships. Defining a broad research domain in such a way enables this at a wider scale. It also permits (1) the understanding of specific sub-areas of content in relation to a content universe, (2) a theoretical structure to content, and (3) specification of relationships to be expected (Hackett, in press).

A mapping sentence format statement will be proposed for the understanding of the consumer in the retail environment. This mapping statement is given in Figure 15.2. The facets are the variable groupings which have been found to affect the understanding of situated consumer behavior. To design research which addresses the whole consumer location, each of these facets would have to be present. However, this would produce an extremely complex and impracticable design. Consequently, the mapping sentence represents the theoretical structure for enquiry. The structure of facets in the mapping sentence along with verbal connectives implies a coherence to the universe of situated consumer behaviors. Thus, a research design which incorporates individual or combinations of these facets may be understood as it may theoretically relate to the total content domain.

The mapping statement further illustrates the multifarious nature of the research area and the need to proceed with caution when attempting to generalize from more simple conceptualizations of the consumer in the retail environment. It is inappropriate to isolate variables within this context as determinants of behavior. Rather, the complexity of the content area must be kept in mind when forming conclusions.

During the course of this chapter we have seen how many features affect the consumer in the retail environment. These features include both those of the physical environment and those internal to consumers themselves. It should be clear by now that consumers and their environments are intimately linked and that this association is synergetic.

What we have attempted to make clear is that the factors which affect consumer behavior in the situation of its occurrence are clearly understandable, that their effects are starting to be understood, and that the investigation of these component parts is steadily increasing. However, it has also been the intention throughout that emphasis should be placed upon the need for the integration of these experimentally separable components. Such an amalgamation, it may be proposed, represents the manner in which social science research may in the future hope to more fully comprehend and to ultimately predict the behavior of the consumer in the retail environment.

Person X possessing a HIGH/LOW (*facet A*) specified personality trait, and a HIGH/LOW (*facet B*) specified attitude, and being a consumer within a WESTERN/EASTERN (*facet C*) culture, CONTROLLED/MARKET (*facet D*) economy, TRADITIONAL/MODERN (*facet E*) physical location type, with GOOD/POOR (*facet F*) access to the location, which comprises MERCHANDISING/DISPLAY (*facet G*) and HIGH/LOW (*facet H*) levels of crowding within an OPEN/CLOSED (*facet I*) setting, engages in consumer behavior which receives HIGH/LOW (*facet J*) emotional reward, HIGH/LOW (*facet K*) performance feedback, and is assessed in terms of the specified range of CONSUMER BEHAVIOR (*facet L*)

The facets are:
A: personality
B: attitude
C: culture
D: economy
E: physical type
F: location
G: physical environmental features
I: openness
J: hedonic reinforcement
K: informational reinforcement
L: consumer behavior range

FIGURE 15.2. General mapping statement for research into consumer behavior in retail environments.

## References

Baum, A., & Paulus, P. B. (1987). Crowding, In D. Stokols & I. Altman (Eds.), *Handbook of environmental psychology* (Vol. 1, pp. 533-570). New York: Wiley.

Belk, R. W. (1974). An exploratory assessment of situational effects in buyer behavior. *Journal of Marketing Research, 11*, 156-163.

Belk, R. W. (1975). Situation variables and consumer behavior. *Journal of Consumer Research, 2*, 157-164.

Borg, I. (1981). Some basic concepts of facet theory. In J. C. Lingoes, E. E. Roskam, & I. Borg (Eds.), *Geometric representations of relational data* (pp. 65-102). Ann Arbor, MI: Mathesis.

Borg, I., & Lingoes, J. C. (1987). *Multidimensional similarity structure analysis*. New York: Springer.

Bowers, D. S. (1973). Situationism in psychology: An analysis and a critique. *Psychological Review, 80*, 307-337.

Buttle, F. (1984). Merchandising. *European Journal of Marketing, 18*(5), 4-25.

Canter, D. (1977). *The psychology of place*. London: Architectural Press.

Canter, D. (1982). Facet approaches to applied social research. *Perceptual and Motor Skills, 55*, 143-154.

Canter, D. (1983a). The potential of facet theory for applied social psychology. *Quantity & Quality, 17*, 35-67.

Canter, D. (1983b). The purposive evaluation of place. A facet approach. *Environment and Behavior, 15*, 659-699.

Canter, D. (Ed.). (1985). *Facet theory: Approaches to social research.* New York: Springer.

Cohen, P. (1981) *Consumer behavior*. New York: Random House.

Donald, I. (1985). The cylindrex of place evaluation. In D. Canter (Ed.), *Facet Theory: Approaches to Social Research*. New York: Springer.

Donovan, R. J., & Rossiter, J. R. (1982). Store atmosphere: An environmental psychology approach. *Journal of Retailing, 58*, 34-57.

Douglas, S. (1976). Cross national comparisons and consumer stereotypes: A case study of working and non-working wives in the U.S. and France. *Journal of Consumer Research, 3*, 12-20.

Fennell, G. (1980). The situation. *Motivation and Emotion, 4*, 299-322.

Foxall, G. R. (1983). *Consumer choice*. London: Macmillan.

Foxall, G. R. (1990). *Consumer psychology in behavioral perspective.* London: Routledge.

Foxall, G. R. (1992). The situated consumer: A behavioral interpretation of purchase and consumption. In R. W. Belk (Ed.), *Research in consumer behavior* (Vol. 5). Greenwich, CT: JAI.

Foxall, G. R., & Hackett, P. M. W. (1992). Consumers' perceptions of micro-retail location: Wayfinding and cognitive mapping in planned and organic shopping environments. *International Review of Retail, Distribution and Consumer Research, 2*, 310-326.

Gagnon, J. P., & Osterhaus, J. T. (1985). Effectiveness of floor displays of retail products. *Journal of Retailing, 61*, 104-116.

Gifford, R. (1987). *Environmental psychology: Principles and practices.* Boston, MA: Allyn & Bacon.

Golledge, R. G. (1987). Environmental cognition. In D. Stokols & I. Altman (Eds.), *Handbook of environmental psychology* (Vol. 1, pp. 131-174). New York: Wiley.

Hackett, P. M. W. (1985). *Birmingham International Airport user evaluation study: A faceted appraisal.* Unpublished doctoral dissertation, University of Aston in Birmingham, U.K.

Hackett, P. M. W. (in press). *Conservation and the consumer: Understanding environmental concern.* London: Routledge.

Hackett, P. M. W., & Foxall, G. R. (1992). *How consumers structure evaluations of satisfaction within complex service and retail locations: A mapping sentence design study of a modern international airport development* (Working papers in consumer behaviour). CRU/92, University of Birmingham, U.K.

Harrell, G., & Hutt, M. (1970). Crowding in retail stores. *MSU Business Topics, 24* (winter).

Harrell, G., Hutt, M., & Anderson, J. (1980). Path analysis of buyer behavior under conditions of crowding. *Journal of Marketing Research, 17*, 45-51.

Hawkins, D. I., Best, R. J., & Coney, K. A. (1983). *Consumer behavior: Implications for marketing strategy.* Plano, TX: Business.

Kakkar, P., & Lutz, R. J. (1975). *Toward a taxonomy of consumption situations.* Combined Proceedings. American Marketing Association.

Kakkar, P., & Lutz, R. J (1981). Situational influence on consumer behavior: a review. In H. H. Kassarjian & T. S. Robertson (Eds.), *Perspectives in consumer behavior.* Glenview, IL: Scott, Foresman & Company.

Kotler, P. (1973). Atmospherics as a marketing tool. *Journal of Retailing, 49*, 48-64.

Leed, T. W., & German, G. A. (1973). *Food merchandising: Principles and practices.* New York: Chain Store Age Books.

Levy, S. (1976). Use of mapping sentences for coordinating theory and research: a cross cultural example. *Quantity and Quality, 10*, 117-125.

Lynch, K. (1960). *The image of the city.* Cambridge, MA: MIT Press.

MacKay, D. B., & Olshavsky, R. W. (1975). Cognitive maps of retail locations. An investigation of some basic issues. *Journal of Consumer Research, 2*, 197-205.

Marans, R. W., & Spreckelmeyer, K. F. (1982). Measuring overall architectural quality: A component of building evaluation. *Environment and Behavior, 14*, 652-670.

May, F. E. (1969). Buying behavior: Some research findings. In J. U. McNeal (Ed.), *Dimensions of Buying Behavior*. New York: Appleton-Century.

Mehrabian, A. (1972). *Nonverbal communication*. Chicago: Aldine-Atherton.

Mehrabian, A., & Russell, J. A. (1974). *An approach to environmental psychology*. Cambridge, MA: MIT Press.

Milgram, S. (1970). The experience of living in cities, *Science, 167*, 1461-1468.

Milliman, R. A. (1982). The effect of background music upon the shopping behavior of supermarket patrons. *Journal of Marketing, 16*, 111-123.

Moeser, S. D. (1988). Cognitive mapping in a complex building. *Environment and Behavior, 20*, 29-49.

Olshavsky, R. W., MacKay, D. B., & Sentell, G. (1975). Perceptual maps of retail locations. *Journal of Applied Psychology, 60*, 80-86.

Patricios, N. N. (1979). Human aspects of planning shopping centers. *Environment and Behavior, 11*, 511-538.

Peled, A. (1974). *A theory of spatiality of situations empirically tested in the experience of passengers in air terminals*. Unpublished doctoral dissertation, University of Strathclyde, U.K.

Russell, J. A., & Mehrabian, A. (1975). Task, setting and personality variables affecting the desire to work. *Journal of Applied Psychology, 60*, 518-520.

Russell, J. A., & Mehrabian, A. (1976). Some behavioral effects of the physical environment. In S. Wapner, S. Cohen, & B. Kaplan (Eds.), *Experiencing the environment* (pp 138-154). New York: Plenum.

Russell, J. A., & Mehrabian, A. (1978). Approach-avoidance and affiliation as functions of the emotion eliciting quality of an environment. *Environment and Behavior, 10*, 355-387.

Sack, R. D., (1988). The consumer's world: Place as context. *Annals of the Association of American Geographers, 78*, 642-664.

Saegert, S. (1973). Crowding: Cognitive overload and behavioral constraint. In W. Preiser (Ed.), *Environmental design research* (Vol 2, pp. 254-261). Stroudsburg, PA: Dowden, Hutchinson & Ross.

Shye, S. (1978). *Theory construction and data analysis in the behavioral sciences.* New York: Jossey Bass.
Soleri, P. (1969). *Arcology: The city in the image of men.* Cambridge, MA: MIT Press.
Sommer, R., Herrick, J., & Sommer, T. R. (1981). The behavioral ecology of supermarkets and farmers' markets. *Journal of Environmental Psychology*, 1, 13-19.
Troye, S. V. (1985). Situationist theory and consumer behavior. In J. N. Sheth (Ed.), *Research in consumer behavior* (Vol. 1, pp. 285-321). Greenwich, CT: JAI.
Van der Ster, W., & Van Wissen, P. (1983). *Marketing & detailhandel.* [Marketing & Retail Trade]. Groningen, The Netherlands: Wolters-Noordhoff.
Van Raaij, W. F. (1983). *Shopping centre evaluation and patronage in the city of Rotterdam.* (Papers on Economic Psychology, No. 27). Rotterdam, The Netherlands: Erasmus University.
Van Raaij, W. F., & Floor, J. M. G. (1983). Retailing developments in the Netherlands. *International Journal of Physical Distribution and Materials Management, 13*(5-6), 128-137.
Verhallen, T. M. M., & Pieters, R. G. M. (1984). Attitude theory and behavioral costs. *Journal of Economic Psychology, 5*, 223-249.
Wicker, A. W., & Kirmeyer, S. (1977). From church to laboratory to national park: A program of research on access and insufficient populations in behavior settings. In D. Stokols (Ed.), *Perspectives on environment and behavior: Theory, research and application* (pp. 69-96). New York: Plenum .
Williams, R. (1981). Outshopping: Problems or opportunity? *Arizona Business, 27*, 9.
Wright, P. L. (1974). The harassed decision maker: Time pressure, distraction and the use of evidence. *Journal of Applied Psychology, 59*, 555-561.

*Behavior and Environment: Psychological and Geographical Approaches*
*T. Gärling and R.G. Golledge (Editors)*



# CHAPTER 16

# Human-Nature Relationships: Leisure Environments and Natural Settings

**John J. Pigram**

The concepts of leisure and recreation defy precise definition. However, an underlying dimension common to many analyses of the terms is the perceived freedom to choose. This discretionary element helps to explain both the growing interest in learning more of why people choose particular settings for their leisure, and the difficulty researchers find in accounting for recreation choice behavior. It might be argued that the choice process for leisure activities is no more complex than that, say, for the selection of a new residence or a shopping trip. Yet, the unbounded nature of leisure, and the subjective, even capricious, characteristics of recreation decision making, make generalization more difficult.

One reaction to this pervasive uncertainty might be to discard attempts at prediction and understanding of recreation behavior, and proceed to provide for leisure pursuits on an ad hoc basis from a management-oriented top-down perspective. Such an approach fails to appreciate the value of gaining insight into the what, the why, and the how of recreation choice behavior. If the essence of leisure is freedom, responses to these questions should contribute to the expansion of choice through the provision of a diverse leisure environment to meet a multiplicity of individual and societal goals.

As with other aspects of human behavior, the recreation choice process is a reflection of how people perceive opportunities, interpret information, and establish preferences for environmental interaction. The meshing of perceptual and behavioral geography as a distinct area of applied research has contributed to a greater understanding of the dynamics of person-environment relationships (Aitken, 1991). A comprehensive review by Timmermans and Golledge (1990) of behavioral research into spatial problems represents further evidence of the insights which behavioral geographers have developed into spatial interaction and spatial relations. At the same time, the review notes the cross-disciplinary emphasis inherent in much behavioral research and the close links which have emerged with behavioral disciplines, in particular environmental psychology.

The study of recreation behavior provides an opportunity to demonstrate the complementarity of research in geography and psychology, and the value of a behavioral approach to the resolution of real-world environmental issues. Understanding of the process of making recreation choices is also important in determining how management can best provide for desired leisure experiences within prevailing economic and resource constraints.

The policy implications of learning more of recreation choice behavior are discussed subsequently in this chapter. Initial discussion is concerned with the human-nature relationship and the reasons why many leisure pursuits appear to reflect a preference for environments of nature.

## Human-Nature Relationships

A perceived preference for the natural world is a basic theme of a recent book by Rachel and Stephen Kaplan (1989). In the book, nature is taken to include wild and pristine places as well as meadows, parks, streetscapes, and backyard gardens. The emphasis is heavily on vegetated landscapes in either a rural or urban context. The Kaplans present convincing empirical evidence that people express a higher preference for environments that reflect natural rather than more human-influenced elements. Preference appears to be related to what the authors call effective functioning: "In an environment that fosters effective functioning, one might expect the individual to experience a sense of both safety and competence ... to feel reasonably comfortable about the situation" (R. Kaplan & S. Kaplan, 1989, p. 68).

In this sense, settings are assessed in terms of their compatibility with human needs and purposes Apparently the immediate reaction of individuals to an environment is to imagine themselves in the setting; the aesthetic response is then influenced by the perceived degree to which "effective functioning" is likely to occur. Yet the process does reflect some common elements which offer enhanced insight into human behavior with nature.

The preference postulated for natural settings suggests there is something inherently attractive in nature which evokes a positive response in humans. The explanation for this attraction, it seems, rests in part with life style changes which have accompanied the emergence of an urbanized, industrialized society (Wearing, 1986). In the pre-industrial era, contact with nature was intimate and inevitable. The farm and the countryside were part of everyday life. One of the consequences of the industrial revolution and attendant social changes is an estrangement between people and nature.

Katz and Kirby (1991, p. 261) deplore "... the way in which the lines between nature and everyday life have been battered by modernity." The result is that nature and society are now separate and even counterpoised. Nature is seen as external to everyday life, something apart and "other." Even, urban parks are seen as a form of internalized "other" imposed on the city; islands of nature inserted into the urban landscape. Katz and Kirby argue for a reconstitution of nature and society so that human social practices are at one with nature. Until this idyllic metamorphosis is achieved, however, it seems that human beings will continue to compensate for the deprivation accompanying a consumer-oriented society by seeking closer affiliation with the natural world.

The tendency for people to seek natural settings to offset the pressures of an urban-industrial existence is well documented and is prompted, in part, by the urbanization process itself. Janiskee (1976) explained the appeal of extra-urban environments in the context of a push-pull model of motivation. Periodically, environmentally undernourished urbanites are pushed from the city because of stresses imposed by their life styles. At the same time, they are pulled into the more natural hinterlands by the opportunity to experience compensatory alternative surroundings. It seems that urban dwellers have a physical and social need to seek novel, irregular, and opposite situations. Natural settings offer the capacity for self-renewal, to exchange routine and escape the boredom and the familiar. Even knowledge that such opportunities exist is considered to act as a psychological safety valve in coping with environmentally induced stress (Iso-Ahola, 1980).

It has been suggested that because human brain and sensory systems evolved over a long period in natural environments, human beings are physiologically and perhaps psychologically better adapted to natural settings (Ulrich et al., 1991). In this sense, humans have an unlearned, genetically coded predisposition to respond positively to natural-environmental content such as vegetation and water (Ulrich, 1983). By contrast, the lack of this evolutionary tuning with respect to urban and built environments makes such settings more stressful and hinders recovery from stress. The implication is that everyday, unthreatening natural environments tend to promote faster more complete recuperation from stress than do urban settings.

The notion of the restorative power of contact with nature is widely acknowledged. R. Kaplan and S. Kaplan (1989) identify four central aspects of restorative settings - being away, extent, fascination, and compatibility. The degree to which these four factors are present is central to "... the importance of the surrounding environment in contributing to the restorative process" (p. 187).

The authors argue that these properties are more likely to occur within the context of nature. The sense of being away, feeling removed from the everyday experience, is readily associated with natural environments; as is the feeling of extent, of being in a larger context and part of another world. Likewise, the content and processes of nature are seen as a rich source of fascination, an important element in the restorative experience. Finally, the feeling of compatibility, of being in harmony with a supportive environment, is more easily achieved in a natural setting:

> It is as if there is a special resonance between the natural environment and human inclinations. Functioning in a natural setting seems for many people to be less effortful than functioning in more civilized settings...(Kaplan & Kaplan, 1989, p. 193)

When these restorative forces are linked to the aesthetic preference, noted earlier, for natural environments, the perceived qualities which people attribute to a natural setting (or perhaps even to a nearby-nature experience in the backyard garden) are more readily explained.

## Leisure and the Natural Environment

Given the widespread appeal which nature apparently holds for people, its importance in the experience of leisure should come as no surprise. Many of the benefits associated with natural settings, generally, are fundamental to the realization of leisure. The opportunity for self-expression and subjective freedom of choice, accepted by many observers as characteristic of leisure, appears to be sought more often in natural, than in created human-dominant landscapes. The intrinsic values derived from experiencing leisure are perceived as being more in keeping with the natural scene and with a minimum of social manipulation. In terms of effective functioning (R. Kaplan & S. Kaplan, 1989), the natural environment would seem to offer greater scope for personal satisfaction through integration of mind and body in the leisure activity itself.

Research carried out on the motivation for participation in outdoor recreation reinforces this view. Several studies reported at a symposium on recreation choice behavior in the U.S.A. highlight the importance of wild settings as the focus for recreation (Stankey & McCool, 1985). Even a study of big game hunting in Montana revealed a similar preoccupation with nature. Two-thirds of the hunters interviewed stated that enjoying nature was an extremely or very important reason for choosing that specific area (Allen, 1985). The centrality of concern for experiencing nature in the context of outdoor recreation is also reported by R. Kaplan and S. Kaplan (1989). In reviewing studies of recreation motivation by Shafer and Mietz (1969), Rossman and Ulehla (1977), and Fly (1986), they note that enjoying the natural surroundings and experiencing nature received the strongest endorsement.

Research by Driver, Brown, Stankey, & Gregoire (1987) further attests to the importance of the natural setting in achieving the desired outcomes from leisure pursuits. In a wide-ranging study of wilderness users in Colorado, the most important experience preference domains were linked to enjoyment of nature. Clearly, the natural environment plays a fundamental part in attaining the outcomes and satisfactions sought from participation in certain forms of recreation.

Whereas the setting remains a major component in the recreation experience, the way people appraise and cognitively organize information about environments is also important (Beaulieu & Schreyer, 1985). Both biophysical and social factors play a role in facilitating or hindering satisfying outcomes from recreation participation. The relative importance of each category will vary depending upon the activity and the expectations of the participants (McCool, Stankey, & Clark, 1985).

Obviously, in particular types of recreation, biophysical components of the environment are basic; water, for instance, is needed for water-based activities such as swimming and boating. Again, in certain circumstances environmental conditions must necessarily be more stringent and closely defined. However, to some observers, the physical setting is merely an external backdrop and it is the *social* milieu in which the recreation activity takes place which is critical (Schreyer, Knopf, & Williams, 1985). This view is supported by Heywood (1989) who believes that social groups play a critical role in defining the appropriateness of recreation activities and experiences within a specific opportunity setting. Recreation meetings need to be defined "... in terms of appropriate modes of behavior and social settings rather than in terms of physical features (Schreyer et al., 1985, p. 17).

If this is so, it suggests that for some forms of recreation, substitution of physical attributes of the setting might be possible without impairing satisfaction, so long as functional similarity is present (Peterson, Stynes, Rosenthal, & Dwyer, 1985; Phillips, 1977). The possibility of substitute settings could be important in the context of people's preference for natural environments. Given that not all environmental attributes are central to the choice process, and the desired attributes of nature can be identified and replicated or simulated in a less pristine setting, pressure on authentic nature-oriented environments may be relieved (Stankey, 1977). Moreover, less demanding types of recreation might well make do with more tenuous links with nature.

The potential for substitution need not be confined to the settings in which recreation takes place. It may arise with different elements in the recreation choice process. Recreation choice may be differentiated by activity categories, by setting categories, or by categories of social organization or interaction (Williams, 1985). Building on Bryan's (1977) concept of specialization, Williams argues that substitution can be appropriate with activities *or* companions *or* settings. The potential for substitution depends upon the content domain to which specialization is linked. Presumably, participants basing their preference for leisure environments on the naturalness of the surroundings would be setting specialists. For such people, the nature of the activity, or the social basis for participation, is subordinate to where recreation takes places. On the other hand, activity specialists may be less sensitive to the setting or the companion components of recreation choice, and be willing to substitute either to retain satisfaction in the activity sought.

Ditwiler (1979) takes the consideration of substitutability further by questioning whether particular resources or environments are necessarily a prerequisite for the leisure experience desired. He argues that the experiences people seek from a natural setting, for example, could well be obtained from an artificial environment designed to have those characteristics of the natural environment required for the purpose. He goes so far to suggest that, in some instances, managers force recreation activity into natural environments and create "...a spurious increase in demand for resource-based recreation sites" (Ditwiler, 1979, p. 440). Certainly, it has been demonstrated that for many visitors to parks and forests, picnicking is the main purpose of the visit and few stray far from access roads (Glytis, 1981). If many supposed wilderness recreationists are more interested in diversion, excitement, or challenge than in nature per se, it should be possible to substitute the utility offered from specifically nature-oriented settings by the creation of artificial environments. Examples of such substitutions are already numerous in theme parks and sporting arenas. Despite skepticism and perhaps resistance from purists, there could be a useful role for technological ingenuity in this way to help alleviate pressure on the natural resource base.

The assumption that recreation experiences are closely related to specific attributes of the recreation setting is central to the concept of the Recreation Opportunity Spectrum. Within this conceptual approach, a recreation opportunity is defined as an opportunity to participate in a preferred activity, in a preferred setting, to realize a desired experience (Driver & Brown, 1978). Environmental and situational attributes may be manipulated to produce different recreation opportunity settings (Clark & Stankey, 1979). The basic premise underlying the concept is that quality recreation experiences can best be assured by making available a diverse set of recreation opportunities open to individual choice. To achieve this, a range of settings or recreation environments is required to provide for the many tastes and preferences that motivate people to participate in outdoor recreation. In many ways the Recreation Opportunity Spectrum concept is an application of behavior setting analysis from environmental psychology (Barker, 1968; Ittelson, Franck, & O'Hanlon, 1976; Levy, 1979). This suggests that all human behavior should be interpreted with reference to the ecological environment or behavior setting in which it occurs. It is further suggested that, given a knowledge of the behavior setting for a specific experience, such as nature-oriented recreation, it should be possible to identify the human values and expectations associated with that experience. Examination of the human and non-human attributes of the behavior setting should then indicate those contributing to and detracting from satisfaction.

As with all human behavior, response to external stimuli is not always simple or direct. Environmental psychologists see people not as passive products of their environment, but as goal-directed individuals acting upon that environment and being influenced by it (Ittelson et al., 1976). All leisure environments affect recreation behavior in some way; it is the dynamic interaction between the environment and users which is crucial to the outcome. There appears to be substantial anecdotal and empirical evidence that natural environments provide opportunity settings conducive to the kind of satisfactions sought from many leisure pursuits.

## Recreation Choice Behavior

Predictions regarding recreation behavior would have greater validity if more was known about attitudes, motivations, and perceptions affecting recreation decision making. This would help explain why certain activities and sites are favoured and how and why alternative recreation opportunities are ranked. The recreation choice process is influenced by the perception of what opportunities are being perceived as being available. In every decision making situation individuals evaluate selected environmental attributes against some predetermined set of criteria to arrive at an overall utility or preference structure (Aitken, 1991). A predisposition for recreation is translated into actual participation through a choice mechanism heavily dependent upon perception of the recreation opportunity and experience on offer (Elson, 1973). Perceptions are mental constructs which are a function of the perceiver's past experiences, present values, motivation, and needs.

Perception operates over several dimensions and various scales in recreation decision making, and initial mental constructs may be confirmed or revised as a result of further spatial search and learning. Information levels, as well as the ability to use that information (including personality characteristics, aversion to risk, etc.) also help structure evaluative beliefs and mental images concerning the nature and quality of anticipated recreation experiences.

Information sources and the credibility of the information itself, are key issues in the choice of leisure settings. The validity of many spatial choice models has been questioned because of the assumption of perfect information and the assumed ability of consumers to evaluate completely all alternatives (Roehl, 1987). In reality, individuals typically consider only a subset of available alternatives. In any choice situation regarding use of natural environments for leisure pursuits, for example, the decision will be influenced by the individual's awareness set. Larger natural settings, with distinctive characteristics, are more likely to be known and considered by potential participants. In an urban context, Roehl demonstrates that smaller neighborhood parks, with fewer facilities, and designed to serve lower-order needs rather than at a community scale are less likely to be in a consumer's awareness set.

Desbarats (1983) notes how the supposedly objective spatial structure of opportunities is narrowed into an effective choice set comprising those (recreation) opportunities that are known to the individual and actively considered. Effective choice sets may represent only a small fraction of objective choice sets because of direct and indirect effects on behavior of constraints stemming from the sociophysical environment. In particular, contraction of the initial choice set may occur because of lack of information about existing options.

The role of information was canvassed in a broad-ranging seminar on recreation planning and management held in Australia recently (Killin, Paradice, & Engel, 1988). Both quality and timing of information were seen as important factors in recreation decision making. Inadequate information and misinformation were identified as constraints in the process of discriminating between alternatives (Krumpe, 1988). The implications for management and policy are obvious and are discussed further below.

Information also helps structure images of the environment to which recreationists respond. However, the cognitive processes involved in image formation are complex (Beaulieu & Schreyer, 1985). The (objective) information flowing from an environment is filtered through the perceiver's set of preferences and values, and cultural interpretations of place meaning. The process is complicated by the personal nature of reactions to external stimuli and by the multifaceted characteristics of the environments being experienced.

Dissection is risky and with nature-oriented environments, it is difficult to reach consensus on what components - landform, water, vegetation, etc. - contribute most to the appeal of the landscape. In any case, these attributes must be mentally fused to complete the totality of the image. Kaplan and Kaplan (1989) note that

> A landscape is more than the enumeration of the things in the scene. A landscape also entails an organization of these components. Both the contents and the organizational patterns play an important role in people's preferences for natural settings (p. 10).

Applying this reasoning to human preference for natural environments, it seems that it is not only the dominance of nature in the scene which is appealing. It is also the spatial configuration of landscape elements which is important to people's reactions. Certain natural settings are favoured because of their openness, their very lack of structure and precise definition, their transparency and the perceived opportunities to enter and move around. Wild environments and impenetrable forests, on the other hand, may evoke less positive responses and feelings of insecurity.

This brief review reveals some of the complexities of the choice process in leisure behavior. As stated at the outset, it is the unbounded subjective nature of leisure and its expression in recreation activity which make explanation so difficult. By definition, recreation is discretionary and any hint of obligation or compulsion must compromise the experience. Moreover, participants in recreation can exercise more control over decisions regarding what, where, and with whom, "... in the design of their desired products and thus the experiences they derive from participation" (Williams, 1985, p. 32).

The types of decisions involved in the recreation choice process are summarized in Table 16.1. Insight into some of the factors underlying these decisions may be gained from a review of empirical studies of targeted groups of recreationists in specific nature-oriented settings.

### *4-Wheel Drive Vehicle Campers*

In a major study on the east coast of Queensland, Australia, 682 4-Wheel Drive (4WD) vehicle campers were interviewed on Fraser Island and in Cooloola National Park (McIntyre, 1990). Both study areas are popular recreation venues because of their relatively undeveloped nature and proximity to the state capital, Brisbane. Camping is possible either on or within a short distance of a long oceanfront beach with firm sand accessible to 4WD vehicles.

TABLE 16.1

*Types of decisions to be made and factors that often weigh in recreation choices*

| Decisions | Factors |
|---|---|
| Go versus do not go | Information and knowledge |
| With whom: | Individual considerations: |
| Primary group | Time/money available |
| Alone | Desire for change |
| Others | Limitations/handicaps |
| Where: | Group Considerations: |
| Specific geographic area | Primary group |
| Macrosite characteristics | Secondary group |
| Competition from others | |
| To do what: | activity considerations: |
| Single or multiple activities | Equipment available |
| Desires of individual or group | Season |
| How: | Place considerations: |
| Mode of travel | Weather/seasons (may impede/facilitate) |
| Style of activity | |
| When: | Opportunities there: |
| Time of day, week | Natural attractions |
| Season | |
| Why: | Management considerations: |
| Satisfactions desired | Rules/regulations |
| Needs, motives | Facilities provided |
| Preferences, etc. | Perceived safety |

From Clark and Downing, 1985.

## Empirical Studies

The study focused on the relationship between the characteristics of recreationists and their preferences for aspects of the recreation setting. It was proposed that preferences for setting characteristics were influenced by the types of personal meanings (defined in the study as affective attachment or enduring involvement) attached to participation in a recreation activity. Additionally, these different meanings were deemed to affect the nature and complexity of the cognitive images associated with participation.

It was demonstrated that recreation involvement, or the attachment of particular meanings to participation, did influence preferences for setting attributes. In turn, the complexity of cognitive imagery also varied with recreation involvement and the focus of specialization, and as a result, participants tended to develop differing types of functional place attachment.

Survey results indicate that the character of the landscape figured highest in the decision to use Fraser Island and Cooloola National Parks as recreation venues. For the sample population as a whole, most frequent mention was made of the qualities of naturalness and lack of commercialization, and the attractions of scenery, tranquillity, peace and quiet, and solitude. The majority of other attributes mentioned related to aspects of the beach which was seen as the focus for a variety of activities. Again, physical attributes of the site and the view were found to be the most important factors in choice of a place to camp. It seems clear that people who come to these areas look for camp sites which will enable them to maximize their appreciation of the natural environment.

In summary, it was concluded that 4WD vehicle campers visit Fraser Island and Cooloola National Park because they perceive them as places of outstanding natural beauty, providing tranquillity and solitude, and opportunities to recreate and use 4WD vehicles. In choice of camp site, although practical considerations were important, aesthetic aspects and the feeling of isolation provided by the site tended to be rated more highly.

Even when the sample population was differentiated into clusters on the basis of recreation involvement, biophysical attributes of the setting rated ahead of other categories in importance. Of the four clusters identified, those campers attracted to camping for the opportunity it gives to achieve personal, self-expressive goals, were also more likely to focus on biophysical aspects of the environment, such as natural beauty and the unique and relatively untouched appearance of the scene. This finding was consistent with the behavioral emphasis of self-expressive campers on relaxing, and their concern with the overall ambience of the camping setting. Members of this cluster were classified as "setting specialists," seeking a recreation experience in an area of high scenic appeal, offering the opportunity to relax and enjoy feelings of solitude and isolation.

A further interesting observation arising from the study related to the influence which various meanings assigned to recreation participation may have on the level of attachment to place. Recent empirical work by Williams and Roggenbuck (1989) has indicated some support for the notion of two major types of place attachment, symbolic attachment linked to what a place means or symbolizes, as with a national park or wilderness, and functional attachment reflecting the value of a place perceived to provide those attributes that facilitate participation in particular experiences.

Although the Fraser Island-Cooloola National Park Study did not specifically seek to measure identification with place, the results suggest that elements of both functional and symbolic attachment to place were present. Functionally, the areas were valued because the natural attributes of the settings maximally supported preferred styles of recreation. On the other hand, the high regard expressed by visitors for the unique, natural qualities of the area reflected significant symbolic place attachment as well.

Once again the Queensland study demonstrates the intensely personal nature of interpretations of leisure and recreation, and of human reaction to identical environmental stimuli (McIntyre & Pigram, 1992). These characteristics serve to make generalizations about environmental preferences and attachment to place difficult and uncertain, and an ongoing challenge to policy makers and management. As noted by McIntyre (1990, p. 152):

> As recreation management matures from a stage of rapid expansion of the allocation of natural areas for the supply of nature-based recreation to a period characterized by accountability, shortage of funds and conflict over land use priorities, the emphasis must change from quantity to quality of provision. This implies that managers must be more aware of what quality means to the recreationists, which in turn necessitates the application of more sophisticated approaches to accessing this information.

## *Risk Recreation*

Risk recreation encompasses those activities which expose the participant to real or perceived dangers typical in a nature-oriented environment. Examples include rock climbing, white-water activities, caving, and hang gliding. Risk recreation, sometimes described as adventure recreation, is on the increase. Sixteen years ago, Dunn and Gulbis (1976) referred to a risk revolution with the emergence of "... new recreation forms characterized by controllable danger, excitement, or thrills ... from the status of rare offerings to mainstream programs" (p. 17). Several researchers have investigated these trends and explored the reasons why increasing numbers of people wish to engage in stress-seeking behavior (Hollenhurst 1988; Johnston, 1987; Robinson, 1990; White, Schreyer, & Downing, 1980). Explanation lies in a search for feelings of competency through the acquisition and experience of particular skills in an environment (oriented to nature) of risk and danger (Ewert & Hollenhurst, 1989).

One of the longer-established manifestations of risk recreation is rock climbing. A study of 148 rockclimbers in eastern Australia was undertaken as part of a larger investigation into specialized behavior in recreation (McIntyre, 1990). Surveys were undertaken at three sites covering a range of climbing grades and styles (McIntyre, 1991). Data analysis established six factors accounting for almost 70 per cent of the variance in motivation for rock climbing: recognition (23%); problem solving (13%); physical setting (11%); competence (8%); escape/ relaxation (7%); and leadership (7%).

When the relative importance of these factors was examined, the most highly rated motive was the physical setting in which participation takes place. This factor related to the aesthetics of the climbing environment, and the support for this motive acknowledges the attraction of natural surroundings as a backdrop to participation in rock climbing. Whereas most climbers preferred natural settings, responses from the one urban site surveyed on the Brisbane River suggest that such preferences can be compromised for the sake of convenience of access and proximity.

Overall, however, the physical setting, and the opportunity to experience wild environments and get close to nature, was the most highly valued among the six motivating factors. This pre-eminence was maintained when assessed relative to individual levels of involvement. As a participant became more involved, the physical setting remained the most highly related factor motivating participation.

The preference revealed for a range of specific risk settings oriented to nature has implications for policy formulation and resources management. Awareness of the needs of those involved, and of the perceived benefits to be gained from participation in risk recreation allows the incorporation of appropriate opportunities within a spectrum of natural leisure settings. Conflict between different forms of risk recreation, and between participants attempting different grades of difficulty, can also be anticipated and managed. It is clear that homogeneous management policies for all sites are not in participants' best interests (Ewert, 1985). With more experience, situations are sought which are more challenging, and less crowded and controlled. Once again, insight into the motives for participation in specific types of risk recreation, and the satisfactions gained, can assist managers in the proper location and degree of development of quality sites.

### *Urban Parks*

In the highly urbanized countries of the western world, the city functions primarily as a place of residence and a base for work commitments. The growing segment of life given over to leisure appears to find only restricted expression in the urban environment. More and more people look beyond the city limits and find their activity space for outdoor recreation identified increasingly with the rural scene. However, for many urban residents, this alternative is not readily accessible so that they must turn towards open space within the city for relief from the deficiencies of the urban environment.

Much of the dissatisfaction with urban living and many of the concomitant social problems can be traced to the apparent inability of the modern city to meet the basic needs of its inhabitants. One of the objectives of urban environmental planning is to produce a more satisfying array of amenity stimuli and responses. The range and intensity of amenity responses are, in turn, a function of the nature, characteristics and location of what Atkisson and Robinson (1969) call amenity precipitants. In an urban situation a fundamental component of the amenity response system is the availability of open space for recreation.

According to Gold (1988), an effective recreation experience in cities calls for opportunities to experience freedom, diversity, self-expression, challenge, and enrichment. Servicing such opportunities provides much of the justification for provision of open space within cities.

This is not to deny that urban open space per se has value apart from a potential recreation role. Demands for lower residential densities in affluent areas and for extensive landscaped sites for public buildings and industrial estates demonstrate a growing social awareness of space as a community asset. Added to this is the acknowledgement of what economists term the existence value of open space and green areas within cities. Nearby residents can develop strong attachments for even rather ordinary local parks which they may rarely use for recreational purposes (Melbourne and Metropolitan Board of Works, 1983).

In any case, not all urban open space is equipped to function as recreation space. Modern planned national capitals such as Brasilia and Canberra are blessed with vast areas of open space, geometrically arranged, trimmed and manicured, yet devoid of any feature which would encourage, facilitate, or even permit leisure activities (Pigram, 1983). In many cases, any recreation function, apart from perhaps passive viewing, is specifically excluded by physical barriers, equally forbidding signage, or other effective means of discouraging participation. Open space it may be, recreation space it is not.

It follows that satisfaction of the leisure needs of urban dwellers requires more than the existence of open space. In the provision of recreation space in cities, is not a matter of how much, but how good that space is. In part, this will reflect the characteristics of urban open space in terms of park size, range of facilities, and accessibility. However, the importance of the natural setting in contrast to the surrounding built-up environment would seem to be paramount.

In a study of urban parks in the City of Melbourne, Australia, the attractiveness and variety of the vegetation, and the presence of water bodies were found to be important factors in accounting for variations in recreational use (Boyle, 1983). At some parks, a strong preference was expressed for peace and quiet in relatively natural areas with few facilities. A significant number of respondents at two native eucalyptus parks, where minimal equipment had been installed, insisted that more facilities were not needed.

A similar preference for natural appearing parks was revealed in a major study of inner city parks in the City of Brisbane, Australia (McIntyre, Cuskelly, & Auld, 1991). The benefits perceived as arising from park visits were explored using a market segmentation approach linked to the Recreation Experience Preference Scale developed for the U.S. Forest Service (Driver, 1977; Manfredo, Driver, & Brown et al., 1983). Factor analysis of responses from 465 interviews revealed five factors explaining 59 per cent of the variance in the data set. The heaviest factor loading of almost 30 per cent was attained by one factor interpreted as nature appreciation. This factor comprised four variables: close to nature; rest and relaxation; viewing the scenery; and relieving tension. It is suggested that the natural setting of inner city parks and green areas provides a venue for rest and tension release for urban residents and an opportunity to appreciate nature.

Cluster analysis of the factor scores for each respondent revealed four distinct homogeneous subgroups or market segments based on their preferences for perceived benefits of park use. The largest cluster made up 42 per cent and demonstrated high mean scores on nature appreciation and the opportunity which natural surroundings provide for physical and mental rest. An important finding of the study was the link between the perceived benefits from a nature-oriented recreation experience and the type of park selected for the visit. The preference revealed for natural settings "... emphasizes the need for the preservation of these 'islands of naturalness' within the cityscape" (McIntyre, Cuskelly, & Auld, 1991, p. 16). It also raises the question of non-use or under-use of urban parks and the importance of matching park settings to the preferences of park users.

These findings have policy implications for the management of urban open space as part of a city's amenity response system. This is not to say that all observed behavior is preferred behavior; rather, it might reflect the constraints under which people are operating (Walmsley, 1988). Personal and social circumstances, along with constraints of time, money, and mobility, may have greater force in leisure pursuits, than for other less discretionary forms of human behavior.

However, knowledge of the range and character of preferred park experiences can provide some input to the setting of priorities for the allocation of scarce resources and expenditure. It can also help redirect development and promotion towards meeting deficiencies in current provision and spatial distribution of recreation opportunities in urban parks.

### *Wilderness*

Increasing attention is being directed towards research into the appeal of what some regard as the ultimate in natural environments - wilderness. For much of history, wilderness held a negative connotation either as waste land, or as some vast hostile and dangerous place to be avoided if at all possible, or else to be tamed, controlled, and exploited. Today, people in many parts of the world have come to think more positively of wilderness as something to be valued, used and managed with care and respect, and preserved for a future world in which it could become increasingly rare.

A broad spectrum of values attached to wilderness has evolved, ranging from the aesthetic to the ecological, the recreational, and the metaphysical (Norton, Common, Mackey, & Moore 1991). Wilderness can have value simply through appreciation of nature in the wild, or for the contribution made to the maintenance of ecological integrity and genetic diversity. Wilderness can also be the focus for special types of recreation activities from which self-confidence can be re-established through physical challenge and reliance on self-sufficiency and subsistence skills.

Much recent research interest on wilderness values has been from the perspective of the experiences that visitors have in these environments and the individual-environment transactions which occur in the wilderness setting. Scherl (1988a) argues that in a wilderness context a very different set of relationships between individuals, or between individuals and the physical environment, exists, and it is for this reason that experiences in these settings are valued. The significance of personal benefits derived from a wilderness experience is also recognized by Driver et al. (1987) (Table 16. 2).

A number of studies have suggested that meaningful changes, with respect to self-perception and self-concept, take place within the individual when entering and undertaking activities within a wilderness setting (Scherl, 1989). These (beneficial) changes have been linked to the notion of perceived control and the need to exert self-control in an environment which cannot (easily) be modified to suit individual purposes. This situation focuses attention on an individual's emotional and physical state, and heightened personal awareness as a component of an environmental transaction. What is central is not the individual or the physical and social environment alone, but the ongoing interaction between both (Scherl, 1988b).

From this perspective, the environment becomes of material relevance through the interplay between some environed object, organism, or process and its milieu; an interaction which is not static, but dynamic and evolving (Pigram, 1979). In a wilderness context, the interaction between an individual and the environment will be mediated by recurring self-appraisal and reassessment of the individual's relationship with the surroundings.

The transactional relationship between the organism (the individual) and the experienced environment was the focus of a study of participants' perception of a wilderness experience based on an Australian Adult Outward Bound Program (Scherl, 1990b). These programs are one of many different ways people can choose to experience a wilderness environment. Data collection was carried out over three demanding programs, each of nine days, in a wilderness setting. Participants recorded their impressions and feelings in log books as each program developed, and the contents were summarized into meaningful categories representing different domains of the wilderness experience.

The relative saliency of the different domains of the wilderness experience was ascertained for each day of the program. The most frequently mentioned categories overall were "description of activities" and "self." When the latter was broken down into subordinate categories, self-awareness was most salient, making up 35 per cent of all self-references. This suggests that the wilderness experience offered by the Outward Bound Program allows people to learn something about themselves or perceive themselves in a different light (Scherl, 1988b).

TABLE 16.2
*Personal Benefits Derived From Wilderness*

DEVELOPMENTAL: changes in users' self-concepts, self-esteem or acquisition of skills;

THERAPEUTIC/HEALING: opportunity for coping with a variety of mental and physical stresses for both clinical and non-clinical populations by experiencing peace and tranquillity and a 'biological fit' (in wilderness we encounter natural rather than artificial stimuli which are more compatible with our ancestral roots);

PHYSICAL HEALTH: opportunities for frequently extended and aerobic activities in an environment free of pollutants. These opportunities can also contribute to one's quality of life;

CLEAR-UNAMBIGUOUS FEEDBACK: opportunities to be involved in activities which generate feedback about oneself which is concrete, clear and inherently reinforcing;

SELF-SUFFICIENCY: opportunities for self-testing and seeking challenges and adventures;

SELF-CONTROL: opportunities to come in close contact with one's emotions and fears and to control these feelings;

SPIRITUAL: chance for spiritually uplifting experiences and for a feeling of unity with the universe;

AESTHETIC/CREATIVE: appreciation and enjoyment of nature;

*educational*: exploring and learning about nature;

SOCIAL IDENTITY: family and friends cohesiveness and solidarity;

SYMBOLIC: importance we attribute to the preservation of wilderness for future generations.

Adapted from Scherl, 1990a.

Analyses of participants' perceptions of the different dimensions of their experiences for each day of the program contributed to an understanding of the process and dynamics of a wilderness experience.

"Description of activities" remained salient throughout, but the underlying characteristics of the dynamics of the program were diversity and change. "Self" and "social setting" emerged as the most consistent categories suggesting, first, that the program was successful in achieving its objectives of promoting an opportunity for self-discovery, self-evaluation, understanding and reflection. Secondly, the growing attention to 'Social Setting' during the course acknowledged the importance of support and dependency, and involvement and interaction with others.

The results of this study suggested that the emotional and/or physical sensations experienced in a wilderness context could be important triggers for enhanced self-understanding. Scherl (1989, p. 132) argues that "...the unique value of the wilderness situation, in contrast to other recreation opportunities, is that it *more easily facilitates* self-relevant feedback, which in turn can contribute to personal growth." The process is incremental: the benefits from a wilderness experience flow from the meshing of individuals' perceptions of the environment, the manner in which these perceptions impinge on transactions with that environment, and the way in which the effects of these transactions evoke consciousness of self and response. Focusing on the human experiential opportunities inherent in wilderness should enhance respect for the environments which make this experiential diversity and complexity possible.

The importance of gaining an understanding of the multidimensional nature of the recreation experience was validated in a subsequent study of visitors to the Great Barrier Reef Marine Park off the Queensland coast of Australia (Scherl, 1991). The study site, Lady Musgrave island and reef, is a nature-oriented environment largely free of human-built structures. Although not a true wilderness, in the sense of the Outward Bound study area, a similar methodological approach was adopted focusing on the nature of the recreation experience and the experiential components of interaction with the reef environment.

Data were collected through on-site interviews with visitors, and a list of categories developed from the summarized content of the interview responses. Several of the domains of a wilderness experience identified in the Outward Bound study were again represented, e.g., "self," "social setting," "activities," and "physical environment." Preliminary results indicate a positive emotional response to the experience in the natural environment of the island and reef. Contemplating nature was the most reported activity. In general, visitors saw a personal and positive interaction with nature as a key part of their experience. This was borne out further by the predominant feeling among respondents that they wished to see no changes to the site, and that development and visits should be restricted (Scherl, 1991).

Both studies benefited from close interaction between managers and researchers from the outset. Involvement of management in the research process is important for understanding of the meaning of parks and nature-oriented recreation resources to people, and what is particularly salient or unique about them. To generate the benefits perceived from participation, more needs to be known about the link between experiences, benefits and setting conditions. In a wilderness experience, where self-awareness has been shown to be an important outcome, insight is required into the experiential circumstances which facilitate such benefits. Awareness of the experiential profiles associated with different wilderness settings should reveal what combination of population attributes and situational attributes (e.g., physical environment, group composition, or structure of activities) is most likely to yield the particular desired type of experiential profile (Scherl, 1988b).

In any setting, the range and quality of recreational opportunities can be diminished because of inadequate understanding of the experiences sought by visitors (Scherl, 1991). Integrating research into resource management decision making, as in the Marine Park study, should encourage the adoption of an experience-based approach to planning for tourism and recreation in the reef environment.

The results of empirical work in wilderness and natural areas support the centrality of appreciation of nature to people's outdoor recreation experiences (Driver et al., 1987). From this perspective the appropriate managerial response would be to maximize opportunities for interaction with nature in the design and planning of settings and infrastructure in harmony with the environment. Moreover, improved understanding of experiences and benefits makes it possible to target the types of information most important in influencing recreationists' behavior. More effective information systems and interpretive programs should be the outcome (Beaulieu & Schreyer, 1984; Roggenbuck & Ham, 1986).

## Conclusion

Consideration of the choice process underlying leisure activities reveals two complementary areas of research interest. From the perspective of environmental psychology, the concern is with appreciation of the reciprocal links between the recreation experience, the benefits perceived, and the environmental setting. Behavioral geographers, while appreciating the importance of the relationship between the individual and the recreation setting, are concerned also with understanding and explaining spatial choice and behavior. The nature of the decision making process, and the way in which preferences for use of leisure reflect perception, evaluation, and choice of alternative opportunities, are central to this task (Lieber & Fesenmaier, 1984).

These are not bipolar perspectives. Knowledge of the benefits derived from a recreation experience, and the functional linkages between perceived benefits and the nature and dynamics of that experience, are fundamental to the explanation of reasons for participation. Recreationists select specific settings for leisure pursuits with specific benefits in mind (Schreyer & Driver, 1990). Recreation behavior in space is the outcome of individual cognitive evaluations of known attributes of recreation settings, and the contribution which it is perceived the environment will make to a rewarding recreation experience. In this context, the demonstrated attraction of natural settings as outlets for leisure is seen as a reflection of a broader human preference for environments dominated by natural rather than human-influenced elements.

The implications for management are obvious. Recreation managers must ensure that their information levels with regard to the product sought from a recreation experience are adequate for an appropriate response to be made. It has been shown that management is not always in touch with visitor motivations and aspirations (Wellman, Roggenbuck, & Smith, 1982). An understanding of user preferences and recreation behavior is all important in planning and in policy formulation, and in the implementation of site-specific management measures. If enjoyment of nature is a basic ingredient as empirical work suggests, then there is an implied obligation on management to build in these desired attributes. In creating a spectrum of fulfilling leisure environments, priority must be given to providing recreation settings which maximize opportunities for interaction with nature and the beneficial outcomes perceived from this experience. Insight into human behavior with environment is the key to providing satisfying leisure experiences in harmony with nature.

## References

Aitken, S. (1991). Person-environment theories in contemporary perceptual and behavioural geography I: Personality, attitudinal and spatial choice theories. *Progress in Human Geography, 15*, 179-193.

Allen, S. (1985). Predicting the impacts of a high-voltage transmission line on big game hunting opportunities in western Montana. In *Proceedings of symposium on recreation choice behavior*. (General Technical Report No. INT-184, pp. 86-100). Ogden, UT: USDA Forest Service.

Atkisson, A., & Robinson, I. (1969). Amenity resources for urban living. In H. Perloff (ed.), *The Quality of the Urban Environment* (pp. 179-201). Washington, D.C.: Johns Hopkins Press.

Barker, R. (1968). *Ecological psychology*. Palo Alto, CA: Stanford University Press.

Beaulieu, J., & Schreyer, R. (1985). Choices of wilderness environments: Differences between real and hypothetical choice situations. In *Proceedings of symposium on recreation choice behavior* (General Technical Report No. INT-184, pp. 38-45). Ogden, UT: USDA Forest Service.

Boyle, R. (1983, November). A survey of the use of small parks. *Australian Parks and Recreation* , pp. 31-6.

Bryan, H. (1977). Leisure value systems and recreation specialization: The case of trout fishermen. *Journal of Leisure Research, 9*, 174-187.

Clark, R., & Downing, K. (1985). Why here and not there: The conditional nature of recreation choice. In *Proceedings of symposium on recreation choice behavior* (General Technical Report No. INT-184, (pp. 61-70). Ogden, UT: USDA Forest Service.

Clark, R., & Stankey, G. (1979). *The recreation opportunity spectrum: A framework for planning, management and research* (General Technical Report No. PNW-98). Seattle, WA: USDA Forest Service.

Desbarats, J. (1983). Spatial choice and constraints on behavior. *Annals of the Association of American Geographers, 73*, 340-357.

Ditwiler, C. (1979). Can technology decrease natural resource use conflicts in recreation? *Search, 10*, 439-441.

Driver, B. (1977). *Item pool for scales designed to quantify the psychological outcomes desired and expected from recreationists participation* (Research Note). Fort Collins: USDA Forest Service.

Driver, B., & Brown, P. (1978). The opportunity spectrum concept and behavioral information in outdoor recreation supply inventories: A rationale. In G. Lund, V. Labau, P. Folliot, & D. Robinson (Eds.), *Integrated Inventories of Renewable Natural Resources* (General Technical Report No. RM-56, pp. 24-31). Fort Collins, CO: USDA Forest Service.

Driver, B., Brown, P., Stankey, G., & Gregoire, T. (1987). The ROS planning system: Evolution, basic concepts and research needed. *Leisure Sciences, 9*, 201-212.

Dunn, D., & Gulbis, J. (1976, August). The risk revolution. *Parks and Recreation*, pp. 12-17.

Elson, M. (1973). Some factors affecting the incidence and distribution of weekend recreation motoring trips. *Oxford Agrarian Studies, 11,* 161-178.
Ewert, A. (1985). Why people climb. *Journal of Leisure Research, 17,* 241-249.
Ewert, A., & Hollenhurst, S. (1989). Testing the adventure model: Empirical support for a model of risk recreation. *Journal of Leisure Research, 21,* 124-139.
Fly, J. (1986). *Nature, outdoor recreation and tourism: The basis for regional population growth in northern lower Michigan.* Unpublished doctoral dissertation, University of Michigan, Ann Arbor.
Glytis, S. (1981). People at play in the countryside. *Geography,* 66, 277-285.
Gold, S. (1988). Urban open space preservation: The American experience. *Australian Parks and Recreation, 24,* 14-19.
Heywood, J. (1989a). Expecting the unexpected: Managing parks for people. *Australian Parks and Recreation, 25,* 21-28.
Heywood, J. (1989b). Recreation opportunity: The social setting. *Australian Parks and Recreation, 25,* 18-20.
Hollenhurst, S. (1988, June). *Recreation specialization: The case of rock-climbers.* Paper presented at the second symposium on social science in resource management, Urbana, IL.
Iso-Ahola, S. (1980). *The social psychology of leisure and recreation.* Dubuque, IO: Brown.
Ittelson, W., Franck, K., & O'Hanlon, T. (1976). The nature of environmental experience. In S. Wapner, S. Cohen, & B. Kaplan (Eds.), *Experiencing the Environment* (pp. 187-206). New York: Plenum.
Janiskee, R. (1976). *On the recreation appeals of extra-urban environments.* Paper presented at the annual meeting of the Association of American Geographers, New York.
Johnston, M. (1987, January). *Risk in mountain recreation: Challenge or danger.* Paper presented at the 14th New Zealand geography conference, Palmerston North.
Kaplan, R., & Kaplan, S. (1989). *The experience of nature: A psychological perspective.* Cambridge: Cambridge University Press.
Katz, C., & Kirby, A. (1991). In the nature of things: The environment and everyday life. *Transactions of the Institute of British Geographers, 16,* 259-271.
Killin, N., Paradice, W., & Engel, M. (Eds.). (1988). Information in planning and management of recreation and tourist services. *Proceedings of Hunter Valley Research Foundation Recreation and Tourism Seminar, Newcastle.*

Krumpe, E. (1988). The role of information in people's leisure decision making process. In N. Killin, W. Paradice, & M. Engel (Eds.), *Information in planning and management of recreation and tourist services*. Newcastle: Hunter Valley Research Foundation.

Levy, J. (1979). A paradigm for conceptualizing leisure behavior. *Journal of Leisure Research, 11*, 48-60.

Lieber, S., & Fesenmaier, D. (1984). Modelling recreation choice: A case study of management alternatives in Chicago. *Regional Studies, 18*, 31-43.

Manfredo, M., Driver, B., & Brown, P. (1983). A test of concepts inherent in experience based setting management for outdoor recreation areas. *Journal of Leisure Research, 15*, 263-83.

McCool, S., Stankey, G., & Clark, R. (1985). Choosing recreation settings: Processes, findings and research directions. *Proceedings of the symposium on recreation choice behavior* (General Technical Report No. INT-184, (pp. 1-8). Ogden, UT: USDA Forest Service.

McIntyre, N. (1990). *Recreation involvement: The personal meaning of participation*. Unpublished doctoral dissertation. University of New England.

McIntyre, N. (in press). Involvement in risk recreation: A comparison of objective and subjective measures of engagement. *Journal of Leisure Research*.

McIntyre, N., Cuskelly, G., & Auld, C. (1991). The benefits of urban parks. *Australian Parks and Recreation, 27*, 11-18.

McIntyre, N., & Pigram, J. (1992). Recreation specialization re-examined: The case of vehicle-based campers. *Leisure Sciences, 14*, 3-15.

Melbourne and Metropolitan Board of Works (1983). *Melbourne parks*. Melbourne: MMBW.

Norton, T., Common, M., Mackey, B., & Moore, I. (1991). *Report to the department of arts, sport, the environment, tourism, and territories concerning the conservation , recreation and tourism values of Australian forests as relevant to the forest and timber enquiry of the resource assessment commission*. Unpublished manuscript, Centre for Resource and Environmental Studies, ANU, Canberra.

Peterson, G., Stynes, D., Rosenthal, D., & Dwyer, J. (1985). Substitution in recreation choice behavior. *Proceedings of the symposium on recreation choice behavior* (General Technical Report No. INT-184, pp. 19-30). USDA Forest Service.

Phillips, S. (1977). *Satisfaction and substitution in recreation: A pilot study*. Ottawa, Canada: Fisheries and Environment.

Pigram, J. (1979, June). *Environment, resources and tourism.* Paper presented to the environmental engineering conference, The Institution of Engineers, Canberra.

Pigram, J. (1983). *Outdoor recreation and resource management.* London: Croom Helm.

Robinson, D. (1990, May). *Stress-seeking behavior in the natural environment: A descriptive model of risk recreation.* Paper presented at the third symposium on social science in resource management, Texas A & M University.

Roehl, W. (1987, April). *An investigation of the perfect information assumption in recreation destination choice models.* Paper presented at the annual conference of the Association of American Geographers, Portland, OR.

Roggenbuck, J., & Ham, S. (1986). Use of information and education in recreation management. In *A literature review - The president's commission on American outdoors* (pp. 59-71). Washington, D.C.: U.S. Government Printing Office.

Rossman, B., & Ulehla, Z. (1977). Psychological reward values associated with wilderness use. *Environment and Behavior*, *9*, 41-66.

Scherl, L. (1988a). *The wilderness experience: Psychological and motivational considerations of a structured experience in a wilderness setting*. Unpublished doctoral dissertation. James Cook University of North Queensland.

Scherl, L. (1988b). The wilderness experience: a psychological evaluation of its components and dynamics. In *The use of wilderness for personal growth, therapy and education*, (General Technical Report No. RM-193, (pp. 11-22). Fort Collins: USDA Forest Service.

Scherl, L. (1989). Self in wilderness: Understanding the psychological benefits of individual-wilderness interaction through self-control. *Leisure Sciences, 11*, 123-35.

Scherl, L. (1990a, May). *Wilderness values and management.* Paper presented at the Institute of Tropical Rainforests Studies workshop, Townsville.

Scherl, L. (1990b, April). *Wilderness benefits from an interactionist perspective.* Paper presented at the first Australasian workshop on recreation benefit measurement, Melbourne.

Scherl, L. (1991, July). *Developing an understanding of recreation experiences in the marine park: Implications for management.* Paper presented at the world leisure research congress, Sydney.

Schreyer, R., & Driver, B. (1990). The benefits of wildland recreation participation: What do we know and where do we go? In B. Driver (Ed.), *Contributions of social scientists to multiple use management: An update*. Fort Collins: USDA Forest Service.

Schreyer, R., Knopf, R., & Williams, D. (1985). Reconceptualizing the motive/environment link in recreation choice behavior. *Proceedings of the symposium on recreation choice behavior* (General Technical Report No. INT.184, (pp. 9-18)). Ogden, UT: USDA Forest Service.

Shafer, E., & Mietz, J. (1969). Aesthetic and emotional experiences rate high with northeast wilderness hikers. *Environment and Behavior, 1*, 187-97.

Stankey, G. (1977). Some social concepts for outdoor recreation planning. *Proceedings of a national symposium on outdoor advances in application of economics* (General Technical Report, WO-2, pp. 154-61). Washington, D.C.: USDA Forest Service.

Stankey, G., & McCool, S. (1985). (Eds.), *Proceedings of the symposium on recreation choice behavior* (General Technical Report No. INT-184, p. 120). Ogden, UT: USDA Forest Service.

Timmermans, H., & Golledge, R. (1990). Applications of behavioral research on spatial problems II: preference and choice. *Progress in Human Geography, 14*, 311-54.

Ulrich, R. (1983). Aesthetic and affective response to natural environment. In I. Altman & J. Wohlwill (Eds.), *Human Behavior and Environment* (pp. 85-125). New York: Plenum.

Ulrich, R., Simons, R., Tosito, B., Fiorito, E., Miles, M. & Zelson, M. (1991). Stress recovery during exposure to natural and urban environments. *Journal of Environmental Psychology, 3*, 201-230.

Vining, J. (1988). *A process tracing approach to recreation choice problems*. Unpublished manuscript. Institute for Environmental Studies, Urbana, IL.

Walmsley, D. J. (1988). *Urban Living*, Harlow, UK: Longman.

Wearing, S. (1986). *Outdoor recreation as a catalyst for change*. Unpublished masters thesis, University of New South Wales.

Wellman, J., Roggenbuck, J., & Smith, A. (1982). Recreatjpion specialization and norms of depreciative behavior among canoeists. *Journal of Leisure Research*, 14, 323-40.

White, R., Schreyer, R., & Downing, K. (1980). Trends in emerging and high risk activities. *Proceedings of the national outdoor recreation trends symposium* (USDA General Technical Report No. NE-57, pp. 199-204). Broomal.

Williams, D. (1985). A developmental model of recreation choice behavior. *Proceedings of the symposium on recreation choice behavior* (General Technical Report No. INT-184, (pp. 31-7). Ogden, UT: USDA Forest Service.

Williams, D., & Roggenbuck, J. (1989). *Measuring place attachment.* Paper presented at the NRPA symposium on leisure research, San Antonio, TX.

*Behavior and Environment: Psychological and Geographical Approaches*
*T. Gärling and R.G. Golledge (Editors)*



# CHAPTER 17

# Psychological Foundations of Nature Experience

**Terry Hartig and Gary W. Evans**

People move among places. They have reasons for doing so, self-generated and externally imposed. People act on places and attach varying sorts of significance to them, just as they are acted upon by these places and imbued with their particular qualities. These interactive realities are common ground for geography and psychology. Geography has traditional interests in patterns of human movement and in people and land as agents of change in one another (Pattison, 1964, 1990). Psychology considers motives for movement and processes in human-environment exchange on the individual level.

Motives for movement engender distinctions between places. Some distinctions are formed by complementary needs. Reciprocal movement between places occurs because people seek to satisfy needs and desires in one place that they see arise in others. Distinctions are reinforced through cycles of movement.

A distinction between natural and built environments is in part based on complementary needs. Consideration of this distinction and factors shaping it will help in understanding environment and behavior relations. This is true particularly for those interested in human relations with the natural world. For the majority of people now living - people in urbanized societies - salient qualities of nature experience are determined by experiences of everyday built environments.

The fundamental organizing principle of this chapter is that the natural-built distinction has a central role in theorizing about nature experience. The chapter has three sections. In the first we address issues met in setting out nature experience as a subject for study. In the second we elaborate on the evolution of the distinction, leading to its establishment as a fundamental categorical device in the language of laypeople and researchers alike. The final section looks at the significance of the natural-built distinction for psychological theories about human-environment relations.

## Definitional Issues

After considering cosmological and ecosystemic meanings for "nature" and "natural," respectively, Wohlwill (1983) concluded that "natural environment" is the most useful term for "psychological analysis of the individual's response to nature. He then defined "natural environment" as "the vast domain of organic and inorganic matter that is not a product of human activity or intervention" (Wohlwill, 1983, p. 7). The human-made world was taken to consist of cities and towns, buildings, and other implements devised for human needs.

Wohlwill identified three problems with defining "natural environment" through exclusion of the human-made. First, some natural environments have no apparent artifacts, yet owe their appearance to human activity. For these cases the recommended criterion is whether evidence of the past activity is discriminable. If not, the setting can be treated as a natural environment. Second, most environments that people will enter have some visible signs of humanity. Here the criterion is whether the natural remains predominant over the built in the given area and the area remains identified as natural or scenic in terms of its use. Third, natural areas and elements are often set within or imported into built settings. Here again predominance of the natural over the built and identification as a natural area by users is the criterion. Variants of the predominance criterion have been employed by other researchers (e.g., S. Kaplan & Talbot, 1983).

Wohlwill acknowledged the arbitrariness of a criterion that permits a developed area within a national park to be classified as natural but denies this classification to a large undeveloped area on a military base. Yet he asserted that a logically precise delimitation of the natural world was not essential for his purposes. Those purposes involved analyzing the stimulus characteristics of large-scale physical environments. He recognized that other views of the distinction between natural and built would not rely on stimulus differences, nor require reference only to large-scale physical environments. Other views might embrace contrasts in patterns of social feedback, or refer to symbols of nature.

The concern here is not only with the differing objective stimulus characteristics. It also encompasses personal, social, and cultural variables that help characterize the natural-built distinction. Because the present approach is not necessarily constrained to experiences of large-scale physical environments, Wohlwill's predominance-of-natural criteria can be applied differently. If the natural predominates over the built in the focus of the person's experience - in the focus of their attention, thought, and feeling - then their experience is also a subject for study. Such experience is more likely to occur in natural environments, but is also possible within built environments. Consistent with this conceptualization, the experience can be momentary or more sustained.

To avoid confusing the experience of the large-scale natural environment itself with experiences of natural features in environments generally, we differentiate here between natural environment experience and nature experience. In the former the person is within a natural environment, suitably defined through use of Wohlwill's criteria. Immersion in wilderness is the exemplar. In nature experience the person has in their experiential focus some part of the surround that is either not of human manufacture or that is a surrogate of something not of human origin. It may be had while gardening just as it might be had in wilderness. It can come while watching a sunset from a city street, or with the feel of a winter wind on the way to the bus. It may visit us indoors through window views and with aquariums, terrariums, houseplants, and pictures. It may come through contemplation of symbols of natural forces, such as those arrayed in Japanese gardens. Nature experience is thus the more encompassing form, and subsumes natural environment experience. For both forms of experience, requirement of some physical referent sets them apart from more purely religious or philosophical experiences.

Corresponding definitions should be set out for the non-natural realm, given that the concern here is for understanding nature experience in light of the natural-built distinction. Accordingly, if the experiential focus is on some human artifact (or on another person, taken as representative of the social environment), it can be referred to as the experience of the built. The experience of the built may be had even in wilderness. The experience of objects representative of humanity or human presence can be distinguished from the experience of some surrounding, large-scale built environment, or built-environment experience. This comes readily with being on the street in the center of a town or city, or through entry into the indoor spaces of homes, stores, workplaces, and so forth. Whether reference is to the built generally or to built environments more specifically, something of human origin is taken to represent social, cultural, and other constructed aspects of human environments.

## The Distinction Between Natural and Built

A better sense of the dynamic underlying the natural-built distinction comes through an analysis of its origin. This analysis supports the point that the distinction has emerged over time and assumed different forms.

The practice of placing natural and built environments in opposition has its origins in the emergence of human material culture. Not until humans had made something was there something to be distinguished as human-made, whether or not they were oriented toward setting it apart as such. Further, not until humans could at least imagine themselves within something they had made could they distinguish a built environment from a natural environment.

As material culture articulated, so also did the means to communicate about what was being made. Some substantial portion of this exchange would have been about values of what had been made relative to demands of existence in the given place. This would also have held true for early built environments, with values attached to them being contrasted with or shown to reflect values attached to some encompassing environment. Communication of this form was and remains integral to a process of design.

In this process the built environment became a stimulus not only for communication about some larger environment, but also for the design of humanity's place in that larger environment. Kluckhohn (1961) asserts that one problem all societies face concerns human relations with nature. Solutions to this problem fall along a range with three key markers: humans as subjugated to nature, humans as within nature, and humans as against or over nature. All societies assume a dominant value orientation that falls within this range. Yet not until members of nascent societies had some means for communication about their relation to nature could there have been a means for those societies to arrive at dominant value orientations toward nature. Coming to terms with the question of human relations with nature required language that enabled discussion of people as beneath, within, or over nature. In the process of designing and building, people created the means not only for discussion of the values of what they were building relative to demands of the larger environment, but also for discussion of their place in the larger environment.

Still, it was not until early humans could communicate about the way in which their built environment actually reflected their value orientation (and so reinforced their being within or separate from some conception of nature) that there could have been the perceived reality of a natural-built distinction. In sum, three conditions were necessary for the emergence of the natural-built distinction: imagined or real built environments, some means for communication about both built environments and human-nature value orientations, and a value orientation that allowed a natural-built distinction to emerge.

As in prehistoric time, historical boundaries between the natural and built have been established by attaching differing values to each. These values configurations have not been stable, as shown by Glacken (1967), Tuan (1974), and others (e.g., Nash, 1982; Thomas, 1983). Over the past two centuries natural environments have been romanticized, while built environments, especially cities, have been stigmatized. This kind of opposition is not new. Tuan (1974) documents a similar pattern in both ancient Greece and ancient China. Such shifting of values speaks to the changing character of the distinction.

A distinction between the natural and the human-made or artificial now functions as a fundamental device for organization. Use of the terms "natural" and "artificial" in reference to objects, processes, concepts, actions, and so forth is widespread and has the character of reflex. This agrees with Wohlwill's (1983) contention that "natural" is an exemplar of a natural category as described by Rosch (1973). As such, it has perceptually salient identifying characteristics that provide a basis for easier learning and better memory of category members. Consistent with their categorical status, the terms each have many connotations, with connotations of "natural" now relatively positive in comparison to those of "artificial."

Subordinate to the larger distinction, the natural-built distinction can be used to readily classify most environments. Wohlwill (1983), citing research by himself and others, asserts that when subjects must spontaneously organize photos of different settings, some form of natural-built distinction or dimension often underlies their organization schemes (see also Ward, 1977; Ward & Russell, 1981; J. Ullrich & M. Ullrich, 1976).

As in language more generally, the natural-built distinction is well established in the language of environment-behavior research. It is commonly referred to without question or analysis. Also, distinctions such as those between indoor and outdoor, urban and rural, metropolitan and nonmetropolitan, urban and wilderness, primitive and urban, and civilized and wild either are encompassed by the natural-built distinction or share important features with it. The development of these more specialized distinctions points to the increasing rootedness of the more encompassing natural-built distinction in the language used to describe human environments.

## The Natural-Built Distinction in Theories About Nature Experience

The natural-built distinction is a cornerstone for a variety of psychological theories. These share a central concern for human relations with the natural world. Theories about aspects of built experience more often do not incorporate the distinction as an aid to explanation. Their insularity follows with the tendency to equate the experience of the built with human experience in general. Concomitants of this tendency are the common view of nature experience as a sort of time-out period and an inability to see the significance of nature experience in some of its more mundane forms, such as exchange with houseplants.

Theories about nature experience are founded on concerns about health and quality of life. Whether implicitly or explicitly, they typically treat nature experience as the potential source of an array of personal benefits for people living in urbanized societies. A personal benefit has been defined as a specific, desirable, improved state or condition, and/or the prevention of a worse state or condition (Driver et al., 1987). Some models relate the potential for benefits to deficits from various taxing conditions in the everyday milieu (e.g., Ulrich, 1983). Others include forms of personal growth among potential benefits, with growth coming through experiences not readily available in everyday built and social settings (e.g., R. Kaplan & S. Kaplan, 1989; Reser & Scherl, 1988). Taken in entirety, then, some theories about values of nature experience are also about deleterious or constraining qualities of the experience of the built. In this they dovetail with much research on environmental stress (cf., Saegert & Winkel, 1990).

Like research on stress, research on nature experience does not pay much attention to positive aspects of the built. Nor does it attend much to negative aspects of nature experience. Stress research and nature experience research assume understanding of positive qualities of built environments and negative qualities of natural environments, respectively, then proceed with their common mission, to find ways to improve conditions in our living environments (cf., Evans & Cohen, 1987 with Knopf, 1987). Yet harsh sides of nature experience have been considered by stress researchers looking at natural disasters (e.g., Baum, Fleming, & Davidson, 1983) and extreme and unusual environments (e.g., Suedfeld, 1987). Also, some researchers more interested in nature experience per se have spoken to the need to acknowledge its less than pleasant aspects when planning studies (Knopf, 1987) and when drawing out the implications of findings (Driver & Greene, 1977). Then, too, some analyses concerned with nature experience incorporate basic assumptions about threats to survival in natural environments during human evolution (e.g., Appleton, 1975; R. Kaplan & S. Kaplan, 1989); however, their treatment of nature experience is by and large positively toned.

Although most researchers share a consistently favorable view of outcomes of nature experience, their discussions of benefits vary in several respects. Of particular relevance here is variation in the treatment of environmental preference. Whether couched in terms of aesthetic response or referred to directly, preference can reflect or imply a positive emotional state. A preference may also signal awareness of something with additional value (R. Kaplan & S. Kaplan, 1989). Thus, the following discussion assumes that preference can have some immediate benefit value and may also be taken as an indicator of the potential for realizing further benefits. Unlike those for preferences, explanations for further benefits typically are constructed on some form of natural-built distinction.

In the remainder of this section we will overview some explanations for benefits of nature experience, setting out differences among them in six areas: (1) the treatment of environmental preference, (2) reference to the natural-built distinction, (3) other intra-individual benefits, (4) the time frame in which benefits are realized, (5) the environmental level on which the encounter takes place (e.g., wilderness experience, exchange with a houseplant), and (6) the conditions specified or implied as antecedent to the realization of benefits. The overview is not exhaustive in its coverage of nature experience benefits, explanations for them, or domains of psychological functioning, but gives a sense of the factors thought to operate in beneficial person-nature interactions. For convenience, it is organized according to the psychological domain(s) emphasized in the given analysis.

### *Perception*

Facts of perception figure prominently in a number of analyses bearing on nature experience and its outcomes. However, an overriding concern with perception is most evident in psychophysical landscape assessment research and in related research by Wohlwill. The goal of the former is to describe mathematical relationships between specified physical characteristics of the landscape (e.g., tree density, tree size, depth of view) and psychological responses (e.g., immediate judgments of preference, aesthetic value, scenic beauty, or fittingness of development) (Daniel & Vining, 1983; Zube, Sell, & Taylor, 1982). By focusing on physical features, statements about likely impacts of human activity on landscape quality are made possible. This is valued by land managers and others responsible for protecting landscape quality. The natural-built distinction may enter into a psychophysical study of landscape quality by way of a perceived naturalness dimension or some analog of it, such as congruity between a human-made feature and its natural surroundings (Daniel & Vining, 1983; Wohlwill, 1982; Wohlwill & Harris, 1980).

Although not all of Wohlwill's work followed a psychophysical approach (Zube et al., 1982), he nonetheless showed a particular interest in physical determinants of perception and behavior (e.g., Wohlwill, 1973). Wohlwill drew on Gibson's (e.g., 1950, 1966) ideas about visual perception and Berlyne's (1960) experimental aesthetics in organizing his thinking about differential response to natural and human-made environments (e.g., Wohlwill, 1973, 1976, 1983).

Gibson (1966) argued for an ecological approach to perception, assuming an information-seeking human moving within an encompassing environment. His treatment of visual information as structure that allows discrimination of objects and events in the environment seems to underlie much of Wohlwill's (1983) effort to differentiate between the natural and non-natural domains on the basis of stimulus characteristics. Gibson proposed that without structure, stimulus energy conveys no information. "The natural structure of information from the near environment conveys information directly" (Gibson, 1966, p. 245). In the case of visual perception, three physical causes of structure are given: illuminated surfaces of the environment that face in different directions, illuminated surface colors of the environment, and variable illumination of the environment. "Ambient light from the terrestrial environment has structure from all three causes in combination" (Gibson, 1966, p. 240); percepts caused by this structure are of "boundaries, textures, patterns, and forms of light."

In an early analysis of differential response to natural and built environments, Wohlwill (1973) discussed the link between the theories of Gibson and Berlyne (1960). Berlyne's (1960) work fills in the aesthetic response part of the story. Aesthetic responses are thought to be a function of collative properties possessed by visual stimuli and of exploratory behavior evoked by those stimuli. Examples of collative properties are novelty and complexity. According to Wohlwill (1976, p. 40):

> The essential aspect of these several stimulus attributes is that all relate to the uncertainty contained within a stimulus, or the conflict it engenders in the individual in attempting to interpret it. Accordingly, a stimulus elicits investigatory or exploratory responses designed to reduce the uncertainty or conflict engendered by it, to the extent that it possesses such collative properties.

Two kinds of exploratory behavior were distinguished by Berlyne (1960). Specific exploration involves a search for information that will help reduce the uncertainty and arousal prompted when a stimulus is encountered. Diversive exploration is directed toward finding a stimulus configuration that promotes optimal levels of uncertainty and arousal. Aesthetic response follows with management of the uncertainty and arousal engendered by stimuli encountered and sought. Also involved in aesthetic response are variables such as fittingness and coherence, which "refer predominantly to structural properties of the configuration of a visual field, and of the elements of the field in relation to one another" (Wohlwill, 1976, p. 58). To the extent these variables operate in perception, a person is able to impose order on the visual stimulus array and thus reduce uncertainty.

In first using the collative properties concept in an analysis of environments, Wohlwill (1968) sought to assess the role of complexity (amount of variation in the stimulus) in determining exploration (number of exposures) of and rated preference for photographic slide stimuli. Included among the test stimuli were pictures of everyday environments. Although no rationale was given for its use, a natural vs. human-made dimension served as one of the five ways chosen to organize test stimuli along the complexity dimension. It was the only content/environmental criterion. The remaining four criteria all concerned more particular aspects of stimulus attributes (i.e., color, shape, texture, direction of dominant lines). Wohlwill found exploratory behavior to increase as a function of complexity, while preference was greatest for an intermediate level of complexity.

In a later analysis, Wohlwill (1983) hypothesized that perceptual differences between the natural and non-natural domains contributed to differences in the diversity and complexity to be experienced in such environments. Among visually perceptible differences, the natural environment's "irregular lines and curvilinear lines and edges, continuous gradations of shape and color, and irregular, rough textures" were contrasted with the "regular lines and rectilinear edges, sharp discontinuities and abrupt transitions, and highly regular, smooth features" of the built environment (Wohlwill, 1983, pp. 14-15). Visual stimulus attributes of natural environments were seen as converging to produce a desirable, intermediate level of complexity, whereas built environments were seen to be relatively high in complexity or low in diversity.

In addition to visual differences, Wohlwill (1983) touched on a variety of other aspects of the stimulus field that might be expected to vary between natural and built settings. His assertions about differences in qualities of movement are relevant to nature experience benefits beyond preference. Movement in natural environments was hypothesized to be of lower intensity and greater predictability than movement in built environments, and the perception of this conducive to relaxation and restoration.

In research on adaptation level, Wohlwill (e.g., 1973, 1974, 1976) elaborated further on the basis for aesthetic and evaluative responses to environments. Adaptation level (Helson, 1964) refers to the aggregated experience an individual brings to bear on perception and evaluation. Thus, a person's experience in and adaptedness to a particular environment should affect the way they perceive and respond to other environments. This idea was supported in a study of people who had just moved to a mid-sized city (Wohlwill & Kohn, 1973). Their evaluations of certain physical and social features of the city (e.g., air pollution, noise, pace of life) reflected the size of the community they had just moved from. For example, those coming from smaller towns tended to view the pace of life in their new city as rushed, while those coming from a larger metropolitan area more often felt the pace of life was relaxed. Adaptation level effects should also hold on the more particular level of collative and structural properties. Wohlwill (1974, p. 137) claimed that optimal levels of stimulation, "rather than representing an intrinsically determined characteristic of the effects of stimulus dimensions [e.g., intensity, diversity, patterning] on the individual, are a function of his history of experience with such dimensions." Affective responses such as expressions of preference are thus also related to the relatively stable adaptation levels. Wohlwill (1973) anticipated the argument that evidence of adaptation level effects could be used in an attempt to undermine claims about environmental determinism. He countered by asserting that adaptation level effects are only meaningful in relation to objective criteria, and that adaptation levels can only mediate perceptions of different environments. Furthermore, adaptation takes place within certain limits of tolerance, established in the course of evolution (Wohlwill, 1974).

In sum, Wohlwill's work is distinctive in its assumptions about adaptation levels and in its reference to molecular, physical features as the basis for a perceptually-based differentiation between natural and built environments. However, like other work on nature experience it joins ideas about the visual stimulus array with a Gibsonian view on perception in arriving at an understanding of aesthetic response to environments. Related ideas about uncertainty, arousal, and exploratory behavior are also common to other models of aesthetic response to the natural environments. Finally, most of the discussion concerns relatively immediate affective outcomes of natural environment experience, with preference treated as the principal dependent variable. Outside of the discussion of adaptation level, there is little analysis of potential long-term effects.

### *Affect and Arousal*

A number of explanations start from the idea that some part of an ability to realize nature experience benefits is, in a sense, built-in. Many thousands of generations of early hominids lived and reproduced in savannah-like natural settings. As their progeny we are genetically best adapted to the demands imposed by such environments. This adaptedness is manifest not only in the physiological systems necessary for survival, but also in psychological systems. Our basic capabilities for apprehending, interpreting, evaluating, and acting upon information from the environment are best suited to the environments from which humans emerged.

Working with these assumptions, evolutionary approaches give first consideration to the benefit value of preferences. Preferences were initially beneficial in that they were adaptive. Individuals able to quickly and unconsciously attach appropriate threat or sustenance values to given environmental conditions were more likely to enjoy opportunities to contribute to the gene pool. This operation of natural selection remains manifest to some degree in contemporary environmental preferences. Although preference responses may now have less significance for biological survival, they retain benefit value in that they signal positive states (e.g., aesthetic satisfaction, lack of anxiety). These states imply the operation of the various psychological and physiological systems evolved for knowing and acting.

Models with an evolutionary basis assume that selection for an ability to exhibit preferences would have taken place while humans were still in natural environments. It follows that in evolutionary times certain natural settings or environmental characteristics would not have been preferred and would have engendered unpleasant feelings when encountered. Thus, an environmental preference expressed now is relative both to unpreferred prehistoric natural environments and to other contemporary environments, whether built or natural.

Although commonly assuming links between preference and evolutionary process, models of this type vary somewhat in their treatment of environmental conditions favored in natural selection. They also vary in the extent to which they go beyond preference to explain other benefits. To the extent that they do this, the role of the natural-built distinction in generating benefits becomes clearer. Then a variety of benefits are seen to come out of nature experience at all levels, realized spontaneously and also over longer periods of time. Finally, they vary in terms of the psychological processes emphasized as agents in the generation of beneficial outcomes. Some, notably the Kaplans and associates (e.g., Herzog, Kaplan, & Kaplan, 1989) emphasize cognitive processes, while others (e.g., Appleton, 1975; Orians, 1980; Ulrich, 1983) emphasize aspects of the emotional response to nature. The better known of the latter explanations will be detailed next.

***Habitat theory.*** As described by Appleton (1975, p. 69), habitat theory would have aesthetic satisfaction arise from "the spontaneous perception of landscape features which, in their shapes, colors, spatial arrangements and other visible attributes, act as sign-stimuli indicative of environmental conditions favorable to survival, whether they really are favorable or not."

This approach is exemplified by Orians' (1980) analysis, which explains environmental preferences through reference to underlying behavioral choice mechanisms. These mechanisms were shaped in the course of evolution by temporal and spatial variability in habitat suitability. Orians analyzes factors operating in the choice process animals might go through in a search for suitable habitat (e.g., knowledge about a potential habitat choice, time available for selecting among choices, variability in relevant environmental features). Assuming that habitat selection typically takes place under conditions of ignorance, Orians argues for the utility of strong, spontaneous emotional responses toward suitable and unsuitable habitats. He groups factors that influenced the suitability of early human habitats into categories of resource availability and protection from predators. The analysis leads to the conclusion that "tropical savannahs, particularly those with irregular relief providing cliffs and caves, should have been the optimal environment for early man" (Orians, 1980, p. 57). Thus, strong positive responses to such settings should have been selected for in the evolution of human habitat choice mechanisms.

Orians (1980, 1986) supports his hypothesis through reference to several lines of evidence: historical accounts of landscape preferences, spending for homes and for recreation access, common practice in the choice and arrangement of aesthetic vegetation, landscape painting, and environmental evaluation research. The evidence marshalled suggests that deeper benefits may accompany these overt expressions of preferences, but Orians does not extend his discussions beyond initial emotional benefits.

Orians (1980) does not clearly indicate the salience of built settings for current manifestations of preference-related behaviors. His main concern is for the persistence of preference responses toward savannah-like landscapes. It is the non-preferred features of prehistoric natural landscapes that are indicated as important to the development of these response orientations. One may, however, consider the possibility that the natural-built distinction matters to people, given their efforts to maintain contact with savannah-like environments even when within built surroundings.

***Prospect-refuge theory.*** Orians (1980) draws conclusions from habitat theory about preferences for savannah-type landscapes with opportunities for shelter. These fit with conclusions arrived at by Appleton (1975) in his presentation of prospect-refuge theory. Yet

Appleton is more specific in treating symbolic aspects of the human-landscape interchange and in setting out landscape characteristics that should influence preference. Indeed, prospect-refuge theory is a reaction to the general nature of habitat theory. Assuming that the ability to move toward a goal while out of the sight of predators would have been of first importance to survival, the environment's potential for supporting this ability should have drawn affective responses before other indicators of survival potential.

The idea of seeing without being seen thus motivates Appleton's analysis of landscape into prospects, refuges, and hazards. Hazard is important to the analysis as the justification of the need for refuge and for seeing without being seen. A hazard can be animate (e.g., a predator) or inanimate (e.g., weather). It can also be seen in an obstacle to free movement (impediment hazard) or in the absence of some desired affordance, such as privacy, or survival requirement, such as water (deficiency hazard).

A refuge may serve as a shelter or as a hiding place. It may be that it does not serve both functions simultaneously; a refuge might offer shelter from a storm yet not hide the occupant from the sight of a predator. Thus, the distinction between shelter and hide assumes importance relevant to the type of hazard. Aside from function, refuges can also be characterized by their accessibility, efficacy, origin (natural vs. artificial), and substance (earth refuges such as caves, vegetation refuges such as trees or grass, and nebulous refuges such as fog).

Prospects, or views outward, are of two general types. Direct prospects are the views available from the presently occupied place, or primary vantage point. Panoramas and vistas are examples, with panoramas not being bounded by objects in the landscape as are vistas. Indirect prospects, such as deflected vistas, imply views that might be attained if one could reach points farther off in the landscape, referred to as secondary vantage points.

In addition to being more specific than habitat theory in its treatment of landscape features, prospect-refuge theory is more explicitly psychological in its emphasis on sign-stimuli and symbols. Although many hazards may no longer be salient, response to landscape is still determined to some extent by prospect and refuge values. Variation in the aesthetic experience of landscape is influenced by variation in the objects that symbolize prospects and refuges, the spatial arrangement of symbols, and the equilibrium between prospect and refuge symbols, among other factors. Furthermore, prospect-refuge symbolism holds on more than one level. It derives not only from the physical characteristics of landscape objects, but also from the imagination and experience of the observer.

Fitting with the emphasis on symbolism is a concern for perception. Prospect-refuge theory could be understood in Gibsonian (1979) terms as entailing description of landscapes in terms of prospect and refuge affordances. Affordances are functional values inherent in physical characteristics of the environment (e.g., a surface may be perceived to afford walking or sitting).

Prospect-refuge theory presents a challenge to understanding the role of the natural-built distinction in guiding landscape preferences. Appleton argues that aesthetic satisfaction derives from functional symbolism adhering to landscape elements and to specific patterns of relations between them. Whether those elements are natural or man-made assumes secondary relevance. However, Appleton does acknowledge some correspondence between the naturalness of landscape elements and their potential preference value in talking about the naturalizing of built elements in the landscape.

Appleton provides fruitful answers to questions regarding what we like about landscape and why. However, prospect-refuge theory has been little used by psychological researchers as a source of hypotheses. Work that has taken up on prospect-refuge theory has been reviewed by Appleton (1984). Of this, the study by Woodcock (1984) is noteworthy for showing similarities between prospect-refuge explanations for preference and explanations offered by other evolutionary approaches. More recent studies have framed environmental choices of teenagers (Owens, 1988) and preschool children (Kirkby, 1989) in prospect-refuge terms.

***Ulrich's psychoevolutionary model.*** Ulrich's (1983; Ulrich et al., 1991) model for affective and aesthetic response to environments has a number of basic assumptions in common with those analyses described above. Rapid-onset emotional responses to certain environmental configurations are assumed to have been adaptive in evolution. Such responses now reflect the play of evolved processes no longer so critical to survival. Exploration and avoidance do, however, continue to be important for maintaining acceptable arousal levels.

Yet Ulrich's efforts are distinctive in important respects. First, he is more deliberate in his treatment of the first moments of an environmental encounter. Cognitive processes have no sway in an initial affective response, nor in the immediately consequent arousal change. Rather, the affective response is assumed to be directly elicited by environmental preferenda. Environmental preferenda are features or stimulus characteristics whose vague nature may preclude cognitive judgments but which still suffice for eliciting generalized affect (after Zajonc, 1980). Ulrich (1983) assumes three basic kinds of preferenda in natural environments: gross structural aspects of settings, gross depth properties that require little inference, and general classes of environmental content. More specifically, affective reactions are evoked by a scene's complexity, focality (degree to which it contains a focal point or an area that attracts the observer's attention), depth, and ground surface texture. Threatening features, deflected vistas, and water also may work in drawing out an initial reaction. In this specification of environmental features, one sees the influence of Berlyne and additional correspondence between Ulrich's model and the analyses of Wohlwill, Orians, and Appleton.

A second distinctive feature of Ulrich's framework is precise description of the underlying affective processes (Figure 17.1). The model starts with recognition of the affective state brought to a new situation. Previous experiences, immediate and more remote, guide attention. What is attended to and visually perceived will elicit an initial affective reaction of a generalized character (e.g., interest or fear). Again, this reaction is assumed to be elicited by environmental preferenda and to take place without cognitive mediation. The affective state then influences psychophysiological arousal, cognition, and motivation. The model additionally portrays culture and experience feeding into cognitive processes operating on the initial affective reaction. It is through the post-cognitive affective state that cognition may thus come to modify psychophysiological arousal. Together with the independent effect of the initial affective state, the post-cognitive states of affect and arousal give the motivational prompt for adaptive behavior or functioning. This may be approach, avoidance, maintenance of on-going activity, or scanning of the scene accompanied by varying degrees of vigilance.

Parsons (1991) speculates on additional neuropsychological details of Ulrich's model. Particular attention is given to the subcortical structures likely to serve as the hard wiring for the pre-cognitive processing implied by the affective primacy assumption. Two components of the limbic system, the amygdala and hippocampus, are viewed as particularly relevant to environmental preference research, given their possible roles in modulating affective reactions and comparing incoming stimuli with stored stimuli. Other research overviewed (e.g., Henry & Meehan, 1981) draws connections between those structures and immune function, and gives Parsons a basis for discussion of the connection between environmental aesthetics and physiological health benefits.

A third feature of Ulrich's work is its unambiguous concern for benefits beyond aesthetic preference, accompanied by an interest in the role of the natural-built distinction in the experience of environment. These joined concerns are furthermore tied in with evolutionary assumptions. The significance of the distinction for emotional and physiological well-being has been examined in studies of stress-reducing effects of natural and urban scenes. An initial study (Ulrich, 1979) measured change in the affective states of individuals experiencing test anxiety. Subjects who viewed slides of nature scenes evidenced a gain in positive affect and a decline in fear arousal, while subjects who saw urban scenes showed an increase in sadness and a decline in attentiveness.

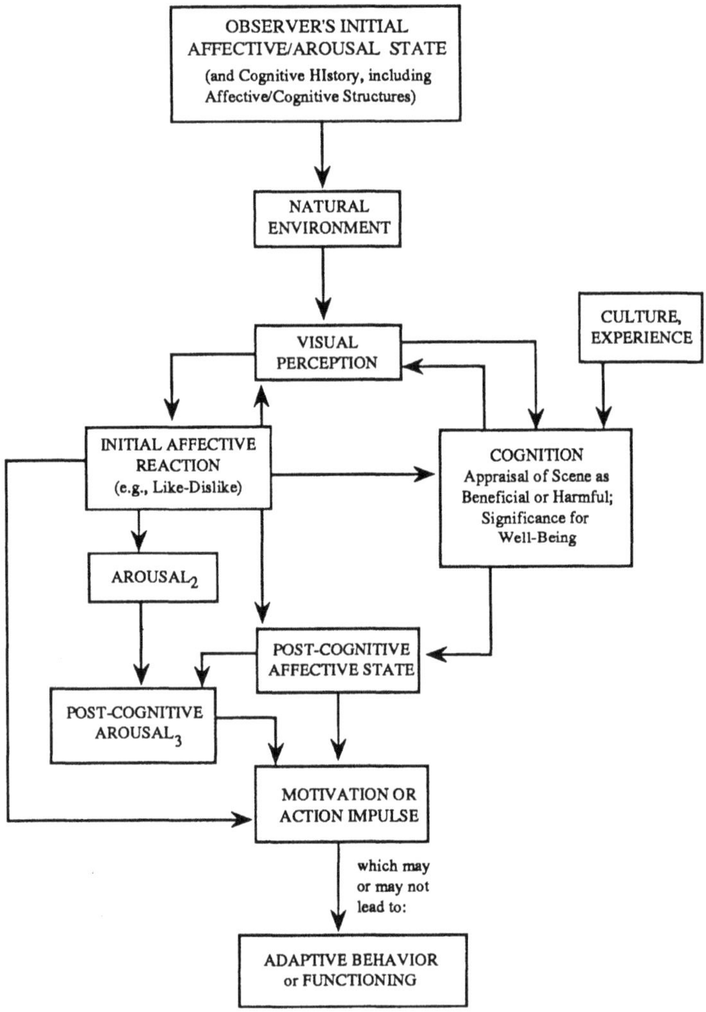


figure 17.1. Ulrich's psychoevolutionary model of affective/arousal response to a natural scene. From Altman & Wohlwill, 1983. Copyright by Plenum. Reprinted by permission.

A hallmark of the subsequent benefits research and a fourth identifying characteristic of Ulrich's work is the use of physiological indices of arousal. Use of physiological measurement methods follows from dictates of arousal theory and the need to monitor arousal level on a continuous basis during the initial period of an environmental encounter. Findings of differences in brain wave activity (Ulrich, 1981), skin conductance, muscle tension, and indices of cardiovascular function (Ulrich et al., 1991), in addition to differences in self-reports of emotion, support the notion that scenes of unspectacular natural environments have greater stress-reducing effects and sustain interest to a greater degree than do scenes of everyday urban environments. Differential effects were documented in unstressed (Ulrich, 1981) as well as stressed (Ulrich et al., 1991) individuals. However, psychophysiological restoration effects of nature experience were only apparent in the latter.

Clearly, the psychoevolutionary framework deals with immediate effects of environmental encounters. An emphasis on short-term encounters is not necessarily a limitation, since, as suggested by Ulrich et al. (1991), most encounters with nature are of a short duration. Moreover, Parsons' (1991) discussion suggests that Ulrich's (1983) framework can encompass some health benefits from temporally extended experiences. He maintains that urban environments "may be uniquely stressful because there is nothing discernibly habitable about them to a low level affective processing system" (Parsons, 1991, p. 16). Consequently, an individual in an urban environment is engaged much of the time in a low-level, subconscious stress response. This is presumably interrupted during a nature experience, whether brief or more extended.

One other feature of Ulrich's work is its specification of conditions antecedent to the realization of nature benefits. Most of the emphasis is on stress, evoked by situations that challenge or threaten well-being. His research shows a particular concern for the negative emotional and physiological arousal components of stress and for stress as a response to threat and urban conditions. He concludes that some restorative effects of nature, such as lowered psychophysiological arousal, are most likely to occur when the individual is stressed. Unstressed individuals may, however, still realize benefits of improved affect and sustained interest and attention. Furthermore, Ulrich (1981) notes that understimulated individuals may benefit more from some contact with urban settings than from contact with nature.

### *Cognition and Affect*

An emphasis on cognitive processes distinguishes the research on preference and benefits by the Kaplans and their associates (e.g., Herzog et al., 1982; R. Kaplan & S. Kaplan, 1989; S. Kaplan & R. Kaplan, 1982; S. Kaplan & Talbot, 1983). The Kaplans do not impose the division between perception and cognition depicted in Ulrich's model. Rather, they assume that perception is inherently cognitive and that thinking in turn depends on the structures that emerge from perception (S. Kaplan & R. Kaplan, 1982).

The Kaplans have long been at the forefront of efforts to build theoretically rigorous explanations for nature experience on evolutionary assumptions (e.g., S. Kaplan, 1972). The cognitive emphasis of their approach is apparent in a conception of human evolution as driven by pressing demands for the acquisition and rapid processing of information (S. Kaplan & R. Kaplan, 1978, 1982). On leaving the trees for savannahs well-populated with predators, prehumans came under selective pressure to build on visual and object perception capabilities in development of an ability to quickly anticipate and respond to events in the environment. For continued survival, sustained in large part by hunting, selection would have favored protohuman abilities to comprehend extended spatial areas and to plan. Selection in favor of these capabilities would help explain the transformation of the small prehuman brain into the relatively large and differentiated mental apparatus we use to support elaborated cognitive representations of environments.

Environmental preferences represent ingrained sensitivity to informational needs (R. Kaplan & S. Kaplan, 1989; S. Kaplan & R. Kaplan, 1982). Early humans are assumed to have been motivated to expand upon the cognitive maps they relied upon for survival. Their success would have been determined to some degree by their responsiveness to conditions which affected way-finding. Aside from ready comprehension of the environment being explored, the possibilities for investigating further would also have worked to establish preferences. Thus, informational qualities of the visual array that supported needs for both understanding and exploration were influential in instituting preferences. The desire to maintain cognitive clarity continues to undergird aesthetic responses. The initial aesthetic response, though unconscious, is cognitive in character, and guides affect (S. Kaplan, 1987a).

Four informational qualities are ordered along a temporal dimension in the Kaplans' preference framework (see Table 17.1). An immediate need for making sense of or understanding the environment is supported by the coherence of its perceived elements. Continuing involvement or exploration is encouraged by the complexity inhering to that set of elements. The potential for making sense in the future is in the legibility of what lies ahead. A legible view suggests one can go further without getting lost. Mystery, the promise of additional information with a change in vantage point, may induce further exploration. It thus signifies future involvement.

As in the preceding analyses, a tension between order and uncertainty is implicated in aesthetic response, a tension that arises from the same (e.g., complexity) or similar factors (cf., mystery with deflected vistas). Sufficient coherence and legibility are needed to make sense of the environment, but their action must be balanced by enough complexity and mystery to engage the individual. Prediction must be possible, but not trivial. Here again, too, aesthetic responses have significance in their links with motivation, exploratory behavior, and survival. Further, in addition to informational qualities, we again see particular contents signaling survival values. In modelling preference, natural elements such as trees and water are designated as primary landscape factors because their very presence appears to have a positive impact. Here the preference framework has common ground with habitat theory. Numerous studies starting from this framework have documented the influences of contents and informational factors on preferences for photographic scenes (reviewed in R. Kaplan & S. Kaplan, 1989).

TABLE 17.1
*The Informational Model of Environmental Preference*

| | Making Sense | Involvement |
|---|---|---|
| Present or Immediate | Coherence | Complexity |
| Future or Promised | Legibility | Mystery |

From S. Kaplan and R. Kaplan, 1982. Reprinted by permission.

The natural-built distinction enters this research both through informational properties and through contents. For example, early research considered the possibility that built environments have greater visual complexity than natural environments (S. Kaplan, R. Kaplan, & Wendt, 1972). Discussion of this possibility led others (e.g., Wohlwill, 1983) to suggest differences between natural and built environments in the ways complexity may be balanced by structural variables such as coherence. As for content, a number of studies indicate a general preference for natural scenes as compared to scenes of built settings (R. Kaplan & S. Kaplan, 1989). Furthermore, built settings with natural elements are likely to be preferred over those without natural elements (e.g., Herzog, 1989; Herzog et al., 1982).

The natural-built distinction also plays in the consideration of environments that serve a restorative function (R. Kaplan & S. Kaplan, 1989; S. Kaplan, 1983; S. Kaplan & Talbot, 1983). A restorative environment helps one replenish the capacity for voluntary attention, or concentration. Heavy demands on this limited capacity may be made in efforts to maintain cognitive clarity while functioning in one's everyday built and social environments. Depletion of the capacity for voluntary attention leads to mental fatigue, a condition resembling overload (e.g., Cohen, 1978; Milgram, 1970; Wohlwill, 1970). Although different from stress, mental fatigue nonetheless may have similar negative emotional, behavioral, interpersonal, and social consequences (S. Kaplan, 1987b). Amelioration of mental fatigue is assumed to follow from a relaxing of demands for voluntary attention and functioning in ways that draw forth involuntary, or effortless, attention. Natural environments are thought to have disproportionately greater restorative potential because functioning in them allows involuntary attention to predominate. This follows from the assumption that people are genetically prepared to handle patterns of information characteristic of natural environments with little attentional effort.

Although restoration may be more likely in natural environments, the explanatory framework for restorative experiences acknowledges the possibility that most environments can aid restoration (Hartig, Mang, & Evans 1991; R. Kaplan & S. Kaplan, 1989; S. Kaplan, 1983; S. Kaplan & Talbot, 1983). The framework attributes restoration to four co-acting factors. Being away denotes geographical and/or psychological distance from the situations or pursuits that are taxing voluntary attention. Fascination refers to the involuntary attention held by environmental contents or engaged in making sense of and exploring the environment. Coherence relies on the structure perceived in the environment, and speaks to an absence of confusion and to a sense of connectedness between the setting occupied and some larger frame of reference. Finally, compatibility lies in the match between one's goals and inclinations and the information and constraints in the setting.

The Kaplans and associates have documented a variety of benefits in keeping with their model of restorative experience. Their research has looked at encounters with nature taking place on different environmental scales and for differing periods of time. Initial studies in a multi-year program of research on a 14-day outdoor challenge program recorded a variety of self-reported improvements from the wilderness experience. Participants showed positive change in areas such as affect, ability to concentrate, outlook on life, and self-concept (R. Kaplan, 1974, 1984). Later studies charted the unfolding and deepening of effects over the course of a briefer, 9-day wilderness experience (S. Kaplan & Talbot, 1983; Talbot & S. Kaplan, 1986). Research on residential satisfaction and other benefits from brief yet frequent contacts with nearby nature bears on more immediately available opportunities for restorative experience (R. Kaplan, 1983, 1985; Talbot, Bardwell, & R. Kaplan, 1987). On an even smaller scale, gardening can be salutary in fostering fascination and tranquility (R. Kaplan, 1973; R. Kaplan & S. Kaplan, 1989).

The Kaplans' restorative experience framework has been the starting point for research by the authors on beneficial effects of natural environment experiences (Hartig et al., 1991). An initial quasi-experimental field study compared emotional and attentional restoration outcomes of wilderness vacation, non-wilderness vacation, and no-vacation conditions. This study used only backpackers as subjects. This helped control for the potential selection bias that has troubled other research on wilderness experience (e.g., Driver et al., 1987). The study also used a behavioral measure of attentional restoration (proofreading performance). Behavioral measures are less subject to extraneous influences than self-reports, and convergence between self-report and behavioral measures allows greater confidence in the validity of results. Post-test proofreading and three-week follow-up scores of happiness indicated that the wilderness vacation condition engendered differentially greater and longer lasting attentional and emotional benefits, respectively. The proofreading results furthermore support the view that attentional processes are at work in restoration.

A second field study reported by Hartig et al. (1991) allowed greater generalizability of findings than was possible with the all-backpackers sample of the first study. Randomly assigned subjects walked through either a natural environment or an urban environment, or sat in a chair reading magazines and listening to music (passive relaxation). Prior to their treatment experience subjects completed a lengthy series of attentionally demanding tasks, thus ensuring comparability across groups in levels of pre-treatment cognitive fatigue. In addition to the self-report and proofreading performance measures used in the initial study, subjects completed a preliminary version of a perceived restorativeness scale (PRS) to evaluate their treatment experience in terms of being away, fascination, coherence, and compatibility (after S. Kaplan & Talbot, 1983). In this way it became possible to examine the match between restoration and operations of the theoretical factors. The natural environment group again showed greater Post-test emotional and attentional restoration than did the other two groups. Furthermore, those outcomes on which the groups differed were reliably correlated with a PRS summary score. Taken together, the two studies offer evidence of emotional and attentional restoration following experiences of different length in natural environments at different degrees of remove from built settings. They also give support for the restorative experience framework.

### *Learning*

Some explanations for nature experience benefits emphasize the shaping of individuals' behavior by perceived contingencies of preceding actions. Learning models posit differences in the reinforcement or feedback shaping individuals' behavior in natural as compared to everyday physical and social environments. The net effect is thought to be change in patterns of behavior and views of self. Personal growth and correction of maladaptive practices are general outcomes. Many more specific outcomes have been claimed, such as improved problem-solving ability, greater self-reliance, and changes in self-concept, self-esteem, body image, and perceived locus of control. Effects typically unfold over the course of days or weeks, with some persisting well beyond the time actually in the environment.

Immersion in a natural environment is indicated or implied by benefits explanations that invoke learning processes. Reference is often made to wilderness environments, and often within discussion of personal growth or therapeutic camping programs. For those wanting to understand natural environment experience, however, the joining of therapeutic program with environmental experience presents some problems. The structure, staffing, and activities of the program may be more salutary for participants than the environment in which the program is being conducted. Natural environments facilitate their conduct, but may not be seen as essential components. When a program is conducted in a natural environment it is difficult to separate environmental influences from program influences. Compounding these difficulties, methodological problems have plagued this area. These points and the details of various programs are discussed in a number of reviews (e.g., Driver et al., 1987; Levitt, 1990). In addition, benefits from a single program experience may be neither as deep nor as lasting as those accruing to wilderness users who are self-motivated and go to wilderness more regularly (Schreyer, Williams R., & Haggard 1990). Yet Driver et al. (1987) present data from aperiodic wilderness users indicating that they do value the personal development outcomes offered by outdoor programs.

In his review of related literature, Knopf (1987) lists five ways natural environments have been differentiated from everyday environments as settings for behavior. Conditions antecedent to the realization of benefits are thus identified through negation. First, a natural environment, wilderness particularly, challenges "accustomed behavior patterns, resources, and problem-solving styles" (Knopf, 1987, p. 787). Second, it is impartial or indifferent, and gives little negative or judgmental feedback (see also Wohlwill, 1983). Third, citing Bernstein (1972), the relative manipulability and predictability of a natural environment obviates being consumed with defensive, coping behaviors. Fourth, it is more allowing of self-expression. Finally, natural settings allow a greater sense of personal control. This last hypothesis has been challenged by S. Kaplan and Talbot (1983), who assert that relaxation of efforts to control the environment was important to participants in their wilderness program. We note here that, although learning explanations are not concerned with issues of environmental preference, accounts of wilderness programs often refer to a liking for that setting relative to everyday settings.

As an example of benefit explanations that invoke learning processes, we can refer to Newman's (1980) model for amelioration of learned helplessness through structured wilderness programs. Learned helplessness follows from the inability to perceive contingency between one's efforts toward a desired outcome and the outcome that actually follows. The person learns to believe they cannot influence outcomes (Seligman, 1975). The condition is attended by emotional, cognitive, motivational, and possibly self-concept deficits, such as depression, impaired problem-solving ability, inability to persist at a task in the face of failure, and low self-esteem (e.g., Abramson, Seligman, & Teasdale, 1978). Causal attributions mediate between expectations of success and the effects of perceptions of effort-outcome contingency. The learned helpless are thought to make attributions of failure to stable, global, internal causes (e.g., persistent, pervasive lack of ability), and to attribute success to external, specific, and possibly unstable causes (e.g., good luck in the particular instance; Abramson et al., 1978; Weiner, 1980).

According to Newman (1980), the structure of Outward Bound style programs and characteristics of their wilderness settings aid the development of clear and realistic patterns of causal attributions and expectations. They also promote acquisition of skills and mastery, encourage a sense of competence or controllability, and help direct perceptions of competence so they positively influence self-concept and self-esteem. Several wilderness characteristics are thought to be instrumental in this. First, in wilderness there are lessened demands on information-processing capabilities. A person freed from having to deal with the usual mental noise may be able to gain needed insight into their attribution patterns. Second, stressful conditions in everyday environments (e.g., noise, crowding, stimulus ambiguity) are either not present or more easily seen as under one's control. Conditions not under one's control (e.g., weather) are readily seen as impartial and out of the control of all people. Third, the novelty and threat values of wilderness evoke close attention and call forth coping efforts. Dealing with manageable doses of confusion and anxiety gives an opportunity to develop a sense of competence in dealing with unexpected situations. Fourth, being in wilderness means engaging in survival activities that promote competence building and give opportunities for improving attributions about success and failure.

Others have made similar observations about ways in which wilderness encounters encourage adaptiveness and personal development, but without placing the encounter in the context of a structured program or referring to the correction of pathological conditions. For example, Reser and Scherl (1988) present a model for person-environment transactions that occur in intrinsically motivating activities such as running or wilderness trekking. They argue that during these activities, person-environment transactions involve feedback that is clear and unambiguous. Because of these qualities, such information has a reward value proportional to the ambiguity and lack of clarity in information drawn from the environment in general. They further assume that feedback obtained from the everyday physical and social environment is typically indirect, ambiguous, routinized, and role prescribed. Their model is also interesting because it integrates aspects of a learning approach with attentional and information processing considerations from evolutionary models such as that of the Kaplans. Clear and unambiguous feedback has reward value in part because of its utility in optimal functioning for a biological information-processing system. Finally, in looking at voluntary participation rather than participation as a form of therapeutic intervention, Reser and Scherl give insight on benefits of continued participation.

## Prospects

The theories described above share some assumptions about the psychological processes responsible for the realization of benefits. Some also have similar views on the implications of the natural-built distinction. Examination of the commonalities suggests that synthesis of different theories is possible.

One possible synthesis would draw on the frameworks of Ulrich (1983) and the Kaplans (1989) to provide a more complete treatment of restorative benefits. Standing alone, their analyses appear to treat different aspects of restoration. Ulrich emphasizes immediate psychophysiological recovery from stressful experiences, whereas the Kaplans' first concern is with replenishment of attentional capacity following cognitive fatigue, which they differentiate from stress. Although the question of whether the models are entirely compatible can be contested, one cannot ignore the relatedness of physiological and cognitive states of well-being.

A second possible synthesis would join the Kaplans' restorative experience framework with key elements of a learning model. Nature experiences may inoculate people against stress and attentional demands met in the following weeks (Hartig et al., 1991). For understanding even longer-term effects of nature experience, a framework which emphasizes both cognitive and learning processes could prove strongest. Such a framework would join ideas about the achievement of cognitive clarity and reflection on one's life with ideas about the shaping and reinforcement of desired, adaptive behavior. Newman's (1980) analysis moves in this direction. Wilderness survival activities are seen doing more than promoting competence building and giving opportunities for improving attributions about success and failure. They also are thought to encourage a sense of personal involvement that reinforces cognitive clarity gained from a reduction in information-processing demands. The model of Reser and Scherl (1988) also integrates learning processes with the sort of cognitive processes handled in the Kaplans' framework.

Other psychological factors related to well-being have received little treatment in the preceding analyses, yet are thought to be sensitive to differences between natural and built environments. For example, developmental processes may be differently affected by natural and urban environments (e.g., Wohlwill & Heft, 1987). Environmental dispositions as dimensions of personality may reflect fairly stable attitudes toward natural and built settings and their suitability for different purposes, as witnessed by findings obtained with the Wildernism-Urbanism scale (e.g., Hendee, Catton, Marlow, & Brockman, 1968) and the Environmental Response Inventory (e.g., McKechnie, 1970). Memory for places may also be sensitive to a natural-built distinction (e.g., Sebba, 1991).

Just as the theories above do not account for the full range of psychological processes that might be sensitive to a natural-built distinction, they do not indicate all features which might distinguish nature experience from the experience of the built. Earlier, reference was made to the dovetailing of stress research with research on restorative experience. We can look to the stress research for signs of other factors that work to create conditions in contrast to which nature experience proves beneficial. Consideration of research in other disciplines, such as geography, can serve the same purpose.

## Acknowledgements

Preparation of this chapter was supported by a Thord-Gray Memorial Fellowship from The American-Scandinavian Foundation to the first author. The first author is grateful for the support of Tommy Gärling and the Department of Psychology at the University of Umeå, his hosts during the fellowship period.

## References

Abramson, L., Seligman, M., & Teasdale, J. (1978). Learned helplessness in humans: Critique and reformulation. *Journal of Abnormal Psychology, 87*, 49-74.

Appleton, J. (1975). *The experience of landscape*. London: Wiley.

Appleton, J. (1984). Prospects and refuges re-visited. *Landscape Journal, 3*, 91-103.

Baum, A., Fleming, R., & Davidson, L. M. (1983). Natural disaster and technological catastrophe. *Environment and Behavior, 15*, 333-354.

Berlyne, D. E. (1960). *Conflict, arousal and curiosity*. New York: McGraw-Hill.

Bernstein, A. (1972). Wilderness as a therapeutic behavior setting. *Therapeutic Recreation Journal, 6*, 160-185.

Cohen, S. (1978). Environmental load and the allocation of attention. In A. Baum, J. Singer, & S. Valins (Eds.), *Advances in environmental psychology* (Vol. 1, pp. 1-29). Hillsdale, NJ: Erlbaum.

Daniel, T. C., & Vining, J. (1983). Methodological issues in the assessment of landscape quality. In I. Altman & J. F. Wohlwill (Eds.), *Human behavior and environment: Advances in theory and research* (Vol. 6, pp. 39-84). New York: Plenum.

Driver, B. L., & Greene, P. (1977). Man's nature: Innate determinants of response to natural environments. In *Children, nature, and the urban environment: Proceedings of a symposium fair* (General Technical Report NE-30, pp. 63-72). Upper Darby, PA: United States Department of Agriculture, Forest Service, Northeastern Forest Experiment Station.

Driver, B. L., Nash, R., & Haas, G. (1987). Wilderness benefits: A state-of-knowledge review. In R. C. Lucas (Ed.), *Proceedings - National Wilderness Research Conference: Issues, state-of-knowledge, future directions* (General Technical Report INT-220; pp. 294-319). Ogden, UT: United States Department of Agriculture, Forest Service, Intermountain Research Station.

Evans, G. W., & Cohen, S. (1987). Environmental stress. In D. Stokols & I. Altman (Eds.), *Handbook of environmental psychology* (Vol. 1, pp. 571-610). New York: Wiley.

Gibson, J. J. (1950). *The perception of the visual world*. Boston: Houghton Mifflin.

Gibson, J. J. (1966). *The senses considered as perceptual systems*. Boston: Houghton Mifflin.

Gibson, J. J. (1979). *The ecological approach to visual perception*. Boston: Houghton Mifflin.

Glacken, C. J. (1967). *Traces on the Rhodian shore: Nature and culture in Western thought from ancient times to the end of the eighteenth century*. Berkeley: University of California Press.

Hartig, T., Mang, M., & Evans, G. W. (1991). Restorative effects of natural environment experiences. *Environment and Behavior, 23*, 3-26.

Helson, H. (1964). *Adaptation-level theory: An experimental and systematic approach to behavior*. New York: Harper and Row.

Hendee, J. C., Catton, W. R., Jr., Marlow, L. D., & Brockman, C. F. (1968). *Wilderness users in the Pacific Northwest - Their characteristics, values, and management preferences* (General Technical Report PNW-61). Portland, OR: United States Department of Agriculture, Forest Service, Pacific Northwest Forest and Range Experiment Station.

Henry, J. P., & Meehan, J. P. (1981). Psychosocial stimuli, physiological specificity, and cardiovascular disease. In H. Weiner, M. A. Hofer, & A. J. Stunkard (Eds.), *Brain, behavior, and bodily disease*. New York: Raven Press.

Herzog, T. R. (1989). A cognitive analysis of preference for urban nature. *Journal of Environmental Psychology, 9*, 27-43.

Herzog, T. R., Kaplan, S., & Kaplan, R. (1982). The prediction of preference for unfamiliar urban places. *Population and Environment, 5*, 43-59.

Kaplan, R. (1973). Some psychological benefits of gardening. *Environment and Behavior, 5*, 145-162.

Kaplan, R. (1974). Some psychological benefits of an Outdoor Challenge Program. *Environment and Behavior, 6*, 101-116.

Kaplan, R. (1983). The role of nature in the urban context. In I. Altman & J. F. Wohlwill (Eds.), *Human behavior and environment: Advances in theory and research* (Vol. 6, pp. 127-161). New York: Plenum.

Kaplan, R. (1984). Wilderness perception and psychological benefits: An analysis of a continuing program. *Leisure Sciences, 6*, 271-289.

Kaplan, R. (1985). Nature at the doorstep: Residential satisfaction and the nearby environment. *Journal of Architectural and Planning Research, 2*, 115-127.

Kaplan, R., & Kaplan, S. (1989). *The experience of nature: A psychological perspective*. New York: Cambridge University Press.

Kaplan, S. (1972). The challenge of environmental psychology: A proposal for a new functionalism. *American Psychologist, 27*, 140-143.

Kaplan, S. (1983). A model of person-environment compatibility. *Environment and Behavior, 15*, 311-332.

Kaplan, S. (1987a). Aesthetics, affect, and cognition: Environmental preference from an evolutionary perspective. *Environment and Behavior, 19*, 3-32.

Kaplan, S. (1987b). Mental fatigue and the designed environment. In J. Harvey & D. Henning (Eds.), *Public environments* (pp. 55-60). Washington, DC: Environmental Design Research Association.

Kaplan, S., & Kaplan, R. (1978). *Humanscape: Environments for people*. Belmont, CA: Duxbury Press (republished Ann Arbor, MI: Ulrich's Books, 1982).

Kaplan, S., & Kaplan, R. (1982). *Cognition and environment: Functioning in an uncertain world*. New York: Praeger.

Kaplan, S., & Talbot, J. F. (1983). Psychological benefits of a wilderness experience. In I. Altman & J. F. Wohlwill (Eds.), *Human behavior and environment: Advances in theory and research* (Vol. 6, pp. 163-203). New York: Plenum.

Kaplan, S., Kaplan, R., & Wendt, J. S. (1972). Rated preference and complexity for natural and urban visual material. *Perception and Psychophysics, 12*, 354-356.

Kirkby, M. (1989). Nature as refuge in children's environments. *Children's Environments Quarterly, 6*, 7-12.

Kluckhohn, F. R. (1961). Dominant and variant value orientations. In C. Kluckhohn & H. A. Murray (Eds.), *Personality in nature, society, and culture* (2nd ed.) (pp. 342-357). New York: Knopf.

Knopf, R. C. (1987). Human behavior, cognition, and affect in the natural environment. In D. Stokols & I. Altman (Eds.), *Handbook of environmental psychology* (Vol. 1, pp. 783-825). New York: Wiley.

Levitt, L. (1988). Therapeutic value of wilderness. In H. R. Freilich (Ed.), *Wilderness Benchmark 1988: Proceedings of the National Wilderness Colloquium* (General Technical Report SE-51, pp. 156-168). Asheville, NC: United States Department of Agriculture, Forest Service, Southeastern Forest Experiment Station.

McKechnie, G. E. (1970). Measuring environmental dispositions with the Environmental Response Inventory. In J. Archea & C. Eastman (Eds.), *EDRA Two: Proceedings of the 2nd Annual Environmental Design Research Association Conference* (pp. 320-326). Stroudsburg, PA: Dowden, Hutchinson, & Ross.

Milgram, S. (1970). The experience of living in cities. *Science, 167*, 1461-1468.

Nash, R. (1982). *Wilderness and the American mind* (2nd ed.). New Haven, CT: Yale University Press.

Newman, R. S. (1980). Alleviating learned helplessness in a wilderness setting: An application of attribution theory to Outward Bound. In L. J. Fyans, Jr. (Ed.), *Achievement motivation: Recent trends in theory and research* (pp. 312-345). New York: Plenum.

Orians, G. H. (1980). Habitat selection: General theory and applications to human behavior. In J. S. Lockard (Ed.), *The evolution of human social behavior* (pp. 49-66). New York: Elsevier.

Orians, G. H. (1986). An ecological and evolutionary approach to landscape aesthetics. In E. C. Penning-Rowsell & D. Lowenthal (Eds.), *Landscape meanings and values* (pp. 4-25). London: Allen and Unwin.

Owens, P. E. (1988). Natural landscapes, gathering places, and prospect refuges: Characteristics of outdoor places valued by teens. *Children's Environments Quarterly, 5*, 17-24.

Parsons, R. (1991). The potential influences of environmental perception on human health. *Journal of Environmental Psychology, 11*, 1-23.

Pattison, W. D. (1990/1964). The four traditions of geography. *Journal of Geography, 89*, 202-206.

Reser, J. P., & Scherl, L. M. (1988). Clear and unambiguous feedback: A transactional and motivational analysis of environmental challenge and self-encounter. *Journal of Environmental Psychology, 8*, 269-286.

Rosch, E. H. (1973). Natural categories. *Cognitive Psychology, 4*, 328-350.

Saegert, S., & Winkel, G. H. (1990). Environmental psychology. *Annual Review of Psychology, 41*, 441-477.

Schreyer, R., Williams, D. R., & Haggard, L. (1990). Periodic versus continued wilderness participation - Implications for self-concept enhancement. In A. T. Easley, J. F. Passineau, & B. L. Driver (Eds.), *The use of wilderness for personal growth, therapy, and education* (General Technical Report RM-193, pp. 23-26). Fort Collins, CO: United States Department of Agriculture, Forest Service, Rocky Mountain Forest and Range Experiment Station.

Sebba, R. (1991). The landscapes of childhood: The reflection of childhood's environment in adult memories and in children's attitudes. *Environment and Behavior, 23*, 395-422.

Seligman, M. (1975). *Helplessness: On depression, development, and death*. San Francisco: Freeman.

Suedfeld, P. (1987). Extreme and unusual environments. In D. Stokols & I. Altman (Eds.), *Handbook of environmental psychology* (Vol. 1, pp. 863-887). New York: Wiley.

Talbot, J. F., & Kaplan, S. (1986). Perspectives on wilderness: Reexamining the value of extended wilderness experiences. *Journal of Environmental Psychology, 6*, 177-188.

Talbot, J. F., Bardwell, L. V., & Kaplan, R. (1987). The functions of urban nature: Uses and values of different types of urban nature settings. *Journal of Architectural and Planning Research, 4*, 47-63.

Thomas, K. (1983). *Man and the natural world: A history of the modern sensibility*. New York: Pantheon Books.

Tuan, Y-F. (1974). *Topophilia: A study of environmental perception, attitudes, and values*. Englewood Cliffs, NJ: Prentice Hall.

Ullrich, J. R., & Ullrich, M. F. (1976). A multidimensional scaling analysis of perceived similarities of rivers in western Montana. *Perceptual and Motor Skills, 43*, 575-584.

Ulrich, R. S. (1979). Visual landscapes and psychological well-being. *Landscape Research, 4*, 17-23.

Ulrich, R. S. (1981). Natural vs. urban scenes: Some psychophysiological effects. *Environment and Behavior*, 13, 523-556.

Ulrich, R. S. (1983). Aesthetic and affective response to natural environment. In I. Altman & J. F. Wohlwill (Eds.), *Human behavior and environment: Advances in theory and research* (Vol. 6, pp. 85-125). New York: Plenum.

Ulrich, R. S., Simons, R. F., Losito, B. D., Fiorito, E., Miles, M. A., & Zelson, M. (1991). Stress recovery during exposure to natural and urban environments. *Journal of Environmental Psychology, 11*, 201-230.

Ward, L. M. (1977). Multidimensional scaling of the molar physical environment. *Multivariate Behavior Research, 12*, 23-42.

Ward, L. M., & Russell, J. A. (1981). The psychological representation of molar physical environments. *Journal of Experimental Psychology: General, 110*, 121-152.

Weiner, B. (1980). *Human motivation*. New York: Holt, Rinehart, and Winston.

Wohlwill, J. F. (1968). Amount of stimulus exploration and preference as differential functions of stimulus complexity. *Perception and Psychophysics, 4*, 307-312.

Wohlwill, J. F. (1970). The concept of sensory overload. In J. Archea & C. Eastman (Eds.), *EDRA Two: Proceedings of the 2nd Annual Environmental Design Research Association Conference* (pp. 340-344). Stroudsburg, PA: Dowden, Hutchinson, & Ross.

Wohlwill, J. F. (1973). The environment is not in the head! In W. F. E. Presier (Ed.), *Environmental Design Research* (Vol. 2, pp. 166-181). Stroudsburg, PA: Dowden, Hutchinson, & Ross.

Wohlwill, J. F. (1974). Human adaptation to levels of environmental stimulation. *Human Ecology, 2*, 127-147.

Wohlwill, J. F. (1976). Environmental aesthetics: The environment as a source of affect. In I. Altman & J. F. Wohlwill (Eds.), *Human behavior and environment: Advances in Theory and research* (Vol. 1, pp. 37-86). New York: Plenum.

Wohlwill, J. F. (1982). The visual impact of development in coastal zone areas. *Coastal Zone Management Journal*, 9, 225-248.

Wohlwill, J. F. (1983). The concept of nature: A psychologist's view. In I. Altman & J. F. Wohlwill (Eds.), *Human behavior and environment: Advances in theory and research* (Vol. 6, pp. 5-37). New York: Plenum.

Wohlwill, J. F., & Harris, G. (1980). Response to congruity or contrast for man-made features in natural-recreation settings. *Leisure Sciences, 3*, 349-365.

Wohlwill, J. F., & Heft, H. (1987). The physical environment and the development of the child. In D. Stokols & I. Altman (Eds.), *Handbook of environmental psychology* (Vol. 1, pp. 281-328). New York: Wiley.

Wohlwill, J. F., & Kohn, I. (1973). The environment as experienced by the migrant: An adaptation level view. *Representative Research in Social Psychology, 4*, 135-164.

Woodcock, D. M. (1984). A functionalist approach to landscape preference. *Landscape Research, 9*, 24-27.

Zajonc, R. B. (1980). Feeling and thinking: Preferences need no inferences. *American Psychologist, 35*, 151-175.

Zube, E. H., Sell, J. L., & Taylor, J. G. (1982). Landscape perception: Research, application, and theory. *Landscape Planning, 9*, 1-33.

# AUTHOR INDEX

# Subject Index

www.ingramcontent.com/pod-product-compliance
Ingram Content Group UK Ltd.
Pitfield, Milton Keynes, MK11 3LW, UK
UKHW020226290926
15470UKWH00001B/392

9 780444 896988